SECOND EDITION

America

A CONCISE HISTORY

Volume 2: Since 1865

SECOND EDITION

America

A CONCISE HISTORY

Volume 2: Since 1865

James A. Henretta
University of Maryland

David Brody
University of California, Davis

Lynn Dumenil
Occidental College

BEDFORD/ST. MARTIN'S
Boston • New York

For Bedford/St.Martin's

Publisher of History: Patricia A. Rossi
Developmental Editors: Gretchen Boger, Jessica Angell
Production Editor: Bridget Leahy
Senior Production Supervisor: Joe Ford
Marketing Manager: Jenna Bookin Barry
Copyeditor: Rosemary Winfield
Text Design: Wanda Kossak
Advisory Editor for Cartography: Michael P. Conzen, University of Chicago
Indexer: Melanie Belkin
Cover Design: Donna Lee Dennison
Cover Art: Urban Freeways. © Wayne Thiebaud/Licensed by VAGA, New York, NY
Composition: TechBooks
Printing and Binding: R.R. Donnelley & Sons Company

President: Charles H. Christensen
Editorial Director: Joan E. Feinberg
Director of Marketing: Karen Melton
Director of Editing, Design, and Production: Marcia Cohen
Managing Editor: Elizabeth M. Schaaf

Library of Congress Control Number: 2001087440

Manufactured in the United States of America.

6   5   4   3   2   1
f   e   d   c   b   a

For information, write: Bedford/St. Martin's, 75 Arlington Street, Boston, MA 02116
(617-399-4000)

ISBN: 0–312–25612–4 (combined edition)
        0–312–25613–2 (Vol. 1)
        0–312–25614–0 (Vol. 2)

For Ellie,
Susan,
Janet, Michael, & Emily

PREFACE

This is the second edition of *America: A Concise History*. In the first edition, our main task was to shorten our comprehensive text, *America's History*, by 40 percent—in effect, to make six words do the work of ten—without compromising the balanced coverage and explanatory power of the original text. Not an easy task, but we are satisfied that *America: A Concise History* met that challenge. In this second edition, our starting point is the concise version itself. And the question we face is the one always confronting textbook authors when they contemplate a new edition: how do we improve on what we have already written? At this juncture, we aspire to make this concise edition a more compelling *narrative* text. What would most please us as authors would be for students to regard *America: A Concise History* as a book to be read, not as a set of assignments to be gotten through.

We remain committed, however, to the historical perspective that has informed this textbook project from its inception. We are bent on a democratic history, one that captures the experiences of ordinary people even as it records the achievements of the great and powerful. Throughout the book, we focus not only on the marvelous diversity of peoples who became Americans but also on the institutions—political, economic, social, and cultural—that forged a common national identity. We want to show how people of all classes and groups make their own history while simultaneously being influenced and constrained by circumstances, by the customs and institutions inherited from the past, and by the distribution of power in the present. We are writing narrative history harnessed to historical argument—not simply a retelling of "this happened and then that happened." The story, we hope, tells not only what happened but *why* it happened.

Features

Accomplishing these goals means first of all grounding *America: A Concise History* in a clear chronology and a strong conceptual framework. Each of the two volumes is divided into three parts, with each corresponding to a distinct phase of development.

Every part begins at a crucial turning point in American history, such as the American Revolution or the cold war, and emphasizes the dynamic forces at work. Part openers contain **Thematic Timelines** that highlight key developments and **Part Essays** that focus on the crucial engines of historical change that create new conditions of life. This part organization helps students to understand the major themes in each period of American history and the larger patterns of development that lend significance to the bits and pieces of historical data.

To put a human face on historical experience, each chapter contains two **American Voices,** first-person excerpts from letters, diaries, autobiographies, and public testimony that paint a vivid picture of the social or political life of the time. One-third of these are new to this edition, including reactions to the contested 2000 presidential election. Each chapter is enhanced by a selection of maps and contemporary illustrations, vibrantly displayed in an all-new four-color design. Coupled with generous margins and a new typeface, this second edition has the feel of a trade book.

America: A Concise History's map and graph program, the most extensive of any brief text, aids students in capturing aspects of American life geographically and in drawing sound conclusions based on statistical analysis. Full-color art, 60 percent of it new to this edition, reinforces students' understanding of history via striking images from the period being discussed. Detailed captions give students context for the images and allow the visual material to extend the text discussion in a substantive and engaging manner. Also new to this edition is **For Further Exploration,** a brief bibliographical essay at the close of each chapter designed to pique the student's interest in reading further. To assist instructors and advanced students, a full bibliography is available on the web at <www.bedfordstmartins.com/henrettaconcise>.

Taken together, these documents and illustrations provide instructors with a trove of teaching materials and allow students to enter the life of the past and see it from within.

Textual Changes

Good narrative history is primarily a product of good sentences and good paragraphs. So our labors have been mostly in the trenches in a line-by-line striving toward the vividness and human presence that are the hallmarks of narrative history. But larger strategies also have been called into play. We have doubled the length of the essays opening each part to afford us more scope for setting the thematic stage for our story. Each chapter now begins with an anecdote or scene selected to capture the reader's interest and establish the chapter's main ideas and topics. Our chapter endings eschew the usual textbook summary in favor of apt statements bringing the discussion to a satisfying close and opening the way for what follows. Within chapters we have been especially attentive to chronology, which sometimes

involved, as in Chapters 18 and 19, major reordering of sections. We have also reduced the numbers of chapters from 33 to 31 to correspond more closely with the
academic calendar. Former Chapters 13 (on sectionalism) and 14 (on the crisis of
union) have been combined, with much of Chapter 13's treatment of southern society, industrialization, and the West shifted to earlier chapters, while former
Chapter 30 (on the politics of the 1960s) has been incorporated into the surrounding
chapters. Changes of this magnitude have a bracing effect, and we are hopeful that
by being forced to think hard about how to organize materials, we have come up
with a stronger periodization and clearer thematic development.

The revising process is also an opportunity to incorporate new scholarship. In
this second edition we have expanded the treatment of Native Americans in the
colonial era, and we have been more attentive to the role of gender and the emergence of a distinctive southern social order before 1820. Our treatment of the coming of the Industrial Revolution shifts the emphasis from industrialization as such
to the extension of markets, in keeping with new scholarship on the market revolution. We have drawn on recent Reconstruction scholarship that sees the transition from slavery to freedom in large part as a battle over labor systems. We have
improved our analysis of Native Americans in the Great Depression and postwar
years and expanded our account of the New Right in the 1970s. The final chapter
not only updates political developments but also discusses the economic prosperity of the late 1990s.

A new feature of this edition of *America: A Concise History* is the Epilogue,
which deals with some of the open, still unresolved questions of our own time and
how the historian thinks about them. The Epilogue invites the student to enter the
historian's world—to participate with us in the act of interpretation that lies behind every historical text, including this one.

Supplements

Since the first edition of *America: A Concise History,* we have been working with instructors from around the country to determine how we can improve our ancillary
package. Instructors stress the growing demand for online resources, particularly
for students, and now more than ever our supplements reflect that request.

ONLINE STUDY GUIDE FOR STUDENTS

By Michael Goldberg, University of Washington, Bothell

We are pleased to offer a new *Online Study Guide* that features up-to-date technology to present students with attractive and highly effective presentations and
learning tools. Written by Michael Goldberg of the University of Washington,
Bothell, this interactive resource has unique self-assessment capabilities. As a student completes a practice test, the *Online Study Guide* immediately assesses her

performance, targets the subject areas that need review, and refers the student back to the appropriate portions of the text. Through a series of multiple-choice, fill-in-the-blank, short-answer, and essay questions, students can gauge whether they have mastered the chapter's key events and themes. Exercises on the maps and on special features in the book encourage critical thinking. This resource is located at <www.bedfordstmartins.com/henrettaconcise>.

Documents Collection

Volume 1 by David L. Carlton (Vanderbilt University) and Volume 2 by Samuel T. McSeveny (Vanderbilt University)

This affordable two-volume *Documents Collection* offers students over 350 primary-source readings on topics covered in *America: A Concise History*. The documents emphasize contested issues in American history that will spark critical thinking and class discussions. Sets of documents highlight different perspectives on the same issue, while added attention has been given to America in the context of the larger world. Each document is preceded by a brief introduction and followed by questions for further thought.

Instructor's Resource Manual

By Bradley T. Gericke (United States Military Academy)

Instructors, too, will benefit from our ancillary package. Bradley Gericke's *Instructor's Resource Manual*, provided free of charge with adoption of the book, offers an extensive collection of tools to aid both first-time and experienced teachers in structuring and customizing the American history course. The *Instructor's Resource Manual* has been revised and expanded to include informative and guiding chapter outlines, lecture strategies, questions to prompt class discussion, and writing assignments involving our American Voices features. This resource also includes map exercises, an extensive film guide, and historiographical essays on topics of particular interest.

Test Bank

Volume 1 by Thomas L. Altherr (Metropolitan State College of Denver) and Volume 2 by Adolph Grundman (Metropolitan State College of Denver)

Our *Test Bank* now places a greater emphasis on thematic concerns within American history. What patterns in religious, cultural, political, and economic history do we see develop over time? How is a specific incident representative of a larger trend? *Test Bank* authors Thomas L. Altherr and Adolph Grundman have revised our first edition with these questions in mind. They have included multiple-choice, fill-in-the-blank, short-answer, essay, and map questions for each chapter. To provide greater ease in using this resource, it is now available on CD-ROM.

TRANSPARENCIES

An expanded set of over 150 full-color acetate transparencies, free to adopters, includes all maps and many tables, graphs, and images from the text.

CD-ROM WITH PRESENTATION MANAGER PRO

For teachers who wish to use electronic media in the classroom, this CD-ROM includes images, maps, graphs, and tables from *America: A Concise History* as well as sound recordings and a collection of supplementary images, in an easy-to-use format that allows instructors to customize their own presentations. The CD-ROM may be used with Presentation Manager Pro or with PowerPoint.

USING THE BEDFORD SERIES IN THE U.S. HISTORY SURVEY, SECOND EDITION

By Scott Hovey

Recognizing that many instructors use a survey text in conjunction with supplements, Bedford/St. Martin's has made the Bedford series volumes available at a discount to adopters of *America: A Concise History.* This short guide gives practical suggestions for using the more than fifty volumes from The Bedford Series in History and Culture and the Historians at Work series with a core text. The guide not only supplies connections between the text and the supplements but also provides ideas for starting discussions focused on a single primary-source volume.

Acknowledgments

The scholars and teachers who reviewed *America: A Concise History* made suggestions that we gratefully incorporated in the new edition. All of our reviewers have used concise texts in their courses, and their classroom experience has helped us to craft a book that meets the needs of today's diverse students. Thanks are due to Michael Goldberg, University of Washington, Bothell; David F. Krugler, University of Wisconsin–Platteville; Connie L. Lester, Mississippi State University; Carl H. Moneyhon, University of Arkansas at Little Rock; Katherine M. B. Osburn, Tennessee Technological University; Glenna R. Schroeder-Lein, University of Tennessee, Knoxville; and Nancy Shoemaker, University of Connecticut.

As the authors of *America: A Concise History,* we know how much this book is the work of other hands and minds. We are grateful to Katherine E. Kurzman and Patricia A. Rossi, who oversaw the project, and Gretchen Boger, who did a splendid job as our history editor (before departing for the Dominican Republic to serve in the Peace Corps). Elizabeth M. Welch offered invaluable insight and guidance along the way. Charles H. Christensen and Joan E. Feinberg have been generous in providing the resources we needed to produce the second edition. Elizabeth M. Schaaf, Joe Ford, and Bridget Leahy have done an outstanding job overseeing the production of the book. Karen Melton and Jenna Bookin Barry in the marketing department have been instrumental in helping this book reach the classroom. We also thank the rest of our editorial and production team for their dedicated efforts: Jessica Angell, Sarah Barrash, Rose Corbett Gordon, William Lombardo, Pembroke Herbert and Sandi Rygiel at Picture Research Consultants, Sandy Schechter, and Rosemary Winfield. Finally, we want to express our appreciation for the invaluable assistance of Patricia Deveneau, Stephanie Murvachik, Norman S. Cohen, and Anastasia Christman, whose work contributed in many ways to the intellectual vitality of this new edition of *America: A Concise History.*

James A. Henretta
David Brody
Lynn Dumenil

CONTENTS

Preface   vii

List of Maps   xxiii

About the Authors   xxv

CHAPTER 15
RECONSTRUCTION, 1865–1877   428

Presidential Reconstruction   429
Johnson's Initiative   429   •   Acting on Freedom   432   •   Congress versus
President   435

Radical Reconstruction   437
Congress Takes Command   437   •   Woman Suffrage Denied   440   •   The South
under Radical Reconstruction   441   •   Sharecropping   445

The Undoing of Reconstruction   448
Counterrevolution   448   •   The Political Crisis of 1877   452

AMERICAN VOICES
A Plea for Land   434
HARRIET HERNANDES: The Intimidation of Black Voters   450

Part Four
A MATURING INDUSTRIAL SOCIETY, 1877–1914   456

CHAPTER 16
THE AMERICAN WEST   460

The Great Plains 460

Indians of the Great Plains 462 • Wagon Trains, Railroads, and Ranchers 463
• Homesteaders 467 • The Fate of the Indians 471

The Far West 475

The Mining Frontier 475 • Hispanics, Chinese, Anglos 478 • Golden
California 482

> AMERICAN VOICES
> IDA LINDGREN: Swedish Emigrant in Frontier Kansas 468
> ZITKALA-SA (GERTRUDE SIMMONS BONNIN): Becoming
> White 474

CHAPTER 17
CAPITAL AND LABOR IN THE AGE OF ENTERPRISE, 1877–1900 487

Industrial Capitalism Triumphant 488

Growth of the Industrial Base 488 • The Railroad Boom 489 • Mass
Markets and Large-Scale Enterprise 492 • The New South 494

The World of Work 497

Labor Recruits 498 • Working Women 499 • Autonomous Labor 502 •
Systems of Control 505

The Labor Movement 506

Reformers and Unionists 507 • The Triumph of "Pure and Simple" Unionism
508 • Industrial War 510 • American Radicalism in the Making 513

> AMERICAN VOICES
> ROSE SCHNEIDERMAN: Getting Organized 501
> JOHN BROPHY: A Miner's Son 503

CHAPTER 18
THE POLITICS OF LATE NINETEENTH-CENTURY AMERICA 516

The Politics of the Status Quo, 1877–1893 517

The National Scene 517 • The Ideology of Individualism 519 • The
Supremacy of the Courts 521

Politics and the People 522

Cultural Politics: Party, Religion, and Ethnicity 522 • Organizational
Politics 524 • Women's Political Culture 526

Race and Politics in the South 528

Biracial Politics 529 • One-Party Rule Triumphant 530 • Resisting
White Supremacy 533

The Crisis of American Politics: The 1890s   536
The Populist Revolt   536   •   Money and Politics   539

AMERICAN VOICES
HELEN POTTER: The Case for Women's Political Rights   528
C. H. JOHNSON: A Black Man on Segregation   533

CHAPTER 19
THE RISE OF THE CITY   545

Urbanization   545
Industrial Sources of City Growth   546   •   City Building   546   •   The City
as Private Enterprise   549   •   A Balance Sheet: Chicago and Berlin   550

Upper Class/Middle Class   551
The Urban Elite   551   •   The Suburban World   553   •   Middle-Class
Families   555

City Life   558
Newcomers   559   •   Ward Politics   562   •   Religion in the City   563   •
City Amusements   566   •   The Higher Culture   569

AMERICAN VOICES
M. CAREY THOMAS: "We Did Not Know . . . Whether Women's
Health Could Stand the Strain of Higher Education"   557
Bintel Brief   561

CHAPTER 20
THE PROGRESSIVE ERA, 1900–1914   573

The Course of Reform   574
The Progressive Mind   574   •   Women Progressives   576   •   Reforming
Politics   581   •   Urban Liberalism   583   •   Racism and Reform   587

Progressivism and National Politics   589
The Making of a Progressive President   589   •   Regulating the Marketplace   591
•   The Fracturing of Republican Progressivism   594   •   Woodrow Wilson and
the New Freedom   596

AMERICAN VOICES
CHARLES EDWARD RUSSELL: Muckraking   578   PAULINE
NEWMAN: Working for the Triangle Shirtwaist Company   584

CHAPTER 21
AN EMERGING WORLD POWER, 1877–1914   601

The Roots of Expansion   602

Diplomacy in the Gilded Age   **602**   •   The Economy of Expansionism   **604**   •   The Making of an Expansionist Foreign Policy   **607**   •   The Ideology of Expansionism   **608**

An American Empire   609

The Cuban Crisis   **610**   •   The Spoils of War   **612**   •   The Imperial Experiment   **615**

Onto the World Stage   620

A Power among Powers   **620**   •   The Open Door in Asia   **623**   •   Wilson and Mexico   **625**   •   The Gathering Storm in Europe   **626**

> AMERICAN VOICES
>
> GEORGE W. PRIOLEAU: Black Soldiers in a White Man's War   **616**   CORPORAL DANIEL J. EVANS: The Water Cure   **619**

Part Five
THE MODERN STATE AND SOCIETY, 1914–1945   **630**

CHAPTER 22
WAR AND THE AMERICAN STATE, 1914–1920   634

The Great War, 1914–1918   636
War in Europe   **636**   •   The Perils of Neutrality   **638**   •   "Over There"   **641**

War on the Home Front   645
Mobilization   **646**   •   Progressive Reform in Wartime   **650**   •   Promoting National Unity   **652**

An Unsettled Peace, 1919–1920   654
The Treaty of Versailles   **654**   •   Racial Strife and Labor Unrest   **657**   •   The Red Scare   **658**

> AMERICAN VOICES
>
> WILLIAM L. LANGER: Trench Warfare   **644**
> A Southern Migrant   **649**

CHAPTER 23
MODERN TIMES: THE 1920s   662

Business-Government Partnership of the 1920s   662
Politics in the Republican "New Era"   **663**   •   The Heyday of Big Business   **665**   •   Economic Power Abroad   **668**

A New National Culture   671

A Consumer Culture   671   •   Mass Media and New Patterns of Leisure   674

Dissenting Values and Cultural Conflict   678

The Rise of Nativism   679   •   Legislating Values: The Scopes Trial and Prohibition   682   •   Intellectual Crosscurrents   684   •   Cultural Clash in the Election of 1928   687

AMERICAN VOICES
Daisy Harriman and Emily Newell Blair: Women Get the Vote   666   Kazuo Kawai: A Foreigner in America   681

CHAPTER 24
THE GREAT DEPRESSION   691

The Coming of the Great Depression   691

Causes of the Depression   692   •   The Worldwide Depression   694

Hard Times   694

The Invisible Scar   695   •   Families Face the Depression   697   •   Popular Culture Views the Depression   702

Harder Times   706

African Americans in the Depression   706   •   Dust Bowl Migrations   708   •   Mexican American Communities   710

Herbert Hoover and the Great Depression   711

Hoover Responds   711   •   Rising Discontent   713   •   The 1932 Election: A New Order   715

AMERICAN VOICES
Larry Van Dusen: A Working-Class Family Encounters the Great Depression   698   Public Assistance Fails a Southern Farm Family   712

CHAPTER 25
THE NEW DEAL, 1933–1939   718

The New Deal Takes Over, 1933–1935   719

Roosevelt's Style of Leadership   719   •   The Hundred Days   720   •   The New Deal under Attack   723

The Second New Deal, 1935–1938   725

Legislative Accomplishments   726   •   Stalemate   728

The New Deal's Impact on Society   731
New Deal Constituencies   731   •   The New Deal and the Land   738   •   The
New Deal and the Arts   739   •   The Legacies of the New Deal   741

AMERICAN VOICES
JOE MARCUS: A New Deal Activist   732
SUSANA ARCHULETA: A Chicana Youth Gets New Deal Work   737

CHAPTER 26
THE WORLD AT WAR, 1939–1945   745

The Road to War   746
Depression Diplomacy   746   •   Aggression and Appeasement   747   •
America and the War   749

Organizing for Victory   752
Defense Mobilization   752   •   Workers and the War Effort   754   •   Politics in
Wartime   756

Life on the Home Front   757
Civilian War Efforts   758   •   Japanese Internment   761

Fighting and Winning the War   763
Wartime Aims and Strategies   764   •   Planning the Postwar World   770

AMERICAN VOICES
MONICA SONE: Japanese Relocation   762
JUANITA REDMOND: An Army Nurse in Bataan   768

Part Six
AMERICA AND THE WORLD, 1945 TO THE PRESENT   **774**

CHAPTER 27
COLD WAR AMERICA, 1945–1960   778

The Early Cold War   778
Descent into Cold War, 1945–1946   780   •   A Policy of Containment   781   •
Containment in Asia   784

Harry Truman and the Cold War at Home   788
Postwar Domestic Challenges   788   •   Fair Deal Liberalism   790   •   The Great
Fear   792

"Modern Republicanism" 795

"I Like Ike" 795 • Emergence of Civil Rights as a National Issue 799 • The "New Look" of Foreign Policy 801 • The Cold War in the Middle East 803 • Domestic Impact of the Cold War 805

> AMERICAN VOICES
> MELVIN RADER: Resisting the Tactics of McCarthyism 796
> RON KOVIC: Memories of a Cold War Childhood 806

CHAPTER 28
THE AFFLUENT SOCIETY AND THE LIBERAL CONSENSUS,
1945–1965 809

The Affluent Society 810

The Economic Record 810 • The Suburban Explosion 812

American Life during the Baby Boom 814

Consumer Culture 814 • The Search for Security: Religion and the Family 815 • Contradictions in Women's Lives 816 • Cultural Dissenters 817

The Other America 820

Urban Migration 821 • The Urban Crisis 822

John F. Kennedy and the Politics of Expectation 823

The New Politics 824 • Activism Abroad and at Home 825 • JFK and Civil Rights 830 • The Kennedy Assassination 833

Lyndon B. Johnson and the Great Society 833

The Momentum for Civil Rights 834 • Enacting the Liberal Agenda 835

> AMERICAN VOICES
> A Woman Encounters the Feminine Mystique 818
> JOHN LEWIS: A Badge of Honor 831

CHAPTER 29
WAR ABROAD AND AT HOME: THE VIETNAM ERA, 1961–1975 840

Into the Quagmire, 1945–1968 841

America in Vietnam: From Truman to Kennedy 841 • Escalation: The Johnson Years 844 • American Soldiers' Perspectives on the War 846

The Cold-War Consensus Unravels 848

Public Opinion on Vietnam 848 • Student Activism and the Counter-culture 850 • The Widening Struggle for Civil Rights 854 • The Legacy of the Civil Rights Movement 856 • The Revival of Feminism 860

The Long Road Home, 1968–1975   863

1968: A Year of Shocks   864   •   Nixon's War   866   •   Détente and the End
of the War   868   •   The Legacy of Vietnam   871

AMERICAN VOICES
DAVE CLINE: A Vietnam Vet Remembers   847
MARY CROW DOG: The Trail of Broken Treaties   859

CHAPTER 30
THE LEAN YEARS, 1969–1980   874

The Nixon Years   875
The Republican Domestic Agenda   875   •   The 1972 Election   876   •
Watergate   877

An Economy of Diminished Expectations   880
Energy Crisis   880   •   Economic Woes   883

Reform and Reaction in the 1970s   885
The New Activism: Environmental and Consumer Movements   885   •   Challenges
to Tradition: The Women's Movement and Gay Rights Activism   887   •   Racial
Minorities   891   •   The Politics of Resentment   895

Politics in the Wake of Watergate   896
Ford's Caretaker Presidency   896   •   Jimmy Carter: The Outsider as
President   897   •   The Reagan Revolution   900

AMERICAN VOICES
ELIZABETH DREW: Watergate Diary   881
DAVID KOPAY: A Gay Athlete Comes Out   892

CHAPTER 31
A NEW DOMESTIC AND WORLD ORDER, 1981–2000   903

The Reagan-Bush Years, 1981–1993   904
Reaganomics   904   •   Reagan's Second Term   905   •   The Bush Presidency   907

Foreign Relations Under Reagan and Bush   909
Interventions in Developing Countries and the End of the Cold War   909   •   War
in the Persian Gulf, 1990–1991   910

Uncertain Times   913
The Economy   913   •   An Increasingly Pluralistic Society   915   •   Backlash
against Women's and Gay Rights   920   •   Popular Culture and Popular
Technology   921

The Clinton Presidency: Public Life Since 1993   923

Clinton's First Term   **923**   •   "The Era of Big Government Is Over"   **927**   •
Second-Term Stalemates   **928**   •   Making Sense of the Late Twentieth
Century   **932**

> AMERICAN VOICES
> CUAUHTÉMOC MENDEZ: The Undocumented Worker   **918**
> JOHN LEWIS: We Marched to Be Counted   **933**

**EPILOGUE: AMERICA AND THE WORLD AT 2001: HOW HISTORIANS
INTERPRET CONTEMPORARY EVENTS AND THEIR LEGACY TO THE
FUTURE**   939

DOCUMENTS   D-1

The Declaration of Independence   D-1

The Articles of Confederation and Perpetual Union   D-4

The Constitution of the United States   D-10

Amendments to the Constitution   D-20

APPENDIX   A-1

Territorial Expansion   A-1

The Labor Force   A-2

Changing Labor Patterns   A-2

American Population   A-3

Presidential Elections   A-4

CREDITS   C-1

INDEX   I-1

LIST OF MAPS

Reconstruction   438
The Barrow Plantation, 1860 and 1881   446
The Natural Environment of the West   461
The Mining Frontier, 1848–1890   476
The Expansion of the Railroad System, 1870–1890   490
The New South, 1900   495
Disfranchisement in the South   531
The Heyday of Western Populism, 1892   537
The Election of 1896   542
Woman Suffrage, 1869–1918   580
The Spanish-American War of 1898   614
The American Empire   622
Policeman of the Caribbean   624
Europe at the Start of World War I   637
U.S. Participation on the Western Front, 1918   643
The Shift from Rural to Urban Population, 1920–1930   679
World War II in Europe   766
World War II in the Pacific   769
Cold War Europe, 1955   783
The Korean War, 1950–1953   786
Metropolitan Growth, 1950–1980   813
The United States and Cuba, 1961–1962   827
The Vietnam War, 1954–1975   843
Racial Unrest in America's Cities, 1965–1968   856
States Ratifying the Equal Rights Amendment   890
American Indian Reservations   893
The Collapse of Communism in Eastern Europe and the Soviet Union   911
U.S. Involvement in the Middle East, 1980–1994   912
Latino and Asian American Population, 1999   916
The Election of 2000   932
The United States   **following the Index**
The World   **following the Index**

ABOUT THE AUTHORS

James A. Henretta is Priscilla Alden Burke Professor of American History at the University of Maryland, College Park. He received his undergraduate education at Swarthmore College and his Ph.D. from Harvard University. He has taught at the University of Sussex, England; Princeton University; UCLA; Boston University; as a Fulbright lecturer in Australia at the University of New England; and at Oxford University as the Harmsworth Professor of American History. His publications include *The Evolution of American Society, 1700–1815: An Interdisciplinary Analysis;* *"Salutary Neglect": Colonial Administration under the Duke of Newcastle; Evolution and Revolution: American Society, 1600–1820;* and *The Origins of American Capitalism.* Recently he co-edited and contributed to a collection of original essays, *Republicanism and Liberalism in America and the German States, 1750–1850,* as part of his larger research project on "The Rise and Transformation of the Liberal State: New York, 1820–1940."

David Brody is Professor Emeritus of History at the University of California, Davis. He received his B.A., M.A., and Ph.D. from Harvard University. He has taught at the University of Warwick in England, at Moscow State University in the former Soviet Union, and at Sydney University in Australia. He is the author of *Steelworkers in America; Workers in Industrial America: Essays on the 20th Century Struggle;* and *In Labor's Cause: Main Themes on the History of the American Worker.* He has been awarded fellowships from the Social Science Research Council, the Guggenheim Foundation, and the National Endowment for the Humanities. He is past president (1991–1992) of the Pacific Coast Branch of the American Historical Association. His current research is on industrial labor during the Great Depression.

Lynn Dumenil is Robert Glass Cleland Professor of American History at Occidental College in Los Angeles. She is a graduate of the University of Southern California and received her Ph.D. from the University of California, Berkeley. She has written *The Modern Temper: American Culture and Society in the 1920s* and *Freemasonry and American Culture: 1880–1930.* Her articles and reviews have appeared in the *Journal of American History,* the *Journal of American Ethnic History, Reviews in American History,* and *the American Historical Review.* She has been a historical consultant to several documentary film projects and is on the Council of the Pacific Coast Branch of the American Historical Association. Her current work, for which she received a National Endowment for the Humanities Fellowship, is on World War I, citizenship, and the state. In 2001–2002 she will be at the University of Helsinki as the Bicentennial Fulbright Chair in American Studies.

SECOND EDITION

America

A CONCISE HISTORY

Chapter 15

RECONSTRUCTION
1865–1877

I felt like a bird out of a cage. Amen. Amen. Amen. I could hardly
ask to feel any better than I did that day.
—HOUSTON H. HOLLOWAY, A FORMER SLAVE
RECALLING HIS EMANCIPATION IN 1865

In his second inaugural address, President Lincoln spoke of the need
to "bind up the nation's wounds." No one knew better than Lincoln how daunting
a task that would be. Foremost, of course, were the terms on which the rebellious
states would be restored to the Union. But America's Civil War had opened more
fundamental questions. Slavery was finished. That much was certain. But what system of labor should replace plantation slavery? What rights should the freedmen
be accorded beyond emancipation itself? How far should the federal government
go to settle these questions? And who should decide—the president or Congress?

While the war was still on, the North began to grope for answers. Taking the
initiative, Lincoln in December 1863 offered a general amnesty to all but high-
ranking Confederates willing to pledge loyalty to the Union and abolish slavery.
When 10 percent of a state's 1860 voters had taken this oath, they could organize
a new government and be restored to the Union. Only states under military occupation—Louisiana, Arkansas, and Tennessee—took advantage of Lincoln's generous offer. Although it reflected Lincoln's conciliatory bent, his Ten Percent Plan was
really aimed at subverting the southern war effort.

What it also did, however, was to reveal the rocky road that lay ahead for Reconstruction. Thus, in Louisiana sugar planters used the restored government to
regain control over the freed slaves, employing curfew laws to restrict their movements and vagrancy regulations to force them back to work. But the Louisiana
freedmen fought back. Led by the well-established free-black community of New
Orleans, they began to agitate for political rights. No less than their former masters, former slaves intended to be actors in the savage drama of Reconstruction.

With the struggle in Louisiana in mind, congressional Republicans proposed a
stricter substitute for Lincoln's Ten Percent Plan. The initiative came from the Radical wing—those bent on a stern peace and full rights for the freedmen—but with
broad support among congressional Republicans generally. The Wade-Davis Bill,
passed on July 2, 1864, laid down, as conditions for the restoration of the rebellious

states to the Union, an oath of allegiance by a majority of each state's adult white men, new state governments formed and operated only by those who had never carried arms against the Union, and permanent loss of voting rights by Confederate leaders. The Wade-Davis Bill served notice that the congressional Republicans were not about to hand reconstruction policy over to the president.

Lincoln was not perturbed. Rather than openly challenging Congress, he executed a "pocket" veto of the Wade-Davis Bill by not signing it before Congress adjourned. At the same time he initiated informal talks with congressional leaders aimed at finding a common ground. The last speech he ever delivered, on April 11, 1865, demonstrated Lincoln's cautious realism. Reconstruction, he pleaded, had to be regarded as a practical, not a theoretical, problem. It could be solved only if Republicans remained united, even if that meant compromising, and only if the defeated South gave its consent, even if that meant forgiveness. What the speech showed, above all, was Lincoln's sense of the fluidity of events, of policy toward the South as an evolving, not a fixed, position.

What course Reconstruction might have taken had Lincoln lived is one of the unanswerable questions of American history. On April 14, 1865—five days after Lee's surrender at Appomattox—Lincoln was shot in the head at Ford's Theater in Washington by a wild-eyed actor named John Wilkes Booth. Ironically, Lincoln might have been spared if the war had dragged on longer, for Booth and his Confederate associates had originally plotted to kidnap the president to force a negotiated settlement. Without regaining consciousness, Lincoln died on April 15.

With one stroke John Wilkes Booth had sent Lincoln to martyrdom, hardened many northerners against the South, and handed the presidency to a man utterly lacking in Lincoln's moral sense and political judgment, Vice President Andrew Johnson.

Presidential Reconstruction

At the end of the Civil War, a big constitutional question remained in dispute—whether, on seceding, the Confederate states had legally left the Union. If so, then they became conquered territory whose fate could be decided only by Congress. If not, if even in rebellion they remained states of the Union, then the terms for their restoration might appropriately be left to the president. This was Andrew Johnson's view, and by an accident of timing he was free to act on it: under leisurely rules that went back to the early republic, the 39th Congress elected in November 1864 was not scheduled to convene until December 1865.

JOHNSON'S INITIATIVE

Andrew Johnson was a self-made man from the hills of eastern Tennessee. A Jacksonian Democrat, he saw himself as the champion of the common man. He hated what he called the "bloated, corrupt aristocracy" of the Northeast, and he was

Andrew Johnson

The president was not an easy man. This photograph of Andrew Johnson (1808–1875) conveys some of the personal qualities that contributed so centrally to his failure to reach an agreement with Republicans on a program of moderate reconstruction. (Library of Congress)

equally disdainful of the wealthy planters, whom he blamed for the poverty of the South's small farmers. It was poor whites he championed; Johnson, a slaveholder himself, had little sympathy for the enslaved blacks. His political career had taken him to the U.S. Senate, where he remained when the war broke out, loyal to the Union. After federal forces captured Nashville, he became Tennessee's military governor. The Republicans nominated him in 1864 for vice president in an effort to promote wartime political unity and to court southern Unionists.

In May 1865, just a month after Lincoln's death, Johnson executed his own plan for restoration. He offered amnesty to all southerners who took an oath of allegiance to the Constitution, except for high-ranking Confederate officials and wealthy property owners, whom he held responsible for secession. Such persons could be pardoned only by the president. Johnson appointed provisional governors for the southern states and, as conditions for their restoration, required only that they revoke their ordinances of secession, repudiate their Confederate debt, and ratify the Thirteenth Amendment, which abolished slavery. Within months all the former Confederate states had met Johnson's requirements for rejoining the Union and had functioning, elected governments.

At first Republicans responded favorably. The moderates among them were sympathetic to Johnson's states-rights argument that it was for the states, not the federal government, to decide what civil and political rights the freedmen should have. Even the Radicals held their fire. They liked the stern treatment of Confederate leaders, and they hoped that the restored governments would show good faith by generous treatment of the freed slaves.

Nothing of the sort happened. The South lay in ruins. But white southerners held fast to the old order. The newly seated legislatures moved to restore slavery in all but name. They enacted laws—known as Black Codes—designed to drive the former slaves back to the plantations and deny them elementary civil rights. The new governments had been formed mostly by southern Unionists, but when it came to racial attitudes, not a lot distinguished these loyalists from the Confederates. The latter, moreover, soon filtered back into the corridors of power. Despite his hard words against them, Johnson forgave ex-Confederate leaders easily so long as he got the satisfaction of making them submit to his personal authority.

His perceived indulgence of their efforts to restore white supremacy emboldened the former Confederates. They packed the delegations to the new Congress with old comrades—nine members of the Confederate Congress, seven former officials of Confederate state governments, four generals and four colonels, and even the vice president of the Confederacy, Alexander Stephens. For Republicans, this was the last straw.

Under the Constitution, Congress is "the judge of the elections, returns and qualifications of its members" (Article 1, Section 5). With this power, the Republican majorities in both houses refused to admit the southern delegations when Congress convened in early December 1865. Although relations with the president had already cooled, the Republicans assumed he would cooperate with them in formulating the new terms on which the South would be readmitted to Congress. To that end, a House-Senate committee—the Joint Committee on Reconstruction—was formed and began public hearings on conditions in the South.

In response, the southern states backed away from the most flagrant of the Black Codes, replacing them with nonracial ordinances whose effect was the same: in practice, they applied to blacks, not to whites. On top of that, a wave of violence erupted across the South against the freedmen. Listening to the graphic testimony of officials, observers and victims, Republicans concluded that the South had embarked on a concerted effort to circumvent the Thirteenth Amendment. The only possible response was for the federal government to intervene.

Back in March 1865, before adjourning, the 38th Congress had established the Freedmen's Bureau to provide emergency aid to former slaves during the chaotic period between war and peace. Now in early 1866, under the leadership of the moderate Republican senator Lyman Trumbull, chairman of the Judiciary Committee, Congress voted to extend the Bureau's life, gave it federal funding for the first time, and authorized its agents to investigate cases of discrimination against blacks.

More extraordinary was Trumbull's proposal for a Civil Rights Bill, declaring all persons born in the United States to be citizens and guaranteeing them—without regard to race—equal rights of contract, of access to the courts, and of protection of persons and property. Trumbull's bill nullified all state laws depriving citizens of these rights, authorized U.S. attorneys to bring enforcement suits in the federal courts, and provided for fines and imprisonment for violators, including public officials. Provoked by an unrepentant South, Republicans of the most moderate persuasion demanded that the federal government accept responsibility for securing the basic civil rights of the freedmen.

ACTING ON FREEDOM

While Congress debated, African Americans acted on their own idea of freedom. News of emancipation left them exultant and hopeful. Freedom meant many things—the reuniting of separated families, the end of punishment by the lash, the ability to move around, the opportunity to begin schools and churches, and, not least, the chance to engage in politics. Across the South, freed slaves held mass meetings, paraded, and formed organizations. Topmost among their demands were equality before the law and the right to vote—"an essential and inseparable element of self-government."

First of all, however, came economic independence, which emancipated blacks believed was the basis for true freedom. During the Civil War they had acted on this assumption whenever Union armies drew near. In the chaotic final months of the war, as plantation owners fled Union forces, freedmen seized control of land where they could. Most famously, General William T. Sherman reserved vast tracts of coastal lands in Georgia and South Carolina—the Sea Islands and the abandoned plantations within 30 miles of the coast—for liberated blacks and settled them on 40-acre tracts. Sherman wanted only to shift the responsibility for the refugees from his army as it marched across the lower South. But the freedmen assumed that Sherman's order meant that the land would be theirs. When the war ended, resettlement became the responsibility of the Freedmen's Bureau, which was charged with distributing confiscated land to "loyal refugees and freedmen." Many black families stayed expectantly on their old plantations. When the South Carolina

Schoolhouse, Port Hudson, Louisiana

This was probably the first schoolhouse built for freedmen by Union forces. In front, African American soldiers from the Port Hudson "Corps d'Afrique" pose with their textbooks. It stood to reason that former slaves who had taken up arms should be first to receive the education so coveted by all freedmen. (Chicago Historical Society)

planter Thomas Pinckney returned, his freed slaves told him, "We ain't going nowhere. We are going to work right here on the land where we were born and what belongs to us."

Johnson's amnesty plan, entitling pardoned Confederates to recover confiscated property, shattered these hopes. In October 1865 President Johnson ordered General Oliver O. Howard, head of the Freedmen's Bureau, to tell Sea Island blacks that they would have to surrender the land they occupied. When Howard reluctantly obeyed, the dispossessed farmers protested: "Why do you take away our lands? You take them from us who have always been true, always true to the Government! You give them to our all-time enemies! That is not right!" (see American Voices, "A Plea for Land"). In the Sea Islands and elsewhere, former slaves resisted efforts to remove them. Led by black veterans of the Union army, they fought pitched battles with plantation owners and bands of former Confederate soldiers. Generally, the local whites prevailed in this land war.

As planters prepared for a new growing season, a great struggle took shape over the labor system that would replace slavery. Convinced that blacks needed supervision, planters insisted on retaining the gang labor of the past, only now with wages replacing the food, clothing, and shelter that their slaves had previously received. The Freedmen's Bureau, although watchful against too exploitative labor contracts, sided with the planters. The Bureau, anxious that former slaves be weaned from the habits of dependency, saw the planters' offer of wage work as a halfstep to independence. But the blacks knew better. It was not only their unequal bargaining power they worried about or even that their former masters' real desire was to reenslave them under the guise of "free" contracts. In their eyes, the condition of wage labor was itself debasing. The rural South was not like the North, where working for wages was the norm and qualified a man as independent. In the South, selling one's labor to another—and in particular, selling one's labor to work another's land—implied not freedom but dependency. To be a "freeman"—a fully empowered citizen—meant heading a household, owning some property, conducting one's own affairs.

So the issue of wage labor cut to the very core of the former slaves' struggle for freedom. Nothing had been more horrifying than the fact that as slaves their persons had been the property of others. In a famous oration celebrating emancipation, the Reverend Henry M. Turner spoke bitterly of the time when his people had "no security of domestic happiness," when "our wives were sold and husbands bought, children were begotten and enslaved by their fathers." That was why formalizing marriage was so urgent a matter after emancipation and why, when hard-pressed planters demanded that freedwomen go back into the fields, they resisted so resolutely. "I seen on some plantations," one former slave recounted, "where the white men would . . . tell colored men that their wives and children could not live on their places unless they worked in the fields. The colored men [answered that] whenever they wanted their wives to work they would tell them themselves; and if he could not rule his own domestic affairs on that place he would leave it and go someplace else."

AMERICAN VOICES

A Plea for Land

*F*ollowing is a painfully written letter by the freed slaves of Edisto Island to President
    Andrew Johnson, pleading for a reversal of his order that the lands they now worked be
returned to the plantation owners.

Edisto Island S.C. Oct 28th, 1865.

To the President of these United States. We the freedmen Of Edisto Island South Carolina
have learned . . . with deep sorrow and Painful hearts of the possibility of government
restoring These lands to the former owners. . . . Here is where secession was born and Nurtured Here is where we have toiled nearly all Our lives as slaves and were treated like dumb
Driven cattle. This is our home, we have made These lands what they are. . . . Shall not we
who Are freedmen and have always been true to this Union have the same rights as are
enjoyed by Others? Have we broken any Law of these United States? have we forfeited our
rights of property In Land?—If not then! are not our rights as A free people and good citizens of these United States To be considered before the rights of those who were Found
in rebellion against this good and just Government. . . . And we who have been abused
and oppressed For many long years But be subject To the will of these large Land owners?
God forbid.

. . . We the freedmen of this Island and the State of South Carolina—Do hereby petition to you as the President of these United States, that some provisions be made by which
Every colored man can purchase land. and Hold as his own. We wish to have A home if It
be but A few acres. . . . May God bless you in the Administration of your duties as the President Of these United States is the humble prayer Of us all.—

	In behalf of the Freedmen
	Henry Bram
Committee	Ishmael. Moultrie
	yates. Sampson

SOURCE: Eileen Boris and Nelson Lichtenstein, eds., *Major Problems in the History of American Workers: Documents and Essays* (Lexington, MA: Heath, 1990), pp. 137–39.

The reader will see the irony in this definition of freedom: it assumed the wife's
subordinate role and designated her labor as the husband's property. But if that was
the price of freedom, freedwomen were prepared to pay it. Far better to take a chance
with their own men than with their former masters.

Many freedpeople voted with their feet, abandoning their old plantations and
seeking better lives and more freedom in the towns and cities of the South. Those
who remained in the countryside refused to work the cotton fields under the hated
gang labor or negotiated tenaciously over the terms of their labor contracts. Whatever system of labor finally might emerge, it was clear that the freedmen and their
families would never settle for anything resembling the old plantation system.

The efforts of former slaves to control their own lives ran counter to deeply entrenched white attitudes. "The destiny of the black race," asserted one Texan, could be summarized "in one sentence—subordination to the white race." Southern whites, a Freedmen's Bureau official observed, could not "conceive of the negro having any rights at all." And when freedmen resisted, white retribution was swift and often terrible. The toll of murdered and beaten blacks mounted into untold thousands. The governments established under Johnson's plan put the stamp of legality on the pervasive efforts to enforce white supremacy. Blacks "would be *just as well* off with no law at all or no Government," concluded a Freedmen's Bureau agent, as with the justice they got under the restored white rule.

In this unequal struggle, blacks turned to Washington. "We stood by the government when it wanted help," a black Mississippian wrote President Johnson. "Now . . . will it stand by us?"

CONGRESS VERSUS PRESIDENT

Andrew Johnson was not, alas, the man to ask. In February 1866 he vetoed the Freedmen's Bureau Bill, declaring it unconstitutional because Congress lacked authority to provide a "system for the support of indigent people" and because the states most directly affected by its provisions were not yet represented in Congress. The Bureau was an "immense patronage," showering benefits on blacks never granted to "our own people." Republicans could not muster enough votes to override his veto. A month later, in a further rebuff to his critics, Johnson vetoed Trumbull's Civil Rights Bill, again arguing that federal protection of black civil rights constituted "a stride toward centralization." His racism, hitherto muted, now blazed forth. In his view, granting blacks the privileges of citizenship was discriminatory, operating "in favor of the colored and against the white race" and fraught with evil consequences, including racial mixing.

Galvanized by Johnson's attack on the Civil Rights Bill, the Republicans went into action. In early April they got the necessary two-thirds majorities in both Houses and enacted the Civil Rights Act of 1866. This was a truly historic event, the first time Congress had prevailed over a presidential veto on a major piece of legislation. The Republican resolve was reinforced by news of mounting violence in the South, culminating in three days of bloody rioting in Memphis. In July an angry Congress renewed the Freedmen's Bureau over a second Johnson veto.

Anxious to consolidate their gains, Republicans moved to enshrine black civil rights in an amendment to the Constitution. The heart of the Fourteenth Amendment was Section 1, which declared that "all persons born or naturalized in the United States" were citizens. No state could abridge "the privileges or immunities of citizens of the United States," deprive "any person of life, liberty, or property, without due process of law," or deny anyone "the equal protection of the laws." These phrases were vague, intentionally so, but they established the constitutionality of the Civil Rights Act and, more important, the basis on which the courts and

Congress could over time erect an enforceable standard of equality before the law in the states.

For the moment, however, the Fourteenth Amendment was most important for its impact on national politics. With the 1866 congressional elections approaching, Johnson somehow figured he had a winning issue in the Fourteenth Amendment. He urged the states not to ratify it. Months earlier, Johnson had begun to maneuver politically against the Republicans, aiming to build a coalition of white southerners, northern Democrats, and conservative Republicans under the banner of National Union. Any hope of creating a new national party, however, was shattered by Johnson's intemperate behavior and by escalating violence in the South. A dissension-ridden National Union convention in July ended inconclusively, and Johnson's campaign against the Fourteenth Amendment became, effectively, a campaign for the Democratic Party.

Republicans responded furiously, unveiling an attack that would become known as "waving the bloody shirt." The Democrats were traitors, charged Indiana governor Oliver Morton; their party was "a common sewer and loathesome receptacle into which is emptied every element of treason." In late August Johnson embarked on a disastrous "swing around the circle"—a railroad tour from Washington to Chicago and St. Louis and back. It was unprecedented for a president to campaign personally for his party, and Johnson made matters worse by engaging in shouting matches with hecklers and insulting the hostile crowds.

The 1866 congressional elections inflicted a humiliating defeat on Johnson. The Republicans won a three-to-one majority in Congress, so that, to begin with, the Republicans considered themselves "masters of the situation," free to proceed "entirely regardless of [Johnson's] opinions or wishes." As a referendum on the Fourteenth Amendment, moreover, the election registered overwhelming popular support for securing the civil rights of the former slaves. The Republican Party emerged with a new sense of unity—a unity coalescing not at the center but on the left, around the unbending program of the Radical minority.

The Radicals represented the abolitionist strain within the Republican Party. Most of them hailed from New England or from the area of the upper Midwest settled by New Englanders. In the Senate they were led by Charles Sumner of Massachusetts; in the House, by Thaddeus Stevens from Pennsylvania. For them, Reconstruction was never primarily about restoring the Union but about remaking southern society. "The foundations of their institutions . . . must be broken up and relaid," declared Stevens, "or all our blood and treasure will have been spent in vain."

Only a handful went as far as Stevens in demanding that the plantations be treated as "forfeited estates of the enemy" and broken up into small farms for the former slaves. About protecting the civil rights of the freedmen and granting them the suffrage, however, there was agreement. In this endeavor Radicals had no qualms about using the powers of the federal government. Nor were there qualms about being aggressively partisan. The Radicals regarded the Republican Party as the instrument of the Lord and black votes as the means by which the party would bring about the regeneration of the South.

At first, in the months after Appomattox, few but the Radicals imagined that so extreme a program had any chance of enactment. Black suffrage especially seemed beyond reach, since the northern states themselves (except in New England) denied blacks the vote at this time. And yet, as fury mounted against the intransigent South, Republicans became ever more radicalized until, in the wake of the smashing victory of 1866, they embraced the Radicals' vision of a reconstructed South.

Radical Reconstruction

Afterward thoughtful southerners admitted that the South had brought radical Reconstruction on itself. "We had, in 1865, a white man's government in Alabama," remarked the man who had been Johnson's provisional governor, "but we lost it." The state's "great blunder" was not to "have at once taken the negro right under the protection of the laws." Remarkably, the South remained defiant even after the 1866 congressional elections. Every state legislature (excepting Tennessee) rejected the Fourteenth Amendment, mostly by virtual acclamation. It was as if they could not imagine that governments installed under the presidential imprimatur and fully functioning might be swept away. But that, in fact, is just what the Republicans intended to do.

CONGRESS TAKES COMMAND

The Reconstruction Act of 1867, enacted in March, organized the South as a conquered land, dividing it (with the exception of Tennessee) into five military districts, each under the command of a Union general (see Map 15.1). The price for reentering the Union was granting the vote to the freedmen and disenfranchising the South's prewar political class. Each military commander was ordered to register all eligible adult men (black as well as white), supervise the election of state conventions, and make certain that the new constitutions guaranteed black suffrage. Congress would readmit a state to the Union if its voters ratified the state constitution, if that document proved acceptable to Congress, and if the new state legislature approved the Fourteenth Amendment (thereby ensuring the three-fourths of the states need for ratification). Johnson vetoed the act, but Congress overrode the veto.

Republicans also restricted President Johnson's room for maneuver. The Tenure of Office Act, companion legislation to the Reconstruction Act, ordered the president not to remove without Senate consent any official whose appointment had required Senate confirmation. Congress chiefly wanted to protect Secretary of War Edwin M. Stanton, a Lincoln hold-over and the only member of Johnson's cabinet who favored radical Reconstruction. In his position Stanton could do much

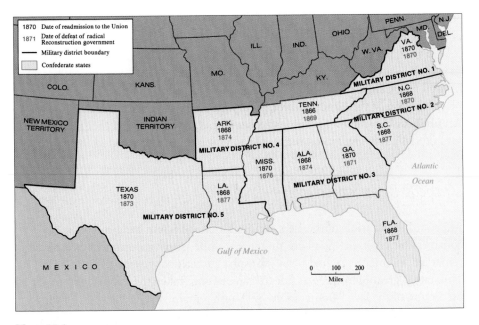

M A P 15.1
Reconstruction

The federal government organized the Confederate states into five military districts during radical Reconstruction. For each state the first date indicates when that state was readmitted to the Union; the second date shows when radical Republicans lost control of the state government. All the ex-Confederate states rejoined the Union from 1868 to 1870, but the periods of radical rule varied widely. Radicals lasted only a few months in Virginia; they held on until the end of Reconstruction in Louisiana, Florida, and South Carolina.

to prevent Johnson from frustrating the goals of Reconstruction. The law also required the president to issue all orders to the army through its commanding general, Ulysses S. Grant. In effect, Congress was attempting to reconstruct the presidency as well as the South.

Seemingly defeated, Johnson appointed generals recommended by Stanton to command the five military districts in the South. But he was just biding his time. In August 1867, after Congress had adjourned, he "suspended" Stanton and replaced him with Grant, believing that the general would be a good soldier and follow orders. Next Johnson replaced four of the commanding generals, including Philip H. Sheridan, Grant's favorite cavalry general. Johnson, however, had misjudged Grant, who publicly registered his opposition to the president's machinations. When the Senate reconvened in the fall, it overruled Stanton's suspension. Grant, now an open enemy of Johnson's, resigned so that Stanton could resume his office.

On February 21, 1868, Johnson dismissed Stanton. The feisty secretary of war barricaded his office and refused to admit the replacement Johnson had appointed.

Resistance in the South

This engraving, entitled *If He Is a Union Man or Freedman: Verdict, Hang the D—Yankee and Nigger,* appeared in *Harper's Weekly* on March 23, 1867, just as the Reconstruction Act was being adopted. Thomas Nast's cartoon encapsulated the outrage at the South's murderous intransigence that led even moderate Republicans to support radical Reconstruction.

(Library of Congress)

Three days later, House Republicans introduced articles of impeachment against President Johnson, employing the power of the Congress under the Constitution to remove high federal officers guilty of "Treason, Bribery, or other high Crimes and Misdemeanors." The House overwhelmingly approved eleven counts of presidential misconduct, nine of which dealt with violations of the Tenure of Office Act.

The case went to the Senate, which acts as the court in impeachment cases, with Chief Justice Salmon P. Chase presiding. After an eleven-week trial, thirty-five senators on May 15 voted for conviction, one vote short of the two-thirds majority required. Seven moderate Republicans broke ranks, voting for acquittal along with twelve Democrats. Congress had removed federal judges from office but never a president. The reluctant Republicans were overwhelmed by the drastic nature of the attack on Johnson. They felt the Tenure of Office Act that Johnson had violated was of dubious validity (in fact, it was subsequently declared unconstitutional by the Supreme Court). The real issue was a political dispute, and removing a president for disagreeing with Congress seemed too extreme, too threatening to the constitutional system of checks and balances, even for the sake of punishing Johnson.

Even without being convicted, however, Johnson had been defanged. For the remainder of his term he was helpless to alter the course of Reconstruction.

The impeachment controversy made Grant, already the North's most popular war hero, a Republican hero as well, and he easily won the party's presidential nomination in 1868. In the fall campaign he supported radical Reconstruction, but he also urged reconciliation between the sections. His Democratic opponent was Horatio Seymour, a former governor of New York and a Peace Democrat who almost declined the nomination, certain that the Democrats could not overcome the stigma of being the party of the disloyal South.

As Seymour feared, the Republicans waved the bloody shirt, stirring up old wartime emotions against the Democrats to great effect. Grant won about the same share of the northern vote (55 percent) that Lincoln had won in 1864 and received 214 of 294 electoral votes. The Republicans also retained two-thirds majorities in both houses of Congress.

In the wake of their smashing victory, the Republicans quickly produced the last major piece of Reconstruction legislation—the Fifteenth Amendment, which forbade either the federal government or the states from denying citizens the right to vote on the basis of race, color, or "previous condition of servitude." The amendment left room for poll taxes and property or literacy tests that could be used to discourage blacks from voting. But its authors did not want to alienate northern states that already relied on such qualifications to keep immigrants and the "unworthy" poor from the polls. A California senator warned that in his state, with its rabidly anti-Chinese sentiment (see Chapter 16), any restriction on that power would "kill our party as dead as a stone."

Despite grumbling by Radical Republicans, the amendment passed without modification in February 1869. Congress required the states still under federal control—Virginia, Mississippi, Texas, and Georgia—to ratify it as a condition of being readmitted to the Union. A year later the Fifteenth Amendment became part of the Constitution.

WOMAN SUFFRAGE DENIED

If the Fifteenth Amendment troubled some proponents of black suffrage, this was nothing as compared to the outrage felt by women's rights advocates. They had fought the good fight for the abolition of slavery for so many years, only to be abandoned by their male allies when their chance finally came; all it would have taken was one more word in the Fifteenth Amendment, so that the protected categories for voting would have read "race, color, *sex,* or previous condition of servitude." Leading suffragists such as Susan B. Anthony and Elizabeth Cady Stanton did not want to hear from Radical Republicans that this was "the Negro's hour" and that women would have to wait for another day. How could the suffrage be granted to former slaves, Elizabeth Cady Stanton demanded, but not to them?

In her despair, Stanton lashed out in ugly terms against "Patrick and Sambo and Hans and Ung Tung," men ignorant of the Declaration of Independence and yet entitled to vote, while the best and most accomplished of American women remained voteless. In 1869 the annual meeting of the Equal Rights Association, the lead organization in the struggle for the rights of blacks and women, broke up in acrimony, and Stanton and Anthony came out against the Fifteenth Amendment.

At this searing moment, a schism opened in the ranks of the women's movement. The majority, led by Lucy Stone and Julia Ward Howe, reconciled themselves to disappointment and accepted the priority of black suffrage. Organized into the American Woman Suffrage Association, these moderates remained allied to the Republican Party in the forlorn hope that once Reconstruction had been settled, it would be time for the woman's vote. The Stanton-Anthony group, however, struck out in a new direction. Stanton declared that woman "must not put her trust in man" in fighting for her rights. The new organization she headed, the New York–based National Women Suffrage Association, accepted only women, focused exclusively on women's rights, and resolutely took up the battle for a federal woman suffrage amendment.

The fracturing of the women's movement obscured the common ground the two sides shared. Both now realized that a broader popular constituency had to be built beyond the small elite of evangelical reformers who had founded the movement. Both elevated suffrage into the preeminent women's issue. And both were energized by a shared anger not evident in earlier times. "If I were to give vent to all my pent-up wrath concerning the subordination of woman," Lydia Maria Child wrote to the Republican warhorse Charles Sumner in 1872, "I might frighten you. . . . Suffice it, therefore, to say, either the theory of our government is *false,* or women have the right to vote." If radical Reconstruction seemed a barren time for women's rights, in fact it had planted the seeds of the modern feminist movement.

THE SOUTH UNDER RADICAL RECONSTRUCTION

Between 1868 and 1871 all the southern states met the congressional stipulations and rejoined the Union. Protected by federal troops and encouraged by northern party leaders, Republican organizations took hold across the South and won control of the newly established Reconstruction governments. These Republican administrations remained in power for periods ranging from a few months in Virginia to nine years in South Carolina, Louisiana, and Florida. Their core support came from African Americans, who constituted a majority of registered voters in Alabama, Florida, South Carolina, Mississippi, and Louisiana and nearly a majority in Georgia, Virginia, and North Carolina.

The southern whites who became Republicans faced the scorn of Democratic former Confederates, who mocked them as *scalawags*—an ancient Scots-Irish term for runty, worthless animals. Whites who had come from the North they denounced as *carpetbaggers*—self-seeking interlopers who carried all their property in cheap cloth suitcases called carpetbags. Such labels glossed over the actual diversity of these groups.

Some carpetbaggers, while motivated by personal gain, also brought capital and skills. Others were Union army veterans taken with the South—its climate, people, and economic opportunities. And interspersed with the self-seekers were many idealists anxious to advance the cause of emancipation.

The scalawags were even more diverse. Some were former slaveowners, ex-Whigs and even ex-Democrats, drawn to Republicanism as the best way to attract northern capital to southern railroads, mines, and factories. In southwest Texas, the large population of Germans was strongly Republican. They sent to Congress Edward Degener, an immigrant and a San Antonio grocer whom Confederate authorities had imprisoned and whose sons had been executed for treason. But most numerous among the scalawags were yeomen farmers from the backcountry who wanted to rid the South of its slaveholding aristocracy. Scalawags had generally fought against (or at least refused to support) the Confederacy; they believed that slavery had victimized whites as well as blacks. "Now is the time," a Georgia scalawag wrote, "for every man to come out and speak his principles publickly and vote for liberty as we have been in bondage long enough."

The Democrats' scorn for black political leaders as ignorant and impressionable field hands was just as ill-founded. The first African American leaders in the South came from an elite of blacks free before the Civil War. They were joined by northern blacks who moved south when radical Reconstruction offered the prospect of meaningful freedom. Some had fought in the antislavery crusade or were Union army veterans; a number were employed by the Freedmen's Bureau or northern missionary societies. Others had escaped from slavery and were returning home, like Blanche K. Bruce, who first taught school in Missouri and then in 1874 became Mississippi's second black U.S. senator.

With the formation of the reconstructed Republican governments, this diverse group of ministers, artisans, shopkeepers, and former soldiers reached out to the freedmen. African American speakers, some financed by the Republican Party, fanned out into the old plantation districts and recruited freed slaves for leadership roles. Still, few among these former slaves had been field hands; most had been preachers or artisans. The literacy of one freedman, Thomas Allen, who was a Baptist minister and shoemaker, helped him win election to the Georgia legislature. "In my county," he recalled, "the colored people came to me for instructions, and I gave them the best instructions I could. I took the *New York Tribune* and other papers, and in that way I found out a great deal, and I told them whatever I thought was right."

Although never proportionate to their size in the population, black office holders held positions of importance throughout the South. In South Carolina African Americans occupied a majority of the seats in one house of the state legislature in 1868. They were heavily represented in states' executive offices, elected three members of Congress, and won a place on the state supreme court. Over the entire course

African American Congressional Delegation, 1872

This Currier and Ives lithograph celebrates one of the notable achievements of radical Reconstruction—the representation that former slaves won, however briefly, in the U.S. Congress. Hiram Revels of Mississippi, the Senate's first African American member, is seated at the extreme left. (Granger Collection)

of Reconstruction twenty African Americans served in the executive branch as governor, lieutenant governor, secretary of state, treasurer, or superintendent of education, more than 600 served as state legislators, and sixteen as Congressmen.

The Republicans who took office had ambitious plans for a reconstructed South. They wanted to end its dependence on cotton agriculture and build instead an industrial economy like the North's. They fell short of achieving this vision but accomplished more than their critics gave them credit for.

The Republicans modernized state constitutions, eliminated property qualifications for the vote, and made more offices elective. They attended especially to the personal freedom of the former slaves, sweeping out the shadow Black Codes that imposed labor discipline on them and limited their mobility. Women also benefited from the Republican defense of personal liberty. Nearly all the new constitutions expanded the rights of married women, enabling them to hold property and personal earnings independent of their husbands. Republican social programs called for hospitals, more humane penitentiaries, and asylums for orphans and the insane.

Reconstruction governments built roads in areas where roads had never existed. They poured money into reviving the region's railroad network. And they did all this without federal financing.

To pay for their ambitious programs, the Republicans copied taxes that Jacksonian reformers had earlier introduced in the North—in particular, general property taxes applying not only to real estate but to personal wealth. The goal was to force planters to pay their fair share of taxes and to force uncultivated land onto the market. In many plantation counties, especially in South Carolina, Louisiana, and Mississippi, former slaves served as tax assessors and collectors, administering the taxation of their onetime owners.

Increasing tax revenues never managed to offset the burgeoning obligations undertaken by the Reconstruction governments. State debts mounted rapidly, and as interest payments on bonds fell into arrears, public credit collapsed. On top of that, much of the spending was wasted or ended in the pockets of state officials. Corruption was endemic to American politics, present in the southern states before the Republicans came on the scene and rampant everywhere in this era, not least in the Grant administration itself. Still, in the free-spending atmosphere of the early Republican regimes, corruption was especially widespread and damaging to the cause of radical Reconstruction.

Nothing, however, could dim the achievement in public education. Here the South had lagged woefully; only Tennessee had a system of public schooling before the Civil War. Republican state governments vowed to make up for lost time, viewing education as the foundation for a democratic order. African Americans of all ages rushed to attend the newly established schools, even when they had to pay tuition. An elderly man in Mississippi explained his desire to go to school: "Ole missus used to read the good book [the Bible] to us . . . on Sunday evenin's, but she mostly read dem places where it says, 'Servants obey your masters.' . . . Now we is free, there's heaps of tings in that old book we is just suffering to learn." By 1875 about half of all the children in Florida, Mississippi, and South Carolina were in classrooms.

The building of schools was part of a larger effort by African Americans to fortify the institutions that had sustained their spirit during the days of slavery. Religious belief had struck deep roots in nineteenth-century slave society. Now, in freedom, the African Americans left the white-dominated congregations, where they had been relegated to segregated balconies and denied any voice in church governance, and built churches of their own. These churches joined together to form African American versions of the Southern Methodist and Southern Baptist denominations, including, most prominently, the National Baptist Convention and the African Methodist Episcopal Church. Everywhere, the robust new churches served not only as places of worship but as schools, social centers, and political meeting halls.

Black ministers were community leaders and often political officeholders. As Charles H. Pearce, a Methodist minister in Florida, declared, "A man in this State cannot do his whole duty as a minister except he looks out for the political interests of his people." Calling for the brotherhood of man and the special destiny of the former slaves as the "Children of Israel," black ministers provided a powerful religious underpinning for the Republican politics of their congregations.

SHARECROPPING

In the meantime, the freedmen were locked in a great economic struggle with their former owners. In 1869 South Carolina established a land commission empowered to buy property and resell it on easy terms to the landless. In this way about 14,000 black families acquired farms. South Carolina's land distribution plan showed what was possible, but it was the exception, not the rule. Despite a lot of rhetoric, Republican regimes elsewhere did little to help the freedmen fulfill their dreams of becoming independent farmers. Federal efforts proved equally feeble. The Southern Homestead Act of 1866 offered 80-acre grants to settlers, limited for the first year to freedmen and southern Unionists. The advantage was mostly symbolic, however, since the public land made available to homesteaders was off the beaten track in swampy, infertile parts of the lower South and since homesteaders lacked the resources to get started. Only about 1,000 homesteading families finally succeeded.

There was no reversing President Johnson's order restoring confiscated lands to the former Confederates. Property rights, it seemed, trumped everything else, even for most radical Republicans. The Freedmen's Bureau, which had earlier championed the land claims of former slaves, now devoted itself to teaching them how to be good agricultural laborers.

So while they yearned for farms of their own, most freedmen started out landless and with no option but to labor for their former owners. But not, they vowed, under the conditions of slavery—no gang work, no overseers, no fines or punishments, no regulation of their private lives or personal freedom. In certain parts of the agricultural South—for example, on the great sugar plantations of Louisiana taken over after the war by northern investors—wage work became the norm. The problem was that cotton planters lacked the money to pay wages, at least not until the crop came in, and sometimes, in lieu of a straight wage, they offered a share of the crop. As a *wage*, this was a bad deal for the freedmen, but if they could be paid in shares for their work, why could they not pay in shares to rent the land they worked?

This form of share tenantry, already familiar in parts of the white South, freedmen now seized on for the independence it offered them. Planters resisted, believing, as one wrote, that "wages are the only successful system of controlling hands." But in a battle of wills that broke out across the cotton South, the planters yielded to "the inveterate prejudices of the freedmen, who desire to be masters of their own time."

Thus there sprang up the distinctive laboring system for cotton agriculture—*sharecropping*, in which the freedmen worked as tenant farmers, exchanging their labor for the use of land, house, implements, sometimes seed and fertilizer, typically turning over half to two-thirds of their harvested crops to the landlord (see Map 15.2). The sharecropping system joined laborers and the owners of land and capital in a common sharing of risks and returns. But it was a very unequal relationship, given the force of southern law and custom on the white landowner's side and given the sharecroppers' dire economic circumstances. Starting out in poverty, they had no way of making it through the first growing season without borrowing for food and supplies.

Country storekeepers stepped in. Bankrolled by their northern suppliers, they "furnished" the sharecropper and took as collateral a *lien* on the crop, effectively assuming ownership of the cropper's share. Under lien laws passed after radical Reconstruction collapsed, sharecroppers received only the proceeds that remained after their debts had been paid. Once indebted at one store, the sharecropper was no longer free to shop around and became an easy target for exorbitant prices, unfair interest rates, and crooked bookkeeping. As cotton prices declined during the 1870s, more and more sharecroppers failed to settle accounts and fell into permanent debt.

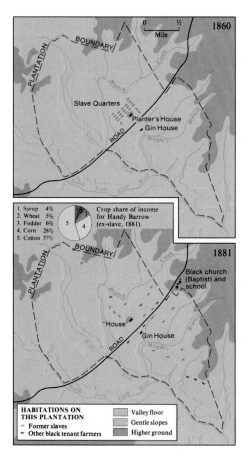

MAP 15.2
The Barrow Plantation, 1860 and 1881

Comparing the 1860 map of this central Georgia plantation with the 1881 map reveals the changing patterns of black residence and farming. In 1860 the slave quarters were clustered near the planter's house, which sat on a small hilltop. The sharecroppers of 1881 built cabins along the spurs or ridges of land between the streams, scattering their community over the plantation. A black church and school were built by this date. A typical sharecropper on the plantation earned most of his income from growing cotton.

Sharecropping

This sharecropping family seems proud of its new cabin and crop of cotton, which it planted in every available bit of ground. But the presence of the white landlord in the background suggests that sharecropping was only a limited kind of economic freedom. (Brown Brothers)

And if the merchant was also the landowner or conspired with the landowner, the debt became a pretext for forced labor, or *peonage*, although evidence now suggests that sharecroppers generally managed to pull up stakes and move on once things became hopeless. Sharecroppers always thought twice about moving, however, because part of their "capital" was being known and well-reputed in their communities. Freedmen who lacked that local standing generally found sharecropping hard going and ended up in the ranks of agricultural laborers.

In the face of all this adversity, the freedpeople struggled to better themselves. The fact that it enabled *family* struggle was, in truth, the saving advantage of sharecropping because it mobilized husbands and wives in common enterprise while shielding both from personal subordination to whites. The trouble with sharecropping, grumbled one planter, was that "it makes the laborer too independent; he becomes a partner, and has to be consulted." By the end of Reconstruction, about one-quarter of sharecropping families had managed to save enough to rent with cash payments, and eventually black farmers owned about a third of the land they cultivated—but rarely the best land and usually at a cost greater than its fertility warranted.

For the freedmen, sharecropping was not the worst choice; it certainly beat wage work for their former owners. But for southern agriculture, the costs were devastating. Sharecropping committed the South inflexibly to cotton, despite soil depletion and unprofitable prices. Crop diversification declined, costing the South its self-sufficiency in grains and livestock. And with farms leased year to year, the tenant had little incentive to improve the property. The crop-lien system lined merchants' pockets with unearned profits that might otherwise have gone into agricultural improvement. The result was a stagnant farm economy, blighting the South's future and condemning it to economic backwardness—a kind of retribution, in fact, for the fresh injustices visited on the people it had once enslaved.

The Undoing of Reconstruction

Former Confederates were blind to the benefits of radical Reconstruction. Indeed, no amount of achievement could have persuaded them that it was anything but an abomination, undertaken without their consent and intended to deny them their rightful place in southern society. Led by the planters, former Confederates staged a massive counterrevolution—one designed to "redeem" the South and restore them to political power under the banner of the Democratic Party. But the Redeemers could not have succeeded on their own. They needed the complicity of the North. The undoing of Reconstruction is as much about northern acquiescence as it is about southern resistance.

COUNTERREVOLUTION

Insofar as they could win at the ballot box, the Democrats took that route. They worked hard to get former Confederates restored to the rolls of registered voters, they appealed to racial solidarity and southern patriotism, and they campaigned against black rule as a threat to white supremacy. But force was equally acceptable. Throughout the Deep South, especially where black voters were heavily concentrated, former Confederate planters and their supporters organized secret societies and waged campaigns of terror against blacks and their white allies.

The most widespread of these groups, the Ku Klux Klan, first appeared in 1866 as a Tennessee social club but quickly became a paramilitary force under Nathan Bedford Forrest, the Confederacy's most decorated cavalry general. Forrest was notorious for a wartime incident at Fort Pillow, Tennessee, when his troops massacred African American soldiers after they had surrendered.

By 1870 the Klan was operating almost everywhere in the South as an armed force serving the Democratic Party. The Klan murdered and whipped Republican politicians, burned black schools and churches, and attacked party gatherings (see American Voices, "The Intimidation of Black Voters"). In October 1870 a group of Klansmen assaulted a Republican rally in Eutaw, Alabama, killing four African Americans and wounding fifty-four. Such terrorist tactics enabled the Democrats to seize power in Georgia and North Carolina in 1870 and make substantial gains

Klan Portrait, 1868

Two armed Klansmen from Alabama pose proudly in their disguises. Northern audiences saw a lithograph based on this photograph in *Harper's Weekly* in December 1868.

(Rutherford B. Hayes Presidential Center, Spiegel Grove, Fremont, Ohio)

elsewhere. An African American politician in North Carolina wrote, "Our former masters are fast taking the reins of government."

Congress responded by passing enforcement legislation, including the Ku Klux Klan Act of 1871, authorizing President Grant to use federal prosecutions, military force, and martial law to suppress conspiracies to deprive citizens of the right to vote, hold office, serve on juries, and enjoy equal protection of the law. Federal agents penetrated the Klan and gathered evidence that provided the basis for widespread arrests; federal grand juries indicted more than 3,000 Klansmen. In South Carolina, where the Klan was most deeply entrenched, federal troops occupied nine counties, driving as many as 2,000 Klansmen from the state.

The Grant administration's assault on the Klan raised the spirits of southern Republicans, but it also emphasized how dependent they were on the federal government. The potency of the Ku Klux Klan Act, a Mississippi Republican wrote, "derived alone from its source" in the federal government. "No such law could be enforced by state authority, the local power being too weak." If Republicans were to prevail over former Confederate terrorists, they needed what one carpetbagger described as "steady, unswerving power from without."

The Intimidation of Black Voters

HARRIET HERNANDES

*T*he *following testimony was given in 1871 by Harriet Hernandes, a black resident of Spartanburg, South Carolina, to the Joint Congressional Select Committee investigating conditions in the South. The terrorizing of black women through rape and other forms of physical violence was among the means of oppression used by the Ku Klux Klan.*

Question: How old are you?
Answer: Going on thirty-four years. . . .
Q: Are you married or single?
A: Married.
Q: Did the Ku-Klux come to your house at any time?
A: Yes, sir; twice. . . .
Q: Go on to the second time. . . .
A: They came in; I was lying in bed. Says he, "Come out here, sir; come out here, sir!" They took me out of bed; they would not let me get out, but they took me up in their arms and toted me out—me and my daughter Lucy. He struck me on the forehead with a pistol, and here is the scar above my eye now. Says he, "Damn you, fall." I fell. Says he, "Damn you, get up." I got up. Says he, "Damn you, get over this fence!" and he kicked me over when I went to get over; and then he went on to a brush pile, and they laid us right down there, both together. They laid us down twenty yards apart, I reckon. They had dragged and beat us along. They struck me right on top of my head, and I thought they had killed me; and I said, "Lord o'mercy, don't, don't kill my child!" He gave me a lick on the head, and it liked to have killed me; I saw stars. He threw my arm over my head so I could not do anything with it for three weeks, and there are great knots on my wrist now.
Q: What did they say this was for?
A: They said, "You can tell your husband that when we see him we are going to kill him. . . ."
Q: Did they say why they wanted to kill him?
A: They said, "He voted the radical ticket [slate of candidates], didn't he?" I said, "Yes," that very way. . . .
Q: When did [your husband] get back home after this whipping? He was not at home, was he?
A: He was lying out; he couldn't stay at home, bless your soul! . . .
Q: Has he been afraid for any length of time?
A: He has been afraid ever since last October. He has been lying out. He has not laid in the house ten nights since October.
Q: Is that the situation of the colored people down there to any extent?
A: That is the way they all have to do—men and women both.
Q: What are they afraid of?
A: Of being killed or whipped to death.
Q: What has made them afraid?

A: Because men that voted radical tickets they took the spite out on the women when they could get at them.

Q: How many colored people have been whipped in that neighborhood?

A: It is all of them, mighty near.

SOURCE: *Report of the Joint Congressional Select Committee to Inquire into the Condition of Affairs in the Late Insurrectionary States, House Reports,* 42d Cong., 2d sess. (Washington, DC: U.S. Government Printing Office, 1972), vol. 5, South Carolina, December 19, 1871.

But northern Republicans were growing weary of Reconstruction and the bloodshed it seemed to produce. Although reelected handily in 1872, Grant did not see his victory as a mandate for an endless war against the white South. Prosecuting Klansmen under the enforcement acts was an uphill battle. U.S. attorneys usually faced all-white juries, and the Justice Department lacked the resources to prosecute effectively. After 1872, prosecutions dropped off, and many Klansmen received hasty pardons; only a small fraction served significant prison terms.

The faltering zeal for Reconstruction stemmed from more than discouragement about prosecuting the Klan, however. The worst depression in the nation's history struck in 1873, and the North became preoccupied with its own economic problems. Northern business interests complained that the turmoil of Reconstruction retarded the South's economic recovery and harmed their investment opportunities. Sympathy for the freedmen also began to wane. The North was flooded with one-sided, often racist reports, such as James M. Pike's *The Prostrate State* (1873), describing extravagant, corrupt Republican rule and a South in the grip of "a mass of black barbarism." In the 1874 elections, the Republicans suffered a crushing defeat, losing control of the House of Representatives for the first time since secession and also losing seven normally Republican states to the Democrats. For party strategists, the political costs in a disillusioned North began to outweigh their hopes for a Republican-dominated South.

In a kind of self-fulfilling prophesy, the unwillingness of the Grant administration to shore up Reconstruction guaranteed that it would fail. Republican governments that were denied federal help found themselves overwhelmed by massive resistance from former Confederates. Democrats overthrew Republican governments in Texas in 1873, in Alabama and Arkansas in 1874, and in Mississippi in 1875.

The Mississippi campaign showed all too clearly what the Republicans were up against. As elections neared in 1875, paramilitary groups such as the Rifle Clubs and Red Shirts operated openly. Often local Democrats paraded armed, as if they were militia companies. They identified black leaders in assassination lists called "dead-books," broke up Republican meetings, provoked rioting that left hundreds of African Americans dead, and threatened voters, who still lacked the protection of the secret ballot. Mississippi's Republican governor, Adelbert Ames, a Congressional Medal of Honor winner from Maine, appealed to President Grant for federal troops, but Grant refused. Ames then contemplated organizing a state militia but ultimately decided against it, believing that only blacks would join and that the state would be plunged into racial war. Brandishing their guns and stuffing the ballot boxs, the Redeemers swept the 1875 elections and took command of Mississippi. Facing impeachment by the new Democratic legislature, Governor Ames resigned his office and returned to the North.

THE POLITICAL CRISIS OF 1877

Northerners were not much troubled by the South's counterrevolution. National politics had moved on, and other concerns absorbed voters. Foremost was the stench of scandal that hung over the White House. In 1875 Grant's secretary of the treasury, Benjamin Bristow, exposed the so-called Whiskey Ring, a network of distillers and government agents who had defrauded the U.S. Treasury of millions of dollars of excise taxes on liquor. The ringleader was a Grant appointee, and Grant's own private secretary, Orville Babcock, had a hand in the thievery. The others went to prison, but Grant stood by Babcock, possibly perjuring himself to save his secretary. On top of this, the economic depression deepened. Grant's administration responded ineffectually, rebuffing the pleas of debtors for relief by increasing the money supply (see Chapter 18).

Among the casualties of the bad economy was the Freedman's Savings and Trust Company, which had been sponsored by the Freedmen's Bureau and held the small deposits of thousands of former slaves. When the bank failed in 1874, Congress refused to compensate the depositors, and many lost their life savings. In denying the depositors' pleas, Congress was signaling that Reconstruction had lost its moral claim on the country.

Abandoning Grant, the Republicans in 1876 nominated Rutherford B. Hayes, governor of Ohio, a colorless figure but untainted by corruption, or by strong convictions—in a word, a safe man. His Democratic opponent was Samuel J. Tilden, governor of New York, a wealthy lawyer with ties to Wall Street and a reform reputation for helping to break the hold of the thieving Tweed Ring over New York City politics. The Democrat Tilden favored "home rule" for the South, but so, more discreetly, did the Republican Hayes. Reconstruction actually did not figure prominently in the campaign and was mostly subsumed under broader Democratic charges of "corrupt centralism" and "incapacity, waste, and fraud." By now, Republicans had written off the South and scarcely campaigned there. They paid little attention to the states still ruled by Reconstruction governments—Florida, South Carolina, and Louisiana.

Once the returns started coming in on election night, however, those three states began to loom very large indeed. Tilden led in the popular vote, and with victories in key northern states, he seemed headed for the White House. But sleepless politicians at Republican headquarters realized that if they kept Florida, South Carolina, and Louisiana, Hayes would win by a single electoral vote. The campaigns in those states had been bitterly fought, with the same kinds of Democratic assaults on blacks that had overturned Republican regimes everywhere else in the South. But Republicans still controlled the election machinery in those states, and citing Democratic fraud and intimidation they could certify Republican victories. Late on election night the audacious announcement came forth from Republican headquarters: Hayes had carried the three southern states and won the election. But newly elected Democratic officials in the three states also sent in electoral votes for Tilden. When Congress met in early 1877, it faced two sets of electoral votes from those states.

The Constitution did not provide for this contingency. All it said was that the President of the Senate (in 1877, a Republican) opens the electoral certificates before the House (Democratic) and the Senate (Republican) and that "The votes shall then be counted." An air of crisis gripped the country. There was talk of inside deals, of a new election, even of a violent coup and civil war. Just in case, the commander of the army, General William T. Sherman, deployed four artillery companies in Washington. Finally, Congress decided to appoint an electoral commission to settle the question. The commission included seven Republicans, seven Democrats, and, as the deciding member, David Davis, a Supreme Court justice not known to have fixed party loyalties. But Davis disqualified himself by accepting an Illinois seat in the Senate. He was replaced by Republican Justice Joseph P. Bradley, and by a vote of 8 to 7, the commission awarded the disputed votes to Hayes.

Outraged Democrats had one more trick up their sleeves. They controlled the House, and they set about stalling a final count of the electoral votes so as to prevent Hayes's inauguration on March 4, 1877. But a week earlier, secret talks had begun between southern Democrats and Ohio Republicans representing Hayes. Other issues may have been on the table, but the main thing was the situation in South Carolina and Louisiana, where rival governments were encamped at the state capitols, with federal soldiers holding the Democrats at bay. Exactly what deal was struck or how involved Hayes himself was will probably never be known, but on March 1 the House Democrats suddenly ended their filibuster, the ceremonial counting of votes went forward, and Hayes was inaugurated on schedule. He soon ordered the Union troops back to their barracks, and the Republican regimes in South Carolina and Louisiana fell. Reconstruction had ended.

In 1877 political leaders on all sides seemed ready to say that what Lincoln had called "the work" was complete. But for the freedmen, the work had only begun. Reconstruction turned out to have been a magnificent aberration, a magnum jump beyond what most white Americans actually felt was due their black fellow citizens. Redemption represented a sad falling back to the norm. Still, something real had been achieved—three rights-defining amendments to the Constitution, some elbow room to advance economically, and, not least, a stubborn confidence among

TIMELINE

Year	Event	Year	Event
1863	Lincoln's Ten Percent Plan	1870	Ku Klux Klan at peak of power
1864	Wade-Davis Bill "pocket"-vetoed by Lincoln.		Congress responds with Enforcement Acts.
			Fifteenth Amendment ratified
1865	Freedmen's Bureau established	1872	Grant reelected president.
	Lincoln assassinated	1873	Panic of 1873 ushers in depression of 1873–77.
	Andrew Johnson becomes President and implements his restoration plan.		
1866	Civil Rights Act passes over Johnson's veto.	1874	Democrats gain majority in House of Representatives.
	Johnson makes disastrous "swing around the circle."	1875	Whiskey Ring scandal undermines Grant administration.
	Congressional elections repudiate Johnson.	1876	Disputed presidential election
1867	Reconstruction Acts	1877	Congressional compromise makes Rutherford B. Hayes president. Reconstruction ends.
1868	Impeachment crisis		
	Fourteenth Amendment ratified		
	Ulysses S. Grant elected president		

blacks that by their own efforts they could lift themselves up. Things would, in fact, get worse before they got better, but the work of Reconstruction was imperishable and could never be erased.

For Further Exploration

The best current book on Reconstruction is Eric Foner's major synthesis, *Reconstruction: America's Unfinished Revolution, 1863–1877* (1988), available also in a shorter version. *Black Reconstruction in America* (1935), by the African American activist and scholar W. E. B. Du Bois, deserves attention as the first book to challenge traditional racist interpretations of Reconstruction and stress the role of blacks in their own emancipation. For the presidential phase of Reconstruction, see Dan T. Carter, *When the War Was Over: The Failure of Self-Reconstruction in the South, 1865–1867* (1985). On the freedmen, Leon F. Litwack, *Been in the Storm So Long: The Aftermath of Slavery* (1979), provides a stirring account. More recent emancipation studies emphasize slavery as a labor system: Julie Saville, *The Work of Reconstruction; From Slave to Wage Laborer in South Carolina, 1860–1870* (1994), and Amy Dru Stanley, *From Bondage to Contract* (1999), which expands the discussion to show what the onset of wage labor meant for freedwomen. Eric Foner, *Nothing But Freedom: Emancipation and Its Legacy* (1983), helpfully places emancipation in a comparative context. William S. McFeely, *Grant: A Biography* (1981), deftly explains the politics of Reconstruction. The emergence of the sharecropping system is explored in Gavin Wright, *Old South, New South* (1986), and Edward Royce *The Origins of Southern Sharecropping* (1993). On the Compromise of 1877, see C. Vann Woodward's classic *Reunion and Reaction* (1956). Two informative websites are <http://womhis .binghampton.edu/intro.htm>, which deals with northern women who assisted the freedpeople, and <1cweb2.loc.gov/ammen/aaohtml/aollist.html>, which provides Library of Congress documents and illustrations on African Americans during Reconstruction.

Part Four

A MATURING INDUSTRIAL SOCIETY
1877–1914

THEMATIC TIMELINE

	ECONOMY	SOCIETY	CULTURE
	THE TRIUMPH OF INDUSTRIALIZATION	RACIAL, ETHNIC, AND GENDER DIVISIONS	THE RISE OF THE CITY
1877	• Andrew Carnegie launches modern steel industry. • Knights of Labor becomes national movement (1878).	• Struggle for black equality defeated • Nomadic Indian life ends.	• National League founded (1876) • Dwight L. Moody pioneers urban revivalism.
1880	• Gustavus Swift pioneers vertically integrated firm. • American Federation of Labor (1886)	• Chinese Exclusion Act (1882) • Dawes Severalty Act divides tribal lands (1887).	• Electrification transforms city life. • First *Social Register* defines high society (1888).
1890	• United States surpasses Britain in iron and steel output. • Economic depression (1893–1897) • Era of farm prosperity begins.	• Black disfranchisement and segregation in the South • Immigration from southeastern Europe rises sharply.	• Settlement houses spread progressive ideas to cities. • William Randolph Hearst's *New York Journal* pioneers yellow journalism.
1900	• Great industrial merger movement • Immigrants dominate factory work. • Industrial Workers of the World (1905)	• Women lead social reform. • Struggle for civil rights revived • Movement to restrict immigration	• Muckraking journalism • Movies begin to overtake vaudeville.
1910	• Henry Ford builds first automobile assembly line.	• NAACP (1910) • Women vote in western states. • World War I ends European migration.	• Urban liberalism

GOVERNMENT	DIPLOMACY
FROM INACTION TO PROGRESSIVE REFORM	AN EMERGING WORLD POWER
• Election of Rutherford B. Hayes ends Reconstruction.	• United States becomes a net exporter.
• Ethnocultural issues dominate state and local politics. • Civil service reform (1883)	• Diplomacy of inaction • Naval buildup begins.
• Populist Party founded (1892) • William McKinley wins presidency; defeats Bryan's free silver crusade (1896).	• Social Darwinism and Anglo-Saxonism promote expansion. • Spanish-American War (1898–1899); conquest of the Philippines.
• Progressivism in national politics • Theodore Roosevelt attacks the trusts. • Hepburn Act regulates railroads (1906).	• Panama cedes Canal Zone to United States (1903). • Roosevelt Corollary to Monroe Doctrine (1904)
• Woodrow Wilson elected (1912) • New Freedom legislation creates Federal Reserve, FTC.	• Taft's diplomacy promotes U.S. business. • Wilson proclaims U.S. neutrality in World War I.

While the nation was absorbed by the political drama of Reconstruction, few people noticed an equally momentous watershed in American economic life. For the first time, as the decade of the 1870s passed, farmers no longer constituted a majority of working Americans. Henceforth, America's future would be linked to its development as an industrial society.

The effects of accelerating industrialization were felt, first of all, in the manufacturing sector itself. Production became increasingly mechanized and increasingly directed at making the capital goods that undergirded economic growth. As the railroad system was completed, modern organizational and management techniques began to dominate American enterprise. The labor movement became firmly established, and as immigration surged, the foreign-born and their children became America's workers. What had been partial and limited now became general and widespread as America turned into a land of factories, corporate enterprise, and industrial workers.

The final surge of western settlement across the Great Plains was largely driven by the pressures of this industrializing economy. Cities demanded new sources of food; factories, the Far West's mineral resources. Defending their way of life, western Indians were ultimately defeated not so much by army rifles as by the unceasing encroachment of railroads, mines, ranches, and proliferating farms. These same forces disrupted the old established Hispanic communities of the Southwest but spurred Asian, Mexican, and European migrations that made for a multiethnic western society.

Industrialization also transformed the nation's urban life. By 1900 one in five Americans lived in cities. That was where the jobs were—as workers in the factories; as clerks and salespeople; as members of a new salaried middle class of managers, engineers, and professionals; and at the apex as a wealthy elite of investors and entrepreneurs. The city was more than just a place to make a living, however. It provided a setting for an urban lifestyle unlike anything seen before in America.

The unfettered, booming economy of the Gilded Age tended at first to marginalize political life. The major parties remained robust not because they stood for much programmatically but because they exploited a culture of popular participation and embraced the ethnocultural interests of their constituencies. The depression of the 1890s triggered a major challenge to the political status quo by the agrarian Populist Party, with its demand for free silver. The election of 1896 turned back that challenge and established the Republicans as the dominant national party.

Still unresolved, however, was the threat that corporate power posed to the marketplace and democratic politics. How to curb the trusts dominated national debate during the Progressive Era. In those years, too, the country took a critical look at its institutions and began to address its social ills. From different angles political reformers, women progressives, and urban liberals went about the business of cleaning up machine politics and making life better for America's urban masses. African Americans, disfranchised and segregated, found allies among white progressives and launched a new drive for racial equality.

Finally, the dynamism of America's economic development decisively altered the country's foreign relations. In the decades after the Civil War, America had been inward-looking, neglectful of its navy and inactive diplomatically. The business crisis of the 1890s, however, brought home the need for a more aggressive foreign policy that would advance the nation's overseas economic interests. In short order the United States went to war with Spain, acquired an overseas empire, and became actively engaged in Latin America and Asia. There was no mistaking America's standing as a Great Power and as World War I approached no evading the responsibilities and entanglements that came with that status.

Chapter 16

THE AMERICAN WEST

Who are to go there? The territory consists of mountains almost inaccessible, and low lands . . . where rain never falls, except during spring. . . . Why, sir, sir, of what use will this be for agricultural purposes? I would not, for that purpose, give a pinch of snuff for the whole territory.

—SENATOR GEORGE MCDUFFIE SPEAKING IN CONGRESS
ABOUT ACQUIRING CALIFORNIA FROM MEXICO, 1843

During the last decades of the nineteenth century American society seemed at odds with itself. From one angle the nation looked like an advanced industrial power, with humming factories and enormous, crowded cities. But from another angle America remained a frontier country, with pioneers streaming onto the Great Plains, repeating the old dramas of "settlement" they had been performing ever since Europeans had first set foot on the continent. Not until the census of 1890 did the federal government declare that a "frontier of settlement" no longer existed: the country's "unsettled area has been so broken into . . . that there can hardly be said to be a frontier line."

That same year, 1890, the country surpassed Great Britain in the production of iron and steel. Newspapers reported Indian wars and labor strikes in the same edition. The last tragic episode in the suppression of the plains Indians, the Sioux massacre at Wounded Knee, South Dakota, occurred only eighteen months before the great Homestead steel strike of 1892. This alignment of events from the distant worlds of factory and frontier was not accidental. The final surge of settlement across the Great Plains and the Far West was driven primarily by the dynamism of American industrialism.

The Great Plains

During the 1860s agricultural settlement reached the western margins of the high-grass prairie country, roughly at the ninety-eighth meridian. Beyond stretched vast, arid plains. It seemed no place for farmers accustomed to forested land and ample rainfall (see Map 16.1).

460

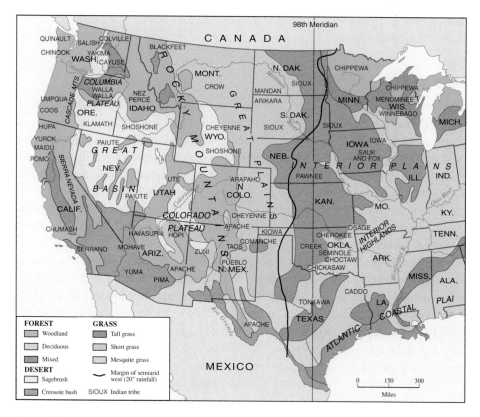

MAP 16.1
The Natural Environment of the West

As settlers pushed into the Great Plains beyond the line of semiaridity, they sensed the over-whelming power of the natural environment. In a landscape without trees for fences and barns and without adequate rainfall, ranchers and farmers had to relearn their business. The Native Americans peopling the plains and mountains had in time learned to live in this environment, but this knowledge counted for little against the ruthless pressure of the settlers to domesticate the West.

The geologic event that created the Great Plains had occurred 60 million years earlier when the Rocky Mountains had been thrust up out of the ocean covering western North America. With no outlet the shallow inland sea to the east dried up, forming a hard pan on which sediment washing down from the mountains built up a loose, featureless surface layer. The mountain barrier also made for a dry cli-mate because the moisture-laden winds from the Pacific spent themselves on the western slopes. Only vegetation capable of withstanding drought and bitter winters could take hold on the plains. Short Gramma grass, the linchpin of this fragile ecosystem, matted the easily blown soil into place and sustained a rich wildlife dom-inated by the grazing antelope and buffalo. What the dry short-grass country had not sustained, until Indians began migrating there three centuries earlier, was human settlement.

INDIANS OF THE GREAT PLAINS

Probably 100,000 Native Americans lived on the Great Plains at mid-nineteenth century. They were a diverse people, divided into six linguistic families and at least thirty tribal groupings. On the eastern margins and along the Missouri River, the Mandans, Arikaras, and Pawnees planted corn and beans and lived in permanent villages. Smallpox and measles brought by Europeans ravaged these settled tribes. Less vulnerable to epidemics were the nomadic tribes that had first arrived on the Great Plains in the seventeenth century: Kiowas and Comanches in the southwest; Arapahos and Cheyennes on the central plains; and to the north Blackfeet, Crows, Cheyennes, and the great Sioux nation.

Originally the Sioux had been eastern prairie people, occupying settlements in the lake country of northern Minnesota. With fish and game dwindling, some Sioux tribes drifted westward and around 1760 began to cross the Missouri River. These Sioux became a nomadic people, living in portable skin tepees and following the buffalo. From tribes to the southwest, they acquired horses. Once mounted, the Sioux became splendid hunters and formidable fighters, claiming the entire Great Plains north of the Arkansas River as their hunting grounds.

The westernmost Sioux—they called themselves the Teton people, or Lakotas (meaning "allies")—made up a loose confederation of seven tribes. In the winter months the tribes broke up into small bands, but each spring they assembled and prepared for the summer hunt and for battle. Raiding parties rode forth intent on capturing ponies and taking scalps, but occasionally long columns of warriors mounted territorial campaigns against rival tribes. The Sioux, it must be remembered, were an invading people who dominated the northern Great Plains by driving out or subjugating longer-settled tribes.

A society that celebrates the warrior virtues is likely to define gender roles sharply. But before the Sioux acquired horses, chasing down the buffalo demanded the cooperation of the entire community, so that hunting could not be an exclusively male enterprise. It took the efforts of both women and men to construct the "pounds" into which, beating the brush side by side, they endeavored to stampede the herds. Once they had horses, the men rode out on the chase while the women remained in the encampment, laboring on the mounting piles of buffalo skins the hunters brought back. This was hard and painstaking work. Fanny Kelly, once a Sioux captive, considered the women's lives "a servitude," but she also noticed their high temper and independence. Subordination to men was not how Sioux women understood their unrelenting labor; it was their allotted share in a partnership on which the proud, nomadic life of the Sioux depended.

Living so close to nature, depending on its bounty for survival, the Sioux saw sacred meaning in every manifestation of the natural world. Unlike Europeans they conceived of a god who was not a supreme being but, in the words of the ethnologist Clark Wissler, was "a controlling power or series of powers pervading the universe"—Wi, the sun; Skan, the sky; Maka, the earth; Inyan, the rock. Below these came the moon, the wind, the buffalo, down through a hierarchy embodying the entire natural order.

By prayer and fasting Sioux prepared themselves to commune with these mysterious powers. Medicine men provided instruction, but the religious experience was personal and open to both sexes. The vision, when a supplicant achieved it, attached itself to some object—a feather, the skin of an animal, or a shell—that was tied into a sacred bundle that became the person's lifelong talisman. In the Sun Dance the entire tribe celebrated the rites of coming of age, fertility, the hunt, and combat, followed by four days of fasting and dancing in supplication to Wi, the sun.

The world of the Teton Sioux was not self-contained. All along they had exchanged pelts and buffalo robes for the produce of agriculturalist Mandans and Pawnees. When white traders appeared on the upper Missouri River during the eighteenth century, the Sioux began to trade with them as well. Although the buffalo remained their staff of life, the Sioux came to rely on manufactured pots, kettles, blankets, knives, and firearms. The trade system they entered was linked to the Euro-American market economy, yet it was also integrated into the Sioux way of life. Everything depended on the survival of the Great Plains as the Sioux had found it—wild grassland on which the antelope and buffalo ranged free.

WAGON TRAINS, RAILROADS, AND RANCHERS

On first encountering the Great Plains, Euro-Americans themselves thought the place best left to the Indians. After exploring a drought-stricken stretch in 1820, Major Stephen H. Long declared it "almost wholly unfit for cultivation, and of course uninhabitable by a people depending upon agriculture for their subsistence."

For years thereafter maps marked the plains region as the Great American Desert. With that notion in mind Congress formally designated the Great Plains in 1834 as permanent Indian country. Trade with the Indians would continue but now closely supervised and licensed by the federal government, with the Indian country otherwise off limits to whites.

Events swiftly overtook the nation's solemn commitment to the native Americans. During the 1840s settlers began moving westward to Oregon and California. Instead of serving as a buffer against the British and Mexicans, the Indian country became a bridge to the Pacific. The first wagon train headed west for Oregon from Missouri in 1842. Soon thousands of emigrants traveled the Oregon Trail to the Willamette Valley or cutting south beyond Fort Hall down into California. Approaching that juncture in 1859, it seemed to Horace Greeley as if "the white coverings of the many emigrant and transport wagons dott[ing] the landscape" gave "the trail the appearance of a river running through great meadows, with many ships sailing on its bosom." Only these "ships" left behind not a trailing wake of foam but a rutted landscape devoid of game and littered with abandoned wagons and rotting garbage.

Talk about the need for a railroad to the Pacific soon began to be heard in Washington. How else could the distant territories formally acquired from Mexico and Britain in 1848 be firmly linked to the Union or the ordeal of overland travel be alleviated? The project languished while North and South argued over the terminus for the route to the Pacific. Meanwhile, the Indian country was crisscrossed by overland freight lines, and pony express riders delivered mail between Missouri and California. In 1861 telegraph lines brought San Francisco into instant communication with the East. The next year, with the South in rebellion and no longer a factor, the federal government finally went forward with the transcontinental project.

No private company could be expected to foot the bill by itself. The construction costs were staggering, and in the short run not much traffic could be expected on the thinly populated route. So the federal government awarded generous land grants along the right of way plus millions of dollars in loans to the two companies that undertook the transcontinental project.

The Union Pacific, building westward from Omaha, made little headway until the Civil War ended but then advanced rapidly across Indian country, reaching Cheyenne, Wyoming, in November 1867. It took the Central Pacific nearly that long, moving eastward from Sacramento, to cross the crest of the Sierra Nevada. Both then worked furiously—since the government subsidy was based on miles of track laid—until, to great fanfare, the tracks met at Promontory Point, Utah, in 1869. No other land-grant railroads made it as far as the Rockies before the Panic of 1873 hit, throwing them into bankruptcy and bringing work to an abrupt halt.

By then, however, railroad tycoons had changed their minds about the Great Plains. No longer did they see it through the eyes of the Oregon-bound settlers—as a place to be gotten through en route to the Pacific. Rail transportation, they realized, was laying the basis for the economic exploitation of the Great Plains. This calculation spurred the railroad boom that followed economic recovery in 1877. Construction soared. During the 1880s, 40,000 miles of track were laid west of the Mississippi, linking southern California via the Southern Pacific Railroad to New Orleans and via the Santa Fe Railroad to Kansas City and linking the Northwest via the Northern Pacific Railroad to St. Paul, Minnesota.

Of all the beckoning opportunities, most obvious was cattle raising. The grazing buffalo made it easy to imagine the Great Plains as cow country. But first the buffalo had to go. A small market for buffalo robes had existed for years. Then in the early 1870s eastern tanneries discovered how to cure the hides, sparking a huge demand from shoe and harness manufacturers. The systematic slaughter of the buffalo began. Already diminished by disease and shrinking pasturage, the great herds almost vanished within ten years. Many people spoke out against this mass killing, but no way existed to stop hunters bent on making a quick dollar. Besides, as General Philip H. Sheridan pointed out, exterminating the buffalo would starve the Indians into submission.

Killing the Buffalo

This woodcut shows passengers shooting buffalo from a Kansas Pacific Railroad train—a small thrill added to the modern convenience of traveling west by rail.

(North Wind Picture Archives)

In south Texas about 5 million head of longhorn cattle grazed on Anglo ranches, hardly worth bothering about because they could not be profitably marketed. In 1865, however, the Missouri Pacific Railroad reached Sedalia, Missouri, far enough west to be accessible across open land to the Texas herds. At the Sedalia railhead, which connected to eastern markets, a longhorn worth $3 in Texas might command $40. With this incentive, Texas ranchers inaugurated the famous Long Drive, hiring cowboys to herd cattle hundreds of miles north to the railroads that were pushing west across Kansas.

At Abilene, Ellsworth, and Dodge City ranchers sold their cattle, and trail-weary cowboys went on a binge. These cattle towns captured the nation's imagination as symbols of the Wild West. The reality was much more ordinary. The cowboys, many of them African Americans and Hispanics, were in fact farm hands on horseback, working long hours under harsh conditions for small pay. Colorful though it seemed, the Long Drive was actually a makeshift means of bridging a gap in the developing transportation system. As soon as railroads reached the Texas range country during the 1870s, ranchers abandoned the Long Drive.

The Texas ranchers owned or leased the land they used, sometimes in huge tracts. North of Texas, where the land was in the public domain, cattlemen simply helped themselves, treating the land as a free commodity for anyone able to put it to use. Hopeful ranchers would spot a likely area along a creek and claim as much land as they could qualify for as settlers under federal homesteading laws, plus what might be added by fraudulent claims taken out by one or two ranch hands. By a custom that quickly became established, ranchers had a "range right" to all the adjacent land rising up to the divide—the point where the land sloped down to the next creek.

The Cowboy at Work

The cowboy, celebrated in dime novels, was really a farm hand on horseback, with the skills to work on the range, including the ability to stay glued to his saddle while lassoing a steer. He earned $25 a month, plus meals and a bed in the bunkhouse, in return for long hours of lonesome, grueling work. But one can see in Charles Russell's vivid painting, *Jerked Down* (1907), why the cowhand could so readily be converted into a western hero.
(Thomas Gilcrease Institute of American History and Art)

News of easy money traveled fast. Calves cost only $5 a head, while steers sold for maybe $60 on the Chicago market. Rail connections were in place or coming in. And the grass was free. Profits of 40 percent per annum seemed sure. The rush was on, attracting from as far away as Europe both shrewd investors and romantics (like the recent Harvard graduate Teddy Roosevelt) eager for a taste of the Wild West. By the early 1880s the plains overflowed with cattle, decimating the grass and trampling the water holes.

A cycle of good weather only postponed the inevitable disaster. When it came— a hard winter in 1885, a severe drought the following summer, then record blizzards and bitter cold—cattle died by the hundreds of thousands. An awful scene of rotting carcasses greeted the cowhands riding out onto the range the following spring. Beef prices plunged when hard-pressed ranchers dumped the surviving cattle on the market. The boom collapsed, and investors fled, leaving behind a more enduring ecological disaster: the native grasses never recovered from the relentless overgrazing in the drought cycle.

Open-range ranching came to an end. Ranchers fenced their land and planted hay for the winter. No longer would cattle be left to fend for themselves on the open range. Hispanic grazers from New Mexico brought sheep in to feed on the mesquite and prickly pear that had replaced the native grasses. Sheep raising, previously scorned by ranchers as unmanly and resisted as a threat to cattle, became a major enterprise in the sparser high country. Some ranchers even sold out to the despised "nesters"—those who wanted to try farming the Great Plains.

HOMESTEADERS

Potential settlers, of course, needed first of all to be persuaded that crops would grow in that dry country. Powerful interests devoted themselves to overcoming the notion of a Great American Desert. Foremost were the railroads, eager to sell off the public land they had been granted—180 million acres of it—and develop traffic for their routes. They advertised aggressively, offered cut-rate tickets, and sold off their land holdings at bargain prices. Land speculators, steamship lines, and the western states and territories did all they could to encourage settlement of the Great Plains. So did the federal government, with its offer under the Homestead Act (1862) of 160 acres of public land to settlers.

"Why emigrate to Kansas?" asked a testimonial in *Western Trail*, the Rock Island Railroad's gazette. "Because it is the garden spot of the world. Because it will grow anything that any other country will grow, and with less work. Because it rains here more than any other place, and at just the right time."

As if to confirm the optimists, an exceptionally wet cycle occurred between 1878 and 1886. "As the plains are settled up we hear less and less of drouth, hot winds, alkali and other bugbears that used to hold back the adventurous," remarked one Nebraska man. Some settlers attributed the increased rainfall to soil cultivation and tree planting. Others credited God. As one settler remarked, "The Lord just knowed we needed more land an' He's gone and changed the climate."

No amount of optimism, however, could dispel the pain of migration. "That last separating word *Farewell!* sinks deeply into the heart," one pioneer woman recorded in her diary, thinking of family and friends left behind. But then came the treeless plains. "Such an air of desolation," wrote a Nebraska-bound woman; and from another woman in Texas, "Such a lonely country." To a Swedish emigrant like Ida Lindgren (see American Voices, "Swedish Emigrant in Frontier Kansas"), no place could have seemed farther from home or offered less hope of seeing family and friends again.

For some women this hard experience had a liberating side. Prescribed gender roles broke down as women shouldered men's work and became self-reliant in the face of danger and hardship. When husbands died or gave up, wives operated farms on their own. Under the Homestead Act, which accorded widows and single women the same rights as men, women filed 10 percent of the claims. "People afraid of coyotes and work and loneliness had better leave ranching alone," advised one woman homesteader. "At the same time, any woman who can stand her own company . . . will certainly succeed; will have independence, plenty to eat all the time, and a home of her own in the end."

Even with a man around, however, women contributed crucially to the farm enterprise. Farming might be thought of as a dual economy, in which men's labor

AMERICAN VOICES

Swedish Emigrant in Frontier Kansas

IDA LINDGREN

L *ike many emigrants, Ida Lindgren did not find it easy to adjust to the harsh new life on the frontier. Her diary entries and letters home show that the adjustment for the first generation was never complete.*

May 15, 1870 [Lake Sibley, Nebraska]

What shall I say? Why has the lord brought us here? Oh, I feel so oppressed, so unhappy! . . . We drove across endless, endless prairies, on narrow roads; no, no, not roads, tracks like those in the fields at home when they harvested grain. No forest but only a few trees which grow along the rivers and creeks. And then here and there you see a homestead and pass a little settlement. . . .

No date [probably written July 1870]

Claus and his wife lost their youngest child at Lake Sibley and it was very sad in many ways. There was no real cemetery but out on the prairie stood a large, solitary tree, and around it they bury their dead, without tolling of bells, without a pastor, and sometimes without any coffin. A coffin was made here for their child, it was not painted black, but we lined it with flowers and one of the men read the funeral service, and then there was a hymn, and that was all.

August 25, 1874 [Manhattan, Kansas]

It has been a long time since I have written, hasn't it? . . . When one never has anything fun to write about, it is no fun to write. . . . We have not had rain since the beginning of June, and then with this heat and often strong winds as well, you can imagine how every- thing has dried out. . . . Then one fine day there came millions, trillions of grasshoppers in great clouds, hiding the sun, and coming down into the fields, eating up everything that was still there, the leaves on the trees, peaches, grapes, cucumbers, onions, cabbage, every- thing, everything. Only the peach stones still hung on the trees, showing what had once been there.

July 1, 1877 [Manhattan, Kansas]

. . . It seems so strange to me when I think that more than seven years have passed since I have seen you all. . . . I can see so clearly that last glimpse I had of Mamma, standing alone amid all the tracks of Eslov station. Oliva I last saw sitting on her sofa in her red and black dress, holding little Brita, one month old, on her lap. And Wilhelm I last saw in Lund at the station, as he rolled away with the train, waving his last farewell to me. . . .

SOURCE: H. Arnold Barton, ed., *Letters from the Promised Land* (Minneapolis: University of Minnesota Press, 1975), pp. 143–45, 150–56.

brought in the big wage at harvest time while women's labor provisioned the family day by day and produced a steady bit of money for groceries. And if the crop failed, it was women's labor that carried the family through. No wonder farming communities placed a high premium on marriage: a mere 2.4 percent of Nebraska women in 1900 had never married.

Male or female, the vision of new land beckoned people onto the plains. By the 1870s the older agricultural states had filled up, and farmers looked hungrily westward. The same excitement took hold in northern Europe. Germans came and also, for the first time, Russians, Norwegians, and Swedes. At the peak of the "American fever" in 1882 over 105,000 Scandinavians emigrated to the United States. Swedish and Norwegian became the primary languages in parts of Minnesota and the Dakotas. Roughly a third of the farmers on the northern plains were foreign-born.

The motivation for most settlers, American or European, was to better themselves economically. But for some southern blacks Kansas briefly represented something more precious—a new promised land of Canaan. In the spring of 1879, with Reconstruction over and federal protection withdrawn, black communities fearful of white vengeance were swept by religious enthusiasm for Kansas. Within a month or so some 6,000 blacks from Mississippi and Louisiana had arrived via St. Louis, most of them with nothing more than the clothes on their backs and faith in the Lord. How many of these Exodusters remained is hard to say, but the 1880 census reported 40,000 blacks in Kansas—by far the largest African American concentration in the West aside from Texas, whose expanding cotton frontier attracted hundreds of thousands of black migrants during the 1870s and 1880s.

No matter where they came from, homesteaders found the plains an alien land. A cloud of grasshoppers might descend and destroy a crop in a day; a brushfire or hailstorm could do the job in an hour. What forested land had always provided—springs for water, lumber for cabins and fencing, ample firewood—was absent. For shelter settlers often cut dugouts into hillsides and, after a season or two, erected sod houses made of turf.

The absence of trees, on the other hand, meant an easier time clearing the land. New technology overcame obstacles once thought insurmountable: steel plows enabled homesteaders to break the tightly matted ground, barbed wire provided cheap fencing against roaming cattle. Strains of hard-kernel wheat tolerant of the extreme temperatures of the plains came from Europe. Homesteaders harvested good crops while the wet cycle held and began to anticipate the wood-frame house, deep well, and full coal bin that might make life tolerable on the plains.

Then in the latter 1880s the dry years came and shattered those hopeful calculations. "From day to day," reported the budding novelist Stephen Crane from Nebraska, "a wind hot as an oven's fury . . . raged like a pestilence," destroying the crops and leaving farmers "helpless, with no weapon against this terrible and inscrutable wrath of nature." Land only recently settled emptied out as homesteaders fled in defeat. The Dakotas lost 50,000 settlers between 1885 and 1890, and comparable departures occurred up and down the drought-stricken plains.

Buffalo Chips

With no trees around for firewood, settlers on the plains had to make do with dried cow and buffalo droppings. Gathering the "buffalo chips" must have been a regular chore for Ada McColl on her homestead near Lakin, Kansas (1893).

(The Kansas State Historical Society, Topeka)

Other settlers held on grimly. Stripped of the illusion that rain followed the plow, the survivors came to terms with the semiarid climate prevailing west of the ninety-eighth meridian. Mormons in the area near the Great Salt Lake (see Chapter 12) had demonstrated how irrigation could turn a wasteland into a garden. But the Great Plains generally lacked the surface water needed for irrigation. The answer lay in dry-farming methods, which involved deep planting to bring subsoil moisture to the roots and quick harrowing after rainfalls to turn over a dry mulch that slowed evaporation. Dry farming developed most fully on the corporate farms that covered up to 100,000 acres in the Red River Valley in North Dakota. But in semiarid country even family farms were not viable with less than 300 acres of cereal crops and machinery for plowing, planting, and harvesting. Dry farming was not for the unequipped homesteader.

By the turn of the century the Great Plains had fully submitted to agricultural development. About half the nation's cattle and sheep, a third of its cereal crops, and nearly three-fifths of its wheat came from the newly settled lands. In this process there was little of the "pioneering" that Americans associated with the westward movement. The railroads came before the settlers, eastern capital financed the ranching bonanza, and agriculture depended on sophisticated dry-farming techniques and modern machinery.

And where was the economic capital of the Great Plains? Far off in Chicago. There, at the hub of the nation's rail system, the wheat pit traded western grain and consigned it to world markets; the great packing houses slaughtered western cattle and supplied the nation with sausage, bacon, and sides of beef. In return western farmers and ranchers got lumber, barbed wire, McCormick reapers, and Sears Roebuck catalogues. Chicago was truly "nature's metropolis."

THE FATE OF THE INDIANS

What of the Native Americans who had inhabited the Great Plains? Basically, their history has been told in the foregoing account of western settlement. "The white children have surrounded me and have left me nothing but an island," lamented the great Sioux chief Red Cloud in 1870, the year after the completion of the transcontinental railroad. "When we first had all this land we were strong; now we are all melting like snow on a hillside, while you are grown like spring grass."

Settlement occurred despite the provisions for a permanent Indian country that had been written into federal law and ratified by treaties with various tribes. As incursions into their lands increased from the late 1850s onward, the Indians resisted as best they could, striking back all along the frontier: the Apaches in the Southwest, the Cheyennes and Arapahos in Colorado, the Sioux in the Wyoming and Dakota territories. Indians hoped that if they resisted stubbornly enough and exacted a high enough price, whites would tire of the struggle and leave them in peace. This reasoning seemed not altogether fanciful, given the country's exhaustion after the Civil War. But the federal government did not give up; instead, it formulated a new reservation policy for dealing with the western Indians.

Few whites questioned the necessity of moving the Native Americans out of the path of settlement and into reservations. That, indeed, had been the fate of the eastern and southern tribes. Now, however, Indian removal included something new: a planned approach for weaning the Indians from their tribal way of life. To this end a peace commission was appointed in 1867 to end the fighting and negotiate treaties by which the western Indians would cede their lands and move to reservations. There, under the guidance of the Office of Indian Affairs, they would be wards of the government until they learned "to walk on the white man's road."

The government set aside two extensive areas. It allocated the southwestern quarter of the Dakota Territory—present-day South Dakota west of the Missouri River—to the Teton Sioux tribes. And it assigned what is now Oklahoma to the southern plains Indians as well as to the Five Civilized Tribes—the Choctaws, Cherokees, Chickasaws, Creeks, and Seminoles—who had been forceably removed there thirty years before (see Chapter 11). Scattered reservations went to the Apaches, Navahos, and Utes in the Southwest and to the mountain Indians in the Rockies and beyond.

That the Indians would resist was inevitable. "You might as well expect the rivers to run backward as that any man who was born a free man should be contented when penned up and denied liberty to go where he pleases," said Chief Joseph of the Nez Percé, who led his people in 1877 on a remarkable 1,500-mile march from eastern Oregon almost to Canada trying to escape confinement on a small reservation.

The U.S. Army was thinly spread, having been cut after the Civil War to a total force of 27,000. But these were seasoned troops, including 2,000 black cavalry-
men of the Ninth and Tenth Regiments, whom Indians called, with grim respect,
"buffalo soldiers." Technology also favored the army. Telegraph communications
and railroads enabled the troopers to concentrate quickly; repeating rifles and
Gatling machine guns increased their firepower. As fighting intensified in the mid-
1870s, a reluctant Congress appropriated funds for more western troopers. Because
of tribal rivalries, the army could always find Indian allies. Worst of all for the
Indians, however, beyond the formidable U.S. Army or their own disunity, was the
overwhelming impact of white settlement.

Resisting the reservations, the Indians fought on for years—in Kansas in 1868
and 1869, in the Red River Valley of Texas in 1874, and sporadically in New Mexico
among the Apaches until the capture of Geronimo in 1886. On the northern plains
the crisis came in 1875, when the Indian Office, despite an 1868 treaty guarantee,
ordered the Sioux to vacate their Powder River hunting grounds and withdraw to
the reservation.

Led by Sitting Bull, Sioux and Cheyenne warriors gathered on the Little Big
Horn River to the west of the Powder River country. In a typical concentrating maneuver, army columns from widely separated forts converged on the Little Big Horn
from three sides. The Seventh Cavalry, commanded by George A. Custer, came upon
the main Sioux encampment on June 25, 1876. Disregarding orders the reckless
Custer sought out battle on his own. He attacked from three sides, hoping to capitalize on the element of surprise. But his forces were stretched too thin. Two groups
fell back to defensive positions, but Custer's force of 256 men was surrounded and
annihilated by Crazy Horse's warriors. It was a great Indian victory but not a decisive one. The day of reckoning was merely postponed.

Pursued by the military and physically exhausted, the Sioux bands one by one
gave up and moved onto the reservation. Last to give up were Sitting Bull's followers. They had retreated to Canada, but in 1881 after five hard years they recrossed
the border and surrendered at Fort Buford, Montana.

Not Indian resistance but white land hunger wrecked the reservation solution. In the mid-1870s prospectors began to dig gold in the Black Hills—sacred
ground to the Sioux and entirely inside their reservation. Unable to hold back
the prospectors or to buy out the Sioux, the government opened up the Black
Hills to gold seekers at their own risk. In 1877 after Sioux resistance had
crumbled, federal agents forced the tribes to cede the western third of their
Dakota reservation.

The Indian Territory of Oklahoma met the same fate. Two million acres in the
heart of the territory had not been assigned to any tribe, and white homesteaders
coveted that fertile land. The "Boomer" movement, stirred up initially by railroads
operating in the Indian Territory, agitated tirelessly to open this so-called Oklahoma
District. In 1889 the government gave in and placed the Oklahoma District under
the Homestead Act. On April 22, 1889, a horde of claimants rushed in and staked

out the entire district within a few hours. Two tent cities—Guthrie with 15,000 people and Oklahoma City with 10,000—were in full swing by nightfall.

The completion of the land-grabbing process was hastened, ironically, by the avowed friends of the Native Americans. The Indians had never lacked sympathizers, especially in the East. After the Civil War reformers created the Indian Rights Association. The movement got a boost from Helen Hunt Jackson's powerful book *A Century of Dishonor* (1881), which told the story of the unjust treatment of the Indians. The reformers, however, had little sympathy for the tribal way of life. They could imagine no other future for the Indian than assimilation into white society (see American Voices, "Becoming White"). And this in turn required that Native Americans enjoy the same rights and have the same benefit of private property as did all American citizens.

The resulting policy called for the division of reservation lands into individually owned parcels. With the blessing of reformers the Dawes Act of 1887 authorized the allotment of tribal lands, with 160 acres for each family head and smaller parcels for individuals. The land would be held in trust by the government for twenty-five years, and the Indians would become U.S. citizens. Remaining reservation lands would be sold off, with the proceeds placed in an Indian education fund.

The Sioux were among the first to bear the brunt of the Dawes Act. The federal government, announcing that it had gained tribal approval, opened their "surplus" land to white settlement on February 10, 1887. But no surveys had been made nor any provision for the Indians living in the ceded areas. On top of these signs of bad faith drought wiped out the Indians' crops. It seemed beyond endurance: they had lost their ancestral lands, they faced a future as farmers that was alien to all their traditions, and immediately confronting them was a winter of starvation.

But news of salvation had also come. An Indian messiah, a holy man who called himself Wovoka, was preaching a new religion on a Paiute reservation in Nevada. In a vision Wovoka had gone to heaven and received God's word that the world would be regenerated. The whites would disappear, all the Indians of past generations would return to earth, and life on the Great Plains would be as it was before the white man appeared. All this would come to pass in the spring of 1891. Awaiting that great day the Indians should follow Wovoka's commandments and practice the Ghost Dance, a daylong ritual that sent the spirits of the dancers rising to heaven. As the frenzy of the Ghost Dance swept through the Sioux encampments in the fall of 1890, resident whites became alarmed and called for army intervention.

Wovoka had an especially fervent following in the Minneconjou tribe, where the medicine man Yellow Bird held sway. But their chief Big Foot had fallen desperately ill with pneumonia, and the Minneconjous agreed to come in under military escort to an encampment at Wounded Knee Creek on December 28. The next morning when the soldiers attempted to disarm the Indians, a battle exploded in the camp. Among the U.S. troopers, 25 died; among the Indians, 146 men, women, and children perished, many of them shot down as they fled.

AMERICAN VOICES

Becoming White

ZITKALA-SA (GERTRUDE SIMMONS BONNIN)

Z itkala-Sa, afterward the author Gertrude Simmons Bonnin, recalled in 1900 her painful transformation from Sioux child to pupil at a mission school.

The first day . . . a paleface woman, with white hair, came up after us. We were placed in a line of girls who were marching into the dining room. These were Indian girls, in stiff shoes and closely clinging dresses. The small girls wore sleeved aprons and shingled hair. As I walked noiselessly in my soft mocassins, I felt like sinking into the floor, for my blanket had been stripped from my shoulders. . . . Late in the morning, my friend Judewin gave me a terrible warning. Judewin knew a few words of English; and she had overheard the paleface woman talk about cutting our long, heavy hair. Our mothers had taught us that only unskilled warriors who were captured had their hair shingled by the enemy. Among our people, short hair was worn by mourners, and shingled hair by cowards! . . . In spite of myself, I was carried downstairs and tied fast in a chair. I cried aloud, shaking my head all the while until I felt the cold blades of the scissors against my neck, and heard them gnaw off one of my thick black braids. Then I lost my spirit. . . .

Now, as I look back upon the recent past, I see it from a distance, as a whole. I remember how, from morning till evening, many specimens of civilized peoples visited the Indian school. The city folks with canes and eyeglass, the countrymen with sunburned cheeks and clumsy feet . . . alike astounded at seeing the children of savage warriors so docile and industrious. . . .

In this fashion many have passed through the Indian schools during the last decade, afterward to boast of their charity to the North American Indian. But few there are who have paused to question whether real life or long lasting death lies beneath this semblance of civilization.

SOURCE: Linda K. Kerber and Jane De-Hart Mathews, eds., *Women's America: Refocusing the Past*, 2d ed. (New York: Oxford University Press, 1987), pp. 254–57.

Wounded Knee was the final episode in the long war of suppression of the plains Indians. The division of communal lands now proceeded without hindrance. In the Dakota Territory the Teton Sioux fared relatively well, and many of the younger generation settled down as small farmers and stock raisers. Ironically, the more fortunate tribes were probably those occupying poor land that did not attract white settlement and thus were spared the allotment process. The flood of whites into South Dakota and Oklahoma, on the other hand, left the Indians as small minorities in lands once wholly theirs—20,000 Sioux in a South Dakotan population of 400,000 in 1900, 70,000 of various tribes in a population of a million when Oklahoma became a state in 1907.

The Far West

On the western edge of the Great Plains, the Rocky Mountains rise up to form a great barrier between the mostly flat eastern two-thirds of the country and the Far West. Beyond the Rockies lie two vast plateaus, the Columbian plateau extending into eastern Oregon and Washington and, flanking the southern Rockies, the Colorado plateau. Where they break off, the plateaus carve out the desertlike Great Basin that covers western Utah and all of Nevada. Separating this arid interior from the Pacific Ocean are two great mountain ranges—the Sierra Nevada and, to the north, the Cascades—beyond which lies a coastal region that is cool and rainy to the north but increasingly dry southward, until in southern California rainfall becomes almost as sparse as in the interior.

What most impressed Americans about this far western country was its sheer inhospitability. The transmountain West could not be occupied in standard American fashion—that is, by a multitude of settlers moving westward along a broad front, blanketing the land and, homestead by homestead, bringing it under cultivation. The wagon trains moving to Oregon's Willamette River Valley adopted an entirely different method of occupation—the planting of scattered settlements in a vast, mostly barren landscape.

New Spain had pioneered this strategy when in 1598 it had sent the first contingents of soldiers and settlers 700 miles northward from Mexico into the upper Rio Grande Valley. When the United States seized the Southwest 250 years later, major Hispanic settlements existed in New Mexico and California, with lesser settlements scattered along the borderlands into south Texas. At that time, aside from Oregon, the only significant Anglo settlement was around the Salt Lake in Utah, where Mormons had moved to escape persecution and plant a New Zion. Fewer than 100,000 Euro-Americans—roughly 25,000 of them Anglo, the rest Hispanic—lived in the entire Far West when it became U.S. territory in 1848.

THE MINING FRONTIER

More emigrants would be coming certainly, but the Far West seemed unlikely to be much of a magnet. California was "hilly and mountainous," noted a U.S. naval officer in 1849, too dry for farming and surely not "susceptible of supporting a very large population." He had not taken account of the recent discovery of gold in the Sierra foothills, however. California would indeed support a very large population, drawn not by the lure of arable land but by dreams of gold.

Extraction of mineral wealth became the basis for the Far West's development (see Map 16.2). This meant, first of all, explosive growth. By 1860, when the Great Plains was still Indian country, California was a booming state with 300,000 residents. There was also a burst of city building. Overnight San Francisco became a bustling metropolis—it had 57,000 residents by 1860—and was the hub of a mining empire that stretched to the Rockies. The distinctive pattern of geographically

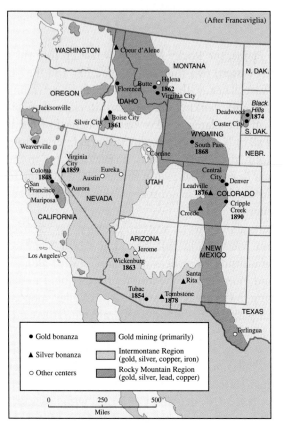

M A P 16.2
The Mining Frontier, 1848–1890

The Far West was America's gold country because of its geological history. Veins of gold and silver form when molten material from the earth's core is forced up into fissures caused by the tectonic movements that create mountain ranges, such as the ones that dominate the far western landscape. It was these veins, the product of mountain-forming activity many thousands of years earlier, that prospectors began to discover after 1848 and furiously exploit. Although widely dispersed across the Far West, the lodes that they found followed the mountain ranges, bisecting the region and bypassing the great plateaus not shaped by the ancient tectonic activity.

dispersed settlement persisted, driven now, however, by a proliferation of mining sites and by people moving not east to west but west to east, coming mainly from California.

By the mid-1850s as easy pickings in the California gold country diminished, prospectors began to pull out and spread across the West in hopes of striking it rich elsewhere. Gold was discovered on the Nevada side of the Sierras, in the Colorado Rockies, and along the Fraser River in British Columbia. New strikes occurred in Montana and Wyoming during the 1860s, a decade later in the Black Hills of South Dakota, and in the Coeur d'Alene region of Idaho during the 1880s.

As the news of each gold strike spread, a wild, remote area turned almost overnight into a mob scene of prospectors, traders, gamblers, prostitutes, and saloon keepers. At least 100,000 fortune seekers flocked to the Pike's Peak area of Colorado in the spring of 1859. Trespassers on government or Indian land, the prospectors made their own law. The mining codes devised at community meetings limited the size of a mining claim to what a person could reasonably work. This kind of informal lawmaking also became an instrument for excluding or discriminating against Mexicans, Chinese, and African Americans in the gold fields. And it turned into hangman's justice for the many outlaws who infested the mining camps.

The heyday of the prospectors at each site was always brief. They were equipped only to skim gold from stream beds and surface outcroppings. Extracting the metal locked in underground lodes required mine shafts and crushing mills—and hence capital, technology, and business organization. The original claim holders quickly sold out when a generous bidder came along, as gold-rush prospecting gave way to entrepreneurial development and large-scale mining. Rough camps turned into big towns.

Nevada's Virginia City, for example, started out as a bawdy, ramshackle mining camp, but with the opening of the Comstock silver lode in 1859 it soon boasted a stock exchange, ostentatious mansions for the mining kings, fancy hotels, and even Shakespearean theater. Virginia City remained a boomtown nevertheless. It was a magnet for job seekers of both sexes: men laboring as miners at $4 a day; the wage-earning women, many of them, becoming dance-hall entertainers and prostitutes because that was the best they could do in Virginia City. In 1870 a hundred saloons operated day and night, brothels lined D Street, and men outnumbered women two to one.

In its final stage the mining frontier entered the industrial economy. At some sites gold and silver proved less profitable than the commoner metals—copper, lead, zinc—for which there was a huge demand in manufacturing industries. Copper mining thrived in the Butte district of Montana. In the 1890s the Coeur d'Alene silver district became the nation's main source of lead and zinc. Entrepreneurs raised capital, built rail connections, devised new extraction methods for the lower-grade copper deposits, constructed smelting facilities, and recruited a labor force.

Western miners were industrial workers, and like other workers they organized trade unions. But relations with management, once they soured during the depressed 1890s, became unusually violent. In 1892 at Coeur d'Alene, Idaho, striking miners fought gun battles with company guards, sent a car of explosive powder careening into the Frisco mine, and threatened to blow up the smelters. Martial law was declared, strikers were crowded into "bullpens" (enclosed stockades), and the strike was broken. Similarly violent strikes took place in 1894 at Cripple Creek, Colorado, in 1896 at Leadville, Colorado, and again at Coeur d'Alene in 1899.

But for its mineral wealth the Far West's history would certainly have been very different. Before the discovery of gold at Sutter's mill Oregon's Willamette River Valley, not dry California, attracted most westward-bound settlers. And without the gold rush California would likely have remained like the Willamette Valley—an economic backwater with no markets for its products and a slow-growing population. In 1860, although already a state, Oregon had scarcely 25,000 inhabitants, and its principal city, Portland, was little more than a village. Booming California and its tributary mining country pulled Oregon from the doldrums by creating a market for the state's produce and timber. During the 1880s Oregon and Washington (which became a state in 1889) grew prodigiously. Where scarcely 100,000 settlers had lived twenty years earlier, there were by 1890 nearly three-quarters of a million. Portland and, even more dramatically, Seattle blossomed into important commercial centers, both prospering from a robust mixed economy of farming, ranching, logging, and fishing.

At a certain point, especially as railroads opened up eastern markets, this diversified growth became self-sustaining. But what had triggered it, what had provided the first markets and underwritten the economic infrastructure, was the bonanza mining economy, at the hub of which stood San Francisco, metropolis for the entire Far West.

HISPANICS, CHINESE, ANGLOS

The first Europeans to enter the Far West—two centuries before the earliest Anglos —were Hispanics moving northward out of Mexico. There, along a 1,500-mile southwestern borderland, outposts had been planted over many years by the viceroys of New Spain. Most populous and best established were the settlements along New Mexico's upper Rio Grande Valley; the main town, Santa Fe, was over 200 years old and contained 4,635 residents in 1860. Farther down the Rio Grande was El Paso, nearly as old but much smaller, and to the west in present-day Arizona, Tucson, an old presidio, or garrison, town. At the western end of this Hispanic crescent, in California, a Spanish-speaking population was spread thinly in presidio towns along the coast and on a patchwork of great ranches.

The economy of the Hispanic Southwest was pastoral, consisting primarily of cattle and sheep ranching. In south Texas there were family-run ranches. Everywhere else the social order was highly stratified. At the top stood an elite, beneficiaries of royal land grants, proudly Spanish, devoted to the traditional life of a landed aristocracy. Below them, with little in between, was a laboring population of servants, artisans, vaqueros (cowboys), and farm hands. New Mexico also contained a large mestizo population—people of mixed Hispanic and Indian blood. They were a Spanish-speaking and Catholic peasantry but still faithful in their village life and farming methods to their Pueblo heritage.

Pueblo Indians, although their dominance of the Rio Grande Valley had long passed, still occupied much of the region, living in the old ways in abobe villages and making the New Mexico countryside a patchwork of Hispanic and Pueblo settlements. To the north a vibrant new people, the Navajos, had appeared, warriors like the Apaches from whom they had sprung but also skilled at crafts and sheep raising.

New Mexico was one place where European and native American cultures managed a successful, if uneasy, coexistence and where the Indian inhabitants were equipped to hold their own against the Anglo challenge. In California, by contrast, the Hispanic occupation was harder on the indigenous hunter-gatherer peoples, undermining their tribal structure, reducing them to coerced labor, and making them easy prey for the aggressive Anglo miners and settlers, who, in short order, nearly wiped out California's once numerous Indian population.

The fate of the Hispanic Southwest after its incorporation into the United States depended on the rate of Anglo immigration. In New Mexico, which remained off the beaten track even after the arrival of railroads in the 1880s, the Santa Fe elite more than held its own, incorporating the Anglo newcomers into Hispanic society through intermarriage and business partnerships. In California, on the other hand, the expropriation of the great ranches was relentless, even though the 1848 peace treaty with Mexico had recognized the property rights of the *californios* and had made them U.S. citizens. Around San Francisco the ranch system disappeared almost in a puff of smoke. Farther south, where Anglos were slow to arrive, the dons held on longer, but by the 1880s just a handful of the original families still retained their Mexican land grants.

The New Mexico peasants found themselves equally embattled. Crucial to their livelihood were grazing rights on communal lands. But these were customary rights that could not withstand legal challenge when Anglo ranchers established title and began putting up fences. The peasants responded resiliently. Their subsistence economy relied on a division of labor that gave women a central productive role in the village economy. Women tended the small gardens, engaged in village bartering, and maintained the households. With the loss of the communal lands the men began migrating seasonally to railway work or the Colorado mines and sugar-beet fields, earning crucial dollars while leaving the village economy in their wives' hands.

Elsewhere, hard-pressed Hispanic inhabitants struck back for what they considered rightfully theirs. When Anglo ranchers began to fence in communal lands in San Miguel County, the New Mexicans long settled there, *los pobres* (the poor ones), organized themselves as masked raiders and in 1889 and 1890 mounted an effective campaign of harassment against the interlopers. After 1900 when Anglo farmers swarmed into south Texas bent on exploiting new irrigation methods, the displaced *Tejanos* responded with sporadic but persistent night-riding attacks. Much of the raiding by Mexican "bandits" from across the border in the years before World War I was really more in the nature of a civil war by embittered *Tejanos* who had lived north of Rio Grande for generations.

But they, like the New Mexico villagers who became seasonal wage laborers, could not avoid being driven into the ranks of a Mexican American working class as the Anglo economy developed. This same development also began to attract increasing numbers of immigrants from Old Mexico.

All along the Southwest borderlands economic activity was picking up in the late nineteenth century. Railroads were being built, copper mines opening in Arizona, cotton and vegetable agriculture developing in south Texas, and fruit growing in southern California. In Texas the Hispanic population increased from about 20,000 in 1850 to 165,000 in 1900. Some came as contract workers for railway gangs and harvest crews; virtually all were relegated to the lowest-paying and most backbreaking work; and everywhere they were discriminated against and reviled by higher-status Anglo workers.

What stimulated the Mexican migration, of course, was the enormous demand for workers by a region undergoing explosive development, which also accounted for the high numbers of European immigrants in the West. In California where they were most heavily concentrated, roughly one-third of the population was foreign-

Mexican Miners

When large-scale mining began to develop in Arizona and New Mexico in the late nineteenth century, Mexicans crossed the border to earn Yankee dollars. In this unidentified photograph from the 1890s the men are wearing traditional clothing, indicating perhaps that they are recent arrivals at the mine. (Wyoming State Archives, Department of State Parks and Cultural Resources)

born, more than twice the level for the country as a whole. Many came from Europe. Most numerous were the Irish, followed by the Germans and British. But there was also another immigrant group unique to the West—the Chinese.

Attracted first by the California gold rush of 1849, 200,000 Chinese came to the United States over the next three decades. In those years they constituted a considerable minority of California's population—around 9 percent—and because virtually all were actively employed, they represented a much larger proportion of the state's labor force, probably a quarter. Elsewhere in the West, at the crest of mining activity, their presence could surge spectacularly—for example, to over 25 percent of Idaho's population in 1870.

The arrival of the Chinese in North America was part of a worldwide Asian migration that began in the mid-nineteenth century. Driven by poverty Chinese went to Australia, Hawaii, and Latin America; Indians went to Fiji and South Africa; and Javanese to Dutch colonies in the Caribbean. Most of these Asians migrated as indentured servants, which in effect made them the property of others. In America, however, indentured servitude was no longer lawful—by the 1820s state courts were ruling that it constituted involuntary servitude—so the Chinese came as free workers. Their passage was financed by a *credit-ticket system,* by which they borrowed passage money from a broker while retaining their personal freedom and right to choose their employers.

Once in America, however, Chinese immigrants normally entered the orbit of the Six Companies—a powerful confederation of Chinese merchants in San Francisco's Chinatown. Most of the arrivals were unattached males eager to earn a stake and return to their native Cantonese villages. The Six Companies acted not only as an employment agency but provided new arrivals with the social and commercial services they needed to survive in an alien world. The few Chinese women—the male to female ratio was thirteen to one—worked mostly as servants and prostitutes, sad victims of the desperate poverty that drove the Chinese to America. Some were sold by impoverished parents; others were tricked by procurers and transported to America.

Until the early 1860s when surface mining played out, Chinese men labored mainly in the California gold fields—as prospectors where the white miners permitted it, as laborers and cooks where they did not. Then, when construction began on the transcontinental railroad, the Central Pacific hired Chinese workers. Eventually they constituted four-fifths of the railroad's labor force, doing most of the pick-and-shovel labor laying the railroad track across the Sierras. Many were recruited directly from around Canton by labor agents to work in gangs run by "China bosses," who not only supervised but fed, housed, paid, and often cheated them.

When the transcontinental railroad was completed in 1869, the Chinese scattered. Some stayed in railway construction gangs, while others labored on swamp-drainage projects in the Central Valley, worked as agricultural workers, and, if they were lucky, became small farmers and orchardists. The mining districts of Idaho, Montana, and Colorado also attracted large numbers of Chinese, but according to the 1880 census nearly three-quarters remained in California. "Wherever we put them, we found them good," remarked Charles Crocker, one of the promoters of the Central Pacific. "Their orderly and industrious habits make them a very desirable class of immigrants."

White workers, however, did not share the employers' enthusiasm for the Chinese. In other parts of the country racism was directed against African Americans; in California, where there were few blacks, it found a target in the Chinese. "They practice all the unnameable vices of the East," wrote the young journalist Henry George. "They are utter heathens, treacherous, sensual, cowardly and cruel." Sadly, this vicious racism was intertwined with labor's republican ideals. The Chinese, argued George, would drive out free labor, "make nabobs and princes of our capitalists, and crush our working classes into the dust . . . substitut[ing] . . . a population of serfs and their masters for that population of intelligent freemen who are our glory and our strength."

The anti-Chinese frenzy climaxed in San Francisco in the late 1870s when mobs ruled the streets. The fiercest agitator, an Irish teamster named Denis Kearney, quickly became a dominant figure in the California labor movement. Under the slogan "The Chinese Must Go!" Kearney led a Workingmen's Party against the state's major parties. Democrats and Republicans, however, jumped on the bandwagon, joining together in 1879 to write a new state constitution replete with anti-Chinese provisions and pressuring Washington to take up the issue. In 1882 Congress finally passed the Chinese Exclusion Act, which barred the further entry of Chinese laborers into the country.

The injustice of this law—no other nationality was similarly targeted—rankled the Chinese. Why us, protested one woman to a federal agent, and not the Irish, "who [are] always drunk and fighting?" Middle-class and American-born Chinese, who were free to come and go, routinely registered a newly born son after each trip to China, enabling many an unrelated "paper son" to enter the country. Even so, resourceful as the Chinese were at evading the exclusion law, the flow of immigrants slowed to a trickle.

But the job opportunities that had attracted the Chinese to America did not subside. If anything, the West's agricultural development intensified the demand for cheap labor, especially in California, which was shifting from wheat, the state's first great cash crop, to fruits and vegetables. Such intensive agriculture required lots of workers—stoop labor, meagerly paid, and mostly seasonal. This was not, as one San Francisco journalist put it, "white men's work." That ugly phrase serves as a touchstone for California agricultural labor as it would thereafter develop—a kind of caste labor system, always drawing some downtrodden, footloose whites, yet basically defined along color lines.

But if not the Chinese, then who? First, Japanese immigrants, who came in increasing numbers and by the early twentieth century constituted half the state's agricultural labor force. Then, when anti-Japanese agitation closed off that population flow in 1908, Mexico became the next, essentially permanent, source of migratory workers for California's booming commercial agriculture.

The irony of the West's social evolution is painful to behold. Here was a land of limitless opportunity, boastful of its democratic egalitarianism, and yet simultaneously, and from its very birth, a racially torn society, at once exploiting and despising the Hispanic and Asian minorities whose hard labor helped make the Far West the enviable land it was.

GOLDEN CALIFORNIA

Life in California contained all that the modern world of 1890 had to offer—cosmopolitan San Francisco, comfortable travel, a high living standard, colleges and universities, even resident painters and writers. Yet California was still remote from the rest of America, still a long journey away, and, of course, differently and spectacularly endowed by nature. Location, environment, and history all conspired to set California somewhat apart from the American nation. And so, in certain ways, did the Californians.

What Californians yearned for was a cultural tradition of their own. Closest to hand was the bonanza era of the forty-niners, captured on paper by one Samuel Clemens. Clemens did a bit of prospecting, became a reporter, and adopted the pen name Mark Twain. Listening to the old miners of Angel's Camp in 1865, Twain jotted one tale down in his notebook, as follows:

> Coleman with his jumping frog—bet stranger $50—stranger had no frog, and C. got him one:—in the meantime stranger filled C's frog full of shot and he couldn't jump. The stranger's frog won.

In Twain's hands, this fragment was transformed in 1875 into a tall tale that caught the imagination of the country and made his reputation as a humorist. "The Celebrated Jumping Frog of Calaveras County" somehow encapsulated the entire world of make-or-break optimism in the mining camps.

In short stories such as "The Luck of Roaring Camp" and "The Outcasts of Poker Flat," Twain's fellow San Franciscan Bret Harte developed this theme in a more literary fashion and firmly implanted it in California's memory. But this past was too raw, too suggestive of the tattered beginnings of so many of the state's leading citizens—in short, too disreputable—for an up-and-coming society.

Then in 1884 Helen Hunt Jackson published her novel *Ramona*. In this story of a half-Indian girl caught between two cultures, Jackson intended to advance the cause of the Native Americans, but she placed her tale in the evocative context of Old California, and that rang a bell. By then the chain of missions planted by the Catholic Church had been long abandoned. The padres were wholly forgotten, their Indian converts scattered and in dire poverty. Now that lost world of "sun, silence and adobe" became all the rage. Sentimental novels and histories appeared in abundance. There was a movement to restore the missions. Many communities began to stage Spanish fiestas, and the mission style of architecture enjoyed a great vogue among developers.

In its Spanish past California found the cultural traditions it needed. The same kind of discovery was taking place elsewhere in the Southwest, although in the case of Santa Fe and Taos there were live Hispanic cultures to celebrate.

All this enthusiasm was, of course, strongly tinged with commercialism. And so was a second distinctive feature of California's development—the exploitation of its climate. While northern California boomed, the southern part of the state was neglected and thinly populated, too dry for anything but grazing and some chancy wheat growing. What it did have, however, was an abundance of sunshine. At the beginning of the 1880s there burst on the country amazing news of the charms of southern California, where "there is not any malaria, hay fever, loss of appetite, or languor in the air; nor any thunder, lightning, mad dogs . . . or cold snaps." This publicity was mostly the work of the Southern Pacific Railroad, which

Kitty Tatch and Friend on Glacier Point, Yosemite

From the time the Yosemite Valley was set aside in 1864 as a place for "public pleasuring, resort, and recreation," it attracted a stream of tourists eager to experience the grandeur of the American West. As is suggested by this photograph taken sometime in the 1890s, the magic of Yosemite was enough to set even staid young ladies dancing.

(Yosemite National Park Research Library, Yosemite National Park, CA)

had reached Los Angeles in 1876 and was eager for business. When the Santa Fe arrived in 1885, a furious rate war broke out, and it became possible to travel by train from Chicago or St. Louis to Los Angeles for $25 or less. Thousands of people, mostly midwesterners, poured in. Los Angeles County, with fewer than 3 percent of the state's population in 1870, had 12 percent by 1900. By then southern California had firmly established itself as the land of sunshine and orange groves. It had found a way to translate climate into riches.

That California was specially favored by nature some Californians knew even as the great stands of redwoods and sugar pine were being hacked down, the streams polluted, and the hills torn apart by reckless mining techniques. Back in 1864 influential Americans who had seen the Sierras prevailed on Congress to grant to the state of California "the Cleft, or Gorge in the granite peak of the Sierra Nevada Mountain, known as Yosemite Valley," which would be reserved "for public pleasuring, resort, and recreation." When the young naturalist John Muir arrived in California four years later, he headed straight for Yosemite. Its "grandeur . . . comes as an endless revelation," he wrote. Muir and others like him became devoted to protecting the High Sierras from "despoiling gain-seekers . . . eagerly trying to make everything immediately and selfishly commercial." One result was the creation of California's national parks in 1890—Yosemite, Sequoia, King's Canyon. Another was the formation in 1892 of the Sierra Club, which became a powerful voice for the defenders of California's wilderness.

They won some and lost some. Advocates of water-resource development insisted that California's irrigated agriculture and thirsty cities could not grow without tapping the abundant snowpack of the Sierras. By the turn of the century Los Angeles faced a water crisis that threatened its growth. The answer was a 238-mile aqueduct to the Owens River in the southern Sierras. A bitter controversy blew up over this immense project, driven by the resistance of local residents to the flooding of the beautiful Owens Valley. More painful for John Muir and his preservationist allies was their failure to save the Hetch Hetchy gorge, north of Yosemite National Park. After years of controversy the federal government in 1913 approved the damming of Hetch Hetchy Valley to serve the water needs of San Francisco.

When the stakes became high enough, nature lovers like John Muir generally came out on the short end. Even so, something original and distinctive had been added to California's heritage—the linking of a society's well-being with the preservation of its natural environment. This realization, in turn, said something important about the nation's relationship to the West. If the urge to conquer and exploit persisted, at least it was now tempered by a sense that nature's bounty was not limitless. And this, more than any announcement by the census that a "frontier line" no longer existed, registered the country's acceptance that the era of heedless westward expansion had ended.

For Further Exploration

The starting point for western history is Frederick Jackson Turner's famous essay, "The Significance of the Frontier in American History" (1893). In recent years there has been a reaction against Turnerian scholarship for being Eurocentric—for seeing western history only through the eyes of frontiersmen and settlers—and for masking the rapacious and environmentally destructive underside of western settlement. Patricia N. Limerick's skillfully argued *The Legacy of Conquest* (1987) opened the debate. Richard White, *"It's Your Misfortune and None of My Own": A New History of the American West* (1991), provides the fullest synthesis. On women's experiences—another primary concern of the new scholarship—a useful introduction is Susan Armitage and Elizabeth Jameson, eds., *The Women's West* (1987). On the plains Indians a lively account is Robert M. Utley, *The Indian Frontier of the American West* (1984). The ecological impact of plains settlement is subtly probed in Frieda Knobloch, *The Culture of Wilderness: Agriculture as Colonization in the American West* (1996). On the integration of the plains economy with the wider world an especially rich book is William Cronon, *Nature's Metropolis: Chicago and the Great West* (1991). Sarah Deutsch, *No Separate*

T I M E L I N E

1848	California is formally acquired from Mexico.	1875	Sioux ordered to vacate Powder River hunting grounds; war breaks out.
1849	California Gold Rush Chinese migration begins.	1876	Battle of Little Big Horn
		1877	San Francisco anti-Chinese riots
1861	Telegraph lines connect San Francisco with the East.	1879	Exoduster migration to Kansas
1862	Homestead Act offers public land to settlers.	1882	Chinese Exclusion Act bars further immigration of Chinese laborers.
1864	Yosemite Valley reserved as public park.	1884	Helen Hunt Jackson's *Ramona*
1865	Long Drive of Texas longhorns begins.	1886	Dry cycle begins on the Great Plains.
1867	Reservation policy for plains Indians	1887	Dawes Act divides tribal land into individual holdings.
1868	Sioux treaty rights to their Powder River hunting grounds confirmed	1889	Oklahoma opened to white settlers.
1869	Union Pacific and Central Pacific transcontinental railroad tracks meet at Promontory Point, Utah.	1890	Indian massacre at Wounded Knee, South Dakota U.S. census declares end of the frontier.
1874	Barbed wire invented.		

Refuge (1987), offers an imaginative treatment of the New Mexican peasantry. On the Asian migration to America the best introduction is Ron Takaki, *Strangers from a Different Shore* (1989). Kevin Starr, *California and the American Dream, 1850–1915* (1973), provides a full account of the emergence of a distinctive California culture. A comprehensive website with many links is <http://americanwest.com/>.

Chapter 17

CAPITAL AND LABOR IN THE AGE OF ENTERPRISE

1877–1900

An almost total revolution has taken place, and is yet in progress, in every branch and in every relation of the world's industrial and commercial system.

—DAVID A. WELLS, *RECENT ECONOMIC CHANGES*, 1899

The year that Reconstruction ended, 1877, also marked the end of the first great crisis of America's industrializing economy. Four years earlier the Panic of 1873 had led to a severe depression that bankrupted 47,000 firms and drove down prices by about 30 percent. Hundreds of thousands of workers lost their jobs, and suffering was widespread. Before long the foundations of the social order began to shake.

On July 16, 1877, disgruntled railroad employees spontaneously stopped work across the Baltimore and Ohio system. After four years of economic depression and relentless wage cuts, they had had enough. In towns along the B&O tracks crowds cheered as the strikers attacked company property and prevented trains from running. The strike spread like wildfire across the entire national rail system. In Pittsburgh the Pennsylvania Railroad's roundhouse went up in flames on July 21. At many rail centers rioters and looters roamed freely. Only the arrival of federal troops restored order. On August 15 President Rutherford B. Hayes wrote in his diary: "The strikers have been put down *by force*." The Great Strike of 1877 had been crushed but only after raising the specter of social revolution.

And then recovery came. Within months the economy was booming again. In the next fifteen years the output of manufactured goods increased more than 150 percent. The nation's confidence in its industrial future rebounded. "Upon [material progress] is founded all other progress," asserted a railroad president in 1888. "Can there be any doubt that cheapening the cost of necessaries and conveniences of life is the most powerful agent of civilization and progress?" How that happened—how scarcity gave way to abundance—is the core event of America's industrial revolution.

Industrial Capitalism Triumphant

Economic historians speak of the late nineteenth century as the age of the Great Deflation. Prices fell steadily, not only in the United States but worldwide. Normally, falling prices signal economic stagnation: there is not enough demand for the available goods and services. For England, a mature industrial power, the Great Deflation did indeed signal economic decline. But not in the United States. Industrial expansion went into high gear (see Figure 17.1) because increasing manufacturing efficiencies enabled American firms to cut prices and yet earn profits for financing still better equipment.

GROWTH OF THE INDUSTRIAL BASE

By the 1870s factories were a familiar sight in America. But the early industries had really been appendages of the agricultural economy. They produced *consumer* goods—textiles, shoes, paper, and furniture—that replaced articles made at home or by individual artisans. Gradually, however, a different kind of demand developed, driven by the country's surging economic growth. Railroads needed locomotives; new factories needed machinery; cities needed trolley lines, sanitation systems, and commercial buildings. Railroad equipment, machinery, and construction materials were *capital* goods—that is, goods that themselves added to the productive capacity of the economy. Although consumer goods remained very important, it was capital goods that now drove America's industrial economy.

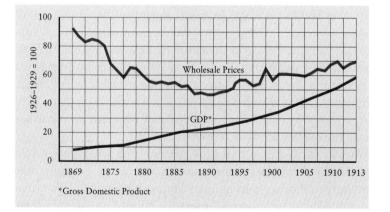

FIGURE 17.1
Business Activity and Wholesale Prices, 1869–1913

This graph shows the key feature of the performance of the late nineteenth-century economy: while output was booming, the price of goods was falling.

Central to this development was a new technology for manufacturing steel. The country already produced large quantities of wrought iron, a malleable metal easily worked by country blacksmiths and farmers. But wrought iron was expensive—it was produced in small batches by skilled puddlers—and not suited for heavy use as railway track. In 1856 the British inventor Henry Bessemer designed a furnace—the Bessemer converter—that refined raw pig iron into an essentially new product, steel, a metal harder and more durable than wrought iron. Bessemer's invention quickly attracted many users, but Andrew Carnegie was the one who fully exploited its revolutionary potential.

An ironmaker and former railroad manager, Carnegie in 1872 erected a massive steel mill outside Pittsburgh, with the Bessemer converter as its centerpiece. The converter broke a bottleneck at the refining stage and enabled Carnegie's engineers to design a mill that functioned on the basis of continuous operation. Iron ore entered the blast furnaces at one end and emerged without interruption at the other end as finished steel rails. Named after Carnegie's admired boss at the Pennsylvania Railroad, the Edgar Thompson Works became a model for the modern steel industry. Large integrated steel plants swiftly replaced the puddling mills that had once dotted western Pennsylvania.

The technological breakthrough in steel spurred the intensive exploitation of the country's rich mineral resources. Once iron ore began to be shipped down the Great Lakes from the rich Mesabi range in northern Minnesota, the industry was assured of an ample supply of its primary raw material. The other key ingredient, coal, came in great abundance from the Appalachian field that stretched from Pennsylvania to Alabama. Of minor importance before the Civil War, coal production doubled every decade after 1870, exceeding 400 million tons a year by 1910.

As steam engines became the nation's energy workhorse, prodigious amounts of coal began to be consumed by railroads and factories. Industries previously dependent on water power rapidly converted to steam. The turbine, utilizing continuous rotation rather than the steam engine's back-and-forth motion, marked another major advance during the 1880s. With the coupling of the steam turbine to the electric generator, the nation's energy revolution was completed, and after 1900 America's factories began a massive conversion to electric power.

THE RAILROAD BOOM

Before the Civil War most goods moved by water, a mode of transportation quite adequate for the country's economic needs at that time. But it was love at first sight when locomotives arrived from Britain in the 1830s. Americans were impatient for the year-round, on-time service that canal barges and riverboats could not provide. By 1860, with a network of tracks already crisscrossing the country east of the Mississippi, the railroad clearly was on the way to being industrial America's preferred mode of transportation (see Map 17.1).

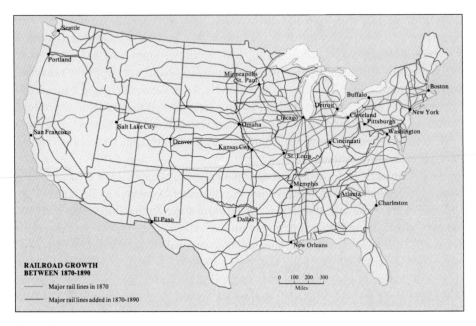

MAP 17.1
The Expansion of the Railroad System, 1870–1890

In 1870 the nation had 53,000 miles of rail track; in 1890, 167,000 miles. That burst of construction essentially completed the nation's rail network, although there would be additional expansion for the next two decades. The main areas of growth were in the South and west of the Mississippi. The Great Plains and the Far West accounted for over 40 percent of all railroad construction in this period.

The question was: Who would pay for it? Railroads could be state enterprises, like the canals, or they could be financed by private investors. Unlike most European countries the United States chose free enterprise. Even so, government played a big role. Anxious for the economic benefits, many states and localities lured railroads with offers of financial aid. The federal government, mainly interested in encouraging interregional development, provided financial credit and land grants; huge tracts went to the transcontinental railroads tying the Far West to the rest of the country.

The most important boost that government gave the railroads, however, was not money or land but a legal form of organization—the corporation—that enabled them to raise private capital in prodigious amounts. Investors who bought stock in the railroads enjoyed *limited liability:* they risked only the money they had invested and were not personally liable for the railroad's debts. Corporations were also empowered to borrow money by issuing interest-bearing bonds, which was how the railroads actually raised most of the money they needed.

Railroad building itself generally was handed over to construction companies, which, despite the name, were primarily another arm of the complex financing system. Hiring contractors and suppliers often involved persuading them to accept the railroad's bonds as payment and, when that failed, wheeling and dealing to raise cash by selling or borrowing on the bonds. Since the railroad promoters actually ran the construction companies, the opportunities for plunder were enormous. The most notorious, the Union Pacific's Credit Mobilier, disbursed probably half its funds into the pockets of the promoters.

The railroad business was not for the faint of heart. Most successful were promoters with the best access to capital, such as John Murray Forbes, a great Boston merchant in the China trade, who developed the Chicago, Burlington, and Quincy Railroad in the Midwest; or Cornelius Vanderbilt, who started with the fortune he had made in the steamboat business. Vanderbilt was primarily a consolidator, linking previously independent lines crossing New York State and ultimately developing the New York Central into a trunk line to Chicago. James J. Hill, who without federal subsidy made the Great Northern into the best of the transcontinental railroads, was certainly the nation's champion railroad builder. In contrast, Jay Gould, at various times owner of the Erie, Wabash, Union Pacific, and Missouri Pacific systems, always remained a stock-market speculator at heart.

Railroad development was often sordid, fiercely competitive, and subject to boom and bust. Yet vast sums of capital were raised, and a network was built exceeding that of the rest of the world combined. By 1900 virtually no corner of the country lacked rail service.

Along with this prodigious growth came increasing efficiency. The early railroads, built by competing local companies, had been a jumble of discontinuous segments. Gauges of track—the width between the rails—varied widely, and at terminal points railroads were not connected. As late as 1880 goods could not be shipped through from Massachusetts to South Carolina. Eight times along the way freight cars had to be emptied, and their contents transferred to other cars across a river or at a different terminal.

In 1883 the railroads rebelled against the jumble of local times that made scheduling a nightmare and, acting on their own, divided the country into the four standard time zones still in use. By the end of the 1880s a standard track gauge (4 feet, 8½ inches) had been adopted everywhere. Fast-freight firms and standard accounting procedures enabled shippers to use the railroad network as if it was a single unit, moving their goods without breaks in transit, transfers between cars, or the other delays that had once bedeviled them.

At the same time, railroad technology was advancing. Durable steel rails permitted heavier traffic. Locomotives became more powerful and capable of pulling more freight cars. To control the greater mass being hauled the inventor George Westinghouse perfected the automatic coupler, the air brake, and the friction gear for starting and stopping a long line of cars. Costs per ton-mile fell by 50 percent between 1870 and 1890, resulting in a steady drop in freight rates for shippers.

The railroads more than met the transportation needs of the maturing industrial economy. For the investors, however, the costs of freewheeling competition and unrestrained growth were painfully high. On the many routes served by too many railroads, competitors fought for the available traffic by cutting rates to the bone. Many were saddled with huge bonded debt from the extravagant construction years; about a fifth of these bonds failed to pay interest, even in a pretty good year like 1889. When the economy turned bad, as it did in the Panic of 1893, a third of the industry went into receivership.

Out of the rubble came a major railroad reorganization. This was primarily the handiwork of Wall Street investment banks such as J. P. Morgan & Co. and Kuhn Loeb & Co., whose main role had been to market railroad stock and bond issues. When railroads failed, the investment bankers stepped in to pick up the pieces. They persuaded investors to accept lower interest rates or put up more money. And they eased competitive pressures by consolidating rivals. By the early twentieth century, a half dozen great regional systems had emerged, and the nerve center of American railroading had shifted to Wall Street.

MASS MARKETS AND LARGE-SCALE ENTERPRISE

Until well into the industrial age, all but a few manufacturers operated on a small scale and mainly for nearby markets. They left distribution to wholesale merchants and commission agents. After the Civil War the scale of economic activity began to change. "Combinations of capital on a scale hitherto wholly unprecedented constitute one of the remarkable features of modern business methods," the economist David A. Wells wrote in 1889. He could see "no other way in which the work of production and distribution can be prosecuted." What was there about the nation's economy that led to Wells's sense that large-scale enterprise was inevitable?

Most of all, the American market. Unlike Europe the United States was not carved up into many national markets; no political frontiers impeded the flow of goods across the continent. The population, swelled by immigration and a high birth rate, jumped from 40 million in 1870 to over 60 million in 1890. People flocked to the cities. The railroads brought these tightly packed markets within the reach of distant producers. The telegraph, fully operational by the Civil War, speeded communications. Nowhere else did manufacturers have so vast and accessible a home market for their products.

How they seized that opportunity is perhaps best revealed in the meat-packing industry. With the opening of the Union Stock Yards in 1865, Chicago became the cattle market for the country. Livestock came in by rail from the Great Plains, was auctioned off at the Chicago stockyards, and then was shipped to eastern cities, where, as before, the cattle were slaughtered in local "butchertowns." Such an arrangement—national distribution but local processing—adequately met the needs of an exploding urban population and could have done so indefinitely. In Europe no further development ever did occur.

But Gustavus F. Swift, a shrewd Chicago cattle dealer from Massachusetts, saw the future differently. He recognized that livestock deteriorated en route to the East and that local slaughterhouses lacked the scale to utilize waste by-products or cut labor costs. If dressed beef could be kept fresh in transit, however, it could be produced in bulk at the Chicago stockyards. Once his engineers developed an effective cooling system, Swift invested in a fleet of refrigerator cars and constructed a central beef-processing plant in Chicago.

This was only the beginning of Swift's innovations. No refrigerated warehouses existed in the cities that received his chilled beef, so Swift built his own network of branch houses. Next, he acquired a fleet of wagons to distribute his products to retail butcher shops. Swift constructed additional facilities to process the fertilizer, chemicals, and other usable by-products from his slaughtering operations. He also began to handle other perishable commodities so that he could fully utilize his refrigerated cars and branch houses. As demand grew, Swift built more packing houses in other stockyard centers, including Kansas City, Fort Worth, and Omaha.

Step by step Swift created a new kind of enterprise—a national company capable of handling within its own structure all the functions of an industry. Swift & Co. was a *vertically integrated* firm, absorbing the functions of many small, specialized enterprises within a single national structure. Swift's lead was followed by several big Chicago packers already operating plants that preserved pork products. By 1900 five firms, all of them nationally organized and vertically integrated, produced nearly 90 percent of the meat shipped in interstate commerce.

In most fields, no single innovation was as decisive as Swift's refrigerator car. But others did share Swift's insight that the essential step was to identify a mass market and then develop a national enterprise capable of serving it. In the petroleum industry John D. Rockefeller built the Standard Oil Company partly by taking over rival firms, but he also built a national distribution system to reach the enormous market for kerosene for lighting and heating homes. The Singer Sewing Machine Company formed its own sales organization, using both retail stores and door-to-door salesmen. Through such distribution systems manufacturers were able also to provide technical information, credit, and repair facilities.

Americans were ready consumers of standardized, mass-marketed goods. Because they were geographically mobile, they lost the local loyalties that were so strong in Europe. Social class in America, though by no means absent, was blurred at the edges and did not, for example, call for class-specific ways of dressing. Foreign visitors often noted that ready-made clothing made it difficult to tell salesgirls from debutantes on city streets.

The American consumer's receptivity to standardized goods should not be exaggerated. Gustavus Swift, for example, encountered great resistance to his Chicago beef. How could it be wholesome weeks later in Boston or Philadelphia? Cheap prices helped, but advertising mattered more. Modern advertising was born in the late nineteenth century, bringing brand names and a billboard-cluttered urban landscape. By 1900 companies spent over $90 million a year for space in newspapers and magazines. Advertisements urged readers to bathe with Pears' soap, eat Uneeda biscuits, sew on a Singer machine, and snap pictures with a Kodak camera. The active molding of demand for brand names became a major function of American business.

Quaker Oats

Like crackers, sugar, and other nonperishable foods, oatmeal had traditionally been marketed to consumers in bulk from barrels. In 1882 the grain merchant Henry P. Cowell completed the first continuous-process mill for oatmeal, cutting production costs and greatly increasing output. He also hit on the idea of selling oatmeal in boxes of standard size and weight to a national market. Broadsides showing the Quaker Oats man soon appeared in every American town, advertising a product of reliable quality and uniform price.

(Division of Political History, Smithsonian Institution)

THE NEW SOUTH

"Shall we dethrone our idols?" Southerners had to ask themselves as they observed the burst of economic activity in the North. For many the answer was a resounding yes. Nostalgia for the Old South had to be put aside, advocates of economic development argued. Led by Henry W. Grady, editor of the Atlanta *Constitution*, they made "the practical wisdom of businessmen" the credo of a "New South."

The plantation economy of the Old South had impeded industrial development. The slave states had few cities, a primitive distribution system, and not much manufacturing. This modest infrastructure, wrecked by the Civil War, was quickly restored. After Reconstruction a railroad boom developed. Track mileage doubled in the next decade, and at least by that measure the South became nearly competitive with the rest of the country (see Map 17.2).

But the South remained overwhelmingly agricultural. Farming and poverty are not necessarily linked, but in the South they were. Tenant systems required a cash crop (see Chapter 15), committing the South to cotton despite soil depletion, low productivity, and unprofitable prices. Wages for southern farm labor fell steadily, down to roughly 75 cents a day by the 1890s.

From this low agricultural wage, surprisingly, sprang the South's hopes for industrialization. Consider, for example, how southern textile mills got started in the Piedmont uplands in the mid-1870s. The mills recruited workers from the surrounding hill farms, where people struggled to make ends meet. To attract them mill wages had to exceed farm earnings but not by much. Paying rock-bottom wages, the new mills had a competitive advantage over the long-established New England industry—as much as 40 percent lower labor costs in 1897.

The labor system that evolved was based on hiring whole families. "Papa decided he would come because he didn't have nothing much but girls and they had to get out and work like men," recalled one woman. It was not Papa, in fact, but his

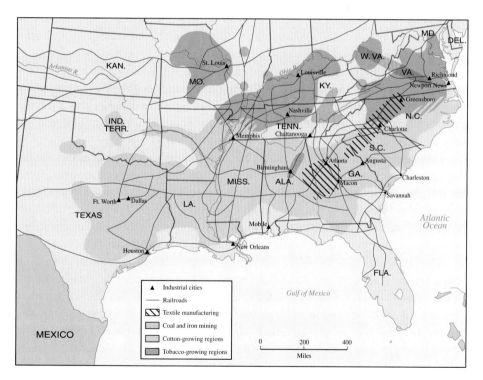

MAP 17.2
The New South, 1900

The economy of the Old South focused on raising staple crops, especially cotton and tobacco. In the New South staple agriculture continued to dominate, but there was marked industrial development as well. Industrial regions emerged, producing textiles, coal and iron, and wood products. By 1900 the South's industrial pattern was well defined.

girls whom the mills wanted, to work as spinners and loom tenders. Only they could not be recruited individually: no right-thinking parent would have permitted that. Hiring by families, on the other hand, was already familiar; after all, everyone had been expected to work on the farm. And so the family system of mill labor developed, with a labor force that was half female and very young. In the 1880s a quarter of all southern textile workers were under fifteen years of age.

The hours were long—twelve hours a day—but life in the mill villages was, in the words of one historian, "like a family." Employers tended to be paternalistic, providing company housing and a variety of services. The mill workers themselves built close-knit, supportive communities, but for whites only. Although blacks sometimes worked as day laborers and janitors, they hardly ever got jobs as operatives in the cotton mills.

Cheap, abundant labor might have been termed the South's most valuable natural resource. But the region was blessed with other resources as well. From its rich soil came tobacco, the South's second cash crop. When cigarettes became fashionable in the 1880s, the young North Carolina entrepreneur James B. Duke seized the new market by taking advantage of a southern invention—James A. Bonsack's machine for producing cigarettes automatically. Blacks stemmed and stripped the leaf as they always had, but Duke followed the textile example and restricted machine tending to white women.

Lumbering, by contrast, was racially integrated, with a labor force evenly divided between black and white men. Cutting down the South's pine forests was a growth business in these years. Alabama's coal and iron ore deposits also attracted investors; by 1890 the Birmingham district was producing nearly a million tons of iron and steel annually.

Despite the South's high hopes, this burst of industrial development did not lift the region out of poverty. In 1900 two-thirds of all southerners made their living from the soil, just as they had in 1870. Moreover, the industries that did develop produced raw materials (forestry and mining) or engaged in the low-tech processing of coarse products. Industry by industry the key statistic—the value added by manufacturing—showed the South consistently lagging behind the North (see Table 17.1).

Southerners tended to blame the North: the South was a "colonial" economy controlled by New York and Chicago. There was some truth to this charge. Much of the capital—by no means all—did come from the North. And the integrating processes of the economy did subordinate regional to national interests. When the railway network moved to a uniform gauge in 1886, the southern railroads converted to the northern standard. Nor did northern interests hesitate to use their muscle to maintain the interregional status quo. Railroads, for example, manipulated freight rates so that it was cheap for southern cotton and timber to flow out and for northern manufactured goods to flow in.

Yet in the end the South's economic backwardness was mostly of its own making. The crowning irony was that the great advantage of the South—its cheap labor—also kept it from becoming a more technologically advanced economy. First, low wages discouraged employers from replacing workers with machinery. Second,

TABLE 17.1
Comparison of Annual Value Added per Worker, South and Non-South, 1910

Type of Industry	South	Non-South
Lumber and timber products	$ 820	$1020
Cotton goods	544	764
Cars and general shop construction by steam railroad companies	657	746
Turpentine and resin	516	—
Tobacco manufactures	1615	1394
Foundry and machine-shop products	1075	1307
Printing and publishing	1760	2100
Cottonseed oil	1715	—
Hosiery and knit goods	461	724
Furniture and refrigerators	732	1052
Iron and steel	1182[a]	1433
Fertilizer	1833	1947

Source: Gavin Wright, *Old South, New South: Revolutions in the Southern Economy Since the Civil War* (New York: Basic Books, 1986), p. 163.
[a]Partially estimated.
Note: This table reveals the consistency with which northern industries (except tobacco manufactures) controlled the more skilled—and hence more value-creating—processes of production.

low wages attracted labor-intensive industry, such as textiles. Third, a cheap labor market inhibited investment in education because of the likelihood that better-educated workers would flee to higher-wage markets.

What distinguished the southern labor market was that it was *insulated* from the rest of the country. Northern workers and European immigrants steered clear of the South because wages were too low and attractive jobs too scarce. Harder to explain is why so few southerners, black or white, left for the higher-wage North prior to World War I. At its core, the explanation is that the South was a place apart, with social and racial mores that discouraged all but the most resourceful from seeking opportunities elsewhere. The result was that a normal flow of workers back and forth did not occur, and wage differentials did not narrow. So long as this isolation persisted, the South would remain a tributary economy, a supplier on unequal terms to the advanced industrial heartland of the North.

The World of Work

In a free-enterprise system, profit drives the entrepreneur. But the industrial order is populated not only by profit makers. It includes—in vastly larger numbers— wage earners. Economic change always affects those who work for wages, but never so drastically as it did in the late nineteenth century.

LABOR RECRUITS

Industrialism invariably set people in motion. Farm folk migrated to cities. Artisans entered factories. An industrial labor force emerged. This happened in the United States just as it did in Europe, but with a difference: the United States did not rely primarily on its own population for a supply of workers.

The demand for labor was ravenous, tripling between 1870 and 1900. Rural Americans were highly mobile in the late nineteenth century, and of those who moved, half ended up in cities. But except in the South native-born whites mostly rejected factory work. They had a basic education, they could read and calculate, and they understood American institutions and ways of doing things. City-bound white Americans found their opportunities in the multiplying white-collar jobs in offices and retail stores.

Modest numbers of blacks began to migrate out of the South—roughly 80,000 between 1870 and 1890, another 200,000 between 1890 and 1910. Most of them settled in cities, but they were restricted to casual labor, janitorial work, and for the women domestic service. Employers turned black applicants away from the factory gates—and away from their one best chance for a fair shake at American opportunity—because immigrant workers already supplied them with as much cheap labor as they needed.

The great migration from the Old World had started in the 1840s, when over a million Irish peasants fled the potato famine. In the following years, as European agriculture became increasingly commercialized, peasant populations lost their hold on the land. The peasant economy failed first in Germany and Scandinavia and then later in the nineteenth century across Austria-Hungary, Russia, Italy, and the Balkans. In Europe's industrial districts new technologies also cut loose many workers in obsolete artisan trades such as hand-loom weaving.

Ethnic origin largely determined the kind of work that the immigrants took in America. Seeking the jobs they had held in the Old World, the Welsh labored as tin-plate workers, the English as miners, the Germans as machinists and traditional artisans (for example, bakers and carpenters), the Belgians as glass workers, and the Scandinavians as seamen on Great Lakes boats. For common labor employers had long counted on the brawn of Irish rural immigrants, although all emigrating groups contributed to the pool of unskilled workers.

As technology advanced, American employers needed fewer European craftsmen, while the demand for ordinary labor skyrocketed. The sources of immigration began to shift, and by 1895 arrivals from southern and eastern Europe far outstripped immigration from western Europe (see Figure 17.2). Italian and Slavic immigrants without industrial skills flooded into American factories. Heavy, low-paid labor became the domain of the recent immigrants. Blast-furnace jobs, a job-seeking investigator heard, were "Hunky work," not suitable for him or any other American.

Not only skill determined where immigrants ended up in American industry. The newcomers, although generally traveling on their own, moved within well-defined net-

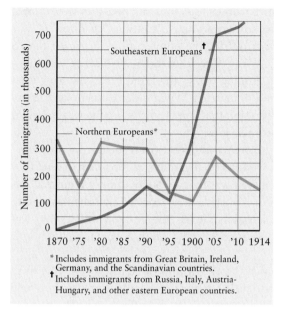

Figure 17.2

American Immigration, 1870–1914

This graph shows the surge of European immigration in the late nineteenth century. While northern Europe continued to send substantial numbers, it was overshadowed after 1895 by south-eastern Europeans pouring into America to work in mines and factories.

works, following relatives or fellow villagers already in America and relying on them to land a job. A high degree of ethnic clustering resulted, even within a single factory. At the Jones and Laughlin steel works in Pittsburgh, for example, the carpentry shop was German, the hammer shop Polish, and the blooming mill Serbian. Immigrants also had different job preferences. Men from Italy, for example, preferred outdoor work, often laboring in gangs under a *padrone* (boss), much as they had in Italy.

Immigrants entered a modern industrial order, but it was not a world they wanted. They were peasants, displaced by the breakdown of the traditional rural economies of eastern and southern Europe. Many had lost their land and fallen into the class of dependent, propertyless servants. They could avoid that bitter fate only if they had money to buy property, and it was that purpose that drove the peasant immigrants who came to America. They never intended to stay permanently. About half did return, departing in great numbers during depression years. No one knows how many left because they had saved enough and how many left for lack of work. For their American employers it scarcely mattered. What mattered was that the immigrants took the worst jobs and were always available when they were wanted. For the new industrial order they made an ideal labor supply.

WORKING WOMEN

Over 4 million women worked for wages in 1900. They made up a quarter of the nonfarm labor force and were increasingly important in the industrial economy. The opportunities they found were shaped by gender. Contemporary beliefs about womanhood largely determined which women took jobs and how they were treated once they became wage earners (see American Voices, "Getting Organized").

Wives were not supposed to work outside the home, and in fact fewer than 5 percent did so in 1890. Only among African Americans did many married women—above 30 percent—work for wages. Among whites the typical working woman at that time was under twenty-four and unmarried. When older women worked, re-marked one observer, it "was usually a sign that something had gone wrong": their husbands had died, deserted, or lost their jobs.

Since women were held to be inherently different from men, it followed that they not be permitted to do "men's work." Nor, regardless of their skills, could they be paid a man's wage. The dominant view was that a woman did not require a "liv-ing wage" because, as one investigator reported, "it is expected that she has men to support her." The occupation that served as the baseline for all women's jobs was domestic service, which was always very poorly paid or, in a woman's own home, not paid at all.

At the turn of the century women's work fell into three categories. One third of women worked as maids or other types of domestic servants. Another third held "female" white-collar jobs in teaching, nursing, sales, and office work. The remain-ing third worked in industry, heavily concentrated in the garment trades and tex-tile mills but present also in many other industries as inspectors, packers, assemblers, and other "light" occupations. Few worked as supervisors, fewer in the crafts, and nearly none as day laborers.

Just how jobs came to be defined as male or female—in sociological terms, the *sex-typing* of occupations—is not easy to explain. Jobs as telephone operator and store clerk, originally male, had by the 1890s become female. Wherever an occupa-tion became female-dominated, people came to think of it as having feminine at-tributes, even though very similar or even identical work elsewhere was done by men. Jobs identified as women's work became unsuitable for men. There were no male telephone operators by 1900.

As with male workers, ethnicity and race played a big part in the distribution of women's jobs. Exclusion from all but the most menial jobs applied as rigidly to black women as it did to black men. White-collar jobs were reserved for native-born women, which in the cities increasingly included the second-generation daughters of immigrants. And as with men ethnicity created clustering patterns in women's jobs or, in the case of Italians, restricted them to sewing or other subcon-tracted tasks that could be done within the family.

Disapproval of wives who took paying jobs, though expressed in sentimental and moral terms, was based on solid necessity. Cooking, cleaning, and tending the children were not income-producing or reckoned in terms of money. But everyone knew that the family household could not function without the wife's contribution. Therefore, her place was in the home.

Working-class families, however, found the going hard on a single income. Only among highly skilled workers, wrote one investigator, "was it possible for the hus-

AMERICAN VOICES

Getting Organized

ROSE SCHNEIDERMAN

*R*ose Schneiderman (1882–1972) typified the young Jewish garment workers who became the firebrands of their industry. Schneiderman went on to an illustrious career as a unionist and reformer.

We had no idea that there was a union in our industry and that women could join it. Nor did we have a full realization of the hardships we were needlessly undergoing. There was the necessity of owning a sewing machine before you could work. Then you had to buy your own thread. But the worst of it was the incredibly inefficient way in which work was distributed. Because we were all pieceworkers, any time lost during the season was a real hardship. . . .

We formed a committee composed of my friend Bessie Mannis, who worked with me, myself, and a third girl. Bravely we ventured into the office of the United Cloth Hat and Cap Makers Union. . . . We were told that we would have to have at least twenty-five women. . . . We waited at the doors of factories and, as the girls were leaving for the day, we would approach them and speak our piece. . . . Within days we had the necessary number, and in January 1903 we were chartered as Local 23, and I was elected secretary. . . .

The only cloud in the picture was mother's attitude toward my becoming a trade union-ist. She kept saying I'd never get married because I was so busy—a prophecy which came true. . . .

That June we decided to put our strength to the test. . . . On Saturdays . . . we women had to hang around until three or four o'clock before getting our pay. I headed a com-mittee which informed Mr. Fox that we wanted to be paid at the same time as the men. . . . He didn't say outright that he agreed; he wouldn't give us that much satisfaction. But on the first Saturday in July, when we went for our pay at twelve noon, there it was ready for us.

SOURCE: Rose Schneiderman, *All for One* (1967), reprinted in Irving Howe and Kenneth Libo, eds., *How We Lived* (New York: New American Library, 1979), pp. 139–41.

band unaided to support his family." The rockiest period came during the child-bearing years, when there were many mouths to feed and only the earnings of the father to provide the food. Thereafter, as the children grew old enough to work, the family income began to increase. Not only unmarried sons and daughters but also the younger children contributed their share. In 1900 one of every five children un-der sixteen worked. "When the people own houses," remarked a printer from Fall River, Massachusetts, "you will generally find that it is a large family all working together."

Switchboard Operators

When the first telephone exchange was set up in Boston in 1878, it was operated by teenage boys, which followed the practice set in the telegraph industry. During the 1880s, however, young women increasingly replaced the boys, and by 1900 switchboard operation was defined strictly as women's work. In this photograph of a telephone exchange in Columbus, Ohio, in 1907, the older woman at left has risen to the position of supervisor, but it is the two men in the picture who are clearly in charge. (Corbis-Bettmann)

By the 1890s all the northern industrial states had passed laws prohibiting child labor and regulating work hours for teenagers. Most of these states also required children under fourteen to attend school for a certain number of weeks each year. Working-class families continued to need more than one income, but this money came increasingly from the wives. After 1890 the proportion of working married women crept steadily upward. About a fifth of the wives of unskilled and semi-skilled men in Chicago held jobs in 1920. Wage-earning wives and mothers were on their way to becoming a primary part of America's labor force.

AUTONOMOUS LABOR

No one supervised the nineteenth-century coal miner (see American Voices, "A Miner's Son"). He was a tonnage worker who was paid for the amount of coal he produced. He provided his own tools, worked at his own pace, and knocked off early when he chose. Such autonomous craft workers—almost all of them men—flourished in many branches of nineteenth-century industry. They were mule spin-

AMERICAN VOICES

A Miner's Son

John Brophy

*J*ohn Brophy (1883–1963), an important mine union official in the twentieth century, recalls what mining was like in his boyhood.

I got a thrill at the thought of having an opportunity to go and work in the mine, to go
and work along side my father. . . . It was a great satisfaction to me that my father was a
skilled, clean workman with everything kept in shape, and the timbering done well. . . .
It's plain that the individual miner in those early days had considerable freedom of judgment. I think that was one of the great satisfactions that a miner had—that he was his
own boss within his workplace. . . .

The miner is always aware of danger, that he lived under dangerous conditions in the
workplace. . . . Then there is the further fact that the miner by and large lived in purely
mining communities which were often isolated. They developed a group loyalty under all
these circumstances. They were both individualists and they were group conscious. . . . You
find time and again miners, in an effort to rescue their fellow workers, taking chances
which quite often meant death for themselves. . . .

Along with that is a sense of justice. There was the very fact the miner was a tonnage
worker and that he could be short weighed and cheated in various ways, and that the only
safeguard against it was organization. . . . The miner in my day in the United States was
aware that all knowledge didn't start with his generation. . . . At least on one side of my
family there are at least four generations of [British] miners, and I say this with a sense of
pride; very much so. I'm very proud of the fact that there is this long tradition of miners
who have struggled with the elements.

SOURCE: Jerold S. Auerbach, ed., *American Labor: The Twentieth Century* (Indianapolis: Bobbs-Merrill,
1969), pp. 44–48.

ners in cotton mills; puddlers and rollers in iron works; molders in stove making;
and machinists, glass blowers, and skilled workers in many other industries.

In the shop they abided by the *stint,* a self-imposed limit on how much they
would produce each day. This informal system of restricting output infuriated
efficiency-minded engineers. But to the worker it signified personal dignity and
"unselfish brotherhood" with fellow employees. The male craft worker took pride
in a "manly" bearing, toward both his fellows and the boss. One day a shop in Lowell, Massachusetts, posted regulations requiring all employees to be at their posts in
work clothes at the opening bell and to remain, with the shop door locked, until
the dismissal bell. A machinist promptly packed his tools, declaring that he had not
"been brought up under such a system of slavery."

The Ironworkers' Noontime

The qualities of the nineteenth-century craft worker—dignity, "unselfish brotherhood," a "manly" bearing—shine through in this painting by Thomas Anshutz. *The Ironworkers' Noontime* became a popular painting when it was reproduced as an engraving in *Harper's Weekly* in 1884. (Fine Arts Museum of San Francisco. Gift of Mr. and Mrs. John D. Rockefeller 3rd, 1979.7.4)

Underlying this ethical code was a keen sense of the craft, each with its own history and customs. Hat finishers—masters of the art of applying fur felting to top hats and bowlers—had a language of their own. When a hatter was hired, he was "shopped"; if fired, he was "bagged"; when he quit work, he "cried off"; and when he took an apprentice, the boy was "under teach." The hatters, most of whom worked in Danbury, Connecticut, or Orange, New Jersey, formed a distinctive, self-contained community.

Women workers found much the same kind of social meaning in their jobs. Department store clerks, for example, developed a work culture and language just as robust as that of any male craft group. The most important fact about wage-earning women was their youth. For many the first job was a chance to be independent, to form friendships with other young women, and to experience, however briefly, a fun-loving time of nice clothes, dancing, and other "cheap amusements."

To some degree, their youthful preoccupations made it easier for working women to accept the miserable terms under which they labored. But this did not mean that they lacked a sense of solidarity or self-respect. A pretty dress might appear frivolous to the casual observer, but it also conveyed the message that the working girl considered herself as good as anyone. Rebellious youth culture sometimes united with job grievances to produce astonishing strike movements, as, for example, by Jewish garment workers in New York and Irish American telephone operators in Boston.

Rarely, however, did women workers wield the kind of craft power that the skilled male worker commonly enjoyed. He hired his own helpers, supervised their work, and paid them from his earnings. In the late nineteenth century, when increasingly sophisticated production called for closer shop-floor supervision, many factory managers deliberately shifted this responsibility to craft workers. In metal-fabricating firms that did precise machining and complex assembling, a system of inside contracting developed, in which skilled employees bid for a production run, taking full responsibility for the operation, paying their crew and pocketing the profits.

Dispersal of authority was characteristic of nineteenth-century industry. The aristocracy of the workers—the craftsmen, inside contractors, and foremen—enjoyed a high degree of autonomy. However, their subordinates often paid dearly for that independence. Any worker who paid his helpers from his own pocket might be tempted to exploit them. In the Pittsburgh area foremen were known as "pushers," notorious for driving their gangs mercilessly. On the other hand, industrial labor in the nineteenth century remained on a human scale. People dealt with each other face to face and often developed cohesive ties within the shop. Striking craft workers commonly received the support of helpers and laborers, and labor gangs sometimes walked out on behalf of a popular foreman.

SYSTEMS OF CONTROL

As technology advanced, workers increasingly lost the proud independence characteristic of nineteenth-century craft work. One cause of this deskilling process was a new system of production—Henry Ford called it *mass production*—that lent itself to mechanization. Agricultural implements, typewriters, bicycles, and after 1900 automobiles were assembled from standardized parts. The machine tools that cut, drilled, and ground these metal parts were originally operated by skilled machinists. But because they produced long runs of a single item, machine tools became more specialized; they became *dedicated* machines—machines set up to do the same job over and over—and the need for skilled operatives disappeared. In the manufacture of sewing machines, one machinist complained in 1883, "the trade is so subdivided that a man is not considered a machinist at all. One man may make just a particular part of a machine and may not know anything whatever about another part of the same machine." Such a worker, noted an observer, "cannot be master of a craft, but only master of a fragment."

Employers were attracted to dedicated machinery because it increased output; the impact on workers was not uppermost in their minds. They recognized that mechanization made it easier to control workers, but that was only an incidental benefit. Gradually, however, the idea took hold that managing workers might itself be a way to reduce the cost of production.

The pioneer in this field was Frederick W. Taylor. An expert on metal-cutting methods, Taylor believed that the engineer's approach might be applied to managing workers, hence the name for his method: *scientific management*. To get the maximum work from the individual worker, Taylor suggested two basic reforms. The first would eliminate the brain work from manual labor. Managers would assume "the burden of gathering together all of the traditional knowledge which in the past has been possessed by the workmen and then of classifying, tabulating, and reducing this knowledge to rules, laws, and formulae." The second reform, a logical consequence of the first, would deprive workers of the authority they had exercised on the shop floor. Workers would "do what they are told promptly and without asking questions or making suggestions. . . . The duty of enforcing . . . rests with the management alone."

Once managers had the knowledge and the power, they would put labor on a "scientific" basis. This meant subjecting each task to *time-and-motion study* by an engineer who would analyze and time each job with a stopwatch. Workers would be paid at a differential rate—that is, a certain amount if they met the stopwatch standard and a higher rate for additional output. Taylor claimed that his techniques would guarantee optimum worker efficiency. His assumption was that only money mattered to workers and that they would automatically respond to the lure of higher earnings.

Scientific management was not, in practice, a roaring success. Implementing it proved very expensive, and workers stubbornly resisted the job-analysis method. "It looks to me like slavery to have a man stand over you with a stopwatch," complained one iron molder. A union leader insisted that "this system is wrong, because we want our heads left on us." Far from solving the labor problem, as Taylor claimed it would, scientific management embittered relations on the shop floor.

Yet Taylor achieved something of fundamental importance. He was a brilliant publicist, and his teachings spread throughout American industry. Taylor's disciples moved beyond his simplistic economic psychology, creating the new fields of personnel work and industrial psychology, whose practitioners purported to know how to extract more and better labor from workers. A threshold had been crossed into the modern era of labor management.

So the circle closed on American workers. With each advance the quest for efficiency cut deeper into their cherished autonomy. The process occurred unevenly. For textile workers the loss had come early. Miners and iron workers felt it much more slowly. Others, such as construction workers, escaped almost entirely. But increasing numbers of workers found themselves in an environment that crushed any sense of mastery or even understanding.

The Labor Movement

Wherever industrialization took hold, workers organized and formed labor unions. However, the movements they built varied from one industrial society to another. In the United States workers were especially uncertain about the path they wanted to take. Only in the 1880s did the American labor movement settle into a steady course.

REFORMERS AND UNIONISTS

Thomas B. McGuire, a New York wagon driver, was ambitious. He had saved $300 from his wages "so that I might become something of a capitalist eventually." But his venture as a cab driver in the early 1880s soon failed:

> Corporations usually take that business themselves. They can manage to get men, at starvation wages, and put them on a hack, and put a livery on them with a gold band and brass buttons, to show that they are slaves—I beg pardon; I did not intend to use the word slaves; there are no slaves in this country now—to show that they are merely servants.

Slave or liveried servant, the symbolic meaning was the same to McGuire. He was speaking of the crushed aspirations of the independent American worker.

What would satisfy the Thomas McGuires of the nineteenth century? Only the establishment of an egalitarian society, one in which every citizen might hope to become economically independent. This republican goal did not mean returning to the agrarian past but rather moving beyond the existing wage system to a more just order that did not distinguish between capitalists and workers. All would be "producers" laboring together in what was commonly called the "cooperative commonwealth." This was the ideal that inspired the Noble and Holy Order of the Knights of Labor.

Founded in 1869 as a secret society of garment workers in Philadelphia, the Knights of Labor spread to other cities and by 1878 emerged as a national movement. The Knights boasted an elaborate ritual and ceremony calculated to appeal to the fraternal spirit of nineteenth-century workers. They enjoyed a sense of comradeship very much like that offered by the Masons or Odd Fellows. For the Knights, however, fraternalism was harnessed to labor reform. The goal was to "give voice to that grand undercurrent of mighty thought, which is today [1880] crystallizing in the hearts of men, and urging them on to perfect organization through which to gain the power to make labor emancipation possible."

But how was "emancipation" to be achieved? Through cooperation, the Knights argued. They intended to set up factories and shops that would be owned and run by the employees. As these cooperatives flourished, American society would be transformed into a cooperative commonwealth. But little was actually done. Instead, the Knights devoted themselves to "education." Their leader, Grand Master Workman Terence V. Powderly, regarded the organization as a vast labor lyceum open to all but lawyers and saloonkeepers. The cooperative commonwealth would arrive in some mysterious way as more and more "producers" became members and learned the group's message from lectures, discussions, and publications. Social evil would not end in a day but "must await the gradual development of educational enlightenment."

The labor reformers expressed the higher aspirations of American workers. Another kind of organization—the trade union—tended to their day-to-day needs. Unions had long been at the center of the lives of craft workers. Apprenticeship rules regulated entry into a trade, and the closed shop—by reserving all jobs for union members—kept out lower-wage and incompetent workers. Union rules specified the terms of work, sometimes in minute detail. The trade union also expressed the social identity of the craft. A Birmingham iron puddler claimed that his union's "main object was to educate mechanics up to a standard of morality and temperance, and good workmanship." Some unions emphasized mutual aid. Because operating trains was a high-risk occupation, the railroad brotherhoods provided accident and death benefits and encouraged members to assist one another.

The earliest unions were local organizations of workers in the same craft and sometimes, more narowly, those in a single ethnic group, such as German bakers or Bohemian cigar makers. As expanding markets intruded, breaking down their ability to control local conditions, unions began to form national organizations. The first was the International Typographical Union in 1852. By the 1870s molders, ironworkers, bricklayers, and about thirty other trades had done likewise. The national union was becoming the dominant organizational form for American trade unionism.

The practical job interests that trade unions espoused might have seemed a far cry from the idealism of the Knights of Labor. But both kinds of motives arose from a single workers' culture. Seeing no conflict, many workers carried membership cards in both the Knights of Labor and a trade union. For many years little separated a trade assembly of the Knights from a local trade union; both engaged in fraternal and job-oriented activities. And because the Knights, once established in a town or city, tended to become politically active and field independent slates of candidates, that too became a magnet attracting trade unionists.

Trade unions generally barred women, and so did the Knights until in 1881 women shoe workers in Philadelphia struck in support of their male coworkers and won the right to form their own local assembly. By 1886 probably 50,000 women belonged to the Knights of Labor. Their courage on the picket line prompted Powderly's rueful remark that women "are the best men in the Order." For a handful, such as the hosiery worker Leonora M. Barry, the Knights provided a rare chance to take up leadership roles as organizers and officials.

Similarly, the Knights of Labor grudgingly expanded the opportunity for black workers to join out of the need for solidarity and, just as important, in deference to the Order's egalitarian principles. The Knights could rightly boast that their "great work has been to organize labor which was previously unorganized."

THE TRIUMPH OF "PURE AND SIMPLE" UNIONISM

In the early 1880s the Knights began to act more and more like trade unions. Boycott campaigns against the products of "unfair" employers achieved impressive results. With the economy booming and workers in short supply, the Knights began to win strikes, including a major victory against Jay Gould's Southwestern railway system in 1885. Workers flocked into the organization, and its membership jumped from 100,000 to perhaps 700,000. For a brief time the Knights stood poised as a potential industrial-union movement capable of bringing all workers into its fold.

The rapid growth of the Knights of Labor frightened the national trade unions. They began to insist on a clear separation of roles, with the Knights confined to labor reform. This was partly a battle over turf, but it reflected also a deepening divergence of labor philosophies.

Samuel Gompers, a cigar maker from New York City, led the ideological assault on the Knights. Gompers hammered out the philosophical position that would become known as "pure and simple" unionism. His starting point was that grand theories and schemes like those that excited the labor reformers should be strictly avoided. Unions, Gompers thought, should focus instead on concrete, achievable gains, and they should organize workers not as an undifferentiated mass of "producers" but by craft and occupation. The battleground should be at the workplace, where workers could best mobilize their power, and not in the quicksands of politics. "No matter how just," Gompers pronounced, "unless the cause is backed up with power to enforce it, it is going to be crushed and annihilated."

Samuel Gompers

This is a photograph of the labor leader in his forties taken when he was visiting striking miners in West Virginia, an area where mine operators resisted unions with special fierceness. The photograph was taken by a company detective.
(The George Meany Memorial Archives Negative #91)

The struggle for the eight-hour day crystallized the conflict between the rival movements. Both, of course, favored a shorter workday, but for different reasons. For the Knights, it was desirable because workers had duties "to perform as American citizens and members of society." Trade unionists took a more hard-boiled view of the eight-hour day: it would spread the available jobs among more workers, protect them against overwork, and give them a better life. When the trade unions set May 1, 1886, as the deadline for achieving the eight-hour day, the leadership of Knights objected. But workers everywhere responded enthusiastically, and as the deadline approached, a wave of strikes and demonstrations broke out.

At one such eight-hour strike, at the McCormick agricultural-implement works in Chicago, a battle erupted on May 3, leaving four strikers dead. Chicago was a hotbed of *anarchism*—the revolutionary advocacy of a stateless society—and local anarchists, most of them German immigrants, called a protest meeting the next evening at Haymarket Square. When police moved in to break it up, someone threw a bomb that killed and wounded several of the police. Despite no proof of their involvement, the anarchists were tried and found guilty of murder and criminal conspiracy. Four were executed, one committed suicide, and the others received long prison sentences. They were victims of one of the great miscarriages of American justice.

Seizing on the antiunion hysteria set off by the Haymarket affair, employers took the offensive. They broke strikes violently, compiled blacklists of strikers, and forced others to sign *yellow-dog contracts* guaranteeing that, as a condition of employment, they would not join a labor organization. If trade unionists needed any further confirmation of the tough world in which they lived, they found it in Haymarket and its aftermath.

In December 1886, having failed to persuade the Knights of Labor to desist from union activity, the national trade unions formed the American Federation of Labor (AFL), with Samuel Gompers as president. The AFL in effect locked into place the trade-union structure as it had evolved by the 1880s. Underlying this structure was the conviction that workers had to take the world as it was, not as they dreamed it might be. At this point, the American movement definitely diverged from the European model, for fundamental to Gompers' AFL was opposition to a political party for workers.

The Knights of Labor never recovered from their defeats after the Haymarket affair. Powderly retreated to the rhetoric of labor reform, but wage earners had lost interest, and he was unable to formulate a viable new strategy. By the mid-1890s, the Knights of Labor had faded away.

INDUSTRIAL WAR

American trade unions were conservative. They accepted the economic order. All they wanted was a larger share for working people. But it was precisely that claim against company profits that made American employers so opposed to collective bargaining. In the 1890s they unleashed a fierce counterattack on the trade-union movement.

In Homestead, Pennsylvania, site of one of Carnegie's great steel mills, the skilled men thought themselves safe from that threat. Mostly homeowners, they elected fellow workers to public office and considered the town very much their community. And they had faith in Andrew Carnegie, who had announced in a famous magazine article that workers had the right to organize and a right to their jobs that employers should honor during labor disputes: it was wrong to bring in strikebreakers.

Espousing high-toned principles made Carnegie feel good, but a healthy bottom line made him feel even better. He decided that collective bargaining had become too expensive, and he was confident that his skilled workers could be replaced by the advanced machinery he was installing. Lacking the stomach for the hard battle, Carnegie fled to a remote estate in Scotland, leaving behind a second-in-command well qualified to do the dirty work. This was Henry Clay Frick, a former coal baron and a veteran of labor wars in the coal fields.

After a brief pretense at bargaining Frick announced that effective July 1, 1892, the company would no longer deal with the Amalgamated Association of Iron and Steel Workers. The plant had already been fortified so that strikebreakers could be brought in to resume operations. At stake for Carnegie's employees now was not just wage cuts but the defense of a way of life. The town mayor, a union man, turned away the county sheriff when he tried to take possession of the plant. The entire community mobilized in defense of the union.

At dawn on July 6 two barges were seen approaching Homestead up the Monogahela River. On board were armed guards hired by the Pinkerton Detective Agency to take control of the steel works on behalf of the company. Behind hastily erected barricades the strikers opened fire and a bloody battle ensued. When the Pinkertons surrendered, they were mercilessly pummeled by the enraged women of Homestead as they retreated to the railway station. Frick appealed to the governor of Pennsylvania, who called out the state militia and placed Homestead under martial law. The great steel works was taken over and opened to strikebreakers, while union leaders and town officials were arrested on charges of riot, murder, and treason.

The Homestead strike ushered in a decade of strife that pitted working people against the formidable power of corporate industry and the even more formidable power of their own government. That hard reality was driven home to workers at a place that seemed an even less likely site for class warfare than Homestead. Pullman, Illinois, was a model factory town built by George M. Pullman, inventor of the sleeping car that brought comfort and luxury to railway travel. When the Panic of 1893 struck, business fell off, and Pullman cut wages but not the rents for company housing. When a workers' committee complained in May 1894, Pullman answered that there was no connection between his roles as employer and landlord. And he fired the workers' committee.

The Pullman Strike

Chicago was the hub of the railway network and the strategic center of the battle between the Pullman boycotters and the trunk line railroads. For the strikers, the crucial thing was to prevent those trains with Pullman cars attached from running; for the railroads, it was to get the trains through at any cost. The arrival of federal troops meant that the trains would move and that the strikers would be defeated. (*Harper's Weekly,* July 21, 1894)

The strike that ensued would have warranted only a footnote in American labor history but for the fact that the Pullman workers belonged to the American Railway Union (ARU), a rapidly growing industrial union of railroad workers. Its leader, Eugene V. Debs, directed ARU members not to handle Pullman sleeping cars, which, although operated by the railroads, were owned and serviced by the Pullman Company. This was a *secondary labor boycott:* force was applied on a second party (the railroads) to bring pressure on the primary target (Pullman). Since the railroads insisted on running the Pullman cars, a far-flung strike soon spread across the country, threatening the entire economy.

Quite deliberately, the railroads maneuvered to bring the federal government into the dispute. Their hook was the U.S. mail cars, which they attached to every train hauling Pullman cars. When strikers stopped these trains, the railroads appealed to President Cleveland to protect the U.S. mail and halt the growing violence. Richard Olney, Cleveland's attorney general, was a former railroad lawyer who unabashedly sided with his former employers. When federal troops failed to get the trains running again, Olney obtained court injunctions prohibiting the ARU leaders from conducting the strike. Debs and his associates, refusing to obey, were charged with contempt of court and jailed. Now leaderless and uncoordinated, the strike quickly disintegrated.

No one could doubt why the great Pullman boycott had failed: it had been crushed by the naked use of government power on behalf of the railroad companies.

AMERICAN RADICALISM IN THE MAKING

Very little in Eugene Debs's background would have suggested that he would one day become the nation's leading socialist. A native of Terre Haute, Indiana, a prosperous railroad town, Debs grew up believing in the essential goodness of American society. A popular young man-about-town, Debs considered a career in politics or business but instead got involved in the local labor movement. In 1880 at the age of twenty-five he was elected national secretary-treasurer of the Brotherhood of Locomotive Firemen, one of the craft unions that represented the skilled operating trades on the railroads.

Troubled by his union's indifference to the low-paid track and yard laborers, Debs unexpectedly resigned from his comfortable post to devote himself to a new organization, the American Railway Union, that would organize all railroad workers irrespective of skill—that is, an *industrial union*.

The Pullman strike visibly changed Debs. Sentenced to six months in the federal penitentiary, Debs emerged an avowed radical, committed to a lifelong struggle against a system that enabled employers to enlist the powers of government to beat down working people. Initially Debs identified himself as a Populist (see Chapter 18), but he quickly gravitated to the socialist camp.

German refugees had brought the ideas of Karl Marx, the radical German philosopher, to America after the failed revolution of 1848 in Europe. Marx postulated a class struggle between capitalists and workers, ending in a revolution that would abolish private ownership of the means of production and bring about a classless society. Little noticed by most Americans, Marxist socialism struck deep roots in the German American communities of Chicago and New York. With the formation of the Socialist Labor Party in 1877, Marxist socialism established itself as a permanent, if narrowly based, presence in American politics.

When Eugene Debs appeared in their midst in 1897, the socialists were in disarray. American capitalism had just gone through its worst crisis, yet they had failed to make much headway. Many blamed the party head, Daniel De Leon, an ideological purist not greatly interested in attracting voters. Debs joined in the revolt against the dogmatic De Leon and helped launch the rival Socialist Party of America in 1901.

A spellbinding campaigner, Debs talked socialism in an American idiom, making Marxism understandable and persuasive to many ordinary Americans. Under him the new party began to break out of its immigrant base and attract American-born voters. In Texas, Oklahoma, and Minnesota socialism exerted a powerful appeal among distressed farmers radicalized by Populism. The party was also highly successful at attracting women activists. Inside of a decade, with a national network of branches and state organizations, the Socialist Party had become a force to be reckoned with in American politics.

For some radical unionists, especially veterans of the fierce labor wars in the West (see Chapter 16), electoral politics seemed too tame. Led by Ed Boyce and "Big Bill" Haywood, the Western Federation of Miners joined with left-wing socialists in 1905 to create a new movement, the Industrial Workers of the World (IWW). The Wobblies, as IWW members were called, fervently supported the Marxist class struggle—but at the workplace rather than in politics. By resistance at the point of production and ultimately by means of a general strike, they believed that the workers would bring about a revolution. A new society would emerge, run directly by the workers through their industrial unions. The term *syndicalism* describes this brand of workers' radicalism.

T I M E L I N E

1869	Knights of Labor founded in Philadelphia First transcontinental railroad completed	1892	Homestead steel strike crushed
		1893	The Panic of 1893 starts the depression of the 1890s. Wave of railroad bankruptcies; reorganization by investment bankers
1872	Andrew Carnegie starts construction of the Edgar Thompson steel works near Pittsburgh.		
		1894	President Cleveland sends troops to break Pullman boycott.
1873	The Panic of 1873 ushers in economic depression.	1895	Frederick W. Taylor launches scientific management. Immigration from southern and eastern Europe exceeds immigration from western Europe for the first time.
1877	Baltimore and Ohio workers initiate a nationwide railroad strike.		
1878	Gustavus Swift introduces the refrigerator train car.		
		1901	Eugene V. Debs helps found the Socialist Party of America.
1883	Railroads establish national time zones.		
1886	Haymarket Square anarchist bombing in Chicago American Federation of Labor (AFL) founded	1905	Industrial Workers of the World (IWW) launched

In both its major forms—politically oriented socialism and the syndicalist IWW—American radicalism flourished after the crisis of the 1890s, but only on a limited basis and never with the possibility of seizing power. Nevertheless, socialists and Wobblies served a larger purpose. The new industrial economy—a wealth-creating machine beyond the world's imagining—was also brutally indifferent to the many who fell by the wayside. American radicalism, by its sheer vitality, bore witness to what was exploitative and unjust in the new industrial order.

For Further Exploration

For students new to economic history, biography offers an accessible entry point into what can be a dauntingly technical subject. The biographical literature is especially rich in American history because of this country's fascination with its great magnates and because of a long-standing debate among historians over what contribution (if any) the business moguls made to America's industrializing economy. The initiating book was Matthew Josephson's classic *The Robber Barons* (1934), which, as the title implies, argued that America's great fortunes were built on the wealth that others had created. The contrary view was taken by the financial historian Julius Grodinsky, whose *Jay Gould: His Business Career, 1867–1892* (1957) explained masterfully how this railroad buccaneer helped shape the transportation system. Since then, there have been superb, mostly sympathetic, business biographies, including Joseph F. Wall, *Andrew Carnegie* (1970); Ron Chernow, *Titan: The Life of John D. Rockefeller* (1998); and Jean Strouse, *Morgan: American Financier* (1999). The founder of scientific management has also recently been the subject of a robust biography: Robert Kanigel, *The One Best Way: Frederick W. Taylor and the Enigma of Efficiency* (1997). On labor's side, the biographical literature is nearly as rich. The founder of the AFL is the subject of a lively brief biography by Harold Livesay, *Samuel Gompers and Organized Labor in America* (1978); Gompers's autobiography, *Seventy Years of Life and Labor* (2 vols., 1925), also makes rewarding reading. His main critic is treated with great insight in Nick Salvatore, *Eugene V. Debs: Citizen and Socialist* (1982). The IWW leader William D. Haywood left a colorful autobiography, *Bill Haywood's Book* (1929), and Haywood is also the subject of Peter Carlson's biography, *Roughneck* (1982). Biography, of course, tends to overlook the foot soldiers of history, but social historians have striven mightily in recent years to tell their story. An excellent example is Paul Krause, *The Battle for Homestead, 1880–1892* (1992), which rescues from obscurity the working people who led that decisive steel strike. There is an excellent website on Andrew Carnegie at <pbs.org/wgbh/amex/pandeoi.html> and a site on the Bessemer converter that established his dominance in steel at <anglia.co.uk/angmulti/indrev/steel5.html>.

Chapter 18

THE POLITICS OF LATE NINETEENTH-CENTURY AMERICA

Politics has now become a gainful profession, like advocacy, stockbroking, [or] the dry goods trade. . . . People go into it to make a living by it.

—James Bryce, *American Commonwealth*, 1888

Ever since the founding of the Republic, foreign visitors had been coming to America to study its political system. Most famous of the early observers was the French aristocrat Alexis de Tocqueville, the author of *Democracy in America* (1835). When an equally brilliant visitor, the Englishman James Bryce, sat down to write his own account fifty years later, he decided that Tocqueville's great book could not serve as his model. For Tocqueville, Bryce noted, "America was primarily a democracy, the ideal democracy, fraught with lessons for Europe." In his own book, *The American Commonwealth* (1888), Bryce was much less rhapsodic. Tocqueville's robust democracy had devolved a half century later into the dreary machine politics of post–Civil War America.

Bryce was anxious, however, that his European readers not misunderstand him. Europeans would find in his book "much that is sordid, much that will provoke unfavourable comment." But they needed to be aware of "a reserve of force and patriotism more than sufficient to sweep away all the evils now tolerated, and to make a politics of the country worthy of its material grandeur and of the private virtues of its inhabitants." Bryce was ultimately an optimist: "A hundred times in writing this book have I been disheartened by the facts I was stating; a hundred times has the recollection of the abounding strength and vitality of the nation chased away these tremours."

Just what Bryce found so disheartening in the practice of American politics is this chapter's first subject. The second is the underlying vitality that Bryce sensed and how it reemerged and began to reinvigorate the nation's politics by the century's end.

The Politics of the Status Quo, 1877–1893

In times of national ferment public life becomes magnified. Leaders emerge. Great issues are debated. The powers of government expand. All this had been true of the Civil War era, when the crises of Union and Reconstruction had severely tested the nation's political structure, not least by the contested presidential election of 1876. In 1877, with Rutherford B. Hayes safely settled in the White House, the era of sectional strife finally ended.

Political life went on, but drained of its earlier drama. In the 1880s there were no Lincolns, no great national debates. An irreducible core of public functions remained and even, as on the question of railroad regulation, grudging acceptance of new federal responsibilities. But the dominant rhetoric celebrated government that governed least, and compared to the Civil War era, American government did govern less.

THE NATIONAL SCENE

There were five presidents from 1877 to 1893: Rutherford B. Hayes (Republican, 1877–1881), James A. Garfield (Republican, 1881), Chester A. Arthur (Republican, 1881–1885), Grover Cleveland (Democrat, 1885–1889), and Benjamin Harrison (Republican, 1889–1893). All were estimable men. Hayes had served effectively as governor of Ohio for three terms, and Garfield had done well as a congressional leader. Arthur, despite his reputation as a hack politician, had shown fine administrative skills as head of the New York customs house. Cleveland had an enviable reputation as reform mayor of Buffalo and governor of New York. None was a charismatic leader, but circumstances, more than personal qualities, explain why these presidents did not make a larger mark on history.

The president's biggest job was to dispense political patronage. Under the spoils system government appointments were treated as rewards for those who had served the victorious party. Reform of this system became urgent after President Garfield was shot in 1881 by Charles Guiteau, a deranged religious fanatic. Although Guiteau's motives were murky, advocates of civil-service reform blamed the poisonous atmosphere of a spoils system that left many disappointed in the scramble for office. The resulting Pendleton Act of 1883 created a list of jobs to be filled on the basis of examinations administered by the new Civil Service Commission. The list originally covered only 10 percent of all federal jobs, however, and patronage remained a preoccupation in the White House. Though standards of public administration did rise, there was no American counterpart to the elite civil services taking shape in Britain and Germany in these years.

The functions of the executive branch were, in any event, very modest. Its biggest job was delivering the mail; of 100,000 federal employees in 1880, 56 percent worked for the Post Office. Even the important cabinet offices—Treasury, State,

PUCK.

-WHERE IS HE?-

"Where Is He?"

This *Puck* cartoon, which appeared two weeks after Benjamin Harrison's defeat for reelection at Grover Cleveland's hands in 1892, is a commentary on Harrison's insignificance as president. The hat in Uncle Sam's hands belonged to Benjamin Harrison's grandfather, President William Henry Harrison. *Puck* started using the hat as a trademark for Benjamin Harrison after he had been elected in 1888. As his term progressed, the hat grew progressively larger, and the president progressively smaller. By the time of his defeat, just the hat is left and Harrison has disappeared altogether.

(Courtesy of the Bancroft Library, University of California at Berkeley. *Puck*, November 16, 1892)

War, Navy, Interior—were sleepy places carrying on largely routine duties. Virtually all federal funding came from customs duties and excise taxes on liquor and tobacco. These sources produced more money than the government spent. How to reduce the federal surplus ranked as one of the most troublesome issues of the 1880s.

On matters of national policy the presidents took a back seat to Congress. But Congress functioned badly. Procedural rules frequently stymied legislative business. Nor were the two parties especially anxious to get things done. Historically, they represented somewhat different traditions. The Democrats favored states' rights, while the Republicans were heirs to the Whig enthusiasm for federally assisted economic development. After Reconstruction, however, the Republicans backed away from that interventionist position, and, in truth, party differences became muddy. On most leading issues of the day—civil-service reform, the currency, and regulation of the railroads—the divisions occurred within the parties, not between them.

Only the tariff remained a fighting issue. From Lincoln's administration onward high duties had protected American industry from imported goods. The

Democrats, free traders by tradition, regularly attacked Republican protectionism. But in practice even the tariff was a negotiable issue, like any other. Congressmen voted their constituents' interests, regardless of party rhetoric. As a result, every tariff bill was a patchwork of bargains among special interests.

Issues were treated gingerly partly because the parties were so equally balanced. The Democrats, in retreat immediately after the Civil War, quickly regrouped and by the end of Reconstruction stood on virtually equal terms with the Republicans. Every presidential election from 1876 to 1892 was decided by a thin margin, and neither party gained permanent command of Congress. Political caution seemed wise; any false move on national issues might tip the scales to the other side.

The weakening of principled politics was evident in the Republicans' retreat from their Civil War legacy. The major unfinished business after 1877 involved the plight of the former slaves. The Republican agenda called for federal funding to combat illiteracy and, even more contentious, federal protection for black voters in southern congressional elections. Neither measure managed to make it through Congress. With little mileage left in Reconstruction politics, Republicans back-pedaled on the race issue and abandoned African Americans to their fate.

That did not stop Republican orators from "waving the bloody shirt" against the Democrats. Service in the Union army gave candidates a strong claim to public office, and veterans' benefits always stood high on the Republican agenda. The Democrats played the same patriotic card in the South as defenders of the Lost Cause.

Alternatively, campaigns could descend into comedy. In the hard-fought election of 1884, for example, the Democrat Cleveland burst on the scene as a reformer, fresh from his victories over corrupt machine politics in New York State. But years earlier Cleveland, a bachelor, had fathered an illegitimate child, and throughout the campaign he was dogged by the ditty, "Maw, Maw, where's my Paw?" (After election day, Cleveland's supporters gleefully responded, "He's in the White House, haw-haw-haw.") Cleveland's opponent, James G. Blaine, already on the defensive for taking favors from the railroads, was weakened by the unthinking charge of a too ardent Republican supporter that the Democrats were the party of "Rum, Romanism and Rebellion." In a twinkling, he had insulted Catholic voters and possibly lost the election for Blaine. In the midst of all the mudslinging, the issues got lost.

THE IDEOLOGY OF INDIVIDUALISM

The characteristics of public life in the 1880s—the inactivity of the federal government, the evasiveness of the political parties, the absorption in politics for its own sake—derived ultimately from the conviction that little was at stake in public affairs. In 1887 Cleveland vetoed a small appropriation for drought-stricken Texas farmers with the remark that "though the people support the Government, the Government should not support the people." Governmental activity was itself considered a bad thing. All that the state could do, said Republican Senator Roscoe

Facing the World

The cover of this Horatio Alger novel (1893) captures the myth of opportunity. Our hero, Harry Vane, is a poor but earnest lad, ready to make his way in the world and, despite the many obstacles thrown in his path, sure to succeed. In some 135 books Horatio Alger repeated this story, with minor variations, for an eager reading public that numbered in the millions.

(Frank and Marie-Therese Wood Print Collections, Alexandria, Virginia)

Conkling, was "to clear the way of impediments and dangers, and leave every class and every individual free and safe in the exertions and pursuits of life." Conkling was expressing the political corollary to the economic doctrine of *laissez-faire*—the belief that the less government did, the better.

A flood of popular writings trumpeted the creed of individualism, from the rags-to-riches tales of Horatio Alger to innumerable success manuals with such titles as *Thoughts for the Young Men of America, or a Few Practical Words of Advice to Those Born in Poverty and Destined to Be Reared in Orphanages* (1871). Self-made men like Andrew Carnegie became cultural heroes. A best seller was Carnegie's *Triumphant Democracy* (1886), which paid homage to a country that enabled a penniless Scottish child to rise from bobbin boy to steel magnate.

From the pulpit came the assurances of the Episcopal bishop William Lawrence of Massachusetts that "Godliness is in league with riches." Bishop Lawrence was voicing a familar theme of American Protestantism: success in one's earthly calling revealed the promise of eternal salvation. It was all too easy for a conservative ministry to make morally reassuring the furious acquisitiveness of industrial America. "To secure wealth is an honorable ambition," intoned the Baptist minister Russell H. Conwell in his lecture "Acres of Diamonds."

The celebration of American acquisitiveness drew strong intellectual support from science. In *The Origin of Species* (1859) the British naturalist Charles Darwin had developed a bold hypothesis to explain the evolution of plants and animals. In nature, Darwin wrote, all living things struggle to survive. Individual members of a species are born with genetic mutations that enable them to compete better in their particular environment—camouflage coloring for a bird, for example, or resistance to thirst in a camel. These survival characteristics, since they are genetically transmissible, become dominant in future generations, and the species evolves. This process of evolution, which Darwin called *natural selection,* created a revolution in biology.

Drawing on Darwin, the British philosopher Herbert Spencer spun out an elaborate analysis of how human society had evolved through competition and "survival of the fittest." Social Darwinism, as Spencer's ideas became known, was championed in America by William Graham Sumner, a sociology professor at Yale. Competition, said Sumner, is a law of nature that "can no more be done away with than gravitation." And who are the fittest? "The millionaires. . . . They may fairly be regarded as the naturally selected agents of society. They get high wages and live in luxury, but the bargain is a good one for society."

Social Darwinists regarded with horror any interference with social processes. "The great stream of time and earthly things will sweep on just the same in spite of us," Sumner wrote in a famous essay, "The Absurd Attempt to Make the World Over" (1894). As for the government, it had "at bottom . . . two chief things . . . with which to deal. They are the property of men and the honor of women. These it has to defend against crime."

THE SUPREMACY OF THE COURTS

Suspicion of government not only paralyzed political initiative; it also shifted power away from the executive and legislative branches. "The task of constitutional government," declared Sumner, "is to devise institutions which shall come into play at critical periods to prevent the abusive control of the powers of a state by the controlling classes in it." Sumner meant the judiciary. From the 1870s onward the courts increasingly accepted the role that he assigned to them, becoming the guardians of the rights of private property against the grasping tentacles of government.

The main target of the courts was the states rather than the national government. This was because, under the federal system as it was understood in the late nineteenth century, the residual powers—those not delegated by the Constitution to the federal government—left to the states primary responsibility for social welfare and economic regulation. They exercised their *police powers* to ensure the health, safety, and morals of their citizens. The leading question in American law was how to strike a balance between state responsibility for the general welfare and the liberty of individuals to pursue their private interests. Most states, caught up in the conservative ethos of the day, were cutting back on expenditures and public services. Even so, there were more than enough state initiatives to alarm vigilant judges. Thus, in the landmark case *In Re Jacobs* (1885), the New York Supreme Court struck down a state law prohibiting cigar manufacturing in tenements on the grounds that such regulation exceeded the police powers of the state.

Increasingly, however, federal judges took up the battle against state activism. The Supreme Court's crucial weapon in this campaign was the Fourteenth Amendment (1868), which prohibited the states from depriving "any person of life, liberty, or property, without due process of law." The due-process clause had been adopted during Reconstruction to protect the civil rights of the former slaves. But due process protected the property rights and contractual liberty of any "person," and legally corporations counted as persons. So interpreted, the Fourteenth Amendment became by the turn of the century a powerful restraint on the states in the use of their police powers to regulate private business.

The Supreme Court similarly hamstrung the federal government. In 1895 the Court ruled that the federal power to regulate interstate commerce did not cover manufacturing and struck down a federal income tax law. And in areas where federal power was undeniable—such as the regulation of railroads—the Supreme Court watched like a hawk for undue interference with the rights of property.

Power conferred status. The law, not politics, attracted the ablest people and held the public's esteem. A Wisconsin judge boasted: "The bench symbolizes on earth the throne of divine justice. . . . Law in its highest sense is the will of God." Judicial supremacy reflected how dominant the ideology of individualism had become in industrial America and also how low American politicians had fallen in the esteem of their countrymen.

Politics and the People

For all the criticism leveled against it, politics figured centrally in the nation's life. Proportionately more voters turned out in presidential elections from 1876 to 1892 than at any other time in American history. People voted Democratic or Republican loyally for a lifetime. National conventions attracted huge crowds. "The excitement, the mental and physical strains," remarked an Indiana Republican after the 1888 convention, "are surpassed only by prolonged battle in actual warfare, as I have been told by officers of the Civil War who later engaged in convention struggles." The convention he described had nominated the colorless Benjamin Harrison on a routine platform. What was all the excitement about?

CULTURAL POLITICS: PARTY, RELIGION, AND ETHNICITY

In the late nineteenth century politics was a vibrant part of the nation's culture. During the election season the party faithful marched in impressive torchlight parades. Party paraphernalia flooded the country—handkerchiefs, mugs, posters, and buttons emblazoned with the Democratic donkey or the Republican elephant, symbols that had been adopted in the 1870s. In the 1888 campaign the candidates were featured on cards, like baseball players, packed into Honest Long Cut tobacco. In an age before movies and radio, politics ranked as one of the great American forms of entertainment.

Party loyalty was a deadly serious matter, however. Long after the killing ended, Civil War emotions ran high. Among family friends in Cleveland, recalled the urban reformer Brand Whitlock, the Republican Party was "a synonym for patriotism, another name for the nation. It was inconceivable that any self-respecting person should be a Democrat"—or, among former Confederates in the South, that any self-respecting person could be a Republican.

Beyond these sectional differences, the most important determinants of party loyalty were religion and ethnicity (see Figure 18.1). Statistically, northern Democrats tended to be foreign-born and Catholic, while Republicans tended to be native-born and Protestant. Among Protestants, the more *pietistic* a person's faith—that is, the more personal and direct the believer's relationship to God—the more likely he or she was to be a Republican and to favor using the powers of the state to uphold social values.

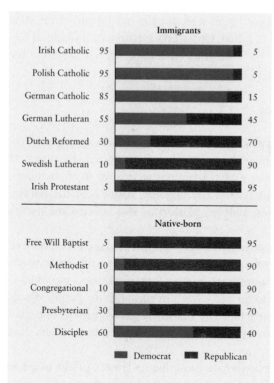

Immigrants

Irish Catholic	95 — 5
Polish Catholic	95 — 5
German Catholic	85 — 15
German Lutheran	55 — 45
Dutch Reformed	30 — 70
Swedish Lutheran	10 — 90
Irish Protestant	5 — 95

Native-born

Free Will Baptist	5 — 95
Methodist	10 — 90
Congregational	10 — 90
Presbyterian	30 — 70
Disciples	60 — 40

■ Democrat   ■ Republican

FIGURE 18.1

Ethnocultural Voting Patterns in the Midwest, 1870–1892

These figures demonstrate how voting patterns among midwesterners reflected ethnicity and religion in the late nineteenth century. Especially striking is the overwhelming preference by immigrant Catholics for the Democratic Party. Among Protestants there was an equally strong preference for the Republican Party by certain groups of immigrants (Swedish Lutherans and Irish Protestants) and native-born (Free Will Baptists, Methodists, and Congregationalists), but other Protestant groups were more evenly divided in their party preferences.

During the 1880s, as ethnic tensions built up in many cities, education became an arena of bitter conflict. One issue was whether instruction would be in English. Immigrant groups often wanted their children taught in their own languages. In St. Louis, a heavily German city, the long-standing policy of teaching German to all students was overturned after a heated campaign. Religion was an even more explosive educational issue. Catholics fought a losing battle over public aid for parochial schools, which by 1900 was prohibited by twenty-three states. In Boston a furious controversy broke out in 1888 over the use of an anti-Catholic history textbook. When the school board withdrew the offending book, angry Protestants threw the moderates off the board and returned the text to the curriculum.

Then there was the regulation of public morals. In many states so-called blue laws restricted activity on Sundays. When Nebraska banned Sunday baseball, the state supreme court approved the law as a blow struck in "the contest between Christianity and wrong." But German and Irish Catholics, who saw nothing evil in a bit of fun on Sunday, considered blue laws a violation of their personal freedom. Ethnocultural conflict also flared over the liquor question. Many states adopted strict licensing and local-option laws governing the sale of alcoholic beverages. Indiana permitted drinking, but only joylessly in rooms containing "no devices for amusement or music . . . of any kind."

Because the hottest social issues of the day—education, the liquor question, and observance of the sabbath—were also party issues, they lent deep significance to party affiliation. And because these issues were fought out mostly at the state and local levels, they hit very close to home. Crusading Methodists thought of Republicans as the party of morality. For embattled Irish and German Catholics the Democratic Party was the defender of their freedoms.

ORGANIZATIONAL POLITICS

Political life was also important because of the organizational activity it generated. By the 1870s both major parties had evolved formal, well-organized structures. At the base lay the precinct or ward, where party meetings were open to all members. County, state, and national committees ran the ongoing business of the parties. Conventions determined party rules, adopted platforms, and selected the party's candidates.

Party administration seemed, on its face, highly democratic, since in theory all power derived from the party members in the precincts and wards. In practice, however, the parties were run by unofficial internal organizations—*machines*—which consisted of insiders willing to do party work in exchange for public jobs or the sundry advantages of being connected. The machines tended toward one-man rule, although the "boss" ruled more by the consent of the secondary leaders than by his own absolute power.

Absorbed in the tasks of power brokerage, party bosses treated public issues as somewhat irrelevant. The high stakes of money, jobs, and influence made for intense factionalism. After Ulysses S. Grant left the White House in 1877, the Republican Party divided into two warring factions—the Stalwarts, who followed Senator Roscoe Conkling of New York, and the Halfbreeds, led by James G. Blaine of Maine. The split was sparked by a personal feud between Conkling and Blaine, but it persisted because of a furious struggle over patronage. The Halfbreeds represented a newer Republican generation that was more favorably disposed than the Stalwarts to political reform and was less committed to shopworn Civil War issues. But issues were secondary in the strife between Stalwarts and Halfbreeds. They were really fighting over the spoils of party politics.

And yet the record of machine politics was not wholly negative. In certain ways the standards of governance got better. Disciplined professionals, veterans of machine politics, proved effective as state legislators and congressmen because they were more experienced in the give-and-take of politics. More important, party machines filled a void in the nation's public life. They did informally much of what the governmental system left undone, especially in the cities (see Chapter 19).

But machine politics never managed to win public approval. Many of the nation's social elite—intellectuals, well-to-do businessmen, and old-line families—resented a politics that excluded people like themselves, the "best men." There was, too, a genuine clash of values. Political reformers called for "disinterestedness" and "independence"—the opposite of the self-serving careerism and party regularity fostered by the machine system. Many of these critics had earned their spurs as Liberal Republicans who had broken from the party and fought President Grant's reelection in 1872.

In 1884 Carl Schurz, Edwin L. Godkin, and Charles Francis Adams Jr. again left the Republican Party because they could not stomach its presidential candidate, James G. Blaine, whom they associated with corrupt politics. Mainly from New York and Massachusetts, these Republicans became known as Mugwumps—a derisive bit of contemporary slang, supposedly of Indian origin, referring to pompous or self-important persons. The Mugwumps threw their support to the Democrat Grover Cleveland and may have ensured his victory by giving him the winning margin in New York State.

After the 1884 election the enthusiasm for reform spilled over into local politics, spawning good-government campaigns across the country. Although they won some municipal victories, the Mugwumps were more adept at molding public opinion than reforming government. Controlling the newspapers and journals read by the educated middle class, the Mugwumps defined the terms of political debate and denied the machine system public legitimacy.

The Mugwumps were reformers, but not on behalf of social justice. The problems of working people did not evoke their sympathy, nor did they favor using the the state to help the poor. As far as the Mugwumps were concerned, that government was best that governed least. Theirs was the brand of "reform" perfectly in keeping with a politics of the status quo.

WOMEN'S POLITICAL CULTURE

The young Theodore Roosevelt, an up-and-coming Republican state politician in 1884, referred to the Mugwumps contemptuously as "man-milliners." The sexual slur was not accidental. In attacking organizational politics the Mugwumps were challenging one of the bastions of male society. At party meetings and conventions men carried on not only the business of politics but also the rituals of male sociability amid cigar smoke and whiskey. Politics was identified with manliness. It was competitive. It dealt in the commerce of power. Party politics, in short, was no place for a woman.

So, naturally, the woman suffrage movement met fierce opposition. Blocked in their efforts to get a constitutional amendment, suffragists concentrated on state campaigns. But except in Wyoming, Idaho, Colorado, and Utah the most they could win was the right to vote for school boards or on tax issues. "Men are ordained to govern in all forceful and material things, because they are men," asserted an anti-suffrage resolution, "while women, by the same decree of God and nature, are equally fitted to bear rule in a higher and more spiritual realm"—that is to say, not in politics.

Yet this invocation of the doctrine of "separate spheres" did open a channel for women to enter public life. "Women's place is Home," acknowledged the journalist Retha Childe Dorr. "But Home is not contained within the four walls of an individual house. Home is the community. The city full of people is the Family. . . . And badly do the Home and Family need their mother." So believing, women had since the early nineteenth century engaged in charitable activities. Women's organizations fought prostitution, assisted the poor, agitated for prison reform, and tried to expand educational and job opportunities for women. Since many of these goals required state intervention, women's organizations of necessity became politically active. Partisan politics, they stressed, was not their game. Quite the contrary: women were bent on creating their own political sphere.

No issue joined home and politics more poignantly than did the liquor question. Just before Christmas in 1873 the women of Hillsboro, Ohio, began to hold vigils in front of the town's saloons, pleading with the owners to close and end the suffering of families of hard-drinking fathers. Thus began a spontaneous uprising of women that spread across the country and closed an estimated 3,000 saloons. From this agitation came the Women's Christian Temperance Union (WCTU), which after its formation in 1874 rapidly blossomed into the largest women's organization in the country.

Because it excluded men, the WCTU was the spawning ground for women leaders. Under the guidance of Frances Willard, who became president in 1879, the WCTU moved beyond temperance and adopted a "Do-Everything" policy. Alcoholism, women recognized, was not simply a personal failing; it stemmed from larger social problems in American society. Willard also wanted to attract women

Wanted, Sober Men

This drawing appeared in a magazine in 1899, twenty-five years after
the women of Hillsboro, Ohio, rose
in revolt against the town's saloonkeepers and launched the Woman's
Christian Temperance Union
(WCTU). But the emotion it expresses had not changed—that the
saloon was the enemy of the family.
(Culver Pictures)

who had no particular interest in the liquor question. By 1889 the WCTU had thirty-
nine departments concerned with labor, prostitution, health, and international
peace as well as temperance.

Most important, the WCTU was drawn to woman suffrage. This was necessary,
Willard argued, "because the liquor traffic is entrenched in law, and law grows out
of the will of majorities, and majorities of women are against the liquor traffic."
The WCTU began by stressing moral suasion and personal discipline—hence the
word "temperance" in its name—but expanded its attack on liquor to include prohibition by law. Women needed the vote, said Willard, to fulfill their social responsibilities *as women* (see American Voices, "The Case for Women's Political
Rights"). This was very different from the claim made by the suffragists—that the
ballot was an inherent right of all citizens *as individuals*—and was less threatening
to masculine pride.

Not much changed in the short run. But by linking women's social concerns
to women's political participation, the WCTU helped lay the groundwork for a
fresh attack on male electoral politics in the early twentieth century. And in the
meantime, even without the vote, the WCTU demonstrated how potent a voice
women could find in the public arena and how vibrant a political culture they
could build.

AMERICAN VOICES

The Case for Women's Political Rights

HELEN POTTER

*I*n 1883 Helen Potter, a New York educator, testified before the Senate Committee on Education and Labor. She meant to speak about the sanitary conditions of the poor in New York City, but in the course of her testimony she delivered a powerful indictment of the unequal treatment of women that spoke volumes about the evolving women's political culture of the late nineteenth century.

The Witness. It is really an important question—this of the condition of women in our community. When I was a young girl I had some ambition, and when I heard a good speaker, or when I read something written by a good writer, I had an ambition to do something of that kind myself. I was exceedingly anxious to preach, but the churches would not have me; why, they said that a woman must not be heard. . . .

Q. What would be the effect of conferring suffrage upon women? Would not the effect be injurious to the moral character and high influence of woman, if she should devote herself to the tricks of the politician's trade, which you very properly criticize so severely?

A. . . . I certainly think it would clean our streets, and I think it would purify politics, at least for the next two hundred years. It would take about that time to get women to understand the tricks of politicians as at present practiced. I do not think that women would be injured by it. . . . This Government is based upon the will of the people—women are "people," yet we have not a word to say about the laws. You will hear women in the course of your acquaintance say they wish they were men; I never heard a man say he wished he was a woman. . . .

Q. What effect do you think the extension of the suffrage to women would have upon their material condition, their wage-earning power and the like?

A. They would get equal pay for equal work of equal value. I do not think a woman ought to be paid the price of an expert, when she is not herself an expert, but I believe there would be a stimulus for a woman to fit herself for the very best work. What stimulus is there for woman to fit herself properly, if she never can attain the highest pay, no matter what sort of work she does? If women had a vote I think larger avenues of livelihood would be opened for them and they would be more respected by the governmental powers.

SOURCE: U.S. Senate, Committee on Education and Labor, *Report upon Relations Between Labor and Capital* (1885), II: 627, 629–32.

Race and Politics in the South

When Reconstruction ended in 1877, so did the promise of racial equality for the South's African Americans. Schooling was strictly segregated. Access to jobs, the courts, and social welfare was racially determined and unequal. But public accommodations were not yet legally segregated, and practices varied a good deal across the South. Only on the railroads, as rail travel became more common, did whites demand that blacks be excluded from first-class cars, with the result that southern railroads became after 1887 the first public accommodation subject to segregation laws.

In politics the situation was still more fluid. Blacks had not been driven from politics. On the contrary, their turnout at elections was not far behind whites. But blacks did not participate on equal terms with whites. In the Black Belt areas where African Americans sometimes outnumbered whites, voting districts were gerry-mandered to ensure that while blacks got some offices, political control remained in white hands. Blacks, moreover, were routinely intimidated during political cam-paigns. Even so, an impressive majority remained staunchly Republican, refusing, as the last black congressman from Mississippi told his House colleagues in 1882, "to surrender their honest convictions, even upon the altar of their personal ne-cessities."

Whatever hopes blacks entertained for better days, however, faded during the 1880s and then, in the next decade, expired in a terrible burst of racial terrorism.

BIRACIAL POLITICS

No democratic society can survive if it does not enable competing economic and social interests to be heard. In the United States the two-party system performs that role. The Civil War crisis severely tested the two-party system because, both North and South, political opposition came to be seen as treasonable. In the North, de-spite the best efforts of the Republicans, the Democrats shed their disgrace after the war and reclaimed their status as a major party. In the defeated South, however, the scars of war cut deep, and Reconstruction cut even deeper. The struggle for "home rule" empowered southern Democrats. They had "redeemed" the South from Re-publican domination; hence the name they adopted: Redeemers. Cloaked in the mantle of the Lost Cause, the Redeemers claimed a monopoly on political legiti-macy.

The Republican Party in the South did not fold up, however. On the contrary, it soldiered on, sustained by tenacious black loyalty, a hard core of white support, patronage from Republican national administrations, and a key Democrat vulner-ability. This was the gap between the universality the Democrats claimed as the party of Redemption and its actual domination by a single interest, the South's eco-nomic elite.

Class antagonism, though masked by sectional patriotism, was never absent from southern society. The Civil War had brought out long-smoldering differences between planters and hill-country farmers, who were called on to shed blood for a slaveholding system in which they had no interest. Afterward class tensions were exacerbated by the spread of farm tenantry and by the emergence of the low-wage factory system. Unable to make their grievances heard, economically distressed southerners broke with the Democratic Party in the early 1880s and mounted insurgent movements across the region. Most notable were the Readjusters, who briefly gained power in Virginia over the issue of speculation in Reconstruction debt: they opposed repayment that would have rewarded bond-holding speculators while leaving the state destitute. After subsiding briefly, this agrarian discontent revived with a vengeance in the late 1880s as tenant farmers now sought political power through farmers' alliances and the newly evolving Populist Party (see p. 537).

As this insurgency against the Democrats accelerated, the question of black participation became critical. Racism cut through southern society and, so some thought, most infected the lowest rungs. "The white laboring classes here," wrote an Alabaman in 1886, "are separated from the Negroes, working all day side by side with them, by an innate consciousness of race superiority." Yet when times got bad enough, hard-pressed whites could also see blacks as fellow victims. "They are in the ditch just like we are," asserted one white Texan. Southern Populists never fully reconciled these contradictory impulses. They did not question the conventions of social inequality. Nor were the interests of white farmers and black tenants and laborers always in concert. But once agrarian protest turned political, the logic of interracial solidarity became hard to deny.

Black farmers had developed a political structure of their own. The Colored Farmers' Alliance operated much less openly than its white counterparts—it could be worth a black man's life to make too open a show of his independence—but nevertheless made black voters a factor in the political calculations of southern Populists. The demands of partisan politics, once the break with the Democrats came, clinched the argument for interracial unity. Where the Populists fused with the Republican Party, as in North Carolina and Tennessee, they automatically became allies of black leaders. Where the Populists fielded separate third-party tickets, they needed to appeal directly to black voters. "The accident of color can make no difference in the interest of farmers, croppers, and laborers," argued the Georgian Tom Watson. "You are kept apart that you may be separately fleeced of your earnings." By making this interracial appeal, even if not always wholeheartedly, the Populists put at risk the foundations of conservative southern politics.

ONE-PARTY RULE TRIUMPHANT

The conservative Democrats struck back with all their might. They played the race card to the hilt, parading as the "white man's party" while denouncing the Populists for promoting "Negro rule." Yet they shamelessly competed for the black vote. In this they had many advantages: money, control of the local power structures, and a paternalistic relationship to the black community. When all else failed, mischief at the polls enabled the Democrats to beat back the Populists. Across the South in the 1892 elections the Democrats snatched victory from defeat by a miraculous vote count of blacks—including many long dead or gone. Thus the Mississippian Frank

Burkitt's bitter attack on the conservatives: they were "a class of corrupt office-seekers" who had "hypocritically raised the howl of white supremacy while they de-bauched the ballot boxes . . . disregarded the rights of the blacks . . . and actually dominated the will of the white people through the instrumentality of the stolen negro vote."

In the midst of these deadly struggles the Democrats decided to settle matters once and for all. Disfranchising the blacks, hitherto suggested hesitantly, now be-came a potent regionwide movement (Map 18.1). In 1890 Mississippi adopted a lit-eracy test that effectively drove the state's blacks out of politics. The motives behind it were cynical, but the literacy test could be dressed up as a reform for white Mis-sissippians tired of electoral fraud and violence. Their children and grandchildren, argued one influential figure, should not be left "with shotguns in their hands, a lie in their mouths and perjury on their lips in order to defeat the negroes." This logic persuaded even some weary Populists: Frank Burkitt, for example, was arguing *for* the Mississippi literacy test in the words quoted in the previous paragraph.

The race issue had helped bring down the Populists; now it helped reconcile them to defeat. Embittered poor whites, deeply ambivalent all along about interra-cial cooperation, turned their fury on blacks. Insofar as disfranchising measures

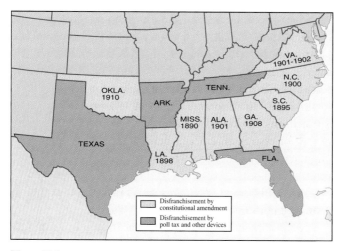

MAP 18.1
Disfranchisement in the South

In the midst of the Populist challenge to Democratic one-party rule in the South, a movement to deprive blacks of the right to vote spread from Mississippi across the South. By 1910 every state in the region except Tennessee, Arkansas, Texas, and Florida had made con-stitutional changes designed to prevent blacks from voting, and these four states accomplished much the same result through poll taxes and other exclusionary methods. For the next half century the political process in the South would be for whites only.

asserted militant white supremacy, poor whites approved. It was important, of course, that their own vulnerability—their own lack of education—be partially offset by lenient enforcement of the literacy test. Thus, to take a blatant instance, Louisiana's grandfather clause exempted from the test those entitled to vote on January 1, 1867 (before the Fifteenth Amendment gave freedmen that right), together with their sons and grandsons. But poor whites were not protected from property and poll-tax requirements, and many stopped voting. Poor whites might have objected more had their spokesmen not been conceded a voice within the Democratic Party. A new brand of demagogic politician came forward to speak for them, appealing not to their class interests but to their racial prejudices. Tom Watson, the fiery Georgia Populist, rebuilt his political career as a brilliant practitioner of race baiting.

The color line, hitherto incomplete, became rigid and comprehensive. Segregated seating in trains, widely adopted in the late 1880s, provided a precedent for the legal separation of the races. The enforcing legislation, known as Jim Crow laws, soon applied to every type of public facility—restaurants, hotels, streetcars, even cemeteries. In the 1890s the South became for the first time a society fully segregated by law.

The U.S. Supreme Court soon ratified the South's decision. In the case of *Plessy v. Ferguson* (1896) the Court ruled that segregation was not discriminatory—that is, it did not violate black civil rights under the Fourteenth Amendment—provided that blacks received accommodations equal to those of whites. The "separate but equal" doctrine ignored the realities of southern life: segregated facilities were rarely if ever "equal" in any material sense, and segregation was itself intended to underscore the inferiority of blacks (see American Voices, "A Black Man on Segregation"). With a similar disregard for reality the Supreme Court in *Williams v. Mississippi* (1898) validated the disfranchising devices of the southern states: so long as race was not a specified criterion for disfranchisement, the Fifteenth Amendment was not being violated even though the practical effect was the virtual exclusion of blacks from politics in the South.

Race hatred manifested itself in a wave of lynchings and race riots, and public vilification of blacks became commonplace. Benjamin R. Tillman, governor of South Carolina and after 1895 a U.S. senator, vilified blacks as "an ignorant and debased and debauched race." This ugly racism stemmed from several sources, including job competition between whites and blacks during the depressed 1890s and white anger against a less submissive black generation born after slavery.

But what had triggered the antiblack impulse was the Populist challenge to one-party rule. From then on white supremacy propped up the one-party system that the Redeemers had been fighting for ever since Reconstruction. If power had to be shared with demagogic poor-white politicians, it would be on terms agreeable to the conservative elite—the exclusion from politics of any serious challenge to the economic status quo.

AMERICAN VOICES

A Black Man on Segregation

C. H. JOHNSON

*W*hen *C. H. Johnson, a porter at an auction house, spoke up before a visiting Senate committee in 1883, the movement for a segregated South was just gathering steam. But even then, Johnson makes clear, southern blacks were not deceived about the fraudulence of "separate but equal."*

Columbus, Ga., November 20, 1883

Question. Do you feel as though your people have had a fair chance to be heard by the committee?

Answer. I do. . . .

Q. And you think they have said all they want to say?

A. Well, I won't say that they did that. . . . It is just like as it was in the time of slavery . . . and they have got the same feelings now, a great many of them, and they want to say things, but they are afraid of the white people. . . .

Q. What do you mean by social equality?

A. . . . If I get on the cars to ride from here to Montgomery, or to Atlanta, although I pay the same fare that you pay—they make me do that—I do not have the same accommodations.

Q. Suppose you have a car just as good as the one white folks have, but are not allowed to go into their car, will that be satisfactory?

A. But that is not going to be done. They are not going to make a law of that kind. . . .

Q. That would be a different case. I am supposing a case where the accommodations provided for the two races are just the same.

A. . . . I would be satisfied. But don't allow a man to come in over my wife, or any other lady that respects herself as a lady, swearing and spitting and cursing around. . . . I do not want to kick up a fuss with any one, or with white people about getting in amongst them . . . but if a colored man comes along and pays the same fare that the white man pays, he has the same rights as the white man. . . .

SOURCE: U.S. Senate, Committee on the Relations Between Capital and Labor, *Report* (1885), IV: 635–38, reprinted in Stanley I. Kutler, ed., *Looking for America* (2nd ed., New York: Norton, 1979), II: 234–38.

RESISTING WHITE SUPREMACY

Southern blacks resisted as best they could. When Georgia adopted the first Jim Crow law applying to streetcars in 1891, Atlanta blacks declared a boycott, and over the next fifteen years blacks boycotted segregated streetcars in at least twenty-five

SOUTHERN HORRORS.

LYNCH LAW

IN ALL

ITS PHASES

Miss IDA B. WELLS,

Price,   ·   ·   ·   Fifteen Cents.

THE NEW YORK AGE PRINT,

1892.

Ida B. Wells

In 1887 Ida B. Wells (Wells-Barnett after she married in 1895) was thrown bodily from a train in Tennessee for refusing to vacate her seat in a section reserved for whites, launching her into a lifetime crusade for racial justice. Her mission was to expose the evil of lynching in the South. This portrait is from the title page of a pamphlet she published in 1892 entitled, "Southern Horrors. Lynch Law in All Its Phases."

(Miriam and Ira D. Wallach Division of Art, Prints and Photographs, The New York Public Library. Astor, Lenox and Tilden Foundations)

cities. "Do not trample on our pride by being 'jim crowed,'" the Savannah *Tribune* urged its readers: "Walk!" Ida Wells-Barnett emerged as the most outspoken black crusader against lynching, so enraging the Memphis white community by the editorials in her newspaper *Free Speech* that she was forced in 1892 to leave the city.

Some blacks were drawn to the Back to Africa movement, abandoning all hope that they would ever find justice in America. But emigration was not a real choice, and African Americans everywhere had to bend to the raging forces of racism and find a way to survive.

Booker T. Washington, the foremost black leader of his day, marked out the path in a famous speech in Atlanta in 1895. Washington retreated from the defiant stand of an older generation of black abolitionists exemplified by Frederick Douglass, who died the same year that the Atlanta speech launched Washington into national prominence. Conciliatory toward the South, Washington considered "the agitation of the question of social equality the extremest folly." He accepted segregation, provided that blacks had equal facilities. He accepted literacy tests and property qualifications for the vote, provided that they applied equally to blacks and whites.

Washington's doctrine came to be known as the Atlanta Compromise. His approach was "accommodationist," in the sense that it avoided a direct assault on white supremacy. Despite the humble face he put on before white audiences, however, Washington did not concede the struggle. Behind the scenes he lobbied hard against Jim Crow laws and disfranchisement. More important, his Atlanta Compromise, while abandoning the field of political protest, opened up a second front of economic struggle.

Booker T. Washington sought to capitalize on a southern dilemma about the economic role of the black population. Racist dogma dictated that blacks be kept down and conform to their image as lazy, shiftless workers. But for the South to prosper it needed an efficient labor force. Washington made this need the target of his efforts. As founder of the Tuskegee Institute in Alabama in 1881, Washington advocated *industrial education*—manual and agricultural training. He preached the virtues of thrift, hard work, and property ownership. Washington's industrial education program won generous support from northern philanthropists and businessmen and, following his Atlanta speech, applause from local proponents of the New South.

Washington assumed that black economic progress would be the key to winning political and civil rights. He regarded members of the white southern elite as crucial allies because only they had the power to change the South. More important, they could see "the close connection between labor, industry, education, and political institutions." When it was in their economic interest, when they had grown dependent on black labor and black enterprise, white men of business and property would recognize the justice of black rights. As Washington put it, "There is little race prejudice in the American dollar."

To what extent black self-help—hard work, industrial education, the husbanding of small resources—might counterbalance race prejudice was the nub of Booker T. Washington's problem. Where the almighty dollar reigned, there was some hope of progress. Elsewhere, as Washington saw it, there was none.

For twenty years after his Atlanta address Washington dominated the organized African American community. In an age of severe racial oppression no black dealt more skillfully with the elite of white America or wielded greater political influence. Black leaders knew Washington as a hard taskmaster. Intensely jealous of his authority, he did not regard opposition kindly. Black politicians, educators, and editors stood up to him at their peril.

Even so, opposition surfaced, especially among younger, educated blacks. They thought Washington was conceding too much. He instilled black pride but of a narrowly middle-class and utilitarian kind. What about the special genius of blacks that W.E.B. DuBois celebrated in his collection of essays, *The Souls of Black Folk* (1903)? And what of the "talented tenth" of the black population, whose promise could only be stifled by manual education? Blacks also became increasingly impatient with

Washington's silence on segregation and lynching. By the time of his death in 1915 Washington's approach had been superseded by a more militant strategy that relied on the courts and political protest, not on black self-help and accommodation.

The Crisis of American Politics: The 1890s

Populism was a catalyst for political crisis not only in the South but across the entire nation. But while in the South the result was preservation of one-party rule, in national politics the effect was the two-party system revitalized.

Ever since Reconstruction national politics had been stalemated by too evenly balanced parties. In the late 1880s this equilibrium began to break down. Benjamin Harrison's election to the presidency in 1888 was the last of the cliff-hanger victories (the Democrat, Grover Cleveland, actually got a larger popular vote). Thereafter, the tide turned against the Republicans. In 1890 Democrats took the House of Representatives decisively and won a number of governorships in normally Republican states. In 1892 Cleveland regained the presidency by the largest margin in twenty years.

Had everything else remained equal, the events of 1890 and 1892 might have inaugurated a long period of Democratic supremacy. But everything else did not remain equal. By the time of Cleveland's inauguration, farm foreclosures and railroad bankruptcies signaled economic trouble. On May 3, 1893, the stock market crashed. In Chicago 100,000 jobless workers walked the streets; nationwide the unemployment rate soared to over 20 percent.

As economic depression set in, which party would prevail—and on what platform—became an open question. The first challenge arrived from the West and South in the form of the Populist Party.

THE POPULIST REVOLT

Farmers were of necessity joiners. They needed organization to overcome their social isolation and provide economic services—hence the appeal of the Granger movement, which had spread across the Midwest after 1867, and, after the Grange's decline, the appeal of farmers' alliances in many rural districts. From these diffuse organizational beginnings two dominant organizations emerged. One was the Farmers' Alliance of the Northwest, confined mainly to the midwestern states. More dynamic was the National (or Southern) Farmers' Alliance, which in the mid-1880s spread rapidly from Texas onto the Great Plains and eastward into the cotton South, as "travelling lecturers" extolled the virtues of cooperative activity and reminded farmers of "their obligation to stand as a great conservative body against the encroachments of monopolies and . . . the growing corruption of wealth and power."

The Texas branch established a massive cooperative, the Texas Exchange, that marketed the crops of cotton farmers and provided them with cheap credit. When cotton prices fell sharply in 1891, the Texas Exchange failed. The Texas Alliance then proposed a new scheme: a subtreasury system that would enable farmers to borrow against their unsold crops from a public fund until their cotton could be profitably marketed. The credit and marketing functions would be as in the defunct Texas Exchange but with a crucial difference: the federal government would play the key role. When the subtreasury plan was rejected by the Democratic Party as too radical, the Texas Alliance decided to strike out in politics independently.

These events in Texas revealed, with special clarity, a process of politicization that engulfed the Alliance movement. Across the South and West, as state alliances grew stronger and more impatient, they began to field independent slates. The confidence gained at the state level led to the formation of the national People's (Populist) Party in 1892. In the elections that year, with the veteran antimonopoly campaigner James B. Weaver as their presidential candidate, the Populists captured a million votes and carried four western states (see Map 18.2). For the first time agrarian protest truly challenged the national two-party system.

Populism was distinguished by the many women in the movement. In the established parties the grassroots political clubs were for men only. Populism, on the other hand, arose from a network of alliances that had formed for largely social purposes and that welcomed women. Although they participated actively and served prominently as speakers and lecturers, few women achieved high office in the alliances, and their role diminished with the shift into politics. In deference to the southern wing the Populist platform was silent on woman suffrage. Still, neither Democrats nor Republicans would have countenanced a spokeswoman such as the fiery Mary Elizabeth Lease, who became famous for calling on farmers "to raise less corn and more hell." Lease insisted just as strenuously on Populism's "grand and

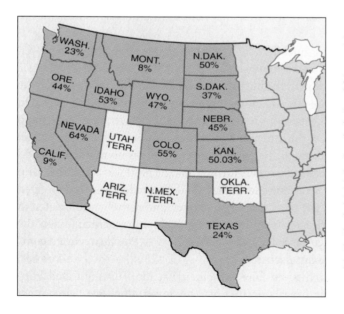

M A P 18.2
The Heyday of Western Populism, 1892

This map shows the percentage of the popular vote won by James B. Weaver, the People's Party candidate, in the presidential election of 1892. Except in California and Montana, the Populists won broad support across the West and genuinely threatened the established parties in that region.

En Route to a Populist Rally, Dickinson County, Kansas

Farm people traveled miles to rallies and meetings for the chance to voice their grievances and socialize with like-minded folks. This tradition infused Populism with a special fervor. Gatherings such as the one these Kansans were heading for were a visible sign of what Populism meant—a movement of the "people." (The Kansas State Historical Society, Topeka)

holy mission . . . to place the mothers of this nation on an equality with the fathers."

Populism was driven as much by ideology as by the quest for political power. The problems afflicting farmers, Populists felt, could stem only from some basic evil. They identified this evil with the business interests controlling the levers of the economic system. "There are but two sides," proclaimed a Populist manifesto. "On the one side are the allied hosts of monopolies, the money power, great trusts and railroad corporations. . . . On the other are the farmers, laborers, merchants and all the people who produce wealth. . . . Between these two there is no middle ground."

By this reasoning farmers and workers formed a single producer class. The claim was not merely rhetorical. Texas railroad workers and Colorado miners cooperated with the farmers' alliances, got their support in strikes, and actively participated in forming state Populist Parties. In its explicit class appeal—in recognizing that "the irrepressible conflict between capital and labor is upon us"—Populism parted company from the two mainstream parties.

In an age dominated by laissez-faire doctrine what most distinguished Populism from the major parties was its positive attitude toward the state. Spokesmen such as Lorenzo Dow Lewelling, Populist governor of Kansas, considered it to be "the business of the government to make it possible to live and sustain the life of my family."

The Omaha Platform, adopted at the founding convention in 1892, called for nationalization of the railroads and communications; protection of the land, including natural resources, from monopoly and foreign ownership; a graduated income tax; the Texas Alliance's subtreasury plan; and the free and unlimited coinage of silver. From this array of issues free coinage of silver emerged as the overriding demand of the Populist Party.

In the early 1890s, reeling from rock-bottom prices, embattled farmers gravitated to free silver because they hoped that an increase in the money supply would raise farm prices and give them some relief. In addition the party's slim resources would be fattened by hefty contributions from silver-mining interests who, scornful though they might be of Populist radicalism, yearned for the day when the government would buy at a premium all the silver they could produce.

Free silver triggered a debate for the soul of the Populist Party. Social democrats such as Henry Demarest Lloyd of Chicago and agrarian radicals such as Georgia's Tom Watson argued that free coinage of silver, if it became the defining party issue, would undercut the broader Populist program and alienate wage earners, who had no enthusiasm for inflationary measures. Any chance of a farmer-labor alliance that might transform Populism into an American version of the social-democratic parties of Europe would be doomed. The practical appeal of free silver, however, was simply too great.

But once Populists made that choice, they had fatally compromised their party's capacity to maintain an independent existence. For free silver was not an issue over which the Populists held a monopoly. Free silver was, on the contrary, a question at the very center of mainstream politics in the 1890s.

MONEY AND POLITICS

In a rapidly developing economy the money supply is bound to be a big political issue. Money has to increase rapidly enough to meet the economy's needs or growth will be stifled. How fast the money supply should grow, however, is a question that creates sharp divisions. Debtors and commodity producers want a larger money supply: more money in circulation inflates prices and reduces the real cost of borrowing. The "sound-money" people—creditors, individuals on fixed incomes, those in the slower-growing sectors of the economy—have an opposite interest.

Before the Civil War the main source of the nation's money supply had been state-chartered banks, several thousand of them, all issuing banknotes to borrowers that then circulated as money. This free-wheeling activity was sharply curtailed by the U.S. Banking Act of 1863. Because the Lincoln administration itself was printing paper money—greenbacks, so-called—to finance the Civil War, the economic impact of the Banking Act was not immediately felt. Afterward the sound-money interests lobbied for a return to the traditional national policy, which was to base the federal currency on the amount of specie—gold and silver—held by the U.S. Treasury. The issue was hotly contested for a decade, but in 1875 the inflationists were defeated, and the circulation of greenbacks as legal tender—that is, backed by nothing more than the good faith of the federal government—came to an end. With state banknotes also in short supply, the country entered an era of chronic deflation and tight credit.

This was the context out of which the silver question emerged. The country had always operated on a bimetallic standard, but the supply of silver had gradually tightened, and, as silver coins became more valuable as metal than as money, they disappeared from circulation. In 1873 silver was officially dropped as a medium of exchange. Soon afterward western mines began producing silver in abundance; silver prices plummeted. Inflationists began to agitate for a resumption of the bimetallic policy: if the government resumed buying at the fixed ratio prevailing before 1873—16 ounces of silver equaling 1 ounce of gold—silver would flow into the Treasury and greatly expand the money in circulation.

With so much at stake for so many people, the currency question became one of the staples of post-Reconstruction politics. Twice the prosilver coalition in Congress won modest victories. First, the Bland-Allison Act of 1878 required the U.S. Treasury to purchase and coin between $2 million and $4 million worth of silver each month. Then in the more sweeping Sherman Silver Purchase Act of 1890 an additional 4.5 million ounces of silver bullion was to be purchased monthly to serve as the basis for new issues of U.S. Treasury notes.

These legislative battles, although hard-fought, cut across the parties in the familiar fashion of post-Reconstruction politics. But when the Panic of 1893 hit, silver suddenly became a burning issue that divided politics along party lines.

As the party in power the Democrats bore the brunt of responsibility for handling the economic crisis. The demands for relief by their own constituencies in agriculture and labor magnified the party's problems. Any Democratic president would have been hard pressed, but the man who actually had the job, Grover Cleveland, could hardly have made a bigger hash of it. When jobless marchers—the so-called Coxey's Army—arrived in Washington in 1894 to appeal for federal relief, Cleveland's response was to disperse them forcibly and arrest their leader, Jacob S. Coxey, for trespassing on the Capitol grounds. Cleveland's brutal handling of the Pullman strike further alienated the labor vote. Nor did he live up to his reputation as a tariff reformer. He lost control of the battle for repeal of the unpopular McKinley Tariff of 1890, allowing weak revisions to be passed into law without his signature.

Most disastrous, however, was Cleveland's rigidity on the silver question. Cleveland was a committed sound-money man. Nothing that happened after the depression set in—not collapsing prices, not the suffering of farmers, not the groundswell of support for free silver within his own party—budged Cleveland. With the government's gold reserves dwindling Cleveland persuaded Congress in

1893 to repeal the Sherman Silver Purchase Act, in effect sacrificing the country's painfully crafted program for maintaining a limited bimetallic standard. Then as his administration's problems deepened, Cleveland turned in 1895 to a syndicate of private bankers led by J. P. Morgan to arrange the gold purchases needed to replenish the Treasury's depleted reserves. The administration's secret negotiations with Wall Street, once discovered, enraged Democrats and completed Cleveland's isolation from his party.

At their Chicago convention in 1896 the Democrats repudiated Cleveland and turned left. The leader of the triumphant silver Democrats was William Jennings Bryan of Nebraska. Bryan was a political phenomenon. Only thirty-six years old, he had already served two terms in Congress and become a passionate advocate of free silver. He was a consummate politician and an inspiring public speaker. Bryan, remarked the journalist Frederic Howe, was "pre-eminently an evangelist," whose zeal sprang from "the Western self-righteous missionary mind." With biblical fervor Bryan swept up his audiences when he joined the debate on free silver at the Democratic convention. He locked up the presidential nomination with a stirring attack on the gold standard: "You shall not press down upon the brow of labor this crown of thorns, you shall not crucify mankind on a cross of gold."

Bryan's nomination meant that the Democrats had become the party of free silver; his "cross of gold" speech meant that he would turn the money question into a national crusade. No one could be neutral on this defining issue. Silver Republicans bolted their party; gold Democrats went for a splinter Democratic ticket or supported the Republican Party. The Populists, meeting after the Democratic convention, accepted Bryan as their candidate. The free-silver issue had become so vital that they could not do otherwise. Although they nominated their own vice-presidential candidate, the Georgian Tom Watson, the Populists found themselves for all practical purposes absorbed into the Democratic silver campaign.

The Republicans took up the challenge. Their party leader was the wealthy Cleveland ironmaker Mark Hanna, a brilliant political manager and an exponent of the new industrial capitalism. Hanna orchestrated an unprecedented money-raising campaign among America's corporate interests. His candidate, William McKinley of Ohio, personified the virtues of Republicanism, standing solidly for high tariffs, honest money, and prosperity. While Bryan broke with tradition and crisscrossed the country in a furious whistle-stop campaign, the dignified McKinley received delegations at his home in Canton, Ohio. Bryan orated with moral fervor; McKinley talked of industrial progress and a full dinner pail.

Not since 1860 had the United States witnessed so hard-fought an election over such high stakes. For the middle class sound money stood symbolically for the soundness of the social order. With jobless workers tramping the streets and bankrupt farmers up in arms, Bryan's fervent assault on the gold standard struck fear in many hearts. Republicans denounced the Democratic platform as "revolutionary and anarchistic" and Bryan's supporters as "social misfits who have almost nothing in common but opposition to the existing order and institutions."

McKinley won handily, with 271 electoral votes to Bryan's 176 (Map 18.3). He kept the ground Republicans had regained in the 1894 midterm elections and pushed into Democratic strongholds, especially in the cities. Boston, New York, Chicago, and Minneapolis, all taken by Cleveland in 1892, went for McKinley in 1896. Bryan ran strongly only in the South, in silver-mining states, and in the Populist West. But the gains his evangelical style brought him in some Republican rural areas did not compensate for his losses in traditionally Democratic urban districts.

The paralyzing equilibrium in American politics ended in 1896. The Republicans had skillfully handled both the economic and the cultural challenges. They persuaded the nation that they were the party of prosperity and convinced many traditionally Democratic urban voters of their sympathy for ethnic diversity. The Republicans had become the nation's majority party. In 1896, too, electoral politics regained its place as an arena for national debate, setting the stage for the reform politics of the Progressive era.

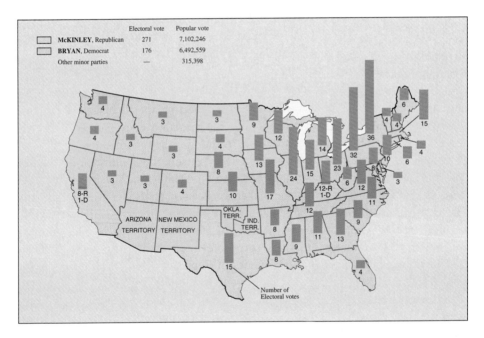

M A P 18.3
The Election of 1896

The 1896 election was one of the truly decisive elections in American history. The Republican Party won by its largest margin since 1872. More important, the Republicans established a firm grip on the key midwestern and Middle Atlantic states—especially New York, Indiana, Ohio, and Illinois—that had been the decisive states in every national election since Reconstruction. The 1896 election broke a party stalemate of twenty years' duration and began a period of Republican domination that would last until 1932.

TIMELINE

1874	Women's Christian Temperance Union founded		Mississippi becomes the first state to adopt a literacy test to disfranchise blacks.
1877	Rutherford B. Hayes inaugurated president; end of Reconstruction	1892	Populist Party founded
1881	President James A. Garfield assassinated; succeeded by Chester A. Arthur	1893	The Panic of 1893 leads to national depression.
1883	Pendleton Act creates a civil-service system.	1894	Coxey's Army
		1895	Booker T. Washington sets out the Atlanta Compromise.
1884	Grover Cleveland the first Democrat elected president since 1856		
1886	Andrew Carnegie's *Triumphant Democracy*	1896	Election of William McKinley; free-silver campaign crushed; era of Republican dominance begins
1887	Florida adopts the first law segregating railroads.		*Plessy v. Ferguson* upholds the constitutionality of "separate-but-equal" segregation.
1888	Benjamin Harrison elected president	1903	W.E.B. DuBois's *The Souls of Black Folk*
1890	Democrats sweep congressional elections, inaugurating a brief era of Democratic Party dominance.		

For Further Exploration

The literature on late nineteenth-century politics offers an embarrassment of riches. On the ideological underpinnings, an older book by Robert G. McCloskey, *American Conservatism in the Age of Enterprise* (1951), still retains its freshness. The mass appeal of Gilded Age politics is incisively explored in Michael E. McGerr, *The Decline of Popular Politics: The American North, 1865–1928* (1986). John G. Sproat, *The "Best Men": Liberal Reformers in the Gilded Age* (1965), is excellent on the Mugwumps. Kathryn Kish Sklar, *Florence Kelley and the Nation's Work* (1995), traces the emergence of women's political culture through the life of a leading reformer. On southern politics the seminal book is C. Vann Woodward, *Origins of the New South, 1877–1913* (1951), which still defines the terms of discussion among historians. The most far-reaching revision is Edward L. Ayers, *The Promise of the New South* (1992). A powerful analysis of southern racism, stressing its psychosocial roots, is Joel Williamson, *A Rage for Order* (1986). The preeminent African American accommodationist is the subject of a superb two-volume biography by Louis B. Harlan, *Booker T. Washington: The Making of a Black Leader* (1973) and *Wizard of Tuskegee* (1983), and equally fine on Washington's main critic is David Levering Lewis, *W.E.B. Du Bois: Biography of a Race 1868–1919* (1993). Richard D. Hofstadter, *The Age of Reform* (1955), stresses the darker side of Populism, in which intolerance and paranoia figure heavily. Hofstadter's thesis, which once dominated debate among historians, has given way to a much more positive assessment. The key book here is Lawrence Goodwyn, *Democratic Promise: The Populist Moment* (1976), which argues that Populism was a broadly based response to industrial capitalism. The most recent synthesis is Robert C. McMath, *American Populism* (1993). Michael Kazin, *The Populist Persuasion* (1995), describes how the language of Populism entered the discourse of mainstream American politics. Much information on the Gilded Age presidents can be found at the website <americanpresident.org/presidentialresources.htm>.

Chapter 19

THE RISE OF THE CITY

> These vast aggregations of humanity, where he who seeks isolation
> may find it more truly than in the desert; where wealth and poverty
> touch and jostle; where one revels and another starves within a few
> feet of each other—they are centers and types of our civilization.
>
> —HENRY GEORGE, 1883

Visiting his fiancée's Missouri homestead in 1894, Theodore Dreiser was struck by "the spirit of rural America, its idealism, its dreams." But this was an "American tradition in which I, alas!, could not share." Said Dreiser, "I had seen Pittsburgh. I had seen Lithuanians and Hungarians in their [alleys] and hovels. I had seen the girls of the city—walking the streets at night." Dreiser would go on to write one of the great American urban novels—*Sister Carrie* (1900)—about one young woman in the army of small-town Americans flocking to the Big City. But the young Dreiser, part of that army, already knew that between rural America and Pittsburgh an unbridgeable chasm had opened up.

In 1820, after 200 years of settlement, fewer than one in twenty Americans lived in urban places of more than 10,000 people. After that, decade by decade, the urban population swelled until by 1900 one of every five Americans lived in cities. Nearly 6.5 million inhabited just three great cities: New York, Chicago, and Philadelphia.

The city was the arena of the nation's vibrant economic life. Here the factories went up, and here the new immigrants settled, constituting in 1900 a third of the residents of the major American cities. Here, too, lived the millionaires and a growing white-collar middle class. For all these people the city was more than a place to make a living. It provided the setting for an urban culture unlike anything seen before in the United States. City people, although differing vastly among themselves, became distinctively and recognizably urban.

Urbanization

The march to the cities seemed inevitable to nineteenth-century Americans. "The greater part of our population must live in cities," declared the Congregational minister Josiah Strong. "In due time we shall be a nation of cities." Urbanization became inevitable because of another inevitability of American life—industrialism.

INDUSTRIAL SOURCES OF CITY GROWTH

Until the Civil War cities were centers of commerce, not industry. They were the places where merchants bought and sold goods for distribution into the interior or out to world markets. Early industry, on the other hand, was largely rural because factories needed water power from streams, access to fuel and raw materials, and workers recruited from the countryside.

But once steam engines came along, mill operators no longer depended on water-driven power. In the iron industry coal replaced charcoal as the primary fuel, so it was not necessary to be near forests. Improved transportation, especially the railroads, allowed entrepreneurs to locate in places most convenient to suppliers and markets. The result was a geographic concentration of industry. Iron makers gravitated to Pittsburgh because of its superior access both to coal and iron ore fields and also to markets for their products. Chicago, ideally situated between live-stock suppliers and consuming markets, became a great meat-packing center.

As factories became bigger, that expansion in itself contributed to urban growth. A plant that employed thousands of workers instantly created a small city in its vicinity. Sometimes this took the form of a company town like Aliquippa, Pennsylvania, which became body and soul the property of the Jones and Laughlin Steel Company. Many firms set up their plants near a large city so they could draw on its labor supply and transportation facilities. Older commercial cities also became more industrial. Warehouse districts could readily be converted to small-scale manufacturing; a distribution network was right at hand. Boston, Philadelphia, Baltimore, and San Francisco became hives of small-scale, labor-intensive industrial activity. New York's enormous pool of immigrant workers made that city a magnet for the garment trades, cigar making, and diversified light industry. New York was, in fact, the nation's largest producer of manufactured goods.

CITY BUILDING

The commercial cities of the early nineteenth century had been compact places, densely settled around harbors or river fronts. As late as 1850, when it had 565,000 people, greater Philadelphia covered only 10 square miles. From the foot of Chestnut Street on the Delaware River a person could walk almost anywhere in the city within forty-five minutes. Thereafter, as it developed, Philadelphia spilled out and, like American cities everywhere, engulfed the surrounding countryside.

A downtown area emerged, usually in what had been the original commercial city. Downtown in turn broke up into shopping, financial, warehousing, manufacturing, hotel and entertainment, and red-light districts. Moving out from the center, industrial development tended to follow the arteries of transportation—railroads, canals, and rivers—and, at the city's outskirts, to create concentrations of heavy industry.

While highly congested at the center, American cities actually had lower population densities than European cities: 22 persons per acre for fifteen American cities in the 1890s, for example, versus 157.6 for a comparable group of German cities. Given their dispersed populations, American cities pressed harder to develop an efficient transport system.

The first innovation, dating back to the 1820s, was the omnibus, an elongated version of the horse-drawn carriage. Much better was the horsecar. The key advantage was that it ran on iron tracks, so that the horses could pull more passengers and move them at a faster clip through congested city streets and out into residential areas. From the 1840s onward horsecars were the mainstay of urban transit across America.

Then came the electric trolley car. Its development was the work primarily of Frank J. Sprague, an engineer once employed by the great inventor Thomas A. Edison. In 1887 Sprague designed an electric-driven system for Richmond, Virginia: a "trolley" carriage running along an overhead power line was attached by cable to streetcars equipped with an electric motor—hence the name trolley car. After Sprague's success the trolley swiftly displaced the horsecar and became the primary mode of transportation in most American cities.

In the great metropolitan centers, however, mounting congestion led to demands that public transit be moved off the streets. In 1879 the first elevated lines went into operation on Sixth and Ninth Avenues in New York City. Powered at first by steam engines, the "els" converted to electricity following Sprague's success with the trolley. Chicago developed elevated transit most fully. New York, meanwhile, turned to the subway. Boston opened a short underground line in 1897, but it was the completion in 1904 of a subway running the length of Manhattan that demonstrated the full potential of the high-speed underground train. Mass transit had become *rapid* transit.

Equally remarkable was the architectural revolution sweeping metropolitan business districts. With steel girders, durable plate glass, and the passenger elevator available by the 1880s, a wholly new way of construction opened up. A steel skeleton supported the building, while the walls, previously weight-bearing, served as curtains enclosing the structure. The sky, so to speak, became the limit.

The first "skyscraper" to be built on this principle was William Jenney's ten-story Home Insurance Building (1885) in Chicago. Although this pioneering effort appeared unremarkable—it looked just like the other downtown buildings—the steel-girdered technology it contained liberated the aesthetic perceptions of American architects. A Chicago school sprang up, dedicated to the design of buildings whose form expressed, rather than masked, their structure and function. Chicago pioneered skyscraper construction, but New York, with its unrelenting need for prime downtown space, took the lead after the mid-1890s. Completed in 1913, the fifty-five story Woolworth Building marked the beginning of the modern Manhattan skyline.

The Chicago Elevated, 1900

This is Wabash Avenue, looking north from Adams Street. For Americans from farms and small towns, this photograph by William Henry Jackson captured something of the peculiarity of the urban scene. What could be stranger than a railroad suspended above the streets in the midst of people's lives? (KEA Publishing Services Ltd.)

For ordinary citizens the electric lights that dispelled the gloom of the city at night offered the most dramatic evidence that times had changed. Gaslight—illuminating gas produced from coal—had been in use since the early nineteenth century, but its 12 candlepower lamps lighted the city's public spaces only dimly. The first use of electricity, once generating technology made it commercially feasible in the 1870s, was for better city lighting. Charles F. Brush's electric arc lamps, installed in Wanamaker's department store in Philadelphia in 1878, threw a brilliant light and soon replaced gaslight on city streets and public buildings across the country. Electric lighting then entered the American home, thanks to Thomas Edison's invention of a serviceable incandescent bulb in 1879. Edison's motto—"Let there be light!"—truly described the experience of the modern city.

Before it had any significant effect on industry, electricity gave the city its modern tempo, lifting elevators, powering streetcars and subway trains, turning night into day. Meanwhile, Alexander Graham Bell's telephone (1876) sped communication beyond anything imagined previously. By 1900, 1.5 million telephones were in use, linking urban people in a network of instant communication.

THE CITY AS PRIVATE ENTERPRISE

City building was very much an exercise in private enterprise. The lure of profit spurred the great innovations—the trolley car, electric lighting, the skyscraper, the elevator, the telephone—and drove urban real-estate development. The investment opportunities looked so tempting that new cities sprang up almost overnight from the ruins of the Chicago fire of 1871 and the San Francisco earthquake of 1906. Real-estate interests, eager to develop subdivisions, often were instrumental in pushing streetcar lines outward from the central districts of cities.

America gave birth to what the urban historian Sam Bass Warner has called the "private city"—shaped primarily by the actions of many individuals, all pursuing their own goals and bent on making money. The prevailing belief was that the sum of such private activity would far exceed what the community could accomplish through public effort. This meant that the city itself handled only functions that could not be undertaken efficiently or profitably by private enterprise.

Even so, American cities compiled an impressive record in the late nineteenth century. Though by no means free of the corruption and wastefulness of earlier days, municipal government became more centralized, better administered, and above all, more expansive in the functions undertaken. Nowhere in the world were there more massive public projects: water aqueducts, sewage systems, street paving, bridge building, extensive park systems.

Yet streets were often filthy and badly maintained. "Three or four days of warm spring weather," remarked a New York journalist, would turn Manhattan's garbage-strewn, snow-clogged streets into "veritable mud rivers." The environment likewise suffered. A visitor to Pittsburgh noted "the heavy pall of smoke which constantly overhangs her . . . until the very sun looks coppery through the sooty haze." As for the lovely hills rising from the rivers, "they have been leveled down, cut into, sliced off, and ruthlessly marred and mutilated." Pittsburgh presented "all that is unsightly and forbidding in appearance, the original beauties of nature having been ruthlessly sacrificed to utility."

Hardest hit by urban growth were the poor. In earlier times they had mainly lived in makeshift wooden structures in alleys and back streets and then, as more prosperous families moved away, in the subdivided homes left behind. As land values climbed after the Civil War, speculators tore down these houses and began to erect buildings specifically designed for the urban masses. In New York City the dreadful result was five- or six-story tenements housing twenty or more families in cramped, airless apartments. In New York's Eleventh Ward an average of 986 persons occupied each acre, a density matched only in Bombay, India.

Reformers recognized the problem but seemed unable to solve it. Some favored model tenements financed by public-spirited citizens willing to accept a limited return on their investment. When private philanthropy failed to make much of a dent, cities turned to housing codes. The most advanced of these was New York's Tenement House Law of 1901, which required interior courts, indoor toilets, and fire safeguards for new structures but did little for existing housing stock. Commercial development had pushed up land values in downtown areas. Only high-density, cheaply built housing could earn a sufficient profit for the landlords of the poor. This economic fact defied nineteenth-century solutions.

It was not that America lacked an urban vision. On the contrary, an abiding rural ideal had influenced American cities for many years. Frederick Law Olmsted, who designed New York's Central Park, wanted cities that exposed people to the beauties of nature. One of Olmsted's projects, the Chicago Columbian Exposition of 1893, gave rise to the influential "City Beautiful" movement. The results included larger park systems, broad boulevards and parkways, and after the turn of the century zoning laws and planned suburbs.

But cities usually heeded urban planners too little and far too late. "Fifteen or twenty years ago a plan might have been adopted that would have made this one of the most beautiful cities in the world," Kansas City's park commissioners reported in 1893. At that time, "such a policy could not be fully appreciated." Nor, even if Kansas City had foreseen its future, would it have shouldered the "heavy burden" of trying to shape its development. The American city had placed its faith in the dynamics of the marketplace, not the restraints of a planned future. The pluses and minuses are perhaps best revealed by comparing a German city and an American city.

A BALANCE SHEET: CHICAGO AND BERLIN

Chicago and Berlin had virtually equal populations in 1900. But they had very different histories. Seventy years earlier, when Chicago had been a muddy frontier outpost, Berlin was already a city of 250,000 and the royal seat of the Hohenzollerns of Prussia.

With German unification in 1871 the imperial authorities rebuilt Berlin on a grander scale. "A capital city is essential for the state, to act as a pivot for its culture," proclaimed the Prussian historian Heinrich von Treitschke. Berlin served that national purpose—"a center where Germany's political, intellectual, and material life is concentrated, and its people can feel united." Chicago had no such pretensions. It was strictly a place of business, made great by virtue of its strategic grip on the commerce of America's industrial heartland. Nothing in Chicago evoked the grandeur of Berlin's boulevards or its monumental palaces and public buildings, nor were Chicagoans ever witness to the pomp and ceremony of the imperial parades up broad, tree-lined Unter den Linden to the national cathedral.

Yet as a functioning city Chicago was in many ways superior to Berlin. Chicago's waterworks pumped 500 million gallons of water a day, or 139 gallons of water per person, while Berliners had to make do with 18 gallons. Flush toilets, a rarity in Berlin in 1900, could be found in 60 percent of Chicago's homes. Chicago's streets were lit by electricity, while Berlin still relied mostly on gaslight. Chicago had a much bigger streetcar system, twice as much acreage devoted to parks, and a public library containing many more volumes. And Chicago had just completed an amazing sanitation project, reversing the course of the Chicago River so that its waters—and the city's sewage—would flow away from Lake Michigan and southward down into the Illinois and Mississippi Rivers.

Giant sanitation projects were one thing; an inspiring urban environment was something else. For well-traveled Americans admiring of things European, the sense of inferiority was palpable. "We are enormously rich," admitted the journalist Edwin L. Godkin, "but . . . what have we got to show? Almost nothing. Ugliness from an artistic point of view is the mark of all our cities." Thus the urban balance sheet: a utilitarian infrastructure that was superb by nineteenth-century standards but "no municipal splendors of any description, nothing but population and hotels."

Upper Class/Middle Class

In the compact city of the early republic class distinctions had been expressed by the way men and women dressed, how they behaved, and the deference they demanded from or granted to others. As the industrial city grew, these interpersonal marks of class began to lose their force. In the anonymity of a large city recognition and deference no longer served as mechanisms for conferring status. Instead people began to rely on external signs: conspicuous display of wealth, membership in exclusive clubs and organizations, and above all choice of neighborhood.

For the poor, place of residence depended, as it always had, on being close to their jobs. But for higher-income urbanites where to live became a matter of personal means and social preference.

THE URBAN ELITE

As early as the 1840s Boston merchants had taken advantage of the new railways to escape the congested city. Fine rural estates appeared in Milton, Newton, and other outlying towns. By 1848 roughly 20 percent of Boston's businessmen were making the trip by train to their downtown offices. Ferries that plied the harbor between Manhattan and Brooklyn or New Jersey served the same purpose for New Yorkers.

As commercial development engulfed downtown residential areas, the exodus by the well-to-do spread across America. In Cincinnati wealthy families settled on the scenic hills rimming the crowded, humid tableland that ran down to the Ohio River. On those hillsides, a traveler noted in 1883, "the homes of Cincinnati's merchant princes and millionaires are found . . . elegant cottages, tasteful villas, and substantial mansions, surrounded by a paradise of grass, gardens, lawns, and tree-shaded roads."

Despite the attractions of country life many of the very richest people preferred the heart of the city. Chicago boasted its Gold Coast; San Francisco, Nob Hill;

Denver, Quality Hill; and Manhattan, Fifth Avenue. The New York novelist Edith Wharton recalled how the comfortable midcentury brownstones gave way to the "'new' millionaire houses," which spread northward on Fifth Avenue along Central Park. Great mansions, emulating the aristocratic houses of Europe, lined Fifth Avenue at the turn of the century.

But great wealth did not automatically confer social standing. An established elite dominated the social heights, even in such relatively raw cities as San Francisco and Denver. It had taken only a generation—and sometimes less—for money made in commerce or real estate to shed its tarnish and become "old" and genteel. In the oldest cities such as Boston, wealth passed intact through several generations, creating a closely knit tribe of Brahmin families that kept moneyed newcomers at bay. Elsewhere urban elites tended to be more open, but only to the socially ambitious who were prepared to make visible and energetic use of their money.

New York City became the home of a national elite as the most ambitious gravitated to this preeminent capital of American financial and cultural life. Manhattan's extraordinary vitality in turn kept the city's high society fluid and relatively open. In Theodore Dreiser's novel *The Titan* (1914) the tycoon Frank Cowperwood reassures his unhappy wife that if Chicago society will not accept them, "there are other cities. Money will arrange matters in New York—that I know. We can build a real place there, and go in on equal terms, if we have money enough." New York thus came to be a magnet for millionaires. The city attracted them not only because of its importance as a financial center but for the opportunities it offered for display and social recognition.

This infusion of wealth shattered the older elite society of New York. Seeking to be assimilated into the upper class, the flood of moneyed newcomers simply overwhelmed it. There followed a curious process of reconstruction, a deliberate effort to define the rules of conduct and identify those who properly "belonged" in New York society.

The key figure was Ward McAllister, a southern-born lawyer who had made a quick fortune in gold-rush San Francisco and then devoted himself to a second career as the arbiter of New York society. In 1888 McAllister compiled the first *Social Register*, which announced that it would serve as a "record of society, comprising an accurate and careful list" of all those deemed eligible for New York society. McAllister instructed the socially ambitious on how to select guests, set a proper table, arrange a party, and launch a young lady into society. He presided over a round of assemblies, balls, and dinners that defined the boundaries of an elite society. At the apex stood "The Four Hundred"—the true cream of New York society. McAllister's list corresponded to those invited to Mrs. William Astor's gala ball of February 1, 1892.

Americans were adept at making money, remarked the journalist Edwin L. Godkin in 1896, but they lacked the aristocratic traditions of Europe for spending it. "Great wealth has not yet entered our manners," Godkin remarked. In their struggle to find the rules and establish the manners, the moneyed elite made an indelible mark on urban life. If there was magnificence in the American city, that was mainly their handiwork. And if there was conspicuous waste and display, that too was their doing.

THE SUBURBAN WORLD

The middle class left a smaller imprint on the public face of urban society. Its members, unlike the rich, preferred privacy and retreated into the domesticity of suburban comfort and family life.

Since colonial times the American economy had spawned a robust middle class of mostly self-employed lawyers, doctors, merchants, and proprietors. This older middle class remained important, but it was joined by a new salaried middle class brought forth by industrialism. Corporate organizations required managers, accountants, and clerks. The new technology called for engineers, chemists, and designers, while the distribution system needed salesmen, advertising executives, and buyers. These salaried ranks increased sevenfold between 1870 and 1910—much faster than any other occupational group. Nearly 9 million people held white-collar jobs in 1910, more than a fourth of all employed Americans.

Some members of this salaried class lived in the row houses of Baltimore and Boston or the comfortable apartment buildings of New York City. But more preferred to escape the clamor and congestion of the city. They were attracted by a persisting "rural ideal," agreeing with the landscape architect Andrew Jackson Downing that "nature and domestic life are better than the society and manners of town." As trolley service expanded out from the central city, middle-class Americans followed the wealthy into the countryside. All sought what one Chicago developer promised for his North Shore subdivision in 1875—"qualities of which the city is in a large degree bereft, namely, its pure air, peacefulness, quietude, and natural scenery."

No major American city escaped suburbanization during the late nineteenth century. City limits everywhere expanded rapidly, but even so, much of the suburban growth took place beyond city limits. By 1900 more than half of Boston's people lived in "streetcar suburbs" outside Boston proper; and nationwide, according to the 1910 census, about 25 percent of the urban population lived in such autonomous suburbs.

The geography of the suburbs was truly a map of class structure because where a family lived told where it ranked. The farther out from the city center, the finer the houses and the larger the lots. Affluent businessmen and professionals had the time and flexibility to travel a long distance into town. People closer in wanted transit lines that went straight into the city center and carried them quickly between home and office. Lower-income commuters were more likely to have more than one wage-earner in the family, less secure employment, and jobs requiring movement around the city. It was better for them to be closer to the city center because they then had access to cross-town lines that afforded the mobility they needed for their work.

Middle-Class Domesticity

For middle-class Americans the home was a place of nurture, a refuge from the world of competitive commerce. Perhaps that explains why their residences were so heavily draped and cluttered with bric-a-brac, every space filled with overstuffed furniture. All of it emphasized privacy and pride of possession. The young woman shown playing the piano symbolizes another theme of American domesticity—wives and daughters as ornaments and as bearers of culture and refinement. (Museum of the City of New York, Byron Collection)

Suburban boundaries were ever shifting, as working-class city residents who wanted to better their lives moved to the cheapest suburbs, prompting an exodus of older residents, who in turn pushed the next higher group farther out in search of space and greenery. Suburbanization was the sum of countless individual decisions. Each family's move represented an advance in living standards—not only more light, air, and quiet but better accommodation than the city afforded. Suburban houses were typically larger for the same money and came equipped with flush toilets, hot water, central heating, and by the turn of the century electricity.

The suburbs also restored an opportunity that rural Americans thought they had lost when they moved to the city. In the suburbs home ownership again became the norm. "A man is not really a true man until he owns his home," propounded the Reverend Russell H. Conwell in his famous sermon on the virtues of making money, "Acres of Diamonds."

The small towns of rural America had fostered community life. Not so the suburbs. The grid street pattern, while efficient for laying out lots, offered no natural focus for group life. Nor did the stores and services that lay scattered along the trolley-car streets. Suburban development conformed to the economics of real estate and transportation, and so did the thinking of middle-class home seekers entering the suburbs. They wanted a house that gave them good value and convenience to the trolley line.

The need for community had lost some of its force for middle-class Americans. Two other attachments assumed greater importance: one was work; the other, family.

MIDDLE-CLASS FAMILIES

In the preindustrial economy farmers, merchants, and artisans generally worked at home. The family included not only blood relatives but everyone living and working in the household. As industrialism progressed, economic activity moved out of the home. For the middle class in particular the family became dissociated from employment. The father left every morning to earn a living, and children spent more years in school. Clothing was bought ready-made; food came increasingly in cans and packages. Middle-class families became smaller, excluding all but nuclear members and consisting typically by 1900 of husband, wife, and three children.

Within this family circle relationships became intense and affectionate. "Home was the most expressive experience in life," recalled the literary critic Henry Seidel Canby of his growing up in the 1890s. "Though the family might quarrel and nag, the home held them all, protecting them against the outside world." In a sense, the family served as a refuge from the competitive, impersonal business world. The quiet, tree-lined streets created a domestic place insulated from the hurly-burly of commerce and enterprise.

The burdens of this domesticity fell heavily on the wife. It was nearly unheard of for her to seek an outside career; that was her husband's role. Her job was to manage the household. "The woman who could not make a home, like the man who could not support one, was condemned," Canby remembered. But with fewer children, the wife's workload declined. Moreover, servants still played an important part in middle-class households. In 1910 there were about 2 million domestic servants, the largest job category for women.

As the physical burdens of household work eased, higher-quality homemaking became the new ideal. This was the message of Catharine Beecher's best-selling book *The American Woman's Home* (1869) and of such magazines as the *Ladies' Home Journal* and *Good Housekeeping*, which first appeared during the 1880s. This advice literature told wives that, in addition to their domestic duties, they were responsible for bringing sensibility, beauty, and love to the household. "We owe to women the charm and beauty of life," wrote one educator. "For the love that rests, strengthens and inspires, we look to women." In this idealized view the wife made the home a refuge for her husband and a place of nurture for their children.

Womanly virtue, even if much glorified, by no means put wives on equal terms with their husbands. Although the legal status of married women—their right to own property, control separate earnings, make contracts, and get a divorce—improved markedly during the nineteenth century, custom still dictated a wife's submission to her husband. She relied on his ability as the family breadwinner, and despite her superior virtues and graces she ranked below him in vigor and intellect. Her mind could be employed "but little and in trivial matters," wrote one prominent physician, and her proper place was as "the companion or ornamental appendage to man" (see American Voices, "We Did Not Know . . . Whether Women's Health Could Stand the Strain of Higher Education").

No wonder that bright, independent-minded women rebelled against marriage. By the late nineteenth century more than 10 percent of women of marriageable age remained single, and the rate was much higher among college graduates and professionals. Married life, remarked the writer Vida Scudder, "looks to me often as I watch it terribly impoverished, for women."

Around 1890 a change set in. Although the birth rate continued to decline, more young people married and at an earlier age. These developments reflected the beginnings of a sexual revolution in the American middle-class family. Experts began to abandon the notion, put forth by one popular medical text, that "the majority of women (happily for society) are not very much troubled by sexual feeling of any kind." In succeeding editions of his book *Plain Home Talk on Love, Marriage, and Parentage* the physician Edward Bliss Foote began to favor a healthy sexuality that gave pleasure to women as well as men.

During the 1890s the artist Charles Dana Gibson created the image of the "new woman" in his drawings for *Life* magazine. The Gibson girl was tall, spirited, athletic, and chastely sexual. She eshewed bustles, hoop skirts, and hourglass corsets, preferring shirtwaists and other natural styles that did not hide or disguise her female form. In the city, women's sphere began to take on a more public character. Among the new urban institutions catering to women, the most important was the department store, which became a temple for their emerging role as consumers.

The children of the middle class experienced their own revolution. In the past American children had been regarded as an economic asset—added hands for the family farm, shop, or countinghouse. Especially for the urban middle class, that no longer held true. Parents stopped expecting their children to be working members of the family. There was such a thing as "the juvenile mind," lectured Jacob Abbott in his book *Gentle Measures in the Management and Training of the Young* (1871). The family was responsible for providing a nurturing environment in which the young personality could grow and mature.

Preparation for adulthood became increasingly linked to formal education. School enrollment went up 150 percent between 1870 and 1900. High school attendance, while still encompassing only a small percentage of teenagers, increased

AMERICAN VOICES

"We Did Not Know . . . Whether Women's Health Could Stand the Strain of Higher Education"

M. CAREY THOMAS

M. *Carey Thomas (1857–1935), president of Bryn Mawr College for many years, recalls her dreams of college as a girl growing up in Baltimore in the 1870s.*

The passionate desire of women of my generation for higher education was accompanied thruout its course by the awful doubt, felt by women themselves as well as by men, as to whether women as a sex were physically and mentally fit for it. . . . I ofen remember praying about it, and begging God that if it were true that because I was a girl I could not successfully master Greek and go to college and understand things to kill me at once, as I could not bear to live in such an unjust world. . . .

We did not know when we began whether women's health could stand the strain of college education. We were haunted in those early days by the clanging chains of that gloomy little specter, Dr. Edward H. Clarke's *Sex in Education.* With trepidation of spirit I made my mother read it, and was much cheered by her remark that, as neither she, nor any of the women she knew, had ever seen girls or women of the kind described in Dr. Clarke's book, we might as well act as if they did not exist. . . .

When . . . I went to Leipzig to study after graduating from Cornell, my mother used to write me that my name was never mentioned to her by the women of her acquaintance. I was thought by them to be as much disgrace to my family as if I had eloped with the coachman. . . .

We are now [1908] living in the midst of great and, I believe on the whole beneficent, social changes which are preparing the way for the coming economic independence of women. . . . The passionate desire of the women of my generation for a college education seems, as we study it now in the light of coming events, to have been part of this greater movement.

SOURCE: Linda K. Kerber and Jane De Hart-Mathews, eds., *Women's America: Refocusing the Past*, 2nd ed. (New York: Oxford University Press, 1987), pp. 263–65.

at the fastest rate. As the years between childhood and adulthood began to stretch out, a new stage of life—adolescence—emerged. While rooted in longer years of family dependency, adolescence shifted much of the socializing role from parents to peer group. A youth culture—one of the hallmarks of American life in the twentieth century—was starting to take shape.

The New Woman

John Singer Sargent's painting *Mr. and Mrs. Isaac Newton Phelps Stokes* (1897) captures on canvas the essence of the "new woman" of the 1890s. Nothing about Mrs. Stokes, neither how she is dressed nor how she presents herself, suggests physical weakness or demure passivity. She confidently occupies center stage, a fit partner for her husband, who is relegated to the shadows of the picture.

(The Metropolitan Museum of Art, New York. Bequest of Edith Minturn Phelps Stokes, 1938 [38.104]. Photograph © 1989 The Metropolitan Museum of Art)

City Life

When the budding writer Hamlin Garland and his brother arrived in Chicago from Iowa in 1881, they knew immediately that they had entered a new world: "Everything interested us. . . . Nothing was commonplace, nothing was ugly to us." In one way or another every city-bound migrant, whether from the American countryside or from a foreign land, experienced something of this sense of wonder.

But with the boundless variety came disorder and uncertainty. The city was utterly unlike the rural world the newcomers had left. In the countryside every person had been known to his or her neighbors. Mark Twain found New York "a splendid desert, where a stranger is lonely in the midst of a million of his race. . . . Every man rushes, rushes, rushes, and never has time to be companionable [or] to fool away on matters which do not involve dollars and duty and business." If rural roles and obligations had been well understood, in the city the only predictable relationships were those dictated by the marketplace.

Rural people could never recreate in the city the communities they had left behind. But they found ways to gain a sense of belonging, they built a multitude of new institutions, and they learned how to function in an impersonal, heterogeneous environment. An urban culture emerged, and through it there developed a new breed of American who was entirely at home in the modern city.

NEWCOMERS

At the turn of the century upwards of 30 percent of the residents of New York, Chicago, Boston, Cleveland, Minneapolis, and San Francisco were foreign-born. The biggest ethnic group in Boston was Irish; in Minneapolis, Swedish; in most other northern cities, German. But by 1910 the influx from southern and Eastern Europe had changed the ethnic complexion of many of these cities. In Chicago Poles took the lead; in New York, Eastern European Jews; in San Francisco, Italians.

As the older "walking cities" disappeared, so did the opportunities for intermingling with the older populations. The later arrivals from southern and eastern Europe had little choice about where they lived; they needed to find cheap housing near their jobs. Some gravitated to the outlying factory districts; others settled in the congested downtown ghettos. The immigrants tended to settle by ethnic group. In New York Italians crowded into the Irish neighborhoods west of Broadway, and Russian and Polish Jews pushed the Germans out of the Lower East Side. A colony of Hungarians lived around Houston Street, and Bohemians occupied the Upper East Side between Fiftieth and Seventy-sixth Streets.

Capitalizing on fellow-feeling within ethnic groups, institutions of many kinds sprang up to meet the immigrants' needs. Wherever substantial numbers lived, newspapers appeared. In 1911 the 20,000 Poles in Buffalo, New York, supported two Polish-langage daily papers. Immigrants throughout the country avidly read *Il Progresso Italo-Americano* and the Yiddish-language *Jewish Daily Forward*, both published in New York City (see American Voices, "Bintel Brief"). Companionship could always be found on street corners, in barbershops and club rooms, and in saloons. Italians marched in saint's day parades, Bohemians gathered in singing societies, and New York Jews patronized a lively Yiddish theater. To provide help in times of sickness and death the immigrants organized mutual-aid societies. The Italians of

Mulberry Street, New York City, c. 1900

The influx of southern and eastern Europeans created teeming ghettos in the heart of New York City and other major American cities. The view is of Mulberry Street, with its pushcarts, street peddlers, and bustling traffic. The inhabitants are mostly Italians, and some of them, noticing the photographer preparing his camera, have gathered to be in the picture.
(Library of Congress)

Chicago had sixty-six of these organizations in 1903, each mostly composed of people from a particular province or district. Immigrants built a rich and functional institutional life in urban America to an extent unimagined in their native villages.

The great African American migration from the rural South to northern cities was just beginning at the turn of the century. The black population of New York increased by 30,000 between 1900 and 1910, making New York second only to Washington, D.C., as a black urban center, but the 91,000 African Americans in New York in 1910 represented fewer than 2 percent of the population, and that was true of Chicago and Cleveland as well.

Despite their relatively small numbers urban blacks could not escape discrimination. They retreated from the scattered black neighborhoods of older times

---

AMERICAN VOICES
Bintel Brief

*T*he Yiddish phrase bintel brief *means "bundle of letters." That was the name of the famous column of the* Jewish Daily Forward *devoted to letters from immigrant readers about their trials and tribulations in America.*

I was born in a small town in Russia, and until I was sixteen I studied in *Talmud Torahs* and *yeshivas,* but when I came to America I developed spiritually and became a freethinker. Yet every year when the time of *Rosh Hashana* and *Yom Kippur* comes around I become very gloomy. . . . So strong are my feelings that I enter the synagogue, not in order to pray to God but to heal and refresh my aching soul by sitting among *landsleit* [countrymen] and listening to the cantor's sweet melodies. The members of my Progressive Society don't understand. They say I am a hypocrite. . . . What do you think? *Answer:* No one can tell another what to do with himself on *Yom Kippur.*

I am a Russian revolutionist and a freethinker. Here in America I became acquainted with a girl who is also a freethinker. We decided to marry, but the problem is that she has Orthodox parents, and if we refuse a religious ceremony we will be cut off from them forever. I don't know what to do. Therefore, I ask you to advise me how to act. *Answer:* There are times when it is better to be kind in order not to grieve old parents.

I am a young man of twenty-five, and I recently met a fine girl. She has a flaw, however—a dimple in her chin. It is said that people who have this lose their first husband or wife. I love her very much. But I'm afraid to marry her lest I die because of the dimple. *Answer:* The tragedy is not that the girl has a dimple in her chin but that some people have a screw loose in their heads.

SOURCE: Irving Howe and Kenneth Libo, eds., *How We Lived* (New York: New American Library, 1979), pp. 88–90.

---

into concentrated ghettos—Chicago's Black Belt on the South Side, for example, or the early outlines of New York's Harlem. Race prejudice likewise cut down job opportunities. Twenty-six percent of Cleveland's blacks had been skilled workers in 1870, but only 12 percent were by 1890, and entire occupations such as barbering (except for those shops that served a black clientele) became exclusively white. Two-thirds of Cleveland's blacks in 1910 worked as domestics and day laborers, with little hope of moving up the job ladder.

In the face of pervasive discrimination urban blacks built their own communities. They created a flourishing press, fraternal orders, a vast array of women's organizations, and a middle class of doctors, lawyers, and small entrepreneurs. Above all there were the black churches—twenty-five in Chicago in 1905, mainly Methodist and Baptist. More than any other institution, remarked one scholar in 1913, it was the church "which the Negro may call his own. . . . A new church may be built . . .

and . . . all the machinery set in motion without ever consulting any white person. . . . [It] more than anything else represents the real life of the race." As in the southern countryside the church was the central institution for city blacks, and the preacher the most important local citizen. Manhattan's Union Baptist Church, housed like many others in a storefront, attracted the "very recent residents of this new, disturbing city" and, ringing with spirituals and fervent prayer, made Christianity come "alive Sunday mornings."

WARD POLITICS

Race and ethnicity tended to divide newcomers and turn them in on themselves. Politics, by contrast, integrated them into urban society. Every migrant to an American city automatically became a ward resident and immediately acquired a spokesman at city hall in the form of his local alderman. Immigrants learned very quickly that if they needed anything from city hall, this was the man to see. That was how streets got paved, water mains extended, or variances granted—so that, for example, in 1888 Vito Fortounescere could "place and keep a stand for the sale of fruit, inside the stoop-line, in front of the northeast corner of Twenty-eight Street and Fourth Avenue" in Manhattan, or the parishioners of Saint Maria of Mount Carmel could set off fireworks at their Fourth of July picnic.

Machine control of political parties, although present at every level, flourished most luxuriantly in the big cities. Urban machines depended on a loyal grassroots constituency, so each ward was divided into election districts of a few blocks. The district captain reported to the ward boss, who was likely also to be the alderman. The main job of these functionaries was to be accessible and, as best they could, serve the needs of the party faithful.

The machine acted as a rough-and-ready social service agency, providing jobs for the jobless, a helping hand for a bereaved family, and intercession against an unfeeling city bureaucracy. The Tammany ward boss George Washington Plunkitt had a "regular system" when fires broke out in his district. He arranged for housing for burned-out families, "fix[ing] them up till they get things runnin' again. It's philanthropy, but it's politics, too—mighty good politics."

The business community was similarly served. Contractors sought city business; gas companies and streetcar lines wanted licenses and privileges; manufacturers needed services and not-too-nosy inspectors; and the liquor trade and numbers racket relied on a tolerant police force. All of them turned to the machine boss and his lieutenants.

Of course, the machine exacted a price for these services. The tenement dweller gave his vote. The businessman wrote a check. Naturally, some of the money that changed hands leaked into the pockets of machine politicians. This "boodle" could be blatantly corrupt—kickbacks by contractors; protection money from gamblers, saloonkeepers, and prostitutes; payoffs from gas and trolley companies. Tammany ward boss Plunkitt, however, insisted that he had no need for kickbacks and bribes.

He favored what he called "honest graft"—the easy profits that came to savvy insiders. Plunkitt made most of his money building wharves on Manhattan's waterfront. One way or another, legally or otherwise, machine politics rewarded its supporters.

For the young and ambitious, this was reason enough to favor the machine system. In the mid-1870s over half of Chicago's forty aldermen were foreign-born, sixteen of them Irish immigrants. The first Italian was elected in 1885, the first Pole in 1888. Blacks did not manage to get on Chicago's board of aldermen until after 1900, but Baltimore's Eleventh Ward elected an African American in 1890, and Philadelphia had three black aldermen by 1899. As a ladder for social mobility machine politics was the most democratic of American institutions.

Ward boss Plunkitt was an Irishman, and so were most of the machine politicians controlling Tammany Hall. But by the 1890s Plunkitt's Fifteenth District was filling up with Italians and Eastern European Jews. In general the New York Irish had no love for these newer immigrants, but Plunkitt played no favorites. On any given day (as recorded in a diary) he might attend an Italian funeral in the afternoon and a Jewish wedding in the evening, and at each he probably paid his respects with a few Italian words or a bit of Yiddish.

In an era when so many forces acted to isolate ghetto communities, politics served an *integrating* function, cutting across ethnic lines and giving immigrants and blacks a stake in the larger urban order.

RELIGION IN THE CITY

For African Americans, as we have seen, the church was a central institution of urban life. So it was for many other city dwellers. But they found the city difficult ground for religious practice. All the major American faiths present at the time—Judaism, Catholicism, Protestantism—had to scramble to reconcile religious belief with the secular demands of the urban world.

About 250,000 Jews, mostly of German origin, were living in America when the Eastern European Jews began arriving in the 1880s. Well-established and prosperous, the German Jews had embraced Reform Judaism, abandoning religious practices—from keeping a kosher kitchen to conducting services in Hebrew—"not adapted to the views and habits of modern civilization." Anxious to preserve their traditional piety, Yiddish-speaking immigrants from Eastern Europe founded their own Orthodox synagogues, often in vacant stores and ramshackle buildings, and practiced Judaism in the old way.

In the villages of Eastern Europe, however, Judaism had involved not only worship and belief but an entire way of life. Insular though it might be, ghetto life in the American city could not recreate the communal environment on which strict religious observance depended. "The very clothes I wore and the very food I ate had a fatal effect on my religious habits," confessed the hero of Abraham Cahan's novel *The Rise of David Levinsky* (1917). "If you . . . attempt to bend your religion to the spirit of your surroundings, it breaks. It falls to pieces." Levinsky shaved off his beard and plunged into the Manhattan clothing business. Orthodox Judaism survived this shattering of faith only by reducing its claims on the lives of the faithful.

Catholics faced much the same problem. The issue, defined within the Roman Catholic Church as "Americanism," turned on the extent to which Catholicism should adapt to American society. Should Catholic children attend parochial or public schools? Should they intermarry with non-Catholics? Should the traditional education for the clergy be changed? Bishop John Ireland of St. Paul, Minnesota, felt that "the principles of the Church are in harmony with the interests of the Republic." But traditionalists, led by Archbishop Michael A. Corrigan of New York, denied the possibility of such harmony and argued in effect for insulating the Church from the pluralistic American environment.

Immigrant Catholics generally supported the Church's conservative wing because of their felt need to preserve what they had known in Europe. But that meant also a desire that church life express their ethnic identities. Settling in ethnically distinct neighborhoods, newly arrived Catholics wanted their own parishes where they could celebrate their customs, speak their languages, and establish their own parochial schools. When they became numerous enough, they also demanded their own bishops. The Catholic hierarchy, which was dominated by Irish Catholics, felt that the integrity of the Church itself was at stake. The demand for ethnic parishes implied local control of church property. And if there were bishops for specific ethnic groups, this would mean disrupting the diocesan structure that unified the Church. Indeed, fifty parishes in 1907 broke away and formed the Polish National Catholic Church of America, which adhered to Catholic ritual without recognizing the pope's authority.

On the whole, however, the Church managed to satisfy the immigrant faithful. It met the demand for representation in the hierarchy by appointing immigrant priests as auxiliary bishops within existing dioceses. Ethnic parishes also flourished. Before World War I American Catholics worshipped in more than 2,000 foreign-language churches, and many others were bilingual. Not without strain, the Catholic Church made itself a central institution for the expression of ethnic identity in urban America.

For the Protestant churches the city posed different but not easier challenges. Every major city retained great downtown churches where wealthy Protestants worshipped. Some of these churches, richly endowed, took pride in nationally prominent pastors, such as Henry Ward Beecher of Plymouth Congregational Church in Brooklyn and Phillips Brooks of Trinity Episcopal Church in Boston. But the eminence of these churches, with their fashionable congregations and imposing edifices, could not disguise the growing remoteness of Protestantism from much of its urban constituency. "Where is the city in which the Sabbath day is not losing ground?" lamented a minister in 1887. The families of businessmen, lawyers, and doctors could be seen in any church on Sunday morning, he noted, "but the workingmen and their families are not there."

Immaculate Heart of Mary Church, 1908

In crowded immigrant neighborhoods the church rose from undistinguished surroundings to assert the centrality of religious belief in the life of the community. This photograph is a view of Immaculate Heart of Mary Church taken from Polish Hill in Pittsburgh in 1908.

(Archives of Industrial Society, University Library System, University of Pittsburgh)

To counter this decline the Protestant churches responded in two ways. They evangelized among the unchurched and indifferent, for example, through the Sunday-school movement. Protestants also made their churches instruments of social uplift. Starting in the 1880s many city churches provided reading rooms, day nurseries, clubhouses, and vocational classes. Some churches linked evangelism and social improvement. The Salvation Army, which arrived from Great Britain in 1879, spread the gospel of repentance among the urban poor and built an assistance program that ranged from soup kitchens to shelters for former prostitutes. When all else failed, the down-and-outers of American cities knew they could count on the Salvation Army.

The social meaning that people sought in religion explained the enormous popularity of a book called *In His Steps* (1896). The author, the Congregational minister Charles M. Sheldon, told the story of a congregation that resolved to live by Christ's precepts for one year. "If the church members were all doing as Jesus would do," Sheldon asked, "could it remain true that armies of men would walk the streets for jobs, and hundreds of them curse the church, and thousands of them find in the saloon their best friend?"

The most potent form of urban evangelism—revivalism—said little about social uplift. From their origins in the eighteenth century revival movements had steadfastly focused on individual redemption. The resolution of earthly problems, revivalists believed, would follow the conversion of the people to Christ. Beginning in the mid-1870s revival meetings swept through the cities.

The pioneering figure was Dwight L. Moody, a former Chicago shoe salesman and YMCA official. After preaching in Britain for two years Moody returned to America in 1875. With his talented chorister and hymn writer, Ira D. Sankey, Moody staged revival meetings that drew thousands. He preached an optimistic, uncomplicated, nondenominational message. Eternal life could be had for the asking, Moody shouted as he held up his Bible. His listeners needed only "to come forward and take, TAKE!"

Many other preachers followed in Moody's path. The most colorful was Billy Sunday, a hard-drinking former outfielder for the Chicago White Stockings who mended his ways and found religion. Like Moody and other city revivalists Sunday was a farm boy. His rip-snorting attacks on fashionable ministers and the "booze traffic" carried the ring of rustic America. By realizing that many people remained villagers at heart, revivalists found a key to bringing city dwellers back into the church.

CITY AMUSEMENTS

City people compartmentalized life's activities, setting workplace apart from home and working time apart from free time. "Going out" became a necessity, demanded not only as solace for a hard day's work but also as proof that life was better in the New World than in the Old. "He who can enjoy and does not enjoy commits a sin," a Yiddish-language paper told its readers. And enjoyment now meant buying a ticket and being entertained.

Amusement parks went up on the outskirts of cities across the country. Most glittering was Luna Park at New York's Coney Island—"an enchanted, storybook land of trellises, columns, domes, minarets, lagoons, and lofty aerial flights. . . . It was a world removed—shut away from the sordid clatter and turmoil of the streets." In fact, escape from everyday urban life explains the appeal of amusement parks. The creators of Luna Park intended it to be "a different world—a dream world . . . where all is bizarre and fantastic . . . gayer and more different from the every-day world."

The theater likewise attracted huge audiences. Chicago had six vaudeville houses in 1896 and twenty-two in 1910. Evolving from tawdry variety and minstrel shows, vaudeville cleaned up its routines, making them suitable for the entire family, and turned into thoroughly professional entertainment handled by national booking agencies. With its standard program of nine singing, dancing, and com-

Amusement Park, Long Beach, California

The origins of the roller coaster go back to LaMarcus Thompson's Switchback Railway, installed at Coney Island in 1884 and featuring gentle dips and curves. By 1900, when Long Beach's Jack Rabbit Race was constructed, the goal was to create the biggest possible thrill. Angelenos journeyed out by trolley to Long Beach not only to take a dip in the ocean but to ride the new roller coaster. The Airplane Ride in the foreground is a further wrinkle on the peculiarly modern notion that the way to have fun is to be scared to death.

(Curt Teich Postcard Archives)

edy acts, vaudeville attained enormous popularity just as the movies arrived. The first primitive films, a minute or so of humor or glimpses of famous people, appeared in 1896 in penny arcades and as filler in vaudeville shows. Within a decade millions of city people were watching films of increasing length and artistry at nickelodeons (named after the five-cent admission charge) across the country.

For young unmarried workers the cheap amusements of the city created a new social space. "I want a good time," a New York clothing operator told an investigator. "And there is no . . . way a girl can get it on $8 a week. I guess if anyone wants to take me to a dance he won't have to ask me twice." Hence the widespread ritual among the urban working class of "treating." The girls spent what money they had dressing up; their beaus were expected to pay for the fun. Parental control over courtship broke down, and amid the bright lights and lively music of the dance hall and amusement park working-class youth forged a more easygoing culture of sexual interaction and pleasure seeking.

The geography of the big city carved out ample space for commercialized sex. Prostitution was not new to urban life, but in the late nineteenth century it became less closeted and more intermingled with other forms of public entertainment. In New York the red-light district was the Tenderloin, running northward from Twenty-third Street between Fifth and Eighth Avenues.

The Tenderloin and the Bowery farther downtown were also the sites of a robust gay subculture. The long-held notion that homosexual life was covert—"in the closet"—in Victorian America appears not to be true, at least not in the country's premier city. Homosexuality was illegal, but as with prostitution the law was mostly a dead letter. In certain corners of the city a gay world flourished, with a full array of saloons, meeting places, and drag balls, which were widely known and patronized by uptown "slummers."

Of all forms of (mostly) male diversion none was more specific to the city or so spectacularly successful as professional baseball. The game's promoters decreed that baseball had been created in 1839 by Abner Doubleday in the village of Cooperstown, New York. Actually, baseball was neither of American origin—it developed from the British game of rounders—nor a product of rural life. The game first appeared in the early 1840s in New York City, where a group of gentlemen enthusiasts competed on an empty lot. Over the next twenty years the aristocratic tone of baseball disappeared. Clubs sprang up across the country, and intercity competition developed on a scheduled basis. In 1868 baseball became openly professional, following the lead of the Cincinnati Red Stockings in signing players to contracts for the season.

Big-time commercial baseball came into its own with the launching of the National League in 1876. The team owners were profit-minded businessmen who shaped the sport to please the fans. Wooden grandstands gave way to the concrete and steel stadiums of the early twentieth century, such as Fenway Park in Boston, Forbes Field in Pittsburgh, and Shibe Park in Philadelphia.

For the urban multitudes baseball grew into something more than an afternoon at the ballpark. By rooting for the home team fans found a way of identifying with the city they lived in. Amid the diversity and anonymity of urban life, the common experience and language of baseball acted as a bridge among strangers.

Most efficient at this task, however, was the newspaper. James Gordon Bennett, founder of the *New York Herald* in 1835, wanted "to record the facts . . . for the great masses of the community." The news was whatever interested city readers, starting with crime, scandal, and sensational events. After the Civil War Charles A. Dana of the *New York Sun* added the human-interest story, which made news of ordinary happenings. Newspapers also targeted specific audiences. A women's page offered recipes and fashion news, separate sections covered sports and high society, and the Sunday supplement helped fill the weekend hours.

The competition for readers became fierce when Joseph Pulitzer, the owner of the *St. Louis Post-Dispatch,* invaded New York in 1883 by buying the *World.* Pulitzer was in turn challenged by William Randolph Hearst, who arrived from San Francisco in 1895 prepared to beat the *New York World* at its own game. Hearst's sensation-alist style of newspaper reporting became known as *yellow journalism*. The term, linked to the first comic strip to appear in color, "The Yellow Kid" (1895), meant a type of reporting in which accuracy was second to eliciting a "Gee Whiz!" feeling in the reader.

"He who is without a newspaper," said the great showman P. T. Barnum, "is cut off from his species." Barnum was speaking of city people and their hunger for in-formation. By meeting this need newspapers revealed their sensitivity to the pub-lic they served.

THE HIGHER CULTURE

In the midst of this popular ferment new institutions of higher culture were tak-ing shape in America's cities. A desire for the cultivated life was not, of course, specifically urban. Before the Civil War the lyceum movement had sent lecturers to the remotest towns, bearing messages of culture and learning. The Chautauqua movement, founded in northern New York in 1874, carried on this work of cul-tural dissemination. However, great institutions such as museums, public libraries, opera companies, and symphony orchestras could flourish only in metropolitan centers.

The nation's first major art museum, the Corcoran Gallery of Art, opened in Washington, D.C., in 1869. New York's Metropolitan Museum of Art started in rented quarters two years later, moved in 1880 to its permanent site in Central Park, and launched an ambitious program of art acquisition. When J. P. Morgan became chairman of the board in 1905, the Metropolitan's preeminence was assured. The Boston Museum of Fine Arts was founded in 1876, and Chicago's Art Institute in 1879.

Symphony orchestras also appeared, first in New York under the conductors Theodore Thomas and Leopold Damrosch in the 1870s and then in Boston and Chicago during the next decade. National tours by these leading orchestras planted the seeds for orchestral societies in many other cities. Public libraries grew from modest collections (in 1870 only seven had as many as 50,000 books) into major urban institutions. The greatest library benefactor was Andrew Carnegie, who announced in 1881 that he would build a library in any town or city that was prepared to maintain it. By 1907 Carnegie had spent more than $32.7 million to establish about a thousand libraries throughout the country.

The late nineteenth century was the great age not only of moneymaking but of money *giving*. Generous with their surplus wealth, new millionaires patronized the arts partly as a civic duty, partly to help establish themselves in society, and also partly out of a sense of national pride.

"In America there is no culture," pronounced the English critic G. Lowes Dickinson in 1909. Science and the practical arts, yes, "every possible application of life to purposes and ends," but "no life for life's sake." Such condescending remarks received a respectful American hearing because of a sense of cultural inferiority to the Old World. In 1873 Mark Twain and Charles Dudley Warner published a novel, *The Gilded Age*, satirizing America as a land of money grubbers and speculators. This enormously popular book touched a nerve in the American psyche. Its title has in fact been appropriated by historians to characterize the late nineteenth century—America's Gilded Age—as an era of materialism and cultural shallowness.

Some members of the upper class, like the novelist Henry James, despaired of the country and moved to Europe. But the more common response was to try to raise the nation's cultural level. The newly rich had a hard time of it. They did not have much opportunity to cultivate a taste for art, and a great deal of what they collected was mediocre and garish. On the other hand, George W. Vanderbilt, grandson of the rough-hewn Cornelius Vanderbilt, was an early champion of French Impressionism, and the coal and steel baron Henry Clay Frick built a brilliant art collection that is still housed, as a public museum, in his mansion in New York City. The enthusiasm of moneyed Americans largely fueled the great cultural institutions that sprang up during the Gilded Age.

A deeply conservative idea of culture sustained this generous patronage. The aim was to embellish life, not to probe or reveal its meaning. "Art," says the hero of the Reverend Henry Ward Beecher's sentimental novel *Norwood* (1867), "attempts to work out its end solely by the use of the beautiful, and the artist is to select out only such things as are beautiful." The idea of culture also took on an elitist cast: Shakespeare, once a staple of popular entertainment (in various bowdlerized versions), was appropriated into the domain of "serious" theater. And simultaneously, the world of culture became feminized. "Husbands or sons rarely share those interests," noted one observer. In American life, remarked the clergyman Horace Bushnell, men represented the "force principle," women the "beauty principle."

The depiction of life, the eminent editor and novelist William Deans Howells wrote, "must be tinged with sufficient idealism to make it all of a truly uplifting character. We cannot admit stories which deal with false or immoral relations. . . . The finer side of things—the idealistic—is the answer for us." The *genteel tradition*, as this literary school came to be known, dominated the nation's elite cultural institutions—its universities and publishers—from the 1860s onward.

But the urban world could not finally be kept at bay. Howells himself resigned in 1881 as editor of the *Atlantic Monthly*, a stronghold of the genteel tradition, and called for a literature that seeks "to picture the daily life in the most exact terms possible." In a series of realistic novels—*A Modern Instance* (1882), *The Rise of Silas Lapham* (1885), and *A Hazard of New Fortunes* (1890)—Howells captured the urban middle class. Stephen Crane's *Maggie: Girl of the Streets* (1893), privately printed because no publisher would touch it, unflinchingly described the destruction of a slum girl. In another urban novel, *The Cliff-Dwellers* (1893), Henry Blake Fuller followed the fortunes of the occupants—"cliff-dwellers"—of a giant Chicago office building.

The city had entered the American imagination and become, by the early 1900s, a main theme of American art and literature. And because it challenged so many assumptions of an older, republican America, the city also became an overriding concern of reformers and a main theater in the drama of the Progressive Era.

For Further Exploration

The starting point for modern urban historiography is Sam Bass Warner's pioneering book on Boston, *Streetcar Suburbs, 1870–1900* (1962). In a subsequent work, *The Private City: Philadelphia in Three Periods* (1968), Warner broadened his analysis to show how private decision making shaped the character of the American city. Innovations in urban construction are treated in Carl Condit, *Rise of the New York Skyscraper, 1865–1913* (1996); Alan

---

TIMELINE

1871	Metropolitan Museum of Art opens in New York City.	1885	William Jenney builds first steel-frame structure, Chicago's Home Insurance Building.
1873	Mark Twain and Charles Dudley Warner's *The Gilded Age*	1887	First electric trolley line constructed in Richmond, Virginia
1875	Evangelist Dwight L. Moody launches urban revival movement.	1888	Ward McAllister compiles the *Social Register*.
1876	Alexander Graham Bell patents the telephone. National Baseball League founded	1893	Chicago Columbian Exposition "City Beautiful" movement begins.
1878	Electric arc-light system installed in Philadelphia	1895	William Randolph Hearst enters New York journalism. The comic strip "The Yellow Kid" appears.
1879	Thomas Edison creates a practical incandescent light bulb. First elevated train lines open in New York City. Salvation Army arrives from Britain.	1897	Boston builds first American subway.
		1904	New York subway system opens.
1881	Andrew Carnegie offers to build a library for every American city.	1913	Woolworth Building completed in New York City
1883	Joseph Pulitzer purchases the New York *World*.		

Trachtenberg, *The Brooklyn Bridge* (1965); and Harold L. Platt, *The Electric City: Energy and the Growth of the Chicago Area, 1880–1930* (1991).

On the social elite, see Frederic C. Jaher, *The Urban Establishment* (1982). Aspects of middle-class life are revealed in Margaret Marsh, *Suburban Lives* (1990); Michael A. Ebner, *Creating Chicago's North Shore: A Suburban History* (1988); Susan Strasser, *Never Done: A History of American Housework* (1983); John F. Kasson, *Rudeness and Civility: Manners in Nineteenth-Century America* (1990); and, on the entry of immigrants into the middle class, Andrew R. Heinze, *Adapting to Abundance* (1990).

On urban life, see especially Gunther Barth, *City People: The Rise of Modern City Culture* (1982); John F. Kasson, *Amusing the Million: Coney Island at the Turn of the Century* (1978); Timothy J. Gilfoyle, *City of Eros: New York City, Prostitution and the Commercialization of Sex, 1790–1920* (1991); Kathy Peiss, *Cheap Amusements: Working Women and Leisure in Turn-of-the-Century New York* (1986). The best introduction to Gilded Age intellectual currents is Alan Trachtenberg, *The Incorporation of America: Culture and Society, 1865–1893* (1983).

On the Columbian Exposition of 1893, an excellent website is "The World's Columbian Exposition: Idea, Experience, Aftermath" at <http://xroads.virginia.edu/~ma96/wce/title>, including detailed guides to every site at the fair and analysis of its lasting impact. "On the Lower East Side" at <http://acad.smumn.edu/history/contents.html> offers a collection of first-rate articles and documents written at the turn of the century about life on New York's Lower East Side, from housing and child labor to ethnic communities and pushcarts.

Chapter 20

THE PROGRESSIVE ERA
1900–1914

Society is looking itself over, in our day, from top to bottom. . . . We
are in a temper to reconstruct economic society.

—WOODROW WILSON, 1913

On the face of it, the political ferment of the 1890s ended with the
election of 1896. After the bitter struggle over free silver the victorious Republicans
had no stomach for political crusades. The McKinley administration devoted itself
to maintaining business confidence: sound money and high tariffs were the order
of the day. The main thing, as party chief Mark Hanna said, was to "stand pat and
continue Republican prosperity."

Yet beneath the surface a deep uneasiness had set in. The depression of the
1890s had unveiled truths not acknowledged in better days—that a frightening
chasm, for example, had opened between America's social classes. In Richard Olney's
view the great Pullman strike of 1894 had brought the country "to the ragged edge
of anarchy." As Cleveland's attorney-general, it had been Olney's job to crush the
strike, which he had done with ruthless efficiency (see Chapter 17). But Olney took
little satisfaction from his success. He asked himself what might be done to avoid
such repressive government actions in the future. His answer was federal regulation
of labor relations on the railroads so that crippling rail strikes would not happen.
As a first step toward Olney's goal Congress adopted the Erdman Mediation Act in
1898. In such ways did the crisis of the 1890s turn the nation's thinking to reform.

The problems themselves, however, were of much older origin. For more than
half a century Americans had been absorbed in building the world's most advanced industrial economy. At the beginning of the twentieth century they paused,
looked around, and began to add up the costs—a frightening concentration of
corporate power, a restless working class, misery in the cities, the corruption of
machine politics. It was as if social awareness reached a critical mass around 1900
and set reform activity in motion as a major, self-sustaining phenomenon. For
this reason the years from 1900 to World War I have come to be known as the
Progressive Era.

The Course of Reform

Historians have sometimes spoken of a progressive "movement." But progressivism was not a movement in any meaningful sense. There was no single progressive constituency, no agreed-upon agenda, no unifying organization. At different times and places different social groups became active. People who were reformers on one issue might be conservative on another. The term *progressivism* embraces a widespread, many-sided effort after 1900 to build a better society. Progressive reformers shared only this objective, plus an intellectual style that can be called "progressive."

THE PROGRESSIVE MIND

If the facts could be known, everything else was possible. That was the starting point for progressive thinking. Hence the burst of enthusiasm for scientific investigation—statistical studies by the federal government of immigration, child labor, and economic practices; social research by privately funded foundations into industrial conditions; vice commissions in many cities looking into prostitution, gambling, and other moral ills of an urban society. Progressives likewise placed great faith in academic expertise. In Wisconsin the state university became a key resource for Governor Robert La Follette's reform administration—the reason, one supporter boasted, for "the democracy, the thoroughness, and the accuracy of the state in its legislation."

The main thing, in the progressive view, was to resist ways of thinking that discouraged purposeful action. Social Darwinists who had so dominated Gilded Age thought (see Chapter 18) were wrong in their belief that society developed according to fixed and unchanging laws. "It is folly," protested the Harvard philosopher William James, "to speak of the 'laws of history,' as of something inevitable, which science only has to discover, and which anyone can then foretell and observe, but do nothing to alter or avert." Man could "shape environmental forces to his own advantage," argued the sociologist Lester F. Ward.

Nowhere were the battle lines more sharply drawn than in economics, where the classical school had long proceeded on the assumption that markets were perfectly competitive and perfectly responsive to supply and demand. Such an imagined world left no room for reform because any interference with the market could only disrupt what was already working perfectly. Critics of classical economics—they called themselves "institutional economists"—turned to statistics and history to reveal how the economy really functioned and why, without trade unions and public regulation, the strong would devour the weak.

Progressives similarly argued against treating questions of law as if they could be answered by eternal and self-evident ideas. An example of this legal reasoning was reliance on the principle of liberty of contract in the *Lochner v. New York* decision (1905): the Supreme Court struck down a state law limiting the working

hours of bakers on the grounds that such a restriction violated the liberty of contract of the bakers (as well as their employers). Nonsense, responded the dissenting Justice Oliver Wendell Holmes. If the choice was between working and starving,
could it really be said that bakers freely accepted jobs requiring them to labor fourteen hours a day or that a law reducing their working hours violated their liberty
of contract?

Legal realism, as Justice Holmes's reasoning came to be known, rested on his
conviction that "the life of the law has not been logic; it has been experience. The
felt necessities of the time, even the prejudices which judges share with their fellow-
men, have had a good deal more to do than logic in determining the rules by which
men shall be governed." The law, moreover, should not claim a false neutrality; on
the contrary, as Holmes's student Felix Frankfurter argued, law should be "a vital
agency for human betterment."

The philosophical underpinnings for legal realism came from William James,
who denied the existence of absolute truths and offered instead a philosophy of
pragmatism, which judged ideas by their consequences. Philosophy should be concerned with solving problems, James insisted, not with contemplating ultimate ends.

Progressives prided themselves on being tough-minded. They had confidence
in people's capacity to take purposeful action. But there was another side to the
progressive mind. It was infused with idealism. Progressives framed their intentions
in terms of high principle. Their cause, proclaimed Theodore Roosevelt, "is based
on the eternal principles of righteousness."

Much of this idealism was rooted in American radical traditions. Many progressives traced their awakening to Henry George's Progress and Poverty (1879),
which asked why, in the midst of fabulous wealth, so many Americans should be
condemned to poverty. His answer was that private control of land siphoned the
community's wealth into the hands of landlords. George's single-tax movement—
advocating a confiscatory tax on the unearned value of land—served as a school
for many budding progressives. Others credited Edward Bellamy's utopian novel
Looking Backward (1888), with its technocratic vision of an orderly, affluent
American socialism, or Henry Demarest Lloyd's Wealth Against Commonwealth
(1894), with its searing indictment of the Standard Oil trust. In later years this radical tradition was transmitted mainly through the Socialist Party, which flourished
after 1900 under the leadership of Eugene V. Debs. Many young reformers passed
through socialism on the way to progressivism, although there were some, like Charlotte Perkins Gilman, who remained faithful to the socialist cause.

The most important source of progressive idealism, however, was religion.
Protestant churches had long been troubled by the plight of the urban poor (see
Chapter 19). Now that concern blossomed into a major doctrine—the Social
Gospel. The Baptist cleric Walter Rauschenbush, its most influential exponent, had
been driven by his ministry in the squalid Hell's Kitchen section of New York City
to become an activist on behalf of his poor parishioners and their neighbors. The
churches had to uphold the "social aims of Jesus," he believed. The Kingdom of God

on Earth would be achieved not by striving for personal salvation but in the cause of social justice.

Progressive leaders characteristically grew up in families imbued with evangelical piety. Many went through a religious crisis, seeking and failing to experience a conversion, and ultimately settling on a career in social work, education, or politics, where religious striving might be translated into secular action. Jane Addams, for example, took up settlement-house work believing that by uplifting the poor she would herself be uplifted: she would experience "the joy of finding Christ" by acting "in fellowship" with the needy.

The progressive mode of thought—idealistic in intent and tough-minded in practice—nurtured a new kind of reform journalism. During the 1890s bright new magazines like *Collier's* and *McClure's* began to find an urban audience for lively, fact-filled reporting. At the turn of the century, almost by accident, editors discovered that what most interested readers was the exposure of mischief in American life.

Lincoln Steffens's article "Tweed Days in St. Louis" in the October 1902 issue of *McClure's* is credited with starting the trend. In a powerful series Steffens wrote about "the shame of the cities"—the corrupt ties between business and political machines. Ida M. Tarbell attacked Standard Oil, and David Graham Phillips told how money controlled the Senate. William Hard exposed industrial accidents in "Making Steel and Killing Men" (1907) and child labor in "De Kid Wot Works at Night" (1908). Hardly a sordid corner of American life escaped the scrutiny of these tireless reporters. They were moralists as well, infusing their factual accounts with personal indignation. "The sights I saw," wrote the pioneering slum investigator Jacob Riis, "gripped my heart until I felt I must tell of them, or burst, or turn anarchist."

Theodore Roosevelt, among many others, thought these journalists went too far. In a 1906 speech he compared them to the man with a muckrake in *Pilgrim's Progress* (by the seventeenth-century English preacher John Bunyan) who was too absorbed with raking the filth on the floor to look up and accept a celestial crown. Thus the term *muckraker* became attached to journalists who exposed the underside of American life. Their efforts were in fact health-giving. More than any other group, the muckrakers called the people to arms (see American Voices, "Muckraking").

WOMEN PROGRESSIVES

Among the first to respond were middle-class women who, in their well-established role as "social housekeepers," had long carried the burden of humanitarian work in American cities. They had been the foot soldiers for the charity organization societies that coordinated private relief after the 1870s, visiting needy families, assessing their problems, and referring them to relief agencies.

After many years of such dedicated labors Josephine Shaw Lowell of New York City concluded that giving assistance to the poor was not enough. "If the working

Ida Tarbell Takes on Rockefeller

A popular biographer of Napoleon and Lincoln in the 1890s, Ida Tarbell turned her journalistic talents to muckraking. Her first installment of "The History of the Standard Oil Company" appeared in *Mc-Clure's* in November 1902. John D. Rockefeller, she wrote, "was willing to strain every nerve to obtain for himself special and illegal privileges from the railroads which were bound to ruin every man in the oil business not sharing them with him." As Tarbell built her case, criticism rained down on Rockefeller. A more sympathetic cartoon in the magazine *Judge* pleads with Rockefeller's critics: "Boys, don't you think you have bothered the old man just about enough?"

(Ida M. Tarbell Collection, Reis Library, Allegheny College, Meadville, Pennsylvania; Culver Pictures)

people had all they ought to have, we should not have the paupers and criminals," she declared. "It is better to save them before they go under, than to spend your life fishing them out afterward." Lowell founded the New York Consumers' League in 1890. Her goal was to improve the wages and working conditions of female clerks in the city's stores.

AMERICAN VOICES
Muckraking
CHARLES EDWARD RUSSELL

*I*n this autobiographical account Charles Edward Russell, a newspaperman, describes how he got into muckraking journalism and what he thought it was all about. He never did, by the way, get back to writing music.

All America had been accustomed to laud and bepraise the makers of great fortunes. . . . Now, of a sudden, men began to discover that these great and adored fortunes had been gathered in ways that not only grazed the prison gate but imposed burdens and disadvantages upon the rest of the community. . . . In the shock of this discovery, a literature of exposition arose. . . .

Pure accident cast me, without the least desire, into the pursuit of this fashion. I had finally withdrawn from the newspaper business, and having enough money to live modestly I was bent upon carrying out a purpose long cherished [to compose music]. Upon this task I was intent when the whole business was upset with a single telegram.

One day, Mr. J. W. Midgley, who was a famous expert on railroad rates and conditions . . . let loose a flood of startling facts about the impositions practised by the owners and operators of refrigerator cars. My friend, Mr. Erman J. Ridgway . . . of *Everybody's Magazine* wired asking me to see Mr. Midgley [who] positively refused all offers to become an exposé writer. [So] Ridgway wire[d] asking me to furnish the article *Everybody's* wanted. I had not the least disposition to do so, except only that Ridgway was my friend. . . . The next thing I knew a muckrake was put into my hand and I was plunged into the midst of the game. . . .

I wrote two or three articles on the refrigerator car scandal and then went on to write a series on the methods of the Beef Trust. . . . We were all up and away, full of the pleasures of the chase . . . and all that business about poetry and music sheets forgotten. It was exhilarating sport, hunting the money octopus.

SOURCE: Charles Edward Russell, *Bare Hands and Stone Walls* (New York, Charles Scribner's Sons, 1933), pp. 135–39.

From these modest beginnings the league spread to other cities and blossomed into the National Consumers' League in 1899. By then the women at its head had lost faith in voluntary action; only the state had the resources to rescue poor urban families. Under the crusading leadership of Florence Kelley, formerly a chief factory inspector in Illinois, the Consumers' League became a powerful lobby for protective legislation for women and children.

Among its achievements none was more important than the *Muller v. Oregon* decision (1908), which upheld an Oregon law limiting the workday for women to ten hours. The Consumers' League recruited the brilliant Boston lawyer Louis D.

Brandeis to defend the Oregon law before the Supreme Court. In his brief Brandeis devoted a scant two pages to the narrow constitutional issue—whether, under its police powers, Oregon had the right to regulate women's working hours. Instead Brandeis rested his case on data gathered by the Consumers' League showing the damage long hours did to women's health and family roles. The *Muller* decision, resting on Brandeis's social brief, cleared the way for a wave of protective laws across the country.

Women's organizations became a mighty lobby on behalf of women and children. Their victories included the first law providing public assistance for mothers with dependent children, in Illinois in 1911; the first minimum wage law for women, in Massachusetts in 1912; more effective child labor laws, in many states; and at the federal level, the Children's and Women's bureaus in the Labor Department, in 1912 and 1920, respectively. The welfare state, insofar as it arrived in America in these years, was what women progressives had made of it; they erected a "maternalist" welfare system.

A parallel path for women's reform came via the settlement-house movement. The seed in America was Hull House, which Jane Addams and Ellen Gates Starr established in 1889 on Chicago's West Side after visiting Toynbee Hall in the London slums. During the progressive years scores of settlement houses sprang up in the poor neighborhoods of the nation's cities. Hull House had meeting rooms, an art gallery, clubs for children and adults, and a kindergarten. Addams herself led battles for garbage removal, playgrounds, better street lighting, and police protection.

Besides the modest good they did in the slum neighborhoods, the settlement houses also satisfied the needs of the middle-class residents for meaningful lives. In a famous essay Jane Addams spoke of the "subjective necessity" of the settlement house. She meant that it was as much for educated young men and women eager to serve as it was a response to the needs of slum dwellers. Addams herself was a case in point. Born in 1860 in Cedarville, Illinois, she grew up in comfortable circumstances and graduated from Rockford College. Then Addams faced an empty future—an ornamental wife if she married, a sheltered spinster if she did not. Hull House became her salvation, enabling her to "begin with however small a group to accomplish and to live."

Almost imperceptibly women activists like Jane Addams and Florence Kelley breathed new life into the suffrage movement. Why, they asked, should a woman who was capable of running a settlement house or lobbying a bill be denied the right to vote? If women had the right to vote, they would demand more enlightened legislation and better government. And by encouraging working-class women to help themselves, women progressives got a whole new class interested in fighting for suffrage.

In 1903 social reformers founded the National Women's Trade Union League. Financed and led by wealthy supporters, the league organized women workers, played a considerable role in their strikes, and trained working-class leaders. One such was Rose Schneiderman, who became a union organizer among New York's garment workers; another was Agnes Nestor, who led Illinois glove workers. Although they often resented the patronizing ways of their well-to-do patrons, such trade-union women identified their cause with the broader struggle for women's rights.

Around 1910 suffrage activity began to quicken, and tactics shifted. In Britain suffragists had begun to picket Parliament, assault politicians, and stage hunger strikes while in jail. Inspired by their example, Alice Paul, a young Quaker once resident in Britain, applied similar confrontational tactics to the American struggle. Although women suffrage had been won in six western states since 1910, Paul rejected the state-by-state route as too slow (see Map 20.1). She advocated a constitutional amendment that in one stroke would grant women everywhere the right to vote. In 1916 Paul organized the militant National Woman's Party.

The National American Woman Suffrage Association (NAWSA), from which Paul had split off, was also rejuvenated. Carrie Chapman Catt, a skilled organizer from the New York movement, took over as national leader in 1915. Under her guidance NAWSA brought a broad-based organization to the campaign for a federal amendment.

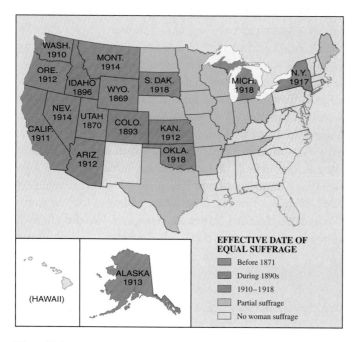

M A P 20.1
Woman Suffrage, 1869–1918

By 1909, after more than sixty years of agitation, only four lightly populated western states had granted women full voting rights. A number of other states offered partial suffrage, limited mostly to voting for school boards and such issues as taxes. Between 1910 and 1918, as the effort shifted to the struggle for a constitutional amendment, eleven states (and Alaska) joined the list granting full suffrage. The most stubborn resistance was in the South.

In the midst of this suffrage struggle something new and more fundamental began to happen. A younger generation of college-educated, self-supporting women refused to be hemmed in by the social constraints of women's "separate sphere." "Breaking into the Human Race" was the intention they proclaimed at a mass meeting in New York in 1914. "We intend simply to be ourselves," declared the chair Marie Jenny Howe, "not just our little female selves, but our whole big human selves."

The women at this meeting called themselves *feminists*, a term that was just coming into use. In this, its first incarnation, feminism meant freedom for full personal development. Thus did Charlotte Perkins Gilman, famous for her advocacy of communal kitchens as a means of liberating women from homemaking, imagine the new woman: "Here she comes, running, out of prison and off the pedestal; chains off, crown off, halo off, just a live woman."

Feminists were militantly prosuffrage, but unlike their more traditional suffragist sisters they had no interest in arguing that women would have an uplifting effect on American politics. Rather they demanded the right to vote because they considered themselves fully equal to men. At the moment the suffrage movement was about to triumph, it was overtaken by a larger revolution that redefined the struggle for women's rights as a battle against all the constraints that prevented women from achieving their potential as human beings.

Feminism brought forth a more radical type of woman social progressive—most notably, Margaret Sanger. As a public health nurse in New York City, Sanger had been repeatedly asked by immigrant women the "secret" of how to avoid having more babies. When one of her patients died of a botched abortion, Sanger decided to devote herself to the cause of birth control. This activity was illegal; nineteenth-century laws treated birth-control literature and contraceptive devices as obscene materials. While the educated middle class had little trouble evading these laws, birth control could reach the poor only by an open campaign of education. Undeterred by police raids or public disapproval, Sanger gave speeches, published pamphlets, and in 1916 opened the first birth-control clinic in the United States. If her ends were the same as Jane Addams's—both wanted to uplift the downtrodden—the means Sanger chose laid down a sharper challenge to the status quo.

REFORMING POLITICS

Like the Mugwumps of the Gilded Age, progressive reformers attacked the boss rule of the party system, but more adeptly and more aggressively. Indeed, because politics was about power, in this realm the motives of progressives were always mixed, with the ideals of civic betterment elbowing uneasily with the drive for self-aggrandizement.

Robert M. La Follette of Wisconsin led the way. Born in 1855, La Follette started as a conventional politician, rising from the Republican ranks to service in Congress for three terms. He was a party regular, never doubting that he was in honorable company until, by his own account, a Republican boss offered him a bribe

Robert M. La Follette

La Follette was transformed into a political reformer when a Wisconsin Republican boss attempted to bribe him in 1891. As he described it in his *Autobiography,* "Out of this awful ordeal came understanding; and out of understanding came resolution. I determined that the power of this corrupt influence . . . should be broken." This photograph captures La Follette at the top of his form, taking his case in 1897 to the people of Cumberland, Wisconsin.
(State Historical Society of Wisconsin, Madison, WI)

to fix a judge in a railroad case. Awakened by this "awful ordeal" La Follette broke with the Wisconsin machine in 1891 and became a tireless exponent of political reform, which for him meant restoring America's democratic ideals. "Go back to the first principles of democracy; go back to the people," he told his audience when he launched his campaign against the state Republican machine. In 1900, after battling for a decade, La Follette won the governorship on a platform of higher taxes for corporations, stricter utility and railroad regulation, and political reform.

The key to party reform, La Follette felt, was to deny the bosses the power to choose the party's candidates. This could be achieved by requiring that nominations be decided not in party conventions but by popular vote. Enacted in 1903, Wisconsin's direct primary expressed La Follette's democratic idealism, but it also suited his particular political talents. The party regulars opposing him were insiders, more comfortable in the caucus room than out on the stump. But that was where La Follette, a superb campaigner, excelled. The direct primary gave La Follette an iron grip on Republican politics in Wisconsin that he did not relinquish until his death twenty-five years later.

What was true of La Follette was more or less true of all successful progressive politicians. They typically described their work as political restoration, frequently confessing that they had converted to reform after discovering how far party politics had drifted from the ideals of representative government. Like La Follette, Albert B. Cummins of Iowa, William U'Ren of Oregon, and Hiram Johnson of California all espoused democratic ideals, and all skillfully used the direct primary as the stepping stone to political power. They practiced a new kind of popular politics, which in a reform age could be a more effective way to power than the backroom techniques of the old-fashioned machine politicians.

Even the most democratizing of reforms espoused by the progressives—the initiative and recall—were really exercises in power politics. The *initiative* enabled citizens to have burning issues placed on the ballot; *recall* empowered them to remove officeholders who had lost the public's confidence. It soon became clear, however, that direct democracy did not supplant organized politics. Initiative and recall campaigns required organization, money, and expertise, and these were attributes not of the people at large but of well-financed interests. Like the direct primary, the initiative and recall had as much to do with power relations as with democratic idealism.

URBAN LIBERALISM

When the Republican Hiram Johnson ran for California governor in 1910, he was the reform candidate of the state's middle class. Famous as prosecutor of the corrupt San Francisco boss Abe Ruef, Johnson pledged to purify California politics and curb the Southern Pacific Railroad—the dominating economic power in the state. By his second term Johnson was championing social and labor legislation. His original base in the middle class had eroded, and he had become the champion of California's immigrant working class.

Johnson's career reflected a shift in the center of gravity of progressivism, which had begun as a movement of the middle class but then took on board America's working people. A new strain of progressive reform emerged that historians have labeled *urban liberalism*. To understand this phenomenon we have to begin with city machine politics.

Thirty minutes before quitting time on Saturday afternoon, March 25, 1911, fire broke out at the Triangle Shirtwaist Company in downtown New York. The flames trapped the workers, mostly young immigrant women. Forty-seven leapt to their deaths; another ninety-nine never reached the windows (see American Voices, "Working for the Triangle Shirtwaist Company"). In the wake of the tragedy, the New York State Factory Commission developed over a four-year period a remarkable program of labor reform: fifty-six laws dealing with fire hazards, unsafe machines, industrial homework, and wages and hours for women and children. The chairman of the commission was Robert F. Wagner; the vice chairman, Alfred E. Smith. Both were Tammany Hall politicians, serving at the time as leaders in the

AMERICAN VOICES

Working for the Triangle Shirtwaist Company

PAULINE NEWMAN

*P*auline Newman was an organizer and educational director for the International Ladies
 Garment Workers Union until her death in 1986. As a child she had worked at the notorious Triangle Shirtwaist factory in New York.

A cousin of mine worked for the Triangle Shirtwaist Company and she got me on there
in October of 1901. . . .

Well, of course, there were [child labor] laws on the books, but no one bothered to enforce them. The employers were always tipped off if there was going to be an inspection.
"Quick," they'd say, "into the boxes!" And we children would climb into the big boxes the
finished shirts were stored in. Then some shirts were piled on top of us, and when the inspector came—no children. The factory always got an okay from the inspector, and I suppose someone at City Hall got a little something, too.

The employers didn't recognize anyone working for them as a human being. . . . If you
went to the toilet and you were there longer than the floor lady thought you should be,
you would be laid off for half a day and sent home. And, of course, that meant no pay.
You were not allowed to have your lunch on the fire escape in the summertime. The door
was locked to keep us in, That's why so many people were trapped when the fire broke
out. . . .

I stopped working at the Triangle Factory during the strike in 1909 and I didn't go back.
The union sent me out to raise money for the strikers. I apparently was able to articulate
my feelings and opinions about the criminal conditions, and they didn't have anyone else
who could do better so they assigned me. . . .

After the 1909 strike I worked with the union, organizing in Philadelphia and Cleveland and other places, so I wasn't at the Triangle Shirtwaist Factory when the fire broke
out, but a lot of my friends were. . . .

Conditions were dreadful in those days. But . . . even when things were terrible, I always had that faith. . . . Only now, I'm a little discouraged sometimes when I see the workers spending their free hours watching television—trash. We fought so hard for those hours
and they waste them. We used to read Tolstoy, Dickens, Shelley, by candlelight, and they
watch the *Hollywood Squares*. Well, they're free to do what they want. That's what we fought
for.

SOURCE: Joan Morrison and Charlotte Fox Zabusky, eds., *American Mosaic: The Immigrant Experience
in the Words of Those Who Lived It* (New York: Dutton, 1980), pp. 9–14. Copyright © 1980 by Joan
Morrison and Charlotte Fox Zabusky. Reprinted by permission.

state legislature. They established the commission, participated fully in its work, and marshaled the party regulars to pass the proposals into law—all with the approval of the Tammany machine.

In thus responding to the Triangle fire, Tammany was conceding that social problems had grown too big to be handled informally by party machines. Only the state could prohibit industrial firetraps or cope with the evils of factory work and slum life. And if that meant a weakening of the traditional bonds of rank-and-file loyalty to Tammany, so be it. Al Smith and Robert Wagner absorbed the lessons of the Triangle investigation. They formed durable ties with such middle-class progressives as the social worker Frances Perkins, who sat on the commission as the representative of the New York Consumers' League, and became urban liberals—advocates of active intervention by the state in uplifting the laboring masses of America's cities.

It was not only altruism that converted seasoned politicians like Smith and Wagner. The city machines faced strong competition from a new breed of middle-class progressive, skilled urban reformers like Mayor Brand Whitlock of Toledo, Ohio, whose administration not only attacked city hall corruption but also provided better schools, cleaner streets, and more social services for Toledo's needy. Combining campaign magic and popular programs, progressive mayors in Cleveland, Jersey City, and elsewhere won over the urban masses and challenged the rule of the machines. Also confronting the bosses was a challenge from the left. The Socialist Party was making headway in the cities, electing Milwaukee's Victor Berger as the nation's first socialist congressman in 1910 and winning municipal elections across the country. The political universe of the urban machines had changed, and they had to pay closer attention to opinion in the precincts.

City machines, always pragmatic, adopted urban liberalism without much ideological struggle. The same could not be said of the trade unions, the other institution that represented American working people. In its early years the American Federation of Labor (AFL) had strongly opposed state interference in labor's affairs. Samuel Gompers preached that workers should not seek from government what they could accomplish by their own economic power and self-help. *Voluntarism*, as trade unionists called this doctrine, did not die out, but it weakened substantially during the progressive years.

One reason was that the labor movement came under severe attack by the courts. In the *Danbury Hatters* case (1908) the Supreme Court declared a boycott by the Hatters' Union against the antiunion D. E. Loewe & Company to be a conspiracy in restraint of trade under the Sherman Act, awarding triple damages that threatened the homes and life savings of hundreds of union members and rendering trade unions vulnerable to antitrust suits. Even worse was the willingness of judges to grant injunctions—court orders—prohibiting unions from carrying on strikes or boycotts. The justification was to prevent "irreparable damage" to an employer while the court was considering the legality of the union's actions. But the effect of this "temporary" measure was invariably to immobilize and defeat the union.

Only a political response could blunt these assaults on labor's economic weapons. In its "Bill of Grievances" of 1906, the AFL demanded that Congress grant unions immunity from antitrust suits and injunctions. Rebuffed, the unions became more politically active, entering campaigns and giving nonpartisan support to candidates who favored their program.

Once into politics the labor movement had difficulty denying the case for social legislation. The AFL, after all, claimed to speak for the entire working class. When muckrakers exposed exploitation of workers and middle-class progressives came forward with solutions, how could the labor movement fail to respond? In state after state organized labor joined the battle for progressive legislation and increasingly became its strongest advocate, including most particularly workers' compensation for industrial accidents.

Accidents took an awful toll at the workplace. Two thousand coal miners were killed every year, dying from cave-ins and explosions at a rate 50 percent higher than in German mines. Liability laws, based on common law, so heavily favored employers that victims of industrial accidents rarely got more than token compensation. The tide turned quickly once the labor movement pushed the issue; between 1910 and 1917 all the industrial states enacted insurance laws covering on-the-job injuries.

Maimed Factory Worker

Lewis Hine, a great photographer of immigrant life, took this undated picture of a disabled factory worker. Two of his four children are in the background. How was he to support them? If his accident occurred before the passage of workers' compensation laws in 1910, they were probably out of luck. (George Eastman House)

The United States hesitated, however, to broaden the attack on the hazards of modern industrial life. Health insurance and unemployment compensation, although popular in Europe, scarcely made it onto the American political agenda. Old-age pensions, which Britain adopted in 1908, got a serious hearing, only to come up against an odd barrier: the United States already had a pension system of a kind, for Civil War veterans, providing benefits to as many as half of all native-born men over sixty-four or their survivors in the early twentieth century.

Not until the Great Depression would the country be ready for social insurance. A secure old age, unemployment payments, health benefits—these human needs of a modern industrial order were beyond the reach of urban liberals in the Progressive Era.

RACISM AND REFORM

The direct primary was the flagship of progressive politics—the crucial reform, as La Follette said, for defeating the party bosses and returning politics to "the people." The primary originated not in Wisconsin, however, but in the South, and by the time La Follette got his primary law in 1903, primaries were already operating in seven southern states. In the South, however, the primary was a *white* primary. Since the Democratic nomination was tantamount to election, excluding African Americans from the nominating process effectively disfranchised them. The southern primary was dressed up as an attack on back-room party rule, but it also served to deprive blacks of their political rights.

Democratic reform and white supremacy thus were wedded together by the racism of the age. In a 1902 book on Reconstruction Professor John W. Burgess of Columbia University denounced the Fifteenth Amendment: granting blacks the vote after the Civil War had been a "monstrous thing." Burgess was southern-born, but he was confident that his northern audience saw the "vast differences in political capacity" between blacks and whites and approved of black disfranchisement. Even the Republican Party offered no rebuttal. Indeed, as president-elect in 1908 William Howard Taft applauded the southern laws as necessary to "prevent entirely the possibility of domination by. . . an ignorant electorate." Taft assured southerners that "the federal government has nothing to do with social equality."

In the North racial tensions were on the rise. Over 200,000 blacks migrated from the South between 1900 and 1910. Their arrival in northern cities invariably sparked white resentment. Attacks on blacks became widespread, capped by a bloody race riot in Springfield, Illinois, in 1908. Equally reflective of racist sentiment was the huge success of D. W. Griffith's epic film *Birth of a Nation* (1915), which depicted Reconstruction as a moral struggle between rampaging blacks and a chivalrous Ku Klux Klan. Woodrow Wilson found the film's history "all so terribly true." His Democratic administration marked a low point for the federal government as the ultimate guarantor of equal rights: during Wilson's tenure segregation of the U.S. civil service would have gone into effect but for an outcry among black leaders and influential white allies.

In these bleak years a core of young black professionals, mostly northern-born, began to fight back. The key figure was William Monroe Trotter, the pugnacious editor of the *Boston Guardian* and an outspoken critic of Booker T. Washington. "The policy of compromise has failed," Trotter argued. "The policy of resistance and aggression deserves a trial." In this endeavor Trotter was joined by W.E.B. Du Bois, a Harvard-trained sociologist and author of *Souls of Black Folk*. In 1906, after breaking with Washington, they called a meeting of twenty-nine supporters at Niagara Falls—but in Canada because no hotel on the U.S. side would admit blacks. The Niagara Movement that resulted from that meeting had an impact far beyond the scattering of members and local bodies it organized. The principles it affirmed would define the struggle for the rights of African Americans: first, encouragement of black pride by all possible means; second, an uncompromising demand for full political and civil equality; and above all the resolute denial "that the Negro-American assents to inferiority, is submissive under oppression and apologetic before insults."

Going against the grain, a handful of white reformers rallied to the African American cause. Among the most devoted was Mary White Ovington, who grew up in an abolitionist family. Like Jane Addams, Ovington became a settlement-house worker but among urban blacks in New York rather than immigrants in a Chicago neighborhood. News of the Springfield race riot of 1908 changed her life. Convinced that her duty was to fight racism, Ovington called a meeting of sympathetic white progressives, which led to the formation of the National Association for the Advancement of Colored People (NAACP) in 1909.

Torn by internal disagreements, the Niagara Movement was breaking up; most of the black activists joined the NAACP. The organization's national leadership was dominated by whites, with one crucial exception. Du Bois became the editor of the NAACP's journal, *The Crisis*. With a passion that only a black voice could provide, Du Bois used that platform to proclaim the demand for equal rights.

In social welfare the National Urban League became the lead organization, uniting in 1911 the many agencies serving black migrants arriving in northern cities. Like the NAACP the Urban League was interracial, including both white reformers such as Ovington and black welfare activists such as William Lewis Bulkley, a New York school principal who was the League's main architect. In the South social welfare was very much the province of black women, mostly working in the churches and schools but also as members of the southern branches of the National Association of Colored Women's Clubs, which had started in 1896. And because their activities seemed unthreatening to white supremacy, black women were able to reach across the color line and find allies and supporters among white women in the South.

Progressivism was a house of many chambers. Most were infected by the racism of the age, but not all. A saving remnant of white progressives rallied to the cause of racial justice. National institutions—the NAACP, the Urban League, and such black organizations as the National Association of Colored Women's Clubs—took shape that would lead the black struggle for a better life over the next half century.

Progressivism and National Politics

The gathering forces of progressivism reached the national scene slowly. Reformers had been spurred by immediate and visible problems, far from Washington. But in 1906 Robert La Follette left Wisconsin for the U.S. Senate. Other seasoned progressives, also ambitious for a wider stage, followed. By 1910 a vocal progressive bloc was making itself heard in both houses of Congress.

Progressivism came to national politics not via Congress, however, but by way of the presidency. This was partly because the White House provided a "bully pulpit"—to use Theodore Roosevelt's phrase. But just as important was the twist of fate that brought Roosevelt to the White House on September 14, 1901.

THE MAKING OF A PROGRESSIVE PRESIDENT

Except for his upper-class background Theodore Roosevelt was cut from much the same cloth as other progressive politicians. Born in 1858 he came from a wealthy old-line New York family, attended Harvard, and contemplated the life of a leisured man of letters. Instead, scarcely out of college, he plunged into Republican politics and entered the New York state legislature. Like many other budding progressives, Roosevelt was motivated by a high-minded, Christian upbringing. He always identified himself—loudly—with the cause of righteousness. But Roosevelt did not scorn power and its uses. Contemptuous of the Mugwump reformers (see Chapter 18), he much preferred the professionalism of party politics. Roosevelt rose in the New York party because he skillfully developed broad popular support and thus forced himself on reluctant state Republican bosses.

Safely back from the Spanish-American War as the hero of San Juan Hill (see Chapter 21), Roosevelt won the New York governorship in 1898. During his single term he clearly signaled his progressivism by pushing through civil-service reform and a tax on corporate franchises. He discharged the corrupt superintendent of insurance over the Republican Party's objections and asserted his confidence in the government's capacity to improve the life of the people.

Hoping to neutralize him the party chieftains promoted Roosevelt in 1900 to what seemed a dead-end job, as William McKinley's vice president. Roosevelt accepted reluctantly. But on September 6, 1901, an anarchist named Leon F. Czolgosz shot the president. When McKinley died eight days later, Roosevelt became president. It was a sure bet, groaned Republican boss Mark Hanna, that "that damn cowboy" would make trouble in the White House.

Roosevelt in fact moved cautiously, attending first of all to politics. He adroitly used the patronage powers of the presidency to gain control of the Republican Party. But he was also uncertain about what reform role the federal government ought to play. At first the new president might have been described as a progressive without a cause.

Even so, Roosevelt displayed his activist bent. An ardent outdoorsman, he emphasized conservation in his first annual message to Congress. Unlike John Muir (see Chapter 16) Roosevelt was not a preservationist wholly opposed to the exploitation of the nation's wilderness. Rather he wanted to conserve the country's resources and make certain that commercial development was mindful of the public interest. In 1902 he backed the Newlands Reclamation Act, which designated the proceeds from public land sales for irrigation in arid regions. His administration expanded the national forests, upgraded land management, and to the chagrin of some Republicans energetically prosecuted violators of federal land laws. In the cause of conservation Roosevelt demonstrated his disdain for those who sought profit "by betraying the public."

That same energetic bent prompted Roosevelt's intervention in the miners' strike of 1902. Hard coal (anthracite) was the main fuel for home heating in those days. As cold weather approached, it became urgent to settle the strike. The United Mine Workers, led by John Mitchell, was willing to submit to arbitration, but the coal operators would have nothing to do with the union. Although lacking any legal grounds for intervening, the president called both sides to a White House conference on October 1, 1902. When the operators balked, Roosevelt threatened a government takeover of the mines. He also persuaded the financier J. P. Morgan to

Theodore Roosevelt at Yellowstone National Park, 1903

President Roosevelt, a devoted conservationist is pictured here about to enter Yellowstone, the first of America's national parks and a favorite of his. The photograph of him on horseback must have delighted Roosevelt. It showed him as he liked to be seen—as a great outdoorsman.

(Picture Research Consultants & Archives)

use his considerable influence. At that point the coal operators caved in. The strike ended with the appointment by Roosevelt of an arbitration commission, another unprecedented step. While not especially sympathetic to organized labor, Roosevelt blamed the crisis on the "arrogant stupidity" of the mine owners.

"Of all the forms of tyranny the least attractive and the most vulgar is the tyranny of mere wealth," Roosevelt wrote in his autobiography. He was prepared to deploy all his presidential authority against the "tyranny" of irresponsible business.

REGULATING THE MARKETPLACE

The economic issue that most troubled Roosevelt was the threat posed by big business to competitive markets. The drift toward large-scale enterprise was itself not new; for many years efficiency-minded entrepreneurs had been building vertically integrated national firms (see Chapter 17). But bigger business, they knew, also meant power to control markets. And when, in the aftermath of the depression of the 1890s, promoters scrambled to merge rival firms, the primary motive was not efficiency but the elimination of competition. These mergers—*trusts,* as they were called—greatly increased business concentration in the economy. By 1910, 1 percent of the nation's manufacturers accounted for 44 percent of the nation's industrial output.

As early as his first annual message, Roosevelt acknowledged the nation's uneasiness with the "real and grave evils" of economic concentration. But what weapons could the president use in response?

The legal principles upholding free competition were already firmly established under common law: anyone injured by monopoly or illegal restraint of trade could sue for damages. With the passage of the Sherman Antitrust Act of 1890, these common-law rights entered the U.S. statute books and could be enforced by the federal government where offenses involved interstate commerce. Neither Cleveland nor McKinley showed much interest, but the Sherman Act was there waiting to be used. Its potential consisted above all in the fact that it incorporated common-law principles of unimpeachable validity. In the right hands the Sherman Act could be a mighty weapon against the abuse of economic power.

Roosevelt made his opening move in 1903 by establishing a Bureau of Corporations empowered to investigate business practices and bolster the Justice Department's capacity to mount antitrust suits. The department had already filed such a suit in 1902 against the Northern Securities Company, a combination of the railroad systems of the Northwest. In a landmark decision the Supreme Court ordered Northern Securities dissolved in 1904.

In the presidential election that year Roosevelt handily defeated a weak conservative Democratic candidate, Judge Alton B. Parker. Now president in his own right, Roosevelt stepped up the attack on the trusts. He took on forty-five of the nation's giant firms, including Standard Oil, American Tobacco, and DuPont. His rhetoric rising, Roosevelt became the nation's trust-buster, a crusader against "predatory wealth."

Jack and the Wall Street Giants

In this vivid cartoon from the humor magazine *Puck* Jack (Theodore Roosevelt) has come to slay the giants of Wall Street. To ordinary Americans trust-busting took on the mythic qualities of the fairy tale—with about the same amount of awe for the fearsome Wall Street giants and hope in the prowess of the intrepid Roosevelt. J. P. Morgan is the giant leering at front right.

(Library of Congress)

But Roosevelt was not antibusiness. He regarded large-scale enterprise as a natural tendency of modern industrialism. Only firms that abused their power deserved punishment. But how would those companies be identified? Under the Sherman Act, following common-law practice, the courts decided whether an act in restraint of trade was "unreasonable"—that is, actually harmed the public interest. In the *Trans-Missouri* decision of 1897, however, the Supreme Court abandoned this discretionary "rule of reason," holding now that actions that restrained or monopolized trade, regardless of the public impact, automatically violated the Sherman Act.

Little noticed at first, *Trans-Missouri* placed Roosevelt in a quandary. He had no desire to hamstring legitimate business activity, but he could not rely on the courts to distinguish between "good" and "bad" trusts. The only solution was for Roosevelt to do so himself, a power he had because as president he decided whether to initiate antitrust prosecutions in the first place. It was his negative power that counted here: he could choose not to prosecute a trust.

In November 1904, with an antitrust suit looming, the United States Steel Corporation's chairman Elbert H. Gary approached Roosevelt with a deal: cooperation in exchange for preferential treatment. The company would open its books to the Bureau of Corporations; if it found evidence of wrongdoing, the company would be warned privately and given a chance to set matters right. Roosevelt accepted this "gentlemen's agreement" because it met his interest in accommodating the realities of the modern industrial order while maintaining his public image as slayer of the trusts.

The railroads posed a different kind of problem. As quasi-public enterprises, they had always been subject to state regulation; after 1887 they came under federal regulation by the Interstate Commerce Commission (ICC). As with the Sherman Act this assertion of federal authority was essentially symbolic at first. Convinced that the railroads needed firmer oversight, Roosevelt pushed through the Elkins Act of 1903, which prohibited discriminatory rates that gave an unfair advantage to preferred or powerful customers; and then, with the 1904 election behind him, he launched a drive for real railroad regulation. In 1906, after nearly two years of wrangling, Congress passed the Hepburn Railway Act, which empowered the ICC to set maximum shipping rates and prescribe uniform methods of bookkeeping. As a concession to the conservative Republican bloc, however, the courts retained broad powers to review the ICC's rate decisions.

The Hepburn Act was a triumph of Roosevelt's skills as a political operator. He had maneuvered brilliantly against determined opposition and come away with the essentials of what he wanted. Despite grumbling by Senate progressives, Roosevelt was satisfied. He had achieved a landmark expansion of the government's regulatory powers over business.

The protection of consumers, another signature issue for progressives, was very much the handiwork of muckraking journalism. What sparked the issue was riveting articles in *Collier's* by Samuel Hopkins Adams exposing the patent-medicine business. For a time industry lobbies stymied legislative action. Then in 1906 Upton Sinclair's novel *The Jungle* appeared. Sinclair thought he was writing about the exploitation of workers in Chicago meat-packing plants, but what caught the nation's attention were his descriptions of rotten meat and filthy conditions. President Roosevelt, weighing into the legislative battle, authorized a federal investigation of the stockyards. Within months the Pure Food and Drug and the Meat Inspection acts passed, and another administrative agency joined the expanding federal bureaucracy: the Food and Drug Administration.

During the 1904 presidential campaign Roosevelt had taken to calling his program the Square Deal. This kind of labeling was new to American politics, emblematic of a political style that dramatized issues, mobilized public opinion, and asserted leadership. After many years of passivity and weakness the federal government was reclaiming the role it had abandoned after the Civil War. Now, however, the target was the new economic order. When companies abused their corporate power, the government would intercede to assure ordinary Americans a "square deal."

THE FRACTURING OF REPUBLICAN PROGRESSIVISM

During his presidency Theodore Roosevelt had struggled to bring a modern corporate economy under public control. He was well aware, however, that his Square Deal was built on nineteenth-century foundations; in particular, antitrust doctrine, which aimed at enforcing competition, seemed inadequate when the economy's tendency was toward industrial concentration. Better for the government to regulate big business than try to break it up. Roosevelt's final presidential speeches dwelt on the need for a reform agenda for the twentieth century. This was the task he bequeathed to his chosen successor, William Howard Taft.

Taft was an estimable man in many ways. An able jurist and superb administrator, he had served Roosevelt loyally as governor-general of the Philippines and as secretary of war. He was an avowed Square Dealer. But he was not by nature a progressive politician. He disliked the give-and-take of politics, he distrusted power, and he revered the processes of law. He could not, for example, have imagined intruding into the 1902 anthracite strike, as Roosevelt had done, or taken so flexible a view of the Sherman Act. He was, in fundamental ways, a conservative.

Taft's Democratic opponent in the 1908 campaign was William Jennings Bryan. This was Bryan's last hurrah, his third attempt at the presidency, and he made the most of it. Eloquent as ever, Bryan attacked the Republicans as the party of the "plutocrats" and outdid them in urging tougher antitrust legislation, lower tariffs, stricter railway regulation, and advanced labor legislation. Bryan's campaign moved the Democratic Party into the mainstream of national progressive politics, but it was not enough to offset Taft's advantages as Roosevelt's candidate.

Taft won comfortably, and he entered the White House with a mandate to pick up where Roosevelt had left off. That was not to be.

By 1909 the ferment of reform had unsettled the Republican Party. On the right the conservatives were girding themselves against further losses. Led by the formidable Senator Nelson W. Aldrich of Rhode Island, they were still a force to be reckoned with. On the left progressive Republicans were rebellious. They had broad popular support—especially in the Midwest—and Robert La Follette, a fiery leader. The progressives felt that Roosevelt had been too easy on business, and with him gone from the White House they intended to make up for lost time. Reconciling these conflicting forces within the Republican Party would have been a daunting task for the most accomplished politician. For Taft it spelled disaster.

First there was the tariff. Progressives considered protective tariffs a major reason that competition had declined and the trusts had taken hold. Although Taft had campaigned for tariff reform, he was won over by the conservative Republican bloc and ended up approving the protectionist Payne-Aldrich Tariff Act of 1909.

Next came the Pinchot-Ballinger affair. U.S. Chief Forester Gifford Pinchot, an ardent conservationist and a chum of Roosevelt's, accused Secretary of the Interior Richard A. Ballinger of conspiring to transfer Alaskan public land—rich in natural resources—to a private syndicate. When Pinchot aired these charges in January

1910, Taft fired him for insubordination. Despite Taft's strong conservationist credentials, in the eyes of the progressives the Pinchot-Ballinger affair marked him for life as a friend of the "interests" bent on plundering the nation's resources.

Taft found himself propelled into the conservative Republican camp, an ally of "Uncle Joe" Cannon, the dictatorial speaker of the House of Representatives. When a House revolt finally broke Cannon's power in 1910, it was regarded as a defeat for the president as well. Galvanized by Taft's defection the reformers in the Republican Party became a dissident faction, calling themselves "Progressives" or in more belligerent moments "Insurgents." Taft answered by backing their conservative foes in the Republican primaries that year.

The Progressives emerged from the 1910 elections stronger and angrier. In January 1911 they formed the National Progressive Republican League and began a drive to take over the Republican Party. Though La Follette was their leader, the Progressives knew that their best chance to topple Taft lay with Theodore Roosevelt.

Home from a year-long safari in Africa, Roosevelt yearned to reenter the political fray. Taft's dispute with the Progressives gave Roosevelt the cause he needed. But Roosevelt was a loyal party man and too astute a politician not to recognize that a party split would benefit the Democrats. He could be spurred into rebellion only by a true clash of principles. On the question of the trusts just such a clash materialized.

By distinguishing between good and bad trusts Roosevelt had managed to reconcile public policy (the Sherman Act) and economic reality (the tendency toward corporate concentration). But this was a makeshift solution that depended on a president who was willing to stretch his powers to the limit. Taft had no such inclination. His legalistic mind rebelled at the notion that he as president should decide which trusts should be prosecuted. The Sherman Act was on the books. "We are going to enforce that law or die in the attempt," Taft promised grimly.

In the *Standard Oil* decision (1911) the Supreme Court eased Taft's problem by reasserting the rule of reason, which meant that, once again, the courts themselves would distinguish between good and bad trusts. With that burden lifted from the executive branch Attorney General George W. Wickersham stepped up the pace of antitrust actions.

United States Steel became an immediate target. Among the charges against the Steel Trust was that it had violated the antimonopoly provision of the Sherman Act by acquiring the Tennessee Coal and Iron Company in 1907. Roosevelt had personally approved the acquisition, believing this was necessary—so U.S. Steel representatives had told him—to prevent a financial collapse on Wall Street. Taft's suit against U.S. Steel thus amounted to an attack on Roosevelt that he could not, without dishonor, ignore.

Ever since leaving the White House Roosevelt had been pondering the trust problem. There was, he concluded, a third way between breaking up big business and submitting to corporate rule. The federal government could be empowered to oversee the nation's industrial corporations to make sure they acted in the public interest. They would be regulated by a federal trade commission as if they were natural monopolies or public utilities.

In a speech in Osawatomie, Kansas, in August 1910 Roosevelt made the case for what he called the New Nationalism. The central issue, he argued, was human welfare versus property rights. In modern society property had to be controlled "to whatever degree the public welfare may require it." The government would become "the steward of the public welfare."

This formulation clarified Roosevelt's thinking about reform. He took up the cause of social justice, adding to his program a federal child labor law, regulation of labor relations, and a national minimum wage for women. Most radical, perhaps, was Roosevelt's attack on the legal system. Insisting that the courts stood in the way of reform, Roosevelt proposed sharp curbs on their powers, even raising the possibility of popular recall of court decisions.

Early in 1912 Roosevelt announced his candidacy for the presidency and immediately swept the Progressive Republicans into his camp. A bitter party battle ensued. Roosevelt won the states that held primary elections, but Taft controlled the party machinery elsewhere. Dominated by the party regulars, the Republican convention chose Taft. Considering himself cheated out of the nomination, Roosevelt led his followers into a new Progressive Party, soon nicknamed the "Bull Moose" Party. In a crusading campaign Roosevelt offered the New Nationalism to the people.

WOODROW WILSON AND THE NEW FREEDOM

While the Republicans battled among themselves, the Democrats were on the move. The scars caused by the free-silver campaign of 1896 had faded, and in the 1908 campaign William Jennings Bryan had established the rejuvenated party's progressive credentials. The Democrats made dramatic gains in 1910, taking over the House of Representatives for the first time since 1892 and capturing a number of traditionally Republican governorships. After fourteen years as the party's standard-bearer, Bryan made way for a new generation of leaders.

The ablest was Woodrow Wilson of New Jersey, a noted political scientist who, as university president, had brought Princeton into the front rank of American universities. In 1910, with no political experience, he accepted the Democratic nomination for governor of New Jersey and won. Wilson compiled a sterling reform record, including the direct primary, workers' compensation, and stringent utility regulation. He went on to win the Democratic presidential nomination in 1912 in a bruising battle.

Wilson possessed, to a fault, the moral certainty that characterized the progressive politician. A brilliant speaker, he instinctively assumed the mantle of righteousness. Only gradually, however, did he hammer out, in reaction to Roosevelt's New Nationalism, a coherent reform program, which he called the New Freedom.

Wilson cast his differences with Roosevelt in fundamental terms of slavery and freedom. "This is a struggle for emancipation," he proclaimed in October 1912. "If

America is not to have free enterprise, then she can have freedom of no sort whatever." Wilson also scorned Roosevelt's social program. Welfare might be benevolent, he declared, but it also would be paternalistic and contrary to the traditions of a free people. The New Nationalism represented a future of collectivism, Wilson warned, whereas the New Freedom would preserve political and economic liberty.

Wilson actually had much in common with Roosevelt. "The old time of individual competition is probably gone by," Wilson admitted. Like Roosevelt he opposed not bigness but the abuse of economic power. Nor did Wilson think that the abuse of power could be prevented without a strong federal government. He parted company from Roosevelt over *how* government should restrain private power.

Despite all the rhetoric the 1912 election fell short of being a referendum on the New Nationalism versus the New Freedom. The outcome turned on a more humdrum reality: Wilson was elected because he kept the traditional Democratic vote, while the Republicans split between Roosevelt and Taft. Despite a landslide in the electoral college, Wilson received only 42 percent of the popular vote. At best the 1912 election signified that the American public was in the mood for reform. Only 23 percent, after all, had voted for the one candidate who stood for the status quo, President Taft. Wilson's own program, however, had received no mandate from the people.

Yet the 1912 election proved decisive in the history of economic reform. The debate between Roosevelt and Wilson had brought forth in the New Freedom a program capable of finally resolving the crisis over corporate power that had gripped the nation for a decade. Just as important the election created a rare legislative opportunity in Washington. With Congress in Democratic hands the time was ripe to act on the New Freedom.

Long out of power the Democrats were hungry for tariff reform. From the prevailing average of 40 percent, the Underwood Tariff Act of 1913 pared rates down to 25 percent. Targeting especially the trust-dominated industries, Democrats confidently expected the Underwood Tariff to spur competition and reduce prices for consumers.

Wilson's administration then turned to the nation's banking system, whose key weakness was the absence of a central bank, or federal reserve. The main function of central banks at that time was to regulate commercial banks and back them up in case they could not meet their obligations to depositors. In the past this back-up role had been assumed by the great New York banks that handled the accounts of outlying banks. If the New York banks weakened, the entire system could collapse. This had nearly happened in 1907, when the Knickerbocker Trust Company failed and panic swept through the nation's financial markets.

While the need for a central bank was clear, the form it should take was hotly disputed. Wall Street wanted a unified system run by the bankers. Rural Democrats and their spokesman, Senator Carter Glass of Virginia, preferred a decentralized network of reserve banks. Progressives in both parties agreed that the essential feature should be strong public control. The bankers, whose practices were already under scrutiny by Congress, were on the defensive.

President Wilson, initially no expert, learned quickly and reconciled the reformers and bankers. The monumental Federal Reserve Act of 1913 gave the nation a banking system that was resistant to financial panic. The act delegated financial functions to twelve district reserve banks, which would be controlled by their member banks. The Federal Reserve Board imposed public regulation on this regional structure. In one stroke the act strengthened the banking system and placed a measure of restraint on the "money trust."

Having dealt with tariff and banking reform, Wilson turned to the big question of how to curb the trusts. In this effort Wilson relied heavily on a new adviser, Louis D. Brandeis, famous as the "people's lawyer" for his public service in many progressive causes (including the landmark *Muller* case). Brandeis denied that bigness meant efficiency. On the contrary, he argued, trusts were wasteful compared with firms that vigorously competed in a free market. The main thing was to prevent the trusts from unfairly using their power to curb competition.

This could be done by strengthening the Sherman Act, but the obvious course—defining with precision what constituted anticompetitive practices—proved hard to implement. Was it feasible to say exactly when interlocking directorates, discriminatory pricing, or exclusive contracts became illegal? Brandeis decided that it was not, and Wilson assented. In the Clayton Antitrust Act of 1914, amending the Sherman Act, the definition of illegal practices was left flexible, subject to the test of whether an action "substantially lessen[ed] competition or tend[ed] to create a monopoly."

This retreat from a definitive antitrust prescription meant that a federal trade commission would be needed to back up the Sherman and Clayton Acts. Wilson was understandably hesitant, given his principled opposition to Roosevelt's powerful trade commission in the campaign. At first Wilson favored an advisory, information-gathering agency. But ultimately, under the 1914 law establishing it, the Federal Trade Commission (FTC) received broad powers to investigate companies and issue "cease and desist" orders against unfair trade practices that violated antitrust law.

Despite a good deal of commotion this arduous legislative process was actually an exercise in consensus building. Wilson himself had opened the debate in a conciliatory way. "The antagonism between business and government is over," he said, and the time ripe for a program representing the "best business judgment in America." Afterward, Wilson felt he had brought the long controversy over corporate power to a successful conclusion, and in fact he had. Steering a course between Taft's conservatism and Roosevelt's radicalism, Wilson had carved out a middle way that brought to bear the powers of government without threatening the constitutional order and curbed abuse of corporate power without threatening the capitalist system.

On social policy, too, Wilson charted a middle way. Having denounced Roosevelt's social program as paternalistic, he was at first unreceptive to what he saw as special-interest demands by labor and farm organizations. On the leading issue—that they be exempt from antitrust prosecution—the most Wilson was willing to accept was cosmetic language in the Clayton Act that did not grant them the immunity they sought.

As his second presidential campaign drew near, Wilson lost some of his scruples about prolabor legislation. In 1915 and 1916 he championed a host of bills beneficial to American workers: a federal child labor law, the Adamson eight-hour law for railroad workers, and the landmark Seamen's Act, which eliminated age-old abuses of sailors aboard ship. Likewise, after earlier resistance, Wilson approved in 1916 the Federal Farm Loan Act, which provided the low-interest rural credit system long demanded by farmers.

Wilson encountered the same dilemma that confronted all successful progressives: the claims of moral principle versus the unyielding realities of political life. Progressives were high-minded but not radical. They saw evils in the system, but they did not consider the system itself to be evil. They also prided themselves on being realists as well as moralists. So it stood to reason that Wilson, like other progressives who achieved power, would find his place at the center. But it would be wrong to underestimate their achievement. Progressives made presidential leadership important again, they brought government back into the nation's life, and they laid the foundation for twentieth-century social and economic policy.

For Further Exploration

The historical literature on the Progressive Era offers an embarrassment of riches. A good entry point is John Milton Cooper, *Pivotal Decades: 1900–1920* (1990). Richard Hofstadter, *Age of Reform* (1955), is an elegantly written interpretation that remains worth reading despite its disputed central arguments. The following books are a sampling of the best that has been written about Progressivism: Robert M. Crunden, *Ministers of Reform, 1889–1920* (1982), on the religious underpinnings; Charles Forcey, *The Crossroads of Liberalism* (1961), on the reform intellectuals; Nancy S. Dye, *As Equals and Sisters* (1980), on working women in the movement; David P. Thelen, *The New Citizenship* (1972), on La Follette and Wisconsin progressivism; John D. Buenker, *Urban Liberalism and Progressive Reform* (1973), on the politics of urban liberalism; Nancy F. Cott, *The Grounding of Modern Feminism* (1987); Naomi Lamoreaux, *The Great Merger Movement in American Business, 1895–1904* (1985); Martin J. Sklar, *The Corporate Reconstruction of American Capitalism, 1890–1916* (1988), on the progressive struggle to fashion a regulatory policy for big business.

Among the stimulating recent books, see Linda Gordon, *Pitied but Not Entitled: Single Mothers and the History of Welfare, 1890–1935* (1994), which uses the current debate over welfare reform as a lens for probing the tangled origins of the American welfare system; Sara Hunter Graham, *Woman Suffrage and the New Democracy* (1996), which treats the battle for the vote as a precocious exercise in modern single-issue politics; Elizabeth Lasch-Quinn, *Black Neighbors* (1993), on the racial conservatism of settlement-house progressives; Glenda Elizabeth Gilmore, *Gender and Jim Crow: Women and the Politics of White Supremacy in*

TIMELINE

Year	Event	Year	Event
1890	Sherman Antitrust Act	1908	*Muller v. Oregon* upholds regulation of working hours for women. William Howard Taft elected president
1899	National Consumers' League founded		
1900	Robert M. La Follette elected Wisconsin governor	1909	National Association for the Advancement of Colored People (NAACP) formed
1901	President McKinley assassinated; Theodore Roosevelt succeeds. United States Steel Corporation formed	1910	Roosevelt announces the New Nationalism. Woman suffrage movement revives; victories in western states begin.
1902	President Roosevelt settles national anthracite strike.	1911	*Standard Oil* decision restores "rule of reason." Triangle Shirtwaist fire
1903	National Women's Trade Union League founded		
1904	Supreme Court dissolves the Northern Securities Company.	1912	Progressive Party formed Woodrow Wilson elected president
1905	*Lochner v. New York* overturns state law restricting workhours for bakers.	1913	Underwood Tariff Act Federal Reserve Act
1906	Hepburn Railway Act Niagara Movement begins the struggle for black equality. AFL adopts Bill of Grievances. Upton Sinclair's *The Jungle*	1914	Clayton Antitrust Act Federal Trade Commission established
		1915	D. W. Griffith's *Birth of a Nation*

North Carolina, 1869–1920 (1996), on black women's political activity in the Progressive Era. The following biographies offer another rewarding avenue into Progressivism: John Milton Cooper, *The Warrior and the Priest* (1983), a joint biography of Roosevelt and Wilson; Allen F. Davis, *American Heroine: Jane Addams* (1973); Kathryn Kish Sklar, *Florence Kelley and the Nation's Work* (1995); Ellen Chesler, *Woman of Valor: Margaret Sanger and the Birth Control Movement* (1992); David Levering Lewis, *W.E.B. DuBois: Biography of a Race, 1868–1919* (1993).

"Votes for Women: NAWSA, 1848–1921" at <http://lcweb2.loc.gov/ammem/naw/nawshome.html> is a searchable archive of over 160 documents from the NAWSA collection. "Theodore Roosevelt: Icon of the American Century" at <http://www.npg.si.edu/exh/roosevelt.htm> presents pictures from the National Portrait Gallery, a biographical narrative, and information on Roosevelt's family and friends. "The Evolution of the Conservation Movement" at <http://memory.loc.gov/ammem/amrvhtml/conshome.html> offers a timeline and archive of materials on the development of the conservation movement from 1850 to 1920.

Chapter 21

AN EMERGING WORLD POWER
1877–1914

God has marked the American people as His chosen nation to
finally lead in the generation of the world. This is the divine mission
of America, and it holds for us all the profit, all the glory, all the
happiness possible to man.

> —SENATOR ALBERT J. BEVERIDGE, ARGUING FOR U.S. ACQUISITION
> OF THE PHILIPPINES, 1900

In 1881 Great Britain sent a new envoy to Washington. He was Sir
Lionel Sackville-West, son of an earl, brother-in-law of the Tory leader Lord Denby,
but otherwise distinguished only as the lover of a celebrated Spanish dancer. His
well-connected friends wanted to park Sir Lionel somewhere comfortable but out
of harm's way. So they made him minister to the United States.

Twenty years later such an appointment would have been unthinkable. All the
European powers had by then elevated their missions in Washington to embassies
and staffed them with top-of-the-line ambassadors. And they treated the United
States, without question, as a fellow Great Power.

In Sir Lionel's day the United States scarcely cast a shadow on world affairs.
America's army in 1881 was smaller than Bulgaria's; its navy ranked thirteenth in
the world and was a threat mainly to the crews manning its unseaworthy ships. By
1900, however, the United States was flexing its muscles. It had just made short
work of Spain in a brief but decisive war and acquired for itself an empire that
stretched from Puerto Rico to the Philippines. America's standing as a rising naval
power was manifest, and so was its muscular assertion of national interest in the
Caribbean and the Pacific.

The European powers could not be sure what America's role would be, since
the United States retained its traditional policy of nonalignment in European affairs. But in foreign offices across the Continent the importance of the United States
was universally acknowledged, and its likely response to every event carefully
assessed.

The Roots of Expansion

In 1880 the United States had a population of 50 million and by that measure ranked with the great European powers. In industrial production the nation stood second only to Britain and was rapidly closing the gap. Anyone who doubted the military prowess of the Americans needed only to recall the ferocity with which they had fought one another in the Civil War. The great campaigns of Lee, Sherman, and Grant had entered the military textbooks and were closely studied by army strategists everywhere.

And when its vital interests were at stake, the United States had not shown itself lacking in diplomatic vigor. The Civil War had put the United States at odds with both France and Britain. The dispute with France involved the establishment in Mexico of a French-sponsored regime under Archduke Maximilian, a move regarded by the United States as a threat to its security in the Southwest. When American troops under General Philip Sheridan began to mass on the Mexican border in 1867, the French military withdrew, abandoning Maximilian to a Mexican firing squad.

With Britain the thorny issue involved damages to Union shipping by the *Alabama* and other Confederate sea raiders operating from English ports. American hopes of taking Canada as compensation were dashed by Britain's grant of dominion status to Canada in 1867. But four years later, after lengthy negotiations, Britain expressed regret for its unneutral acts and agreed to the arbitration of the *Alabama* claims, settling to America's satisfaction the last outstanding diplomatic issue of the Civil War.

DIPLOMACY IN THE GILDED AGE

In the years that followed the United States lapsed into diplomatic inactivity, not out of weakness but for lack of any clear national purpose in world affairs. The business of building the nation's industrial economy absorbed Americans and turned their attention inward. And though the new international telegraphic cables provided the country with swift overseas communication after the 1860s, wide oceans still kept the world at a distance and gave Americans a sense of isolation and security.

In these circumstances, with no external threat to be seen, what was the point of maintaining a big navy? After the Civil War the fleet gradually deteriorated. Of the 125 ships on the navy's active list, only about twenty-five were seaworthy at any one time. No effort was made to keep up with European advances in weaponry or battleship design; the American fleet consisted mainly of sailing ships and obsolete ironclads modeled on the *Monitor* of Civil War fame.

During the administration of Chester A. Arthur (1881–1885) the navy began a modest upgrading program, commissioning new ships, raising the standards for the officer corps, and founding the Naval War College. But the fleet remained small, without a unified naval command and with little more to do than maintain coastal defenses.

The conduct of diplomacy was likewise of little account. Appointment to the foreign service was mostly through the spoils system. American envoys and consular officers were a mixed lot, with many idlers and drunkards among the hardworking and competent. Domestic politics, moreover, made it difficult to develop a coherent foreign policy. Although diplomacy was a presidential responsibility, the U.S. Senate jealously guarded its constitutional right to give "advice and consent" on treaties and diplomatic appointments. For its part the State Department tended to be inactive, exerting little control over either policy or its missions abroad. In distant places the American presence was likely to be Christian missionaries proselytizing among the native populations of Asia, Africa, and the Pacific Islands.

In the Caribbean the expansionist enthusiasms of the Civil War era subsided. Nothing came of the grandiose imperial plans of William H. Seward, Andrew Johnson's secretary of state, or of President Grant's efforts to purchase Santo Domingo (the future Dominican Republic) in 1870, and the Senate regularly blocked later moves to acquire bases in Haiti, Cuba, and Venezuela. The long-cherished interest in an interoceanic canal across Central America also faded. Despite its claims of exclusive rights the United States stood by when a French company headed by the builder of the Suez Canal, Ferdinand de Lesseps, started to dig across the Isthmus of Panama in 1880. That project failed after a decade, but the reason was bankruptcy, not American opposition.

Diplomatic activity quickened when the energetic James G. Blaine became secretary of state in 1881. He got involved in a border dispute between Mexico and Guatemala, tried to settle a war Chile was waging against Peru and Bolivia, and called the first Pan-American conference. Blaine's interventions in Latin American disputes went badly, however, and his successor cancelled the Pan-American conference after Blaine left office in late 1881.

Pan-Americanism—the notion of a community of American states—took root, however, and Blaine, returning in 1889 for a second stint at the State Department, took up the plans of the outgoing Cleveland administration for a new Pan-American conference. But little came of it except for provisions for an agency in Washington that became the Pan-American Union. Any Latin American goodwill won by Blaine's efforts was soon blasted by the humiliation the United States visited on Chile because of a riot against American sailors in the port of Valparaiso in 1891. Threatened with war, Chile was forced to apologize to the United States and pay an indemnity of $75,000.

In the Pacific American interest centered on Hawaii. With a climate ideal for raising sugarcane the islands had become a magnet for American planters and investors. Nominally an independent nation, Hawaii fell increasingly under American control. Under an 1875 treaty Hawaiian sugar gained duty-free entry to the American market, and the islands were declared off limits to other powers. A second treaty in 1887 granted the United States naval rights at Pearl Harbor.

When Hawaii's favored access to the American market was abruptly cancelled by the McKinley Tariff of 1890, sugar planters began to plot an American takeover of Hawaii. They organized a revolt in January 1893 against Queen Liliuokalani and quickly negotiated a treaty of annexation with the Harrison administration. Before the Senate could approve, however, Grover Cleveland returned to the presidency and withdrew the treaty. To annex Hawaii, he declared, would violate both America's "honor and morality" and an "unbroken tradition" against acquiring territory far from the nation's shores.

Meanwhile, the American presence elsewhere in the Pacific was growing. The purchase of Alaska from imperial Russia in 1867 gave the United States not only a huge territory with vast natural resources but an unlooked-for presence stretching across the northern Pacific. And far to the south, in the Samoan Islands, the United States secured rights in 1878 to a coaling station at Pago Pago harbor—a key link on the route to Australia—and established an informal protectorate there. In 1889, after some jostling with Germany and Britain, the rivalry over Samoa ended in a tripartite protectorate, with America retaining its rights in Pago Pago.

American diplomacy in these years has been characterized as a series of incidents, not the pursuit of a foreign policy. Many things happened, but intermittently and without any well-founded conception of national objectives. This was possible because, as the Englishman James Bryce remarked in 1888, America still sailed "upon a summer sea." In the stormier waters that lay ahead a different kind of diplomacy would be required.

THE ECONOMY OF EXPANSIONISM

"A policy of isolation did well enough when we were an embryo nation," remarked Senator Orville Platt of Connecticut in 1893. "But today things are different. . . . We are 65 million people, the most advanced and powerful on earth, and regard to our future welfare demands an abandonment of the doctrines of isolation." What especially demanded that Americans look outward was their prodigious economy.

America's gross domestic product—the total value of goods and service—quadrupled between 1870 and 1900. But were there markets big enough to absorb the output of America's farms and factories? Over 90 percent of American goods in the late nineteenth century was consumed at home. Even so, foreign markets mattered. Roughly a fifth of the nation's agricultural output was exported, and as the industrial economy expanded, so did factory exports. Between 1880 and 1900 the industrial share of total exports jumped from 15 percent to over 30 percent.

American firms began to establish themselves overseas. As early as 1868 the Singer Sewing Machine Company established its first foreign factory in Glasgow, Scotland. The giant among American firms doing business abroad was Rockefeller's Standard Oil, with European branches operating tankers and marketing kerosene across the continent. In Asia, Standard Oil cans, converted into utensils and roofing tin, became a visible sign of American market penetration.

The Singer Sewing Machine

The sewing machine was an American invention that swiftly found markets abroad. The Singer Company, the dominant firm, not only exported large quantities but produced 200,000 machines annually at a Scottish plant that employed 6,000 workers. Singer's advertising rightly boasted of its prowess as an international company and of a product that was "The Universal Machine." (New-York Historical Society)

Foreign trade was important partly for reasons of international finance. As a developing economy, the United States attracted a lot of foreign capital. The result was a heavy outflow of dollars to pay interest and dividends to foreign investors. To balance this account the United States needed to export more goods than it imported. In fact, a favorable import-export balance was achieved in 1876 (Figure 21.1). But because of its dependence on foreign capital America had to be constantly vigilant about its export trade.

Even more important, however, was the relationship that many Americans perceived between foreign markets and the nation's social stability. Hard times always sparked agrarian unrest and labor trouble. The problem, many thought, was that the nation's capacity to produce was outrunning its capacity to consume. When the economy slowed, cutbacks in domestic demand drove down farm prices and caused layoffs across the country. The answer was to make sure there would always be enough buyers for America's surplus products, and this meant, more than anything else, buyers in foreign markets.

How did these concerns about overseas trade relate to America's foreign policy? The bulk of American exports in the late nineteenth century—over 80 percent—went to Europe and Canada. In these countries the normal instruments of diplomacy sufficed to protect the nation's economic interests. But in Asia, Latin America, and other regions that Americans considered "backward" a tougher brand

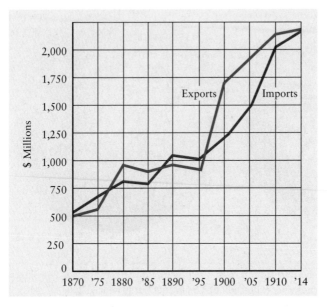

FIGURE 21.1
Balance of U.S. Imports, 1870–1914

By 1876 the United States had become a net export-ing nation. The brief reversal after 1888 aroused fears that the United States was losing its for-eign markets and helped fuel the expansionist drive of the 1890s.

of intervention seemed necessary because there the United States was competing with other industrial powers.

Asia and Latin America represented only a modest part of America's export trade—roughly an eighth of the total in the late nineteenth century. Still, this trade was growing—it was worth $200 million in 1900—and parts of it mattered a great deal to specific industries (for example, the Chinese market for American textiles). The real importance of these non-Western markets, however, was not so much their current value as their future promise. China especially exerted a powerful hold on the American mercantile imagination. Many felt that the China trade, although quite small at the time, would one day be the key to American prosperity. There-fore, China and other beckoning markets must not be closed to the United States.

In the mid-1880s the pace of European imperialism picked up. After the Berlin Conference of 1884 Africa was rapidly carved up by the European powers. In a burst of modernizing energy Japan transformed itself into a major power and began to challenge China's dominance in Korea. In the Sino-Japanese War of 1894–1895, Japan won an easy victory and started a scramble among the great powers, includ-ing Russia, to divide China into spheres of influence. In Latin America U.S. interests began to be challenged more aggressively by Britain, France, and Germany.

On top of all this came the Panic of 1893, setting in motion industrial strikes and agrarian protests that Cleveland's secretary of state, Walter Q. Gresham, like many other Americans, took to be "symptoms of revolution." With the nation's sta-bility seemingly at risk, securing the markets of Latin America and Asia became an urgent necessity, inspiring the expansionist diplomacy of the 1890s.

THE MAKING OF AN EXPANSIONIST FOREIGN POLICY

"Whether they will or no, Americans must now begin to look outward. The growing production of the country requires it." So wrote Captain Alfred T. Mahan, America's leading naval strategist, in his book *The Influence of Seapower upon History* (1890), which argued that the key to imperial power was control of the seas. From this insight Mahan developed a naval analysis that became the cornerstone of American strategic thinking.

The United States should regard the oceans not as barriers, Mahan argued, but as "a great highway . . . over which men pass in all directions." Traversing that highway required a robust merchant marine (America's had fallen on hard times since its heyday in the 1850s), a powerful navy to protect American commerce, and strategic overseas bases. Having converted from sails to steam, navies required coaling stations far from home. Without such stations, Mahan warned, warships were "like land birds, unable to fly far from their own shores."

Mahan called for a canal across Central America to connect the Atlantic and Pacific oceans. Such a canal would enable the eastern United States to "compete with Europe, on equal terms as to distance, for the markets of East Asia." The canal's approaches would need to be guarded by bases in the Caribbean Sea. And Hawaii would have to be annexed to extend American power into the Pacific. What Mahan envisioned was a form of colonialism different from Europe's—not rule over territories and populations but control over strategic points in defense of America's trading interests.

Other exponents of a powerful America flocked to Mahan, including such up-and-coming politicians as Theodore Roosevelt and Henry Cabot Lodge. The influence of these men, few in number but well connected, increased during the 1890s. They pushed steadily for what Lodge called a "large policy." But mainstream politicians also accepted Mahan's underlying logic, and from the inauguration of Benjamin Harrison in 1889 onward a surprising consistency began to emerge in the conduct of American foreign policy.

The next year Congress appropriated funds for three battleships as the first installment on a two-ocean navy. Battleships might be expensive, said Benjamin F. Tracy, Harrison's ambitious secretary of the navy, but they were "the premium paid by the United States for the insurance of its acquired wealth and its growing industries." The battleship took on a special aura for those—like the young Roosevelt—who had grand dreams for the United States. "Oh, Lord! if only the people who are ignorant about our Navy could see those great warships in all their majesty and beauty, and could realize how [well fitted they are] to uphold the honor of America!"

The incoming Cleveland administration was less spread-eagled and by canceling Harrison's scheme for annexing Hawaii established its antiexpansionist credentials. But after hesitating briefly, Cleveland picked up the naval program of his Republican predecessor, pressing Congress just as forcefully for more battleships (five were authorized) and making the same basic argument. The nation's commercial vitality—"free access to all markets," in the words of Cleveland's second secretary of state, Richard Olney—depended on its naval power.

While rejecting the territorial aspects of Mahan's thinking, Cleveland absorbed the underlying strategic arguments about where America's vital interests lay. This explains the remarkable crisis that suddenly blew up in 1895 over Venezuela.

For years a border dispute had simmered between Venezuela and British Guiana. Now the United States demanded that it be resolved. The European powers were carving up Africa and Asia. How could the United States be sure that Europe did not have similar designs on Latin America? Secretary of State, Olney made that point in a bristling note to London on July 25, 1895, insisting that Britain accept arbitration or face the consequences. Invoking the Monroe Doctrine, Olney warned that the United States would brook no challenge to its vital interests in the Caribbean. These vital interests were America's, not Venezuela's; Venezuela was not consulted during the entire dispute.

Despite its suddenness, the pugnacious stand of the Cleveland administration was no aberration but a logical step in the new American foreign policy. Once the British realized that Cleveland meant business, they agreed to arbitration of the boundary dispute. Afterward Olney remarked with satisfaction that as a great industrial nation the United States needed "to accept [a] commanding position" and take its place "among the Powers of the earth." Other countries would have to accommodate America's need for access to "more markets and larger markets for the consumption and products of the industry and inventive genius of the American people."

THE IDEOLOGY OF EXPANSIONISM

As policymakers hammered out a new foreign policy, a sustaining ideology took shape. One source of expansionist dogma was the Social Darwinist theory that dominated the political thought of this era (see Chapter 17). If, as Charles Darwin had shown, animals and plants evolved through the survival of the fittest, so did nations. "Nothing under the sun is stationary," warned the American social theorist Brooks Adams in *The Law of Civilization and Decay* (1895). "Not to advance is to recede." By this criterion the United States had no choice; if it wanted to survive, it had to expand.

Linked to Social Darwinism was a spreading belief in the inherent superiority of the Anglo-Saxon "race." In the late nineteenth century Great Britain basked in the glory of its representative institutions, industrial prosperity, and far-flung empire—all ascribed to the supposed racial superiority of its people and, by extension, of their American cousins as well. On both sides of the Atlantic Anglo-Saxonism was in vogue. Thus did John Fiske, an American philosopher and historian, lecture the nation on its future responsibilities: "The work which the English race began when it colonized North America is destined to go on until every land on the earth's surface that is not already the seat of an old civilization shall become English in its language, in its religion, in its political habits, and to a predominant extent in the blood of its people."

Fiske titled his lecture "Manifest Destiny." A half century earlier this term had expressed the sense of national mission—America's "manifest destiny"—to sweep aside the Native American peoples and occupy the continent. In his widely read book *The Winning of the West* (1896) Theodore Roosevelt drew a parallel between the expansionism of his own time and the suppression of the Indians. To Roosevelt what happened to "backward peoples" mattered little because their conquest was "for the benefit of civilization and in the interests of mankind." More than historical parallels, however, linked the Manifest Destiny of the past and present.

In 1890 the U.S. Census reported the end of the westward movement on the North American continent: there was no longer a frontier beyond which land remained to be conquered. The psychological impact of that news on Americans was profound, spawning among other things a new historical interpretation that stressed the importance of the frontier in shaping the nation's character. In a landmark essay setting out this thesis—"The Significance of the Frontier in American History" (1893)—the young historian Frederick Jackson Turner suggested a link between the closing of the frontier and overseas expansion. "He would be a rash prophet who should assert that the expansive character of American life has now entirely ceased," Turner wrote. "Movement has been its dominant fact, and, unless this training has no effect upon a people, the American energy will continually demand a wider field for its exercise." As Turner predicted, Manifest Destiny did turn outward.

Thus a strong current of ideas, deeply rooted in American experience and traditions, justified the new diplomacy of expansionism. The United States was eager to step onto the world stage. All it needed was the right occasion.

An American Empire

Ever since Spain had lost its South American empire in the early nineteenth century, still-subjugated Cubans yearned to join their mainland brothers and sisters in freedom. In February 1895 Cuban patriots rebelled and began a guerrilla war. A standoff developed; the Spaniards controlled the towns, the insurgents much of the countryside. In early 1896 the newly appointed Spanish commander, Valeriano Weyler, adopted a harsh policy of *reconcentration,* forcing entire populations into guarded camps. Because no aggressive pursuit followed, reconcentration only inconvenienced the guerrilla fighters. The toll on civilians, however, was devastating. Out of a population of 1,600,000 as many as 200,000 died of starvation, exposure, or dysentery.

THE CUBAN CRISIS

Rebel leaders recognized that their best hope was not military but political: they had to draw the United States into their struggle. A key group of exiles, the *junta,* set up shop in New York to make the case for *Cuba Libre.* Their timing was lucky. William Randolph Hearst had just purchased the *New York Journal,* and he was in a hurry to build readership. Cuba was ideal for Hearst's purposes. Locked in a furious circulation war with Joseph Pulitzer's *New York World,* Hearst elevated Cuba's agony into flaming front-page headlines.

Across the country powerful sentiments stirred: humanitarian concern for the suffering Cubans, sympathy with their aspirations for freedom, and, as anger against Spain rose, a superheated patriotism that became known as *jingoism.* Congress began calling for Cuban independence.

Grover Cleveland, still in office when the rebellion broke out, took a cooler view of the situation. His concern was with America's vital interests, which, he told Congress, were "by no means of a wholly sentimental or philanthropic character." The Cuban civil war was disrupting the sizable trade between the two countries and harming American property interests, especially in Cuban sugar plantations. Cleveland was also worried that Spain's troubles might draw other European powers into the situation. A chronically unstable Cuba was incompatible with America's strategic interests, in particular a planned interoceanic canal whose Caribbean approaches would have to be safeguarded. If Spain could put down the rebellion, that was fine with Cleveland. But there was a limit, he felt, to how long the United States could tolerate Spain's impotence.

The McKinley administration, on taking office in March 1897, adopted much the same pragmatic line. Like Cleveland, McKinley was motivated by a conception of the United States as the dominant Caribbean power, with vital interests that had to be defended. McKinley, however, was inclined to be tougher on the Spaniards. He was appalled by their "uncivilized and inhumane conduct" in Cuba. And he had to contend with rising jingoism in the Senate. But the notion, long held by historians, that McKinley was swept along against his better judgment by popular opinion and by a Republican war faction led by Henry Cabot Lodge, Alfred J. Beveridge, and other aggressive advocates of a "large policy" was not true. McKinley was very much his own man. He was a skilled politician and a canny, if undramatic, president. In particular, McKinley was sensitive to business fears of any rash action that might disrupt an economy just recovering from depression.

On September 18, 1897, the American minister in Madrid informed the Spanish government that it was time to "put a stop to this destructive war." If Spain could not ensure an "early and certain peace," the United States would take whatever steps it "should deem necessary to procure this result." At first America's hard line seemed to work. The conservative regime fell, and a liberal government, on taking office in October 1897, moderated its Cuban policy. Spain recalled General Weyler, backed away from reconcentration, and offered Cuba a degree of self-rule but not inde-

"*Remember the* Maine!"

In late January 1898 the *Maine* entered Havana harbor on a courtesy call. On the evening of February 15 a mysterious blast sent the U.S. battlecruiser to the bottom. This dramatic lithograph conveys something of the impact of that event on American public opinion. Although no evidence ever linked the Spanish authorities to the explosion, the sinking of the *Maine* fed the emotional fires that prepared the nation for war with Spain. (Granger Collection)

pendence. Madrid's incapacity soon became clear, however. In January 1898 Spanish loyalists in Havana rioted against the offer of autonomy. The Cuban rebels, encouraged by the prospect of American intervention, demanded full independence.

On February 9, 1898, Hearst's *New York Journal* published a private letter of Dupuy de Lôme, the Spanish minister to the United States. In it de Lôme called President McKinley "weak" and "a bidder for the admiration of the crowd." Worse, his letter suggested that the Spanish government was not taking the American demands seriously. De Lôme immediately resigned, but the damage had been done.

A week later the U.S. battlecruiser *Maine* blew up and sank in Havana harbor, with the loss of 260 seamen. "Whole Country Thrills with the War Fever," proclaimed the *New York Journal*. From that moment onward popular passions against Spain became a major factor in the march toward war.

McKinley kept his head. He assumed that the sinking had been accidental. A naval board of inquiry, however, issued a damaging report. Disagreeing with a Spanish inquiry, the American board concluded improbably that the sinking had been caused by a mine. (A 1976 naval inquiry faulted the ship's design, which located the explosive magazines too close to coal bunkers that were prone to spontaneous fires.) No evidence linked the Spanish to the purported mine. But if a mine did sink the ship, then the Spanish were responsible for not protecting a peaceful American vessel within their jurisdiction.

President McKinley had no stomach for the martial spirit engulfing the country. He was not swept along by the calls for blood to avenge the *Maine*. But he did have to attend to an aroused public opinion. Hesitant business leaders now also became impatient for the dispute with Spain to end. War was preferable to the unresolved Cuban crisis. On March 27 McKinley cabled to Madrid what was in effect an ultimatum: an immediate armistice for six months, abandonment of the practice of reconcentration, and, with the United States as mediator, peace negotiations with the rebels. A telegram the next day added that only Cuban independence would be regarded as a satisfactory outcome to the negotiations. Spain categorically rejected these humiliating demands.

On April 11 McKinley asked Congress for authority to intervene to end the fighting in Cuba. His motives were as he described them: "In the name of humanity, in the name of civilization, in behalf of endangered American interests which give us the right and the duty to speak and to act, the war in Cuba must stop." The War Hawks in Congress—a mixture of Republicans and western Democrats—chafed under McKinley's cautious progress. But the president did not lose control, and he defeated the War Hawks on the crucial issue of recognizing the rebel republican government, which would have greatly reduced the administration's freedom of action in dealing with Spain.

The resolutions authorizing intervention in Cuba contained an amendment by Senator Henry M. Teller of Colorado disclaiming any intention by the United States of taking possession of Cuba. No European government should say that "when we go out to make battle for the liberty and freedom of Cuban patriots, that we are doing it for the purpose of aggrandizement." This had to be made clear with regard to Cuba, "whatever," Senator Teller added, "we may do as to some other islands."

Did McKinley contemplate "some other islands"? Was this really a war of aggression, secretly motivated by a desire to seize strategic territory from Spain? In a strict sense, almost certainly no. It was not *because* of expansionist ambitions that McKinley forced Spain into a corner. But once war came, McKinley saw it as an opportunity. As he wrote privately after hostilities began: "While we are conducting war and until its conclusion, we must keep all we get; when the war is over we must keep what we want." Precisely what would be forthcoming, of course, depended on the fortunes of battle.

THE SPOILS OF WAR

Hostilities formally began when Spain declared war on April 24, 1898. Across the country regiments began to form up. Theodore Roosevelt immediately resigned as assistant secretary of the navy, ordered a fancy uniform, and was commissioned lieutenant colonel in a volunteer cavalry regiment that would become famous as the Rough Riders. Raw recruits poured into makeshift bases around Tampa, Florida. Confusion reigned. Tropical uniforms did not arrive; the food was bad, the sanitation worse; and rifles were in short supply. No provision had been made for getting the troops to Cuba; the government hastily began to collect a miscellaneous fleet of yachts, lake steamers, and commercial boats. Fortunately, the small regular army was a disciplined, highly professional force, and its 28,000 seasoned troops provided a nucleus for the 200,000 civilians who had to be turned into soldiers inside of a few weeks.

The navy was in better shape. Spain had nothing to match America's seven battleships and armored cruisers, and the ships it did have were undermanned and ill-prepared for battle. The Spanish admiral, Pascual Cervera, gloomily expected that his fleet would "like Don Quixote go out to fight windmills and come back with a broken head."

On April 23, acting on plans already drawn up, Commodore George Dewey's small Pacific fleet set sail from Hong Kong for the Philippines. Here, at this Spanish possession in the far Pacific, not in Cuba, the decisive engagement of the war took place. On May 1 American ships cornered the Spanish fleet in Manila Bay and destroyed it (Map 21.1). The victory produced euphoria in the United States. Immediately, part of the army being trained for the Cuban campaign was diverted to the Philippines. Manila, the Philippine capital, fell on August 13, 1898.

With Dewey's naval victory American strategic thinking clicked into place. "We hold the other side of the Pacific and the value to this country is almost beyond imagination," declared Senator Lodge. "We must on no account let the [Philippine] Islands go." President McKinley agreed, and so did his key advisers. Naval strategists had long coveted an anchor in the western Pacific. At this time, too, the Great Powers were carving up China into spheres of influence. If American merchants wanted a crack at that glittering market, the United States would have to project its power into Asia.

Once the decision for a Philippine base had been made, other decisions followed almost automatically. The question of Hawaii was quickly resolved. After stalling the previous year, Hawaiian annexation went through Congress by joint resolution in July 1898. Hawaii had suddenly acquired a crucial strategic value: it was a halfway station on the way to the Philippines. The navy pressed for a coaling base in the central Pacific; that meant Guam, a Spanish island in the Marianas. There was need also for a strategically located base in the Caribbean; that meant Puerto Rico. By July, before the assault on Cuba, the full scope of McKinley's war aims had crystallized.

The campaign in Cuba was something of an anticlimax. Santiago, where the Spanish fleet was anchored, became the key to the military campaign. Half trained and ill equipped, the American forces moving on the city might have been checked by a determined opponent.

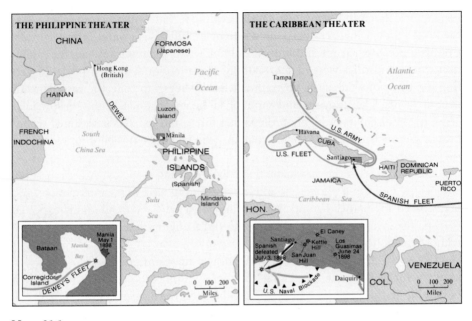

MAP 21.1
The Spanish-American War of 1898

The swift American victory in the Spanish-American War resulted from overwhelming naval superiority. Dewey's destruction of the Spanish fleet in Manila harbor doomed the Spaniards in the Philippines. In Cuba, American ground forces won a hard victory on San Juan Hill, for they were ill equipped and poorly supplied. With the United States in control of the seas, the Spaniards saw no choice but to give up the battle for Cuba.

The main battle, on July 1, occurred near Santiago on the heights commanded by San Juan Hill. Roosevelt's dismounted Rough Riders (there had been no room for horses on the transports) seized Kettle Hill. Then the frontal assault against the San Juan heights began. Four black regiments took the brunt of the fighting. White observers grudgingly credited much of the victory to the "superb gallantry" of the black soldiers (see American Voices, "Black Soldiers in a White Man's War"). In fact, it was not quite a victory. The Spaniards, driven from their forward positions, retreated to a well-fortified second line. The exhausted Americans had suffered heavy casualties; whether they could have mounted a second assault was questionable. They were spared this test, however, by the Spanish. On July 3 Cervera's fleet in Santiago harbor made a daylight attempt to run the American blockade and was destroyed. A few days later, convinced that Santiago could not be saved, the Spanish forces surrendered.

The two nations signed an armistice in which Spain agreed to liberate Cuba and cede Puerto Rico and Guam to the United States. American forces occupied Manila pending a peace treaty.

The Battle of San Juan Hill

On July 1, 1898, the key battle for Cuba took place on heights overlooking Santiago. African American troops bore the brunt of the fighting. Although generally overlooked, the black role in the San Juan battle is done justice in this contemporary lithograph, without the demeaning stereotypes by which blacks were normally depicted in an age of intensifying racism. Even so, the racial hierarchy is maintained. The blacks are the foot soldiers; their officers are white. (Library of Congress)

THE IMPERIAL EXPERIMENT

The big question was the Philippines, an archipelago of over 7,000 islands populated—as William R. Day, McKinley's secretary of state, put it in the racist language of that era—by "eight or nine millions of absolutely ignorant and many degraded people." Not even the most avid American expansionists had advocated colonial rule over subject peoples—that was European-style imperialism, not the strategic bases that Mahan and his followers had in mind. Both Mahan and Lodge initially advocated keeping only Manila. It gradually became clear, however, that Manila was not defensible without the whole of Luzon, the large island on which the city was located.

McKinley and his advisers surveyed the options. One possibility was to return most of the islands to Spain, but the reputed evils of Spanish rule made that a "cowardly and dishonorable" solution. Another possibility was to partition the Philippines with one or more of the Great Powers. But as McKinley observed, to turn

AMERICAN VOICES

Black Soldiers in a White Man's War

GEORGE W. PRIOLEAU

George W. Prioleau, the chaplain of the Ninth Cavalry regiment, expresses his bitterness against the racism experienced by black troopers in the South on their way to battle in Cuba.

Hon. H. C. Smith
Editor, *Gazette*

Dear Sir:

All the way from northwest Nebraska this regiment was greeted with cheers and hurrahs. At places where we stopped the people assembled by the thousands. While the Ninth Cavalry band would play some national air the people would raise their hats, men, women, and children would wave their handkerchiefs, and the heavens would resound with their hearty cheers. . . . These demonstrations, so enthusiastically given, greeted us all the way until we reached Nashville. . . . From there until we reached Chattanooga there was not a cheer given us. . . .

The prejudice against the Negro soldier and the Negro was great, but it was of heavenly origin to what it is in this part of Florida. . . . The southerners have made their laws and the Negroes know and obey them. They never stop to ask a white man a question. He (Negro) never thinks of disobeying. . . . Talk about fighting and freeing poor Cuba and of Spain's brutality; of Cuba's murdered thousands, and starving reconcentradoes. Is America any better than Spain? Has she not subjects in her very midst who are murdered daily without a trial of judge or jury? Has she not subjects in her own borders whose children are half-fed and half-clothed, because their father's skin is black. . . . Yet the Negro is loyal to his country's flag. . . .

The four Negro regiments are going to help free Cuba, and they will return to their homes, some then mustered out and begin again to fight the battle of American prejudice. . . .

Yours truly,
Geo. W. Prioleau, Chaplain, Ninth Cavalry

SOURCE: *Cleveland Gazette* (May 13, 1898), reprinted in Willard B. Gatewood, *"Smoked Yankees" and the Struggle for Empire, 1898–1902* (Urbana: University of Illinois Press, 1971), pp. 27–29.

over valuable territory to "our commercial rivals in the Orient—that would have been bad business and discreditable."

Most plausible was the option of granting the Philippines independence. As in Cuba, Spanish rule had already stirred up a rebellion, led by the fiery patriot Emilio Aguinaldo. An arrangement might have been possible like the one being negotiated with the Cubans over Guantanamo Bay: the lease of a naval base to the Americans as the price of freedom. But after some hesitation McKinley was persuaded that "we could not leave [the Filipinos] to themselves—they were unfit for self-rule—and they would soon have anarchy and misrule over there worse than Spain's was."

As for the Spaniards, they had little choice against what they considered "the immoderate demands of a conqueror." In the Treaty of Paris they ceded the Philippines to the United States for a payment of $20 million. The treaty encountered harder going at home and was ratified by the Senate (requiring a two-thirds majority) on February 6, 1899, with only a single vote to spare.

The administration's narrow margin signaled the revival of an antiexpansionist tradition that had been briefly silenced by the patriotic passions of a nation at war. In the Senate opponents of the treaty invoked the country's republican principles. Under the Constitution, argued the conservative Republican George F. Hoar, "no power is given to the Federal Government to acquire territory to be held and governed permanently as colonies" or "to conquer alien people and hold them in subjugation." The alternative—making 8 million Filipinos American citizens—was equally unpalatable to the antiimperialists, who were no more champions of "these savage people" than were the expansionists who denigrated the self-governing capacity of the Filipinos.

Emilio Aguinaldo

At the start of the war with Spain, U.S. military leaders brought the Filipino patriot Aguinaldo back from Singapore because they thought he would stir up a popular uprising that would help defeat the Spaniards. Aguinaldo came because he thought the Americans favored an independent Philippines. These differing intentions—it has remained a matter of dispute what assurances Aguinaldo received— were the root cause of the Filipino insurrection that proved far costlier in American and Filipino lives than the war with Spain that preceded it. (Corbis-Bettmann)

Leading citizens enlisted in the anti-imperialist cause, including the steelmaker Andrew Carnegie, who offered a check for $20 million to purchase the independence of the Philippines; the labor leader Samuel Gompers, who feared the competition of cheap Filipino labor; and Jane Addams, who believed that women should stand for peace. The key group, however, was a social elite of old-line Mugwump reformers such as Carl Schurz, Charles Eliot Norton, and Charles Francis Adams. In November 1898 a Boston group formed the first of the Anti-Imperialist leagues that began to spring up around the country.

Although skillful at publicizing their cause, the anti-imperialists never developed a popular movement. They shared little but their anti-imperialism and, within the Mugwump core, lacked the common touch. Nor was anti-imperialism easily translated into a viable political cause because the Democrats, once the treaty had been adopted, waffled on the issue. Although an outspoken anti-imperialist, William Jennings Bryan, the Democratic standard-bearer, confounded his friends by favoring ratification of the treaty and afterward hesitated to stake his party's future on a crusade against a national policy he privately believed to be irreversible. Still, if it was an accomplished fact, Philippine annexation lost the moral high ground because of the grim events that began to unfold in the Philippines.

On February 4, 1899, two days before the Senate ratified the treaty, fighting broke out between American and Filipino patrols on the edge of Manila. Confronted by American annexation, Aguinaldo asserted his nation's independence and turned his guns on the occupying American forces.

The ensuing conflict far exceeded in ferocity the war just concluded with Spain. Fighting tenacious guerrillas, the U.S. Army resorted to the reconcentration tactic the Spaniards had employed in Cuba, moving people into towns, carrying out indiscriminate attacks beyond the perimeters, and burning crops and villages (see American Voices, "The Water Cure"). Atrocities became commonplace on both sides. In three years of warfare 4,200 Americans and many thousands of Filipinos died. The fighting ended in 1902, and William Howard Taft, who had been appointed governor-general, set up a civilian administration. He intended to make the Philippines a model of American road building and sanitary engineering.

McKinley's convincing victory over William Jennings Bryan in the 1900 election, though by no means a referendum on American expansionism, suggested popular satisfaction with America's overseas adventure. Yet a strong undercurrent of misgivings was evident. Americans had not anticipated the brutal methods needed to subdue the Filipino guerrillas. "We are destroying these islanders by the thousands, their villages and cities," protested the philosopher William James. "No life shall you have, we say, except as a gift from our philanthropy after your unconditional surrender to our will. . . . Could there be any more damning indictment of that whole bloated ideal termed 'modern civilization'?"

There were, moreover, disturbing constitutional issues to be resolved. Did the Constitution extend to the acquired territories? Did their inhabitants automatically become U.S. citizens? In 1901 the Supreme Court ruled negatively on both ques-

AMERICAN VOICES

The Water Cure

CORPORAL DANIEL J. EVANS

*I*n 1902, after the fighting had ceased, the U.S. Senate held hearings on the conduct of the war in the Philippines. This is the testimony of Corporal Daniel J. Evans, Twelfth Infantry, about his service on the island of Luzon.

Question: The committee would like to hear . . . whether you were the witness to any cruelties inflicted upon the natives of the Philippine Islands; and if so, under what circumstances.—*Answer:* The case I had reference to was where they gave the water cure to a native in the Ilicano Province at Ilocos Norte . . . about the month of August 1900. There were two native scouts with the American forces. They went out and brought in a couple of insurgents. . . . They tried to get from this insurgent . . . where the rest of the insurgents were at that time. . . . The first thing one of the Americans—I mean one of the scouts for the Americans—grabbed one of the men by the head and jerked his head back, and then they took a tomato can and poured water down his throat until he could hold no more. . . . Then they forced a gag into his mouth; they stood him up . . . against a post and fastened him so that he could not move. Then one man, an American soldier, who was over six feet tall, and who was very strong, too, struck this native in the pit of the stomach as hard as he could. . . . They kept that operation up for quite a time, and finally I thought the fellow was about to die, but I don't believe he was as bad as that, because finally he told them he would tell, and from that time on he was taken away, and I saw no more of him. . . .

Question: What is your observation as to the treatment of the people engaged in peaceable pursuits, as to kindness and consideration, or the reverse, from the American officers and the men?—*Answer:* They were never molested if they seemed to be peaceable natives. They would not be molested unless they showed some signs of hostility. . . . If we struck a part of the island where the natives were hostile and they would fire on our soldiers or even cut the telegraph lines, the result would be that their barrios would probably be burned.

SOURCE: Henry F. Graff, ed., *American Imperialism and the Philippine Insurrection* (Boston: Little, Brown, 1969), pp. 80–84.

tions; these were matters for Congress to decide. A special commission appointed by McKinley recommended independence for the islands after an indefinite period of U.S. rule, during which the Filipinos would be prepared for self-government. In 1916 the Jones Act formally committed the United States to granting Philippine independence but set no date.

The ugly business in the Philippines rubbed off some of the moralizing gloss but left undeflected America's global aspirations. In a few years the United States had acquired the makings of an overseas empire: Hawaii, Puerto Rico, Guam, the

Philippines, and finally, in 1900, several of the Samoan Islands that had been jointly administered with Germany and Britain. The United States, remarked the legal scholar John Bassett Moore in 1899, had moved "from a position of comparative freedom from entanglements into a position of what is commonly called a world power."

Onto the World Stage

In Europe the flexing of America's muscles against Spain caused a certain amount of consternation. At the instigation of Kaiser Wilhelm II of Germany, the major powers had tried before war broke out to intercede on Spain's behalf—but tentatively because no one was looking for trouble with the Americans. President McKinley had listened politely to their envoys and had then proceeded with his war.

The decisive outcome confirmed what the Europeans already suspected. After Dewey's naval victory the semiofficial French paper *Le Temps* observed that "what passes before our eyes is the appearance of a new power of the first order." And the London *Times* concluded: "This war must . . . effect a profound change in the whole attitude and policy of the United States. In the future America will play a part in the general affairs of the world such as she has never played before."

A POWER AMONG POWERS

The politician most ardently agreeing with the London *Times*'s vision of America's future was the man who, with the assassination of William McKinley, became president on September 14, 1901. Theodore Roosevelt was an avid student of world affairs, widely traveled and acquainted with many of the European leaders. He had no doubt about America's role in the world.

It was important, first of all, to uphold the country's honor in the community of nations. Nor should the country shrink from righteous battle. "All the great masterful races have been fighting races," Roosevelt declared. But when he spoke of war, Roosevelt had in mind actions by the "civilized" nations against "backward peoples." Roosevelt felt "it incumbent on all the civilized and orderly powers to insist on the proper policing of the world." That was why Roosevelt sympathized with European imperialism and how he justified American dominance in the Caribbean.

As for the "civilized and orderly" policemen of the world, the worst thing that could happen was for them to fall to fighting among themselves. Roosevelt had an acute sense of the fragility of world peace, and he was farsighted about the likelihood—in this he was truly exceptional among Americans—of a catastrophic world war. He believed in American responsibility for helping to maintain the balance of power.

The cornerstone of Roosevelt's thinking was Anglo-American amity. The British, increasingly isolated in world affairs, eagerly reciprocated. In the Hay-Pauncefote Agreement (1901) they gave up their treaty rights to participate in any Central American canal project, clearing the way for a canal under exclusive U.S.

The Panama Canal

The Canal Zone was acquired through devious means from which Americans could take little pride (and which led in 1978 to the Senate's decision to restore the property to Panama). But the building of the Panama Canal itself was a triumph of American ingenuity and drive. Dr. William C. Gorgas cleaned out the malarial mosquitoes that had earlier stymied the French. Under Colonel George W. Goethals the U.S. Army overcame formidable obstacles in a mighty feat of engineering. This photograph shows the massive effort underway in December 1904 to excavate the Culebra Cut so that oceangoing ships would be able to pass through. (Corbis-Bettmann)

control. And two years later the last of the vexing U.S.-Canadian border disputes—this one involving British Columbia and Alaska—was settled, again to American satisfaction. No formal alliance was forthcoming, but Anglo-American friendship had been placed on such a firm basis that after 1901 the British admiralty designed its war plans on the assumption that America was "a kindred state with whom we shall never have a parricidal war."

Among nations, however, what counted was strength, not merely goodwill. Roosevelt wanted "to make all foreign powers understand that when we have adopted a line of policy we have adopted it definitely, and with the intention of backing it up with deeds as well as words." As Roosevelt famously said: "Speak softly and carry a big stick." By a "big stick" he meant above all naval power. Under Roosevelt the battleship program went on apace. By 1904 the U.S. Navy stood fifth in the world; by 1907 it was third. At the top of Roosevelt's agenda was a canal across Central America.

Having secured Britain's surrender of its joint canal rights in 1901, Roosevelt proceeded to the more troublesome task of leasing from Colombia the needed strip of land across Panama, a Colombian province. Furious when the Colombian legislature voted down the proposed treaty, Roosevelt contemplated outright seizure of Panama but settled on a more devious solution. With an independence movement brewing in Panama, the United States lent covert assistance that ensured the success of a bloodless revolution against Colombia. On November 7, 1901, the United States recognized Panama and received two weeks later a perpetually renewable lease on a canal zone. Roosevelt never regretted the victimization of Colombia, although the United States, as a kind of conscience money, paid Colombia $25 million in 1922.

Building the canal, one of the heroic engineering feats of the century, involved a swamp-clearing project to rid the area of malaria and yellow fever, the construction of a series of great locks, and the excavation of 240 million cubic yards of earth. It took the U.S. Army Corps of Engineers eight years to finish the huge project. When the Panama Canal opened in 1914, it gave the United States a commanding commercial and strategic position in the Western Hemisphere (Map 21.2).

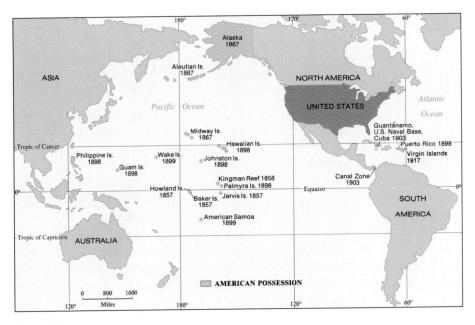

M A P 21.2
The American Empire

In 1890 Alfred T. Mahan wrote that the United States should regard the oceans as "a great highway" across which America would carry on world trade. That was precisely what resulted from the empire the United States acquired after the Spanish-American War. The Caribbean possessions, the strategically located Pacific Islands, and in 1903 the Panama Canal Zone gave the United States commercial and naval access to a wider world.

Next came the task of making the Caribbean basin secure. The countries there, said Secretary of State Elihu Root, had been placed "in the front yard of the United States" by the Panama Canal. Therefore, as Roosevelt put it, they had to "behave themselves." Believing that instability in the Caribbean invited the intervention of European powers, Roosevelt announced in 1904 that the United States would act as "policeman" of the region, stepping in, "however reluctantly, in flagrant cases . . . of wrong doing or impotence." This policy became known as the Roosevelt Corollary to the Monroe Doctrine. It transformed what had been a broad principle of opposition against European expansionist ambitions in Latin America into an unrestricted American right to regulate Caribbean affairs. The Roosevelt Corollary was not a treaty with other states; it was a unilateral declaration sanctioned only by American power and national interest.

Citing the Roosevelt Corollary, the United States intervened regularly in the internal affairs of Caribbean states. In the case of Cuba a condition for its independence had been a 1902 proviso in its constitution called the Platt amendment, which gave the United States the right to intervene if Cuba's independence or internal order was threatened. Elsewhere there was not even this semblance of legality. American authorities took over the customs and debt management of the Dominican Republic in 1905, of Nicaragua in 1911, and of Haiti in 1916. When domestic order broke down, the U.S. Marines occupied Cuba in 1906, Nicaragua in 1909, and Haiti and the Dominican Republic in later years (Map 21.3).

THE OPEN DOOR IN ASIA

In China the occupying powers quickly instituted discriminatory trade regulations in their zones of control. Fearful of being frozen out, U.S. Secretary of State John Hay in 1899 sent them an "open-door" note claiming the right of equal trade access—an open door—for all nations that wanted to do business in China. Despite its Philippine bases the United States lacked real leverage in East Asia and elicited only noncommittal responses from the occupying powers. But Hay chose to interpret them as accepting the American open-door position.

When a secret society of Chinese nationalists, the Boxers, rebelled against the foreigners in 1900, the United States joined the multinational campaign to break the Boxers' siege of the diplomatic missions in Peking (Beijing). America took this opportunity to assert a second principle of the open door: that China would be preserved as a "territorial and administrative entity." As long as the legal fiction of an independent China survived, so would American claims to equal access to the China market.

The European powers had acceded to American preeminence in the Caribbean. But Britain, Germany, France, and Russia were strongly entrenched in East Asia and not inclined to defer to American interests. The United States also confronted a powerful Asian nation—Japan—that had its own vital interests. Although the open-door policy was important to him, Roosevelt perceived in the Pacific a deadlier game calling for American involvement.

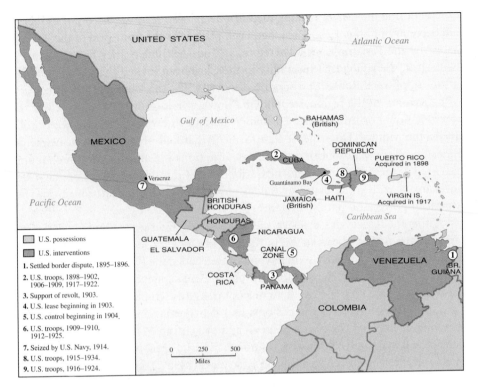

M AP 21.3
Policeman of the Caribbean

After the Spanish-American War the United States vigorously asserted its interest in the affairs of its neighbors to the south. As the record of interventions shows, the United States truly became the "policeman" of the Caribbean.

Japan had unveiled its military strength in the Sino-Japanese War of 1894–1895. A decade later, provoked by Russian rivalry in Manchuria and Korea, Japan suddenly attacked the tsar's fleet at Port Arthur, Russia's leased port in China. In a series of brilliant victories the Japanese smashed the Russian forces in Asia. Anxious to restore some semblance of a balance of power, Roosevelt mediated a settlement of the Russo-Japanese War at Portsmouth, New Hampshire, in 1905. Japan emerged as the predominant power in East Asia.

Contemptuous of other Asian nations, Roosevelt admired the Japanese—"a wonderful and civilized people . . . entitled to stand in absolute equality with all the other peoples of the civilized world." He conceded that Japan had "a paramount interest in what surrounds the Yellow Sea, just as the United States has a paramount interest in what surrounds the Caribbean." But American strategic and commercial interests in the Pacific had to be accommodated. The United States approved of Japan's protectorate over Korea in 1905 and then of its declaration of full sovereignty six years later. However, a surge of anti-Asian feeling in California complicated Roosevelt's efforts. In 1906 San Francisco's school board placed all Asian students in a segregated school, infuriating Japan. The "gentlemen's agreement" of 1907, in which Japan agreed to restrict immigration to the United States, smoothed matters over, but periodic racist slights by Americans made for continuing tensions with the Japanese.

Roosevelt meanwhile moved to balance Japan's military power by increasing American naval strength in the Pacific. American battleships visited Japan in 1908 on a global tour that impressively displayed U.S. sea power. Late that year, near the end of his administration, Roosevelt achieved a formal accommodation with Japan. The Root-Takahira Agreement confirmed the status quo in the Pacific, as well as the principles of free oceanic commerce and equal trade opportunity in China.

William Howard Taft, however, entered the White House in 1909 convinced that the United States had been shortchanged. He pressed for a larger role for American investors, especially in the railroad construction going on in China. An exponent of *dollar diplomacy*—the aggressive coupling of American political and economic interests abroad—Taft hoped that American capital would counterbalance Japanese power and pave the way for increased commercial opportunities. When the Chinese Revolution of 1911 toppled the ruling Manchu dynasty, Taft supported the victorious Chinese Nationalists, who wanted to modernize their country and liberate it from Japanese domination. The United States thus entered a long-term rivalry with Japan that would end in war thirty years later.

The United States had become embroiled in a distant struggle that promised many future liabilities but few of the fabulous profits that had lured Americans to Asia.

WILSON AND MEXICO

When Woodrow Wilson became president in 1913, he was bent on reforming American foreign policy no less than domestic politics. Wilson did not really differ with his predecessors on the importance of economic development overseas. He applauded the "tides of commerce" that would arise from the Panama Canal. But he opposed dollar diplomacy, which he believed bullied weaker countries financially and gave undue advantage to American business. It seemed to Wilson "a very perilous thing to determine the foreign policy of a nation in terms of material interest."

The United States, Wilson insisted, should conduct its foreign policy in conformity with its democratic principles. He intended to foster the "development of constitutional liberty in the world" and above all in the nation's neighbors in Latin America. Wilson vowed that the United States would "never again seek one additional foot of territory by conquest." He was committed to advancing "human rights, national integrity, and opportunity" in Latin America. To do otherwise would make "ourselves untrue to our own traditions."

Mexico became the primary object of Wilson's ministrations. A cycle of revolutions had begun there in 1911. The dictator Porfirio Diaz was overthrown by Francisco Madero, who spoke much as Wilson did about liberty and constitutionalism. But before Madero got very far with his reforms, he was deposed and murdered in February 1913 by one of his generals, Victoriano Huerta. Other powers quickly recognized Huerta's provisional government but not the United States. Wilson abhorred Huerta; he called him a murderer and pledged "to force him out."

By intervening in this way, "we act in the interest of Mexico alone. . . . We are seeking to counsel Mexico for its own good." Wilson meant that he intended to put the Mexican revolution back on the constitutional path started by Madero. Wilson was not deterred by the fact that American business interests, with big investments in Mexico, favored Huerta.

The emergence of armed opposition in northern Mexico under Venustiano Carranza strengthened Wilson's hand. But Carranza's Constitutionalist movement, ardently nationalist, had no desire for American intervention in Mexican affairs. Carranza angrily rebuffed Wilson's efforts to bring about elections by means of a compromise with the Huerta government. He also vowed to fight any intrusion of U.S. troops in his country. All he wanted from Wilson, Carranza asserted, was recognition of the Constitutionalists' belligerent status, so they could purchase arms in the United States. In exchange for vague promises to respect property rights and "fair" foreign concessions, Carranza finally got his way in 1914. American weapons began to flow to his troops.

When it became clear that Huerta was not about to fall, the United States threw its own forces into the conflict. On the pretext of a minor insult to the U.S. Navy at Tampico, Wilson ordered the occupation of the port of Veracruz on April 21, 1914, at the cost of 19 American and 126 Mexican lives. At that point the Huerta regime began to crumble. Carranza nevertheless condemned the United States, and his forces came close to engaging the Americans. When he entered Mexico City in triumph in August 1914, Carranza had some cause to thank the Yankees. But if any sense of gratitude existed, it was overshadowed by the anti-Americanism inspired by Wilson's insensitivity to Mexican pride and revolutionary zeal.

THE GATHERING STORM IN EUROPE

In the meantime Europe had begun to drift toward world war. There were two main sources of tension. One was the rivalry between Germany, the new military and economic superpower of Europe, and the European states threatened by its might—above all France, which had been humiliated in the Franco-Prussian War of 1870. The second danger zone was the Balkans, where the Ottoman empire was disintegrating and where, in the midst of explosive ethnic rivalries, Austria-Hungary and Russia were maneuvering for dominance. Out of these conflicts an alliance system had emerged, with Germany, Austria-Hungary, and Italy (the Triple Alliance) on one side and France and Russia (the Dual Alliance) on the other.

The tensions in Europe were partially released by European imperial adventures, especially by France in Africa and by Russia in Asia. These activities placed France and Russia in opposition to imperial Britain, effectively excluding Britain from the European alliance system. Fearful of Germany, however, Britain in 1904 resolved her differences with France, and the two countries reached a friendly understanding, or *entente*. When Britain came to a similar understanding with Russia in 1907, the basis was laid for the Triple Entente. A deadly confrontation between two great European power blocs became possible.

In these European quarrels Americans had no obvious stake nor any inclination, in the words of a cautionary Senate resolution, "to depart from the traditional American foreign policy which forbids participation . . . [in] political questions which are entirely European in scope." But on becoming president Theodore Roosevelt took a lively interest in European affairs and was eager, as the head of a Great Power, to make a contribution to the cause of peace there. In 1905 he got his chance.

The Anglo-French entente of the previous year was based partly on an agreement over spheres of influence in North Africa: the Sudan went to Britain, Morocco to France. Then Germany suddenly challenged France over Morocco—a disastrous move, conflicting with Germany's self-interest in keeping France's attention diverted from Europe. The German ruler, Kaiser Wilhelm, turned to Roosevelt for help. Roosevelt arranged an international conference, which was held in January 1906 at Algeciras, Spain. With U.S. diplomats playing a key role, the crisis was defused. Germany got a few token concessions, but France's dominance over Morocco was sustained.

Algeciras marked an ominous turning point—the first time the power blocs that would become locked in battle in 1914 first squared off against one another. But in 1906 the outcome of the conference seemed a diplomatic triumph. Roosevelt's secretary of state, Elihu Root, boasted of America's success in "preserv[ing] world peace because of the power of our detachment."

Root's words prefigured how the United States would define its role among the Great Powers: it would be the apostle of peace, distinguished by its lack of selfish interest in European affairs. Opposing this internationalist impulse, however, was America's traditional isolationism.

Americans had applauded the international peace movement launched by the Hague Peace Conference of 1899. The Permanent Court of Arbitration that resulted offered new hope for the peaceful settlement of international disputes. Both the Roosevelt and the Taft administrations negotiated arbitration treaties with other countries, pledging to submit their disputes to the Hague Court, only to have the treaties emasculated by a Senate unwilling to permit any erosion of the nation's sovereignty. Nor was there any sequel to Roosevelt's initiative at Algeciras. It was coolly received in the Senate and by the nation's press.

When Wilson became president, he chose William Jennings Bryan to be secretary of state. An apostle of world peace, Bryan devoted himself to negotiating a series of "cooling off" treaties with other countries—so called because the parties agreed to wait one year while disputed issues were submitted to a conciliation process. Although admirable these bilateral agreements had no bearing on the explosive power politics of Europe. As tensions there reached the breaking point in 1914, the United States remained effectively on the sidelines.

Yet at Algeciras Roosevelt had correctly anticipated what the future would demand of America. So did the French journalist Andre Tardieu, who remarked in 1908:

> The United States is . . . a world power. . . . Its power creates for it . . . a duty— to pronounce upon all those questions that hitherto have been arranged by agreement only among European powers. . . . The United States intervenes thus in the affairs of the universe. . . . It is seated at the table where the great game is played, and it cannot leave it.

T I M E L I N E

1875	Treaty brings Hawaii within U.S. orbit.	**1901**	Theodore Roosevelt becomes president; "big stick" diplomacy.
1881	Secretary of State James G. Blaine inaugurates Pan-Americanism.		Hay-Pauncefote Agreement
			United States recognizes Panama and receives grant of Canal Zone.
1889	Germany, Britain, and United States share protectorate in Samoa.	**1902**	Platt amendment gives United States right of intervention in Cuba.
1890	Alfred Thayer Mahan's *The Influence of Seapower upon History*		
		1904	Roosevelt Corollary
1893	Annexation of Hawaii fails.	**1905–**	United States mediates Franco-German
	Frederick Jackson Turner's "The Significance of the Frontier in American History"	**1906**	crisis over Morocco at Algeciras.
		1907	Gentlemen's Agreement restricts Japanese immigration.
	Panic of 1893 ushers in economic depression.		
1894	Sino-Japanese war begins breakup of China into spheres of influence.	**1908**	Root-Takahira Agreement
		1909	William Howard Taft becomes president; dollar diplomacy.
1895	Venezuela crisis	**1913**	Wilson asserts new principles for American diplomacy.
1898	Outbreak of Spanish-American War in Cuba and Philippines		Intervention in the Mexican Revolution
	Hawaii annexed		
	Anti-imperialist movement launched	**1914**	Panama Canal opens.
			World War I begins.
1899	Hague Peace Conference		
	Guerrilla war in the Philippines		
	Open-door policy in China		

For Further Exploration

Walter LaFeber, *The American Search for Opportunity, 1865–1913* (1993), is an excellent, up-to-date synthesis. LaFeber emphasizes economic interest—the need for overseas markets—as the source of American expansionism. His immensely influential *The New Empire, 1860–1898* (1963) initiated the scholarly debate on this issue. A robust counterpoint is Fareed Zakaria's recent *From Wealth to Power* (1998), which asks why the United States was so slow (compared to other imperial nations) to translate its economic power into international muscle. The debate can be explored at greater depth in Thomas J. McCormick, *China Market: America's Quest for Informal Empire, 1893–1901* (1967); Michael Hunt, *Ideology and U.S. Foreign Policy* (1987); and Mark R. Shulman, *Navalism and the Emergence of American Sea Power, 1882–1893* (1995). On the war with Spain the liveliest narrative is still Frank Freidel, *A Splendid Little War* (1958). For fuller treatments see David S. Trask, *The War with Spain in 1898* (1981); Ivan Musicant, *Empire by Default* (1998); and Lewis Gould, *The Spanish-American War and President McKinley* (1982), which emphasizes McKinley's strong leadership. Ernest R. May, *Imperial Democracy: The Emergence of America as a Great Power* (1961), exemplifies the earlier view that McKinley was a weak figure driven to war by jingoistic pressures. On the Mexican involvement see John S. D. Eisenhower, *Intervention! The United States and the Mexican Revolution* (1993). The revolution as experienced by the Mexicans is brilliantly depicted in John Womack, *Zapata and the Mexican Revolution* (1968).

The Library of Congress maintains an excellent website, "The Spanish-American War," at <lcweb.loc.gov/rr/hispanic/1898/> with separate sections on the war in Cuba, the Philippines, Puerto Rico, and Spain. "American Imperialism" at <http://boondocksnet.com> includes an extensive collection of stereoscopic images, political cartoons, maps, photographs, and documents from the period.

Part 5

THE MODERN STATE AND SOCIETY
1914–1945

THEMATIC TIMELINE

	GOVERNMENT	DIPLOMACY	ECONOMY
	THE RISE OF THE STATE	FROM ISOLATION TO WORLD LEADERSHIP	PROSPERITY, DEPRESSION, AND WAR
1914	• Wartime agencies expand power of the federal government.	• United States enters World War I (1917). • Wilson's Fourteen Points (1918)	• Shift from debtor to creditor nation • Agricultural glut
1920	• Republican ascendancy • Prohibition (1920–1933) • Business-government partnership • Nineteenth Amendment gives women the vote.	• Treaty of Versailles rejected by U.S. Senate (1920) • Washington Conference sets naval limits (1922).	• Economic recession (1920–1921) • Booming prosperity (1922–1929) • Rise in welfare capitalism
1930	• Franklin D. Roosevelt becomes president (1933). • The New Deal: unprecedented government intervention in economy, social welfare, arts	• Roosevelt's Good Neighbor Policy toward Latin America (1933) • Abraham Lincoln Brigade fights in Spanish Civil War. • U.S. neutrality proclaimed (1939)	• Great Depression (1929–1941) • Rise of labor movement • Married women increasingly participate in the workforce.
1940	• Government mobilizes industry for war production and rationing.	• United States enters World War II (1941). • Allies defeat Axis powers; bombing of Hiroshima (1945).	• War mobilization ends depression.

SOCIETY	CULTURE
NATIVISM, MIGRATION, AND SOCIAL CHANGE	A MASS NATIONAL CULTURE EMERGES
• Southern blacks begin migration to northern cities.	• Silent screen; Hollywood becomes movie capital of the world.
• Rise of nativism • National Origins Act (1924) • Mexican American immigration increases.	• Consumer culture—advertising, radio, magazines, movies—flourishes. • Consumer culture promotes image of emancipated womanhood, the Flapper.
• Farming families migrate from Dust Bowl states to California and the West. • Indian New Deal • Increased use of birth control leads to smaller families.	• Documentary impulse • Federal patronage of the arts
• Rural whites and blacks migrate to war jobs in cities. • Cival rights movement revitalized	• Film industry enlisted to aid war effort

By 1914 industrialization, economic expansion abroad, massive immigration, and the growth of a vibrant urban culture had set the foundations for a distinctly modern American society. In all facets of politics, the economy, and daily life, American society was becoming more organized, more bureaucratic, and more complex. By 1945, after Americans had fought in two world wars and weathered a dozen years of economic depression, the edifice of the new society was largely complete.

A strong national state, an essential building block of modern society, came late and haltingly to America compared to industrialized countries of Western Europe. American participation in World War I called forth an unprecedented mobilization of the domestic economy, but policymakers quickly dismantled the centralized wartime bureaucracies in 1919. During the 1920s the Harding and Coolidge administrations embraced a philosophy of business-government partnership, believing that unrestricted corporate capitalism would provide for the welfare of the American people. Ultimately the Great Depression, with its uncounted business failures and unprecedented levels of unemployment, overthrew that long-cherished idea. Franklin D. Roosevelt's New Deal dramatically expanded federal responsibility for the economy and the welfare of ordinary citizens. An even greater expansion of the national state resulted from the massive mobilization necessitated by America's entry into World War II. Unlike the experience after World War I, the new state apparatus remained in place when the war ended.

America was slowly and somewhat reluctantly drawn into a position of world leadership, which it continues to hold today. World War I provided the major impetus: before 1914 the world had been dominated by Europe, but from that point on the United States increasingly dominated the world. In 1918 American troops provided the margin of victory for the Allies, and President Wilson helped shape the treaties that ended the war. The United States, however, refused to join the League of Nations created by those treaties. America's dominant economic position guaranteed an active role in world affairs in the

1920s and 1930s nonetheless. The globalization of America accelerated in 1941, when the nation threw all its energies into a second world war that had its roots in the imperfect settlement of the first one. Of all the powers that participated in this most devastating of global conflagrations, only America emerged physically unscathed. The country was also the only one to possess a dangerous new weapon—the atomic bomb. Within wartime decisions lay the roots of the cold war that followed.

In this period the American economy also took on its modern contours. Between 1914 and 1945 the nation's industrial economy was the most productive in the world. The Great Depression, which slashed the nation's gross national product and left millions unemployed and destitute, hit the United States harder than any other industrialized nation. Yet although it had a powerful effect on the country's politics and culture, it did not permanently affect its global economic standing. Indeed, throughout the period American businesses successfully competed in world markets, and American financial institutions played the leading role in international economic affairs. Large-scale corporate organizations replaced smaller family-run businesses. White-collar jobs, ranging from managerial to clerical, expanded dramatically and contributed to the growing presence of women in the workforce. The automobile industry symbolized the ascendancy of mass-production techniques. Many workers shared in the general prosperity but also bore the brunt of economic downturns. These uncertainties fueled the dramatic growth of the labor movement in the 1930s.

American society was transformed by the great wave of European immigration and the movement from farms to cities. The growth of metropolitan areas gave the nation an increasingly urban tone, and geographical mobility broke down regional differences. Many old-stock white Americans viewed these processes with alarm; in 1924 nativists succeeded in all but eliminating immigration from everywhere but other Western Hemisphere nations, as migration across the border from Mexico continued to shape the West and Southwest. Internal migration also changed the face of America, as African Americans moved north and west to take factory jobs and Dust Bowl farmers in the 1930s moved to the Far West to find better livelihoods. World War II accelerated these migration patterns even more.

Finally, modern America saw the emergence of a mass national culture. By the 1920s Americans were increasingly drawn into a web of interlocking cultural experiences. Advertising and the new entertainment media—movies, radio, and magazines—disseminated the new values of consumerism; the movies exported this vision of the American experience worldwide. Not even the Great Depression could divert Americans from their desire for leisure, self-fulfillment, and consumer goods. The emphasis on consumption and a quest for a rising standard of living would define the American experience for the rest of the twentieth century.

Chapter 22

WAR AND THE AMERICAN STATE
1914–1920

It is not an army we must shape and train for war, it is a nation.

WOODROW WILSON, 1917

"It's Up to You—Protect the Nation's Honor—Enlist Now." "Turn Your Silver into Bullets at the Post Office." "Rivets Are Bayonets—Drive Them Home!" "Women! Help America's Sons Win the War: Buy U.S. Government Bonds." "Food Is Ammunition—Don't Waste It." At every turn during the eighteen months of U.S. participation in the Great War—at the movies, in schools and libraries, in shop windows and post offices, at train stations and factories—Americans encountered dramatic posters urging them to do their bit. More than colorful reminders of a bygone era, these propaganda tools were meant to unify the American people in voluntary, self-sacrificing service to the nation. They suggest not only that the federal government had increased its presence in the lives of Americans but also that in modern war victory demanded more than armies. On the home front, businessmen, workers, farmers, housewives, and even children had important roles to play. The story of the United States' involvement in World War I, then, is a story of battles and diplomacy abroad and mobilization at home, all of which would have lasting impact on the nation's future.

The American decision to enter the conflict in 1917 confirmed one of the most important shifts of power in the twentieth century. Before the outbreak of the Great War in 1914, the world had been dominated by Europe; the postwar world was increasingly dominated by the United States. The historian Akira Iriye calls this broad transformation the "globalization" of America. Increasingly, the United States became "involved in security, economic, and cultural affairs in all parts of the world." This development, which is usually thought to begin with World War II and its aftermath, actually started in 1917.

Related changes that shaped the country for the rest of the twentieth century also emerged at home. New federal bureaucracies had to be created to coordinate the efforts of business, labor, and agriculture—a process that hastened the emergence of a national administrative state. War meant new opportunities, albeit

America and the War Effort

Popular magazines like *Leslie's Illustrated Weekly Newspaper* teamed up with the federal government to promote food conservation. If a patriotic reader affixed a 1 cent stamp to the cover's top right corner, the magazine would be sent to soldiers or sailors at the front.

(*Leslie's*, September 29, 1917/Picture Research Consultants & Archives)

temporary, for white women and for members of ethnic minorities. It also meant new divisions among Americans and new hatreds, first of Germans and Austrians and then of "Bolshevik" Reds. When the war ended, the United States was forced to confront the deep class, racial, and ethnic divisions that had surfaced during wartime mobilization.

The Great War, 1914–1918

When war erupted in August 1914, most Americans saw no reason to involve them-selves in the struggle among Europe's imperialistic powers. No vital U.S. interests were at stake. Indeed, the United States had a good relationship with both sides, and its industries benefited from providing war material for the combatants. Many Americans placed their faith in what historians call "U.S. exceptionalism"—the be-lief that their superior democratic values and institutions made their country im-mune from the corruption and chaos of other nations. Horrified by the carnage and sympathetic to the suffering, Americans nevertheless expected that they would be able to follow their president's dictum "to be neutral in fact as well as in name."

WAR IN EUROPE

Almost from the moment France, Russia, and Britain formed the Triple Entente in 1907 to counter the Triple Alliance of Germany, Austria-Hungary, and Italy (see Chapter 21), European leaders began to prepare for what they saw as an inevitable conflict. The spark that ignited the war came in Europe's perennial tinderbox, the Balkans, where Austria-Hungary and Russia competed for power and influence. Austria's seizure of the provinces of Bosnia and Herzegovina in 1908 had enraged Russia and its client, the independent state of Serbia. Serbian terrorists responded by recruiting Bosnians to agitate against Austrian rule. On June 28, 1914, a nineteen-year-old Bosnian student, Gavrilo Princip, assassinated Franz Ferdinand, the heir to the Austro-Hungarian throne, and his wife, the Duchess of Hohenberg, in the town of Sarajevo.

After the assassination the complex European alliance system, which had for years maintained a fragile peace, drew all the major powers into war. Austria-Hungary, blaming Serbia for the assassination, declared war on Serbia on July 28. Russia, which had a secret treaty with Serbia, mobilized its armies; Germany re-sponded by declaring war on Russia and its ally, France, and by invading neutral Belgium. The brutality of the invasion, and Britain's commitment to Belgian neu-trality, prompted Great Britain to declare war on Germany on August 4. Within a few days all the major European powers had formally entered the conflict.

The combatants were divided into two rival blocs. The Allied Powers—Great Britain, France, Japan, Russia, and, in 1915, Italy—were pitted against the Central Powers—Germany, Austria-Hungary, Turkey, and, in 1915, Bulgaria (see Map 22.1).

M A P 22.1
Europe at the Start of World War I

In early August 1914 a complex set of interlocking alliances drew the
major European powers into war. At first the United States avoided
the conflict. Not until April 1917 did America enter the war on the
Allied side.

Because the alliance system encompassed competing imperial powers, the conflict
spread to parts of the world far beyond Europe, including the Middle East, Africa,
and China. Its worldwide scope gave it the name the Great War, or later, World
War I.

The term "Great War" also suggested the terrible devastation the conflict produced. It was the first modern war in which extensive harm was done to civilian
populations. New military technology, much of it from the United States, made
armies more deadly than ever before. Soldiers carried long-range, high-velocity
rifles that could hit a target at 1,000 yards—a vast improvement over the 300-yard
range of the rifle-musket used in the American Civil War. Another innovation was
the machine gun, whose American-born inventor, Hiram Maxim, moved to Great
Britain in the 1880s to follow a friend's advice: "If you want to make your fortune,
invent something which will allow those fool Europeans to kill each other more
quickly."

The concentrated firepower of rifles and machine guns gave troops in defensive positions a tremendous advantage. For four bloody years, between 1914 and
1918, the Allies and the Central Powers faced each other on the Western Front, a

The Landscape of War

World War I devastated the countryside: this was the battleground at Ypres in 1915. The carnage of trench warfare also scarred the soldiers who served in these surreal settings, causing the "gas neurosis," "burial-alive neurosis," and "soldiers' heart"—all symptoms of shell shock. (Imperial War Museum, London)

narrow swath of territory in Belgium and northern France crisscrossed by 25,000 miles of heavily fortified trenches, protected by deadly barbed wire. Trench warfare produced unprecedented numbers of casualties. If one side tried to break the stalemate by venturing into the "no man's land" between the trenches, its soldiers, caught in the sea of barbed wire, were mowed down by artillery fire or poison gas, first used by the Germans at Ypres in April 1915. Between February and December 1916, the French suffered 550,000 casualties and the Germans 450,000, as Germany tried to break through the French lines at Verdun. The front did not move.

THE PERILS OF NEUTRALITY

As the bloody stalemate continued, the United States grappled with its role in the international conflagration. Two weeks after the outbreak of war in Europe, President Woodrow Wilson had made the American position clear. In a message widely printed in the newspapers, the president called on Americans to be "neutral in fact as well as in name, impartial in thought as well as in action." Wilson wanted to keep the nation out of the war partly because he believed that if America kept aloof from the quarrel, he could arbitrate—and influence—its ultimate settlement.

The nation's divided loyalties also influenced Wilson's policy. Many Americans, including Wilson, felt deep cultural ties to the Allies, especially Britain and France. Yet most Irish Americans resented Britain's centuries-long occupation of their homeland and the cancellation of Home Rule in 1914. Pro-German sentiments drew strength from America's 10 million immigrants from Germany and Austria-Hungary. Indeed, German Americans made up one of the largest and best-established ethnic groups in the United States, and many aspects of German culture, including classical music and the German university system, were widely admired. Wilson could not easily have rallied the nation to the Allied side in 1914.

Many Americans had no strong sympathy for either side. Some progressive leaders—both Republicans and Democrats—vehemently opposed American participation in the European conflict. Newly formed pacifist groups, among them the American Union against Militarism and the Women's Peace Party, both founded in 1915, also mobilized popular opposition. Virtually the entire political left, led principally by Eugene Debs and the Socialist Party, condemned the war as imperialistic. African American leaders such as A. Philip Randolph viewed it as a conflict of the white race only. And some prominent industrialists bankrolled antiwar activities. In December 1915 Henry Ford spent almost half a million dollars to send more than a hundred men and women to Europe on a "peace ship" in an attempt to negotiate an end to the war.

All these factors might have kept the nation neutral if the conflict had not spread to the high seas. Here the United States wished to assert its neutrality rights—freedom to trade with nations on both sides of a conflict. But the warring nations would not long let America trade in peace. By the end of August 1914 the British had imposed a naval blockade on the Central Powers, hoping to cut off military supplies and starve the German people into submission. But their actions also prevented neutral nations like the United States from trading with Germany and its allies. The United States chafed at the infringement of its neutral rights but chose to do little besides complain, largely because the war had produced a spectacular increase in trade with the Allies that more than made up for the lost commerce with the Central Powers. American trade with Britain and France grew from $824 million in 1914 to $3.2 billion in 1916. By 1917 U.S. banks had lent the Allies $2.5 billion. In contrast, American trade with and loans to Germany totaled only $29 million and $27 million, respectively, by 1917. This trade imbalance translated into closer U.S. ties with the Allies, despite the nation's official posture of neutrality.

To challenge British control of the seas, the German navy launched a devastating new weapon, the U-boat. In April 1915 the German embassy in the United States had issued a warning to civilians that all ships flying the flags of Britain or its allies were liable to destruction. A few weeks later, on May 7, a German U-boat off the coast of Ireland torpedoed the British luxury liner *Lusitania,* killing 1,198 people, 128 of them Americans. The attack on the unarmed passenger vessel (which was later revealed to have been carrying munitions) incensed Americans—newspapers branded it a "mass murder"—and prompted President Wilson to send a series of strongly worded protests to Germany. Mounting tension between the two nations temporarily subsided in September 1915, when Germany announced its submarines would no longer attack passenger ships without warning.

The *Lusitania* crisis was one factor that prompted Wilson to rethink his opposition to preparedness. He was further discouraged by the failure of his repeated attempts in 1915 and 1916 to mediate an end to the European conflict through his aide, Colonel Edward House. With neither side apparently interested in serious peace negotiations, Wilson worried that the potential for the United States to be drawn into the conflict was deepening. In the fall of 1915 he endorsed a $1 billion buildup of the army and the navy, and by 1916 armament was well under way.

Nevertheless, public opinion still ran against entering the war, a factor that profoundly shaped the election of 1916. The Republican Party passed over the belligerently prowar Theodore Roosevelt in favor of Supreme Court Justice Charles Evans Hughes, a former governor of New York. The Democrats renominated Wilson, whose campaign emphasized his progressive reform record (see Chapter 20) but whose telling campaign slogan was, "He kept us out of war." Wilson won reelection by only 600,000 popular votes and by 23 votes in the electoral college, a slim margin that limited his options in mobilizing the nation for war.

The events of early 1917 diminished Wilson's lingering hopes of staying out of the conflict. On January 31 Germany announced the resumption of unrestricted submarine warfare, a decision dictated by the impasse in the land war. In response, Wilson broke off diplomatic relations with Germany on February 3. A few weeks later, newspapers published an intercepted communication from Germany's foreign secretary, Arthur Zimmermann, to the German minister in Mexico City, in which Zimmermann urged Mexico to join the Central Powers in the war. In return, Germany promised to help Mexico recover "the lost territory of Texas, New Mexico, and Arizona." This threat to the territorial integrity of the United States jolted both congressional and public opinion, especially in the West, where opposition to entering the war was strong. Combined with the resumption of unrestricted submarine warfare, the Zimmermann telegram inflamed anti-German sentiment. Although the likelihood of Mexico's reconquering the border states was small, the continued instability there in the final phases of the Mexican Revolution (see Chapter 21) had led to border raids that killed sixteen U.S. citizens in January 1916 and made American policymakers take the German threat seriously.

Throughout March, U-boats attacked American ships without warning, sinking three on March 18 alone. On April 2, 1917, after consulting his cabinet, Wilson appeared before a special session of Congress to ask for a declaration of war. The rights of the nation had been trampled, and its trade and citizens' lives imperiled, he charged. But while U.S. self-interest shaped the decision to go to war, Americans' long-standing sense of their exceptionalism, coupled with Progressive Era zeal to right social injustices, also played a part. Believing that the United States, in sharp contrast to other nations, was uniquely high minded in the conduct of its international affairs, many Americans accepted Wilson's claim that America had no selfish aims: "We desire no conquest, no dominion. We seek no indemnities for ourselves, no material compensation for the sacrifices we shall freely make. We are but one of the champions of the rights of mankind." In a memorable phrase intended to ennoble the nation's role, Wilson proposed that U.S. participation in the war would make the world "safe for democracy."

Four days after Wilson's speech, on April 6, 1917, the United States declared war on Germany. Reflecting the divided feelings of the country as a whole, the vote was far from unanimous. Six senators and fifty members of the House voted against the action, including Representative Jeannette Rankin of Montana, the first woman elected to Congress. "I want to stand by my country," she declared, "but I cannot vote for war."

"OVER THERE"

To native-born Americans, Europe seemed a great distance away—literally "over there," as the lyrics of George M. Cohan's popular song described it. After the declaration of war many citizens were surprised to learn that the United States planned to send troops to Europe, optimistically having assumed that the nation's participation could be limited to military and economic aid.

In May 1917 General John J. Pershing traveled to London and Paris to determine how the United States could best support the war effort. The answer, as Marshal Joseph Joffre of France put it, was clear: "Men, men, and more men." The problem was that the United States had never maintained a large standing army in peacetime. To field a fighting force strong enough to enter a global war, the government turned to conscription. The passage of the Selective Service Act in May 1917 demonstrated the increasing impact of the state on ordinary citizens. Though draft resistance had been common during the Civil War, no major riots occurred in 1917. The Selective Service System worked in part because it combined central direction from Washington with local administration and civilian control and thus did not tread on the nation's tradition of individual freedom and local autonomy. Draft registration also demonstrated the potential bureaucratic capacity of the American state. On a single day, June 5, 1917, more than 9.5 million men between the ages of twenty-one and thirty were processed for military service in their local voting precincts. By the end of the war almost 4 million men, plus a few thousand female navy clerks and army nurses, were in uniform. Another 300,000 men, called "slackers," evaded the draft, and 4,000 were classified as conscientious objectors.

Wilson chose Pershing to head the American Expeditionary Force (AEF). But the newly raised army did not have an immediate impact on the fighting. The fresh recruits had to be trained and outfitted and then wait for transport across the submarine-infested Atlantic. The nation's first main contribution was to secure the safety of the seas. Aiming for safety in numbers in the face of mounting German submarine activity, the government began sending armed convoys across the Atlantic. The plan worked: no American soldiers were killed on the way to Europe, and Allied shipping losses were cut dramatically.

Meanwhile, trench warfare on the Western Front continued its deadly grind. Allied commanders pleaded for American reinforcements, but Pershing was reluctant to put his soldiers under foreign commanders, preferring to delay introducing American troops until the AEF could be brought up to strength and ready to fight. Thus, until May 1918 the brunt of the fighting continued to fall on the French and British. Their burden increased when the Eastern Front collapsed after the Russian Revolution in November 1917. Under the Treaty of Brest-Litovsk, the new Bolshevik regime under Vladimir Ilych Lenin surrendered about one-third of Russia's territories, including Russian Poland, Ukraine, and the Baltic provinces, in return for an end to hostilities.

Once hostilities with Russia had ended, the Germans launched a major offensive against the Allies on the Western Front on March 21, 1918. By May the German army had advanced to the Marne River, within 50 miles of Paris, and was attempting to subdue the city by bombardment. When Allied leaders intensified their calls for American troops, Pershing committed about 60,000 Americans to help the French repel the Germans in the battles of Château-Thierry and Belleau Wood (see Map 22.2).

American reinforcements now began to arrive in large numbers. Slowly they worked their way to the front through the clogged French transportation system. Augmented by American troops, the Allied forces brought the German offensive to a halt in mid-July. The counteroffensive began with a successful campaign to drive the Germans back from the Marne. In mid-September 1918, American and French troops led by General Pershing forced the Germans to retreat at St. Mihiel (see American Voices, "Trench Warfare"). The last major assault of the war began on September 26, when Pershing pitted over a million American soldiers against vastly outnumbered and exhausted German troops. The Meuse-Argonne campaign pushed the enemy back across the Selle River near Verdun and broke the German defenses, at a cost of over 26,000 American lives.

World War I ended on November 11, 1918, when German and Allied representatives signed an armistice in the railway car of Marshal Ferdinand Foch of France. The flood of American troops and supplies during the last six months of the war had helped secure the Allied victory. The nation's decisive contribution signaled a shift in international power as European diplomatic and economic dominance declined and the United States emerged as a world leader.

About 2 million American soldiers were in France at the war's end. Two-thirds of them had seen action at least briefly on the Western Front, but most had escaped the horrors of sustained trench warfare that sapped the morale of Allied and German

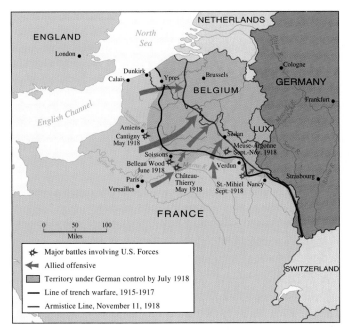

M A P 22.2
U.S. Participation on the Western Front, 1918

When American troops reached the European front in significant numbers in 1918, the Allied and Central Powers had been grinding each other down in a war of attrition for almost four years. The influx of American troops and supplies broke the stalemate. Successful offensive maneuvers by the American Expeditionary Force included those at Belleau Wood and Château-Thierry, and the Meuse-Argonne campaign.

troops. During the eighteen months in which the United States fought, 48,000 American servicemen were killed in action or died from wounds. Another 27,000 died from other causes, mainly the influenza epidemic that swept the world in 1918 and 1919. But the nation's casualties were minimal compared with the 8 million soldiers lost by the Allies and Central Powers. The French lost far more soldiers in the siege of Verdun than the United States did in the entire war.

After the armistice the war lived on in the minds of the men and women who had gone "over there." Many members of the AEF, especially those who had been spared the horror of sustained battle, experienced the war more as tourists than as soldiers. Before joining the army, most had barely traveled beyond their hometowns; for them the journey across the ocean was a monumental, once-in-a-lifetime event. Their letters described "old cathedrals, chateaux and ancient towns . . . quite wonderful . . . to eyes so accustomed to the look of the New World." In 1919 a group of former AEF officers formed the American Legion, "to preserve the memories and incidents of our association in the great war." The word *legion* captured the

AMERICAN VOICES

Trench Warfare

WILLIAM L. LANGER

Sergeant William L. Langer, of Battery E, 1st Gas Regiment, describes the effort to work through the trenches to get to the front lines to set up devices for launching bombs at the Germans at the battle of St. Mihiel in September 1918.

There was not much activity in the trenches, certainly not enough to give reason to suppose that a large scale attack was about to start. The enemy, to be sure, kept up his Vérey lights and fired at intervals. Still, most of us were quite startled and surprised when, about 1:00 in the morning, the sky lit up behind us and the American barrage began. . . .

After depositing our loads at the position we started back for another. . . . And going back was quite a different proposition than going, for, as if by magic, the trenches had filled with men, most of them Marines . . . and troops of the 9th Infantry . . . who were to go over the top with the first wave. Those rows of cold, shivering men, equipped with grenades and with bayonets fixed, crouching in the mud of the trenches and waiting for the crucial moment, is another sight we shall never forget. . . .

We were just about to start back for the trenches [with a second load of bombs] when the Boche suddenly opened up with a concentrated bombardment of the town. Everywhere the shells were bursting. For a moment we were undecided, but then we set out on a run. . . . We reached the trenches without mishap. The first wave was just about to go over, and our machine guns had just opened a rolling barrage to precede it. For green men it was a novel experience—this stuttering breathless chatter of the machine guns behind one. The trenches were in places so congested that to get through would have been impossible had we not struck on a rather clever idea. "Heads up, men, high explosives, watch these sacks";—shouting words to that effect worked like magic and we secured an easy passage.

SOURCE: Frank Freidel, *Over There: The Story of America's First Great Overseas Crusade* (McGraw-Hill, rev. ed. 1990), 127–28.

romantic, almost chivalric memories many veterans held of their wartime service. Only later did disillusionment over the contested legacy of World War I set in.

For African Americans, the war experience had never been very romantic. Encouraged by black leaders to enlist as a means of proving their loyalty and achieving first-class citizenship, black soldiers instead suffered continued discrimination. Placed in segregated units under white officers, they served in the most menial positions as laborers, stevedores, and messboys. Many African Americans emerged from the war determined to stand up for their rights and contributed to a spirit of black militancy that characterized the early 1920s.

Portrait of a Corporal

Black soldiers such as this corporal in the 15th New York Infantry received segregated and unequal treatment at every level of military service. Yet their pride in serving their country remained strong, as this 1918 painting by Raymond Desvarraus suggests.

(West Point Museum, United States Military Academy, West Point, NY)

War on the Home Front

Fighting World War I required extraordinary economic mobilization on the home front in which corporations, workers, and the general public all cooperated. Although the federal government did expand its power and presence during the emergency, the watchword was voluntarism. The government avoided compulsion as much as possible. Ambivalence about expanding state power, coupled with the pressures of wartime mobilization, severely damaged the impetus for progressive reforms that had characterized the prewar era. Yet even in the context of international crisis, some reformers expected that the war could serve the cause of improving American society.

MOBILIZATION

The continuing impact of the prewar progressive reform movement was evident in the financing of the war, the cost of which would eventually mount to $33 billion. The government paid for the war in part by using the Federal Reserve System established in 1913 (see Chapter 20) to expand the money supply, making it easier to borrow money. Two-thirds of the funds came from loans, especially the popular liberty bonds. Treasury Secretary William McAdoo encouraged the small, heavily advertised bond sales as a way of widening support for the war and demonstrating the voluntary self-sacrifice of the nation's citizenry. To augment the funds raised by bonds, McAdoo increased the federal income tax. Income taxes had been instituted by Congress after the passage of the Sixteenth Amendment to the Constitution in 1913. Now the War Revenue Bills of 1917 and 1918 transformed the tax into the foremost method of federal fund raising. The Wilson administration took a progressive approach, rejecting a tax on all wages and salaries in favor of a tax on corporations and wealthy individuals. The excess-profits tax signaled a direct and unprecedented intrusion of the state into the workings of corporate capitalism. By 1918 U.S. corporations were paying over $2.5 billion in excess-profits taxes per year—more than half of all federal taxes.

The revenue bills should not mask the fact that the federal government for the most part took a collaborative rather than a coercive approach to big business during the war. To the dismay of many progressives who had hoped that the war emergency would increase federal regulation of business, the government suspended antitrust laws to encourage cooperation and promote efficiency. For economic expertise the administration turned to those who knew the capacities of the economy best—the nation's business leaders. Executives flocked to Washington, where they served with federal officials on a series of boards and agencies that sought a middle ground between total state control of the economy and total freedom for business.

The central agency for mobilizing wartime industry was the War Industries Board (WIB), established in July 1917. In March 1918, after a fumbling start that showed the limits of voluntarism in a national emergency, the Wilson administration reorganized the board under the direction of Bernard Baruch, a Wall Street financier. The WIB produced an unparalleled expansion of the federal government's economic powers: it allocated scarce resources, gathered economic data and statistics, controlled the flow of raw materials, ordered the conversion from peacetime to war production, set prices, imposed efficiency and standardization procedures, and coordinated purchasing. Though the board had the authority to compel compliance, Baruch preferred to win voluntary cooperation by industry, often through personal intervention. Business generally supported this governmental oversight because it coincided with its own interests in improving efficiency and productivity. Despite higher taxes, corporate profits soared, aided by the suspension of antitrust laws and the institution of price guarantees for war work. War profits produced an economic boom that continued without interruption until 1920.

The reliance on voluntarism was best exemplified in the Food Administration, created in August 1917 and led by Stanford-trained engineer Herbert Hoover, who proposed to "mobilize the spirit of self-denial and self-sacrifice in this country." Using the slogan "Food will win the war," Hoover encouraged farmers to expand production of wheat and other grains from 45 million acres in 1917 to 75 million in 1919. Although the Food Administration issued reams of rules and regulations for producers and retailers, at no time did the government contemplate domestic food rationing. Rather, Hoover sent women volunteers from door to door to secure housewives' cooperation in observing "wheatless" Mondays, "meatless" Tuesdays, and "porkless" Thursdays and Saturdays—a campaign that resulted in substantial voluntary conservation of food resources.

In some instances, new federal agencies took dramatic, decisive action. In the face of the severe winter of 1917 to 1918, which led to coal shortages in northeastern cities and industries, the Fuel Administration ordered all factories east of the Mississippi River to shut down for four days. An even more striking example of the temporary use of federal power came in December 1917. When a massive railroad traffic snarl interfered with the transport of troops, the Railroad War Board, which coordinated the nation's sprawling transportation system, took over the railroads. Guaranteeing railroad owners a "standard return" equal to their average earnings between 1915 and 1917, the board promised that the carriers would be returned to private control no later than twenty-one months after the end of the war. Although reformers hoped to continue this experiment in government control on behalf of labor and consumers, the government fulfilled its pledge.

With the signing of the armistice in November 1918, the United States scrambled to dismantle wartime controls. Wilson, determined to "take the harness off," disbanded the WIB on January 1, 1919, resisting suggestions that the board would help stabilize the economy during demobilization. Like most Americans, Wilson could tolerate government planning power during an emergency but not as a permanent feature of the economy.

Although the nation's participation in the war lasted just eighteen months, it left an enduring legacy, the modern bureaucratic state. Entire industries had been organized as never before, linked to a maze of government agencies and executive departments. A modern system of income taxation had been established, with the potential for vastly increasing federal reserves. Finally, the collaboration between business and government had been mutually beneficial, teaching both partners a lesson they would put to use in state building in the 1920s and afterward.

Besides mobilizing armies and businesses to wage war, the federal government also needed to ensure a reliable workforce, especially in war industries. Acute labor shortages, caused by the demands of the draft, the abrupt decline in European immigration, and the urgency of war production, had enhanced workers' bargaining power. The National War Labor Board (NWLB), formed in April 1918, also helped to improve labor's position. Composed of representatives of labor, management, and the public, the NWLB established an eight-hour day for war workers, with time and a half for overtime, and endorsed equal pay for women workers. Workers were not allowed to disrupt war production through strikes or other disturbances. In return, the NWLB supported the workers' right to organize unions, required employers to deal with shop committees, and arbitrated labor disputes.

Wartime Opportunities

Women took on new jobs during the war, working as mail carriers, police officers, drill-press operators, and farm laborers attached to the Women's Land Army. These three women clearly enjoyed the camaraderie of working in a railroad yard in 1918. When the war ended, women usually lost such employment. (National Archives, photo by M. Rudolph Vetter)

AMERICAN VOICES
A Southern Migrant

*T*he Great Migration of southern African Americans to the cities of the North disrupted
  communities and families, but the migrants kept in touch with friends and kin through
letters and visits. While cities like Chicago offered new opportunities and experiences, as this
letter indicates, migrants often found churches that provided important continuity with their
southern past.

My dear Sister: I was agreeably surprised to hear from you and to hear from home. . . .
I got here in time to attend one of the greatest revivals in the history of my life—over 500
people joined the church. . . . It was snowing some nights and if you didnt hurry you could
not get standing room. Please remember me kindly to any who ask of me. The people are
rushing here by the thousands and I know if you come and rent a big house you can get
all the roomers you want. You write me exactly when you are coming. I am not keeping
house yet I am living with my brother and his wife. . . . I can get a nice place for you to
stop until you can look around and see what you want. I am quite busy. I work in Swifts
packing Co. in the sausage department. My daughter and I work for the same company—
We get $1.50 a day and we pack so many sausages we don't have much time to play but it
is a matter of a dollar with me and I feel that god made the path and I am walking therein.
    Tell your husband work is plentiful here and he wont have to loaf if he want to
work. . . . Well goodbye from your sister in Christ.

SOURCE: *Journal of Negro History*, vol. 4, no. 4, 1919, p. 457.

After years of federal hostility toward labor, the NWLB's actions brought a welcome change in labor's status and power. From 1916 to 1919 AFL membership grew
by almost 1 million workers, reaching over 3 million at the end of the war. Few of the
wartime gains lasted, however. Like other agencies, the NWLB was quickly disbanded.
Wartime inflation ate up most of the wage hikes, and a virulent postwar antiunion
movement caused a rapid decline in union membership that lasted into the 1930s.
    While the war emergency benefited labor, it had a special effect on workers who
were traditionally excluded from many industrial jobs. For the first time, northern
factories actively recruited African Americans, spawning the "Great Migration" from
the South. The lure of decent jobs was potent. As one Mississippi man said in an-
ticipation of working in northern meat-packing houses: "You could not rest in your
bed at night for thoughts of Chicago." Over 400,000 African Americans moved
northward to cities such as St. Louis, Chicago, New York, and Detroit during the
war. Though they encountered discrimination there as well, they found new opportunities and an escape from the repressive southern agricultural system (see
American Voices, "A Southern Migrant").

Mexican Americans in California, Texas, New Mexico, and Arizona also found new opportunities. Wartime labor shortages prompted many Mexican Americans to leave farm labor for industrial jobs in rapidly growing southwestern cities. Continuing political instability in Mexico following the revolution encouraged many Mexicans to relocate, temporarily or permanently, across the border, a process facilitated by newly opened railroad lines. At least 100,000 Mexicans entered the United States between 1917 and 1920, often settling in segregated neighborhoods (barrios) in urban areas, meeting discrimination similar to that faced by African Americans.

Women were the largest group to take advantage of new wartime opportunities. White women and, to a lesser degree, black and Mexican American women found that factory jobs usually reserved for men had been opened to them. About 1 million women joined the labor force for the first time, while many of the 8 million women who already held jobs switched from low-paying fields like domestic service to higher-paying industrial work. Americans soon got used to the sight of female streetcar conductors, train engineers, and defense workers. But everyone—including most working women—believed that those jobs would return to men after the war.

PROGRESSIVE REFORM IN WARTIME

Supporters of woman suffrage hoped that the war would reinvigorate reform. The National American Woman Suffrage Association (NAWSA) continued to lobby for the proposed woman suffrage amendment to the Constitution. It also threw the support of its 2 million members behind the Wilson administration, encouraging women to do their part to win the war. Women in communities all over the country labored exhaustively to promote food conservation, to protect children and women workers, and to distribute emergency relief through organizations like the Red Cross. Many agreed with Carrie Chapman Catt, president of NAWSA, that women's patriotic service could advance the cause of woman's suffrage.

Alice Paul and the National Woman's Party (NWP) took a more militant tack. To the dismay of NAWSA leaders, NWP militants began picketing the White House in July 1917 to protest their lack of the vote. Arrested and sentenced to seven months in jail, Paul and other women prisoners went on a hunger strike, which prison authorities met with forced feeding. Public shock at the women's treatment made them martyrs, drawing attention to the issue of woman's suffrage.

The combination of NWP's and NAWSA's policy of patient persuasion finally brought results. In January 1918 Woodrow Wilson withdrew his opposition to a federal woman suffrage amendment. The constitutional amendment quickly passed the House but took eighteen months to get through the Senate. Then came another year of hard work for ratification by the states. Finally, on August 26, 1920, Tennessee gave the Nineteenth Amendment the last vote it needed. The goal that had first been declared publicly at the Seneca Falls convention in 1848 was finally achieved seventy-two years later, in large part because of women's contributions to the war effort. The suffragists had posed a simple but effective moral challenge: how could the United States fight to make the world safe for democracy while denying half its citizens the right to vote?

Throughout the mobilization period, reformers pushed for a wide range of social reforms. In the name of army efficiency, or "keeping fit to fight," the federal government launched an ambitious campaign against sexually transmitted diseases, forcing the shutdown of "red-light" districts in cities with military training camps. With the cooperation of the YMCA and the YWCA, the government undertook a far-reaching sex education program, designed to enlighten both men and women about the dangers of sexual activity and the value of "social purity." Other reformers addressed the welfare of children, whom they characterized as the nation's most valuable resource. The Women's Council of National Defense, a voluntary organization with federal backing, proclaimed 1918 the year of the child, conducted a nationwide growth-monitoring program, and disseminated information about child health and nutrition. All of these idealistic crusaders described the war as just the start of a continuing battle for social welfare.

Especially active were temperance advocates, who viewed alcoholic beverages as the key social evil. In the early twentieth century, many Americans viewed the legal prohibition of alcohol as a progressive reform, not a denial of individual freedom. Urban reformers, concerned about good government, poverty, and public morality, supported a nationwide ban on drinking. The drive for Prohibition also had substantial backing in rural communities. Many people equated liquor with all the sins of the city: prostitution, crime, immigration, machine politics, and public disorder. The churches with the greatest strength in rural areas, including the Methodists, the Baptists, and the Mormons, also strongly condemned drinking. Protestants from rural areas dominated the membership of the Anti-Saloon League, which supplanted the Women's Christian Temperance Union as the leading proponent of Prohibition early in the century.

Temperance advocates were right in identifying cities as the sites of resistance to Prohibition. Alcoholic beverages, especially beer and whiskey, played an important role in the social life of certain ethnic cultures in the nation's heavily urbanized areas, especially those of German Americans and Irish Americans. Most saloons were in working-class neighborhoods and served as gathering places for workers. Machine politicians indeed conducted much of their business in bars. Thus many immigrants and working-class people opposed Prohibition, not only as an attack on drinking but as an attempt to impose middle-class cultural values on them.

Numerous states—mostly southern and midwestern states without a significant immigrant presence—already had prohibition laws, but World War I offered the impetus for national action. Because several major breweries had German names (Pabst and Busch, for example), beer drinking became unpatriotic in many people's minds. To conserve food, Congress prohibited the use of foodstuffs such as hops and barley in breweries and distilleries. Finally, in December 1917, Congress passed the Eighteenth Amendment, which would prohibit the "manufacture, sale, or transportation of intoxicating liquors." Ratified in 1919 and effective on January 16, 1920, the Eighteenth Amendment demonstrated the widening influence of the state in matters of personal behavior.

The Eighteenth Amendment was an example of how "progressive" reform efforts could benefit from the climate of war. But despite the stimulus the Great War gave to some types of reform, for the most part it blocked rather than furthered reforms. Though many Progressives had anticipated that the stronger federal presence in wartime would lead to stronger economic controls and corporate regulation, federal agencies were quickly disbanded once the war was over, reflecting the unease most Americans felt about a strong bureaucratic state. The wartime collaboration between government and business gave corporate leaders more influence in shaping the economy and government policy, not less.

PROMOTING NATIONAL UNITY

For the liberal reformers convinced that the war for democracy could promote a more just society at home, perhaps the most discouraging development was the campaign to promote "One Hundred Percent Americanism," which meant an insistence on conformity and an intolerance of dissent. It was Woodrow Wilson who had predicted what came to pass: "Once lead this people into war, and they'll forget there ever was such a thing as tolerance." But the president also recognized the need to manufacture support for the war. Ironically, his efforts to drum up support for the war themselves encouraged a repressive spirit hostile to reform.

In April 1917 Wilson formed the Committee on Public Information (CPI) to promote public support for the war. This government propaganda agency, headed by the journalist George Creel, quickly attracted progressive reformers and muckraking journalists. Professing lofty-sounding goals such as educating citizens about democracy, promoting national unity, assimilating immigrants, and breaking down the isolation of rural life, the committee also acted as a nationalizing force by promoting the development of a common ideology.

During the war the CPI touched the lives of practically every American. It distributed 75 million pieces of patriotic literature and sponsored speeches at local movie theaters, reaching cumulative audiences estimated at more than 300 million—three times the population of the United States at the time. In its zeal, the committee often ventured into hatemongering. In early 1918, for example, it encouraged speakers to use inflammatory stories of alleged German atrocities to build support for the war effort.

As a spirit of conformity pervaded the home front, many Americans found themselves targets of suspicion. Local businesses paid for newspaper and magazine ads that asked citizens to report to the Justice Department "the man who spreads pessimistic stories, cries for peace, or belittles our efforts to win the war." Posters encouraged Americans to be on the lookout for German spies. And quasi-vigilante groups such as the American Protective League mobilized about 250,000 self-appointed agents, furnished with badges issued by the Justice Department, to spy on neighbors and coworkers.

The CPI also urged ethnic groups to give up their Old World customs in the spirit of One Hundred Percent Americanism. German Americans bore the brunt of this campaign. In an orgy of hostility generated by propaganda about German militarism and atrocities, everything associated with Germany became suspect. German music, especially opera, was banished from the concert halls. Publishers removed pro-German references from textbooks, and many communities banned the teaching of the German language. Sauerkraut was renamed "liberty cabbage," and hamburgers were transformed into "liberty sandwiches." Though anti-German hysteria dissipated when the war ended, hostility toward the "hyphenated" American survived into the 1920s.

In law enforcement, officials tolerated little criticism of established values and institutions, as the suffragists picketing the White House during wartime had discovered. The main legal tools for curbing dissent were the Espionage Act of 1917 and the Sedition Act of 1918. The Espionage Act imposed stiff penalties for anti-war activities and allowed the federal government to ban treasonous materials from the mails. The postmaster general revoked the mailing privileges of groups considered to be radical, virtually shutting down their publications.

Individuals suffered as well. Because these acts defined treason and sedition loosely, they led to the conviction of more than a thousand people. The Justice Department focused particularly on socialists, who criticized the war and the draft, and on radicals like the Industrial Workers of the World (see Chapter 17), whose attacks on militarism threatened to disrupt war production in the western lumber and copper industries. Socialist party leader Eugene Debs was sentenced to ten years in jail for stating that the master classes declared war while the subject classes fought the battles. (Debs was pardoned by President Warren G. Harding in 1921.) Victor Berger, a Milwaukee socialist who had been jailed under the Espionage Act, was twice prevented from taking the seat to which he had been elected in the U.S. House of Representatives.

The courts rarely resisted these wartime excesses. In *Schenck v. United States* (1919), the Supreme Court upheld the conviction of the general secretary of the Socialist Party, Charles T. Schenck, who had been convicted of mailing pamphlets urging draftees to resist induction. In a unanimous decision, Justice Oliver Wendell Holmes ruled that an act of speech uttered under circumstances that would "create a clear and present danger to the safety of the country" could be constitutionally restricted. Because of the national war emergency, then, the Court upheld limits on freedom of speech that would not have been acceptable in peacetime. In wartime, the drive for conformity reigned, dashing reformers' optimistic hopes that war could be what philosopher John Dewey had called a "plastic juncture," in which the country would be more open to reason and progressive ideas.

An Unsettled Peace, 1919–1920

The war's end did not bring the tranquillity Americans had hoped for. Demobilization proceeded with little planning, in part because Wilson was so preoccupied with the peacemaking process. Spending only ten days in the United States between December 1918 and June 1919, for more than six months he was virtually an absentee president. Unfortunately, many urgent domestic issues demanded strong leadership that never emerged. In particular, racial, ethnic, and class tensions racked the nation as it attempted to adjust to a postwar order.

THE TREATY OF VERSAILLES

In January 1917 Woodrow Wilson had proposed a "peace without victory," since only a "peace among equals" could last. His goal was "not a balance of power, but a community of power; not organized rivalries, but an organized common peace." The keystone of Wilson's postwar plans was a permanent league of nations. But he would first have to win over a Senate that was Republican controlled and openly hostile to the treaty he had brought home.

President Wilson brought to the 1919 peace negotiations in France an almost missionary zeal. Confident in his own vision for a new world order, he believed that if necessary, "I can reach the peoples of Europe over the heads of their rulers." He scored an early victory when the Allies accepted his Fourteen Points as the basis for the peace negotiations that began in January 1919. In this blueprint for the postwar world, the president called for open diplomacy, "absolute freedom of navigation upon the seas," arms reduction, the removal of trade barriers, and an international commitment to national self-determination. Essential to Wilson's vision was the creation of a multinational organization "for the purpose of affording mutual guarantees of political independence and territorial integrity to great and small States alike." The League of Nations became Wilson's obsession.

The Fourteen Points were imbued with the spirit of progressivism. Widely distributed as propaganda during the final months of the war, Wilson's plan proposed to extend the ideals of America—democracy, freedom, and peaceful economic expansion—to the rest of the world. The League of Nations, acting as a kind of international Federal Trade Commission, would supervise disarmament and—according to the crucial Article X of its covenant—curb aggressor nations through collective military action. More grandiosely, Wilson anticipated that the League would mediate disputes between nations, preventing future wars, and thus ensuring that the Great War would be "the war to end all wars." By emphasizing these lofty goals, Wilson guaranteed disappointment: his ideals for world reformation were too far-reaching to be practical or attainable.

Twenty-seven countries sent representatives to the peace conference in Versailles, near Paris. Distrustful of the new Bolshevik regime in Russia and its call for proletarian revolution against capitalism and imperialism, the allies deliberately excluded its representatives. Nor was Germany invited. The Big Four—Wilson, Prime Minister David Lloyd George of Great Britain, Premier Georges Clemenceau of France, and Prime Minister Vittorio Orlando of Italy—did most of the negotiating. The three European leaders sought a peace that differed radically from Wilson's plan. They wanted to punish Germany and treat themselves to the spoils of war by demanding heavy reparations. In fact, before the war ended, Britain, France, and Italy had already made secret agreements to divide up the German colonies.

It is a tribute to Wilson that he managed to influence the peace settlement as much as he did. He was able to soften some of the harshest demands for reprisal against Germany. National self-determination, a fundamental principle of Wilson's Fourteen Points, bore fruit in the creation of the independent states of Austria, Hungary, Poland, Yugoslavia, and Czechoslovakia from the defeated empires of the Central Powers. The establishment of the new nations of Finland, Estonia, Lithuania, and Latvia not only upheld the principle of self-determination but also served Wilson's (and the Allies') desire to isolate Soviet Russia from the rest of Europe.

Wilson had less success in achieving other goals. He won only limited concessions regarding the colonial empires of the defeated powers. The old Central and Eastern European colonial empires were dismantled, but instead of becoming independent countries the colonies were assigned to victorious Allied nations to administer as trustees, a far cry from Wilson's ideal of national self-determination. Certain topics, such as freedom of the seas and free trade, never even appeared on the agenda because of Allied resistance. Finally, Wilson had only partial success in scaling back French and British demands for reparations from Germany, which eventually were set at $33 billion.

In the face of these disappointments, Wilson consoled himself with the negotiators' commitment to his proposed League of Nations. He acknowledged that the peace treaty had defects but expressed confidence that they could be resolved by a permanent international organization dedicated to the peaceful resolution of disputes.

On June 28, 1919, representatives gathered in the Hall of Mirrors at the Palace of Versailles to sign the peace treaty. Wilson sailed home to a public enthusiastic about a league of nations in principle. Major newspapers and the Federal Council of Churches of Christ of America supported the treaty, and even an enemy of the proposed League, Henry Cabot Lodge, acknowledged that "[T]he people of the country are very naturally fascinated by the idea of eternal preservations of the world's peace."

But by the time Wilson presented the treaty to the Senate on July 10, it was clear that the treaty was in trouble, with support in the Senate being far short of the two-thirds vote necessary for ratification. Wilson had not paid much attention to the political realities of building support for the League of Nations and the treaty in the Senate. He had failed to include a prominent Republican in the American commission that represented the United States at Versailles. Stubbornly convinced of his own rectitude and ability, he had kept the negotiations firmly in his own hands. When the Senate balked at the treaty, Wilson adamantly refused to compromise. "I shall consent to nothing," he told the French ambassador. "The Senate must take its medicine."

The Senate, however, did not oblige. And despite the president's attempt to make the 1918 congressional elections a referendum for his peace plans, Americans returned a Republican majority to Congress. Wilson and the League faced stiff opposition in the Senate. Some progressive senators, who endorsed the idea of American internationalism, felt that the peace agreement was too conservative, that it served to "validate existing empires" of the victorious Allies. The "irreconcilables," including progressive senators William E. Borah of Idaho, Hiram W. Johnson of California, and Robert M. La Follette of Wisconsin, disagreed fundamentally with the premise of permanent U.S. participation in European affairs. More influential was a group of Republicans led by Senator Henry Cabot Lodge of Massachusetts. They proposed a list of amendments that focused on Article X, the section of the League covenant that called for collective security measures when a member nation was attacked. This provision, they argued, would restrict Congress's constitutional authority to declare war and would limit the freedom of the United States to pursue a unilateral foreign policy.

Wilson refused to budge, especially not to placate Lodge, his hated political rival. Hoping to mobilize support for the treaty, in September 1919 the president launched an extensive speaking tour during which he brought large audiences to tears with his impassioned defense of the treaty. But the tour had to be cut short when the ailing sixty-two-year-old president collapsed in Pueblo, Colorado, late in September. One week later, in Washington, Wilson suffered a severe stroke that paralyzed one side of his body. While his wife, Edith Bolling Galt Wilson, his physician, and the various cabinet heads oversaw the routine business of government, Wilson slowly recovered, but he was never the same again.

From his sickbed, Wilson remained inflexible in his refusal to compromise, ordering Democratic senators to vote against all Republican amendments. The treaty came up for a vote in November 1919 but was not ratified. When another attempt in March 1920 fell seven votes short, the issue was dead. Wilson died in 1924, "as much a victim of the war," David Lloyd George noted, "as any soldier who died in the trenches."

The United States never ratified the Versailles treaty or joined the League of Nations. Many wartime issues were only partially resolved, notably Germany's future, the fate of the colonial empires, and rising nationalist demands for self-determination. These unsolved problems played a major role in the coming of World War II; some, like the competing ethnic nationalisms in the Balkans, remain unresolved today.

RACIAL STRIFE AND LABOR UNREST

Shortly after the end of the war, an author in the popular periodical *World's Work* observed that "the World War has accentuated all our differences. It has not created those differences, but it has revealed and emphasized them." Nowhere was this more evident than in race relations. Many African Americans emerged from the war determined to stand up for their rights and they contributed to a spirit of black militancy that characterized the early 1920s. The volatile mix of black migration and blacks' raised expectations as a result of service in World War I combined to exacerbate white racism. In the South the number of lynchings rose from forty-eight in 1917 to seventy-eight in 1919. Several African American men were lynched while wearing military uniforms. In the North, race riots broke out in more than twenty-five cities, with one of the first and most deadly occurring in 1917 in East St. Louis, Illinois, where nine whites and more than forty blacks died in a conflict sparked by competition over jobs at a defense plant.

By the summer of 1919, the death toll from racial violence had reached 120. One of the worst race riots in American history took place in Chicago in July, where five days of rioting left twenty-three blacks and fifteen whites dead. A variety of tensions were at work in cities where violence erupted. Black voters often determined the winners of close elections, thereby enraging white racists who resented black political influence. Blacks also competed with whites for jobs and scarce housing. Even before the July riot, blacks in Chicago had suffered the bombing of their homes and other forms of harassment. They did not sit meekly by as whites destroyed their neighborhoods: they fought back in self-defense and for their rights as citizens. Wilson's rhetoric about democracy and self-determination had raised their expectations, too.

Workers of all races harbored similar hopes for a better life after the war. The war years had brought them higher pay, shorter hours, and better working conditions. Yet many native-born Americans continued to identify unions with radicalism and foreigners, and soon after the armistice many employers resumed their attacks on union activity. In addition, rapidly rising inflation—in 1919 the cost of living was 77 percent higher than its prewar level—threatened to wipe out workers' wage increases. Nevertheless, workers hoped to hold onto and perhaps even expand their wartime gains.

The result of workers' determination—and employers' resistance—was a dramatic wave of strikes. More than 4 million workers—one in every five—went on strike in 1919, a proportion never since equaled. The year began with a walkout by shipyard workers in Seattle, a strong union town. Their action spread into a general strike that crippled the city. Another hard-fought strike disrupted the steel industry when 350,000 steel workers demanded union recognition and an end to twelve-hour shifts and the seven-day workweek. And in the fall the Boston police force shocked many Americans by going on strike. Governor Calvin Coolidge of

Massachusetts propelled himself into the political spotlight by declaring, "There is no right to strike against the public safety by anybody, anywhere, any time." Coolidge fired the entire police force, and the strike failed. The public supported this harsh reprisal, and Coolidge was rewarded with the Republican vice presidential nomination in 1920.

THE RED SCARE

A crucial factor in organized labor's failure to win many of its strikes in the postwar period was the pervasive fear of radicalism. This concern coincided with mainstream Americans' long-standing anxiety about unassimilated immigrants—an anxiety that the war had made worse. The Russian Revolution of 1917 so alarmed the Allies that Wilson sent several thousand troops to Russia in the summer of 1918 in hopes of weakening the Bolshevik regime. When the Bolsheviks founded the Third International (or Comintern) in 1919 to export communist doctrine throughout the world, American fears deepened. As domestic labor unrest increased, Americans began to see radicals everywhere. Hatred of the German Hun was quickly replaced by hostility toward the Bolshevik Reds.

Ironically, as public concern about domestic Bolshevism increased, radicals were rapidly losing members and political power. No more than 70,000 Americans belonged to either the fledgling U.S. Communist Party or the Communist Labor Party in 1919. Both the IWW and the Socialist Party had been weakened by wartime repression and internal dissent. Yet the public and the press continued to blame almost every disturbance, especially labor conflicts, on alien radicals. "REDS DIRECTING SEATTLE STRIKE—TO TEST CHANCE FOR REVOLUTION," warned a typical newspaper headline.

Tensions mounted with a series of bombings in the early spring. "The word 'radical' in 1919," the historian Robert Murray observed, "automatically carried with it the implication of dynamite." In June a bomb detonated outside the Washington townhouse of the recently appointed attorney general, A. Mitchell Palmer. His family escaped unharmed, but the bomber was blown to bits. Angling for the presidential nomination, Palmer capitalized on the event, fanning fears of domestic radicalism.

In November 1919, on the second anniversary of the Russian Revolution, the attorney general staged the first of what became known as "Palmer raids." Federal agents stormed the headquarters of radical organizations, capturing supposedly revolutionary booty such as a set of blueprints for a phonograph (at first thought to be sketches for a bomb). The dragnet pulled in thousands of aliens who had committed no crime but were suspect because of their anarchist or revolutionary beliefs or their immigrant backgrounds. Lacking the protection of U.S. citizenship, they faced deportation without formal trial or indictment. In December 1919 the U.S.S. *Buford,* nicknamed the "Soviet Ark," embarked for Finland and the Soviet state with a cargo of 294 deported radicals.

The peak of Palmer's power came with his New Year's raids in January 1920. In one night, with the greatest possible publicity, federal agents rounded up 6,000 radicals, invading private homes, union headquarters, and meeting halls and arresting citizens and aliens alike. Palmer was riding high in his ambitions for the presidency, but then he overstepped himself. He predicted that on May Day 1920 an unnamed conspiracy would attempt to overthrow the U.S. government. State militia units and police went on twenty-four-hour alert to guard the nation against the threat of revolutionary violence, but not a single incident occurred. As the summer of 1920 passed without major labor strikes or renewed bombings, the hysteria of the Red Scare began to abate.

The wartime legacy of antiradicalism and anti-immigrant sentiment, however, persisted well into the next decade. In May 1920, at the height of the Red Scare, Nicola Sacco, a shoemaker, and Bartolomeo Vanzetti, a fish peddler, were arrested for the robbery and murder of a shoe company's paymaster in South Braintree, Massachusetts. The two men, self-proclaimed anarchists and alien draft evaders, were both armed at the time of their arrest.

Convicted in 1921, Sacco and Vanzetti sat on death row for six years while supporters appealed their verdicts. Although new evidence suggesting their innocence surfaced, Judge Webster Thayer denied a motion for a new trial. Scholars still debate the question of their guilt, but most agree that the two anarchists did not receive a fair trial, that both the evidence and procedures were tainted. The verdict stemmed as much from their status as radicals and immigrants as it did from evidence. As future Supreme Court jurist Felix Frankfurter said at the time, "The District Attorney invoked against them a riot of political passion and patriotic sentiment." Nevertheless, shortly before his execution in the electric chair on August 23, 1927, Vanzetti claimed triumph:

> If it had not been for these thing, I might have live out my life among scorning men. I might have die, unmarked, unknown, a failure. . . . Never in our full life can we hope to do such work for tolerance, for justice, for man's understanding of man, as now we do by an accident.

This oft-quoted elegy captures the eloquence and tolerance of a man caught in the last spasm of antiradicalism and fear that capped America's participation in the Great War.

That participation left other legacies as well. World War I did not have the catastrophic effect on the United States that it did on European countries. With relatively few casualties and no physical destruction at home, America emerged from the conflict stronger than ever before. Consolidating developments that had begun with the Spanish-American War, the United States became a major international power, both economically and politically. Increased efficiency and technological advancements fostered exceptional industrial productivity, making the United States the envy of the rest of the world in the postwar decade. And though mobilization

TIMELINE

1914	Outbreak of war in Europe		Armistice ends war.
	United States declares neutrality.		U.S. troops intervene in Russia.
1915	German submarine sinks *Lusitania*.	1919	Treaty of Versailles
			Chicago race riot
1916	Woodrow Wilson reelected president		Steel strike
1917	U.S. enters World War I.		Red Scare and Palmer raids
	Selective Service Act passed		*Schenck v. United States*
	War Industries Board established		American Legion founded
	Suffrage militancy		League of Nations defeated in Senate
	East St. Louis race riot		Eighteenth Amendment (Prohibition)
	Espionage Act passed		ratified
	Bolshevik Revolution		War Industries Board disbanded
	Committee on Public Information established	1920	Nineteenth Amendment (woman suffrage)
1918	Wilson proposes Fourteen Point peace plan.		Sacco and Vanzetti arrested
	Meuse-Argonne campaign	1924	Woodrow Wilson dies.
	Eugene Debs imprisoned under Sedition Act		

was accompanied by an insistence on as much voluntarism as possible, the war emergency did leave a legacy of a stronger federal government and an enlarged bureaucracy. Finally, the war—especially the nationalism that accompanied it—contributed to a climate that was inhospitable to liberal social reforms, a climate that would persist until the crisis of the Great Depression.

For Further Exploration

Meirion Harries and Susie Harries, *The Last Days of Innocence: America at War, 1917–1918* (1997), is a recent overview that admirably captures America's war experience at home and abroad. Frank Freidel, *Over There: The Story of America's First Great Overseas Crusade* (1990), offers soldiers' vivid firsthand accounts of the war. William M. Tuttle Jr., *Race Riot: Chicago in the Red Summer of 1919* (1970), provides a moving and thoughtful analysis of that devastating riot, as well as a good summary of the "Great Migration" of African Americans. For the war in fiction begin with William March, *Company K* (1993), and Ernest Hemingway's *In Our Time* (1925) and *A Farewell to Arms* (1929). *Pale Horse, Pale Rider* (1939) by Katherine Anne Porter offers insight to the war on the homefront.

The Library of Congress website, "American Leaders Speak: Recordings from World War I and the 1920 Election," available at <http://memory.loc.gov/ammem/nfhome.html>, offers voice recordings of John J. Pershing and other key figures of the World War I era. "The

Diary of Bugler Benjamin Edgar Cruzan," Battery F, 341st Field Artillery, 89th Division, 3rd Army, in which an ordinary soldier poignantly discusses his battle experiences, friendships, and the peace negotiations, is provided at <http://www2.mo-net.com/~mcruzan/diary .htm>. "World War I Documents Archive" at <http://www.lib.byu.edu/~rdh/wwi> provides extensive primary documents as well as a series of World War I links. The Public Broadcasting Service's "The Great War and the Shaping of the Twentieth Century" at <http://www.pbs.org/greatwar/index.html> is a companion to the documentary series. Its rich offerings, which emphasize the European context of the war, include bibliographies and maps.

Chapter 23

MODERN TIMES
The 1920s

> Modern life is everywhere complicated, but especially so in the
> United States. . . . The tendency to seize upon new types of
> machines, rich natural resources and vast driving power, have
> hurried us dizzily away from the days of the frontier into a whirl of
> modernisms which almost passes belief.
>
> —REPORT OF THE PRESIDENT'S COMMISSION
> ON RECENT SOCIAL TRENDS, 1933

In 1924 the sociologists Robert Lynd and Helen Merrell Lynd arrived in
Muncie, Indiana, to study the life of a small American city. They observed how the
citizens of Middletown (the fictional name they gave the city) made a living, maintained a home, educated their young, practiced their religion, organized community
activities, and spent their leisure time. As the Lynds' fieldwork proceeded, they were
struck by how much had changed over the past thirty-five years—the lifetime of a
middle-aged Middletown resident—and decided to contrast the Muncie of the 1890s
with the Muncie of the 1920s. When *Middletown* was published in 1929, this "study
in modern American culture" became an unexpected best seller. Its success spoke to
Americans' desire to understand the forces that were transforming their society.

This transformation had begun with World War I. The United States emerged
from the war as a powerful modern state and a major player in the world economy.
The 1920s, however, rather than World War I were the watershed in the development of a mass national culture. Only then did the Protestant work ethic and the
old values of self-denial and frugality begin to give way to the fascination with consumption, leisure, and self-realization that is the essence of modern American culture. In economic organization, political outlook, and cultural values, the 1920s had
more in common with the United States today than with the industrializing America
of the late nineteenth century.

Business-Government Partnership of the 1920s

The business-government partnership fostered by World War I continued on an informal basis throughout the 1920s. As the *Wall Street Journal* enthusiastically proclaimed, "Never before, here or anywhere else, has a government been so completely

662

fused with business." From 1922 to 1929 the nation's prosperity seemed to confirm the economy's ability to regulate itself with minimal government intervention. Gone or at least submerged was the reform impulse of the Progressive Era. Business leaders were no longer villains but respected public figures. President Warren G. Harding captured the prevailing political mood when he offered the American public "not heroics but healing, not nostrums but normalcy."

POLITICS IN THE REPUBLICAN "NEW ERA"

Except for Woodrow Wilson's two terms, the Republican Party had controlled the presidency since 1896. When Wilson's progressive coalition floundered in 1918, the Republicans had a chance to regain the White House. With the ailing Wilson out of the picture, in the 1920 election the Democrats nominated Governor James M. Cox of Ohio for president and Assistant Secretary of the Navy Franklin D. Roosevelt as vice president. The Democratic platform called for U.S. participation in the League of Nations and a continuation of Wilson's progressivism. The Republicans, led by Warren G. Harding and Calvin Coolidge, promised a return to "normalcy," which meant a strong probusiness stance and conservative cultural values. Harding and Coolidge won in a landslide, marking the beginning of a Republican dominance that would last until 1932.

Central to what Republicans termed the "New Era" was business-government cooperation. Although Republican administrations generally opposed expanding state power to promote progressive reforms, they had no qualms about using federal policy and power to assist corporations. Thus, Harding's secretary of the treasury, financier Andrew W. Mellon, engineered a tax cut that undercut the wartime Revenue Acts, benefiting wealthy individuals and corporations. The Republican-dominated Federal Trade Commission (FTC) for the most part ignored the antitrust laws rather than using federal power to police industry. In this the Commission followed the lead of the Supreme Court, which in 1920 had dismissed the long-pending antitrust case against U.S. Steel, ruling that largeness in business was not against the law as long as some competition remained.

Perhaps the best example of government-business cooperation emerged in the Department of Commerce, headed by Herbert Hoover, who was a believer in what historian Ellis Hawley has called the "associative state." Hoover thought that with the offer of government assistance, businessmen would voluntarily work in behalf of the public interest, thereby benefiting the entire country. Under Hoover the Commerce Department expanded dramatically, offering new services like the compilation and distribution of trade and production statistics to American business. It also assisted private trade associations in their efforts to rationalize and make more efficient major sectors of industry and commerce by cooperating in such areas as product standardization and wage and price controls.

Unfortunately, not all government-business cooperation was as high-minded as Hoover had anticipated. President Harding was basically an honest man, but some of his political associates were not. When Harding died suddenly of a heart attack in San Francisco in August 1923, evidence of widespread fraud and corruption in his administration had just come to light. In 1924 a particularly damaging scandal concerned the secret leasing of government oil reserves in Teapot Dome, Wyoming, and in Elk Hills, California, without competitive bidding. Secretary of the Interior Albert Fall was eventually convicted of taking $300,000 in bribes; he became the first cabinet officer in American history to serve a prison sentence.

After Harding's death the taciturn vice president, Calvin Coolidge, moved into the White House. In contrast to his predecessor's political cronyism and outgoing style, Coolidge personified an austere rectitude. As vice president "Silent Cal" often sat through official functions without uttering a word. A dinner partner once challenged him by saying, "Mr. Coolidge, I've made a rather sizable bet with my friends that I can get you to speak three words this evening." Responded Coolidge icily, "You lose." Although Coolidge was quiet and unimaginative, his image of unimpeachable integrity reassured voters, and he soon announced his candidacy for the presidency in 1924.

When the Democrats gathered that July in the sweltering heat of New York City, they faced a divided party that drew its support mainly from the South and from northern urban political machines like Tammany Hall in New York. These two constituencies often collided. They disagreed mightily over Prohibition, immigration restriction, and most seriously the mounting power of the racist and anti-immigrant Ku Klux Klan. The resolutions committee remained deadlocked for days over whether the party should condemn the Klan, eventually reaching a weak compromise that affirmed its general opposition to "any effort to arouse religious or racial dissension."

With this contentious background, the convention took 103 ballots to nominate John W. Davis, a Wall Street lawyer, for the presidency. To attract rural voters, the Democrats chose as their vice presidential candidate Governor Charles W. Bryan of Nebraska, William Jennings Bryan's brother. But the Democrats could not mount an effective challenge to their more popular and better-financed Republican rivals, whose strength came chiefly from the native-born Protestant middle class, augmented by small-business people, skilled workers, farmers, northern blacks, and wealthy industrialists. Until the Democrats could overcome their sectional and cultural divisions and build an effective national organization to rival that of the Republicans, they would remain a minority party.

The 1924 campaign also featured a third-party challenge by Senator Robert M. La Follette of Wisconsin, who ran on the Progressive Party ticket. La Follette's candidacy mobilized reformers and labor leaders as well as disgruntled farmers in an effort to reinvigorate the reform movement both major parties had abandoned. Their platform called for nationalization of railroads, public ownership of utilities, and the right of Congress to overrule Supreme Court decisions. It also favored the direct election of the president by the voters rather than by indirect election through the electoral college.

In an impressive Republican victory Coolidge received 15.7 million popular votes to Davis's 8.4 million and won a decisive margin in the electoral college. La Follette chalked up almost 5 million popular votes, but he carried only Wisconsin in the electoral college. Perhaps the most significant aspect of the election was the low voter turnout. Only 52 percent of the electorate cast their ballots in 1924, compared to more than 70 percent in presidential elections of the late nineteenth century. Newly enfranchised women voters were not to blame, however; a long-term drop in voting by men, rather than apathy among women, caused the decline.

Instead of resting after their suffrage victory, women increased their political activism in the 1920s. African American women struggled for voting rights in the Jim Crow South and pushed unsuccessfully for a federal antilynching law. Many women tried to break into party politics, but Democrats and Republicans granted them only token positions on party committees. Women were more influential as lobbyists. The Women's Joint Congressional Committee, a Washington-based coalition of ten major white women's organizations, including the newly formed League of Women Voters, lobbied actively for reform legislation (see American Voices, "Women Get the Vote"). Its major accomplishment was the passage in 1921 of the Sheppard-Towner Federal Maternity and Infancy Act, which appropriated $1.25 million for well-baby clinics, educational programs, and visiting-nurse projects. Such major reform legislation was rare in the 1920s, however, and its success short-lived. Once politicians realized that women did not vote as a bloc, they stopped listening to the women's lobby, and in 1929 Congress cut off the act's funding.

The roadblocks women activists faced were part of a broader public antipathy to ambitious reforms. Although some states—such as New York, where an urban liberalism was coalescing under leaders like Al Smith—did enact a flurry of legislation that promoted workmen's compensation, public health programs, and conservation measures, on the national level reforms that would strengthen federal power made little headway. After years of progressive reforms and an expanded federal presence in World War I, Americans were unenthusiastic about increased taxation or more governmental bureaucracy. The Red Scare had given ammunition to opponents of reform by making it easy to claim that legislation calling for governmental activism was the first step toward Bolshevism. The general prosperity of the 1920s further hampered the reform spirit. With a strong economy, the Republican policy of an informal partnership between business and government seemed to work and made reforms regulating corporations and the economy seem unnecessary and even harmful.

THE HEYDAY OF BIG BUSINESS

Although prosperity and the 1920s seem almost synonymous, the decade got off to a bumpy start in the transition from a wartime to a peacetime economy. In the immediate postwar years the nation suffered rampant inflation: prices jumped by a third in 1919, accompanied by feverish business activity. Federal efforts to halt

AMERICAN VOICES
Women Get the Vote
DAISY HARRIMAN AND EMILY NEWELL BLAIR

*I*n her autobiography, Daisy Harriman recounted the comments of another activist woman, Emily Newell Blair, about the difficulties of encouraging newly enfranchised women to vote. Both Blair and Harriman hoped to harness these potential new voters to promote a broad agenda of social reform and women's rights. Of particular concern, as this passage indicates, was the plight of working women.

Men and women are just alike, human beings with the same hopes and instincts, [yet] still we have to go on talking about "the woman vote" as though it were something separate, because we are all so interested in going after women who never have taken the slightest interest in politics, and in introducing them for the first time to the political sphere. And to do this, since most women work and live in "the home," one has to have a special organization to reach "women" as they bend over cradles and roll out the biscuits on the breadboard, as they darn Pa's socks or wash up the family dishes. Women are still separate, not only biologically, which doesn't count for so much in politics, but economically. They are the vast body of homeworkers, sometimes sweated and sometimes petted. The American wife is supposed to be a member of the great leisure-class and I suppose it is true that more American wives have more time to waste or to pursue culture than any other people in the world. . . . [But] of all statistics the ones that have impressed and shocked me the most are those that Margaret Hinchey, the laundry worker, once gave me,—that in New York alone more than 14,000 old women over sixty-five years of age are dependent upon their own labors for support. I suppose most of those 14,000 old women spent the best part of their lives doing domestic service for some man. I look forward to a time when women, even if they keep on at the old business of having for their main job the making of man comfortable, and themselves too,—sometimes, of course,—will use the vote in order to make the world a more pleasant place to be thrown on, and to work in, when their heads are gray and their joints stiff.

SOURCE: Mrs. J. Borden Harriman, *From Pinafores to Politics* (London: Allen & Unwin, [1923?]), p. 353.

inflation—through spending cuts and a contraction of the supply of credit—produced the recession of 1920 and 1921, the sharpest short-term downturn the United States had ever faced. Unemployment reached 10 percent. Foreign trade dropped by almost half as European nations resumed production after the disruptions of war. Prices fell dramatically—more than 20 percent—and reversed much of the wartime inflation.

The recession was short. In 1922, stimulated by an abundance of consumer products, particularly automobiles, the economy began a recovery that continued with only brief interruptions through 1929. Between 1922 and 1929 the gross national product (GNP) grew from $74.1 billion to $103.1 billion, approximately 40 percent. Per capita income rose from $641 in 1921 to $847 in 1929. Soon the federal government was recording a budget surplus. This economic expansion provided the backdrop for the partnership between business and government.

As industries churned out an abundance of new consumer products—cars, appliances, chemicals, electricity, radios, aircraft, and movies—manufacturing output expanded 64 percent. Behind the growth lay new techniques of management and mass production, which brought a 40 percent increase in workers' productivity. The demand for goods and services kept unemployment low in most industries throughout the decade. High employment rates, combined with low inflation, enhanced the spending power of many Americans, especially skilled workers and the middle class.

The economy, however, had some weaknesses. Income distribution reflected significant disparity: 5 percent of the nation's families received one-third of all income. In addition, a number of industries were unhealthy. Agriculture never fully recovered from the 1920 and 1921 recession. During the inflationary period of 1914 to 1920 farmers had borrowed heavily to finance mortgages and equipment in response to government incentives, increased demand, and rising prices. When the war ended, European countries resumed agricultural production, glutting the world market. The price of wheat dropped 40 percent as the government withdrew wartime price supports. Corn prices fell 32 percent, and hog prices 50 percent. Farmers were not the only ones whose incomes plunged. Certain "sick industries," such as coal and textiles, had also expanded in response to wartime demand, which dropped sharply at war's end. Their troubles foreshadowed the Great Depression of the 1930s.

But for the most part, despite these ominous signs, the nation was in a confident mood about the economy and the corporations that shaped it. Throughout the decade business leaders enjoyed enormous popularity and respect; their reputations often surpassed those of the era's lackluster politicians. The most revered businessman of the decade was Henry Ford, whose rise from poor farm boy to corporate giant embodied both the traditional value of individualism and the triumph of mass production. Success stories like Ford's prompted President Calvin Coolidge to declare solemnly, "The man who builds a factory builds a temple. The man who works there worships there."

In this apotheosis of big business the 1920s saw the triumph of the managerial revolution that had been reshaping American business since the late nineteenth century (see Chapter 17), as large-scale corporate organizations with bureaucratic structures of authority replaced family-run enterprises. There were more mergers in the 1920s than at any time since the flourishing of business combinations in the 1880s and 1890s, with the largest number occurring in rapidly growing industries like chemicals, electrical appliances, and automobiles. By 1930 the 200 largest corporations controlled almost half the nonbanking corporate wealth in the United States. Rarely did any single corporation monopolize an entire industry; instead, oligopolies, in which a few large producers controlled an industry, became the norm, as in auto manufacturing, oil, and steel. The nation's financial institutions expanded and consolidated along with its corporations. Total bank assets rose dramatically as mergers between Wall Street banks enhanced New York's role as the financial center of the world. In 1929 almost half the nation's banking resources were controlled by 1 percent of American banks (250 banks).

Most Americans benefited from corporate success in the 1920s. Although unskilled African Americans and immigrants participated far less fully in the prosperity of the decade, many members of the working class enjoyed higher wages and a better standard of living. A shorter workweek (five full days and a half day on Saturday) and paid vacations gave many more leisure time. But despite those benefits labor had less power in the workplace. Scientific management techniques, first introduced in 1895 by Frederick W. Taylor but widely implemented only in the 1920s, reduced workers' control over their labor.

The 1920s were also the heyday of "welfare capitalism," a system of labor relations that stressed management's responsibility for employees' well-being. At a time when unemployment compensation and government-sponsored pensions did not exist, large corporations offered workers stock plans, health insurance, and old-age pension plans. Employee security was not, however, the primary aim of the programs, which were established mainly to deter the formation of unions. The approach reflected the conservative values of the 1920s, which placed the responsibility for economic welfare in the private sector to avoid government interference on the side of labor. Coupled with an aggressive drive for what corporate leaders called the American Plan (or an open, nonunion shop) and with Supreme Court decisions that limited workers' ability to strike, welfare capitalism helped to erode the unions' strength. Membership dropped from 5.1 million in 1920 to 3.6 million in 1929—about 10 percent of the nonagricultural workforce—and the number of strikes also fell dramatically from the level in 1919. Technology and management had combined to undermine workers' power.

ECONOMIC POWER ABROAD

The power of American corporations emerged also in the international arena. During the 1920s the United States was the most productive country in the world, with an enormous capacity to compete in foreign markets that eagerly desired American consumer products such as radios, telephones, automobiles, and sewing machines. The demand for U.S. capital was just as great. American investment abroad more than doubled between 1919 and 1930: by the end of the 1920s American corporations had invested $15.2 billion in foreign countries. Soon the United States became the world's largest creditor nation, reversing its pre–World War I status as a debtor and causing a dramatic shift of power in the world's capital markets.

A wide variety of American companies aggressively sought investment opportunities abroad. General Electric built plants in Latin America, China, Japan, and Australia; Ford had major facilities throughout the British empire. The United Fruit Company developed plantations in Costa Rica, Honduras, and Guatemala. American capital ran sugar plantations in Cuba and rubber plantations in the Philippines, Sumatra, and Malaya. Standard Oil of New Jersey led American oil companies in acquiring oil reserves in Mexico and Venezuela.

American power abroad was also evident in the country's new role as a creditor nation. European countries, particularly Germany, needed American capital to

Bananas

... a good mixer
with every fruit that grows

Oranges, apples, grapefruit, pineapples, pears, melons, grapes—all these and many others—blend perfectly with bananas. The distinctive flavor of the banana, when added to a fruit cup, a fruit salad, or any fruit combination, brings out the flavor of the other fruits and makes them taste better.

"Ripe bananas are good for little children."

"EAT plenty of fresh fruits" is now an accepted principle of diet—and the mere sight of mellow, luscious bananas is an invitation to serve many delicious and nourishing fruit combinations.

All year round from the tropics ... Easter, Fourth of July, Thanksgiving, Christmas—every season, every day—bananas are available. Thanks to the nearness and all-year-round productiveness of the tropics, they always can be had at your grocery or fruit store.

Children crave the temptingly flavored banana instinctively. And it is well that they do, for bananas are one of the most important energy-producing foods. Doctors and dietitians consider the banana not only one of the most valuable foods, but also one of the most easily digested ... as beneficial for grown-ups as for children.

Serve bananas with other fruits, with cereals, with milk or cream ... or serve them plain. But always be sure they are fully ripe (generously flecked with brown spots). If they are not at the proper stage of ripeness when you buy them, let them ripen at room temperature. Never place them in the ice-box.

UNIFRUIT   BANANAS
Reg. U. S. Pat. Off.
A United Fruit Company Product
Imported and Distributed by Fruit Dispatch Company
17 Battery Place, New York, N. Y.

American Companies Abroad

United Fruit was one of the many American companies that found opportunities for investment in South America in the 1920s. Bananas were such a new and exotic fruit that advertisements had to tell consumers such facts as how to tell when bananas are ripe and how to store them (never refrigerate).

(Duke University Library, Special Collections)

finance their economic recovery following World War I. Germany had to rebuild its economy and pay reparations to the Allies; Britain and France had to repay wartime loans. As late as 1930 the Allies still owed the United States $4.3 billion. American political leaders, responding to voters' disenchantment with the cost of the war, rigidly demanded payment. "They hired the money, didn't they?" President Coolidge scoffed.

European countries had difficulty repaying their debts because the United States was maintaining high protective tariffs against foreign-made goods. The Fordney-McCumber Tariff of 1922 and the Hawley-Smoot Tariff of 1930 advanced the long-standing Republican policy of protectionism and economic nationalism. Most American manufacturers favored high tariffs because they feared foreign competition would reduce their profits. But the difficulty of selling goods in the United States hindered European nations' efforts to pay off their debts in dollars.

In 1924, at the prodding of the United States, the nations of France, Great Britain, and Germany joined with the United States in a plan to promote European financial stability. The Dawes Plan (named for Charles G. Dawes, the Chicago banker who negotiated the agreement) offered Germany substantial loans from American banks and a reduction in the amount of reparations owed to the Allies. But the Dawes Plan did not provide a permanent solution because the international economic system was inherently unstable. It depended on the flow of American capital to Germany, reparations payments from Germany to the Allies, and the repayment of the Allies' debts to the United States. If the outflow of capital from the United States were to slow or stop, the international financial structure could collapse.

American efforts to shore up the international economy belie the common view of U.S. foreign affairs as isolationist in the interwar period—as representing a time when the United States, disillusioned after World War I, willfully retreated from involvement in the rest of the world. In fact, the United States played an active role in world affairs during this period. Expansion into new markets was fundamental to the prosperity of the 1920s. U.S. officials ardently sought a stable international order to facilitate American investments in Latin American, European, and Asian markets.

They continued the quest for peaceful ways to dominate the Western Hemisphere both economically and diplomatically but retreated slightly from military intervention in Latin America. U.S. troops withdrew from the Dominican Republic in 1924 but remained in Nicaragua almost continuously from 1912 to 1933 and in Haiti from 1915 to 1934. Relations with Mexico remained tense, a legacy of U.S. intervention during the Mexican Revolution and of U.S. resentment over the Mexican government's efforts to wrest control of its oil and mineral deposits away from foreign owners, a policy that particularly alarmed American oil companies.

There was little popular or political support, however, for entangling diplomatic commitments to allies, European or otherwise. The United States never joined the League of Nations or the Court of International Justice (the World Court). International cooperation had to come through other forums, such as the 1921 Washington Naval Arms Conference. At that meeting, the leading naval powers—Britain, the United States, Japan, Italy, and France—agreed to halt construction of large battleships for ten years and to limit their future shipbuilding to a set ratio between the five nations of 5 to 5 to 3 to 1.75 to 1.75, respectively. By placing limits on naval expansion, policymakers hoped to encourage stability in areas like the Far East and to protect the fragile postwar economy from an expensive arms race. A thinly veiled agenda was to contain Japan, whose expansionist tendencies in Asia were alarming other nations.

Seven years later, in a similar spirit of international cooperation the United States joined other nations in condemning militarism through the Kellogg-Briand Peace Pact. Fifteen nations signed the pact in Paris in 1928; forty-eight more approved it later. The signatories agreed to "condemn recourse to war for the solution of international controversies, and renounce it as an instrument of national policy." U.S. peace groups such as the Women's International League for Peace and Freedom enthusiastically supported the pact, and the U.S. Senate ratified it eighty-five to one. Yet critics complained that it lacked mechanisms for enforcement, calling it nothing more than an "international kiss."

In the end, fervent hopes and pious declarations were no cure for the massive economic, political, and territorial problems created by World War I. U.S. policymakers vacillated, as they would in the 1930s, between wanting to play a larger role in world events and fearing that treaties and responsibilities would limit their ability to act unilaterally. Their diplomatic efforts ultimately proved inadequate to the mounting crises that followed in the wake of the war.

A New National Culture

The 1920s represented an important watershed in the development of a mass national culture. A new emphasis on leisure, consumption, and amusement characterized the era, although their benefits were more accessible to the middle class than to disadvantaged groups. Automobiles, paved roads, the parcel post service, movies, radios, telephones, mass-circulation magazines, brand names, chain stores—all linked mill towns in the southern Piedmont, rural outposts on the Oklahoma plains, and ethnic enclaves on the coasts in an expanding web of national experience. In fact, with the exportation of automobiles, radios, and movies to consumers throughout the world, the American experience became a global model.

A CONSUMER CULTURE

In homes across the country Americans sat down to a breakfast of Kellogg's corn flakes and toast from a General Electric toaster. Then they got into a Ford Model T to go about their business, perhaps shopping at one of the chain stores that had sprung up across the country, such as Safeway or A&P. In the evening the family gathered to listen to radio programs like *Great Moments in History* or to read the latest issue of the *Saturday Evening Post;* on weekends they might go to see the newest Charlie Chaplin film at the local theater. Millions of Americans, in other words, now shared similar daily experiences.

Yet participation in commercial mass culture was not universal, nor did it necessarily mean total conversion to mainstream values, as is often assumed. The historian Lizabeth Cohen concluded that "Chicago's ethnic workers were not transformed into more Americanized, middle-class people by the objects they consumed. Buying an electric vacuum cleaner did not turn Josef Dobrowolski into *True Story's* Jim Smith." What is more, the unequal distribution of income limited many consumers' ability to buy the enticing new products. At the height of the nation's prosperity in the 1920s about 65 percent of families had incomes of less than $2,000 a year, which barely supported a decent standard of living. Poor minority families in particular were isolated from the new consumerism. Many Americans stretched their incomes by buying on the newly devised install-ment plan: in 1927 two-thirds of the cars in the United States had been bought "on time." Once consumers saw how easily they could finance a car, they bought radios, refrigerators, and sewing machines on credit. "A dollar down and a dollar forever," one cynic remarked.

Many of the new products were household appliances made feasible by the rapid electrification of American homes. Such technological advances had a dra-matic impact on women's lives, for despite enfranchisement and participation in the workforce the primary role for most women continued to be that of housewife. Electric appliances made housewives' chores less arduous. Plugging in an electric iron was far easier than heating an iron on the stove; using a vacuum cleaner was quicker and easier than wielding a broom and a rug beater. Paradoxically, however, the new products did not dramatically increase women's leisure time. Instead, more middle-class housewives began to do their own housework and laundry, replacing human servants with electric ones. The new gadgets also raised standards of clean-liness, encouraging women to spend more time doing household chores.

Few of the new consumer products could be considered necessities. But the ad-vertising industry, which became big business in this period, spent billions of dol-lars annually to entice consumers into buying automobiles, cigarettes, radios, and refrigerators. Advertisers appealed to people's social aspirations by projecting im-ages of successful and elegant sophisticates who smoked a certain brand of ciga-rette or drove a recognizable make of car. Ad writers also sold products by preying on people's insecurities, coming up with a variety of socially unacceptable "dis-eases," from "office hips" and "ashtray breath" to the dreaded "B.O." (body odor).

Yet consumers were not merely passive victims. Advertisers recognized that the buying public made choices and struggled to offer messages that appealed to their targeted audiences. In the process they made consumption a cultural ideal for most of the middle class. Character, religion, and social standing, once the main criteria for judging self-worth, became less important than the gratification of personal needs through the acquisition of more and better possessions.

No possession typified the new consumer culture better than the automobile. "Why on earth do you need to study what's changing this country?" a Muncie, Indiana, resident asked the sociologists Robert and Helen Lynd. "I can tell you what's happening in just four letters: A-U-T-O!" The showpiece of modern capitalism, the automobile revolutionized the way Americans spent their money and leisure time. In the wake of the automobile the isolation of rural life broke down. Cars touched so many aspects of American life that the word *automobility* was coined to describe their impact on production methods, the landscape, and American values.

Mass production of cars stimulated the prosperity of the 1920s. Before the introduction of the moving assembly line in 1913, Ford workers took twelve and a half hours to put together an auto; on an assembly line they took only ninety-three minutes. By 1927 Ford was producing a car every twenty-four seconds. Auto sales climbed from 1.5 million in 1921 to 5 million in 1929, a year in which Americans spent $2.58

All in a Day's Work

Parked in the testing ground at Ford's huge River Rouge plant in Dearborn, Michigan, sit 1,000 assembled chassis, a single day's production. (From the Collections of the Henry Ford Museum and Greenfield Village)

billion on new and used cars. By the end of the decade Americans owned about 80 percent of the world's automobiles—an average of one car for every five people.

The success of the auto industry had a ripple effect on the American economy. In 1929, 3.7 million workers owed their jobs to the automobile, either directly or indirectly. Auto production stimulated the steel, petroleum, chemical, rubber, and glass industries. Highway construction became a billion-dollar-a-year enterprise, financed by federal subsidies and state gasoline taxes. Car ownership also spurred the growth of suburbs, contributed to real-estate speculation, and in 1924 spawned the first shopping center, Country Club Plaza in Kansas City. Not even the death of 25,000 people a year in traffic accidents—70 percent of them pedestrians—could dampen America's passion for the automobile.

The auto also changed the way Americans spent their leisure time. They took to the roads, becoming a nation of tourists. The American Automobile Association, founded in 1902, reported that in 1929 about 45 million people—almost a third of the population—took vacations by automobile, patronizing the "autocamps" and tourist cabins that were the forerunners of motels. And like movies and other products of the new mass culture, cars changed the dating patterns of young Americans. Contrary to many parents' views, premarital sex was not invented in the backseat of a Ford, but a Model T offered more privacy and comfort than did the family living room or the front porch and contributed to increased sexual experimentation among the young.

MASS MEDIA AND NEW PATTERNS OF LEISURE

Equal in importance to the automobile in transforming American culture were the increasingly significant mass media. The movie industry probably did more than anything else to disseminate common values and attitudes. In contrast to Europe where cinema developed as an avant-garde, highbrow art form, in America movies were part of popular culture almost from the start. They began around the turn of the century in nickelodeons, where for a nickel the mostly working-class audience could see a one-reel silent film like the spectacularly successful *The Great Train Robbery* (1903). Because the films, mostly comedies and melodramas, were silent, they could be understood by immigrants who did not speak English. Both democratic and highly lucrative, the new medium quickly became popular.

By 1910 the movie-making industry had concentrated in southern California, which had cheap land, plenty of sunshine, and varied scenery—mountains, deserts, cities, and the Pacific Ocean—within easy reach. Another attraction was Los Angeles's reputation as an antiunion town. By war's end the United States was producing 90 percent of the world's films. Foreign distribution of Hollywood films stimulated the market for the material culture so lavishly displayed on the screen.

As directors turned to feature films and began exhibiting them in large, ornate theaters, movies quickly outgrew their working-class audiences and began to appeal to the middle class. Early movie stars—the comedians Buster Keaton, Charlie

Chaplin, and Harold Lloyd; Mary Pickford ("America's Sweetheart," though born in Canada); and dashing leading men Douglas Fairbanks, Wallace Reid, and John Gilbert—became national idols who helped to set national trends in clothing and hairstyles. Then a new cultural icon, the flapper, burst on the scene to represent emancipated womanhood. Clara Bow, the It Girl (*It* represented "sex appeal"), was Hollywood's favorite flapper, a bobbed-haired "jazz baby" who rose to stardom almost overnight. Decked out in short skirt and rolled-down silk stockings, the flapper wore makeup (once assumed to be a sign of sexual availability in lower-class women), smoked, and danced to jazz, flaunting her liberated lifestyle. Like so many cultural icons, the flapper represented only a tiny minority of women. Yet the movies, along with advertising, mass-marketed this symbol of women's emancipation, suggesting it was the norm.

Movies became even more powerful cultural influences with the advent of the "talkies." Warner Brothers' *The Jazz Singer* (1927), starring Al Jolson, was the first feature-length film to offer sound. Two years later all the major studios had made

The Flapper

The flapper phenomenon was not limited to Anglos. This 1921 photograph of a young Mexican American woman shows how mainstream fads and fashions reached into Latino communities across the country.

(Arizona Historical Society)

the transition to talkies. By the end of the 1920s the nation had almost 23,000 movie theaters, including elaborate picture palaces built by the studios in major cities. Movie attendance rose from 60 million in 1927 to 90 million in 1930. In two short decades movies had become thoroughly entrenched as the most popular—and probably the most influential—form of urban-based mass media.

That the first talkie was *The Jazz Singer* was perhaps no coincidence. Jazz was such an important part of the new mass culture that the 1920s are often referred to as the Jazz Age. An improvisational style whose notes were (and are) rarely written down, jazz originated in the dance halls and bordellos of New Orleans around the turn of the century. A synthesis of African American music forms, such as ragtime and the blues, it also drew on African and European styles. Most of the early jazz musicians were blacks who brought to Chicago, New York, and other northern cities music that had originated in the South. Some of the best-known performers were the composer-pianist Ferdinand "Jelly Roll" Morton; the trumpeter Louis Armstrong; the singer Bessie Smith, the "Empress of the Blues"; and composer-bandleader Edward "Duke" Ellington. Phonograph records increased the appeal of jazz by capturing its spontaneity and distributing it to a wide audience; jazz, in turn, boosted the infant recording industry. Soon this uniquely American art form had caught on in Europe, especially in France. That jazz, which expressed black dissent in the face of mainstream white values, also appealed to white audiences signifies the role that African Americans played in shaping the contours of American popular culture.

Other forms of mass media also helped to establish national standards of taste and behavior. In 1922 ten magazines claimed a circulation of at least 2.5 million, including the *Saturday Evening Post,* the *Ladies' Home Journal, Collier's Weekly,* and *Good Housekeeping. Reader's Digest, Time,* and the *New Yorker,* still found today in homes throughout the country, all started publication in the 1920s. Tabloid newspapers also became part of the national scene. Thanks to syndicated newspaper columns and features people across the United States could read the same articles. They could also read the same books, preselected by a board of expert judges for the Book-of-the-Month Club, founded in 1926.

The newest instrument of mass culture, professional radio broadcasting, began in 1920. By 1929 about 40 percent of the nation's households owned a radio. More than 800 stations, most affiliated with the Columbia Broadcasting Service (CBS) or the National Broadcasting Company (NBC), were on the air. Unlike European networks, which were government monopolies, American radio stations operated for profit. Though the federal government licensed the stations, their revenue came primarily from advertisers and corporate sponsors.

Americans loved radio. They listened avidly to the World Series and other sports events and to variety shows sponsored by advertisers. One of the most popular radio shows of all time, *Amos 'n' Andy,* premiered on NBC in 1928, featuring two white actors playing stereotypical black characters. Soon fractured phrases from *Amos 'n' Andy,* such as "Check and double check," became part of everyday speech. So many

CRAZY BLUES

By PERRY BRADFORD

MAMIE SMITH AND HER JAZZ HOUNDS

Get this number for your phonograph on Okeh Record No. 4169

PUBLISHED BY
PERRY BRADFORD
MUSIC PUB CO.
1547 BROADWAY, N. Y. C.

All That Jazz

The phonograph dramatically expanded the popularity and market for jazz recordings like this one by Mamie Smith and her Jazz Hounds. The success of "Crazy Blues" convinced record companies that there was a market to be tapped in black communities for what were called "race records," and Mamie Smith skyrocketed to fame with this 1920 recording.
(Division of Political History, Smithsonian Institution, Washington, DC)

people "tuned in" (another new phrase of the 1920s) that the country seemed to come to a halt during popular programs—a striking example of the pervasiveness of mass media.

The automobile and new forms of entertainment like movies and radio pointed to a new emphasis on leisure. As the workweek shrank and some workers won the right to paid vacations, Americans had more time and energy to spend on recreation. Like so much else in the 1920s leisure became increasingly tied to consumption and mass culture. Public recreation flourished as cities and suburbs built baseball diamonds, tennis courts, swimming pools, and golf courses. Americans not only played sports but had the time and money to watch professional athletes perform in increasingly commercialized enterprises. They could see a game in a comfortable stadium, or they could listen to it on the radio or catch highlights in the newsreel at the local movie theater.

Americans reveled vicariously in the accomplishments of the superb athletes of the 1920s. Baseball continued to be the national pastime, drawing as many as 10 million fans a year. Tarnished in 1919 by the "Black Sox" scandal, in which some Chicago White Sox players took bribes to throw the World Series, baseball bounced back with the rise of stars like Babe Ruth of the New York Yankees. African Americans, however, had different heroes. Excluded from the white teams, black athletes like Satchel Paige played in Negro leagues formed in the 1920s.

Thanks to the media's attention, the popularity of sports figures rivaled that of movie stars. In football Red Grange of the University of Illinois was a major star, while Jack Dempsey and Gene Tunney attracted a loyal following in boxing and Bobby Jones helped to popularize golf. Bill Tilden dominated men's tennis, while Helen Wills and Suzanne Lenglen reigned in the women's game. The decade's best-known swimmer was Gertrude Ederle, who crossed the English Channel in 1926 in just over fourteen hours.

The decade's most popular hero, however, was neither an athlete nor a movie star. On May 20, 1927, aviator Charles Lindbergh, flying the small plane *The Spirit of St. Louis,* made the first successful nonstop solo flight between New York and Paris, a distance of 3,610 miles, in $33^1/2$ hours. Returning home to tickertape parades and effusive celebrations, he became *Time* magazine's first Man of the Year in 1928. Lindbergh captivated the nation by combining his mastery of the new technology (the airplane) with the pioneer virtues of individualism, self-reliance, and hard work. He symbolized Americans' desire to enjoy the benefits of modern industrialism without renouncing their traditional values.

Dissenting Values and Cultural Conflict

As movies, radio, advertising, and mass-production industries helped to transform the country into a modern, cosmopolitan nation, many Americans welcomed them as exciting evidence of progress. But others were uneasy. Flappers dancing to jazz, youthful sexual experimentation in the back of Ford Model Ts, hints of a decline in religious values: these harbingers of a new era worried more tradition-minded folk. In the nation's cities the powerful presence of immigrants and African Americans suggested the waning of white Protestant cultural dominance. Beneath the clichés of the Roaring Twenties were deeply felt tensions that surfaced in conflicts over immigration, religion, Prohibition, and race relations.

THE RISE OF NATIVISM

Tensions between the fast-paced city and the traditional, small-town values of the country partially explain the decade's conflicts. As farmers struggled with severe economic problems, rural communities lost residents to the cities at an alarming rate. The 1920 census revealed that for the first time in the nation's history city people outnumbered rural people: 52 percent of the population lived in urban areas, compared with just 28 percent in 1870. Though the census exaggerated the extent of urbanization—its guidelines classified towns with only 2,500 people as cities—there was no mistaking the trend (see Map 23.1). By 1929 ninety-three cities had populations over 100,000. The mass media generally reflected the cosmopolitan values of these urban centers, and many old-stock Americans worried that the cities and the immigrants who clustered there would soon dominate the culture.

Yet the polarities between city and country should not be overstated. Rural and small-town people were affected by the same forces that influenced urban residents. Much of the new technology—especially automobiles—enhanced rural life. Country people, like their urban counterparts, were tempted by the materialistic new

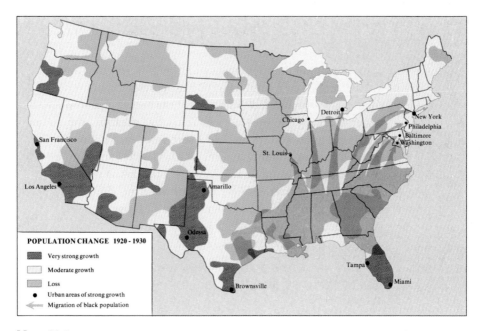

M A P 23.1
The Shift from Rural to Urban Population, 1920–1930

Despite the increasingly urban tone of modern America after 1920, regional patterns of population growth and decline were far from uniform. Cities in the South and West grew most dramatically as southern farmers moved to more promising areas with familiar climates. An important factor in the growth of northern cities, such as New York and Chicago, was the migration of southern blacks set in motion by World War I.

values proclaimed on the radio, in magazines, and in movies. Moreover, many urban residents—immigrant Catholics, for example—were just as alarmed about declining moral standards as rural Protestants were. A simplified urban-rural
dichotomy misrepresents the complexity of the decade's cultural conflicts.

These conflicts often centered on the question of growing racial and ethnic pluralism. When native-born white Protestants—both rural and city dwellers—looked
at their communities in 1920, they saw a nation that had changed dramatically in
only forty years. During that time more than 23 million immigrants had come to
America, many of them Jews or Catholics, most of peasant stock. Senator William
Bruce of Maryland branded them "indigestible lumps" in the "national stomach,"
implying that mainstream society could not absorb their large numbers and foreign customs. This sentiment, termed *nativism*, was widely shared.

Nativist animosity fueled a new drive against immigration. The Chinese had
been excluded in 1882, and Theodore Roosevelt had negotiated a "gentleman's
agreement" to limit Japanese immigration in 1908 (see American Voices, "A Foreigner in America"). Yet efforts to restrict European immigration did not meet with
much success until after World War I, which had heightened suspicion of "hyphenated" Americans. During the Red Scare, nativists had played up the supposed
association of the immigrants with radicalism and labor unrest, charging that
Southern and Eastern European Catholics and Jews were incapable of becoming
true Americans.

In response Congress passed an emergency bill in 1921, limiting the number
of immigrants to 3 percent of each national group as represented in the 1910 census. President Woodrow Wilson refused to sign it, but the bill was reintroduced and
passed under Warren Harding. In 1924 a more restrictive measure, the National
Origins Act, reduced immigration until 1927 to 2 percent of each nationality's representation in the 1890 census—which had included relatively small numbers of
people from Southeastern Europe and Russia. After 1927 the law set a cap of 150,000
immigrants per year and continued to tie admission into the United States to a
quota system that intentionally limited immigration from those regions. Japanese
immigrants were excluded entirely.

One remaining loophole in immigration law permitted unrestricted immigration from countries in the Western Hemisphere. This source became increasingly
significant over the years (see Figure 23.1), as Mexicans and Central and South
Americans crossed the border to fill jobs made available by the cutoff of immigration from Europe and Asia. Over 1 million Mexicans entered the United States between 1900 and 1930. Nativists and representatives of organized labor, who viewed
Mexican immigrants as unwanted competition, lobbied Congress to close the loophole but were unsuccessful until the 1930s when the economic devastation of the
Great Depression minimized the need for immigrant labor.

Another expression of nativism in the 1920s was the revival of the Ku Klux
Klan. Shortly after the premiere of *Birth of a Nation* in 1915, a popular film glori-
fying the Reconstruction-era Ku Klux Klan, a group of southerners had gathered on

A Foreigner in America

KAZUO KAWAI

*A*sian immigrants' experience of prejudice was much sharper than that of Europeans, but nonetheless Japanese immigrant Kazuo Kawai's experience echoes the problems that many young ethnic Americans in the 1920s had as they recognized that they did not belong in the old country, nor were they accepted as "One Hundred Percent Americans."

But it hurt because I couldn't say: "This is my own, my native land." What was my native land? Japan? True, I was born there. But it had seemed a queer, foreign land to me when I visited it. America? I had, until now, thought so. I had even told my father once that even in case of war between Japan and America, I would consider America as my country. In language, in thought, in ideals, in custom, in everything, I was American. But America wouldn't have me. She wouldn't recognize me in high school. She put the pictures of those of my race at the tail end of the year book. (I was a commencement speaker, so they had to put my picture near the front.) She won't let me play tennis on the courts in the city parks of Los Angeles, by city ordinance. She won't give me service when I go to a barber's shop. She won't let me own a house to live in. She won't give me a job, unless it is a menial one that no American wants. I thought I was American, but America wouldn't have me. Once I was American, but America made a foreigner out of me—Not a Japanese, but a foreigner—a foreigner to any country, for I am just as much a foreigner to Japan as to America.

SOURCE: *Stanford Survey of Race Relations* (Stanford University, 1924), Hoover Institute Archives.

Stone Mountain outside Atlanta to revive the racist organization. Taking as its motto "Native, white, Protestant supremacy," the modern Klan appealed to both urban and rural folk, though its largest "klaverns" were in urban areas. Spreading out from its southern base, the group found significant support in the Far West, the Southwest, and the Midwest, especially Oregon, Indiana, and Oklahoma. Unlike the Klan that was founded after the Civil War, the Klan of the 1920s did not limit its harassment to blacks; Catholics and Jews were just as likely to be its targets. Many of its tactics, however, were the same: arson, physical intimidation, and economic boycotts. The new Klan also turned to politics, succeeding in electing hundreds of Klansmen to public office. At the height of its power in 1925 the Klan had over 3 million members—including a strong contingent of women who pursued a political agenda that combined racism, nativism, and equal rights for white Protestant women.

After 1925 the Klan declined rapidly. Internal rivalries and the disclosure of rampant corruption hurt the group's image. Especially damaging was the revelation that Grand Dragon David Stephenson, the Klan's national leader, had kidnapped

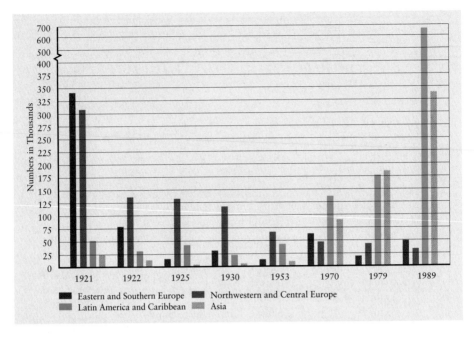

FIGURE 23.1
American Immigration after World War I

Legislation reflecting nativism slowed the influx of immigrants after 1920, as did the dislocations brought on by depression and war in the 1930s and 1940s. Note the higher rate of non-European immigration since the 1970s.

and sexually assaulted his former secretary, driving her to suicide. And the passage of the National Origins Act in 1924 reduced the nativist fervor, robbing the Klan of its most potent issue.

LEGISLATING VALUES: THE SCOPES TRIAL AND PROHIBITION

Other cultural tensions erupted over religion. The debate between modernist and fundamentalist Protestants, which had been simmering since the 1890s (see Chapter 19), came to a boil in the 1920s. Modernists, or liberal Protestants, tried to reconcile religion with Charles Darwin's theory of evolution and recent technological and scientific discoveries. Fundamentalists clung to a literal interpretation of the Bible. At the same time most major Protestant denominations, especially the Baptists and the Presbyterians, experienced heated internal conflicts. However, the most conspicuous evangelical figures came from outside mainstream denominations. Popular preachers like Billy Sunday and Aimee Semple McPherson used revivals, storefront churches, and open-air preaching to popularize their own blends of charismatic fundamentalism and traditional values.

Religious controversy soon entered the political arena when fundamentalists, worried about increasing secularism and declining morality, turned to the law to shore up their vision of a righteous Protestant nation. Some states enacted legislation to block the teaching of evolution in the schools. In 1925, for instance, Tennessee passed a law declaring that "it shall be unlawful . . . to teach any theory that denies the story of the Divine creation of man as taught in the Bible, and to teach instead that man has descended from a lower order of animals." In a test case involving John T. Scopes, a high school biology teacher in Dayton, Tennessee, the fledgling American Civil Liberties Union (ACLU) challenged the constitutionality of that law. Clarence Darrow, the famous criminal lawyer, defended Scopes; the spellbinding orator William Jennings Bryan, three-time presidential candidate and ardent fundamentalist, was the most prominent member of the prosecution's team.

The Scopes trial was quickly dubbed the "monkey trial," referring both to Darwin's theory that human beings and primates share a common ancestor and to the circus atmosphere in the courtroom. In July 1925 more than 100 journalists crowded the sweltering courthouse in Dayton, Tennessee, giving massive publicity to the knotty questions of faith and scientific theory that the trial addressed. The jury took only eight minutes to deliver its verdict: guilty. Though the Tennessee Supreme Court later overturned the conviction on a technicality, the reversal prevented further appeals of the case, and the controversial law remained on the books more than thirty years. Historically, the trial symbolizes the conflict between the two competing value systems, cosmopolitan and traditional, that clashed in the 1920s. It suggests that despite the period's image as a frivolous and decadent time, religion continued to matter deeply to many Americans.

Like the dispute over evolution, Prohibition involved the power of the state to enforce social values. Americans did drink less overall after passage of the Eighteenth Amendment, which took effect in January of 1920 (see Chapter 22). Yet more than any other issue, Prohibition gave the decade its reputation as the Roaring Twenties. In major cities, whose ethnic populations had always opposed Prohibition, noncompliance was widespread. People imitated rural moonshiners by distilling "bathtub gin." Illegal saloons called "speakeasies" sprang up everywhere—more than 30,000 of them in New York City alone. Liquor smugglers operated with ease along borders and coastlines. Organized crime, already a presence in major cities, supplied a ready-made distribution network for the bootleg liquor, using the "noble experiment," as Prohibition was called, to entrench itself more deeply in city politics. Said the decade's most notorious gangster, Al Capone, "Everybody calls me a racketeer. I call myself a businessman. When I sell liquor, it's bootlegging. When my patrons serve it on a silver tray on Lake Shore Drive, it's hospitality."

By the middle of the decade, Prohibition was clearly failing. Government appropriations for its enforcement were woefully inadequate; the few highly publicized raids hardly made a dent in the liquor trade. Forces for repeal—the "wets," as opposed to the "drys," who continued to support the Eighteenth Amendment—began the long process to obtain the necessary votes in Congress and state

Scopes Trial

As this picture of a stall selling antievolution material in Dayton, Tennessee, suggests, the Scopes trial in 1925 became a focus of the antievolution movement. Pitting the old-time religion of rural America against modern values, the trial symbolized much of the cultural conflict of the 1920s and demonstrated the continued importance of religion to many Americans. (Corbis-Bettmann)

legislatures to amend the Constitution once more. The wets argued that Prohibition had undermined respect for the law and had seriously impinged on individuals' liberty. The onset of the Great Depression hastened the repeal process, as politicians began to see alcohol production as a way to create jobs and prop up the faltering economy. On December 5, 1933, the Eighteenth Amendment was repealed. Ironically, drinking became more socially acceptable, though not necessarily more widespread, than it had been before the experiment began.

INTELLECTUAL CROSSCURRENTS

The most articulate and embittered dissenters of the 1920s were writers and intellectuals disillusioned by the horrors of World War I and the crass materialism of the new consumer culture. Some artists were so repelled by what they saw as the complacent, moralistic, and anti-intellectual tone of American life that they settled in Europe—some temporarily, like the novelists Ernest Hemingway and F. Scott Fitzgerald, others permanently, like writer Gertrude Stein. Prominent African American artists, such as dancer Josephine Baker and writer Langston Hughes, sought temporary escape from racism in France. The poet T. S. Eliot, who left the United States before the war, ultimately became a British citizen. His despairing poem *The Waste Land* (1922), with its images of a fragmented civilization in ruins after the war, influenced a generation of writers. Other writers too made powerful antiwar statements, including John Dos Passos, whose first novel, *The Three Soldiers* (1921), was inspired by the war, and whose *1919* (1932), the second volume of his magnificent *USA* trilogy, railed against the obscenity of "Mr. Wilson's war." Ernest Hemingway's novels *In Our Time* (1924), *The Sun Also Rises* (1926), and *A Farewell to Arms* (1929) also powerfully described the dehumanizing consequences and the futility of war.

But the artists and writers who migrated to Europe, particularly Paris, were not simply a "lost generation" fleeing America. They were also drawn to Paris as the cultural and artistic capital of the world and a beacon of modernism. Paris, as Gertrude Stein put it, was "where the twentieth century was happening." Indeed, the modernist movement, which was marked by skepticism and technical experimentation in literature, art, and music, invigorated American writing both abroad and at home. Many American writers, whether they settled in Paris or remained in their home country, joined the movement, which had begun before the war as intellectuals reacted with excitement to the cultural and social changes that science, industrialization, and urbanization had brought. In the 1920s the business culture and political corruption of the Harding years caused intellectuals to cast a more critical eye on American society. One of the sharpest critics, the Baltimore journalist H. L. Mencken, directed his mordant wit against mass culture, small-town America with its guardians of public morals, and the "booboisie," his contemptuous term for the middle class. In the *American Mercury,* the journal he founded in 1922, Mencken championed writers like Sherwood Anderson, Sinclair Lewis, and Theodore Dreiser, who satirized the provincialism of American society.

The literature of the 1920s was rich and varied. Poetry enjoyed a renaissance in the works of Robert Frost, Wallace Stevens, Marianne Moore, and William Carlos Williams. Edith Wharton won a Pulitzer Prize—the first woman so honored—for *The Age of Innocence* (1920). Influenced by Freudian psychology, William Faulkner achieved his first critical success with *The Sound and the Fury* (1929), set in the fictional Mississippi county of Yoknapatawpha, where inhabitants clung to the values of the old agrarian South as they struggled to adjust to modern industrial capitalism. Playwright Eugene O'Neill also showed the influence of Freudian psychology in his experimental plays, including *The Hairy Ape* (1922) and *Desire Under the Elms* (1924). Although both Faulkner and O'Neill went on to produce additional major works in the 1930s, on the whole the creative energy of the literary renaissance of the 1920s did not survive into the 1930s. The Great Depression, social and ideological unrest, and the rise of totalitarianism would reshape the intellectual landscape.

A different kind of cultural affirmation took place in the African American community of Harlem in the 1920s. In the words of the Reverend Adam Clayton Powell Sr., pastor of the influential Abyssinian Baptist Church, Harlem loomed as "the symbol of liberty and the Promised Land to Negroes everywhere." One aspect of this hope was the Harlem Renaissance, a movement of young writers and artists who broke with older genteel traditions of black literature to reclaim a cultural identity with African roots. Alain Locke, editor of the anthology *The New Negro* (1926), summed up the movement when he stated that, through art, "Negro life is seizing its first chances for group expression and self-determination." Authors like Claude McKay, Jean Toomer, Jessie Fauset, and Zora Neale Hurston explored the black experience and represented the "New Negro" in fiction. Countee Cullen and Langston Hughes turned to poetry, and Augusta Savage to sculpture. Their outpouring of artistic expression gave voice to the African American struggle to find a way, as W. E. B. Du Bois put it, "to be both a Negro and an American."

The vitality of the Harlem Renaissance was short-lived. Although the NAACP's magazine *The Crisis* provided a forum for the Harlem writers, the black middle class and Harlem's intellectual elite were relatively small and could not adequately support its efforts. The movement had depended on white patronage for financial backing and access to publication. During the Jazz Age, when Harlem was in vogue, publishing houses courted Harlem writers, but when the stock market crashed in 1929, their interest in funding black writers withered, and the movement waned as the Depression deepened. But the works of the Harlem Renaissance would influence a new generation of black writers when black intellectuals rediscovered them during the civil rights movement of the 1960s.

Although the Harlem Renaissance had little impact on the masses of African Americans, other movements built racial pride and challenged white political and cultural hegemony. The most successful was the Universal Negro Improvement Association (UNIA), which championed black separatism under the leadership of the Jamaican-born Marcus Garvey. Based in Harlem, the UNIA was the black working class's first mass movement. At its height it claimed 4 million followers, many of whom were recent migrants to northern cities. Like several nineteenth-century reformers, Marcus Garvey urged blacks to return to Africa because, he reasoned, blacks would never be treated justly in countries ruled by whites. Although he did not anticipate a massive migration, he did envision a strong black Africa that could use its power to protect blacks everywhere. Garvey's wife, Amy Jacques Garvey, appealed to black women by combining black nationalism with an emphasis on women's contributions to culture and politics.

The UNIA grew rapidly in the early 1920s. It published a newspaper called *Negro World* and undertook extensive business ventures to support black enterprise. The most ambitious project, the Black Star Line steamship company, was supposed to ferry cargo between the West Indies and the United States and take African Americans back to Africa. Irregularities in fund raising for the project, however, led to Garvey's conviction for mail fraud in 1925, and he was sentenced to five years in prison. President Coolidge commuted his sentence in 1927, but Garvey was deported to Jamaica. Without his charismatic leadership, the movement collapsed.

CULTURAL CLASH IN THE ELECTION OF 1928

The works of the lost generation and the Harlem Renaissance touched only a small minority of Americans in the 1920s, but emotionally charged issues like Prohibition, fundamentalism, and nativism eventually spilled over into national politics. The Democratic Party, which attracted both rural Protestants in the South and the West and ethnic minorities in northern cities, was especially vulnerable to the cultural conflicts of the time. The 1924 Democratic National Convention had revealed an intensely polarized party, split between the urban machines and its rural wing.

In 1928 the urban wing held sway and succeeded in nominating New York's Governor Alfred E. Smith, a descendant of Irish immigrants and a product of Tammany Hall. Proud of his background, Smith adopted "The Sidewalks of New York" as his campaign song. His candidacy troubled many voters, however. His heavy New York accent, his brown derby, and his colorful style highlighted his urban working-class origins, and his early career in Tammany Hall suggested—incorrectly—that he was little more than a cog in the machine. Smith's stand on Prohibition—although he promised to enforce it, he wanted it repealed—alienated even more voters.

An additional handicap, however, was his religion. In 1928 most Protestants were not ready for a Catholic president. Although Smith insisted that his religion would not interfere with his duties as president, his perceived allegiance to Rome cost him the support of Democrats and Republicans alike. Protestant clergymen, who already opposed Smith because he supported the repeal of Prohibition, led the drive against him. "No Governor can kiss the papal ring and get within gunshot of the White House," declared one Methodist bishop.

Smith's candidacy met with much opposition, but for his supporters he embodied a new America. Throughout the decade, attacks on immigrants, Catholics, and Jews had repeatedly labeled them as unwelcome outsiders. Ethnic and religious leaders and communities had vehemently countered these criticisms by offering a more inclusive vision of citizenship. One Catholic bishop summed it up neatly in 1921, stating that "National aspirations constitute Americanism. We are the blend of all the peoples of the world, and I think we are much the better for that. Americanism is not a matter of birth, Americanism is a matter of faith, of consecration to the ideals of America." That Al Smith, a man of Catholic immigrant stock, could be the Democratic Party's nominee for president suggested to many in 1928 that the country might yet embrace a more pluralistic conception of American identity.

Just as Smith was a new kind of presidential candidate for the Democrats, so was Herbert Hoover for the Republicans. As a professional administrator and engineer who had never before been elected to political office, Hoover embodied the new managerial and technological elite that was restructuring the nation's economic order. During his campaign, in which he gave only seven speeches, Hoover asserted that his vision of individualism and cooperative endeavor would banish poverty from the United States. That rhetoric, as well as his reputation for organizing a drive for humanitarian relief during the war, caused many voters to see him as more progressive than Smith.

Hoover won a stunning victory, receiving 58 percent of the popular vote to Smith's 41 percent and 444 electoral votes to Smith's 87. The election reflected important underlying political changes. Despite the overwhelming loss, the Democrats' turnout increased substantially in urban areas. Smith won the industrialized states of Massachusetts and Rhode Island and carried the nation's twelve largest cities. The Democrats were on their way to fashioning a new identity as the party of the urban masses, a reorientation the New Deal completed in the 1930s.

It is unlikely that any Democratic candidate, let alone a Catholic, could have won the presidency in 1928. With a seemingly prosperous economy, national consensus on foreign policy, and strong support from the business community, the Republicans were unbeatable. Ironically, Herbert Hoover's victory would put him in the unenviable position of leading the United States when the Great Depression struck in 1929. Having claimed credit for the prosperity of the 1920s, the Republicans could not escape blame for the depression; twenty-four years would pass before a Republican won the presidency again.

But as Hoover began his presidency in early 1929, most Americans expected progress and prosperity to continue. The New Era the Republicans had touted meant more than Republican ascendancy in politics, more than business-government cooperation, and more than a decline in the progressive reform movement. To most Americans, the New Era embodied the industrial productivity and technological advances that made consumer goods widely available and the movies and the radio an exciting part of American life. At home and abroad the nation seemed unprecedentedly vigorous and powerful. Despite disruptive cultural conflicts and a changing workplace that undermined workers' power, despite inequities in the racial order and in the distribution of income, the general tone was one of optimism, of faith in the modern society the country had become. That faith made the harsh realities of the Great Depression that would follow all the more shocking.

TIMELINE

1920	Eighteenth Amendment takes effect (January) and outlaws alcohol (repealed in 1933).			U.S. troops withdraw from the Dominican Republic.
	First commercial radio broadcast			Teapot Dome scandal
	Republican Warren G. Harding elected president			National Origins Act further limits immigration.
	Census reveals a population shift from farms to cities.		1925	Height of power for the Ku Klux Klan
				Scopes trial
	Edith Wharton's *The Age of Innocence*		1926	Alain Locke's *The New Negro*
1920–1921	National economic recession			The Book-of-the-Month Club is founded.
1921	Sheppard-Towner Act appropriates money for women's and infants' health.		1927	*The Jazz Singer* becomes the first "talkie."
	Immigration Act limits immigration.			Charles Lindbergh flies solo across the Atlantic.
	Washington Conference supports naval disarmament.		1928	Herbert Hoover defeats Al Smith for the presidency.
1922	T. S. Eliot's *The Waste Land*			Kellogg-Briand Peace Pact condemns the use of war.
1922–1929	Record economic expansion			*Amos 'n' Andy* premieres on NBC radio.
1923	Harding dies in office and is succeeded by Calvin Coolidge as president.		1929	*Middletown* is published.
				Ernest Hemingway's *A Farewell to Arms*
1924	Dawes Plan reduces German reparations payments.			William Faulkner's *The Sound and the Fury*

For Further Exploration

A recent overview of the decade that pays extensive attention to racial, religious, and ethnic pluralism is Lynn Dumenil, *The Modern Temper: American Culture and Society in the 1920s*. Invaluable collections of primary documents include Alain Locke, ed., *The New Negro* (1925), which features authors of the Harlem Renaissance; Loren Baritz, ed., *The Culture of the Twenties* (1970), which covers such diverse topics as the Lost Generation and Ku Klux Klan; and Freda Kirchwey, ed., *Our Changing Morality: A Symposium* (1924), which brings together a series of 1920s essays on women. For fiction, in addition to the titles offered in the text, see Sinclair Lewis's two classic midwestern novels, *Babbitt* (1922) and *Mainstreet* (1920); Sherwood Anderson's dark stories in *Winesburg, Ohio* (1919); and Nella Larsen's novel *Quicksand* (1928) about an African American woman's conflicted identity.

The State University of New York at Binghamton's page on "Women and Social Movements in the United States, 1830–1930" at <http://womhist.binghamton.edu/> is especially rich on the 1920s, with material on conflicts between African American and white women activists, women in the peace movement, and women's participation in partisan politics. The Library of Congress's American Memory Collection, *Prosperity and Thrift: The Coolidge Era and the Consumer Economy, 1921–1929,* at <http://memory.loc.gov/ammem/coolhtml/ coolhome.html> is an extensive site with original documents, film footage, and scholarly insights on a variety of topics dealing with the 1920s. Douglas O. Linder of University of Missouri–Kansas City, maintains a "Famous Trials" website at <http://www.law.umkc.edu/ faculty/projects/ftrials/scopes/scopes.htm> that offers photos, cartoons, biographies of the participants, and firsthand accounts of the Scopes trial. "Greatest Films of the 1920s" at <http://www.filmsite.org/20sintro.html> is an informative site that provides summaries and reviews of such significant movies as *King of Kings* (1927) and *The Sheik* (1921).

Chapter 24

THE GREAT DEPRESSION

Mass unemployment is both a statistic and an empty feeling in the stomach. To fully comprehend it, you have to both see the figures and feel the emptiness.

—CABELL PHILLIPS

Our images of the 1920s and the decade that followed are polar opposites. Flappers and movie stars, admen and stockbrokers, caught up in what F. Scott Fitzgerald called the "world's most expensive orgy"—these are our conceptions of the Jazz Age. The 1930s we remember in terms of bread lines and hobos, dust bowl devastation and hapless migrants piled into dilapidated jalopies. Almost all our impressions of that decade are black and white, in part because widely distributed photographs taken by Farm Security Administration photographers etched this dark visual image of depression America on the popular consciousness.

But this contrast between the flush times of the 1920s and the hard times of the 1930s is too stark. The vaunted prosperity of the 1920s was never as widespread or as deeply rooted as many believed. Though America's mass-consumption economy was the envy of the world, many people lived on its margins. Nor was every American devastated by the depression. Those with a secure job or a fixed income survived the economic downturn in relatively good shape. Yet few could escape the depression's wide-ranging social, political, and cultural effects. Whatever their personal situation was, Americans understood that the nation was deeply scarred by the pervasive struggle to survive and overcome "hard times."

The Coming of the Great Depression

Booms and busts are a permanent feature of the business cycle in capitalist economies. Since the beginning of the Industrial Revolution early in the nineteenth century, the United States had experienced recessions or panics at least once every twenty years. But none was as severe as the Great Depression of the 1930s. The country would not recover from the depression until World War II put American factories and people back to work.

CAUSES OF THE DEPRESSION

The downturn began slowly and almost imperceptibly. After 1927 consumer spending declined, and housing construction slowed. Soon inventories piled up; in 1928 manufacturers began to cut back production and lay off workers, reducing incomes and buying power and reinforcing the slowdown. By the summer of 1929 the economy was clearly in recession.

Yet stock-market activity continued unabated. By 1929 the stock market had become the symbol of the nation's prosperity, an icon of American business culture. In a *Ladies' Home Journal* article titled "Everyone Ought to Be Rich," the financier John J. Raskob advised that $15 a month invested in sound common stocks would grow to $80,000 in twenty years. Not everyone was playing the market, however. Only about 4 million Americans, or roughly 10 percent of the nation's households, owned stock in 1929.

Stock prices had been rising steadily since 1921, but in 1928 and 1929 they surged forward, rising on average over 40 percent. At the time market activity was essentially unregulated. Margin buying in particular proceeded at a feverish pace, as customers were encouraged to buy stocks with a small down payment and finance the rest with a broker loan. But then on "Black Thursday," October 24, 1929, and again on "Black Tuesday," October 29, the bubble burst. On those two bleak days, more than 28 million shares changed hands in frantic trading. Overextended investors, suddenly finding themselves heavily in debt, began to sell their portfolios. Waves of panic selling ensued. Practically overnight stock values fell from a peak of $87 billion (at least on paper) to $55 billion.

The impact of what became known as the Great Crash was felt far beyond the trading floors of Wall Street. Commercial banks had invested heavily in corporate stock. Speculators who had borrowed from banks to buy their stocks could not repay their loans because they could not sell their shares. Throughout the nation bank failures multiplied. Since bank deposits were uninsured, a bank collapse meant that depositors lost all their money. The sudden loss of their life savings was a tremendous shock to members of the middle class, many of whom had no other resources to cope with the crisis. More symbolically the crash destroyed the faith of those who viewed the stock market as the crowning symbol of American prosperity, precipitating a crisis of confidence that prolonged the depression.

Although the stock-market crash precipitated the Great Depression, long-standing weaknesses in the economy accounted for its length and severity. Agriculture, in particular, had never recovered from the recession of 1920 and 1921. Farmers faced high fixed costs for equipment and mortgages, which they had incurred during the inflationary war years. When prices fell because of overproduction, many farmers defaulted on their mortgage payments, risking foreclosure. Because farmers accounted for about a fourth of the nation's gainfully employed workers in 1929, their difficulties weakened the general economic structure.

Certain basic industries also had economic setbacks during the prosperous 1920s. Textiles, facing a steady decline after the war, abandoned New England for cheaper labor in the South but suffered still from decreased demand and overproduction. Mining and lumbering, which had expanded in response to wartime demand, confronted the same problems. And the railroad industry, damaged by stiff competition from trucks, faced shrinking passenger revenues and stagnant freight levels, worsened by inefficient management. While these older sectors of the economy faltered, newer and more successful consumer-based industries, such as appliances and food processing, proved not yet strong enough to lead the way to recovery.

The unequal distribution of the nation's wealth was another underlying weakness of the economy. During the 1920s the share of national income going to families in the upper- and middle-income brackets increased. The tax policies of Secretary of the Treasury Andrew Mellon contributed to a concentration of wealth by lowering personal income tax rates, eliminating the wartime excess-profits tax, and increasing deductions that favored corporations and the affluent. In 1929 the lowest 40 percent of the population received only 12.5 percent of aggregate family income, while the top 5 percent of the population received 30 percent. Once the depression began, this skewed income distribution left the majority of people unable to spend the amount of money that was needed to revive the economy.

The Great Depression became self-perpetuating. The more the economy contracted, the longer people expected the depression to last. The longer they expected it to last, the more afraid they became to spend or invest their money, if they had any. The economy showed some improvement in the summer of 1931, when low prices encouraged consumption, but plunged again late that fall.

The nation's banks, already weakened by the stock-market crash, contributed to the worsening contraction. When agricultural prices and income fell more steeply than usual in 1930, many farmers went bankrupt, causing rural banks to fail. By December 1930 so many rural banks had defaulted on their obligations that urban banks too began to collapse. The wave of bank failures frightened depositors, who withdrew their savings, deepening the crisis.

In 1931 a change in the nation's monetary policy compounded the banks' problems. In the first phase of the depression, the Federal Reserve System had reacted cautiously. But in October 1931 the Federal Reserve Bank of New York significantly increased the discount rate—the interest rate charged on loans to member banks—and reduced the amount of money placed in circulation through the purchase of government securities. This miscalculation squeezed the money supply, forcing prices down and depriving businesses of funds for investment. In the face of the money shortage, the American people could have pulled the country out of the depression only by spending faster. But because of falling prices, rising unemployment, and a troubled banking system, Americans preferred to keep their dollars, stashing them under the mattress rather than depositing them in the bank, further limiting the amount of money in circulation. Economic stagnation solidified.

THE WORLDWIDE DEPRESSION

President Hoover later blamed the severity of the depression on the international economic situation. Although domestic factors far outweighed international causes of America's protracted decline, Hoover was correct in surmising that economic problems in the rest of the world affected the United States, and vice versa. Indeed, the international economic system had been out of kilter since World War I. It functioned only as long as American banks exported enough capital to allow European countries to repay their debts and to buy U.S. manufactured goods and foodstuffs. By the late 1920s European economies were staggering under the weight of huge debts and trade imbalances with the United States, which effectively undercut their recovery from the war. By 1931 most European economies had collapsed.

In an interdependent world, the economic downturn in America had enormous repercussions. When U.S. companies cut back production, they also cut their purchases of raw materials and supplies abroad, devastating many foreign economies. When American financiers sharply reduced their foreign investment and consumers bought fewer European goods, debt repayment became even more difficult, straining the gold standard, the foundation of international commerce in the interwar period. As European economic conditions worsened, demand for American exports fell drastically. Finally, when the Hawley-Smoot Tariff of 1930 went into effect, raising rates to all-time highs, foreign governments retaliated by imposing their own trade restrictions, further limiting the market for American goods and intensifying the worldwide depression.

No other nation was as hard hit as the United States. From the height of its prosperity before the stock-market crash in 1929 to the depths of the depression in 1932 and 1933, the U.S. gross national product (GNP) was cut almost in half, declining from $103.1 billion to $58 billion in 1932. Consumption expenditures dropped by 18 percent, construction by 78 percent; private investment plummeted 88 percent, and farm income, already low, was more than halved. In this period 9,000 banks went bankrupt or closed their doors, and 100,000 businesses failed. The consumer price index (CPI) declined by 25 percent, and corporate profits fell from $10 billion to $1 billion.

Most tellingly, unemployment rose from 3.2 percent to 24.9 percent, affecting approximately 12 million workers. Statistical measures at the time were fairly crude, so the figures were probably understated. At least one in four workers was out of a job, and even those who had jobs faced wage cuts, work for which they were overqualified, or layoffs. Their stories put a human face on the almost incomprehensible dimensions of the economic downturn.

Hard Times

"We didn't go hungry, but we lived lean." That statement sums up the experiences of many families during the Great Depression. The vast majority of Americans were neither very rich nor very poor. For most the depression did not mean losing thousands of dollars in the stock market or pulling children out of boarding school; nor did it mean going on relief or living in a shantytown. In a typical family in the 1930s the husband still had a job, and the wife was still a homemaker. Families usually managed to "make do." But life was far from easy, and most Americans worried about an uncertain future that might bring even harder times into their lives.

THE INVISIBLE SCAR

"You could feel the depression deepen," recalled the writer Caroline Bird, "but you could not look out the window and see it." Many people never saw a bread line or a man selling apples on the corner. The depression caused a private kind of despair that often simmered behind closed doors. "I've lived in cities for many months broke, without help, too timid to get in bread lines," the writer Meridel LeSueur remembered. "A woman will shut herself up in a room until it is taken away from her, and eat a cracker a day and be as quiet as a mouse."

Many variables—race, ethnicity, age, class, and gender—influenced how Americans experienced the depression. Blacks, Mexican Americans, and others already on the economic margins saw their opportunities shrink further. Hard times weighed heavily on the nation's senior citizens of all races, many of whom faced total destitution. Many white middle-class Americans now experienced downward mobility for the first time. An unemployed man in Pittsburgh told the journalist Lorena Hickok, "Lady, you just can't know what it's like to have to move your family out of the nice house you had in the suburbs, part paid for, down into an apartment, down into another apartment, smaller and in a worse neighborhood, down, down, down, until finally you end up in the slums." People like this, who strongly believed in the Horatio Alger ethic of upward mobility through hard work, suddenly found themselves floundering in a society that no longer had a place for them. Thus, the depression challenged basic American tenets of individualism and success. Yet even in the midst of pervasive unemployment, many people blamed themselves for their misfortune. This sense of damaged pride pervaded letters written to President Franklin D. Roosevelt and his wife Eleanor, summed up succinctly in one woman's plea for assistance: "Please don't think me unworthy."

After exhausting their savings and credit, many families faced the humiliation of going on relief. Seeking aid from state or local government hurt their pride and disrupted the traditional custom of turning to relatives, neighbors, church, and mutual-aid society in time of need. Even if families endured the demeaning process of certification for state or local relief, the amount they received was a pittance. In New York State, where benefits were among the highest in the nation, a family on relief received only $2.39 a week. Such hardships left a deep wound: Caroline Bird described it as the "invisible scar." For the majority of Americans, even those who were not forced onto the relief rolls, the fear of losing control over their lives was the crux of the Great Depression.

The Bread Line

Some of the most vivid images from the depression were bread lines and men selling apples on street corners. Note that all the people in this bread line are men. Women rarely appeared in bread lines, often preferring to endure private deprivation rather than violate standards of respectable behavior.

(Franklin D. Roosevelt Library, Hyde Park, NY)

FAMILIES FACE THE DEPRESSION

Sociologists who studied family life during the 1930s found that the depression usually intensified existing behavior. If a family had been stable and cohesive before the depression, then members pulled together to overcome the new obstacles. But if a family had shown signs of disintegration, the depression made the situation worse. On the whole, far more families hung together than broke apart.

Men and women experienced the Great Depression differently, partly because of the gender roles that governed male and female behavior in the 1930s. From childhood men had been trained to be breadwinners; they considered themselves failures if they could no longer support their families (see American Voices, "A Working-Class Family Encounters the Great Depression"). But while millions of men lost their jobs, few of the nation's 28 million homemakers lost their positions in the home. In contrast to men, women's sense of self-importance increased as they struggled to keep their families afloat. The sociologists Robert and Helen Lynd noticed this phenomenon in their follow-up study of *Middletown* (Muncie, Indiana), published in 1937:

> The men, cut adrift from their usual routine, lost much of their sense of time and dawdled helplessly and dully about the streets; while in the homes the women's world remained largely intact and the round of cooking, housecleaning, and mending became if anything more absorbing.

Even if a wife took a job when her husband lost his, she retained almost total responsibility for housework and child care. To economize women sewed their own clothes and canned fruits and vegetables. They bought day-old bread and heated several dishes in the oven at once to save fuel. Women who had once employed servants did their own housework. Eleanor Roosevelt described the stressful effects of the depression on these women's lives: "It means endless little economies and constant anxiety for fear of some catastrophe such as accident or illness which may completely swamp the family budget." Housewives' ability to watch every penny often made the difference in a family's survival.

Despite hard times Americans as a whole maintained a fairly high level of consumption. As in the 1920s households in the middle-income range—in 1935 the 50.2 percent of American families with an income of $500 to $1,500—did much of the buying. Several trends allowed those families to maintain their former standard of living despite pay cuts and unemployment. Between 1929 and 1935 deflation lowered the cost of living almost 20 percent. And buying on the installment plan increased in the 1930s, permitting many families to stretch their reduced incomes.

Americans spent their money differently in the depression, though. Telephone use and clothing sales dropped sharply, but cigarettes, movies, radios, and newspapers, once considered luxuries, became necessities. The automobile proved one of

A Working-Class Family Encounters the Great Depression

LARRY VAN DUSEN

Although many families endured the privations of the Great Depression with equanimity, others, like Larry Van Dusen's family, experienced tremendous strains. In this passage from his oral history account to journalist Studs Terkel, he describes the pressures on male wage earners and their children.

My father led a rough life: he drank. During the Depression, he drank more. There was more conflict in the home. A lot of fathers—mine among them—had a habit of taking off. They'd go to Chicago to look for work. To Topeka. This left the family at home, waiting and hoping that the old man would find something. And there was always the Saturday night ordeal as to whether or not the old man would get home with his paycheck. Everything was sharpened and hurt more by the Depression.

Heaven would break out once in a while, and the old man would get a week's work. I remember he'd come home at night, and he'd come down the path through the trees. He always rode a bicycle. He'd stop and sometimes say hello, or give me a hug. And that smell of fresh sawdust on those carpenter overalls, and the fact that Dad was home, and there was a week's wages. . . . That's the good you remember.

And then there was always the bad part. That's when you'd see your father coming home with the toolbox on his shoulder. Or carrying it. That meant the job was over. The tools were home now, and we were back on the treadmill again.

I remember coming back home, many years afterwards. Things were better. It was after the Depression, after the war. To me, it was hardly the same house. My father turned into an angel. They weren't wealthy, but they were making it. They didn't have the acid and the recriminations and the bitterness that I had felt as a child.

SOURCE: Studs Terkel, *Hard Times* (New York: Pantheon Books, 1986), pp. 107–08.

the most depression-proof items in the family budget. Though sales of new cars dropped, gasoline sales held stable, suggesting that families bought used cars or kept their old models running longer.

Another measure of the impact of the depression on family life was the change in demographic trends. The marriage rate fell from 10.14 per thousand persons in 1929 to 7.87 per thousand in 1932. The divorce rate decreased as well because couples could not afford the legal expense of dissolving failed unions. And between 1930 and 1933 the birth rate, which had fallen steadily since 1800, dropped from 21.3 live births per thousand to 18.4, a dramatic 14 percent decrease. The new level would have produced a decline in population if maintained. Though it rose slightly after 1934, by the end of the decade it was still only 18.8. (In contrast, at the height of the baby boom following World War II, the birth rate was 25 per thousand.)

The drop in the birth rate during the Great Depression could not have happened without increased access to effective contraception. In 1936, in *United States v. One Package of Japanese Pessaries*, a federal court struck down all federal restrictions on the dissemination of contraceptive information. The decision gave doctors wide discretion in prescribing birth control for married couples, making it legal everywhere except the heavily Catholic states of Massachusetts and Connecticut. While abortion remained illegal, the number of women who underwent the procedure increased. Because many abortionists operated under unsafe or unsanitary conditions, between 8,000 and 10,000 women died each year from the illegal operations.

Margaret Sanger played a major role in encouraging the availability and popular acceptance of birth control. Sanger began her career as a public health nurse

Women Face the Depression

Most information for the 1930 census, conducted just as the depression gripped the nation, was gathered in personal interviews. This well-dressed census taker, Marie Cioffi, was probably lucky to get the job. The woman she is interviewing on East 112th Street in New York City, Margaret Napolitana, was likely a homemaker and, from her attire and expression, a struggling one. Meanwhile her daughter is not quite sure what to make of the two women's conversation.

(Corbis-Bettmann)

in the 1910s in the slums of New York City. At first she joined forces with social-ists trying to help working-class families to control their fertility. In the 1920s and 1930s, however, she appealed to the middle class for support, identifying those fam-ilies as the key to the movement's success. Sanger also courted the medical profes-sion, pioneering the establishment of professionally staffed birth control clinics and winning the American Medical Association's endorsement of contraception in 1937. As a result of Sanger's efforts, birth control became less a feminist issue and more a medical question. And in the context of the depression it became an economic issue as well, as financially pressed couples sought to delay or limit their child-bearing while they weathered hard times.

One way for families to make ends meet was to send an additional member of the household to work. At the turn of the century that additional member was of-ten a child or a young, unmarried adult. The married working woman was most likely to be an African American, employed in domestic service. In the 1930s the most striking changes were that married white women expanded their presence in the labor market and the total number of married women employed outside the home rose 50 percent. The 1940 census reported almost 11 million women in the workforce—approximately a fourth of the nation's workers—and a small increase over 1930.

Working women, especially white married women, encountered sharp re-sentment and outright discrimination in the workplace. After calculating that the number of employed women roughly equaled total unemployment in 1939, the editor Norman Cousins suggested this tongue-in-cheek remedy: "Simply fire the women, who shouldn't be working anyway, and hire the men. Presto! No un-employment. No relief rolls. No depression." Many people agreed with the idea. When asked in a 1936 Gallup poll whether wives should work when their hus-bands had jobs, 82 percent of those interviewed said no. Such public disapproval encouraged restrictions on women's right to work. From 1932 to 1937 the fed-eral government would not allow a husband and a wife to hold government jobs at the same time. Many states adopted laws that prohibited married women from working.

Married or not, most women worked because they had to. A sizable minority were the sole support of their families because their husbands had left home or lost their jobs. Single, divorced, deserted, or widowed women had no husbands to sup-port them. This was especially true of poor black women. A survey of Chicago re-vealed that two-fifths of adult black women in the city were single. These working women rarely took jobs away from men. "Few of the people who oppose married women's employment," observed one feminist in 1940, "seem to realize that a coal miner or steel worker cannot very well fill the jobs of nursemaids, cleaning women, or the factory and clerical jobs now filled by women." Custom made crossovers from one field to another rare.

The division of the workforce by gender gave white women a small edge dur-ing the depression. Many fields where they had concentrated—including clerical, sales, and service and trade occupations—reinforced the traditional stereotypes of female work but suffered less from economic contraction than heavy industry, which employed men almost exclusively. As a result unemployment rates for white women, although extremely high, were somewhat lower than those for their male counterparts. This small bonus came at a high price, however. When the depression ended, women were even more concentrated in low-paying, dead-end jobs than when it began. White women also benefited at the expense of minority women. To make ends meet white women willingly sought jobs usually held by blacks or other minority workers—domestic service jobs, for example—and employers were quick to act on their preference for white workers.

White men also took jobs once held by minority males. Contemporary observers' concerns about the crisis of the male breadwinner or married women in the workforce rarely extended to blacks. Most commentators paid scant attention to the impact of the depression on the black family, for example, focusing instead on the perceived threats to the stability of white households. As historian Jacqueline Jones explains it, few leaders worried "over the baneful effects of economic independence on the male ego when the ego in question was that of a black husband."

During the Great Depression there were few feminist demands for equal rights, at home or on the job. On an individual basis, women's self-esteem probably rose because of the importance of their work to family survival. Most men and women, however, continued to believe that the two sexes should have fundamentally different roles and responsibilities and that a woman's life cycle should be shaped by marriage and her husband's career.

The depression hit another segment of the family—the nation's 21 million young people—especially hard. Though small children often escaped the sense of bitterness and failure that gripped their elders, hard times made children grow up fast. About 250,000 young people became so demoralized that they took to the road as hobos and "sisters of the road," as female tramps were called. Others chose to stay in school longer: public schools were free, and they were warm in the winter. In 1930 less than half the nation's youth attended high school, compared with three-fourths in 1940, at the end of the depression. College, however, remained the privilege of a distinct minority. About 1.2 million young people, or 7.5 percent of the population between eighteen and twenty-four, attended college in the 1930s. Forty percent of them were women. After 1935 college became slightly more affordable when the National Youth Administration (NYA) gave part-time employment to more than 2 million college and high school students. The government agency also provided work for 2.6 million out-of-school youths.

College students worked hard in the 1930s; financial sacrifice encouraged seriousness of purpose. Interest in fraternities and sororities declined as many students became involved in political movements. Fueled by disillusionment with World War I, thousands of youth took the "Oxford Pledge" never to support United States involvement in a war. In 1936 the Student Strike Against War drew support from several hundred thousand students across the country.

Although many youths enjoyed more education in the 1930s, the depression damaged their future prospects. Studies of social mobility confirm that young men who entered their twenties during the depression era had less successful careers than those who came before or after. After extensive interviews with these youths all over the nation, the writer Maxine Davis described them as "runners, delayed at the gun," adding, "The depression years have left us with a generation robbed of time and opportunity just as the Great War left the world its heritage of a lost generation."

POPULAR CULTURE VIEWS THE DEPRESSION

Americans turned to popular culture to alleviate some of the trauma of the Great Depression. In June 1935 a Chicago radio listener wrote station WLS, "I feel your music and songs are what pulled me through this winter." She explained that "Half the time we were blue and broke. One year during the depression and no work. Kept from going on relief but lost everything we possessed doing so. So thanks for the songs, for they make life seem more like living." Mass culture flourished in the 1930s, offering not just entertainment but commentary on the problems that beset the nation. Movies and radio served as a forum for criticizing the system—especially politicians and bankers—as well as vehicles for reaffirming traditional ideals.

Despite the closing of one-third of the country's theaters by 1933, the movie industry and its studio system flourished. Sixty percent of Americans—some 60 to 75 million people—flocked to the cinema each week, seeking solace from the pain of the depression. In the early thirties moviegoers might be titillated or scandalized by Mae West, who was noted for her sexual innuendos: "I used to be Snow White, but I drifted." But in response to public outcry against immorality in the movies, especially from the Protestant and Catholic churches, the industry established a means of self-censorship, the Production Code Administration. After 1934 somewhat racy films were supplanted by sophisticated, fast-paced, screwball comedies like *It Happened One Night,* which swept the Oscars in 1934. The musical comedies of Fred Astaire and Ginger Rogers, including *Top Hat* (1935) and *The Gay Divorcee* (1934), in which the two dancers seemed to glide effortlessly through opulent sets, provided a stark contrast with most movie-goers' own lives.

But Hollywood, which produced 5,000 films during the decade, offered much more than what on the surface might seem to be escapist entertainment. Many of its movies contained complex messages that reflected a real sense of the societal crisis that engulfed the nation. The cultural historian Lawrence W. Levine has argued that depression-era films were "deeply grounded in the realities and intricacies of the Depression" and thus offer "a rich array of insights" into the period. Even if they did not deal specifically with the economic or political crisis, many films reaffirmed traditional values like democracy, individualism, and egalitarianism. They

Dancing Cheek to Cheek

During the Great Depression, Americans turned to inexpensive recreational activities such as listening to the radio and going to the movies. One of the most popular attractions in Hollywood movies was the dance team of Fred Astaire and Ginger Rogers, who starred together in ten movies. (Steve Schapiro)

also contained criticisms—suggestions that the system was not working or that law and order had broken down. Thus, popular gangster movies, such as *Public Enemy* (1931), with James Cagney, or *Little Caesar* (1930), starring Edward G. Robinson, could be seen as perverse Horatio Alger tales, in which the main character struggled to succeed in a harsh environment. Often these movies suggested that incompetent or corrupt politicians, police, and businessmen were as much to blame for organized crime as the gangsters themselves.

Depression-era films repeatedly portrayed politicians as cynical and corrupt. In *Washington Merry-Go-Round* (1932), lobbyists manipulated weak congressmen to undermine democratic rule. The Marx Brothers' irreverent comedies more humorously criticized authority—and most everything else. In *Duck Soup* (1933) Groucho Marx played Rufus T. Firefly, president of the mythical Freedonia, who sings gleefully:

> The last man nearly ruined this place,
> He didn't know what to do with it.
> If you think this country's bad off now,
> Just wait till I get through with it.

Few filmmakers left more of a mark on the decade than Frank Capra. An Italian immigrant who personified the possibilities for success the United States offered, Capra made films that spoke to Americans' idealism. In movies like *Mr. Deeds Goes to Town* (1936) and *Mr. Smith Goes to Washington* (1939), he pitted the virtuous small-town hero against corrupt urban shysters—businessmen, politicians, lobbyists, and newspaper publishers—whose machinations subverted the nation's ideals. Though the hero usually prevailed, Capra was realistic enough to suggest that the victory was not necessarily permanent and that the problems the nation faced were serious.

Radio occupied an increasingly important place in popular culture during the 1930s. At the beginning of the decade about 13 million households had radios; by the end 27.5 million owned them. Listeners tuned in to daytime serials like *Ma Perkins,* picked up useful household hints on the *The Betty Crocker Hour,* or enjoyed the Big Band "swing" of Benny Goodman, Duke Ellington, and Tommy Dorsey. Weekly variety shows featured Jack Benny; George Burns and Gracie Allen, and the ventriloquist Edgar Bergen and his impudent dummy, Charlie McCarthy. And millions of listeners followed the adventures of the Lone Ranger (with his cry "Heigh-ho, Silver"), Superman, and Dick Tracy.

Like movies, radio offered Americans more than escape. A running gag in comedian Jack Benny's show was his stinginess; audiences could identify with an unwillingness—or inability—to spend money. Even more relevant was Benny's distrust of banks. He kept his money in an underground vault guarded by a pet polar bear named Carmichael—presumably a more reliable place than the nation's financial institutions. *Amos 'n' Andy* (see Chapter 23) is remembered primarily for its racial stereotyping. But the exceptionally popular show also dealt with hard times, often referring explicitly to the depression. A central theme was the contrast between Amos's hard work and Andy's more carefree approach to life. Amos, tending to believe that the nation's economic crisis had been brought about by the extravagant spending of the 1920s, criticized his friend's fiscal irresponsibility. As the historian Arthur Frank Wertheim notes, "The way that the characters' hopes for monetary success were turned into business failures mirrored the lives of many Americans." Though *Amos 'n' Andy* reinforced racial stereotypes, it also reaffirmed the traditional values of "diligence, saving, and generosity."

Mr. Smith Goes to Washington

In director Frank Capra's classic 1939 film, *Mr. Smith Goes to Washington,* actor Jimmy Stewart plays an idealistic young senator who exposes the unscrupulous political machine that dominates his home state. In response, the machine frames Senator Smith for corruption. Although he is eventually vindicated, in this scene the despairing Smith encounters the avalanche of hostile mail generated against him by his crooked opponents. (MOMA-Film Stills Archive)

Americans did not spend all their leisure time in commercial entertainment. In a resurgence of traditionalism, attendance at religious services rose, and the home again became a center for pleasurable pastimes. Amateur photography and stamp collecting enjoyed tremendous vogues, as did the board game Monopoly. Reading aloud from books borrowed from the public library was another affordable diversion. But Americans bought books, too. Taking advantage of new manufacturing processes that made books cheaper, they made best sellers of Margaret Mitchell's *Gone with the Wind* (1936), James Hilton's *Lost Horizon* (1933), and Pearl Buck's *The Good Earth* (1932). Finally, "talking was the Great Depression pastime," recalled the columnist Russell Baker. "Unlike the movies, talk was free."

Harder Times

Much writing about the 1930s has focused on white working-class or middle-class families caught suddenly in a downward spiral. For African Americans, farmers, and Mexican Americans, times had always been hard; during the 1930s they got much harder. As the poet Langston Hughes noted, "The depression brought everybody down a peg or two. And the Negroes had but few pegs to fall."

AFRICAN AMERICANS IN THE DEPRESSION

The African American worker had always known discrimination and limited opportunities and thus viewed the depression differently from most whites. "It didn't mean too much to him, the Great American Depression, as you call it," one man remarked. "There was no such thing. The best he could be is a janitor or a porter or shoeshine boy. It only became official when it hit the white man." The novelist and poet Maya Angelou, who grew up in Stamps, Arkansas, recalled, "The country had been in the throes of the Depression for two years before the Negroes in Stamps knew it. I think that everyone thought the Depression, like everything else, was for the white folks."

Despite the black migration to northern cities, which had begun before World War I, as late as 1940 more than 75 percent of African Americans still lived in the South. Nearly all black farmers lived in the South, their condition scarcely better than it had been at the end of Reconstruction. Only 20 percent of black farmers owned their own land; the rest toiled at the bottom of the South's exploitative agricultural system as tenant farmers, farm hands, and sharecroppers. African Americans rarely earned more than $200 a year, less than a quarter of the annual average wages of a factory worker. In one Louisiana parish black women averaged only $41.67 a year picking cotton.

Throughout the 1920s southern agriculture had suffered from falling prices and overproduction. The depression made an already desperate situation worse. Some black farmers tried to protect themselves by joining the Southern Tenant Farmers Union (STFU), which was founded in 1934. The STFU was one of the few southern groups that welcomed both blacks and whites. Landowners, however, had a stake in keeping sharecroppers from organizing, and they countered the union's efforts with repression and harassment. In the end the STFU could do little to reform an agricultural system that depended on a single crop—cotton.

All blacks faced harsh social and political discrimination throughout the South. In a celebrated 1931 case in Scottsboro, Alabama, two white women who had been riding a freight train claimed to have been raped by nine black youths, all under twenty years old. The two women's stories contained many inconsistencies, and one woman later recanted. But in the South when a white woman claimed to have been raped by a black, she was taken at her word. Two weeks later juries composed entirely of white men found all nine defendants guilty of rape; eight were sentenced to death. (One defendant escaped the death penalty because he was a minor.) Though the U.S. Supreme Court overturned the sentences in 1932 and ordered new trials on grounds that the defendants had been denied adequate legal counsel, five of the men eventually were reconvicted and sentenced to long prison terms.

The hasty trials and the harsh sentences, especially given the defendants' young age, stirred public protest, prompting the International Labor Defense (ILD), a labor organization tied closely to the Communist Party, to take over the defense. Though the Communist Party had targeted the struggle against racism as a priority in the early 1930s, it was making little headway recruiting African Americans. "It's bad enough being black, why be red?" was a common reaction. White southerners resented radical groups' interference, noting that almost all those involved in the Scottsboro defense were northerners and Jews. Declared a local solicitor, "Alabama justice cannot be bought and sold with Jew money from New York."

The Scottsboro case received wide coverage in black communities across the country. Along with an increase in lynching in the early 1930s (twenty blacks were lynched in 1930, twenty-four in 1933), it gave black Americans a strong incentive to head for the North and the Midwest. Harlem, one of their main destinations, was already strained by the enormous influx of African Americans in the 1920s. The depression only aggravated the housing shortage. Residential segregation kept blacks from moving elsewhere, so they paid excessive rents to live in deteriorating buildings where crowded living conditions fostered disease and premature death. As whites clamored for jobs traditionally held by blacks—as waiters, domestic servants, elevator operators, and garbage collectors—unemployment in Harlem rose to 50 percent, twice the national rate. At the height of the depression, shelters and soup kitchens staffed by the Divine Peace Mission, under the leadership of the charismatic black religious leader Father Divine, provided 3,000 meals a day for Harlem's destitute.

In March 1935 Harlem exploded in the only major race riot of the decade. Anger about the lack of jobs, a slowdown in relief services, and economic exploitation of the black community had been building for years. Although white-owned stores were entirely dependent on black trade, store owners would not employ blacks. The arrest of a black shoplifter, followed by rumors that he had been severely beaten by white police, triggered the riot. Four blacks were killed, and $2 million worth of property was damaged.

There were some signs of hope for African Americans in the 1930s. Partly in response to the 1935 riot but mainly in return for growing black allegiance to the

Lynching

The threat of lynching remained a terrifying part of life for African Americans in the 1930s, and not just in the South. Artist Joe Jones set this canvas in 1933, perhaps influenced by the fact that twenty-four blacks were lynched that year. He gave it the ironic title of *American Justice, 1933 (White Justice).* (Collection of Philip J. and Suzanne Schiller)

Democratic Party (see Chapter 25), the New Deal would channel significant amounts of relief money toward blacks outside the south. And the National Association for the Advancement of Colored People (NAACP) continued to challenge the status quo of race relations. Though calls for racial justice went largely unheeded during the depression, World War II and its aftermath would further the struggle for black equality.

DUST BOWL MIGRATIONS

A distressed agricultural sector had been one of the causes of the Great Depression. In the 1930s conditions only got worse, especially for farmers on the Great Plains. In the semiarid states of Oklahoma, Texas, New Mexico, Colorado, Arkansas, and

Kansas, farmers had always risked the ravages of drought (see Chapter 16), but the years 1930 to 1941 witnessed the worst drought in the country's history. Low rainfall alone did not create the Dust Bowl, however. National and international market forces, like the rising demand for wheat during World War I, had caused farmers to push the farming frontier beyond its natural limits. To capture a profit they had stripped the land of its natural vegetation, destroying the delicate ecological balance of the plains. When the rains dried up and the winds came, nothing remained to hold the soil. Huge clouds of dust rolled over the plains, causing streetlights to blink on as if night had fallen. Dust seeped into houses and "blackened the pillow around one's head, the dinner plates on the table, the bread dough on the back of the stove."

The ecological disaster prompted a mass exodus from the plains. Their crops ruined, their lands barren and dry, their homes foreclosed for debts they could not pay, at least 350,000 Okies (so-called whether or not they were from Oklahoma) loaded their belongings into beat-up Fords and headed west, encouraged by handbills distributed by growers that promised good jobs in California. Some went to metropolitan areas, but about half settled in rural areas where they worked for low wages as migratory farm laborers. John Steinbeck's novel *The Grapes of Wrath* (1939) immortalized them and their journey. In the novel the Joads abandon their land not only because of drought but also as a result of the economic transformation of American agriculture that had begun during World War I. By the 1930s large-scale commercialized farming had spread to the plains, where family farmers still used draft animals. In Steinbeck's novel, after the bank forecloses on the Joads' farm, a gasoline-engine tractor, the symbol of mechanized farming, plows under their crops and demolishes their home. Though it was a powerful novel, *The Grapes of Wrath* did not convey the diversity of the westward migration. Not all Okies were destitute dirt farmers; perhaps one in six was a professional, a business proprietor, or a white-collar worker. For most the drive west was fairly easy. Route 66 was a paved two-lane road; in a decent car, the journey from Oklahoma or Texas to California took only three to four days.

Before the 1930s Californians had developed a different type of agriculture from that practiced in the Southwest and Midwest. Basically industrial in nature, California agriculture was large-scale, intensive, and diversified, ironically requiring a massive irrigation system that would lay the groundwork for serious future environmental problems. The key crops were specialty foods—citruses, grapes, potatoes—whose staggered harvests required a great deal of transient labor during short picking seasons. A steady supply of cheap migrant labor provided by Chinese, Mexicans, Okies, Filipinos, and, briefly, East Indians made this type of farming economically feasible.

The migrants had a lasting impact on California culture. At first they met outright hostility from old-time Californians—a demoralizing experience for white native-born Protestants, who were ashamed of the Okie stereotype. But they stayed, filling important roles in California's expanding economy. Soon some communities in the San Joaquin Valley—Bakersfield, Fresno, Merced, Modesto, and Stockton—took on a distinctly Okie cast, identifiable by southern-influenced evangelical religion and the growing popularity of country music.

MEXICAN AMERICAN COMMUNITIES

As Okies arrived in California, many Mexican Americans were leaving. In the depths of the depression, with fear of competition from foreign workers at a peak, perhaps a third of the Mexican American population, most of them immigrants, returned to Mexico. The federal government's deportation policy—fostered by racism and made feasible by the proximity of Mexico—was partly responsible for the exodus, but many more Mexicans left voluntarily when work ran out and local relief agencies refused to assist them. Los Angeles lost approximately one-third of its Mexican community of 150,000—the largest concentration of Mexicans outside Mexico—during the deportations, which separated families, disrupted children's education, and caused extreme financial hardship during the worst years of the depression. Although forced repatriation slowed after 1932, for those who remained in America deportation was still a constant threat, an unmistakable reminder of their fragile status in the United States.

Discrimination and exploitation were omnipresent in the Mexican community. The harsh experiences of migrant workers influenced a young Mexican American named César Chávez, who would become one of the twentieth century's most influential labor organizers. In the mid-1930s, Chávez's father became involved in several bitter labor struggles in California's Imperial Valley. Thirty-seven major agricultural strikes occurred in California in 1933 alone, including one in the San Joaquin Valley that mobilized 18,000 cotton pickers—the largest agricultural strike to date. All these strikes failed, but they gave the young Chávez a background in labor organizing, which he would use to found a national farm workers' union in 1962.

Not all Mexican Americans were migrant farm workers. Many worked as miners; others held industrial jobs, especially in steel mills, meat-packing plants, and refineries, where they established a vibrant tradition of labor activism. In California, Mexican Americans also found employment in fruit- and vegetable-processing plants. Young single women especially preferred the higher-paying cannery work to domestic service, needlework, and farm labor. In plants owned by corporate giants like Del Monte, McNeill, and Libby, Mexican American women earned around $2.50 a day, while their male counterparts received $3.50 to $4.50. Labor unions came to the canneries in 1939 with the formation of the United Cannery, Agricultural, Packing, and Allied Workers of America, an unusually democratic union in which women, the majority of the rank-and-file workers, played a leading role.

Activism in the fields and factories demonstrated how a second generation of Mexican Americans, born in the United States, had turned increasingly to the struggle for political and economic justice in the United States rather than retaining primary allegiance to Mexico. According to the historian George Sánchez, they were creating "their own version of Americanism without abandoning Mexican culture." Joining American labor unions and becoming more involved in American politics (see Chapter 25) were important steps in the creation of a distinct Mexican American ethnic identity.

Herbert Hoover and the Great Depression

Had Herbert Hoover been elected in 1920 instead of 1928, he probably would have been a popular president. As the director of successful food conservation programs at home and charitable food relief abroad during World War I, he was respected as an intelligent and able administrator. Although Hoover's name frequently emerged as a possible candidate in 1920, he did not run for president until the end of the decade. Timing was against him. Although his optimistic predictions in the 1928 campaign—that "the poorhouse is vanishing from among us" and that America was "nearer to the final triumph over poverty than ever before in the history of any land"—reflected beliefs that many Americans shared, that prosperity and Hoover's reputation were soon to be dramatically undermined. When the stock market crashed in 1929, he stubbornly insisted that the downturn was only temporary. In June 1930 he greeted a business delegation with the words "Gentlemen, you have come sixty days too late. The Depression is over." As the country hit rock bottom in 1931 and 1932, the president finally acted, but by then it was too little, too late.

HOOVER RESPONDS

Hoover's approach to the Great Depression was shaped by his priorities as secretary of commerce. Hoping to avoid coercive measures on the part of the federal government, he turned to the business community for leadership in overcoming the economic downturn. Hoover asked business executives to maintain wages and production levels voluntarily and to work with the government to build people's confidence in the economic system.

Hoover did not rely solely on public pronouncements, however; he also used public funds and federal action to encourage recovery. Soon after the stock-market crash he cut federal taxes and called on state and local governments to increase their expenditures on public construction projects. He signed the 1929 Agricultural Marketing Act, which gave the federal government an unprecedented role in stabilizing agriculture. In 1930 and the first half of 1931 Hoover raised the federal budget for public works to $423 million, a dramatic increase in expenditures not traditionally considered to be the federal government's responsibility. Hoover also eased the international crisis by declaring a moratorium on the payment of Allied debts and reparations early in the summer of 1931. The depression continued, however. When

Public Assistance Fails a Southern Farm Family

When times were bad, even public assistance could be bad for a family in dire straits. Here a young mother living in the farming community of Commerce, Georgia, relates how relief efforts ironically proved to be a burden to her family of eight.

I've just met with a problem I cannot solve alone. I am a Mother of six children the oldest is only 11 years old the youngest 18 months and I'm expecting another in March. We couldn't get any crop for 1936 because we could neither furnish ourselves or had any stock. So here we are having made out on a little work once in a while all summer. And then in Aug I had to have a serious operation and now I'm not able to feed & clothe our six children as my husband couldnt find anything at all to do was compelled to get on relief job at $1.28 a day 16 days a month. Well you take 8 meals 3 times a day out of $1.28 and what will you have left is 24 meals and what kind of meals do you have? We have to buy everything we eat. We have nothing except what we buy. Our bedclothes are threadbare our clothes the same. No shoes and no money to buy yet the relief say that cant help us as he is working. Can he work naked. Can he sleep cold. I don't know of any one at all that can help me and I know we cant go on like this. . . .

I hate to be like this but can a person that is willing to work for a living and that honest and disable to help themselves sit idle and see their small children suffer day after day without enough food or clothes to keep their bodies warm when there are thousands of people with plenty to give if they knew your need.

How it hurts to know that you are almost starving in the land of plenty.

SOURCE: Julia Kirk Blackwelder, "Letters from the Great Depression," in *Southern Exposure* 6, no. 3 (Fall 1978), p. 77.

---

the president asked Congress for a 33 percent tax increase to balance the budget, the ill-advised move choked investment and, to a lesser extent, consumption, contributing significantly to the continuation of the depression.

Hoover's most innovative program—one the New Deal would later draw on—was the Reconstruction Finance Corporation (RFC), approved by Congress in January 1932. Modeled on the War Finance Corporation of World War I and developed in collaboration with the business and banking communities, the RFC was the first federal institution created to intervene directly in the economy during peacetime. To alleviate the credit crunch for business, the RFC would provide federal loans to railroads, financial institutions, banks, and insurance companies in a strategy that has been called *pump priming*. In theory, money lent at the top of the economic structure would stimulate production, creating new jobs and increasing consumer spending. These benefits would eventually "trickle down" to the rest of the economy.

Unfortunately, the RFC lent its funds too cautiously to make a significant difference. Nonetheless, it represents a watershed in American political history and the growth of the federal government. When voluntary cooperation failed, the president had turned to federal action to stimulate the economy. Yet Hoover's break with the past had clear limits. In many ways, his support of the RFC was just another attempt to encourage business confidence. Compared with previous chief executives—and in contrast to his popular image as a "do-nothing" president—Hoover responded to the national emergency on an unprecedented scale. But the nation's needs were also unprecedented, and Hoover's programs failed to meet them (see American Voices, "Public Assistance Fails a Southern Farm Family").

In particular, federal programs fell short of helping the growing ranks of the unemployed. Hoover remained adamant in his refusal to consider any plan for direct federal relief to those out of work. Throughout his career he had believed that privately organized charities were sufficient to meet the nation's social welfare needs. During World War I he had headed the Commission for Relief of Belgium, a private group that distributed 5 million tons of food to Europe's suffering civilian population. And in 1927 he had coordinated a rescue and cleanup operation after a devastating flood of the Mississippi River left 16.5 million acres of land under water in seven states. The success of these and other predominantly voluntary responses to public emergencies had confirmed Hoover's belief that private charity, not federal aid, was the "American way" of solving social problems. He would not undermine the country's hallowed faith in individualism, even in the face of evidence that charities and state and local relief agencies could not meet the needs of a growing unemployed population.

RISING DISCONTENT

As the depression deepened, many citizens came to hate Herbert Hoover. Once the symbol of business prosperity, he became the scapegoat for the depression. "In Hoover we trusted, now we are busted," declared the hand-lettered signs carried by the down and out. New terms entered the vocabulary: Hoovervilles (shantytowns where people lived in packing crates and other makeshift shelters), Hoover flags (empty pockets turned inside out), Hoover blankets (newspapers). Hoover's declarations that nobody was starving, that hobos were better fed than ever before, seemed cruel and insensitive. His apparent willingness to bail out businesses and banks while leaving individuals to fend for themselves added to his reputation for cold-heartedness.

As the country entered the fourth year of depression, signs of rising discontent and rebellion emerged. Farmers were among the most vocal protestors, banding together to harass the bank agents and government officers who enforced evictions and foreclosures and to protest the low prices they received for their

Hoovervilles

By 1930 shantytowns had sprung up in most of the nation's cities. In New York City squatters camped out along the Hudson River railroad tracks, built makeshift homes in Central Park, or lived in the city dump. This scene from the old reservoir in Central Park looks east toward the fancy apartment buildings of Fifth Avenue and the Metropolitan Museum of Art, at left.
(Grant Smith/Corbis)

crops. Midwestern farmers had watched the price of wheat fall from $3 a bushel in 1920 to barely 30 cents in 1932. Now they formed the Farm Holiday Association, barricaded local roads, and dumped milk, vegetables, and other farm produce in the dirt rather than accept prices that would not cover their costs. Nothing better captured the cruel irony of maldistribution than farmers destroying food at a time when thousands were going hungry.

Protest was not confined to rural America, however. Bitter labor strikes occurred in the depths of the depression, despite the threat that strikers would lose their jobs. In Harlan County, Kentucky, in 1931 miners struck over a 10 percent wage cut. Their union was crushed by mine owners and the National Guard. In 1932 at Ford's River Rouge factory outside Detroit a demonstration provoked violence from police and Ford security forces; three demonstrators were killed, and fifty more seriously injured. Later some 40,000 people viewed the coffins under a banner charging that "Ford Gave Bullets for Bread."

In 1931 and 1932 violence broke out in the nation's cities. Groups of the unemployed battled local authorities over inadequate relief, staging rent riots and hunger marches. Some of these actions were organized by the Communist Party—still a tiny organization with only 12,000 members—as a challenge to the capitalist system, such as "unemployment councils" that agitated for jobs and food and a hunger march on Washington, D.C., in 1931. Though the marches were well attended and often got results from local and federal authorities, they did not necessarily win converts to communism.

Not radicals but veterans staged the most publicized—and most tragic—protest. In the summer of 1932 the "Bonus Army," a ragtag group of about 15,000 unemployed World War I veterans, hitchhiked to Washington to demand immediate payment of their bonuses, originally scheduled for distribution in 1945. While their leaders lobbied Congress, the Bonus Army camped out in the capital. "We were heroes in 1917, but we're bums now," one veteran complained bitterly. When the marchers refused to leave their Anacostia Flats camp, Hoover called out riot troops to clear the area. Led by General Douglas MacArthur, assisted by Major Dwight D. Eisenhower and Major George S. Patton, the troops burned the encampment to the ground. In the fight that followed, more than a hundred marchers were injured. Newsreel footage captured the deeply disturbing spectacle of the U.S. Army moving against its own veterans, and Hoover's popularity plunged even lower.

THE 1932 ELECTION: A NEW ORDER

Despite the evidence of discontent, the nation overall was not in a revolutionary mood as it approached the 1932 election. Having internalized Horatio Alger's ideal of the self-made man, many Americans initially blamed themselves rather than the system for their hardship. Despair and apathy, not anger, was their mood. The Republicans, who could find no credible way to dump an incumbent president, unenthusiastically renominated Hoover. The Democrats turned to Governor Franklin Delano Roosevelt of New York, who won the nomination by capitalizing on that state's reputation for innovative relief and unemployment programs.

Roosevelt, born into a wealthy New York family in 1882, had attended Harvard College and Columbia Law School. He had served in the New York State legislature and as assistant secretary of the navy in the Wilson administration, a post that had earned him the vice-presidential nomination on the Democratic ticket in 1920. Roosevelt's rise to the presidency was interrupted in 1921 by an attack of polio that left both his legs paralyzed for life. But he fought back from illness, emerging from the ordeal a stronger, more resilient man. "If you had spent two years in bed trying to wiggle your toe, after that anything would seem easy," he explained. His wife, Eleanor Roosevelt, strongly supported his return to public life and helped to mastermind his successful campaign for the governorship of New York in 1928.

The 1932 campaign for the presidency foreshadowed little of the New Deal. Roosevelt hinted only vaguely at new approaches to alleviating the depression: "The country needs and, unless I mistake its temper, the country demands bold, persistent experimentation." He won easily, receiving 22.8 million votes to Hoover's 15.7

million. Despite the nation's economic collapse, Americans remained firmly committed to the two-party system. The Socialist Party candidate, Norman Thomas, got fewer than a million votes, and the Communist Party candidate, party leader William Z. Foster, drew only 100,000 votes.

The 1932 election marked a turning point in American politics, the emergence of a Democratic coalition that would help to shape national politics for the next four decades. Roosevelt won the support of the Solid South, which returned to the Democratic fold after defecting in 1928 because of Al Smith's Catholicism and his views on Prohibition. Roosevelt drew substantial support in the West and in the cities, continuing a trend first noticed in 1928, when the Democrats appealed successfully to recent immigrants and urban ethnic groups. However, Roosevelt's election was hardly a mandate to reshape American political and economic institutions. Many people voted as much against Hoover as for Roosevelt.

Having spoken, the voters had to wait until Roosevelt's inauguration in March 1933 to see him put his ideas into action. (The four-month interval between the election and the inauguration was shortened by the Twentieth Amendment in 1933.) In the worst winter of the depression, Americans could do little but hope that things would get better. According to the most conservative estimates, unemployment stood at 20 to 25 percent nationwide. The rate was 50 percent in Cleveland, 60 percent in Akron, and 80 percent in Toledo—cities dependent on manufacturing jobs in industries that had essentially shut down. The nation's banking system was so close to collapse that many state governors closed banks temporarily to avoid further panic.

By the winter of 1932 to 1933 the depression had totally overwhelmed public welfare institutions. Private charity and public relief, both of whose expenditures had risen dramatically, still reached only a fraction of the needy. Hunger haunted cities and rural areas alike. When a teacher tried to send a coal miner's daughter home from school because she was weak from hunger, the girl replied, "It won't do any good . . . because this is sister's day to eat." In New York City hospitals reported ninety-five deaths from starvation. This was the America that Roosevelt inherited when he took the oath of office on March 4, 1933.

For Further Exploration

The 1930s are particularly rich in document collections of oral histories and other primary sources. Robert S. McElvaine's *Down and Out in the Great Depression* (1983) offers poignant letters written by ordinary people to the Roosevelts, Herbert Hoover, and other government officials. Studs Terkel's *Hard Times: An Oral History of the Great Depression* (1970) is an invaluable collection, as is Ann Banks, ed., *First-Person America*. See also Russell Baker's memoir about his depression-era childhood, *Growing Up* (1982). Similarly, there is much to choose from in the literature of the decade. The most familiar novel is John Steinbeck's *The Grapes of Wrath* (1939), but see also the radical novel *Pity Is Not Enough* (1933) by Josephine

TIMELINE

1929	Stock market crash		Franklin Delano Roosevelt is elected president.
1930	Midwestern drought (through 1941)		
	Hawley-Smoot Tariff slashes demand for U.S. imports.	**1933**	Unemployment rises to its highest level.
1931	Scottsboro case		Birth rate drops to its lowest level.
	Hoover declares a moratorium on Allied war debts.		Marx Brothers' *Duck Soup*
	Miners strike in Harlan County, Kentucky.	**1934**	Southern Tenant Farmers Union founded
	Communist-led hunger marches		*It Happened One Night* sweeps the Oscars.
1932	Reconstruction Finance Corporation created	**1935**	National Youth Administration created
	Bonus Army war veterans dispersed by U.S. Army troops		Harlem race riot
	Height of deportation of Mexican migrant workers	**1936**	Margaret Mitchell's *Gone with the Wind*
	Pearl S. Buck's *The Good Earth*		Birth control legalized
	Farm Holiday Association founded	**1939**	John Steinbeck's *The Grapes of Wrath*
	Violent strike at Ford's River Rouge plant in Michigan		Frank Capra's *Mr. Smith Goes to Washington*

Herbst and Richard Wright's *Native Son* (1940), his classic novel about Bigger Thomas, a young African American man in Chicago mired in a life of poverty and violence. A haunting account of southern poverty is *Let Us Now Praise Famous Men* (1940) by James Agee, with photographs by Walker Evans. For a collection of poetry, fiction, and nonfiction writing, see Harvey Swados, *The American Writer and the Great Depression* (1966).

The University of Virginia's "America in the 1930s" is a comprehensive site. See especially "On the Air," which offers audio clips of *Amos 'n' Andy* and other series at <http://xroads.virginia.edu/~1930s/home_1.html>. Much valuable material can be found on the University of Utrecht's "American Culture in the 1930s" site at <http://www.let.ruu.nl/ams/xroads/1930proj.htm>, which in turn points to other sites dealing with literature, film, and other aspects of American culture during the depression. The Library of Congress's American Memory collection has extensive material on the Depression, including a multimedia presentation, "Voices from the Dust Bowl: The Charles L. Todd and Robert Sonkin Migrant Worker Collection, 1940–41," at <http://lcweb2.loc.gov/ammem/afctshtml/tshome.html>.

Chapter 25

THE NEW DEAL
1933–1939

I have been seeing people who, according to almost any standard, have practically nothing to look forward to or hope for. But there is hope; confidence, something intangible and real: the president won't forget us.

—MARTHA GELHORN, GASTON COUNTY, NORTH CAROLINA, 1934

In his bold inaugural address on March 4, 1933, President Franklin Delano Roosevelt told a despondent, impoverished nation, "The only thing we have to fear is fear itself." That memorable phrase rallied a nation that had already endured almost four years of the worst economic contraction in its history—with no end in sight. His demeanor grim and purposeful, Roosevelt preached his first inaugural address like a sermon. Issuing ringing declarations of his vision of governmental activism—"This Nation asks for action, and action now"—he repeatedly compared combating the Great Depression to fighting a war. The new president was willing to ask Congress for "broad Executive power to wage a war against the emergency, as great as the power that would be given to me if we were in fact invaded by a foreign foe." He promised to "assume unhesitatingly the leadership of this great army of our people dedicated to a disciplined attack upon our common problems."

To wage this war, Roosevelt proposed the New Deal—a term that he first used in his acceptance speech at the Democratic National Convention in 1932 and that eventually came to stand for his administration's complex set of responses to the nation's economic collapse. The New Deal was never a definitive plan of action but rather evolved and expanded over the course of Roosevelt's presidency. In a time of major crisis it was meant to relieve suffering and conserve the nation's political and economic institutions through unprecedented activity on the part of the national government. Its legacy would be an expanded federal presence in the economy and in the lives of ordinary citizens.

The New Deal Takes Over, 1933–1935

The Great Depression destroyed Herbert Hoover's political reputation and helped to make Roosevelt's. Although some Americans—especially wealthy conservatives—hated FDR, he was immensely popular and beloved by many. Ironically, the ideological differences between Hoover and Roosevelt were not that vast. Both were committed to maintaining the nation's basic institutional structure. Both believed in the basic morality of a balanced budget and extolled the values of hard work, cooperation, and sacrifice. But Roosevelt's personal charisma, his political savvy, and his willingness to experiment made all the difference. Above all, his New Deal programs put people to work, instilling hope and restoring the nation's confidence.

ROOSEVELT'S STYLE OF LEADERSHIP

While the New Deal represented many things to many people, one unifying factor was the personality of Franklin Roosevelt. A superb and pragmatic politician, Roosevelt crafted his administration's program in response to shifting political and economic conditions rather than according to a set ideology or plan. He experimented with an idea; if it did not work, he tried another. "I have no expectation of making a hit every time I come to bat," Roosevelt told his critics. "What I seek is the highest possible batting average."

Roosevelt established an unusually close rapport with the American people. "Mr. Roosevelt is the only man we ever had in the White House who would understand that my boss is a son of a bitch," remarked one worker. Many ordinary citizens credited Roosevelt with the positive changes in their lives, saying. "He gave me a job" or "He saved my home." Roosevelt's masterful use of the new medium of radio, typified by the "fireside chats" he broadcast during his first two terms, fostered this personal identification. In the week after the inauguration more than 450,000 letters, many of which addressed Roosevelt as a friend or a member of the family, poured into the White House. An average of 5,000 to 8,000 arrived weekly for the rest of the decade. Whereas one person had handled public correspondence during the Hoover administration, a staff of fifty was required under Roosevelt.

Roosevelt's personal charisma allowed him to continue the expansion of presidential power begun in the administrations of Theodore Roosevelt and Woodrow Wilson. From the beginning he dramatically expanded the role of the executive branch in initiating policy, thereby helping to create the modern presidency. For policy formulation he turned to his talented cabinet, which included Secretary of the Interior Harold Ickes, Frances Perkins at Labor, Henry A. Wallace at Agriculture, and an old friend, Henry Morgenthau Jr., at Treasury. During the interregnum (the period between election and inauguration) Roosevelt relied so heavily on the advice of the Columbia University professors Raymond Moley, Rexford Tugwell, and Adolph A. Berle Jr. that the press dubbed them the "Brain Trust."

FDR

President Franklin Delano Roosevelt was a consummate politician who loved the adulation of a crowd, such as this one greeting him in Warm Springs, Georgia, in 1933. He consciously adopted a cheerful mien to keep people from feeling sorry for him because of his infirmity, knowing that he could not be a successful politician if the public pitied him.
(Corbis-Bettmann)

THE HUNDRED DAYS

The first problem the new president confronted was the banking crisis. Since the stock-market crash about 9 million people had lost their savings. On the eve of the inauguration thirty-eight states had closed their banks, and the remaining ten had restricted their hours of operation. On March 5, the day after the inauguration, the president declared a national "bank holiday"—a euphemism for closing all the banks—and called Congress into special session. Four days later Congress, which responded enthusiastically to most early New Deal legislative proposals, passed Roosevelt's proposed emergency banking bill, which permitted banks to reopen beginning on March 13—but only if a Treasury Department inspection showed they had sufficient cash reserves. The House approved the plan after only thirty-eight minutes of debate.

The Emergency Banking Act, which Roosevelt developed in consultation with banking leaders, was a conservative document that mirrored Herbert Hoover's proposals. The difference was the public's reaction. On the Sunday evening before the banks reopened, Roosevelt broadcast his first fireside chat to a radio audience estimated at 60 million. In simple terms he reassured citizens that the banks were safe, and Americans believed him. When the banks reopened on Monday morning, deposits exceeded withdrawals. "Capitalism was saved in eight days," observed Raymond Moley, who had served as Roosevelt's speechwriter in the 1932 campaign. By using the federal government to investigate the nation's banks and restore confidence in the system, the banking act did its job. Though more than 4,000 banks failed in 1933—the vast majority in the months before the law took effect—only 61 closed their doors in 1934.

The Banking Act was the first of fifteen pieces of major legislation enacted by Congress in the opening months of the Roosevelt administration. This legislative session, known as the "Hundred Days," remains one of the most productive ever. Congress created the Home Owners Loan Corporation to refinance home mortgages threatened by foreclosure. A second banking law, the Glass-Steagall Act, curbed speculation by separating investment banking from commercial banking and created the Federal Deposit Insurance Corporation (FDIC), which insured deposits up to $2,500. Another act established the Civilian Conservation Corps (CCC), which sent 250,000 young men to do reforestation and conservation work. The Tennessee Valley Authority (TVA) received legislative approval for its innovative plan of government-sponsored regional development and public energy. And in a move that lifted public spirits immeasurably, Roosevelt legalized beer in April. Full repeal of Prohibition came eight months later in December 1933.

To speed economic recovery the Roosevelt administration targeted three pressing problems—agricultural overproduction, business failures, and unemployment relief. Roosevelt considered a healthy farming sector crucial to the nation's economic well-being. As he put it in 1929, "If farmers starve today, we will all starve tomorrow." Thus, he viewed the Agricultural Adjustment Act (AAA) as a key step toward the nation's recovery. The AAA established a system for seven major commodities (wheat, cotton, corn, hogs, rice, tobacco, and dairy products) that provided cash subsidies to farmers who cut production—a tradition that continues to the present day. These benefits were financed by a tax on processing (such as the milling of wheat), which was passed on to consumers. New Deal planners hoped prices would rise in response to the federally subsidized scarcity, spurring a general recovery.

Though the AAA stabilized the agricultural sector, its benefits were distributed unevenly. Subsidies for reducing production went primarily to the owners of large and medium-size farms, who often cut production by reducing their renters' and sharecroppers' acreage rather than their own. In the South, where many sharecroppers were black and the landowners and government administrators white, that strategy had racial overtones. As many as 200,000 black tenant farmers were displaced from their land by the AAA. Thus, New Deal agricultural policies fostered the migration of marginal farmers in the South and Midwest to northern cities and California, while they consolidated the economic and political clout of larger land-holders.

The New Deal's major response to the problem of economic recovery, the National Industrial Recovery Act, launched the National Recovery Administration (NRA). The NRA established a system of industrial self-government to handle the problems of overproduction, cutthroat competition, and price instability that had caused business failures. For each industry a code of prices and production quotas, similar to those for farm products, was hammered out. In effect, these legally enforceable agreements suspended the antitrust laws. The codes also established minimum wages and maximum hours and outlawed child labor. One of the most far-reaching provisions, Section 7(a), guaranteed workers the right to organize and bargain collectively, "through representatives of their own choosing." These union rights dramatically spurred the growth of the labor movement in the 1930s.

General Hugh Johnson, a colorful if erratic administrator, headed the NRA. Johnson supervised negotiations for more than 600 NRA codes, ranging from large industries such as coal, cotton, and steel to small ones such as dog food, costume jewelry, and even burlesque theaters. Trade associations, controlled by large companies, tended to dominate the code-drafting process, thus solidifying the power of large businesses at the expense of smaller enterprises. Labor had little input, and consumer interests almost none.

The early New Deal also addressed the critical problem of unemployment. In the fourth year of the depression the total exhaustion of private and local sources of charity made some form of federal relief essential. Reluctantly, Roosevelt moved toward federal assumption of responsibility for the unemployed. The Federal Emergency Relief Administration (FERA), set up in May 1933 under the direction of Harry Hopkins, a social worker from New York, offered federal money to the states for relief programs. FERA was designed to keep people from starving until other recovery measures took hold. In his first two hours in office Hopkins distributed $5 million. Over the program's two-year existence FERA spent $1 billion.

Roosevelt and his advisers maintained a strong distaste for the dole. As Hopkins worried, "I don't think anybody can go year after year, month after month, accepting relief without affecting his character in some ways unfavorably. It is probably going to undermine the independence of hundreds of thousands of families." Whenever possible New Deal administrators promoted work relief over cash subsidies, and they consistently favored jobs that would not compete directly with the private sector. When the Public Works Administration (PWA), under Secretary of the Interior Harold L. Ickes, received a $3.3 billion appropriation in 1933, Ickes's cautiousness in initiating public works projects limited the agency's effectiveness. But in November 1933 Roosevelt established the Civil Works Administration (CWA) and named Harry Hopkins its head. Within thirty days the CWA had put 2.6 million men and women to work; at its peak in January 1934 it employed 4 million in jobs such as repairing bridges, building highways, constructing public buildings, and setting up community projects. The CWA, regarded as a stopgap measure to get the country through the winter of 1933 to 1934, lapsed the next spring after spending all its funds.

Many of these early emergency measures were deliberately inflationary. They were designed to trigger price increases, which were thought necessary to stimulate recovery and halt the steep deflation. Another element of this strategy was Roosevelt's executive order of April 18, 1933, to abandon the international gold standard and allow gold to rise in value like any other commodity. As the price of gold rose, administrators hoped, so too would the prices of manufactured and agricultural goods. Though removing the country from the gold standard did not have much impact on the American economy, it did provide the Federal Reserve System freedom to pursue domestic goals such as stable prices and full employment without being tied to the value of gold on the international market. Now it could manipulate the value of the dollar in response to fluctuating economic conditions.

When an exhausted Congress recessed in June 1933, much had been accomplished. Rarely had a president so dominated a legislative session. A mass of "alphabet soup agencies," as the New Deal programs came to be known, had been created. But though they gave the impression of action and initiated a slight economic upturn, they did not turn the economy around.

After the Hundred Days, with no end to the depression in sight, Roosevelt and Congress continued to pass legislation to promote recovery and restore confidence. Much of it focused on reforming business practices to prevent future depressions. In 1934 Congress established the Securities and Exchange Commission (SEC) to regulate the stock market and prevent insider trading, fraud, and other abuses. The Banking Act of 1935 authorized the president to appoint a new Board of Governors of the Federal Reserve System, placing control of interest rates and other money-market policies at the federal level rather than with regional banks. By requiring all large state banks to join the Federal Reserve System by 1942 to take advantage of the federal deposit insurance system, the law further encouraged centralization of the nation's banking system.

THE NEW DEAL UNDER ATTACK

As Congress and the president consolidated the New Deal, their work came under attack from several quarters. Although Roosevelt billed himself as the savior of capitalism, noting that "to preserve we had to reform," his actions provoked strong hostility from many Americans. To the wealthy Roosevelt became simply "that man," a traitor to his class. Business leaders and conservative Democrats formed the Liberty League in 1934 to lobby against the New Deal and its "reckless spending" and "socialist" reforms.

The conservative majority on the Supreme Court also disagreed with the direction of the New Deal. On "Black Monday," May 27, 1935, the Supreme Court struck down the NRA in *Schechter v. United States,* ruling unanimously that the National Industrial Recovery Act represented an unconstitutional delegation of legislative power to the executive. The so-called sick-chicken case concerned a Brooklyn, New York, firm convicted of violating NRA codes by selling diseased poultry. In its decision the court also ruled that the NRA regulated commerce within states, while the Constitution limited federal regulation to interstate commerce. Roosevelt protested that the Court's narrow interpretation would return the Constitution "to the horse-and-buggy definition of interstate commerce" and worried privately that the Court might invalidate the entire New Deal.

Other citizens thought the New Deal had not gone far enough. Francis Townsend, a Long Beach, California, doctor, spoke for the nation's elderly. Many Americans feared poverty in old age because few had pension plans and many had lost their life savings in bank failures. In 1933 Townsend proposed the Old Age Revolving Pension Plan, which would have given $200 a month—a considerable sum at the time—to citizens over the age of sixty. To receive payments the elderly would have had to retire from their jobs, thus opening their positions to others, and would also have had to agree to spend the money within a month. Townsend Clubs soon sprang up across the country, particularly in the Far West.

Father Charles Coughlin also challenged Roosevelt's leadership, attracting a large following, especially in the Midwest. A parish priest in the Detroit suburb of Royal Oak, Coughlin had turned to the radio in the mid-1920s to enlarge his pastorate. In 1933 about 40 million Americans listened regularly to the Radio Priest's broadcasts. At first Coughlin supported the New Deal, but he soon broke with Roosevelt over the president's refusal to support the nationalization of the banking system and expansion of the money supply. In 1935 Coughlin organized the National Union for Social Justice to promote his views, billing them as an alternative to those of "Franklin Double-Crossing Roosevelt." Because he was Canadian-born and a priest, Coughlin was not likely to make a run for president, but his rapidly growing constituency threatened to complicate the 1936 election.

The most direct threat to Roosevelt came from Senator Huey Long. In a single term as governor of Louisiana the flamboyant Long had achieved stunning popularity. He had increased the share of state taxes paid by corporations and had embarked on a program of public works that included construction of new highways, bridges, hospitals, and schools. But Long's accomplishments came at a price: to push through his reforms he had seized almost dictatorial control of the state government. He maintained control over Louisiana's political machine even after his election to the U.S. Senate in 1930. Though he supported Roosevelt in 1932, he made no secret of his own presidential ambitions.

In 1934 Senator Long broke with the New Deal, arguing that its programs did not go far enough. Like Coughlin he established his own national movement, the Share Our Wealth Society, which boasted over 4 million followers by 1935. Arguing that the unequal distribution of wealth in the United States was the fundamental cause of the depression, Long advocated taxing 100 percent of all incomes over $1

The Kingfish

Huey Long, the Louisiana governor and senator, was one of the most controversial figures in American political history. He took his nickname "Kingfish" from a character in the popular radio show *Amos 'n' Andy*. Long inspired one of the most powerful political novels of all time, Robert Penn Warren's *All the King's Men*, which won a Pulitzer Prize in 1946. (UPI/Corbis-Bettmann)

million and all inheritances over $5 million, distributing the money to the rest of the population. He knew his plan was unworkable but confided privately, "When they figure that out, I'll have something new for them."

Like Coughlin, Long offered simple solutions to the nation's economic ills. Their extreme proposals alarmed liberals. Coughlin's rhetoric, furthermore, often had anti-Semitic overtones, and both men showed little regard for the niceties of representative government. Coughlin had actually promised to dictate if necessary to preserve democracy. And the demagogic Long had dismissed complaints about his unconstitutional interference with the Louisiana legislative process by announcing, "I'm the Constitution around here." Long's and Coughlin's ideas and their rapid rise in popularity suggested strong currents of public dissatisfaction with the Roosevelt administration. The president's strategists feared that Long might join forces with Coughlin and Townsend to form a third party, enabling the Republicans to win the 1936 election.

The Second New Deal, 1935–1938

As the depression continued and attacks on the New Deal mounted, Roosevelt and his advisers embarked on a new course, which historians have labeled the Second New Deal. By 1935, frustrated by his inability to win the support of big business, Roosevelt began to openly criticize the "money classes," proudly stating that "We have earned the hatred of entrenched greed." Pushed to the left by the popularity of movements like Long's as well as by signs of militancy among workers, Roosevelt, his eye fixed firmly on the 1936 election, began to construct a new coalition and broaden the scope of his response to the depression. Unlike the First New Deal, which focused on recovery, the Second New Deal emphasized reform and promoted legislation to increase the role of the federal government in providing for the welfare of citizens.

LEGISLATIVE ACCOMPLISHMENTS

The first beneficiary of Roosevelt's change in direction was the labor movement. The rising number of strikes in 1934—about 1,800 involving a total of 1.5 million workers—reflected the dramatic growth of rank-and-file militancy. After the Supreme Court declared the NRA unconstitutional in 1935, invalidating Section 7(a), labor representatives demanded effective legislation. The Wagner Act (1935), named for its sponsor, Senator Robert F. Wagner of New York, offered a degree of protection to labor. It upheld the right of industrial workers to join a union (farm workers were not covered) and outlawed many unfair labor practices used to squelch unions, such as firing workers for union activities. The act also established the non-partisan National Labor Relations Board (NLRB) to protect workers from employer coercion, supervise elections for union representation, and guarantee the process of collective bargaining.

The Social Security Act signed by Roosevelt on August 14, 1935, was partly a response to the political mobilization of the nation's elderly through the Townsend and Long movements. But it also reflected prodding from social reformers like Grace Abbott, head of the Children's Bureau, and Secretary of Labor Frances Perkins. The Social Security Act provided pensions for most workers in the private sector, although originally agricultural workers and domestics were not covered. Pensions were to be paid out of a federal-state fund to which both employers and employees would contribute. The act also established a joint federal-state system of unemployment compensation, funded by an unemployment tax on employers.

The Social Security Act was a milestone in the creation of the modern welfare state. Now the United States joined industrialized countries like Great Britain and Germany in providing old-age pensions and unemployment compensation to citizens. (The Roosevelt administration chose not to push for national health insurance, even though most other industrialized nations offered such protection.) The act also mandated categorical assistance to the blind, deaf, and disabled and to dependent children—the so-called deserving poor, who clearly could not support themselves. Categorical assistance programs, only a small part of the New Deal, gradually expanded over the years until they became an integral part of the American welfare system.

Roosevelt was never enthusiastic about large expenditures for social welfare programs. But in the sixth year of the depression 10 million Americans were still out of work, creating a pressing moral and political issue for FDR and the Democrats. Un-

"Gulliver's Travels"

So many new agencies flooded out of Washington in the 1930s that one almost needed a score-card to keep them straight. Here a July 1935 *Vanity Fair* cartoon by William Gropper substitutes Uncle Sam for Captain Lemuel Gulliver, tied to the ground by Lilliputians, in a parody of Jonathan Swift's *Gulliver's Travels.*

(Courtesy Vanity Fair. © 1935 [renewed 1963] by The Conde Nast Publications, Inc.)

der Harry Hopkins the Works Progress Administration (WPA) became the main fed-eral relief agency for the rest of the depression. While FERA had supplied grants to state relief programs, the WPA put relief workers directly onto the federal payroll. Between 1935 and 1943 the WPA employed 8.5 million Americans, spending $10.5 billion. The agency's employees constructed 651,087 miles of roads, 125,110 public buildings, 8,192 parks, and 853 airports and built or repaired 124,087 bridges.

Though the WPA was an extravagant operation by the standards of the 1930s (it inspired nicknames such as "We Putter Around" and "We Poke Along"), it never reached more than a third of the nation's unemployed. The average wage of $55 a month—well below the government-defined subsistence level of $100 a month—barely enabled workers to eke out a living. In 1941 the government cut the pro-gram severely. It ended in 1943 when the economy returned to full employment during World War II.

The Revenue Act of 1935, a tax reform bill that increased estate and corporate taxes and instituted higher personal income tax rates in the top brackets, showed Roosevelt's willingness to push for reforms that were considered too controversial earlier in his presidency. Much of the business community had already turned violently against Roosevelt in reaction to the NRA, the Social Security Act, and the Wagner Act. Wealthy conservatives quickly labeled the measure an attempt to "soak the rich." Roosevelt, seeking to defuse the popularity of Huey Long's Share Our Wealth plan, was just as interested in the political mileage of the tax bill as its actual results, which increased federal revenue by only $250 million a year.

As the 1936 election approached, the broad range of New Deal programs (Table 25.1) brought new voters into the Democratic coalition. Many had been personally helped by federal programs; others benefited because their interests had found new support in the federal expansion. Roosevelt could count on a potent coalition of urban-based workers, organized labor, northern blacks, farmers, white ethnic groups, Catholics, Jews, liberals, intellectuals, progressive Republicans, and middle-class families concerned about unemployment and old-age dependence. The Democrats also held on, though with some difficulty, to their traditional constituency of white southerners.

The Republicans realized that they could not directly oppose Roosevelt and the New Deal. To run against the president they chose the progressive governor of Kansas, Alfred M. Landon, who accepted the general precepts of the New Deal. Landon and the Republicans concentrated on criticizing the inefficiency and expense of many New Deal programs, stridently accusing FDR of harboring dictatorial ambitions.

Roosevelt's victory in 1936 was one of the biggest landslides in American history. The assassination of Huey Long in September 1935 had deflated the threat of a serious third-party challenge; the candidate of the combined Long-Townsend-Coughlin camp, Congressman William Lemke of North Dakota, garnered fewer than 900,000 votes (1.9 percent) for the Union Party ticket. Roosevelt received 60.8 percent of the popular vote and carried every state except Maine and Vermont. The New Deal was at high tide.

STALEMATE

From this high point the New Deal soon slid into retrenchment, controversy, and stalemate. The first setback came when Roosevelt attempted to make fundamental changes in the structure of the Supreme Court. Shortly after finding the NRA unconstitutional in *Schechter v. United States,* the Court had struck down the Agricultural Adjustment Act, a coal conservation act, and New York State's minimum wage law. With the Wagner Act, the TVA, and Social Security coming up on appeal, the future of New Deal reform measures seemed in doubt.

Roosevelt's response, two weeks after his second inauguration, was to propose the addition of one new justice for each sitting justice over the age of seventy—a

TABLE 25.1
Major New Deal Legislation

Agriculture

1933	Agricultural Adjustment Act (AAA)
1935	Resettlement Administration (RA)
	Rural Electrification Administration
1937	Farm Security Administration (FSA)
1938	Agricultural Adjustment Act of 1938

Business and Industry

1933	Emergency Banking Act
	Glass-Steagall Act (FDIC)
	National Industrial Recovery Act (NIRA)
1934	Securities and Exchange Commission (SEC)
1935	Banking Act of 1935
	Revenue Act (wealth tax)

Conservation and the Environment

1933	Tennessee Valley Authority (TVA)
	Civilian Conservation Corps (CCC)
1936	Soil Conservation and Domestic Allotment Act

Labor and Social Welfare

1933	Section 7(a) of NIRA
1935	National Labor Relations Act (Wagner Act)
	National Labor Relations Board (NLRB)
	Social Security Act
1937	National Housing Act
1938	Fair Labor Standards Act (FLSA)

Relief

1933	Federal Emergency Relief Administration (FERA)
	Civil Works Administration (CWA)
	Public Works Administration (PWA)
1935	Works Progress Administration (WPA)
	National Youth Administration (NYA)

scheme that would have increased the number of justices from nine to fifteen. Roosevelt's opponents quickly protested that he was trying to "pack" the Court with justices who favored the New Deal. The president's proposal was also regarded as an assault on the principle of the separation of powers. But the issue became a moot one when the Supreme Court upheld several key pieces of New Deal legislation and a series of resignations created vacancies on the Court. Within four years Roosevelt managed to reshape the Supreme Court to suit his liberal philosophy through seven new appointments, including Hugo Black, Felix Frankfurter, and William O. Douglas.

Yet his handling of the court issue was a costly blunder at a time when his second-term administration was vulnerable to the lame-duck syndrome. No one yet suspected that FDR would break with tradition by seeking a third term.

Congressional conservatives had long opposed the direction of the New Deal, but the court-packing episode galvanized them by demonstrating that Roosevelt was no longer politically invincible. Throughout Roosevelt's second term a conservative coalition composed mainly of southern Democrats and Republicans from rural areas blocked or impeded social legislation. Two pieces of reform legislation that did win passage were the National Housing Act of 1937, which mandated the construction of low-cost public housing, and the Fair Labor Standards Act of 1938, which made permanent the minimum wage, maximum hours, and anti–child labor provisions in the NRA codes.

The "Roosevelt recession" of 1937 to 1938 dealt the most devastating blow to the president's political standing in the second term. Until that point the economy had made steady progress. From 1933 to 1937 the gross national product had grown at a yearly rate of about 10 percent, and by 1937 industrial output and real income had finally returned to 1929 levels. Unemployment had declined from 25 percent to 14 percent. Many Americans agreed with Senator James F. Byrnes of South Carolina that "the emergency has passed."

The steady improvement of the economy cheered Roosevelt, who had never been comfortable with large federal expenditures. Accordingly, Roosevelt slashed the federal budget in 1937. Between January and August Congress cut the WPA's funding in half, causing layoffs of about 1.5 million workers. The Federal Reserve, fearing inflation, tightened credit, creating a sharp drop in the stock market. Unemployment soared to 19 percent. Roosevelt soon found himself in the same situation that had confounded Hoover. Having taken credit for the recovery between 1933 and 1937, he had to take the blame for the recession.

Shifting gears, Roosevelt spent his way out of the downturn. Large WPA appropriations and a resumption of public works projects poured enough money into the economy to lift it out of the recession by early 1938. Roosevelt and his economic advisers were groping their way toward the general theory advanced by John Maynard Keynes, a British economist who proposed that governments use deficit spending to stimulate the economy when private spending proves insufficient. But Keynes's theory would not be widely accepted until a dramatic increase in defense spending for World War II finally ended the Great Depression.

Still struggling with attacks on the New Deal, Roosevelt decided to "purge" the Democratic Party of some of his most conservative opponents as the 1938 election approached. In the spring primaries he campaigned against members of his own party who had been hostile or unsympathetic to New Deal initiatives. The purge failed abysmally and widened the liberal-conservative rift in the party. In the general election of 1938 Republicans capitalized on the "Roosevelt recession" and the backlash against the court-packing attempt to pick up eight seats in the Senate and eighty-one in the House. The Republicans also gained thirteen governorships.

Even without these political reversals the reform impetus of the New Deal probably would not have continued. Roosevelt had always set clear limits on how far he was willing to go. His instincts were basically conservative, not revolutionary; he had wanted only to save the capitalist economic system by reforming it. The new activism of the Second New Deal was a major step beyond the informal, one-sided business-government partnership of the preceding decade—a step Roosevelt took only because the emergency of the depression had pushed him in that direction.

The New Deal's Impact on Society

Despite the limits of the New Deal, it had a tremendous impact on the nation and fundamentally altered Americans' relationship to their government. With an optimistic faith in using government for social purposes, New Dealers sponsored programs in the arts. They created vast projects to conserve the country's natural beauty and resources and to make them more accessible to its citizens. The "broker state" that emerged in the New Deal also brought the voices of more citizens—women, blacks, labor, Mexican Americans—into the public arena, helping to promote the view that Roosevelt and his party represented and mediated for the common people.

NEW DEAL CONSTITUENCIES

The New Deal accelerated the expansion of the federal bureaucracy that had been under way since the turn of the century. In a decade the number of civilian government employees increased 80 percent, exceeding a million by 1940. The number of federal employees who worked in Washington grew at an even faster rate, doubling between 1929 and 1940. Power was increasingly centered in the nation's capital, not in the states (see American Voices, "A New Deal Activist").

The growth of the federal government increased the potential impact of its decisions (and spending) on various constituencies. During the 1930s the federal government operated as a broker state—mediating between contending pressure groups seeking power and benefits. Democrats recognized the importance of satisfying certain blocs of voters to cement their allegiance to the party. Even before the depression they had begun to build a coalition based on urban political machines and white ethnic voters. In the 1930s organized labor, women, African Americans, and other groups joined that coalition, receiving increased attention from the Democrats and the federal government they controlled.

During the 1930s labor relations became a legitimate arena for federal action and intervention, and organized labor claimed a place in national political life. Labor's dramatic growth in the 1930s represented one of the most important social and economic changes of the decade—an enormous contrast to its demoralized state at the end of the 1920s. Several factors encouraged the growth of the labor movement—the inadequacy of welfare capitalism in the face of the depression, New

AMERICAN VOICES
A New Deal Activist
JOE MARCUS

As an economist working for Harry Hopkins, Joe Marcus was one of thousands who formed the growing New Deal bureaucracy. Marcus's account, as told to Studs Terkel, captures some of the excitement that the New Deal generated. Marcus also suggests the way in which Roosevelt's administration expanded opportunities for Jews and other "outsiders."

I graduated college in '35. I went down to Washington and started to work in the spring of '36. The New Deal was a young man's world. Young people, if they showed any ability, got an opportunity. . . . In a few months I was made head of the department. We had a meeting with hot shots: What's to be done? I pointed out some problems: let's define what we're looking for. They immediately had me take over. . . .

The climate was exciting. You were part of a society that was on the move. You were involved in something that could make a difference. Laws could be changed. So could the conditions of people.

The idea of being involved close to the center of political life was unthinkable, just two or three years before all this happened. Unthinkable for someone like me, of lower middle-class, close to ghetto, Jewish life. Suddenly you were a significant member of society. It was not the kind of closed society you had lived in before. . . .

You were really part of something, changes could be made. Bringing *immediate* results to people who were starving. You could do something about it: that was the most important thing. . . .

We weren't thinking of remaking society. That wasn't it. I didn't buy this dream stuff. What was happening was a complete change in social attitudes at the central government level. The question was: How can you do it within this system? . . . The basic feeling—and I don't think this is just nostalgia—was one of excitement, of achievement, of happiness. Life was important, life was significant.

SOURCE: Studs Terkel, *Hard Times* (New York: Pantheon, 1986), pp. 265–66.

Deal legislation like the Wagner Act, the rise of the Congress of Industrial Organizations (CIO), and the growing militancy of rank-and-file workers. By the end of the decade the number of unionized workers had tripled to almost 9 million, or 23 percent of the nonfarm workforce. Organized labor won the battle not only for union recognition but for higher wages, seniority systems, and grievance procedures.

The CIO served as the cutting edge of the union movement by promoting industrial unionism—that is, organizing all the workers in an industry, both skilled and unskilled, into one union. John L. Lewis, leader of the United Mine Workers (UMW) and a founder of the CIO in 1935, was the foremost exponent of industrial unionism. Lewis began to detach himself from the American Federation of Labor (AFL), which favored organizing workers on a craft-by-craft basis, in 1935; by 1938 the break was complete.

The CIO achieved some of its momentum through the presence in its ranks of members of the Communist Party. The rise of fascism in Europe had prompted the Soviet Union to mobilize support in democratic countries. In Europe and the United States communist parties called for a "popular front," welcoming the cooperation of any group concerned about the threat of fascism to civil rights, organized labor, and world peace. Under the popular front communists softened their revolutionary rhetoric and concentrated on becoming active leaders in many CIO unions. While few workers actually joined the Communist Party, its influence in labor organizing in the thirties was far greater than its numbers, which in 1936 reached 40,000.

The CIO's success also stemmed from the recognition that to succeed unions must be more inclusive. The CIO worked deliberately to attract new groups to the labor movement. Mexican Americans and African Americans found the CIO's commitment to racial justice a strong contrast to the AFL's long-established patterns of

Organize

The Steel Workers Organizing Committee was one of the most vital labor organizations contributing to the rise of the CIO. Though steelworkers were all male, women workers in other sectors of the economy also joined the CIO in large numbers.

(Library of Congress)

exclusion and segregation. And about 800,000 women workers also found a limited welcome in the CIO. Few blacks, Mexican Americans, or women held leadership positions, however.

The CIO scored its first major victory in the automobile industry. On December 31, 1936, General Motors workers in Flint, Michigan, staged a sit-down strike, vowing to stay at their machines until management agreed to collective bargaining. The workers lived in the factories and machine shops for forty-four days before General Motors recognized their union, United Automobile Workers (UAW). Shortly thereafter the CIO won another major victory, at the U.S. Steel Corporation. Despite a long history of bitter opposition to unionization (as demonstrated in the 1919 steel strike—see Chapter 22), Big Steel executives capitulated without a fight and recognized the Steel Workers Organizing Committee (SWOC) on March 2, 1937.

Labor's new vitality spilled over into political action. The AFL generally had stood aloof from partisan politics, but the CIO quickly allied itself with the Democratic Party, hoping to use its influence to elect candidates sympathetic to labor and social justice. Through Labor's Nonpartisan League, the CIO gave $770,000 to Democratic campaigns in 1936. Labor also provided solid support for Roosevelt's plan to reorganize the Supreme Court.

Despite the breakthroughs of the New Deal the labor movement never developed into a dominant force in American life. Roosevelt never made the growth of the labor movement a high priority, and many workers remained indifferent or even hostile to unionization. And although the Wagner Act guaranteed unions a permanent place in American industrial relations, it did not revolutionize working conditions. The right to collective bargaining, rather than redistributing power in American industry, merely granted labor a measure of legitimacy. Management even found that unions could be used as a buffer against rank-and-file militancy. New Deal social welfare programs also tended to diffuse some of the pre-1937 radical spirit by channeling economic benefits to workers whether or not they belonged to unions. The road to union power, even with New Deal protection, continued to be a rocky and uncertain one.

Like organized workers white women achieved new influence in the experimental climate of the New Deal, as unprecedented numbers of them were offered positions in the Roosevelt administration. Frances Perkins, the first woman named to a cabinet post, served as secretary of labor throughout Roosevelt's presidency. Molly Dewson, a social reformer turned politician, headed the Women's Division of the Democratic National Committee, where she pushed an issue-oriented program that supported New Deal reforms. Roosevelt's appointments of women included the first female director of the mint, the head of a major WPA division, and a judge on a circuit court of appeals. Many of those women were close friends as well as professional colleagues and cooperated in an informal network to advance feminist and reform causes.

Eleanor Roosevelt exemplified the growing prominence of women in public life. In the 1920s she had worked closely with other reformers to increase women's power in political parties, labor unions, and education. The experience proved an invaluable apprenticeship for her White House years, when her marriage to FDR developed into one of the most successful political partnerships of all time. He was the pragmatic politician, always aware of what could be done; she was the idealist, the gadfly, always pushing him—and the New Deal—to do more. Eleanor Roosevelt served as the conscience of the New Deal.

Despite the advocacy of a female political network for equal opportunity for women, grave flaws still marred New Deal programs. A fourth of the NRA codes set a lower minimum wage for women than for men performing the same jobs. New Deal agencies like the Civil Works Administration and the Public Works Administration gave jobs almost exclusively to men: only 7 percent of CWA workers were female. And the CCC excluded women entirely, prompting critics to ask, "Where is the 'she-she-she'?"

When they did hire women, New Deal programs tended to reinforce the broader society's gender and racial attitudes. Thus program administrators resisted placing women in nontraditional jobs. Under the WPA sewing rooms became a sort of dumping ground for unemployed women. African American and Mexican American women, if they had access to work relief at all, often found themselves shunted into training as domestics, whose work was not covered by the Social Security and Fair Labor Standards Acts.

Just as the New Deal did not seriously challenge gender inequities, it did little to battle racial discrimination. In the 1930s the vast majority of the American people did not regard civil rights as a legitimate area for federal intervention. Indeed, many New Deal programs reflected prevailing racist attitudes. CCC camps segregated blacks and whites, and many NRA codes did not protect black workers. Most tellingly, Franklin Roosevelt repeatedly refused to support legislation to make

Eleanor Roosevelt and Civil Rights

One of Eleanor Roosevelt's greatest legacies was her commitment to civil rights. For example, she publicly resigned from the Daughters of the American Revolution (DAR) in 1939 when the group refused to let the black opera singer Marian Anderson perform at Constitution Hall. Roosevelt developed an especially close working relationship with Mary McLeod Bethune of the National Youth Administration, shown here at a conference on black youth in 1939. (AP/Wide World Photos)

lynching a federal crime, claiming it would antagonize southern members of Congress whose support he needed to pass New Deal measures.

Nevertheless, blacks did receive significant benefits from those New Deal relief programs that were directed toward the poor regardless of their race or ethnic background. Blacks made up about 18 percent of the WPA's recipients, although they constituted only 10 percent of the population. The Resettlement Administration, established in 1935 to help small farmers buy land and to resettle sharecroppers and tenant farmers on more productive land, fought for the rights of black tenant farmers in the South—until angry southerners in Congress drastically cut its appropriations. Still, many blacks reasoned that the tangible aid from Washington outweighed the discrimination that marred many federal programs.

African Americans were also pleased to see blacks appointed to federal office. Mary McLeod Bethune, an educator who ran the Office of Minority Affairs of the National Youth Administration, headed the "black cabinet." This informal network worked for fairer treatment of blacks by New Deal agencies, in the same way the women's network advocated feminist causes. Both groups benefited greatly from the support of Eleanor Roosevelt. The first lady's promotion of equal treatment for blacks ranks as one of her greatest legacies.

Help from the WPA and other New Deal programs and a belief that the White House—or at least Eleanor Roosevelt—cared about their plight, caused a dramatic change in African Americans' voting behavior. Since the Civil War blacks had voted Republican, a loyalty based on Abraham Lincoln's freeing of the slaves. As late as 1932 black voters in northern cities overwhelmingly supported Republican candidates. But in 1936 black Americans outside the South (where blacks were still largely prevented from voting) gave Roosevelt 71 percent of their votes. In Harlem, where relief dollars increased dramatically in the wake of the 1935 riot (see Chapter 24), their support was an extraordinary 81.3 percent. Black voters have remained overwhelmingly Democratic ever since.

The election of Franklin Roosevelt also had an immediate effect on Mexican American communities, demoralized by the depression and the deportations of the Hoover years. In cities like Los Angeles and El Paso Mexican Americans qualified for relief more easily under New Deal guidelines, and there was more relief to go around (see American Voices, "A Chicana Youth Gets New Deal Work"). Even though New Deal guidelines prohibited discrimination based on an immigrant's legal status, the new climate encouraged a marked rise in requests for naturalization papers. Mexican Americans also benefited from New Deal labor policies; for many, joining the CIO was an important stage in becoming an American. Inspired by New Deal rhetoric about economic recovery and social progress through cooperation, Mexican Americans increasingly identified with the United States rather than with Mexico. This shift was especially evident among American-born children of Mexican immigrants (see Chapter 24). Participating in the political system increasingly became part of Mexican American life. Los Angeles activist Beatrice Griffith noted, "Franklin D. Roosevelt's name was the spark that started thousands of Spanish-speaking persons

AMERICAN VOICES

A Chicana Youth Gets New Deal Work

SUSANA ARCHULETA

A *lthough African Americans and Chicanos often experienced discrimination in New Deal programs, many did find opportunities in New Deal agencies like the Civilian Conservation Corps, the National Youth Administration, or the Works Progress Administration. And they attributed the help they received directly to Franklin Delano Roosevelt's election, as Susana Archuleta's reminiscence of life in Wyoming suggests.*

I was born in New Mexico, on a farm up North in Mora County. I was the fifth of eight children. When I was very little, my dad moved us all to Wyoming. You see, he heard that they had free textbooks in Wyoming, while here in New Mexico the parents had to pay for the books. Daddy didn't have much money, and he felt that we all needed an opportunity for education. We left the farm—the animals, the machinery, everything—and he went to work in the mines up in Rock Springs, Wyoming. . . .

During the Depression, things got bad. My dad passed away when I was about twelve, leaving my mother with eight children and no means of support. There wasn't any welfare. My mother took in washings to make a living, and our job was to pick up the washings on the way home from school. We'd pick up clothes from the schoolteachers, the attorney, and what-have-you. Then, at night, we'd help iron them and fold them. . . .

When I was a teenager, the Depression began to take a turn. Franklin Roosevelt was elected, and the works projects started. The boys and young men who'd been laid off at the mines went to the CCC camps, and the girls joined the NYA. When school was over, we'd go and work right there in the school building. We'd help out in the office, do filing and other things. Actually, we didn't do much work—it was our first job. But we learned a lot. It was good experience.

They paid us about twenty-one dollars a month. Out of that we got five and the other sixteen was directly issued to our parents. The same was true of the boys working in the camps. They got about thirty dollars a month. They were allowed to keep five of it. The rest was sent to their families. All of us were hired according to our family income. If a man with a lot of children was unemployed, he was given preference over someone who had less children. They also had projects for women who were widows. They made quilts and mattresses. Those programs were great. Everybody got a chance to work. I think there should be more training programs like that, instead of giveaway programs like welfare. . . .

SOURCE: Nan Elsasser, "Susana Archuleta," in Nan Elsasser et al., *Las Mujeres: Conversations from a Hispanic Community* (New York: Feminist Press, 1980), pp. 36–37.

to the polls." The Democrats made it clear that they welcomed Mexican American voters and considered them an important part of the New Deal coalition.

But what about groups that did not mobilize politically or were not recognized as key participants in the New Deal coalition? Native Americans were one of the nation's most disadvantaged and powerless minorities. The average annual income of a Native American in 1934 was only $48; the unemployment rate among Native Americans was three times the national average. Concerned New Deal administrators like Secretary of the Interior Harold Ickes and Commissioner of the Bureau of Indian Affairs John Collier tried to correct some of those inequities. The Indian Section of the Civilian Conservation Corps brought needed money and projects to reservations throughout the West. Indians also received benefits from FERA and CWA work relief projects.

More ambitious was the Indian Reorganization Act of 1934, sometimes called the "Indian New Deal." That law reversed the Dawes Severalty Act of 1887 by promoting more extensive self-government through tribal councils and constitutions. The government also abandoned the attempt to force Native Americans to assimilate into mainstream society in favor of promoting cultural pluralism. The New Deal pledged to help preserve Indian languages, arts, and traditions and to restore some lands lost in the allotment program (see Chapter 16).

Despite the intention to redress some of the ills produced by earlier government policies, the Indian New Deal was profoundly flawed. Reflecting Collier's paternalistic approach, it tended to treat all tribes as identical, with the same needs and structures. Its imposition of American-style democracy did not always mesh with Native Americans' consensus style of decision making. The Seneca, for example, argued that the Indian Reorganization Act violated their treaty rights and the system of self-government they had adopted in 1848. Only 174 nations accepted the reorganization policy, while 78 refused to participate. While some native groups may have benefited from the Indian New Deal, the problems of Native Americans were so severe that these changes in federal policy did little to improve their lives or reinvigorate tribal communities.

THE NEW DEAL AND THE LAND

Concern for the land was one of the dominant motifs of the New Deal, and the shaping of the public landscape was among its most visible legacies. The expansion of federal responsibilities in the 1930s created a climate conducive to conservation efforts, as did public concern heightened by the dramatic images of drought and devastation in the Dust Bowl. Although the long-term success of New Deal resources policy was mixed, it innovatively stressed scientific management of the land, conservation instead of commercial development, and the aggressive use of public authority to safeguard both private and public holdings.

The most extensive New Deal environmental undertaking was the Tennessee Valley Authority. The need for dams to control flooding and erosion in the Tennessee River Basin, a seven-state area with some of the country's heaviest rainfall, had been recognized since World War I. But not until 1933 was the Tennessee Valley Authority established to develop the region's resources under public control. The TVA was the ultimate watershed demonstration area, integrating flood control, reforestation, and agricultural and industrial development, including the production of chemical fertilizers. A hydroelectric grid provided cheap electric power for the valley's residents.

The Dust Bowl helped to focus attention on land management and ecological balance. Agents from the Soil Conservation Service in the Department of Agriculture taught farmers the proper technique for tilling hillsides. Government agronomists also tried to remove marginal land from cultivation and to prevent soil erosion through better agricultural practices. One of their most widely publicized programs was the creation of the Shelterbelts, which involved the planting of 220 million trees running along roughly the ninety-ninth meridian from Abilene, Texas, to the Canadian border. Planted as a windbreak, the trees also prevented soil erosion. Another priority of the Roosevelt administration was helping rural Americans to stay on the land. The Rural Electrification Administration, established in 1935, brought power to farms in an attempt to improve the quality of rural life.

Today New Deal projects affecting the environment can be seen throughout the country. CCC and WPA workers built the Blue Ridge Parkway, which connects the Shenandoah National Park in Virginia with the Great Smoky Mountain National Park in North Carolina. In the West government workers built the San Francisco Zoo, Berkeley's Tilden Park, and the canals of San Antonio. The CCC helped to complete the East Coast's Appalachian Trail and the West Coast's Pacific Crest Trail through the Sierras. In state parks across the country cabins, shelters, picnic areas, lodges, and observation towers, built in a style that has been called *government rustic,* are witness to the New Deal ethos of recreation coexisting with conservation.

Although the New Deal was ahead of its time in its attention to conservation, its legacy to later environmental movements in mixed. Many of the tactics used in New Deal projects—damming rivers, blasting fire roads, altering the natural landscape through the construction of buildings and shelters—are now considered intrusive. In the 1970s the TVA came under attack for its longstanding practice of strip mining and the pollution caused by its power plants and chemical factories. Because of environmental concerns a project as massive as the TVA probably could not be built today—an ironic comment on what was once hailed as an enlightened use of government power.

THE NEW DEAL AND THE ARTS

In the arts, the depression dried up traditional sources of patronage. Like most Americans creative artists had nowhere to turn but Washington. A WPA project known as "Federal One" put unemployed artists, actors, and writers to work, but its spirit and purpose extended far beyond relief. New Deal administrators wanted to redefine the relationship between artists and the community so that art would no longer be the exclusive province of the elite. "Art for the millions" became a popular New Deal slogan.

The Federal Art Project (FAP) gave work to many of the twentieth century's leading painters, muralists, and sculptors at a point in their careers when the lack of private patronage might have prevented them from continuing their artistic production. Under the direction of Holger Cahill, an expert on American folk art, the FAP commissioned murals for public buildings and post offices across the country. Jackson Pollock, Alice Neel, Willem de Kooning, and Louise Nevelson all received support from the FAP.

The Federal Music Project employed 15,000 musicians under the direction of Nicholas Sokoloff, the conductor of the Cleveland Symphony Orchestra. Government-sponsored orchestras toured the country, presenting free concerts of both classical and popular music. Like many New Deal programs the Music Project emphasized American themes. The composer Aaron Copland wrote his ballets *Billy the Kid* (1938) and *Rodeo* (1942) for the WPA, basing the compositions on western folk motifs. The distinctive "American" sound and athletic dance style of these works made them immensely appealing to audiences. The federal government also employed the musicologist Charles Seeger and his wife, the composer Ruth Crawford Seeger, to catalog hundreds of American folk songs.

The former journalist Henry Alsberg headed the Federal Writers' Project (FWP), which at its height employed about 5,000 writers. Young FWP employees who later achieved fame included Saul Bellow, Ralph Ellison, Tillie Olsen, and John Cheever. The black folklorist and novelist Zora Neale Hurston finished three novels while on the Florida FWP, among them *Their Eyes Were Watching God* (1937). And Richard Wright won the 1938 *Story* magazine prize for the best tale by a WPA writer. Wright used his spare time to complete his novel *Native Son* (1940).

Of all the New Deal arts programs the Federal Theatre Project (FTP) was the most ambitious. American drama thrived in the 1930s, the only time at which the United States had a federally supported national theater. Under the gifted direction of Hallie Flanagan, former head of Vassar College's Experimental Theater, the Theatre Project reached an audience of 25 to 30 million people in the four years of its existence. Talented directors, actors, and playwrights, including Orson Welles, John Huston, and Arthur Miller, offered their services.

The WPA arts projects were influenced by a broad artistic trend called the *documentary impulse*. Combining social relevance with distinctively American themes, this approach—which presented actual facts and events in a way that aroused the interest and emotions of the audience—characterized the artistic expression of the 1930s. The documentary, probably the decade's most distinctive genre, influenced practically every aspect of American culture—literature, photography, art, music, film, dance, theater, and radio. It is evident in John Steinbeck's fiction (see Chapter 24) and in John Dos Passos's *USA* trilogy, which used actual newspaper clippings, dispatches, and headlines in its fictional story. *The March of Time* newsreels, which movie audiences saw before feature films, presented the news of the world for the pretelevision age. The filmmaker Pare Lorentz commissioned the composer Virgil Thompson to create music that set the mood for documentary movies such as *The Plow That Broke the Plains* (1936) and *The River* (1936). The new photojournalism magazines, including *Life* and *Look,* also reflected this documentary approach. And the New Deal institutionalized the trend by sending investigators like the journalist Lorena Hickok and the writer Martha Gellhorn into the field to report on the conditions of people on relief.

Finally, the federal government played a leading role in compiling the photographic record of the 1930s. The Historical Section of the Resettlement Administration had a mandate to document and photograph the American scene for the government. Through their haunting images of sharecroppers, Dust Bowl migrants, and the urban homeless, the photographers Dorothea Lange, Walker Evans, Ben Shahn, and Margaret Bourke-White permanently shaped the image of the Great Depression. The government hired photographers solely for their professional skills, not to provide them relief, as in Federal One projects. Their photographs, collected by the Historical Section, which in 1937 became part of the newly created Farm Security Administration (FSA), rank as the best visual representation of life in the United States during the depression years.

THE LEGACIES OF THE NEW DEAL

The New Deal set in motion far-reaching changes, notably the growth of a modern state of significant size. For the first time people experienced the federal government as a concrete part of everyday life. During the 1930s more than a third of the population received direct government assistance from new federal programs, including Social Security payments, farm loans, relief work, and mortgage guarantees. Furthermore, the government had made a commitment to intervene in the economy when the private sector could not guarantee economic stability. New legislation regulated the stock market, reformed the Federal Reserve system by placing more power in the hands of Washington policymakers, and brought many practices of modern corporate life under federal regulation. Thus, the New Deal accelerated the pattern begun during the Progressive Era of using federal regulation to bring order and regularity to economic life, a pattern that would persist for the rest of the twentieth century, despite recurring criticism about the increased presence of the state in American life.

One particularly important arena of expansion was the development of America's welfare state—that is, the federal government's acceptance of primary responsibility for the individual and collective welfare of the people. But although the New Deal offered more benefits to American citizens than they had ever received before, its safety net had many holes, especially in comparison with the far more extensive welfare systems of Western Europe. The Social Security Act did not include national health care. Another serious defect of the emerging welfare system was its failure to reach a significant minority of American workers, including domestics and farm workers, for many years. And since state governments administered the programs, benefits varied widely, with southern states consistently providing the lowest amounts.

To its credit the New Deal recognized that poverty was an economic problem, not a matter of personal failure. Reformers assumed that once the depression was over, full employment and an active economy would take care of the nation's welfare needs and poverty would wither away. It did not. When later administrations confronted the persistence of inequality and unemployment, they grafted welfare programs onto the jerrybuilt system left over from the New Deal. Thus the American welfare system would always be marked by its birth during the crisis atmosphere of the Great Depression.

Even if the depression-era welfare system had some serious flaws, it was brilliant politics. The Democratic Party courted the allegiance of citizens who benefited from New Deal programs. Organized labor aligned itself with the administration that had made it a legitimate force in modern industrial life. Blacks voted Democratic in direct relation to the economic benefits that poured into their communities. At the grassroots level, the Women's Division of the Democratic National Committee mobilized 80,000 women who recognized what the New Deal had done for their communities. The unemployed also looked kindly on the Roosevelt administration. According to one of the earliest Gallup polls, 84 percent of those on relief voted the Democratic ticket in 1936.

But the Democratic Party did not attract only the down-and-out. Roosevelt's magnetic personality and the dispersal of New Deal benefits to families throughout the social structure brought middle-class voters, many of them first- or second-generation immigrants, into the Democratic fold. Thus the New Deal completed the transformation of the Democratic Party that had begun in the 1920s toward a coalition of ethnic groups, city dwellers, organized labor, blacks, and a broad cross-section of the middle class. Those voters would form the backbone of the Democratic coalition for decades to come and would provide support for liberal reforms that extended the promise of the New Deal.

The New Deal coalition contained potentially fatal contradictions, involving mainly the issue of race. Because Roosevelt depended on the support of southern white Democrats to pass New Deal legislation, he was unwilling to challenge the economic and political marginalization of blacks in the South. At the same time New Deal programs were changing the face of southern agriculture by undermining the sharecropping system and encouraging the migration of southern blacks to northern and western cities. Outside the South blacks were not prevented from voting, guaranteeing that civil rights would enter the national agenda. The resulting fissures would eventually weaken the coalition that seemed so invincible at the height of Roosevelt's power.

With all its shortcomings the New Deal nonetheless had a profound impact on the nation, all the more remarkable in light of its short duration. After 1936 the only

TIMELINE

1933	FDR's inaugural address and first fireside chat		Works Progress Administration (WPA)
			Huey Long assassinated
	The Emergency Banking Act begins the Hundred Days.		Congress of Industrial Organizations (CIO) is formed.
	Glass-Steagall Act establishes FDIC.	1935–1939	Communist Party at height of influence
	Civilian Conservation Corps (CCC)		Supreme Court finds the Agricultural Adjustment Act unconstitutional.
	Agricultural Adjustment Act (AAA)		
	National Industrial Recovery Act (NIRA)		Rural Electrification Administration (REA)
	Tennessee Valley Authority (TVA)		
	United States abandons the gold standard.		*The Plow That Broke the Plains* and *The River*
	Townsend Clubs participate in an Old Age Revolving Pension Plan.		
	Prohibition is repealed.	1936	General Motors sit-down strike
1934	Securities and Exchange Commission	1937	FDR's attempted Supreme Court reorganization fails.
	Indian Reorganization Act		
	Share Our Wealth Society established by Senator Huey Long	1937–1938	"Roosevelt recession"
1935	Supreme Court finds the NRA unconstitutional in *Schechter v. United States*.	1938	Aaron Copland's *Billy the Kid*
			Fair Labor Standards Act (FLSA)
	National Union for Social Justice (Father Charles Coughlin)	1939	The Federal Theatre Project is terminated.
	National Labor Relations (Wagner) Act		
	Social Security Act		

major pieces of reform legislation passed were the National Housing Act of 1937 and the Fair Labor Standards Act of 1938. While the Supreme Court–packing scheme, the "Roosevelt recession," and the political successes of Republicans in 1938 helped to bring an end to the New Deal, the darkening international scene also played a part. As Europe moved toward war and Japan flexed its muscles in the Far East, Roosevelt became increasingly preoccupied with international relations and placed domestic reform further and further into the background. After the United States entered the war in 1941, Roosevelt made the end of his depression program official when he announced in 1943 that it was time for "Dr. Win the War" to take the place of "Dr. New Deal." But in reality the New Deal had long ceased to propel the nation toward social reform.

For Further Exploration

A valuable synthesis of the New Deal is Robert S. McElvaine, *The Great Depression* (1984). An older but still engaging account of FDR is James MacGregor Burns, *Roosevelt* (1956). Insights into Eleanor Roosevelt's life are compellingly offered in Blanche Wiesen Cook's two-volume biography, *Eleanor Roosevelt* (vol. 1, 1992; vol. 2, 1999). For other New Dealers, see Katie Loucheim, ed., *The Making of the New Deal: The Insiders Speak* (1983). For contemporary material from the Federal Writers' Project, see *These Are Our Lives* (1939). Photography of the New Deal era is presented and analyzed in Carl Fleischhauer, ed., *Documenting America 1935–1943* (1988).

"The New Deal Network," sponsored by the Franklin and Eleanor Roosevelt Institute and the Institute for Learning Technologies, has an impressive site at <http://www .newdeal.feri.org/> with extensive images, features such as "Work-Study-Live: The Resident Youth Centers of the NYA," and links to other New Deal sites. The Library of Congress page on the "Federal Theater 1933–1939" at <http://memory.loc.gov/ammem/fedtp/fthome .html> offers scripts, still photographs, costumes, and production materials for several plays put on by the Federal Theater Project. See also the library's excellent posting of over 55,000 photographs from the Farm Security Administration and Office of War Information Collection at <http://www.nara.gov/exhall/newdeal/newdeal.html>. The National Archives' site at <http://memory.loc.gov/ammem/fsowhome.html> contains "A New Deal for the Arts," which covers folklore, music, writing, photography, film, and painting sponsored by New Deal agencies.

A number of sites offer resources for local and state history. An excellent example is the Michigan State History Museum's "The Great Depression," with material on the Flint sit-down strike and New Deal relief programs at <http://www.sos.state.mi.us/history/museum/ explore/museums/hismus/hismus.html>.

Chapter 26

THE WORLD AT WAR
1939–1945

> The great majority of the American people understand very well
> that this war is not a war only, but an end and a beginning—an end
> to things known and a beginning of things unknown.
>
> —ARCHIBALD MACLEISH, *ATLANTIC,* 1943

Times Square, New York City, on August 15, 1945, was awash with people celebrating V-J (Victory over Japan) Day. World War II was over. Civilians and soldiers "jived in the streets and the crowd was so large that traffic was halted and sprinkler trucks were used to disperse pedestrians." The spontaneous street party seemed a fitting end to what had been the country's most popular war. For many Americans World War II had been what one man described to journalist Studs Terkel as "an unreal period for us here at home. Those who lost nobody at the front had a pretty good time."

Americans had many reasons to view World War II as the "good war." Shocked by the Japanese attack on Pearl Harbor on December 7, 1941, they united in their determination to fight German and Japanese totalitarianism in defense of their way of life. When evidence of the grim reality of the Jewish Holocaust came to light, U.S. participation in the war seemed even more just. And despite their sacrifices, many people found the war a positive experience because it ended the devastating Great Depression, bringing full employment and prosperity. The unambiguous nature of the victory and the subsequent emergence of the United States as an unprecedentedly powerful nation further contributed to the sense of the war as one worth fighting.

But the good war had other sides. The period brought significant social disruption, accompanied by widespread anxiety about women's presence in the workforce and a rise in juvenile delinquency. In a massive violation of civil liberties over 100,000 people of Japanese ancestry were incarcerated in internment camps, victims of racially based hysteria. African Americans served in a segregated military and, with Chicanos, faced discrimination and violence at home. World War II also fostered the rise of a military industrial complex and unleashed the terrible potential of the atomic bomb. Finally, another enduring legacy developed out of the unresolved issues of the wartime alliance: the debilitating cold war, which would dominate American foreign policy for decades.

The Road to War

The rise of fascism in Europe and Asia in the 1930s threatened the fragile peace that had prevailed since the end of World War I. When the League of Nations proved too weak to deal with the emerging crises, President Roosevelt foresaw the possibility of America's participation in another war. An internationalist at heart, he wanted the United States to play a prominent role in world affairs to foster the long-term prosperity necessary for a lasting peace. Hampered at first by the pervasive isolationist sentiment in the country, by 1939 he was leading the nation toward war.

DEPRESSION DIPLOMACY

During the early years of the New Deal America's involvement in international affairs, especially those in Europe, remained limited. One of Roosevelt's few diplomatic initiatives had been the formal recognition of the Soviet Union in November 1933. A second significant development was the Good Neighbor Policy, under which the United States voluntarily renounced the use of military force and armed intervention in the Western Hemisphere. This policy was predicated on the recognition that the friendship of Latin American countries was essential to the security of the United States. One practical outcome came in 1934 when Congress repealed the Platt Amendment, a relic of the Spanish-American War, which asserted the United States' right to intervene in Cuba's affairs. Indicating the limits to the Good Neighbor Policy, the U.S. Navy kept (and still maintains) a major base at Cuba's Guantanamo Bay and continued to meddle in Cuban politics. And in numerous Latin American countries U.S. diplomats frequently resorted to economic pressure to solidify the influence of the United States and benefit its international corporations.

Roosevelt and his secretary of state, Cordell Hull, might have hoped to pursue more far-reaching diplomatic initiatives. But isolationism had been building in both Congress and the nation throughout the 1920s, a product in part of disillusionment with American participation in World War I. In 1934 Gerald P. Nye, a Republican senator from North Dakota, began a congressional investigation into the profits of munitions makers during World War I and then widened the investigation to determine the influence of economic interests on America's decision to declare war. Nye's committee concluded that war profiteers, whom it called "merchants of death," had maneuvered the nation into World War I for financial gain.

Though most of the committee's charges were dubious or simplistic, they gave momentum to the isolationist movement, contributing to the passage of the Neutrality Act of 1935. Designed explicitly to prevent a recurrence of the events that had pulled the United States into World War I, the act imposed an embargo on arms trading with countries at war and declared that American citizens traveled on the ships of belligerent nations at their own risk. In 1936 Congress expanded the Neutrality Act to ban loans to belligerents, and in 1937 it adopted a "cash-and-carry" provision: if a country at war wanted to purchase nonmilitary goods from the United States, it had to pay for them in cash and pick them up in its own ships.

The same year Congress explicitly reinforced earlier bans on sales of arms to Spain, where a bloody civil war had erupted in 1936. There Francisco Franco, strongly supported by the fascist regimes in Germany and Italy, was leading a rebellion against the democratically elected republican government. Backed officially only by the Soviet Union and Mexico, the republicans, or Loyalists, relied heavily on individual volunteers from other countries, including the American Lincoln Brigade, which fought courageously and sustained heavy losses throughout the war. The governments of the United States, Great Britain, and France, despite their Loyalist sympathies, remained neutral, a policy that dismayed many American intellectuals and activists and virtually ensured a fascist victory.

AGGRESSION AND APPEASEMENT

The nation's neutrality was soon challenged by the aggressive actions of Germany, Italy, and Japan, all determined to expand their borders and their influence. The first crisis was precipitated by Japan, a country whose militaristic regime was intent on dominating the Pacific basin. In 1931 Japan occupied Manchuria, the northernmost province of China; then in 1937 it launched a full-scale invasion of China. In both instances the League of Nations condemned Japan's action but was helpless to stop the aggression. Japan simply served the required one-year notice of withdrawal from the League.

Japan's defiance of the League encouraged a fascist dictator half a world away. Italy's Benito Mussolini had long been unhappy with the Versailles treaty, which had not awarded Italy any formerly German or Turkish colonies. In 1935 Italy invaded Ethiopia, one of the few independent countries left in Africa. The Ethiopian emperor, Haile Selassie, appealed to the League of Nations, which condemned the invasion and imposed sanctions but to little effect. By 1936 the Italian subjugation of Ethiopia was complete.

Not Italy but Germany presented the gravest threat to the world order in the 1930s. There huge reparations payments, runaway inflation, fear of communism, labor unrest, and rising unemployment fueled the rise of Adolf Hitler and his National Socialist (Nazi) Party. In 1933 Hitler became chancellor of Germany and assumed dictatorial powers. Aiming at nothing short of world domination, as he made clear in his book *Mein Kampf* (My Struggle), Hitler sought to overturn the territorial settlements of the Versailles treaty, to "restore" all the Germans of Central and Eastern Europe to a single greater German fatherland, and to annex large areas of Eastern Europe. In his warped vision "inferior races" such as Jews, Gypsies, and Slavs as well as "undesirables" such as homosexuals and the mentally impaired

This is the Enemy

WINNER R. HOE & CO., INC. AWARD – NATIONAL WAR POSTER COMPETITION
HELD UNDER AUSPICES OF ARTISTS FOR VICTORY, INC. – COUNCIL FOR DEMOCRACY – MUSEUM OF MODERN ART

Why We Fight

This 1942 award-winning litho-graph by Karl Koehler and Victor Ancona painted a sinister, menac-ing portrait of a Nazi officer, leav-ing little room for doubt as to why it was necessary to end Nazism. (National Museum of American Art, Smithsonian Institution, Washington, DC)

would have to make way for the "master race." In 1933 Hitler established the first concentration camp at Dachau and opened a campaign of persecution against Jews, which expanded to a campaign of extermination once the war began.

Hitler's strategy for gaining territory through the use of troops and intimida-tion provoked a series of crises that gave Britain and France no alternative but to let him have his way or risk war. British Prime Minister Neville Chamberlain was a particularly insistent proponent of what became known as "appeasement." Germany withdrew from the League of Nations in 1933; two years later Hitler an-nounced that he planned to rearm the nation in violation of the Versailles treaty. Not willing to risk war, no one stopped him. In 1936 Germany reoccupied the Rhineland, a region that had been declared a demilitarized zone under the treaty. Once again France and Britain took no action. Later that year Hitler and Mussolini joined forces in the Rome-Berlin Axis, a political and military alliance. When the Spanish Civil War broke out, Germany and Italy armed the Spanish fascists. The same year Germany and Japan signed the Anti-Comintern Pact, a precursor to the military alliance between Japan and the Axis that was formalized in 1940.

In 1938 Hitler's ambitions expanded: he sent troops to annex Austria, while si-multaneously scheming to seize part of Czechoslovakia. Because Czechoslovakia had an alliance with France, war seemed imminent. But at the Munich Conference in September 1938 Britain and France capitulated, agreeing to let Germany annex the Sudetenland—the German-speaking border areas of Czechoslovakia—in return for Hitler's pledge to seek no more territory.

Within six months, however, Hitler's forces had overrun the rest of Czechoslovakia and were threatening to march into Poland. Britain and France realized that their policy of appeasement had been disastrous and prepared to take a stand. Then in August 1939 Hitler shocked the world by signing the Nonaggression Pact with the Soviet Union, which assured Germany it would not have to wage war on two fronts at once. On September 1, 1939, German troops attacked Poland; two days later Britain and France declared war on Germany. World War II had begun.

AMERICA AND THE WAR

Because the United States had become a major world power, its response would affect the course of the European conflict. Two days after the war started the United States officially declared its neutrality. Roosevelt made no secret of his sympathies, however. He pointedly rephrased Woodrow Wilson's declaration of 1914: "This nation will remain a neutral nation, but I cannot ask that every American remain neutral in thought as well." The overwhelming majority of Americans supported the Allies (Britain and France) over the Nazis, but most Americans did not want to be drawn into another world war.

At first the need for American intervention seemed remote. After the German conquest of Poland in September 1939, a false calm settled over Europe. But then on April 9, 1940, Nazi tanks overran Denmark. Norway fell to the Nazi Blitzkrieg ("lightning war") next, then the Netherlands, Belgium, and Luxembourg. Finally, on June 22, 1940, France fell. Britain stood alone against Hitler's plans for world domination.

In America the developments in Europe stirred debate over neutrality. The journalist William Allen White and his Committee to Defend America by Aiding the Allies led the interventionists. Isolationists, including the aviator Charles Lindbergh, formed the America First Committee to keep the nation out of the war. They attracted the support of the *Chicago Tribune,* the Hearst newspapers, and other conservative publications.

Despite the isolationist pressure in 1940 the United States moved closer to involvement in the war. In May Roosevelt began putting the economy and the government on a defense footing by creating the National Defense Advisory Commission and the Council of National Defense. During the summer he traded fifty World War I destroyers to Great Britain in exchange for the right to build military bases on British possessions in the Atlantic, thus circumventing the nation's neutrality law by executive order. In October Congress approved a large increase in defense spending and instituted the first peacetime draft registration and conscription in American history.

While the war expanded in Europe, Asia, North Africa, and the Middle East, the United States was preparing for the 1940 presidential election. The conflict had convinced Roosevelt that he should seek an unprecedented third term. Despite some conservative opposition Roosevelt chose the liberal secretary of agriculture Henry A. Wallace as his running mate. The Republicans nominated Wendell Willkie of Indiana, a former Democrat who supported many New Deal policies. The two parties' platforms differed only slightly. Both pledged aid to the Allies but stopped short of calling for American participation in the war. Though Willkie's spirited campaign resulted in a closer election than those of 1932 or 1936, Roosevelt and the Democrats won 55 percent of the popular vote and a lopsided total in the electoral college.

With the election behind him Roosevelt concentrated on persuading the American people to increase aid to Britain, whose survival he viewed as the key to American security. In November 1939 FDR had won a bitter battle in Congress to amend the Neutrality Act of 1935 to allow the Allies to buy weapons from the United States—but only on the cash-and-carry basis established for nonmilitary goods in 1937. In March 1941, with German submarines sinking British ships faster than they could be replaced and Britain no longer able to afford to pay cash for arms, Roosevelt convinced Congress to pass the Lend-Lease Act. The legislation authorized the president to "lease, lend, or otherwise dispose of" arms and other equipment to any country whose defense was considered vital to the security of the United States. After Germany invaded the Soviet Union in June 1941 (abandoning the Nazi-Soviet pact of two years earlier), the United States extended lend-lease to the Soviet Union, which became part of the Allied coalition.

In his State of the Union address to Congress in January 1941 Roosevelt had connected lend-lease to the defense of democracy at home as well as in Europe. He spoke about what he called "four essential human freedoms everywhere in the world"—freedom of speech and expression, freedom of worship, freedom from want, and freedom from fear. Although Roosevelt avoided stating explicitly that America had to enter the war to protect those freedoms, he intended to justify exactly that, for he regarded the United States' entry in the war as inevitable. And indeed the implementation of lend-lease marked the unofficial entrance of the United States into the European war.

The United States became even more involved in August 1941, when Roosevelt and the British prime minister, Winston Churchill, conferred secretly to discuss goals and military strategy. Their joint press release, which became known as the Atlantic Charter, provided the ideological foundation of the Western cause and of the peace to follow. Like Wilson's Fourteen Points the Charter called for economic collaboration and guarantees of political stability after the war ended to ensure that "all men in all the lands may live out their lives in freedom from fear and want." The Charter also supported free trade, national self-determination, and the principle of collective security.

As in World War I, when Americans started supplying the Allies, Germany attacked American and Allied ships. By September 1941 Nazi submarines and American vessels were fighting an undeclared naval war in the Atlantic, unknown to the American public. Without a dramatic enemy attack, however, and with the public reluctant to enter the war, Roosevelt hesitated to ask Congress for a declaration of war.

The final provocation came not from Germany but from Japan. Throughout the 1930s Japanese military advances in China had upset the balance of political and economic power in the Pacific, where the United States had long enjoyed the economic benefits of the open-door policy. After the Japanese invasion of China in 1937 Roosevelt had denounced "the present reign of terror and international lawlessness," suggesting that aggressors such as Japan be "quarantined" by peace-loving nations. Despite such rhetoric, however, the United States avoided taking a stand. During the brutal sack of Nanking in 1937 the Japanese had sunk an American gunboat, the *Panay,* in the Yangtze River. The crisis was smoothed over, however, when the United States accepted Japan's apology and more than $2 million in damages.

Japan soon became more expansionist in its intentions, signing the Tri-Partite Pact with Germany and Italy in 1940. In the fall of 1940 Japanese troops occupied the northern part of French Indochina. The United States retaliated by restricting trade with Japan and placing an embargo on aviation fuel and scrap metal. Despite mounting tensions Roosevelt hoped to avoid war with Japan. But in July 1941 Japanese troops occupied the rest of Indochina. Roosevelt responded by freezing Japanese assets in the United States and instituting an embargo on trade with Japan, including vital oil shipments that accounted for almost 80 percent of Japanese consumption.

In September 1941 the government of Prime Minister Hideki Tojo began secret preparations for war against the United States. By November American military intelligence knew that Japan was planning an attack but did not know where it would come. Early on Sunday morning, December 7, 1941, Japanese bombers attacked Pearl Harbor in Hawaii, killing more than 2,400 Americans. Eight battleships, three cruisers, three destroyers, and almost two hundred airplanes were destroyed or heavily damaged.

Although the attack was devastating, it infused the American people with a determination to fight. Pearl Harbor Day is still etched in the memories of millions of Americans who remember precisely what they were doing when they heard about the attack. The next day Roosevelt went before Congress. Calling December 7 "a date which will live in infamy," he asked for a declaration of war against Japan. The Senate voted unanimously for war, and the House concurred by a vote of 388 to 1. The lone dissenter was Jeannette Rankin of Montana, who had also opposed American entry into World War I. Three days later Germany and Italy declared war on the United States, and the United States in turn declared war on those nations.

Organizing for Victory

The task of fighting a global war accelerated the growing influence of the state on all aspects of American life. A dramatic expansion of power occurred at the presidential level when Congress passed the War Powers Act of December 18, 1941, giving Roosevelt unprecedented authority over all aspects of the conduct of the war. Coordinating the changeover from civilian to war production, raising an army, and assembling the necessary workforce taxed government agencies to the limit. Mobilization on such a scale demanded cooperation between business executives and political leaders in Washington, solidifying a partnership that had been growing since World War I.

DEFENSE MOBILIZATION

Defense mobilization had a powerful impact on the federal government's role in the economy. During the war the federal budget expanded by a factor of ten, and the national debt grew sixfold, peaking at $258.6 billion in 1945. At the same time the national government became more closely tied to its citizens' pocketbooks. The Revenue Act of 1942 continued the income tax reform that had begun during World War I by taxing not just wealthy individuals and corporations but average citizens as well. Tax collections rose from $2.2 billion to $35.1 billion, facilitated by payroll deductions and tax withholding, instituted in 1943. This system of mass taxation, a revolutionary change in the financing of the modern state, was sold to the taxpayers as a way to express their patriotism.

The war also brought significant changes in the federal bureaucracy. The number of civilians employed by the government increased almost fourfold, to 3.8 million—a far more dramatic growth than the New Deal period had witnessed. Leadership of federal agencies also changed as the Roosevelt administration turned to business executives to replace the reformers who had staffed New Deal relief agencies in the 1930s. The executives became known as "dollar-a-year men" because they volunteered for government service while remaining on the corporate payroll.

Many wartime agencies extended the power of the federal government. One of the most important was the War Production Board (WPB), which awarded defense contracts, evaluated military and civilian requests for scarce resources, and oversaw the conversion of industry to military production. The WPB used the carrot more often than the stick. To encourage businesses to convert to war production, the board granted generous tax write-offs for plant construction and approved contracts with cost-plus provisions that guaranteed a profit and promised that businesses could keep the new factories after the war. As Secretary of War Henry Stimson put it, in capitalist countries at war "you had better let business make money out of the process or business won't work."

In the interest of efficiency and maximum production the WPB preferred to deal with major corporations rather than with small businesses. The fifty-six largest corporations got three-fourths of the war contracts; the top ten a third. This system of allocating contracts, along with the suspension of antitrust prosecution during the war, hastened the trend toward large corporate structures. In 1940 the hundred largest companies manufactured 30 percent of the nation's industrial output; by 1945 their share was 70 percent. These very large businesses would form the core of the military-industrial complex of the postwar years, which linked the federal government, corporations, and the military in an interdependent partnership (see Chapter 27).

Together business and government turned out an astonishing amount of military goods. By 1945 the United States had turned out 86,000 tanks, 296,000 airplanes, 15 million rifles and machine guns, 64,000 landing craft, and 6,500 ships. Mobilization on this gigantic scale gave a tremendous boost to the economy, causing it to more than double, rising from a gross national product in 1940 of $99.7 billion to $211 billion by the end of the war. After years of depression Americans' faith in the capitalist system was restored. But it was a transformed system that relied heavily on the federal government's participation in the economy.

An expanded state presence was also evident in the government's mobilization of a fighting force. By the end of World War II the armed forces of the United States numbered more than 15 million men and women. Draft boards had registered about 31 million men between the ages of eighteen and forty-four. More than half the men failed to meet the physical standards: many were rejected because of defective teeth or poor vision. The military also tried to screen out homosexuals, but its attempts were ineffectual. Once in service homosexuals found opportunities to participate in a gay subculture more extensive than that in civilian life.

Racial discrimination prevailed in the armed forces, directed mainly against the approximately 700,000 blacks who fought in all branches of the armed forces in segregated units. Though the National Association for the Advancement of Colored People (NAACP) and other civil rights groups chided the government with reminders such as "A Jim Crow army cannot fight for a free world," the military continued to segregate African Americans and to assign them the most menial duties. In contrast, Mexican Americans were never officially segregated. Unlike blacks they were welcomed into combat units, and seventeen Mexican Americans won the Congressional Medal of Honor. Native Americans also served in nonsegregrated combat, and some, like the Navajo Code Talkers, played a unique role in circumventing Japanese code-breaking efforts by using their native language to send military messages.

About 350,000 American women enlisted in the armed services and achieved a permanent status in the military, serving in agencies such as the WACS (Women's Army Corps) and the WAVES (Women Appointed for Volunteer Emergency Service). The armed forces limited the types of duty assigned to women, as it did with black men. Women were barred from combat, although nurses and medical personnel sometimes served close to the front lines, risking capture or death. Most of the jobs women did—clerical work, communications, and health care—reflected stereotypes of women's roles in civilian life.

WORKERS AND THE WAR EFFORT

When millions of citizens entered military service, the United States faced a critical labor shortage, which the War Manpower Commission sought to remedy. Well-organized government propaganda urged women into the workforce. "Longing won't bring him back sooner . . . GET A WAR JOB!" one poster beckoned, and the artist Norman Rockwell's famous "Rosie the Riveter" appealed to women from the cover of the *Saturday Evening Post*. Although the government directed its propaganda at housewives, women who were already employed gladly abandoned low-paying "women's" jobs as domestic servants or file clerks for higher-paying jobs in the defense industry. Suddenly the nation's factories were full of women working as riveters, welders, and drill press operators. Women made up 36 percent of the labor force in 1945, compared with 24 percent at the beginning of the war. Despite their new opportunities, women war workers faced much discrimination on the job. In shipyards women with the most seniority and responsibility earned $6.95 a day, while the top men made as much as $22.

When the men came home from war and the nation's plants returned to peacetime operations, Rosie the Riveter was out of a job. But many women refused to put on aprons and stay home. Though women's participation in the labor force dropped temporarily when the war ended, it rebounded steadily for the rest of the 1940s, especially among married women (see Chapter 27).

Wartime Workers

The photographer Dorothea Lange captured these shipyard construction workers coming off their shift at a factory in Richmond, California, in 1942. Note the large number of women workers and the presence of minority workers. Several of the workers prominently display their union buttons.

(Copyright by the Dorothea Lange Collection, Oakland Museum of California, City of Oakland. Gift of Paul S. Taylor)

Wartime mobilization also opened up opportunities to advance the labor movement. Organized labor responded to the war with an initial burst of patriotic unity. On December 23, 1941, representatives of the major unions made a "no-strike" pledge—though it was nonbinding—for the duration of the war. In January 1942 Roosevelt set up the National War Labor Board (NWLB), composed of representatives of labor, management, and the public. The NWLB established wages, hours, and working conditions and had the authority to order government seizure of plants that did not comply. Forty plants were seized during the war.

During its tenure the NWLB handled 17,650 disputes affecting 12 million workers. It resolved the controversial issue of union membership through a compromise. New hires did not have to join a union, but those who already belonged had to maintain their membership over the life of a contract. Agitation for wage increases caused a more serious disagreement. Because managers wanted to keep production running smoothly and profitably, they were willing to pay higher wages. However, pay raises would conflict with the government's efforts to combat inflation, which drove prices up dramatically in the early war years. Incomes rose as much as 70 percent during the war because workers earned overtime pay, which was not covered by wage ceilings.

Although incomes were higher than anyone could have dreamed during the depression, many union members felt cheated as they watched corporate profits soar in relation to wages. Dissatisfaction peaked in 1943. That year a nationwide railroad strike was narrowly averted, and John L. Lewis led more than half a million United Mine Workers out on strike, demanding an increase in wages over that recommended by the NWLB. Though Lewis won concessions, he alienated Congress; and because he had defied the government, he became one of the most disliked public figures of the 1940s.

Congress countered Lewis's action by overriding Roosevelt's veto of the Smith-Connally Labor Act of 1943, which required a thirty-day cooling-off period before a strike and prohibited entirely strikes in defense industries. Nevertheless, about 15,000 walkouts occurred during the war. Though less than one-tenth of 1 percent of working hours were lost to labor disputes, the public perceived the disruptions to be far more extensive. Thus although union membership increased dramatically during the war, from 9 million to almost 15 million workers—a third of the nonagricultural workforce—the labor movement also evoked significant public and congressional hostility that would hamper it in the postwar years.

Just as labor sought to benefit from the war, African Americans manifested a new mood of militancy. "A wind is rising throughout the world of free men everywhere," Eleanor Roosevelt wrote during the war, "and they will not be kept in bondage." Black leaders pointed out parallels between anti-Semitism in Germany and racial discrimination in America and pledged themselves to a "Double V" campaign: victory over Nazism abroad and victory over racism and inequality at home.

Even before Pearl Harbor black activism was on the rise. In 1940 only 240 of the nation's 100,000 aircraft workers were black, and most of them were janitors.

Black leaders demanded that the government require defense contractors to integrate their workforces. When the government took no action, A. Philip Randolph, head of the Brotherhood of Sleeping Car Porters, a black union, announced plans for a "March on Washington" in the summer of 1941. Though Roosevelt was not a strong supporter of civil rights, he feared the embarrassment of a massive public protest. Even more, he worried about a disruption of the nation's war preparations.

In June 1941, in exchange for Randolph's cancellation of the march, Roosevelt issued Executive Order 8802, declaring "that there shall be no discrimination in the employment of workers in defense industries or government because of race, creed, color, or national origin," and established the Fair Employment Practices Commission (FEPC). Though this federal commitment to minority employment rights was unprecedented, it was limited in scope; for instance, it did not affect segregation in the armed forces. Moreover, the FEPC could not require compliance with its orders and often found that the needs of defense production took precedence over fair employment practices. The committee resolved only about a third of the more than 8,000 complaints it received.

Encouraged by the ideological climate of the war years, civil rights organizations increased their pressure for reform. The League of United Latin American Citizens (LULAC) built on their community's patriotic contributions to national defense and the armed services to challenge long-standing patterns of discrimination and exclusion. In Texas, where it was still common to see signs reading, "No Dogs or Mexicans Allowed," the organization protested segregation in schools and public facilities. African American groups also flourished. The NAACP grew ninefold to 450,000 by 1945. Although the NAACP generally favored lobbying and legal strategies, a student chapter of the NAACP at Howard University used direct tactics. In 1944 it forced several restaurants in Washington, D.C., to serve blacks after picketing them with signs that read "Are You for Hitler's Way or the American Way? Make Up Your Mind." In Chicago James Farmer helped to found the Congress of Racial Equality (CORE), a group that became known nationwide for its use of direct action like demonstrations and sit-ins. These wartime developments—both federal intervention and resurgent African American militancy—laid the groundwork for the civil rights revolution of the 1950s and 1960s.

POLITICS IN WARTIME

Although the federal government expanded dramatically during the war years, there was little attempt to use the state to promote social reform on the home front, as in World War I. An enlarged federal presence was justified only insofar as it assisted war aims. During the early years of the war Roosevelt rarely pressed for social and economic change, in part because he was preoccupied with the war but also because he wanted to counteract Republican political gains. Republicans had picked up ten seats in the Senate and forty-seven seats in the House in the 1940 elections, thus bolstering conservatives in Congress who sought to roll back New

Deal measures. With little protest Roosevelt agreed to drop several popular New Deal programs, including the Civilian Conservation Corps and the National Youth Administration, which were less necessary once war mobilization brought full employment.

Later in the war Roosevelt began to promise new social welfare measures. In his State of the Union address in 1944, he called for a second bill of rights, which would serve as "a new basis of security and prosperity." This extension of the New Deal identified jobs, adequate food and clothing, decent homes, medical care, and education as basic rights. But the president's commitment to them remained largely rhetorical; congressional support for this vast extension of the welfare state did not exist in 1944. Some of those rights did become realities for veterans, however. The Servicemen's Readjustment Act (1944), known as the GI Bill of Rights, provided education, job training, medical care, pensions, and mortgage loans for men and women who had served in the armed forces during the war.

Roosevelt's call for more social legislation was part of a plan to woo Democratic voters. In the 1942 election Republicans gained seats in both houses of Congress and increased their share of state governorships. The Democrats realized they would have to work hard to maintain their strong coalition in 1944. Once again Roosevelt headed the ticket, reasoning that the continuation of the war made a fourth term necessary. Democrats, concerned about Roosevelt's health and the need for a successor, dropped Vice President Henry Wallace, whose outspoken support for labor, civil rights, and domestic reform was too extreme for many party leaders. In his place they chose Senator Harry S Truman of Missouri.

The Republicans nominated Governor Thomas E. Dewey of New York. Only forty-two years old, Dewey had won fame fighting organized crime as a U.S. attorney. He accepted the broad outlines of the welfare state and was among those Republicans who rejected isolationism in favor of an internationalist stance. The 1944 election was the closest since 1916: Roosevelt received only 53.5 percent of the popular vote. The Democrats lost ground among farmers, but most ethnic minorities remained solidly Democratic. The party's margin of victory came from the cities: in urban areas of more than 100,000 people the president drew 60 percent of the vote. A significant segment of this urban support came from organized labor. The CIO's Political Action Committee made substantial contributions to the party, canvassed door to door, and conducted voter registration campaigns—a role organized labor would continue to play after the war.

Life on the Home Front

Although the United States did not suffer the physical devastation that ravaged much of Europe and the Pacific, the war affected the lives of those who stayed behind. Every time relatives of a loved one overseas saw the Western Union boy on his bicycle, they feared a telegram from the War Department saying that their son, husband, or father would not be coming home. All Americans tolerated small deprivations daily. "Don't you know there's a war on?" became the standard reply to any request that could not be fulfilled. People accepted the fact that their lives would be different "for the duration." They also accepted, however grudgingly, the increased role of the federal government in shaping their daily lives.

CIVILIAN WAR EFFORTS

Just like the soldiers in uniform people on the home front had a job to do. They worked on civilian defense committees, collected old newspapers and scrap material, and served on local rationing and draft boards. About 20 million home "Victory gardens" produced 40 percent of the nation's vegetables. All these endeavors were encouraged by various federal agencies, especially the Office of War Information (OWI), which strove to disseminate information and promote patriotism. Working closely with advertising agencies, the OWI urged them to link their clients' products to the "four freedoms," explaining that patriotic ads would not only sell goods but would "invigorate, instruct and inspire [the citizen] as a functioning unit in his country's greatest effort."

Popular culture, especially the movies, reinforced the connections between the home front and troops serving overseas. Average weekly movie attendance soared to over 100 million during the war. Demand was so high that many theaters operated around the clock to accommodate defense workers on the swing and night shifts. Many movies, encouraged in part by the OWI, had patriotic themes; stars such as John Wayne, Anthony Quinn, and Spencer Tracy portrayed the heroism of American fighting men in films like *Back to Bataan* (1945), *Guadalcanal Diary* (1943), and *Thirty Seconds over Tokyo* (1945). Other movies, such as *Watch on the Rhine* (1943), warned of the danger of fascism at home and abroad, while the Academy Award–winning *Casablanca* (1943) demonstrated the heroism and patriotism of ordinary citizens. *Since You Went Away* (1943), starring Claudette Colbert as a wife who took a war job after her husband left for war, was one of many films that portrayed struggles on the home front. Newsreels accompanying the feature films kept the public up to date on the war, as did on-the-spot radio broadcasts by commentators such as Edward R. Murrow. Thus popular culture reflected America's new international involvement at the same time that it built morale on the home front.

Perhaps the major source of Americans' high morale was wartime prosperity. Federal defense spending had solved the depression; unemployment had disappeared, and per capita income had risen from $691 in 1939 to $1,515 in 1945. Despite geographical dislocations and shortages of many items, about 70 percent of Americans admitted midway through the war that they had personally experienced "no real sacrifices." A Red Cross worker put it bluntly: "The war was fun for America. I'm not talking about the poor souls who lost sons and daughters. But for the rest of us, the war was a hell of a good time."

For many Americans the major inconveniences of the war were the limitations placed on their consumption. In contrast to the largely voluntaristic approach used during World War I, federal agencies such as the Office of Price Administration subjected almost everything Americans ate, wore, or used during World War II to rationing or regulation. In response to depleted domestic gasoline supplies and a shortage of rubber the government restricted the sale of tires, rationed gas, and imposed a nationwide speed limit of 35 miles per hour. By 1943 the amount of meat, butter, sugar, and other foods Americans could buy was also regulated. Most people cooperated with the complicated system of restrictions, but almost a fourth occasionally bought items on the black market, especially meat, gasoline, and cigarettes.

The war and the government affected not only what people ate, drank, and wore, but where they lived. When men entered the armed services, their families often followed them to training bases or points of debarkation. The lure of high-paying defense jobs encouraged others—Native Americans on reservations, white southerners in the hills of Appalachia, African Americans in the rural South—to move. About 15 million Americans changed residence during the war years, half of them moving to another state.

As a center of defense production California was affected by wartime migration more than any other state. The western mecca welcomed nearly 3 million new residents during the war, a 53 percent growth in population. "The Second Gold Rush Hits the West," headlined the *San Francisco Chronicle* in 1943. During the war one-tenth of all federal dollars went to California, and the state turned out one-sixth of the total war production. People went where the defense jobs were—to Los Angeles, San Diego, and the San Francisco Bay area. Some towns grew practically overnight: just two years after the Kaiser Corporation opened a shipyard in Richmond, the population quadrupled.

Migration and relocation often caused strains. In many towns with defense industries housing was scarce, and public transportation inadequate. Conflicts over public space and recreation erupted between old-timers and newcomers. Of special concern were the young people the war had set adrift from traditional community safeguards. Newspapers were filled with stories of "latchkey" children who stayed home alone while their mothers worked in defense plants. Adolescents were even more of a problem. Teenage girls who hung around army bases looking for a good time became known as "victory girls." In 1942 and 1943 juvenile delinquency seemed to be reaching epidemic proportions.

Another significant result of the growth of war industries was the migration of more than a million African Americans to defense centers in California, Illinois, Michigan, Ohio, and Pennsylvania. The migrants' need for jobs and housing led to racial conflict in several cities. Early in 1942 black families encountered resistance and intimidation when they tried to move into the Sojourner Truth housing project, in the Polish community of Hamtramck near Detroit—the new home of a large number of southern migrants, both black and white. In June 1943 similar tensions erupted in Detroit itself, where a major race riot left thirty-four people dead. Racial conflicts broke out in forty-seven cities across the country during 1943.

Other Americans also experienced racial violence. In Los Angeles male Latinos who belonged to *pachuco* (youth) gangs dressed in "zoot suits"—broad-brimmed felt hats, pegged trousers, and clunky shoes—wore their long hair slicked down and carried pocket knives on gold chains. The young women they hung out with favored long coats, huarache sandals, and pompadour hairdos. Blacks and some working-class white teenagers in Los Angeles, Detroit, New York, and Philadelphia also wore zoot suits as a symbol of alienation and self-assertion. To adults and to many Anglos, however, the zoot suit symbolized wartime juvenile delinquency.

In Los Angeles white hostility toward Mexican Americans had been smoldering for some time, and zoot-suiters soon became the targets. In July 1943 rumors that a *pachuco* gang had beaten a white sailor set off a four-day riot, during which white servicemen entered Mexican American neighborhoods and attacked zoot-suiters, taking special pleasure in slashing their pegged pants. The attacks occurred in full view of white police officers, who did nothing to stop the violence.

Although racial confrontations and zoot-suit riots recalled the widespread racial tensions of World War I, the mood on the home front was generally calm in the

Zoot Suits

Zoot suits gained wide popularity among American youth during the war. In 1943 this well-dressed teenager greased his hair in a duck-tail and wore a loosely cut coat with padded shoulders ("finger-tips") that reached midthigh, baggy pleated pants cut tight ("pegged") around the ankles, and a long gold watch chain. (Corbis-Bettmann)

1940s. German Americans generally did not experience the intense prejudice of World War I nor did Italian Americans, though some aliens in both groups were interned. Leftists and communists faced little repression, mainly because after Pearl Harbor the Soviet Union became an ally of the United States.

JAPANESE INTERNMENT

The internment of Japanese Americans on the West Coast was a glaring exception to this record of tolerance, a reminder of the fragility of civil liberties in wartime. California had a long history of antagonism toward both Japanese and Chinese immigrants (see Chapters 16 and 21). The Japanese Americans, who clustered together in highly visible communities, were a small, politically impotent minority, numbering only about 112,000 in the three coastal states. Unlike German and Italian Americans the Japanese stood out. "A Jap's a Jap," snapped General John DeWitt. "It makes no difference whether he is an American citizen or not." This sort of sentiment, coupled with fears of the West Coast's vulnerability to attack and the inflammatory rhetoric of newspapers and local politicians, fueled mounting demands that the region be rid of supposed Japanese spies.

In early 1942, in Executive Order 9066, Roosevelt approved a War Department plan to intern Japanese Americans in relocation camps for the rest of the war. Despite the lack of any evidence of their disloyalty or sedition—no Japanese American was ever charged with espionage—few public leaders opposed the plan. The announcement shocked Japanese Americans, more than two-thirds of whom were native-born American citizens. (They were *Nisei*, children of the foreign-born *Issei*.) Most had to sell their property and possessions at cut-rate prices and were then rounded up in temporary assembly centers and sent by the War Relocation Authority to internment camps in California, Arizona, Utah, Colorado, Wyoming, Idaho, and Arkansas—places "where nobody had lived before and no one has lived since," a historian commented (see American Voices, "Japanese Relocation").

Almost every Japanese American in California, Oregon, and Washington was involuntarily detained for some period during World War II. Ironically, the Japanese Americans who made up one-third of the population of Hawaii, and presumably posed a greater threat because of their numbers and proximity to Japan, were not interned. Less vulnerable to suspicion because of the islands' multiracial heritage, the Japanese also provided much of the unskilled labor on the islands. The Hawaiian economy simply could not function without them.

Cracks soon appeared in the relocation policy. A labor shortage in farming led the government to furlough seasonal agricultural workers from the camps as early as 1942. About 4,300 young people who had been in college when they were interned were allowed to return to school if they would transfer out of the West Coast military zone. Another route out of the camps was enlistment in the armed ser-

AMERICAN VOICES

Japanese Relocation

MONICA SONE

*M*onica (Itoi) Sone's autobiography, Nisei Daughter (1953) tells the story of Japanese relocation from the perspective of a young woman in Seattle, Washington. Here she describes the Itoi family's forced evacuation to a temporary encampment called Camp Harmony; later they were moved to a settlement in Idaho. Although her parents spent the entire war in the camp, Monica Sone was allowed to leave in 1943 to attend college in Indiana.

All through the night I heard people getting up, dragging cots around. I stared at our little window, unable to sleep. I was glad Mother had put up a makeshift curtain on the window for I noticed a powerful beam of light sweeping across it every few seconds. The lights came from high towers placed around the camp where guards with Tommy guns kept a twenty-four hour vigil. I remembered the wire fence encircling us, and a knot of anger tightened in my breast. What was I doing behind a fence like a criminal? If there were accusations to be made, why hadn't I been given a fair trial? Maybe I wasn't considered an American anymore. My citizenship wasn't real, after all. Then what was I? I was certainly not a citizen of Japan as my parents were. On second thought, even Father and Mother were more alien residents of the United States than Japanese nationals for they had little tie with their mother country. In their twenty-five years in America, they had worked and paid their taxes to their adopted government as any other citizen.

Of one thing I was sure. The wire fence was real. I no longer had the right to walk out of it. It was because I had Japanese ancestors. It was also because some people had little faith in the ideas and ideals of democracy. They said that after all these were but words and could not possibly insure loyalty. New laws and camps were surer devices. I finally buried my face in my pillow to wipe out burning thoughts and snatch what sleep I could.

SOURCE: Monica Sone, *Nisei Daughter* (Boston: Little, Brown, 1953), pp. 176–78.

vices. The 442d Regimental Combat Team, a segregated unit composed almost entirely of Nisei volunteers, served in Europe and became one of the most decorated units in the armed forces.

The Supreme Court upheld the constitutionality of internment as a legitimate exercise of power during wartime in *Hirabayashi v. United States* (1943) and in *Korematsu v. United States* (1944). It was not until 1988 that Congress decided to issue a public apology and to give $20,000 in cash to each of the 80,000 surviving internees—small restitution indeed. Though with each generation the memory of internment grows dimmer, this shameful episode has been burned into the national conscience.

Behind Barbed Wire

As part of the forced relocation of 120,000 Japanese Americans, Los Angeles photographer Toyo Miyatake and his family were sent to Manzanar, a camp in the California desert east of the Sierra Nevada. Miyatake secretly began shooting photographs of the camp, although he eventually received permission from the authorities to document life in the camp. This photograph of three young boys behind barbed wire with a watchtower in the distance must have been shot with official sanction because the photographer is on the other side of the barbed wire. It gives new meaning to the phrase "prisoners of war." (Toyo Miyatake)

Fighting and Winning the War

World War II, noted the military historian John Keegan, was "the largest single event in human history." Fought on six continents at a cost of 50 million lives, it was far more global than World War I. At least 405,000 Americans were killed and 671,000 wounded in the global fighting—less than half of 1 percent of the U.S. population. In contrast the Soviets lost as many as 21 million soldiers and civilians during the war, or about 8 percent of their population.

WARTIME AIMS AND STRATEGIES

The Allied coalition was composed mainly of Great Britain, the United States, and the Soviet Union; other nations, notably China and France, played lesser roles. President Franklin Roosevelt, Britain's Prime Minister Winston Churchill, and Premier Joseph Stalin of the Soviet Union took the lead in setting overall strategy. The Atlantic Charter, which Churchill and Roosevelt had drafted in August 1941, formed the basis of the Allies' vision of the postwar international order. But Stalin had not been part of that agreement, a fact that would later cause disagreements over its goals.

One way to wear down the Germans would have been to open a second front on the European continent, preferably in France. The Russians argued strongly for this strategy because it would draw German troops away from Russian soil. The issue came up so many times that the Soviet foreign minister, Vyacheslav Molotov, was said to know only four English words: yes, no, and second front. Though Roosevelt assured Stalin informally that a second front would be opened in 1942, British opposition and the need to raise American war production to full capacity stalled the effort. At a conference in Teheran, Iran, in late November 1943 Churchill and Roosevelt agreed to open a second front within six months in return for Stalin's promise to join the fight against Japan after the war in Europe ended. Both sides kept their promises. However, the long delay in creating a second front meant that for most of the war the Soviet Union bore the brunt of the land battle against Germany. Roosevelt and Churchill's foot-dragging angered Stalin, who was suspicious about American and British intentions. His mistrust and bitterness carried over into the cold war that followed the Allied victory.

During the first six months of 1942 the military news was so bad it threatened to swamp the Grand Alliance. The Allies suffered severe defeats on land and sea in both Europe and Asia. German armies pushed deeper into Soviet territory, reaching the outskirts of Moscow and Leningrad. Simultaneously, they began an offensive in North Africa aimed at seizing the Suez Canal. At sea German submarines were crippling American convoys carrying vital supplies to Europe.

The major turning point of the war in Europe occurred in the winter of 1942 to 1943, when the Soviets halted the German advance in the Battle of Stalingrad. By 1944 Stalin's forces had driven the German army out of the Soviet Union. Meanwhile, the Allies launched a major offensive in North Africa, Churchill's substitute for a second front in France. Between November 1942 and May 1943 Allied troops under the leadership of General Dwight D. Eisenhower and General George S. Patton defeated Germany's crack *Afrika Korps*, led by General Erwin Rommel.

From Africa the Allied command moved to attack the Axis through what Churchill called its "soft underbelly": Sicily and the Italian peninsula. In July 1943 Benito Mussolini's fascist regime fell, and Italy's new government joined the Allies. The Allied forces fought bitter battles against the German army during the Italian campaign, finally entering Rome in June 1944 (see Map 26.1). The last German forces in Italy did not surrender until May 1945, however.

The long-promised invasion of France came on D-Day, June 6, 1944. That morning, after an agonizing delay caused by bad weather, the largest armada ever assembled moved across the English Channel. Over the next few days, under the command of General Dwight Eisenhower, more than 1.5 million American, British, and Canadian soldiers crossed the Channel. In August Allied troops helped to liberate Paris; by September they had driven the Germans out of most of France and Belgium.

The Germans were not yet ready to give up, however. In December 1944 their forces in Belgium mounted an attack that began the Battle of the Bulge, so called because their advance made a large balloon in the Allied line on war maps. After ten days of heavy fighting in what was to be the final German offensive of the war, the Allies regained their momentum and pushed the Germans back across the Rhine River. American and British troops led the drive from the west toward Berlin, while Soviet troops advanced from the east through Poland, arriving there first. On April 30, with much of Berlin in rubble from intense Allied bombing, Hitler committed suicide in his bunker. Germany surrendered on May 8, 1945, the date that became known as V-E (Victory in Europe) Day.

When Allied troops advanced into Germany in the spring of 1945, they came face to face with Hitler's "final solution of the Jewish question": the extermination camps where 6 million Jews had been put to death, along with another 6 million Poles, Slavs, Gypsies, homosexuals, and other "undesirables." Photographs of the Nazi death camps at Buchenwald, Dachau, and Auschwitz, showing bodies stacked like cordwood and survivors so emaciated they were barely alive, horrified the American public. But government officials could not claim that no one knew about the camps before the German surrender. The Roosevelt administration had had reliable information about the death camps as early as November 1942.

The lack of response by the U.S. government to the systematic near annihilation of European Jewry ranks as one of the gravest failures of the Roosevelt administration. So few Jews escaped the Holocaust because the United States and the rest of the world would not take them in. State Department policies allowed only 21,000 refugees to enter the United States during the war. The War Refugee Board, established in 1944 with little support from the Roosevelt administration, eventually helped to save about 200,000 Jews, who were placed in refugee camps in countries such as Morocco and Switzerland.

Several factors combined to inhibit U.S. action: anti-Semitism; fears of economic competition from a flood of refugees to a country just recovering from the depression; the failure of the media to grasp the magnitude of the story and to publicize it accordingly; and the failure of religious leaders, Jews and non-Jews alike, to speak out. In justifying the American course of action Roosevelt claimed that winning the war would be the strongest contribution America could make to liberating the camps. But one cannot escape the conclusion that the United States could have done much more to lessen the Holocaust's terrible human toll.

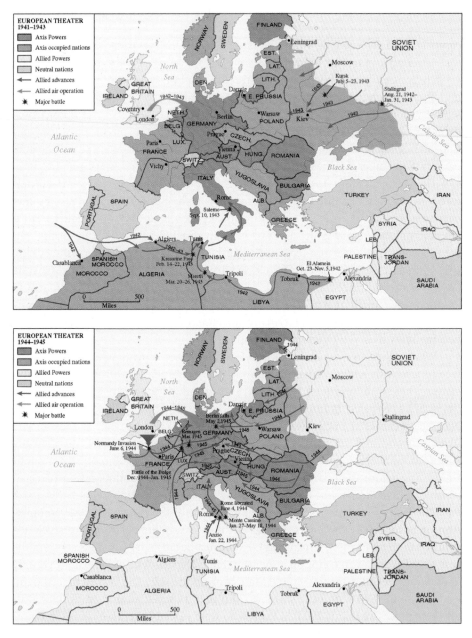

M A P 26.1
World War II in Europe

1941–1943 Hitler's Germany reached its greatest extent in 1942, when Nazi forces stalled at Leningrad and Stalingrad. The tide of battle turned in the fall, when the Soviet army launched a massive counterattack at Stalingrad and Allied forces began to drive the Germans from North Africa. In 1943 the Allies invaded Sicily and the Italian mainland. **1944–1945** On June 6, 1944 (D-Day), the Allies finally invaded France. It took almost a year for the Allied forces to close in on Berlin—the Soviets from the east and the Americans, British, and French from the west. Germany surrendered on May 8, 1945.

Hitting the Beach at Normandy

These American soldiers, part of almost 150,000 Allied troops, stormed the beaches of
Normandy, France, on D-Day, June 6, 1944. More than a million Allied troops came ashore
during the next month. Filmmaker Stephen Spielberg recreated the carnage and confusion
of the landing in the opening scene of *Saving Private Ryan* (1998). (Library of Congress)

After the victory in Europe the Allies still had to defeat Japan. American forces
bore the brunt of the fighting in the Pacific, just as the Russians had done in the
land war in Europe. In early 1942 the news from the Pacific was uniformly grim.
In the wake of Pearl Harbor Japan had scored quickly with seaborne invasions of
Hong Kong, Wake Island, and Guam. Japanese forces soon conquered much of
Burma, Malaya, the Philippines, and the Solomon Islands and began to threaten
Australia and India (see American Voices, "An Army Nurse in Bataan"). But on May
7 and 8, 1942, in the Battle of the Coral Sea near southern New Guinea, American
naval forces halted the Japanese offensive against Australia. In June at the island of
Midway the Americans inflicted crucial damage on the Japanese fleet. With that
success the American military command, led by General Douglas MacArthur and
Admiral Chester W. Nimitz, took the offensive in the Pacific. For the next eighteen
months American forces advanced arduously from one island to the next. In October
1944 the reconquest of the Philippines began with a victory in the Battle of Leyte
Gulf, a massive naval encounter in which the Japanese lost practically their entire
fleet, while the Americans suffered only minimal losses (see Map 26.2).

By early 1945 victory over Japan was in sight. The campaign in the Pacific
moved slowly toward what military leaders anticipated would be a massive and

AMERICAN VOICES
An Army Nurse in Bataan
JUANITA REDMOND

A rmy Nurse Juanita Redmond recounts her experiences as one of the last nurses to remain in Bataan in the Philippines as the Japanese advanced. She was evacuated shortly
before the Americans surrendered on May 6, 1942. Her description reveals both the horror of
warfare and the extraordinary service performed by military nurses.

[The bomb] landed at the hospital entrance and blew up an ammunition truck that was
passing. The concussion threw me to the floor. There was a spattering of shrapnel and
pebbles and earth on the tin roof. Then silence for a few minutes.

I heard the corpsmen rushing out with litters, and I pulled myself to my feet. Precious
medicines were dripping to the ground from the shattered dressing carts, and I tried to
salvage as much as possible.

The first casualties came in. The boys in the ammunition truck had been killed, but the
two guards at the hospital gate had jumped into their foxholes. By the time they were ex-
tricated from the debris that filled up the holes they were both shell-shock cases.

There were plenty of others. . . .

Only one small section of my ward remained standing. Part of the roof had been blown
into the jungle. There were mangled bodies under the ruins; a blood-stained hand stuck
up through a pile of scrap; arms and legs had been ripped off and flung among the rub-
bish. Some of the mangled torsos were almost impossible to identify. One of the few corpsmen who had survived unhurt climbed a tree to bring down a body blown into the top
branches. Blankets, mattresses, pajama tops hung in the shattered trees.

We worked wildly to get to the men who might be buried, still alive, under the mass
of wreckage, tearing apart the smashed beds to reach the wounded and the dead. These
men were our patients, our responsibility; I think we were all tortured by an instinctive,
irrational feeling that we had failed them.

SOURCE: Judy Barrett Litoff and David C. Smith, eds., *American Women in a World at War: Contemporary Accounts from World War II* (Wilmington, DE: Scholarly Resource Books, 1997), pp. 85–86.
Reprinted from Juanita Redmond, *I Served on Bataan* (Philadelphia: Lippincott, 1943), pp. 106–22.

costly invasion of Japan. In some of the fiercest fighting of the war, American
marines won the battles for Iwo Jima and Okinawa, where they sustained more than
52,000 casualties, including 13,600 dead. The closer U.S. forces got to the Japanese
home islands, the more fiercely the Japanese fought. On Iwo Jima almost all the
21,000 Japanese died.

By mid-1945 Japan's army, navy, and air force had suffered devastating losses.
American bombing of the mainland had killed about 330,000 civilians and
crippled the Japanese economy. In a last-ditch effort to stem the tide, Japanese

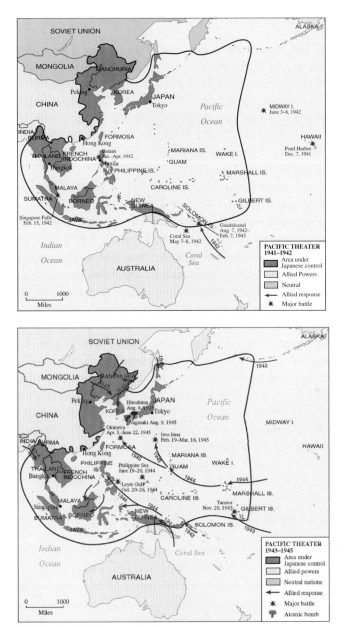

MAP 26.2
World War II in the Pacific

1941–1942 After the attack on Pearl Harbor in December 1941 the Japanese rapidly extended their domination in the Pacific. The Japanese flag soon flew as far east as the Marshall and Gilbert Islands and as far south as the Solomon Islands and parts of New Guinea. Japan also controlled the Philippines, much of Southeast Asia, and parts of China, including Hong Kong. American naval victories at the Coral Sea and Midway stopped further Japanese expansion.

1943–1945 Allied forces retook the islands in the Central Pacific in 1943 and 1944 and the Philippines early in 1945. The capture of Iwo Jima and Okinawa put U.S. bombers in position to attack Japan itself. The Japanese offered to surrender on August 10, after the United States dropped atomic bombs on Hiroshima and Nagasaki.

pilots began flying suicidal kamikaze missions, crashing their planes and boats into American ships. This desperate action, combined with the Japanese military leadership's refusal to surrender, suggested to military strategists that Japan would continue to fight despite overwhelming losses. American commanders grimly predicted millions of casualties in the upcoming invasion.

PLANNING THE POSTWAR WORLD

When Roosevelt, Churchill, and Stalin met in February 1945 at Yalta, a resort on the Black Sea, victory in Europe and the Pacific was in sight, but no agreement had been reached on the peace to come. Roosevelt focused on maintaining Allied unity, the key to postwar peace and stability. The fate of British colonies such as India, where an independence movement had already begun, caused friction between Roosevelt and Churchill. Some of the tensions with the Russians were resolved when, in return for additional possessions in the Pacific, Stalin agreed to enter the war against Japan within three months of the German surrender.

A more serious source of conflict was Stalin's desire for a band of Soviet-controlled satellite states to protect the Soviet Union's western border. With Soviet armies in control of much of Eastern Europe Stalin had become increasingly inflexible on the issue of Eastern Europe, insisting that he needed friendly (that is, Soviet-dominated) governments there to provide a buffer zone that would guarantee the Soviet Union's national security. Roosevelt acknowledged the legitimacy of that demand but, with the Atlantic Charter's principle of self-determination in mind, hoped for democratically elected governments in Poland and the neighboring countries. Unfortunately, the two goals proved mutually exclusive.

At Yalta Roosevelt and Churchill agreed in principle on the idea of a Soviet sphere of influence in Eastern Europe but deliberately left its dimensions vague. Stalin in return pledged to hold "free and unfettered elections" at an unspecified time. (Those elections never took place.) The compromise the three leaders reached at Yalta was open to multiple interpretations. Admiral William D. Leahy, Roosevelt's chief military aide, described the agreement as "so elastic that the Russians can stretch it all the way from Yalta to Washington without ever technically breaking it."

At Yalta the three leaders proceeded with plans to divide Germany into four zones to be controlled by the United States, Great Britain, France, and the Soviet Union. The capital city, Berlin, which lay in the middle of the Soviet zone, would also be partitioned among the four powers. The issue of German reparations remained unsettled.

The Big Three made further progress toward the establishment of an international organization in the form of the United Nations. They agreed that the Security Council of the United Nations would include the five major Allied powers—the United States, Britain, France, China, and the Soviet Union—plus six other nations elected on a rotating basis. They also decided that the permanent members of the Security Council should have veto power over decisions of the General Assembly, in which all nations would be represented. Roosevelt, Churchill, and Stalin announced that the United Nations would convene in San Francisco on April 25, 1945.

Roosevelt returned to the United States in February, visibly exhausted by his 14,000-mile trip. He neglected to inform the American public of the concessions he had made to maintain the increasingly fragile wartime alliance. When he reported to Congress on the Yalta agreements, he made an unusual acknowledgment of his physical infirmity. Referring to the heavy steel braces he wore on his legs, he asked Congress to excuse him for giving his speech while sitting down. The sixty-three-year-old president was a sick man, suffering from heart failure and high blood pressure. On April 12, 1945, during a short visit to his vacation home in Warm Springs, Georgia, Roosevelt suffered a cerebral hemorrhage and died.

When Harry S Truman took over the office, he learned about the top-secret Manhattan Project, charged with developing an atomic bomb. The project, which cost $2 billion and employed 120,000 people, culminated in Los Alamos, New Mexico, where the country's top physicists assembled the first bomb. Not until the first test—at Alamogordo, New Mexico, on July 16, 1945—did scientists know that the bomb would work. A month later Truman ordered the dropping of atomic bombs on two Japanese cities, Hiroshima on August 6 and Nagasaki on August 9.

Many later questioned why the United States did not warn Japan about the attack or choose a noncivilian target; the rationale for dropping the second bomb was even less clear. Some historians have argued that American policymakers, already worried about potential conflicts with the Soviets over the postwar order, used the bomb to intimidate the Soviets. Others have suggested that the fact that the Japanese were a nonwhite race facilitated the momentous decision to use the new, alarming weapon. At the time, however, the belief that Japan's military leaders would never surrender unless their country was utterly devastated convinced policymakers that they had to deploy the atom bomb. One hundred thousand people died at Hiroshima, 60,000 at Nagasaki; tens of thousands more died slowly of radiation poisoning. Japan offered to surrender on August 10 and signed a formal treaty of surrender on September 2, 1945.

Franklin Roosevelt's death and the dropping of the atomic bomb came at a critical juncture in world affairs. Many issues had been left deliberately unresolved, in hopes of keeping the wartime alliance intact through the transition to peace. But as the war ended, issues such as the fates of Poland and Germany demanded action. The resulting compromises, not all of which were fully reported to the American people, tended to promote spheres of influence, rather than the ideals of national self-determination and economic cooperation laid out in the Atlantic Charter, as the new basis of international power.

Once the common enemies had been defeated, the wartime alliance became strained and then began to split apart in ways so fundamental that Roosevelt could not likely have kept it together had he lived. Perhaps the greatest legacy of World War II, then, was the cold war that followed.

For Further Exploration

An engaging overview of war on the homefront that emphasizes social and cultural conflicts embodied in the war effort is John Morton Blum, *V Was for Victory* (1976). An anthology that focuses on popular culture—including an analysis of glamorous movie icons

T I M E L I N E

1935	Italy invades Ethiopia.		Atlantic Charter
1935–1937	U.S. Neutrality Acts		Japanese attack Pearl Harbor.
		1942	Battles of Coral Sea and Midway halt Japanese advance.
1936	Germany reoccupies Rhineland demilitarized zone.		Women recruited for war industries
	Rome-Berlin Axis established		Internment of Japanese Americans
	Japan and Germany sign Anti-Comintern Pact.	**1942–1945**	Rationing
1937	Japan invades China.	**1943**	Race riots in Detroit and Los Angeles
1938	Munich agreement		Fascism falls in Italy.
1939	Nazi-Soviet Nonaggression Pact	**1944**	D-Day
	Germany invades Poland.		GI Bill of Rights
	Britain and France declare war on Germany.	**1945**	Yalta Conference
			Battles of Iwo Jima and Okinawa
1940	Conscription reinstated		Germany surrenders.
	Tri-Partite Pact signed by Germany, Italy, and Japan		Harry S Truman becomes president after Roosevelt's death.
1941	Roosevelt promulgates Four Freedoms.		United Nations convenes.
	Germany invades Soviet Union.		Atomic bombs dropped on Hiroshima and Nagasaki
	Lend-Lease Act passed		Japan offers to surrender.
	Fair Employment Practices Commission		

like Betty Grable—as a means to understanding the wartime experience is Lewis A. Erenberg and Susan E. Hirsch, eds., *The War in American Culture* (1996). Stephen J. Ambrose offers insight into military life from the ordinary man's point of view with *Citizen Soldiers* (1997). Two oral history collections are indispensable. Studs Terkel, *The Good War* (1984), examines the notion that in contrast to America's more recent war in Vietnam World War II is largely remembered in positive terms. Sherna B. Gluck, *Rosie the Riveter Revisited* (1988), offers compelling accounts by women war workers. Powerful novels inspired by the war include James Jones, *From Here to Eternity* (1951), Norman Mailer, *The Naked and the Dead* (1948), and John Hersey, *Bell for Adano* (1944).

The National Archives Administration at <http://www.nara.gov/exhall/exhibits.html> has two World War II sites. "A People at War" offers a number of documents, including a letter about the Navajo Code Talkers. "Powers of Persuasion: Poster Art from World War II" contains thirty-three color posters and a sound file of the song "Any Bonds Today." The Library of Congress at <http://lcweb.loc.gov/exhibits/wcf/wcf0001.html> has an online exhibit, "Women Come to the Front: Journalists, Photographers, and Broadcasters During World War II," that features articles, biographies, and photographs of eight women who covered the war. See also "Rosie Pictures: Select Images Relating to American Women Workers

During World War II" at <http://lcweb.loc.gov/rr/print/126_rosi.html>. There are many sites on Japanese internment. The University of Washington provides a particularly interesting one at <http://www.lib.washington.edu/exhibits/harmony/default.htm> on the experiences of the Seattle Japanese American community's incarceration at the Puyallup Assembly Center; it includes letters, photographs, and other documents. The Rutgers Oral History Archive of World War II at <http://history.rutgers.edu/oralhistory/orlhom.htm> offers over 100 oral histories that cover not just the interviewees' war experiences but their life histories as well, providing valuable insights into community life in depression and wartime New Jersey.

Part Six

AMERICA AND THE WORLD
1945 to the Present

THEMATIC TIMELINE

	DIPLOMACY	GOVERNMENT	ECONOMY
	THE COLD WAR ERA— AND AFTER	REDEFINING THE ROLE OF THE STATE	UPS AND DOWNS OF U. S. ECONOMIC DOMINANCE
1945	• Truman Doctrine (1947) • Marshall Plan (1948) • NATO (1949)	• Harry Truman's Fair Deal liberalism • Taft-Hartley Act (1947)	• Bretton Woods system established: World Bank, IMF, GATT
1950	• Permanent mobilization: NSC-68 (1950) • Korean War (1950–1953)	• Eisenhower's modern Republicanism • Warren Court activism	• Rise of military-industrial complex • Service sector expands.
1960	• Cuban missile crisis (1962) • Nuclear test ban treaty (1963) • Vietnam War escalates (1965).	• Great Society, War on Poverty • Richard Nixon ushers in conservative era.	• Kennedy-Johnson tax cut, military expenditures fuel economic growth.
1970	• Nixon visits China (1972). • SALT initiates détente (1972). • Paris Peace Accords (1973)	• Watergate scandal; Nixon resigns (1974). • Deregulation begins under Gerald Ford and Jimmy Carter.	• Arab oil embargo (1973–1974); inflation surges. • Unemployment in "Rustbelt." • Income stagnation
1980	• Ronald Reagan begins arms buildup. • Berlin Wall falls (1989).	• Reagan Revolution • Supreme Court conservatism	• Reaganomics • Deficits soar. • Savings and loan bailout
1990– 2000	• War in the Persian Gulf (1990) • Cold war ends. • U.S. peacekeeping forces in Bosnia	• Republican Congress shifts federal government tasks to states. • George W. Bush narrowly elected President	• Corporate down-sizing • NAFTA (1993) • Recovery from recession

In 1945 the United States entered an era of unprecedented international power and influence. Unlike the period after World War I, American leaders did not avoid international commitments: instead, they aggressively pursued U.S. interests abroad, vowing to contain communism around the globe. The consequences of that struggle profoundly influenced the nation's domestic economy, political affairs, and social and cultural trends for the next half-century.

SOCIETY	CULTURE
SOCIAL MOVEMENTS AND DEMOGRAPHIC DIVERSITY	CONSUMER CULTURE AND THE INFORMATION REVOLUTION
• Urban migration • Armed forces desegregated (1948)	• End of wartime rationing • Rise of television
• *Brown v. Board of Education* (1954) • Montgomery bus boycott (1955)	• Growth of suburbia • Baby boom
• Student activism • Civil Rights Act (1964) • Voting Rights Act (1965) • Revival of feminism	• Shopping malls spread. • Youth counterculture
• *Roe v. Wade* (1973) • New Right urges conservative agenda.	• Gasoline shortages • Apple introduces first personal computer (1977).
• New Hispanic and Asian immigration	• MTV debuts. • AIDS epidemic
• Affirmative action challenged • Welfare reform	• Health-care crisis • Information superhighway

First and most important, the United States took a leading, or hegemonic, role in global diplomatic and military affairs. When the Soviet Union challenged America's vision of postwar Europe, the Truman administration responded by crafting the policies and alliances that came to define the cold war. That bipolar struggle lasted for more than forty years, spawned two "hot" wars in Korea and Vietnam, and fueled a terrifying and debilitating nuclear arms race. Althouh the moderate policy of détente pursued by Richard Nixon and later presidents helped ease tensions, the cold-war mentality prevailed until the collapse of the Soviet Union in 1991.

America's global commitments had dramatic consequences for American government and politics. Until the national consensus fractured over the Vietnam War, liberals and conservatives agreed on keeping the country in a state of permanent mobilization and maintaining a large and well-equipped military establishment. The end of the cold war brought modest cutbacks in defense spending, but an explosion of ethnic and religious conflicts in the former Yugoslavia, Africa, and other areas required U.S. military participation in several international peacekeeping missions in the 1990s. In the area of economic policy all administrations, Republican and Democratic, were willing to intervene in the economy when private initiatives could not maintain steady growth. But liberals also pushed for a larger role for the federal government in the areas of social welfare and environmental protection. Under Harry S Truman, John F. Kennedy, and especially Lyndon B. Johnson, the government went beyond the New Deal by erecting an extensive federal and state apparatus to provide for the social well-being of the people. In subsequent years, particularly under the presidency of Ronald Reagan in the 1980s and Republican control of Congress in the mid-1990s, conservatives cut back on many of the major programs and tried to delegate federal powers to the states. By the turn of the century the long-term significance of the efforts to end the "era of big government" were not yet clear.

Thanks to the growth of a military industrial complex of enormous size and the expansion of consumer culture, the quarter-century after 1945 repre-sented the heyday of American capitalism. Economic dominance abroad translated into unparalleled affluence at home. A heady sense of unlimited progress and affluence lasted until the early 1970s, when slow growth, environmental problems, and foreign competition undermined America's economic supremacy. For the next two decades many American workers experienced high unemployment, declining real wages, stagnant incomes, and a standard of living that could not match that of their parents. Following this period of global economic restructuring, the U.S. economy rebounded in the mid-1990s, reclaiming its position of undisputed dominance. Underlying the optimism about this extraordinary national prosperity, however, were fears that it was too dependent on consumer confidence and a potentially volatile stockmarket and concerns that disparities in wealth and opportunity were growing.

The victory over fascism in World War II led to renewed calls for America to make good on its promise of liberty and equality for all. In great waves of protests in the 1950s and 1960s African Americans—and then women, Latinos, and other groups—challenged the political status quo. The resulting hard-won reforms brought concrete gains for many Americans, but in the 1980s and 1990s conservatives challenged many of these initiatives. And as immigration from Latin America and Asia swelled, new tensions arose over cultural and ethnic pluralism. As the new century began, the promise of social justice and equality remained unfulfilled.

American economic power in the postwar era accelerated the development of a consumer society based on suburbanization and technology. As millions of Americans migrated to new suburban developments after World War II, growing baby-boom families provided an expanded market for household products of all types. Among the most significant were new technological devices—television, video recorders, personal computers—that helped break down the isolation of suburban and rural living. In the 1990s the popularization of the Internet initiated an "information revolution," which both expanded and challenged the power of corporate-sponsored consumer culture.

Today, more than half a century after the end of World War II, Americans are living in an increasingly interwoven network of national and international forces. Outside events shape ordinary lives in ways that were inconceivable a century ago. As the cold war era fades into history, the United States remains the sole military superpower, but it shares economic leadership in the new interdependent global system.

Chapter 27

COLD WAR AMERICA
1945–1960

We have been in the process of fighting monsters without stop for a generation and half, looking all that time into the nuclear abyss. And the abyss has looked back into us.

— DANIEL ELLSBERG, 1971

When Harry Truman arrived at the White House on April 12, 1945, after Franklin Roosevelt died, he asked the president's widow, "Is there anything I can do for you?" Eleanor Roosevelt responded, "Is there anything we can do for you? For you are the one in trouble now." Truman inherited the presidency at one of the most perilous times in modern history. Unscathed by bombs and battles on the home front, U.S. industry and agriculture had grown rapidly during World War II. The nation wielded enormous military power as the sole possessor of the atomic bomb. The most powerful country in the world, the United States had become a preeminent force in the international arena. Only the Soviet Union represented an obstacle to American *hegemony,* or dominance, in global affairs. Soon the two superpowers were locked in a cold war of economic, political, and military rivalry but no direct engagement on the battlefield.

Soviet-American confrontations during the postwar years had important domestic repercussions. The cold war boosted military expenditures, fueling a growing arms race. It fostered a climate of fear and suspicion of "subversives" in government, education, and the media who might undermine American democratic institutions. But the economic benefits of internationalism also gave rise to a period of unprecedented affluence and prosperity during which the United States enjoyed the highest standard of living in the world (see Chapter 28). That prosperity helped to continue and in some cases to expand federal power, perpetuating the New Deal state in the postwar era.

The Early Cold War

The defeat of Germany and Japan did not bring stability to the world. Six years of devastating warfare had destroyed prewar governments and geographical bound-

Postwar Devastation, 1945

Cologne, Germany, was one of many European cities reduced to rubble during World War II. Here one of the 120,000 remaining inhabitants of Cologne (from a prewar population of 780,000) sits homeless with all of her belongings amid the ruins of this once beautiful and prosperous city. U.S. policymakers worried that physical devastation and economic disorder would make many areas of Europe vulnerable to communist influence.

(Johnny Florea, LIFE Magazine, © 1945 Time, Inc.)

aries, creating new power relationships that helped to dissolve colonial empires. Even before the war ended, the United States and the Soviet Union were struggling for advantage in those unstable areas; after the war they engaged in a protracted global conflict. Hailed as a battle between communism and capitalism, the cold war was in reality a more complex power struggle covering a range of economic, strategic, and ideological issues. As each side tried to protect its own national security and way of life, its actions aroused fear in the other, contributing to a cycle of distrust and animosity that would shape U.S.-Soviet relations for decades to come.

DESCENT INTO COLD WAR, 1945–1946

During the war Franklin Roosevelt had worked effectively with Soviet leader Joseph Stalin and had determined to continue good relations with the Soviet Union in peacetime. In particular, he hoped that the United Nations would provide a forum for resolving postwar conflicts. Avoiding the disagreements that had doomed American membership in the League of Nations after World War I, the Senate approved America's participation in the United Nations in December 1945. Coming eight months after Roosevelt's death, the vote was in part a memorial to the late president's hopes for peace.

Shortly before his death, however, Roosevelt had been disturbed by Soviet actions in Eastern Europe. As the Soviet army drove the Germans out of Russia and back through Eastern Europe, the USSR sponsored provisional governments in the occupied countries. Since the Soviet Union had been a victim of German aggression in both world wars, Stalin was determined to prevent the rebuilding and rearming of its traditional foe, and he insisted on a security zone of friendly governments in Eastern Europe for further protection. At the Yalta Conference in February both America and Britain had agreed to recognize this Soviet "sphere of influence," with the proviso that "free and unfettered elections" would be held as soon as possible. But in succeeding months the Soviets made no move to hold elections and rebuffed western attempts to reorganize the Soviet-installed governments.

When Truman assumed the presidency after Roosevelt's death, he took a belligerent stance toward the Soviet Union. Recalling Britain's disastrous appeasement of Hitler in 1938, he had decided that the United States had to take a hard line against Soviet expansion. "There isn't any difference in totalitarian states," he said. "Nazi, Communist, or Fascist." At a meeting held shortly after he took office, the new president berated the Soviet foreign minister, V. M. Molotov, over the Soviets' failure to honor their Yalta agreement (see Chapter 26) to support free elections in Poland. Truman used what he called "tough methods" that July at the Potsdam Conference, which brought together the United States, Britain, and the Soviet Union. After learning of the successful test of America's atomic bomb, Truman "told the Russians just where they got off and generally bossed the whole meeting," recalled British Prime Minister Winston Churchill. Negotiations on critical postwar issues deadlocked, revealing serious cracks in the Grand Alliance.

One issue tentatively resolved at Potsdam was the fate of occupied Germany. At Yalta the defeated German state had been divided into four zones of occupation, controlled by the United States, France, Britain, and the Soviet Union. At Potsdam the Allies agreed to disarm the country, dismantle its military production facilities, and permit the occupying powers to extract reparations from the zones they controlled. Plans for future reunification stalled, however, as the United States and the Soviet Union each worried that a united Germany would fall into the other's sphere. The foundation was thus laid for what would become the political division into East and West Germany four years later.

As tensions over Europe divided the former allies, hopes of international co-operation in the control of atomic weapons faded as well. In the Baruch Plan, sub-mitted to the United Nations in 1946, the United States proposed a system of international control that relied on mandatory inspection and supervision but pre-served American nuclear monopoly. The Soviets rejected the plan categorically and worked assiduously to complete their own bomb. Meanwhile, the Truman admin-istration pursued plans to develop nuclear energy and weapons further. Thus the failure of the Baruch Plan signaled the beginning of a frenzied nuclear arms race between the two superpowers.

A POLICY OF CONTAINMENT

As tensions mounted between the superpowers, the United States increasingly per-ceived Soviet expansionism as a threat to its own interests, and a new American policy, called *containment*, began to take shape. The most influential expression of the policy came in February 1946 from George F. Kennan in an 8,000-word cable, dubbed the "long telegram," from his post at the U.S. Embassy in Moscow to his superiors in Washington. Kennan, who was identified only as "X," warned that the USSR was moving "inexorably along the prescribed path, like a persistent toy au-tomobile wound up and headed in a given direction, stopping only when it meets unanswerable force." To stop Soviet expansionism, Kennan argued, the United States should pursue a policy of "firm containment . . . at every point where [the Russians] show signs of encroaching upon the interests of a peaceful and stable world."

The emerging policy of containment crystallized in 1947 over a crisis in Greece. In the spring of 1946, several thousand local communist guerrillas, whom Ameri-can advisers mistakenly believed were taking orders from Moscow, launched a full-scale civil war against the government and the British occupation authorities. In February 1947 the British informed Truman that they could no longer afford to assist anticommunists in Greece. American policymakers worried that Soviet in-fluence in Greece threatened American and European interests in the eastern Mediterranean and the Middle East, especially in strategically located Turkey and the oil-rich state of Iran.

In response the president announced what would be known as the Truman Doctrine. In a speech to the Republican-controlled Congress on March 12, he re-quested large-scale military and economic assistance to Greece and Turkey. If Greece fell to communism, Truman warned, the effects would be serious not only for Turkey but for the entire Middle East. This notion of an escalating communist contagion was an early version of what Dwight Eisenhower would later call the "domino the-ory." Not just Greece but freedom itself was at issue, Truman declared: "If we fal-ter in our leadership, we may endanger the peace of the world," and "we shall surely endanger the welfare of our own nation." Despite the open-endedness of this mil-itary commitment, Congress quickly approved Truman's request for $300 million in aid to Greece and $100 million for Turkey. The appropriation reversed the postwar trend toward sharp cuts in foreign spending and marked a new level of commitment to the emerging cold war.

During this period Secretary of State George Marshall proposed a plan to provide economic as well as military aid to Europe. In June 1947 Marshall urged the nations of Europe to construct a comprehensive recovery program and then ask the United States for aid. In Truman's words the Marshall Plan was "the other half of the walnut" (the first half being the aggressive containment of communism). By bolstering European economies devastated by war, Marshall and Truman believed, the United States could forestall severe economic dislocation, which might give rise to communism. American economic self-interest was also a contributing factor; the legislation required that foreign-aid dollars be spent on U.S. goods and services. A revitalized Europe centered on a strong West German economy would provide a better market for U.S. goods.

Truman's pledge of economic aid to European economies, however, met with significant opposition in Congress. Republicans castigated the Marshall Plan as a huge "international W.P.A." But in the midst of the congressional stalemate, on February 25, 1948, came a communist coup in Czechoslovakia. A stark reminder of the menace of Soviet expansion in Europe, the coup rallied congressional support for the Marshall Plan. In March 1948 Congress voted overwhelmingly to approve funds for the program. Like most other foreign-policy initiatives of the 1940s and 1950s, the Marshall Plan won bipartisan support despite the opposition of an isolationist wing of the Republican Party.

Over the next four years the United States contributed nearly $13 billion to a highly successful recovery effort. Western European economies revived, and industrial production increased 64 percent, opening new opportunities for international trade. The Marshall Plan did not specifically exclude Eastern Europe or the Soviet Union, but it required that all participating nations exchange economic information and work toward the elimination of tariffs and other trade barriers. Denouncing those conditions as attempts to draw Eastern Europe into the American orbit, Soviet leaders forbade the satellite states of Czechoslovakia, Poland, and Hungary to participate.

The Marshall Plan accelerated American and European efforts to rebuild and unify the West German economy. In June 1948, after agreeing to fuse their zones of occupation, the United States, France, and Britain initiated a program of currency reform in West Berlin. The economic revitalization of Berlin, located deep within the Soviet zone of occupation, alarmed the Soviets, who feared a resurgent Germany aligned with the West. As a response, they imposed a blockade on all highway, rail, and river traffic to West Berlin. Truman countered with an airlift: for nearly a year American and British pilots, who had been dropping bombs on Berlin only four years earlier, flew in 2.5 million tons of food and fuel—nearly a ton for each resident. On May 12, 1949, Stalin lifted the blockade, which had made West Berlin a symbol of resistance to communism.

The coup in Czechoslovakia and the crisis in Berlin convinced U.S. policy-makers of the need for a collective security pact. In April 1949, for the first time since the end of the American Revolution, the United States entered into a peace-time military alliance, the North Atlantic Treaty Organization (NATO). Truman asked Congress for $1.3 billion in military assistance to NATO and authorized the basing of four U.S. army divisions in Western Europe. Under the NATO pact, twelve nations—the United States, Canada, Britain, France, Italy, Belgium, the Netherlands, Luxembourg, Denmark, Norway, Portugal, and Iceland—agreed that "an armed at-tack against one or more of them in Europe or North America shall be considered an attack against them all." In May 1949 those nations also agreed to the creation of the Federal Republic of Germany (West Germany), which joined NATO in 1955 (Map 27.1).

In October 1949, in response to the creation of NATO, the Soviet Union tight-ened its grip on Eastern Europe by creating a separate government for East Germany, which became the German Democratic Republic. The Soviets also organized an economic association, the Council for Mutual Economic Assistance (COMECON) in 1949, and a military alliance for Eastern Europe, the Warsaw Pact, in 1955. The postwar division of Europe was nearly complete.

New impetus for the policy of containment came in September 1949, when American military intelligence detected a rise in radioactivity in the atmosphere—proof that the Soviet Union had detonated an atomic bomb. The American atomic monopoly, which some military and political advisers had argued would last for decades, had ended in just four years, forcing a major reassessment of the nation's foreign policy.

MAP 27.1
Cold War Europe, 1955

In 1949 the United States sponsored the creation of the North Atlantic Treaty Organization—an al-liance of ten European nations, the United States, and Canada. West Ger-many was formally ad-mitted to NATO in May 1955. A few days later the Soviet Union and seven other communist nations established a rival al-liance, the Warsaw Pact.

To devise a new diplomatic and military blueprint Truman turned to the National Security Council (NSC), an advisory body established in 1947 to set defense and military priorities. In April 1950 the NSC delivered its report, known as NSC-68, to the president. Filled with alarmist rhetoric and exaggerated assessments of Soviet capabilities, the document made several specific recommendations, including the development of a hydrogen bomb, an advanced weapon a thousand times more destructive than the atomic bombs that had destroyed Hiroshima and Nagasaki. (The United States would explode its first hydrogen bomb in November 1952; the Soviet Union its first in 1953.) NSC-68 also supported increases in U.S. conventional forces and the establishment of a strong system of alliances. Most important, it called for increased taxes to finance "a bold and massive program of rebuilding the West's defensive potential to surpass that of the Soviet world."

Though Truman was an aggressive anticommunist, he was reluctant to commit to a major defense buildup, fearing that it would overburden the budget. But the Korean War, which began just two months after NSC-68 was completed, helped to transform the report's recommendations into reality, as the cold war spawned a hot war.

CONTAINMENT IN ASIA

As mutual suspicion deepened between the United States and the Soviet Union, cold-war doctrines began to influence the American position in Asia as well. American policy there was based on Asia's importance to the world economy as much as on the desire to contain communism. At first American plans for the region centered on a revitalized China, but political instability there prompted the Truman administration to focus on developing the Japanese economy instead. After dismantling Japan's military forces and weaponry, American occupation forces under General Douglas MacArthur began the job of transforming the country into a bulwark of Asian capitalism. MacArthur drafted a democratic constitution and oversaw the rebuilding of the economy, paving the way for the restoration of Japanese sovereignty in 1951.

In China the situation was more precarious. Since the 1930s a civil war had been raging, as communist forces led by Mao Zedong (Mao Tse-tung) and Zhou Enlai (Chou En-lai) contended for power with conservative Nationalist forces under Jiang Jieshi (Chiang Kai-shek). Although dissatisfied with the corrupt and inefficient Jiang regime, officials for the Truman administration did not see Mao as a good alternative, and they resigned themselves to working with the Nationalists. Between 1945 and 1949 the United States provided more than $2 billion to Jiang's forces but to no avail. In 1947 General Albert Wedemeyer, who had tried to work with Jiang, reported to President Truman that, until the "corrupt, reactionary, and inefficient Chinese National government" undertook "drastic political and economic reforms," the United States could not accomplish its purpose. In August 1949, when those reforms did not occur, the Truman administration cut off aid to the

Nationalists, sealing their fate. The People's Republic of China was formally established under Mao on October 1, 1949, and what was left of Jiang's government fled to Taiwan.

Many Americans viewed Mao's success as a defeat for the United States. A pro-Nationalist "China lobby," supported by the powerful publisher Henry R. Luce and by Republican senators Karl Mundt of South Dakota and William S. Knowland of California, protested that under Truman's newly appointed secretary of state, Dean Acheson, the State Department was responsible for the "loss of China." The China lobby's influence led to the United States' refusal to recognize what it called "Red China"; instead, the nation recognized the exiled Nationalist government in Taiwan. The United States also used its influence to block China's admission to the United Nations. For almost twenty years U.S. administrations treated mainland China, the world's most populous country, as a diplomatic nonentity.

In Korea as in China cold-war confrontation grew out of World War II roots. Both the United States and the Soviet Union had troops in Korea at the end of the war. As a result Korea was divided at the thirty-eighth parallel into competing spheres of influence. The Soviets supported a communist government, led by Kim Il Sung, in North Korea; the United States backed a longtime Korean nationalist, Syngman Rhee, in South Korea. Soon sporadic fighting broke out along the thirty-eighth parallel, and a civil war began.

On June 25, 1950, the North Koreans launched a surprise attack across the thirty-eighth parallel (Map 27.2). The initiative for Korean reunification came from Kim Il Sung, but Stalin supported the mission (although the extent of Soviet involvement was unknown at the time). Soviet and North Korean leaders may have expected Truman to ignore this armed challenge, but the president felt that the United States must take a firm stance against the spread of communism. "There's no telling what they'll do if we don't put up a fight now," he said. Truman immediately asked the U.N. Security Council to authorize a "police action" against the invaders. Because the Soviet Union was temporarily boycotting the Security Council to protest the exclusion of the People's Republic of China from the United Nations, it could not veto Truman's request. Three days after the Security Council voted to send what was called a "peacekeeping force," Truman ordered U.S. troops to Korea.

Though fourteen other noncommunist nations sent troops, the rapidly assembled United Nations army in Korea was overwhelmingly American. At the request of the Security Council President Truman named General Douglas MacArthur to head the U.N. forces. At first the North Koreans held an overwhelming advantage, controlling practically the entire peninsula except for the area around Pusan. But on September 15, 1950, MacArthur launched a surprise amphibious attack at Inchon, far behind the North Korean front line, while U.N. forces staged a breakout from Pusan. Within two weeks the U.N. forces controlled Seoul, the South Korean capital, and almost all the territory up to the thirty-eighth parallel.

Encouraged by this success MacArthur sought the authority to lead his forces across the thirty-eighth parallel and into North Korea. Truman's initial plan had

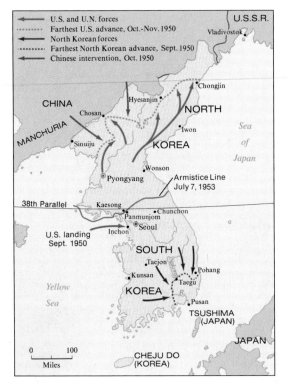

MAP 27.2

The Korean War, 1950–1953

The first months of the Korean War featured dramatic shifts in control up and down the 600-mile peninsula. From June to September 1950 North Korean troops overran most of the territory south of the thirty-eighth parallel. On September 15, U.N. forces under General Douglas MacArthur counterattacked behind enemy lines at Inchon and pushed north almost to the Chinese border. Massive Chinese intervention forced the U.N. troops to retreat to the thirty-eighth parallel in January 1951, and the war was a stalemate for the next two years.

been to restore the 1945 border, but he managed to win U.N. support for the broader goal of creating "a unified, independent and democratic Korea." Though the Chinese government in Beijing warned repeatedly that such a move would provoke retaliation, American officials ignored the warnings. MacArthur's troops crossed the thirty-eighth parallel on October 9, reaching the Chinese border at the Yalu River by the end of the month. Just after Thanksgiving a massive Chinese counterattack of almost 300,000 troops forced MacArthur to retreat to the thirty-eighth parallel. Then on January 4, 1951, communist troops reoccupied Seoul.

Two months later American forces and their allies counterattacked, regained Seoul, and pushed back to the thirty-eighth parallel. Then stalemate set in. Public support in the United States had dropped after Chinese intervention increased the likelihood of a long war. A poll revealed in early January 1951 that 66 percent of Americans thought the United States should withdraw; 49 percent felt intervening in the war had been a mistake. Given domestic opinions and the stalemate in Korea, Truman and his advisers decided to work for a negotiated peace. They did not want to tie down large numbers of U.S. troops in Asia, far from what were considered more strategically important trouble spots in Europe and the Middle East.

MacArthur disagreed. Headstrong, arrogant, and brilliant, the general fervently believed that the nation's future lay in Asia, not Europe. Disregarding Truman's

The Korean War

These men of the Second Infantry battalion, shown here in Korea in 1950, helped pave the way for the formal integration of all U.S. Army units by 1954. The Korean War marked the first time in the nation's history that all troops served in racially integrated combat units. (National Archives)

instructions MacArthur traveled to Taiwan and urged the Nationalists to join in an attack on mainland China. He pleaded for permission to use the atomic bomb against China. In an inflammatory letter to the House minority leader, Republican Joseph J. Martin of Massachusetts, he denounced the Korean stalemate. "We must win," MacArthur declared. "There is no substitute for victory."

Martin released MacArthur's letter on April 6, 1951, as part of a concerted Republican campaign to challenge Truman's conduct of the war. The strategy backfired. On April 11 Truman relieved MacArthur of his command in Korea and Japan, accusing him of insubordination—a decision the Joint Chiefs of Staff supported. Truman's decision was nonetheless highly unpopular. The allure of decisive victory under a charismatic military leader temporarily overshadowed the public's doubts about the war. Returning to tumultuous receptions in San Francisco, Chicago, and New York, the general delivered an impassioned address to a joint session of Congress. But when the shouting subsided, Truman had the last word. After failing to win the Republican presidential nomination in 1952, MacArthur faded from public view.

The war dragged on for more than two years after MacArthur's dismissal. Truce talks began in Korea in July 1951, but a final armistice was not signed until July

1953. Approximately 45 percent of American casualties were sustained during this period. The final settlement left Korea divided very near the original border at the thirty-eighth parallel, with a demilitarized zone between the two countries. North Korea remained firmly allied with the Soviet Union; South Korea signed a mutual defense treaty with the United States in 1954.

The Korean War had a lasting impact on the conduct of American foreign policy. Calling it a "police action" rather than a war, Truman had committed troops to Korea without congressional approval, arguing that he had the power to do so as commander in chief of the armed forces and as executor of the treaty binding the United States to the United Nations. His act expanded executive power and set a precedent for other undeclared wars. The Korean War also widened American involvement in Asia, transforming containment into a truly global policy. During and after the war the United States stationed large numbers of troops in South Korea and increased military aid to the Nationalist Chinese forces in Taiwan and to French forces fighting communist insurgents in Indochina (see Chapter 29). American foreign policy had become more global, more militarized, and more costly. Even in times of peace the United States functioned in a state of permanent mobilization.

Harry Truman and the Cold War at Home

Harry S Truman brought a complex personality to the presidency. Alternately humble and cocky, he had none of Roosevelt's patrician ease and was a distinctly unpopular president. Yet he handled affairs with an assurance and a crisp dispatch that have endeared him to later generations. "If you can't stand the heat, stay out of the kitchen," he liked to say of presidential responsibility. The major domestic issues he faced were reconversion to a peacetime economy and fears of communist infiltration and subversion—fears his administration played a part in perpetuating.

POSTWAR DOMESTIC CHALLENGES

The public's main fear in 1945—that the depression would return once war production had ended—proved unfounded. Despite a drop in government spending after the war, consumer spending increased; workers had amassed substantial wartime savings and were eager to spend them. The Servicemen's Readjustment Act of 1944, popularly known as the GI Bill, also put money into the economy by providing educational and economic assistance to returning veterans. Despite some temporary dislocations as war production shifted back to civilian production and veterans entered the workforce, unemployment did not soar.

But the transition was hardly trouble free. The main domestic problem was inflation. Consumers wanted to end wartime restrictions and price rationing, but Truman feared economic chaos if he lifted all controls immediately. In the summer of 1945 he eased industrial controls but retained the wartime Office of Price

Administration (OPA). When he disbanded the OPA and lifted almost all the remaining controls in the following year, prices soared, producing an annual inflation rate of 18.2 percent. Rising prices and persistent shortages of food and household goods irritated consumers.

The rapidly rising cost of living prompted workers' demands for higher wages. Under government-sanctioned agreements the labor movement had held the line on salary increases during the war. But after the war ended, union leaders expressed frustration. Corporate profits had doubled while real wages had declined as a result of inflation and the loss of overtime pay. Determined to make up for their war-induced sacrifices, workers mounted crippling strikes in the automobile, steel, and coal industries. General strikes effectively closed down business in more than a half dozen cities in 1946. By the end of that year 5 million workers had idled factories and mines for a total of 107,476,000 workdays.

Truman responded dramatically. In the face of a devastating railway strike he used his executive authority to place the nation's railroad system under federal control and asked Congress for the power to draft striking workers into the army—a move that infuriated labor leaders but pressured strikers to go back to work. Three days later he seized control of the nation's coal mines to end a strike by the United Mine Workers. Such actions won Truman support from many Americans but outraged organized labor, an important partner in the Democratic coalition.

These domestic upheavals did not bode well for the Democrats at the polls. In 1946 the Republicans gained control of both houses of Congress and set about undoing New Deal social welfare measures, especially targeting labor legislation. In 1947 Congress passed the Taft-Hartley Act, a rollback of several provisions of the 1935 National Labor Relations Act. Unions especially disliked Section 14b of Taft-Hartley, which outlawed the closed shop and allowed states to pass "right-to-work" laws that further limited unions' operations. The act also restricted unions' political power by prohibiting use of their dues for political activity and allowed the president to declare an eighty-day cooling-off period in strikes that had a national impact. Truman issued a ringing veto of the Taft-Hartley bill in June 1947, calling it "bad for labor, bad for management, and bad for the country." Congress easily overrode the veto, but Truman's actions countered some of workers' hostility to his earlier antistrike activity and kept labor in the Democratic fold.

Most observers believed that Truman faced an impossible task in the presidential campaign of 1948. The Republicans were united, and with Thomas E. Dewey, the politically moderate governor of New York, as their candidate once again, they had a good chance of attracting traditional Democratic voters. To increase their appeal in the West the Republicans nominated Earl Warren, governor of California, for vice president. In their platform they promised to continue most New Deal reforms and to support a bipartisan foreign policy.

Truman, in contrast, led a party in disarray. Both the left and the right wings of the Democratic Party split off and nominated their own candidates. Henry A. Wallace, a former New Deal liberal whom Truman had fired as secretary of commerce in 1946 because he was perceived as too "soft" on communism, ran as the candidate of the new Progressive Party. Wallace advocated increased government intervention in the economy, more power for labor unions, and cooperation with the Soviet Union. The right-wing challenge came from the South. At the Democratic national convention, northern liberals such as Mayor Hubert H. Humphrey of Minneapolis had pushed through a platform calling for the repeal of the Taft-Hartley Act and increased federal commitment to civil rights. Southern Democrats, unwilling to tolerate federal interference in race relations, bolted the convention and created the States' Rights Party, popularly known as the Dixiecrats. They nominated Governor J. Strom Thurmond of South Carolina for president.

Truman responded to these challenges with one of the most effective presidential campaigns ever waged. He launched a strenuous cross-country speaking tour in which he hammered away at the Republicans' support for the antilabor Taft-Hartley Act. He also criticized Republicans for opposing legislation for housing, medical insurance, and civil rights. By combining these issues with attacks on the Soviet menace abroad, Truman began to salvage his troubled campaign. At his rallies enthusiastic listeners shouted, "Give 'em hell, Harry!"

Truman won a remarkable victory, receiving 49.6 percent of the vote to Dewey's 45.1 percent. The Democrats also regained control of both houses of Congress. Strom Thurmond carried only four southern states, and Henry Wallace failed to win any electoral votes. Truman retained the support of organized labor. Jewish and Catholic voters in the big cities and black voters in the North offset his losses to the Dixiecrats. Most important, Truman appealed effectively to people like himself from the farms, towns, and small cities in the nation's heartland.

FAIR DEAL LIBERALISM

Shortly after becoming president, Truman had proposed to Congress a twenty-one-point plan for expanded federal programs based on individual "rights," including the right to a "useful and remunerative" job, controls over monopolies, good housing, "adequate medical care," "protection from the economic fears of old age," and a "good education." Later, Truman added support for civil rights and in his 1949 State of the Union address christened his program the Fair Deal. Although to some extent the Fair Deal represented an extension of the New Deal's liberalism—with faith in the positive influence of government and the use of federal power to ensure public welfare—it also took some new directions. Its attention to civil rights reflected the growing importance of African Americans to the Democratic Party's coalition of urban voters. And the desire to extend a high standard of living and other benefits of capitalism to an ever-greater number of citizens reflected a new liberal vision of the role of the state. Economically, the liberals of Truman's era were more moderate than the Progressive Era and New Deal reformers who had proposed extensive federal regulation of corporations and intrusive planning of the economy. They believed that the essential role of the federal government was to manage the economy indirectly through fiscal policy. Drawing on the Keynesian notion of using government spending to spur economic growth, they expected that welfare programs not only would provide a safety net for disadvantaged citizens but also would maintain consumer purchasing power, keeping the economy healthy.

Truman's agenda met with a generally hostile Congress, despite the Democratic majority. The same conservative coalition that had blocked Roosevelt's initiatives in his second term and dismantled or cut popular New Deal programs during wartime continued to fight against Truman's proposals. Only parts of the Fair Deal won adoption: the minimum wage was raised; the Social Security program was extended to cover 10 million new workers; and Social Security benefits were increased by 75 percent. The National Housing Act of 1949 called for the construction of 810,000 units of low-income housing, but only half that number were actually built.

Interest groups successfully opposed other key items in the Fair Deal. The American Medical Association (AMA) quashed a labor-backed movement for national health insurance by denouncing it as the first step toward "socialized medicine." Catholics successfully opposed aid to education because it did not include subsidies for parochial schools. Trade associations, the National Association of Manufacturers, and other business groups also actively opposed what they called "creeping socialism." Though most corporate leaders recognized that some state involvement in the economy was necessary and even beneficial to business interests, they felt the Fair Deal went too far. As a lobbyist for the National Association of Real Estate Boards explained, "In our country we prefer that government activity shall take the form of assisting and aiding private business rather than undertake great public projects of a governmental character." Through extensive lobbying and public relations campaigns, business groups agitated not only to defeat specific pieces of Fair Deal legislation but also to forestall increased taxes, antitrust activity, and other unwanted federal interference in corporate affairs. Their activities helped to block support for enlarged federal responsibilities for economic and social welfare.

Truman's record on civil rights illustrates still other obstacles that faced the Fair Deal. Black demands for justice, which had accelerated during World War II, continued into the postwar years, spurred by symbolic victories such as Jackie Robinson's breaking through the color line in major league baseball by joining the Brooklyn Dodgers in 1947. Truman offered some support for modest civil rights measures, in part because of his desire to solidify the Democrats' hold on African American voters as they migrated from the South, where they were effectively disfranchised, to northern and western cities. Truman was also concerned about America's image abroad, especially since the Soviet Union often compared the segregation of southern blacks with the Nazis' treatment of the Jews. The desire to gain the allegiance of emerging African nations and of India provided further incentive for the United States to address the problem of racial discrimination.

Lacking a popular mandate on civil rights Truman turned to executive action. In 1946 he appointed a National Civil Rights Commission, which in its 1947 report called for an expanded federal role in civil rights that foreshadowed much of the civil rights legislation of the 1960s. He ordered the Justice Department to prepare an *amicus curiae* ("friend of the court") brief in the Supreme Court case of *Shelley v. Kraemer* (1948), which struck down as unconstitutional restrictive covenants that enforced residential segregation by barring home buyers of a certain race or religion. In the same year Truman signed an executive order to desegregate the armed forces. His administration also proposed a federal antilynching law, federal protection of voting rights (such as an end to poll taxes), and a permanent federal agency to guarantee equal employment opportunity, but a filibuster by southern conservatives blocked the legislation.

The outbreak of the Korean War in 1950 also limited the chances of the Fair Deal being passed by diverting national attention and federal funds from domestic affairs. So did the nation's growing paranoia concerning internal subversion, the most dramatic manifestation of the cold war's effect on American life.

THE GREAT FEAR

As American relations with the Soviet Union deteriorated, fear of communism at home fueled a widespread campaign of domestic repression. Americans often call this phenomenon "McCarthyism," after Senator Joseph R. McCarthy of Wisconsin, the decade's most vocal anticommunist, but more was involved than the work of just one man. The Great Fear built on the longstanding distrust of radicals and foreigners that had exploded in the Red Scare after World War I. Worsening cold-war tensions intersected with both those deep-seated anxieties and partisan politics to spawn an obsessive concern with internal subversion. Ultimately, few Communists were found in positions of power; far more Americans became innocent victims of false accusations and innuendos.

The roots of postwar anticommunism dated back to 1938, when Congressman Martin Dies of Texas and other conservatives launched the House Committee on Un-American Activities (HUAC) to investigate alleged fascist and communist influence in labor unions and New Deal agencies. HUAC gained heightened visibility after the war, especially after revelations in 1946 of a Soviet spy ring operating in Canada and the United States accentuated fears of Soviet subversion.

In 1947 HUAC helped launch the Great Fear by holding widely publicized hearings on alleged communist infiltration in the film industry. A group of writers and directors, soon dubbed the Hollywood Ten, went to jail for contempt of Congress when they cited the First Amendment in refusing to testify about their past associations. Hundreds of other actors, directors, and writers whose names had been mentioned in the HUAC investigation or whose associates and friends the committee had labeled as "reds" were unable to get work, victims of an unacknowledged but very real blacklist honored by industry executives. HUAC also investigated playwrights, authors, university professors, labor activists, organizations, and government officials thought to be "left wing."

Although HUAC bore much of the responsibility for spawning the witch hunt, its effects spread far beyond the congressional committee. In March 1947 President Truman issued an executive order initiating a comprehensive investigation into the loyalty of federal employees. Following Washington's lead, many state and local governments, universities, political organizations, churches, and businesses undertook their own antisubversion campaigns, including the requirement that employees take loyalty oaths. In the labor movement, which Communists had been active in organizing in the 1930s, charges that Soviet-led Communists were taking over American unions led to a purge of Communist members. Civil rights organizations such as the NAACP and the National Urban League also expelled Communists or "fellow travelers." Thus the Great Fear was particularly devastating to the political left; accusations of guilt by association affected progressives of all stripes.

The anticommunist crusade intensified in 1948 when HUAC began an investigation of Alger Hiss, a former New Dealer and a State Department official who had accompanied Franklin Roosevelt to Yalta. A former Communist, Whittaker Chambers, claimed that Hiss was a member of a secret Communist cell operating within the government and had passed him classified documents in the 1930s. Hiss categorically denied the allegations and denied even knowing Chambers. HUAC's investigation was orchestrated by Republican Congressman Richard M. Nixon of California. Because the statute of limitations on the crime Hiss was accused of had expired, he was charged instead with perjury for lying about his communist affiliations and acquaintance with Chambers. In early 1950 Hiss was found guilty and sentenced to five years in federal prison. Although recently released evidence from Soviet archives has helped to harden the case against Hiss, the question of his guilt continues to be a contentious one among historians and journalists.

Hiss's conviction fueled the paranoia about a Communist conspiracy in the federal government, contributing to the meteoric rise of Senator Joseph McCarthy of Wisconsin. In February 1950 McCarthy delivered a bombshell during a speech in Wheeling, West Virginia: "I have here in my hand a list of the names of 205 men that were known to the Secretary of State as being members of the Communist Party and who nevertheless are still working and shaping the policy of the State Department." McCarthy later reduced his numbers, first to fifty-seven, then to one "policy risk," and he never released any names or proof, but he had gained the attention he sought. For the next four years he was the central figure in a virulent campaign of anticommunism. Like other Republicans in the late 1940s McCarthy leveled accusations of Communist subversion in the government to embarrass President Truman and the Democratic Party. Critics who disagreed with him exposed themselves to charges of being "soft" on communism. Because McCarthy charged that his critics were themselves part of "this conspiracy so immense," few political leaders challenged him. Truman called McCarthy's charges "slander, lies, character assassination" but could do nothing to curb them. When the Republican Dwight D. Eisenhower was elected president in 1952, he refrained from publicly challenging his party's most outspoken senator.

Despite McCarthy's failure to identify a single Communist in government, a series of national and international events allowed him to retain credibility. Besides the Hiss case, the sensational 1951 espionage trial of Julius and Ethel Rosenberg fueled McCarthy's allegations. Convicted of passing atomic secrets to the Soviet Union in a highly controversial trial, the Rosenbergs were executed in 1953. (As in the case of Hiss their convictions continue to be debated; the recent release of declassified documents from a top-secret intelligence mission has provided some new evidence of Julius Rosenberg's guilt.) The Korean War, which embroiled the United States in a frustrating fight against communism in a faraway land, also made Americans susceptible to McCarthy's claims. Blaming disloyal individuals rather than complex international factors for the problems of the cold war undoubtedly helped many Americans make sense of a disordered world of nuclear

McCarthy's Assault on Civil Liberties

Senator Joseph McCarthy's reckless attacks on alleged Communists in the U.S. government stirred widespread public fears of Soviet subversion in the 1950s. His critics, such as cartoonist Al Hirschfeld, expressed alarm at what they saw as McCarthy's assault on American liberty.

(© Al Hirschfeld. Drawing reproduced by special arrangement with The Margo Feiden Galleries, NY)

bombs, "police actions," and other world crises that seemed to come with alarming regularity.

In early 1954 McCarthy overreached himself by launching an investigation into possible subversion in the U.S. Army. When the lengthy televised hearings brought McCarthy's smear tactics and leering innuendos into the nation's living rooms, support for him declined. The end of the Korean War and the death of Stalin in 1953 also undercut public interest in McCarthy's red-baiting campaign. In December 1954 the Senate voted sixty-seven to twenty-two to censure McCarthy for unbecoming conduct. He died an alcoholic three years later at the age of forty-eight, his name forever attached to a period of political repression of which he was only the most flagrant manifestation (see American Voices, "Resisting the Tactics of McCarthyism").

"Modern Republicanism"

In 1952, in the middle of the Korean stalemate and at the height of the Great Fear, a newly elected president, Dwight D. Eisenhower, succeeded Harry Truman, ousting the Democrats from the White House. Eisenhower set the tone for what historians have called "modern Republicanism," an updated party philosophy that emphasized a slowdown, rather than a dismantling, of federal responsibilities. Compared with their predecessors in the 1920s and their successors in the 1980s and 1990s, modern Republicans were more tolerant of government intervention in social and economic affairs, though they did seek to limit the scope of federal action. More important to the average voter than Eisenhower's political philosophy, however, was his proven leadership in trying times; he seemed the right man to guide the nation through the perils of the cold war.

"I LIKE IKE"

Eisenhower's status as a war hero was his greatest political asset. Born in 1890 and raised in Abilene, Kansas, he had graduated from the U.S. Military Academy at West Point in 1915. Rising quickly through the ranks, during World War II he became Supreme Commander of Allied Forces in Europe. To hundreds of thousands of soldiers and to the millions of civilians who followed the war on newsreels, he was simply "Ike," the best known and best liked of the nation's military leaders.

As a professional military man Eisenhower claimed to stand "above politics." While in the army he had never voted, insisting that such political activity represented an intrusion of the military into civilian affairs. Many Democrats had hoped to make him their candidate for president in 1948 and again in 1952. Eisenhower did want the office but as a Republican. After winning several primaries, he secured the Republican nomination and asked Senator Richard M. Nixon of California to be his running mate. Nixon, young, tirelessly partisan, and with a strong

AMERICAN VOICES

Resisting the Tactics of McCarthyism

MELVIN RADER

*I*n addition to Congress's House Un-American Activities Committee, many states had their
own committees investigating alleged Communists. In Washington State the Canwell committee scrutinized the loyalty of faculty at the University of Washington. In 1948 a witness before the committee identified Professor Melvin Rader as having attended a secret communist
school in New York during the 1930s. Rader took the unusual course of filing perjury charges
against his accuser, George Hewitt, and eventually not only cleared his name but helped to
discredit the Canwell committee's methods and accusations. Despite his vindication the anticommunist crusade extracted a heavy toll on Rader and his family, as this account of the response to Hewitt's charges suggests.

The number of anonymous telephone calls we received [during this time] was upsetting.
I could never know, when I answered the phone, whether I was about to be denounced by
some unidentified person as "a Communist rat." . . . Even when we talked to friends, we
felt constrained for fear that our line was being tapped.

The newspapers and radio had spread the news of the hearing far and wide. Wherever
we went, to the drugstore or the grocery, to the university or the theater, people knew about
Hewitt's charges. Many were friendly, but some were hostile. . . .

[My wife] Virginia and I spent many hours racking our memories. She or I would wake
up excitedly in the middle of the night with the sudden recollection of something we had
done in those distant summers. But it is difficult to remember and even harder to prove
what you were doing eight, nine, or ten years ago. For weeks and even months we investigated every lead that occurred to us. We interrogated every storekeeper who might have
kept invoices of our purchases; checked with the gas and electric and telephone companies to see if they had kept records; . . . went to the County-City Building to look up
voting registrations; interviewed innumerable friends and acquaintances who might remember my presence in the Seattle area during the three summers in question. Many kindly
persons and even total strangers cooperated in our search. A heroic librarian, Dolly Cooper,
searched thousands of books in the University of Washington Library to find in the back
pocket of the books withdrawal cards, dated by a librarian, that I had signed, and was successful in discovering several crucial signatures and dates. . . . Virginia and I were disappointed to discover that most memories are short and most records are not kept for longer
than five or six years, but we were heartened by the fact that so many cooperated in our
search.

SOURCE: Melvin Rader, *False Witness* (Seattle: University of Washington Press, 1969), pp. 91–93.

anticommunist record from his crusade against Alger Hiss, brought an aggressive campaign style as well as regional balance to the Republican ticket.

The Democrats never seriously considered renominating Harry Truman, who by 1952 was a thoroughly discredited leader. Lack of popular enthusiasm for the Korean War had dealt the most severe blow to Truman's support, but a series of scandals involving federal officials in bribery, kickback, and influence-peddling schemes had caused a public outcry about the "mess in Washington." With a certain relief the Democrats turned to Governor Adlai E. Stevenson of Illinois, who enjoyed the support of respected liberals such as Eleanor Roosevelt and of organized labor. To appease southern voters who feared Stevenson's liberal agenda, the Democrats nominated Senator John A. Sparkman of Alabama for vice president.

Throughout the 1952 campaign Stevenson advocated New Deal and Fair Deal policies with an almost literary eloquence. But Eisenhower's artfully unpretentious speeches and "I Like Ike" slogan were more effective with voters. Eager to win the support of the broadest electorate possible, Eisenhower played down specific questions of policy. Instead, he attacked the Democrats with the "K_1C_2" formula—"Korea, Communism, and Corruption." In a campaign pledge that ultimately clinched the election, he vowed to go to Korea, with the implication that he would end the stalemated war if elected.

The Republican campaign was temporarily set back by the revelation that wealthy Californians had set up a secret "slush fund" for Richard Nixon. Eisenhower contemplated dropping Nixon from the ticket, but Nixon adroitly used a televised speech to convince voters that he had not misused campaign funds. Nixon did admit to accepting one gift—a puppy his young daughters had named Checkers. That gift he would not give back, he declared earnestly. Nixon's televised speech turned an embarrassing incident into an advantage, as sympathetic viewers flooded Republican headquarters with supportive telegrams and phone calls. Outmaneuvered, Republican leaders had no choice but to keep Nixon on the ticket. The "Checkers speech" showed how the powerful new medium of television could be used to a politician's advantage.

That November Eisenhower won 55 percent of the popular vote, carrying all the northern and western states and four southern states. Republican candidates for Congress did not fare quite as well. They regained the Senate from the Democrats but took the House of Representatives by a slender margin of only four seats. In 1954 they would lose control of both houses to the Democrats. Even though the enormously popular Eisenhower would easily win reelection over Adlai Stevenson in 1956, the Republicans would remain in the minority in Congress.

The political scientist Fred Greenstein has characterized Eisenhower's style of leadership as the "hidden-hand presidency," pointing out that the president maneuvered deftly behind the scenes while seeming not to concern himself in public with partisan questions. Seeking a middle ground between liberalism and conservatism, Eisenhower did his best to set a quieter national mood, hoping to decrease the need for federal intervention in social and economic issues, while avoiding conservative demands for a complete roll back of the New Deal.

Eisenhower nonetheless presided over new increases in federal activity. When the Soviet Union launched the first satellite, *Sputnik,* in 1957, Eisenhower supported a U.S. space program to catch up in this new cold-war competition. The National Aeronautics and Space Administration (NASA) was founded the following year. Alarmed that the United States was falling behind the Soviets in technological expertise, the president also persuaded Congress to appropriate additional money for college scholarships and for research and development at universities and in industry. After 1954, when the Democrats took over control over Congress, the Eisenhower administration also acceded to legislation promoting social welfare. Federal outlays for veterans' benefits, unemployment compensation, housing, and Social Security were increased, and the minimum wage was raised from 75 cents an hour to $1. The creation of the new Department of Health, Education, and Welfare (HEW) in 1953 consolidated government control of social welfare programs, confirming federal commitments in that area. Congress also passed the Interstate Highway Act of 1956, which authorized $26 billion over a ten-year period for the construction of a nationally integrated highway system. This enormous public works program surpassed anything undertaken during the New Deal.

The Sputnik *Crisis*

The Soviet launching of the *Sputnik* space satellite in 1957 precipitated a crisis of confidence in American science and education. That sense of crisis was reflected in a 1950s "Space Race" card game, in which those dealt the *Sputnik* card would lose two turns.

(The Michael Barson Collection/Past Perfect)

Thus Republicans, though they resisted the unchecked expansion of the state, did not generally cut back federal power. In social welfare programs and defense expenditures modern Republicanism signaled an abandonment of the traditional Republican commitment to limited government. When Eisenhower retired from public life in 1961, the federal government had become an even greater presence in everyday life than it had been when he took office. Some of the most controversial federal initiatives occurred in the area of civil rights.

EMERGENCE OF CIVIL RIGHTS AS A NATIONAL ISSUE

The civil rights movement was arguably the most important force for change in postwar America, and its accelerating momentum had profound implications for the federal government. Legal segregation of the races still governed southern society in the early 1950s. In most southern states in the 1950s whites and blacks could not eat in the same rooms at restaurants and luncheonettes or use the same waiting rooms and toilets at bus and train stations. All forms of public transportation were rigidly segregated by custom or by law. Even drinking fountains were labeled "White" and "Colored."

Beginning with World War II the National Association for the Advancement of Colored People (NAACP) had redoubled its efforts to combat segregation in housing, transportation, and other areas. The first significant victory came in 1954, when the Supreme Court handed down its most far-reaching decision in *Brown v. Board of Education of Topeka*. The NAACP's chief legal counsel, Thurgood Marshall, had argued that the segregated schools mandated by the Board of Education in Topeka, Kansas, were inherently unconstitutional because they stigmatized an entire race, denying black children the "equal protection of the laws" guaranteed by the Fourteenth Amendment. In a unanimous decision announced on May 17, 1954, the Supreme Court, following the lead of Chief Justice Earl Warren (see Chapter 30), agreed with Marshall and overturned the longstanding "separate but equal" doctrine of *Plessy v. Ferguson* (see Chapter 19).

Over the next several years, in response to NAACP suits, the Supreme Court used the *Brown* precedent to overturn segregation in city parks, public beaches, and golf courses; in interstate and intrastate transportation; and in public housing. In the face of these Court decisions white resistance to integration solidified. In 1956, 101 members of Congress signed the Southern Manifesto, denouncing the *Brown* decision as "a clear abuse of judicial power" and encouraging their constituents to defy it. That same year, 500,000 southerners joined White Citizens' Councils dedicated to blocking school integration and other civil rights measures. Some whites revived old tactics of violence and intimidation, swelling the ranks of the Ku Klux Klan to levels not seen since the 1920s.

Unlike Harry Truman, Eisenhower showed little interest in civil rights. Though he proved extremely reluctant to intervene in what was widely seen as a state issue, entrenched southern resistance to federal authority eventually forced his hand. In

1957 the governor of Arkansas, Orval Faubus, defied a federal court order to desegregate Little Rock's Central High School. Faubus called out the National Guard
to bar nine black students who were attempting to enroll in the all-white school.
After scenes of vicious mobs harassing the determined students aired on television, President Eisenhower reluctantly intervened, sending 1,000 federal troops
and 10,000 nationalized members of the Arkansas National Guard to protect the
students. Eisenhower thus became the first president since Reconstruction to use
federal troops to enforce the rights of blacks.

White resistance to the *Brown* decision, as well as Eisenhower's hesitancy to act
in Little Rock, showed that court victories were not enough to overturn segregation. In 1955 one tiny but monumental act of defiance gave black leaders an
opportunity to implement a new strategy, nonviolent protest. On December 1 Rosa
Parks, a seamstress and a member of the NAACP in Montgomery, Alabama, refused
to give up her seat on a city bus to a white man. "I felt it was just something I had
to do," Parks stated. She was promptly arrested and charged with violating a local
segregation ordinance. When the black community in Montgomery met to discuss

Integration at Little Rock, Arkansas

With chants such as "Two-four-six-eight, we ain't gonna integrate," angry crowds taunted
Elizabeth Eckford (shown here walking past white students and National Guardsmen) and
eight other black students who tried to register at the previously all-white Central High School
in Little Rock, Arkansas, on September 4, 1957. The court-ordered integration proceeded only
after President Eisenhower reluctantly nationalized the Arkansas National Guard to protect the
students. (Francis Miller, LIFE Magazine, © Time, Inc.)

the proper response, they turned to the Reverend Martin Luther King Jr., who had become the pastor at a local church the year before. King endorsed a plan by a Montgomery black women's organization to boycott the city's bus system until it was integrated. For the next 381 days members of a united black community formed carpools or walked to work. The bus company neared bankruptcy, and downtown stores saw their business decline. But not until the Supreme Court ruled in November 1956 that bus segregation was unconstitutional did the city of Montgomery finally relent, prompting one woman boycotter to proclaim, "My feets is tired, but my soul is rested."

The Montgomery bus boycott catapulted King to national prominence. In 1957, with the Reverend Ralph Abernathy and other southern black clergy, he founded the Southern Christian Leadership Conference (SCLC), based in Atlanta. The black church had long been the center of African American social and cultural life. Through the SCLC the church lent its moral and organizational strength, as well as the voices of its most inspirational preachers, to the civil rights movement. Black churchwomen flocked to the movement, transferring the skills they had honed through years of church work to the fight for racial change. Soon the SCLC had joined the NAACP as one of the major advocates for racial justice. While the two groups achieved only limited victories in the 1950s, they laid the organizational groundwork for the dynamic civil rights movement that would emerge in the 1960s.

THE "NEW LOOK" OF FOREIGN POLICY

Eisenhower felt far more comfortable exercising leadership in military and diplomatic affairs than in civil rights. One of his first acts as president was to put that skill to use in negotiating an end to the Korean War. As he had pledged in the campaign, he visited Korea in December 1952. The final settlement was signed in July 1953, after the parties reached a compromise on the tricky issue of prisoner exchange.

Once the Korean War was settled, Eisenhower turned his attention to Europe. Stalin's death in March 1953 precipitated an intraparty struggle in the Soviet Union, which lasted until 1956, when Nikita S. Khrushchev emerged as Stalin's successor. Although Khrushchev surprised westerners by calling for "peaceful coexistence" between communist and capitalist societies, he made certain that the USSR's Eastern European satellites did not deviate too far from the Soviet path. When nationalists revolted in Hungary in 1956 and moved to take the country out of the Warsaw Pact, Soviet tanks moved rapidly into Budapest—an action the United States could condemn but could not realistically resist. Soviet repression of the Hungarian revolt showed that American policymakers had few, if any, options for rolling back Soviet power in Eastern Europe, short of going to war with the USSR.

Although Eisenhower strongly opposed communism, he hoped to keep the cost of containment at a manageable level. Under his "New Look" defense policy,

Eisenhower and Secretary of State John Foster Dulles decided to economize by developing a massive nuclear arsenal as an alternative to more expensive conventional forces. Nuclear weapons delivered "more bang for the buck," explained Defense Secretary Charles E. Wilson. To that end the Eisenhower administration expanded its commitment to the hydrogen bomb, approving extensive atmospheric testing in the South Pacific and in western states such as Nevada, Colorado, and Utah. To improve the nation's defenses against an air attack from the Soviet Union the administration made a commitment to develop the long-range bombing capabilities of the Strategic Air Command and installed the Distant Early Warning line of radar stations in Alaska and Canada in 1958.

Those measures did little to improve the nation's security, however, as the Soviets matched the United States weapon for weapon in an escalating arms race. The Soviet Union carried out atmospheric tests of its own of hydrogen bombs between 1953 and 1958 and developed a fleet of long-range bombers. By 1958 both nations had intercontinental ballistic missiles (ICBMs). When an American nuclear submarine launched an atomic-tipped Polaris missile in 1960, Soviet engineers raced to produce an equivalent weapon. While the arms race boosted the military-industrial sectors of both nations, it debilitated their social welfare programs by funneling immense resources into soon-to-be-obsolete weapons systems.

The New Look policy also extended collective security agreements between the United States and its allies. To complement the NATO alliance in Europe, for example, Secretary of State Dulles orchestrated the creation of the Southeast Asia Treaty Organization (SEATO), which in 1954 linked America and its major European allies with Australia, Pakistan, Thailand, New Zealand, and the Philippines. This extensive system of defense tied the United States to more than forty other countries.

U.S. policymakers tended to support stable governments, no matter how repressive, as long as they were overtly anticommunist. Some of America's staunchest allies—the Philippines, Iran, Cuba, South Vietnam, and Nicaragua—were governed by dictatorships or repressive right-wing regimes that lacked broad-based popular support. In fact, Dulles often resorted to covert interventions against governments that were, in his opinion, too closely aligned with communism.

For such tasks he used the newly formed Central Intelligence Agency (CIA), which had moved beyond its original mandate of intelligence gathering into active, albeit covert, involvement in the internal affairs of foreign countries, even to the extent of overthrowing several governments. When Iran's nationalist premier, Muhammad Mossadegh, seized British oil properties in 1953, CIA agents helped the young shah of Iran, Muhammad Reza Pahlavi, depose him. In 1954 the CIA supported a coup in Guatemala against the popularly elected Jacobo Arbenz Guzman, who had expropriated 250,000 uncultivated acres held by the American-owned United Fruit Company and accepted arms from the communist government of Czechoslovakia. Eisenhower specifically approved those efforts. "Our traditional ideas of international sportsmanship," he wrote privately in 1955, "are scarcely applicable in the morass in which the world now flounders."

THE COLD WAR IN THE MIDDLE EAST

American leaders had devised the policy of containment in response to Soviet expansion in Eastern Europe, but they soon extended it to new nations emerging in the developing world. Before World War II nationalism, socialism, and religion had inspired powerful anticolonial movements; in the 1940s and 1950s those forces intensified and spread, especially in the Middle East, Africa, and the Far East. Between 1947 and 1962 the British, French, Dutch, and Belgian empires all but disintegrated. Seeking to draw the new countries into an American-led world system, U.S. policymakers encouraged the development of stable market economies in those areas. They also sought to further the ideal of national self-determination that had shaped American participation in both world wars. But influenced by their polarized perspective of the cold war both the Truman and the Eisenhower administrations often failed to recognize that indigenous nationalist or socialist movements in emerging nations had their own goals and were not, as they assumed, necessarily under the control of either local communists or the Soviet Union. Their failure to appreciate the complexity of local conditions limited the effectiveness of American policies and often had devastating effects on the very people they were intended to help.

The Middle East, an oil-rich area that was playing an increasingly central role in strategic planning, presented one of the most complicated challenges. After World War II many Jewish survivors of Nazi extermination camps had resettled in Palestine, where with U.N. assistance and despite Arab resistance, they established the nation of Israel in 1948. President Truman quickly recognized the new state, alienating the Arabs but winning crucial support from Jewish Americans in the 1948 election.

Egypt was another site of conflict with the Arab nations, one that reflected the way in which developing countries became embroiled in the cold war. When Gamal Abdel Nasser came to power in Egypt in 1954, two years after his nation won independence from Britain, he pledged to lead not just Egypt but the entire Middle East out of its dependent colonial relationship with the West through a form of pan-Arab socialism. From the Soviet Union Nasser obtained arms and promises of economic assistance, including help in building the Aswan Dam on the Nile. Secretary of State Dulles countered with an offer of American assistance, but Nasser refused to distance himself from the Soviets, declaring Egypt's neutrality in the cold war. Unwilling to accept this stance of nonalignment, Dulles abruptly withdrew his offer in July 1956.

A week later Nasser retaliated against the withdrawal of Western financial aid by seizing control of the Suez Canal, over which Britain had retained administrative authority and through which three-quarters of Western Europe's oil passed. After several months of fruitless negotiation, Britain and France, in alliance with Israel, attacked Egypt and retook the canal. Their attack occurred at the same time as the Soviet repression of the Hungarian revolt, placing the United States in the potentially awkward position of denouncing Soviet aggression while tolerating a similar action by its own allies. President Eisenhower and the United Nations

Testing an Atomic Bomb

Throughout the 1950s the Atomic Energy Commission conducted above-ground tests of atomic and hydrogen bombs. Thousands of soldiers were exposed to fallout during the tests, such as this one at Yucca Flats, Nevada, in April 1952. The AEC, ignoring or suppressing medical evidence to the contrary, mounted an extensive public relations campaign to convince local residents that the tests did not endanger their health. (FPG International)

condemned the European actions in Egypt, forcing France and Britain to pull back. Egypt retook the canal and proceeded to build the Aswan Dam with Soviet support. In the end the Suez crisis increased Soviet influence in the developing world, intensified antiwestern sentiment in Arab countries, and produced dissension among leading members of the NATO alliance.

In early 1957, in the aftermath of the Suez crisis, the president persuaded Congress to approve the Eisenhower Doctrine. Addressing concerns over declining British influence in the Middle East, the joint policy stated that American forces would assist any nation in the region "requiring such aid, against overt armed aggression from any nation controlled by International Communism." Later that year Eisenhower invoked the doctrine when he sent the U.S. Sixth Fleet to the Mediterranean to aid King Hussein of Jordan. A year later he landed 8,000 troops to back a pro–United States government in Lebanon.

The attention the Eisenhower administration paid to developments in the Middle East in the 1950s reflected the nation's growing desire for access to steady supplies of oil—a desire that increasingly affected foreign policy. Indeed, by the late 1950s the Middle East contained about 65 percent of the world's known reserves. But more broadly, attention to the Middle East confirmed the global scope of American interests. Just as the Korean War had stretched the application of the containment policy from Europe to Asia, the Eisenhower Doctrine revealed the U.S. intention to bring the Middle East into its sphere as well.

DOMESTIC IMPACT OF THE COLD WAR

While the cold war extended to the most distant corners of the globe, it also had a devastating impact on the health of American citizens at home, some of whom became unwitting guinea pigs in the nation's nuclear weapons program. In the late 1950s a small but growing number of citizens became concerned about the effects of radioactive fallout from above-ground bomb tests. In later years federal investigators documented a host of illnesses, deaths, and birth defects among families of veterans who had worked on weapons tests and among "downwinders"—people who lived near nuclear test sites and weapons facilities. The most shocking revelations, however, came to light in 1993, when the Department of Energy released millions of previously classified documents on human radiation experiments conducted in the late 1940s and 1950s under the auspices of the Atomic Energy Commission (AEC) and other federal agencies. Many of the subjects were irradiated without their consent or understanding.

The nuclear arms race affected all Americans by fostering a climate of fear and uncertainty. Bomb shelters, civil defense drills, and other survival measures provided a daily reminder of the threat of nuclear war (see American Voices, "Memories of a Cold War Childhood"). Eisenhower himself had second thoughts about a nuclear policy based on the premise of annihilating the enemy, even if one's own country was destroyed—the aptly named acronym MAD (Mutual Assured Destruction) policy. He also found spiraling arms expenditures a serious hindrance to balancing the federal budget, one of his chief fiscal goals. Consequently, Eisenhower tried to negotiate an arms-limitation agreement with the Soviet Union. Progress along those lines was cut short, however, when on May 5, 1960, the Soviets shot down an American U-2 spy plane over their territory and captured and imprisoned its pilot, Francis Gary Powers. Eisenhower at first denied that the plane was engaged in espionage but later admitted that he had authorized the mission and other secret flights over the USSR. In the midst of the dispute a proposed summit meeting was canceled, and Eisenhower's last chance to negotiate an arms agreement evaporated.

When Eisenhower left office in January 1961, he used his final address to warn against the growing power of what he termed the "military-industrial complex," which by then employed 3.5 million Americans. Its pervasive influence, he noted,

---

AMERICAN VOICES

Memories of a Cold War Childhood

RON KOVIC

*T*he menacing threat of the atom bomb, the looming presence of the Soviet Union, and *the fear of internal subversion were part of everyday life in the 1950s. In his autobiog-raphy,* Born on the Fourth of July, *Ron Kovic conveys the anxiety Americans felt when the Soviets launched the satellite* Sputnik, *revealing that Americans were behind in the race to conquer outer space.*

We joined the cub scouts and marched in parades on Memorial Day. We made contin-gency plans for the cold war and built fallout shelters out of milk cartons. We wore space-suits and space helmets. We made rocket ships out of cardboard boxes. And one Saturday afternoon in the basement Castiglia [a friend] and I went to Mars on the couch we had turned into a rocket ship. . . . And the whole block watched a thing called the space race begin. On a cold October night Dad and I watched the first satellite, called *Sputnik,* mov-ing across the sky above our house like a tiny bright star. I still remember standing out there with Dad looking up in amazement at that thing moving in the sky above Massape-qua. It was hard to believe that this thing, this *Sputnik,* was so high up and moving so fast around the world, again and again. Dad put his hand on my shoulder that night and with-out saying anything I quietly walked back inside and went to my room thinking that the Russians had beaten America into space and wondering why we couldn't even get a rocket off the pad. . . .

The Communists were all over the place back then. And if they weren't trying to beat us into outer space, Castiglia and I were certain they were infiltrating our schools, trying to take over our classes and control our minds. We were both certain that one of our teach-ers was a secret Communist agent and in our next secret club meeting we promised to re-port anything new he said during our next history class. We watched him very carefully that year.

SOURCE: Ron Kovic, *Born on the Fourth of July* (New York: Pocket Books, 1976), pp. 56–57.

---

was "felt in every city, every statehouse, every office of the Federal Government." Even though his administration had fostered the growth of the defense establish-ment, Eisenhower was gravely concerned about its implications for a democratic people. "We must guard against the acquisition of unwarranted influence, whether sought or unsought, by the military-industrial complex," he warned. "We must never let the weight of this combination endanger our liberties or democratic processes." With those words Dwight Eisenhower showed how well he understood the major transformations that the cold war had wrought in the nation. The conflict between the Soviet Union and the United States not only had far-reaching international implications; it had powerful effects on domestic politics, the economy, and cul-tural values, and it permanently altered the contours of the modern state.

T I M E L I N E

1945	Yalta and Potsdam conferences	**1950**	Alger Hiss convicted of perjury
	Harry S Truman succeeds Roosevelt as president.		Joseph McCarthy's "list" of Communists in government
	End of World War II		NSC-68 calls for permanent
	Senate approves U.S. participation in United Nations.		mobilization.
		1952	Dwight D. Eisenhower elected president
1946	Kennan sends "long telegram" outlining containment policy.		United States detonates hydrogen bomb.
	Baruch Plan for international control of atomic weapons fails.	**1953**	Soviet Union explodes hydrogen bomb.
1947	Taft-Hartley Act limits union power.	**1954**	Army-McCarthy hearings on army subversion
	Jackie Robinson joins Brooklyn Dodgers.		*Brown v. Board of Education of Topeka*
	House Un-American Activities Com-mittee (HUAC) investigates film industry.	**1955**	Montgomery bus boycott begins.
	Truman Doctrine		Warsaw Pact
	Marshall Plan	**1956**	Crises in Hungary and Suez
			Southern Manifesto defies *Brown*.
1948	Communist coup in Czechoslovakia		Interstate Highway Act
	Executive order desegregating armed forces	**1957**	Eisenhower Doctrine commits aid to Middle East.
	State of Israel created		Eisenhower sends U.S. troops to enforce integration of Little Rock Central High School.
	Stalin blockades West Berlin; Berlin airlift begins.		
1949	North Atlantic Treaty Organization (NATO) founded		Southern Christian Leadership Conference founded
	Berlin airlift ends.		Soviet Union launches *Sputnik*.
	National Housing Act	**1958**	National Aeronautics and Space Admin-istration (NASA) established
	Soviet Union detonates atomic bomb.		
	Mao Zedong establishes People's Republic of China.	**1960**	U-2 spy plane shot down over Soviet Union
1950–1953	Korean War		

For Further Exploration

An excellent overview of the diplomatic history of the cold war is Stephen Ambrose and Douglas Brinkley, *Rise to Globalism* (8th ed., 1997). A good introduction to the Great Fear is the collection of documents in Ellen Schrecker, ed., *The Age of McCarthyism* (1994), which offers primary sources covering court cases, Hollywood, spy scandals, the Rosenbergs, and other topics. Another valuable set of sources that help to explain the early stages of the cold war is Ernest R. May, ed., *American Cold War Strategy: Interpreting NSC 68* (1993), which includes essays by both American and foreign scholars. David Halberstam's *The Fifties* (1993) offers a brief but searing account of CIA covert activities in Iran and Guatemala. For a powerful fictional account of growing up with the bomb see Tim O'Brien, *The Nuclear Age* (1996). Taylor Branch's biography of Martin Luther King Jr., *Parting the Waters: American in the King Years, 1954–1963* (1988), while focusing on King's leadership, provides an engaging account of the early civil rights movement.

The Woodrow Wilson International Center for Scholars has established the "Cold War International History Project" at <http://cwihp.si.edu/default.htm>, an exceptionally rich website offering documents on the cold war, including materials from former communist-bloc countries. The Center for the Study of the Pacific Northwest's site, "The Cold War and Red Scare in Washington State" at <http://www.washington.edu/uwired/outreach/cspn/curcan/main.html> provides detailed information on how the Great Fear operated in one state. Its bibliography includes books, documents, and videos. "Project Whistlestop: Harry Truman" at <http://whistlestop.org>, a program sponsored by the U.S. Department of Education, is a searchable collection of images and documents from the Harry S Truman Presidential Library. The site is organized into categories such as the origins of the Truman Doctrine, the Berlin airlift, the desegregation of the armed forces, and the 1948 presidential campaign. Users can also browse through the president's correspondence.

Chapter 28

THE AFFLUENT SOCIETY AND THE LIBERAL CONSENSUS
1945–1965

The nation of the well-off must be able to see through the wall of affluence and recognize the alien citizens on the other side. And there must be vision in the sense of purpose, of aspiration. . . . there must be a passion to end poverty, for nothing less than that will do.

—MICHAEL HARRINGTON, *THE OTHER AMERICA* (1962)

In 1959 Vice President Richard Nixon traveled to Moscow to open the American National Exhibit, one of several efforts to reduce cold-war tensions in the period. While touring the kitchen of a model American home, Nixon and Soviet Premier Nikita Khrushchev got into a heated debate about the relative merits of Soviet and American societies. Instead of discussing rockets, submarines, and missiles, however, they talked dishwashers, toasters, and televisions. In what was quickly dubbed the "kitchen debate," Nixon used the exhibit and its representation of American affluence and mass consumption to assert the superiority of capitalism over communism and inevitable American victory in the cold war.

During the postwar era millions of Americans, enjoying the highest standard of living in the nation's history, pursued the promise of consumer society in the burgeoning suburbs. But affluence was never as widespread as the Moscow exhibit implied. The middle-class suburban lifestyle was beyond the reach of many poor and nonwhite Americans, particularly those in the decaying central cities. Hoping to spread the abundance of a flourishing economy to greater numbers of Americans, the Democratic administrations of the early 1960s pressed for the expansion of New Deal social welfare programs. The administrations of John F. Kennedy and—to a much greater extent—Lyndon B. Johnson tried to use federal power to ensure the public welfare in areas such as health care, education, and civil rights. In the Great Society program—a burst of social legislation in 1964 and 1965 that marked the high tide of postwar liberalism—the Johnson administration attempted to use the fiscal powers of the state to redress the imbalances of the economy without directly challenging capitalism.

Liberal politicians also pursued an activist stance abroad. Continuing and in some cases expanding the cold-war policies of Truman and Eisenhower, the Kennedy and Johnson administrations took aggressive action against communist influence in Europe, the Caribbean, Vietnam (see Chapter 29), and other areas. The growing financial and political costs of that ambitious agenda, however, hampered further progress on the domestic front and revealed ominous cracks in the postwar liberal coalition.

The Affluent Society

By the end of 1945 war-induced prosperity had made the United States the richest country in the world, a preeminence that would continue unchallenged for twenty years. U.S. corporations and banking institutions so dominated the world economy that the period has been called the *Pax Americana* (American peace). U.S. military policy and foreign aid, as well as the absence of major economic competitors, were vital factors in extending the global reach of American corporate capitalism, which enjoyed remarkable growth in productivity and profits. American economic leadership abroad translated into affluence at home. As many Americans, especially whites, moved to home ownership in new suburban communities, it was clear that domestic prosperity was benefiting a wider segment of society than anyone would have dreamed possible in the dark days of the Great Depression.

THE ECONOMIC RECORD

These years witnessed the heyday of modern American capitalism, characterized by the consolidation of economic and financial resources by *oligopolies*—a few large producers that controlled the national and, increasingly, the world market. In 1970, for example, the top four American firms produced 91 percent of the motor vehicles sold in the domestic market. Large firms maintained their dominance by diversifying. Combining companies in unrelated industries, these *conglomerates* ensured for themselves protection from instability in any single market, making them more effective international competitors. International Telephone and Telegraph became a diversified conglomerate by acquiring companies in unrelated industries, including Continental Baking, Sheraton Hotels, Avis Rent-a-Car, Levitt and Sons home builders, and Hartford Fire Insurance. This pattern of corporate acquisition developed into a great wave of mergers that peaked in the 1960s.

The development of giant corporations also depended on the penetration of foreign markets. Unlike the Soviet Union, Western Europe, and Japan, America emerged physically unscathed from the war, with its defense industries eager to convert to consumer production. The weakness of the competition enabled American business to enter foreign regions when domestic markets became saturated or when

American recessions cut into sales. Soon American companies provided products and services for war-torn European and Asian markets, giving the nation a trade surplus close to $5 billion in 1960.

America's global economic supremacy stemmed in part from institutions created at a monetary conference of twenty-eight nations at Bretton Woods, New Hampshire, in 1944. The International Bank for Reconstruction and Development (known commonly as the World Bank) provided private loans for the reconstruction of war-torn Europe as well as for the development of Third World countries. The International Monetary Fund (IMF), designed to stabilize the value of currencies, helped to guide the world economy after the war. Backed by the United States' money and influence, these international organizations tended to favor American-style internationalism over the economic nationalism traditional in most other countries.

U.S. economic supremacy abroad helped boost the domestic economy, creating millions of new jobs. One of the fastest-growing groups was salaried office workers, whose numbers increased by 61 percent between 1947 and 1957. Growing corporate bureaucracies and increased access to a college education through the GI Bill helped expand the male white-collar ranks. These "organization men," as sociologist William Whyte called them, were joined by millions of women who moved into clerical work and other lower-paying service-sector occupations. Although the percentage of blue-collar manufacturing jobs declined slightly during this period, the power of organized labor reached an all-time high. In 1955 the Congress of Industrial Organizations made a formal alliance with its old adversary, the American Federation of Labor. That merger created a single organization—the AFL-CIO—which represented more than 90 percent of the nation's 17.5 million union members. In exchange for labor peace and stability—that is, fewer strikes—corporate managers often cooperated with unions, agreeing to contracts that gave many workers secure, predictable, and steadily rising incomes, guaranteeing them a share in the new prosperity.

As the income of many American workers grew, consumer spending soared. That spending, combined with federal outlays for defense and domestic programs, seemed to promise a continuously rising standard of living. The gross national product (GNP) grew from $213 billion in 1945 to more than $500 billion in 1960. With the inflation rate under 3 percent in the 1950s this steady economic growth meant a 25 percent rise in real income between 1946 and 1959. American homeownership rates reflected the rising standard of living: in 1940, 43 percent of American families owned their homes; by 1960, 62 percent did. The postwar boom was marred, however, by periodic bouts of recession and unemployment that particularly hurt low-income and nonwhite workers. Moreover, the rising standard of living was not accompanied by a redistribution of income: the top 10 percent of Americans still earned more than the bottom 50 percent. Nevertheless, most Americans had more money to spend than ever before.

THE SUBURBAN EXPLOSION

Although Americans had been gravitating toward urban areas throughout the twentieth century, the postwar period was characterized by two new patterns: one was a shift away from older cities in the Northeast and Midwest and toward newer urban centers in the South and West; the other, a mass defection from the cities to the suburbs. Both processes were stimulated by the dramatic growth of a car culture and the federal government's support of housing and highway initiatives.

At the end of World War II many cities were surrounded by pastures and working farms, but just five to ten years later those cities were surrounded by tract housing, factories, and shopping centers. By 1960 more Americans—particularly whites—lived in suburbs than in cities. People flocked to the suburbs in part because they followed the available housing. Few new dwellings had been built during the depression or war years, and the returning veterans and their families faced a critical housing shortage. The difficulty was partly resolved by an innovative Long Island building contractor. Arthur Levitt revolutionized the suburban housing market by applying mass-production techniques to home construction. Levitt's company could build 150 homes per week. In Levittown a basic four-room house, complete with kitchen appliances and an attic that a handy homeowner could convert into two additional bedrooms, was priced at less than $10,000 in 1947. Other developers soon followed suit in subdivisions all over the country, hastening the exodus from the farm and central city.

Many families financed their homes with mortgages from the Federal Housing Administration (FHA) and the Veterans Administration at rates dramatically lower than those offered by private lenders. In 1955 those two agencies wrote 41 percent of all nonfarm mortgages. Such lending demonstrated the quiet yet revolutionary way in which the federal government was entering and influencing daily life.

The new suburban homes—and much of the FHA and Veterans Administration loan funds—were reserved almost exclusively for whites. Levittown homeowners had to sign a covenant prohibiting occupation "by members of other than the Caucasian Race"; Levitt did not sell houses directly to blacks until 1960. Other communities adopted similar covenants to exclude Jews or Asians. Although the Supreme Court had ruled in *Shelley v. Kraemer* (1948) that restrictive covenants were illegal, the custom continued informally until the civil rights laws of the 1960s banned private discrimination.

The new patterns of growth and development were most striking in the South and West, where open space allowed for sprawling suburban-style expansion. Fueled by World War II defense spending, the postwar development of the southern and western cities accelerated as industry took advantage of inexpensive land, unorganized labor, low taxes, and warm climates (now made more bearable through the new technology of air conditioning). Some of the most explosive growth occurred in Florida, Texas, and California—states that would become the industrial leaders of the emerging Sun Belt economy (Map 28.1). Spurred by massive defense spend-

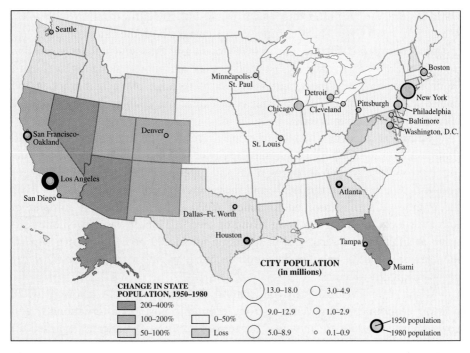

M A P 28.1
Metropolitan Growth, 1950–1980

A metropolitan area is generally defined as a central city that in combination with its surrounding territory forms an integrated economic and social unit. The U.S. Census Bureau
introduced the Standard Metropolitan Statistical Area (SMSA) in 1950, but later changes in the
definition of SMSA make it difficult to generalize from the 1950 figures. This map compares
the population of central cities in 1950 with population figures for the more broadly defined
metropolitan areas in 1980 to illustrate the extent and geographical distribution of metropolitan growth in the postwar period.

ing, California grew the most rapidly, adding 2.6 million people in the 1940s and
3.1 million more in the 1950s.

Automobiles were essential both to suburban growth and to the development
of the Sun Belt states of the South and the West. Suburbanites throughout the country needed cars to get to work and to take their children to school and piano lessons.
In 1945 Americans owned 25 million cars; by 1965 the number had tripled to 75
million. As the car culture that first emerged in the 1920s expanded dramatically
in the 1950s, cars—extravagant gas guzzlers with elaborate tail fins and ostentatious chrome detail—became symbols of status and success.

More cars required more highways, which were funded largely by the federal
government. In 1947 Congress authorized the construction of 37,000 miles of highways; the National Interstate and Defense Highway Act of 1956 increased this commitment by another 42,500 miles. One of the largest civil engineering projects in

world history, the new interstate system would link the entire country with roads at least four lanes wide. The interstate system changed both the cities and the countryside. It rerouted traffic away from small towns and through rural areas, creating isolated pockets of gas stations, fast-food outlets, and motels along highway exits. In urban areas new highways cut wide swaths through old neighborhoods and caused air pollution and traffic jams; critics complained about "autosclerosis," a hardening of the urban arteries.

Highway construction had far-reaching effects on patterns of consumption and shopping. Instead of taking a train into the city or walking to a corner grocery store, people drove to suburban shopping malls and supermarkets. The first mall had appeared in Kansas City in the 1920s, and there were still only eight in 1945; by 1960 the number had mushroomed to almost 4,000. When a 110-store complex at Roosevelt Field on suburban Long Island opened in 1956, it was conveniently situated at an expressway exit and had parking for 11,000 cars. Downtown department stores and other retail outlets soon declined, helping to precipitate the decay of American central cities.

At the time few Americans understood that tradeoffs were involved in the postwar economic boom. With a strong economic position internationally and government spending to help fuel expansion at home, Americans expected an unending trajectory of progress. Their faith led to complacency—an unwillingness to look beneath the surface for the hidden implications of the forces that were transforming America.

American Life during the Baby Boom

Hula Hoops and poodle skirts, sock hops and rock 'n' roll, shiny cars and gleaming appliances—all signify the "fifties," a period that really stretched from 1945 through the early 1960s. The postwar years are remembered as a time of affluence and stability, a time when Americans enjoyed an optimistic faith in progress and technology and a serene family-centered culture, reflected in a booming birth rate known as the baby boom and enshrined in television sitcoms such as *Father Knows Best*. This powerful myth, like many myths, has some truth to it, but there were other sides to the story. Focusing solely on affluence, popular culture, and consumption does not do justice to this complex period of economic and social transformation, which included challenges to the status quo as well as conformity.

CONSUMER CULTURE

The new prosperity of the 1950s was aided by a dramatic increase in consumer credit, which enabled families to stretch their incomes. Between 1946 and 1958 short-term consumer credit rose from $8.4 billion to almost $45 billion. The Diners Club introduced the first credit card in 1950, followed by the American Express card and Bank Americard in 1959. By the 1970s the omnipresent plastic credit card had revolutionized personal and family finances.

Aggressive advertising contributed to the massive increase in consumer spending. In 1951 businesses spent more on advertising ($6.5 billion) than taxpayers did on primary and secondary education ($5 billion). The 1950s gave Americans the Marlboro man; M&Ms that "melt in your mouth, not in your hand"; Wonder Bread to "build strong bodies in twelve ways"; and the "Does she or doesn't she?" Clairol woman.

Consumers had more free time in which to spend their money than ever before. In 1960 the average worker put in a five-day week, with eight paid holidays a year (double the 1946 standard) plus a two-week paid vacation. Americans took to the interstate highway system by the millions, encouraging dramatic growth in motel chains, roadside restaurants, and fast-food eateries. (The first McDonald's restaurant opened in 1954 in San Bernardino, California; the Holiday Inn motel chain started in Memphis in 1952.) Among the most popular destinations were state and national parks and Disneyland, which opened in Anaheim, California, in 1955.

Perhaps the most significant hallmark of postwar consumer culture was television. TV's leap to cultural prominence was swift and overpowering. There were only ten broadcasting stations in the country and a meager 7,000 sets in American homes in 1947. By 1960, 87 percent of American families had at least one television set. Soon television supplanted radio as the chief diffuser of popular culture, its national programming promoting shared interests and tastes and reducing regional and ethnic differences.

What Americans saw on television, besides the omnipresent commercials, was an overwhelmingly white, middle-class world of nuclear families living in suburban homes. *Leave It to Beaver, Ozzie and Harriet,* and similar sitcoms featured characters who adhered to clear-cut gender roles and plots based on minor family crises that were always happily resolved by the end of the show. Programs such as *The Honeymooners,* starring Jackie Gleason as a Brooklyn bus driver, and *Life of Reilly,* a situation comedy featuring a California aircraft worker, were rare in their treatment of working-class lives. Nonwhite characters appeared mainly as servants, such as comedian Jack Benny's black "houseboy" Rochester or the Latino gardener with the anglicized name "Frank Smith" on *Father Knows Best.* Although the new medium did offer some serious programming, notably live theater and documentaries, Federal Communications Commissioner Newton Minow concluded in 1963 that television was "a vast wasteland." Its reassuring images of family life and postwar society, however, dovetailed with the social expectations of many Americans.

THE SEARCH FOR SECURITY: RELIGION AND THE FAMILY

The dislocations of the depression and war years made Americans yearn for security and a reaffirmation of traditional values. Some of this sentiment was expressed in a renewed emphasis on religion. Church membership rose from 49 percent of the population in 1940 to 69 percent in 1960. All the major denominations shared in the growth, which was accompanied by an ecumenical movement to bring Catholics, Protestants, and Jews together. The stress on religion meshed with cold-war Americans' view of themselves as a righteous people opposed to "godless communism." In 1954 the phrase "under God" was inserted into the Pledge of Allegiance, and in 1956 Congress added "In God We Trust" to all U.S. coins.

Beyond patriotism religion also served more deeply felt needs. In his popular television program Bishop Fulton Sheen asked, "Is life worth living?" He and countless others optimistically answered in the affirmative. None was more positive than Norman Vincent Peale, whose best-selling book *The Power of Positive Thinking* (1952) embodied the trend toward the therapeutic use of religion to assist men and women in coping with the stresses of modern life. Evangelical religion also experienced a resurgence, most evident in the dramatic rise to popularity of the Reverend Billy Graham, who used television, radio, advertising, and print media to spread the gospel. Although critics suggested that middle-class interest in religion stemmed not so much from a renewed spirituality as from a surging impulse toward conformity, the revival nonetheless spoke to Americans' search for spiritual meaning in uncertain times.

Even more dramatic testimony to the desire for stability in the postwar era was the emphasis Americans placed on the family and children. As one popular advice book put it, "The family is the center of your living. If it isn't, you've gone far astray." Family demographics between 1940 and 1960 moved notably away from depression and war trends. Marriages were remarkably stable; not until the mid-1960s did the divorce rate begin to rise sharply. But the average age at marriage fell during the period, to twenty-two for men and twenty for women. In 1951 a third of all women were married by age nineteen. More important, the drop in the average age at marriage resulted in a surge of young married couples who produced a bumper crop of children. After a century and a half of declining family size, the birth rate shot up and peaked in 1957: more babies were born between 1948 and 1953 than had been born in the previous thirty years. As a result of this trend and a lengthened life expectancy because of improvements in diet, public health, and medicine, the American population rose dramatically from 140 million in 1945 to 179 million in 1960, and to 203 million in 1970.

The baby boom had a broad and immediate impact on American society. It prompted a major expansion of the nation's educational system: by 1970 school expenditures were double those of the 1950 level. In addition, babies' consumer needs fueled the economy as families bought food, diapers, toys, and clothing for their expanding broods. Together with federal expenditures on national security, family spending on consumer goods fueled the unparalleled prosperity and economic growth of the 1950s and 1960s.

CONTRADICTIONS IN WOMEN'S LIVES

The parents of baby boomers experienced multiple economic and social pressures. In addition to providing for their children materially and emotionally, they were expected to adhere to rigid gender roles as a way of maintaining the family and undergirding the social order. The mass media, educators, and experts urged men to conform to a masculine ideal that emphasized their role as responsible bread-winners. Women's proper place, they advised, was in the home. Endorsing what Betty Friedan has called the "feminine mystique" of the 1950s—the ideal that "the highest value and the only commitment for women is the fulfillment of their own femininity"—many psychologists pronounced motherhood the only "normal" fe-male gender role and berated mothers who worked outside the home, charging that they damaged their children's development.

Though the power of these ideas stunted the lives of many women, not all housewives were unhappy or neurotic, as Friedan would later charge in her 1963 best seller, *The Feminine Mystique.* Many working-class women embraced their new roles as housewives; unlike their mothers and unmarried sisters, they were not com-pelled to take low-paid employment outside the home. But not all Americans could or did live by the norms of suburban domesticity, ideals that were out of reach of or irrelevant to many racial minorities, inner-city residents, recent immigrants, rural Americans, and homosexuals. At the height of the postwar period, more than one-third of American women held jobs outside the home (see American Voices, "A Woman Encounters the Feminine Mystique"). The increase in the number of work-ing women coincided with another change of equal significance—a dramatic rise in the number of older, married middle-class women who took jobs.

How could the society of the 1950s cling so steadfastly to the domestic ideal while an increasing number of wives and mothers worked? Often women justified their jobs as an extension of their family responsibilities, enabling their families to enjoy more of the fruits of the consumer culture. Working women also still bore full responsibility for child care and household management, allowing families and society to avoid facing the implications of their new roles. Thus the reality of women's lives departed significantly from the cultural stereotypes glorified in advertising, sitcoms, and women's magazines.

CULTURAL DISSENTERS

Beneath the surface of family togetherness lay other tensions—those between par-ents and children. Dating back to the 1920s the emergence of a mass youth culture had its roots in the democratization of education, the growth of peer culture, and the increasing purchasing power of teenagers in an age of affluence. Youth, eager to escape the climate of suburban conformity of their parents, had become a dis-tinct new market that advertisers eagerly exploited. In 1956 advertisers projected an adolescent market of $9 billion for items such as transistor radios (introduced in 1952), clothing, and fads such as Hula Hoops (1958).

What really defined this generation's youth culture, however, was its music. Rejecting the rigid boundaries of traditional popular music, teenagers in the 1950s discovered rock 'n' roll, an amalgam of white country and western music and the black urban music known as rhythm and blues. The Cleveland disc jockey Alan

AMERICAN VOICES

A Woman Encounters the Feminine Mystique

T *he power of the feminine mystique in the 1950s made it difficult for middle-class women who challenged the view that women's proper place was in the home. In this oral history account, "Sylvia" describes her struggle to pursue a career as an ophthalmologist.*

We sat on a bench in the middle of the lobby there—I remember it looked like a train station—and he [her professor] said, "Do you plan to get pregnant or married?" I promised him I wouldn't do either. I felt like I was about ten years old. They gave me a year's trial in the research department and after that I could get a residency. Most people there, the men, had a three-year residency. I was only the second woman they'd ever accepted, and I was the only woman out of twenty men.

I had a fellowship, so when I finished with my work I'd have to go over to see how my research projects were coming along. I never, never, goofed off. These guys were watching me all the time and complaining that I wasn't doing my work. It was hard enough to be a first-year resident, where you're the bottom person who gets kicked by everybody. I had no friends. My fellow physicians were constantly telling me I should switch to obstetrics or pediatrics, I should be home having babies, that a man could earn a wonderful living for his family in my place. Finally I was at my wits' end and I called my old ophthalmology professor and told him I didn't know if I could psychologically take this for another two and a half years. He said, "You know, if you give up now I'll never be able to get another woman in there." So I went on.

SOURCE: Brett Harvey, *The Fifties: A Women's Oral History* (New York: Harper, 1993), pp. 154–55.

Freed played a major role in introducing white America to the new African American sound by playing rhythm and blues records on white radio stations beginning in 1954. Young white performers such as Bill Haley, Buddy Holly, and especially Elvis Presley incorporated the new mixture into their own music and capitalized on the new youth market. Between 1953 and 1959 record sales increased from $213 million to $603 million, with 45-rpm rock-'n'-roll records as the driving force. The new teen music shocked many white adults, who saw rock 'n' roll as an invitation to race-mixing, sexual promiscuity, and juvenile delinquency.

The youth rebellion was only one aspect of a broader undercurrent of discontent with the conformist culture of the 1950s. In major cities across the nation, gay men and women, many of whom had served in the military during World War II, fought back against homophobic laws and personal attacks. In Los Angeles homosexual men founded the Mattachine Society, a gay-rights organization, in 1951, and in 1954 lesbians established the Daughters of Bilitis. While for the most part the gay subculture remained closeted, this did not stop gay baiting or local police raids on gay bars. And because homosexuals were viewed as emotionally unstable or vulnerable to blackmail, they were assumed to be security risks. As a result of publicity attached to raids, as well as government investigations, many gays lost their jobs, a testament to the perceived threat they represented to mainstream sexual and cultural norms.

Postwar artists, musicians, and writers expressed their alienation from mainstream society through intensely personal, introspective art forms. In New York Jackson Pollock and other painters rejected the social realism of the 1930s for an unconventional style that became known as abstract expressionism. Swirling and splattering paint onto giant canvases, Pollock emphasized self-expression in the act of painting, capturing the chaotic atmosphere of the nuclear age.

A similar trend developed in jazz, as black musicians originated a hard-driving improvisational style known as bebop. Black jazz musicians found eager fans not only in the African American community but among young white Beats in New York and San Francisco. Disdaining middle-class conformity, corporate capitalism, and suburban materialism, the Beats were a group of writers and poets who were

A Woman's Dilemma in Postwar America

This 1959 cover of the *Saturday Evening Post* depicts some of the difficult choices facing women in the postwar era. Women's consignment to low-paid, dead-end jobs in the service sector encouraged many to become full-time homemakers. Once back in their suburban homes, however, many middle-class women felt isolated and trapped amid endless rounds of cooking, cleaning, and diaper changing. (© The Curtis Publishing Company)

Elvis Presley

The young Elvis Presley shown here on the cover of his first album in 1956, embodied cultural rebellion against the conservatism and triviality of adult life in the 1950s. (© 1956 BGM Music)

both literary innovators and outspoken social critics. In his poem "Howl" (1956), which became a manifesto of the Beat generation, Allen Ginsberg lamented: "I saw the best minds of my generation destroyed by madness, starving hysterical naked, dragging themselves through the angry streets at dawn looking for an angry fix." In works such as Jack Kerouac's novel *On the Road* (1957) the Beats glorified spontaneity, sexual adventurism, drug use, and spirituality. Although they were most often apolitical—their rebellion was strictly cultural—in the 1960s they inspired a new generation of rebels who would champion both political and cultural change.

The Other America

As middle-class whites flocked to the suburbs, a diverse group of poor and working-class migrants, many of them nonwhite, moved into the central cities. With jobs and financial resources flowing to the suburbs, urban newcomers inherited a declining economy and a decaying environment. To those enjoying new prosperity, *The Other America*—as the social critic Michael Harrington called it in 1962—remained largely invisible.

URBAN MIGRATION

Newly arrived immigrants were one of several groups moving into the nation's cities in the postwar era. Although until 1965 U.S. immigration policy followed the restrictive national origins quota system set up in 1924 (see Chapter 23), Congress modified the law during and after World War II. The War Brides Act of 1945, permitting the entry and naturalization of the wives and children of Americans living abroad (mainly servicemen), brought thousands of new immigrants between 1950 and 1965, including some 17,000 Koreans. Three years later the Displaced Persons Act admitted approximately 415,000 European refugees. The repeal of the Chinese Exclusion Act in 1943, in deference to America's wartime alliance with China, and the passage of the McCarran-Walter Act in 1952 ended the exclusion of Chinese, Japanese, Korean, and Southeast Asian immigrants. Finally, in recognition of the freeing of the Philippines from American control in 1946, Filipinos received their own quota.

One of the largest groups of postwar migrants came from Mexico. Nearly 275,000 Mexicans came in the 1950s, and almost 444,000 in the 1960s. They moved primarily to western and southwestern cities such as Los Angeles, El Paso, and Phoenix, where they found jobs as migrant workers or in the expanding service sector. Before World War II most Mexican Americans had lived in rural areas and engaged in agricultural work; by 1960 a majority were living in urban areas where they joined more settled communities of service and manufacturing workers.

Part of the stimulus for Mexican immigration was the reinstitution of the *bracero* program from 1951 to 1964. Originally devised as a means of importing temporary labor during World War II, the program brought 450,000 Mexican workers to the United States at its peak in 1959. But even as the federal government welcomed braceros, it deported those who stayed on illegally. In response to the recession of 1953 to 1954 and the resulting high rate of unemployment throughout the nation, federal authorities deported nearly 4 million Mexicans in a program called "Operation Wetback." The deportations discouraged illegal immigration for a few years, but the level increased again after the bracero program ended.

Another group of Spanish-speaking migrants came from the American-controlled territory of Puerto Rico. Residents of that island had been American citizens since 1917, so their migration was not subject to immigration laws. The inflow from the territory increased dramatically after World War II, when mechanization of the island's sugarcane industry pushed many rural Puerto Ricans off the land. When airlines began to offer cheap direct flights between San Juan and New York City (in the 1940s the fare was about $50, or two weeks' wages), Puerto

Ricans—most of whom settled in New York—became this country's first group to immigrate by air.

Cuban refugees constituted the third large group of Spanish-speaking immigrants. In the six years after communist Fidel Castro's overthrow of the Batista dictatorship in 1959, an estimated 180,000 people fled Cuba for the United States. The Cuban refugee community grew so quickly that it turned Miami into a cosmopolitan, bilingual city almost overnight. Unlike most new immigrants Miami's Cubans prospered, in large part because they had arrived with more resources.

Internal migration from rural areas also brought large numbers of people to the cities, especially African Americans, continuing a trend that had begun during World War I (see Chapter 22). Although both whites and blacks left the land, the starkest decline was among black farmers. Their migration was hastened by the transformation of southern agriculture, especially by the introduction of innovations like the mechanical cotton-picker, which significantly reduced the demand for farm labor.

Some of the migrants settled in southern cities, where they found industrial jobs. White southerners from Appalachia moved north to "hillbilly" ghettos such as Cincinnati's Over the Rhine neighborhood and Chicago's Uptown. As many as 3 million blacks headed to Chicago, New York, Washington, Detroit, Los Angeles, and other cities between 1940 and 1960. So pervasive were the migrants that certain sections of Chicago seemed like the Mississippi Delta transplanted. By 1960 about half of the nation's black population was living outside the South, compared with only 23 percent before World War II.

In western cities an influx of Native Americans also contributed to the rise in the nonwhite urban population. Seeking to end federal responsibility for Indian affairs, Congress in 1953 authorized a "Termination" program aimed at liquidating the reservation system and integrating Native Americans into mainstream society. The program, which reflected a cold-war preoccupation with conformity and assimilation, enjoyed strong support from mining, timber, and agricultural interests that wanted to open reservation lands for private development. The Bureau of Indian Affairs encouraged voluntary relocation to urban areas with a program subsidizing moving costs and establishing relocation centers in San Francisco, Denver, Chicago, and other cities. The relocation program proved problematic, however, as many Indians found it difficult to adjust to an urban environment and culture. Although forced termination was halted in 1958, by 1960 some 60,000 Indians had moved to the cities. Despite the program's stated goal of assimilation, most Native American migrants settled together in poor urban neighborhoods alongside other nonwhite groups.

THE URBAN CRISIS

American cities thus saw their nonwhite populations swell at the same time that whites were flocking to the suburbs. From 1950 to 1960 the nation's twelve largest cities lost 3.6 million whites and gained 4.5 million nonwhites. As affluent whites left the cities, urban tax revenues shrank, leading to the decay of services and infrastructure, which, coupled with growing racial fears, accelerated white suburban flight in the 1960s.

By the time that blacks, Latinos, and Native Americans moved into the inner cities, urban America was in poor shape. Housing continued to be a crucial problem. City planners, politicians, and real-estate developers responded with urban renewal programs, razing blighted city neighborhoods to make way for modern construction projects. Local residents were rarely consulted about whether they wanted their neighborhoods "renewed," and redevelopment programs often produced grim high-rise housing projects that destroyed community bonds and created anonymous open areas that were vulnerable to crime. Between 1949 and 1967 urban renewal demolished almost 400,000 buildings and displaced 1.4 million people.

Postwar urban areas were increasingly becoming places of last resort for the nation's poor. Lured to the cities by the promise of plentiful jobs, migrants found that many of those opportunities had relocated to the suburban fringe, putting steady employment out of reach for those who needed it most. Migrants to the city, especially blacks, also faced racial hostility and institutional barriers to mobility—biased school funding, hiring and promotion decisions, and credit practices. Two separate Americas were emerging: a largely white society in suburbs and peripheral areas and an inner city populated by blacks, Latinos, and other disadvantaged groups.

The stereotypes of boundless affluence and contentment in the 1950s—of "Happy Days"—are thus misleading, for they hide those persons who did not share equally in the American dream—displaced factory workers, destitute old people, female heads of households, blacks and other racial minority groups. In the turbulent decade to come the contrast between suburban affluence and the "other America," between the lure of the city for the poor and minorities and its grim, segregated reality, and between a heightened emphasis on domesticity and the widening opportunities for women would spawn growing demands for social change that the nation's leaders in the 1960s could not ignore.

John F. Kennedy and the Politics of Expectation

In his 1961 inaugural address President John Fitzgerald Kennedy challenged a "new generation of Americans" to take responsibility for the future: "Ask not what your country can do for you, ask what you can do for your country." Few presidents came to Washington more primed for action than John F. Kennedy. His New Frontier program promised to "get America moving again" through vigorous governmental activism at home and abroad. But the legislative achievements of Kennedy's New Frontier, particularly in domestic affairs, were modest.

THE NEW POLITICS

The Republicans would have been happy to renominate Dwight D. Eisenhower for president, but the Twenty-second Amendment prevented them from doing so. Passed in 1951 by a Republican-controlled Congress to prevent a repetition of Franklin Roosevelt's four-term presidency, the amendment limited future presidents to two full terms. So in 1960 the Republicans turned to Vice President Richard M. Nixon, who campaigned for an updated version of Eisenhower's policies but was hampered by lukewarm support from the popular president.

The Democrats chose Senator John F. Kennedy of Massachusetts, with the Senate majority leader, Lyndon B. Johnson of Texas, as the vice-presidential nominee. First elected to Congress in 1946, John Kennedy moved to the Senate in 1952. Ambitious and hard-driven, Kennedy launched his campaign in 1960 with a platform calling

The Kennedy Magnetism

John Kennedy, the Democratic candidate for president in 1960, used his youth and personality to attract voters. Here the Massachusetts senator draws an enthusiastic crowd on a campaign stop in Elgin, Illinois. (AP/Wide World Photos)

for civil rights legislation, health care for the elderly, aid to education, urban renewal, expanded military and space programs, and containment of communism abroad.

At forty-three Kennedy was poised to become the youngest man ever elected to the presidency and the nation's first Catholic chief executive. Turning his age into a powerful campaign asset, Kennedy practiced what came to be called the "new politics," an approach that emphasized youthful charisma, style, and personality more than issues and platforms. Using the power of the media—particularly television—to reach voters directly, practitioners of the new politics relied on professional media consultants, political pollsters, and mass fund raising.

A series of four televised debates between the two principal candidates, a major innovation of the 1960 campaign, showed how important television was becoming to political life. Nixon, far less photogenic than Kennedy, looked sallow and unshaven under the intense studio lights. Kennedy, in contrast, looked vigorous, cool, and self-confident on screen. Polls showed that television did sway political perceptions: voters who listened to the first debate on the radio concluded that Nixon had won, but those who viewed it on TV judged in Kennedy's favor.

Despite the edge Kennedy enjoyed in the debates, he won only the narrowest of electoral victories, receiving 49.7 percent of the popular vote to Nixon's 49.5 percent. Kennedy successfully appealed to the diverse elements of the Democratic coalition, attracting large numbers of Catholic and black voters and a significant sector of the middle class; the vice-presidential nominee, Lyndon Johnson, brought in southern white Democrats. Yet only 120,000 votes separated the two candidates, and the shift of a few thousand votes in key states such as Illinois (where there were confirmed cases of voting fraud) would have reversed the outcome.

ACTIVISM ABROAD AND AT HOME

Kennedy's greatest priority as president was foreign affairs. A resolute cold warrior, Kennedy took a hard line against communist expansionism. In contrast to Eisenhower, whose cost-saving New Look program had built up the American nuclear arsenal at the expense of conventional weapons, Kennedy proposed a new policy of "flexible response," stating that the nation must be prepared "to deter all wars, general or limited, nuclear or conventional, large or small." Congress quickly granted Kennedy's military requests, and by 1963 the defense budget reached its highest level as a percentage of total federal expenditures in the cold-war era, greatly expanding the military-industrial complex.

Flexible response measures were designed to deter direct attacks by the Soviet Union. To prepare for a new kind of warfare, evident in the wars of national liberation that had broken out in many developing countries, Kennedy adopted a new military doctrine of *counterinsurgency*. Soon U.S. Army Special Forces, called Green Berets for their distinctive headgear, were receiving intensive training in repelling the random, small-scale attacks typical of guerrilla warfare. Vietnam would soon provide a testing ground for counterinsurgency techniques (see Chapter 29).

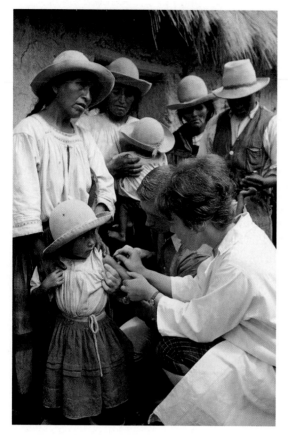

The Peace Corps

The Peace Corps, a New Frontier program initiated in 1961, attracted thousands of idealistic young Americans to volunteer in development projects overseas. Volunteers Rita Helmkamp and Ed Dennison worked in a vaccination program in Bolivia.

(David S. Boyer/National Geographic Society Image Collection)

Another of Kennedy's projects, the Peace Corps, established in 1961, embodied the commitment to public service that the president had called for in his inaugural address. Thousands of men and women agreed to devote two or more years to programs that had them teaching English to Filipino schoolchildren or helping African villagers obtain adequate supplies of water. Embodying the idealism of the early 1960s, the Peace Corps was also a cold-war weapon intended to bring developing countries into the American orbit and away from communist influence.

For the same reason Kennedy pushed for economic aid to developing countries. The State Department's Agency for International Development coordinated foreign aid for the Third World, including surplus agricultural products distributed to developing nations through its Food for Peace program. In Latin America the Alliance for Progress provided funds for food, education, medicine, and other services, although it did little to enhance economic growth or improve social conditions there.

Latin America was the site of Kennedy's first major foreign policy initiative and one of his biggest failures—an effort to overthrow the new Soviet-supported regime in Cuba. The United States had long exercised nearly total economic and political dominance of the island. But on New Year's Day in 1959 the revolutionary Fidel Castro overthrew the corrupt and unpopular dictator Fulgencio Batista. When Castro began agrarian reforms and nationalized American-owned banks and industries, relations with Washington deteriorated. By early 1961 the United States had declared an embargo on all exports to Cuba, cut back on imports of Cuban sugar, and broken off diplomatic relations with Castro's regime.

Isolated by the United States, Cuba turned increasingly toward the Soviet Union for economic and military support. Concerned about Castro's growing friendliness with the Soviets, in early 1961 Kennedy used plans originally drawn up by the Eisenhower administration to dispatch Cuban exiles living in Nicaragua to foment an anti-Castro uprising. Although the invaders had been trained by the Central Intelligence Agency (CIA), they were ill prepared for their task and had little popular support. After landing at Cuba's Bay of Pigs on April 17, the tiny force of 1,400 men was crushed by Castro's troops (Map 28.2).

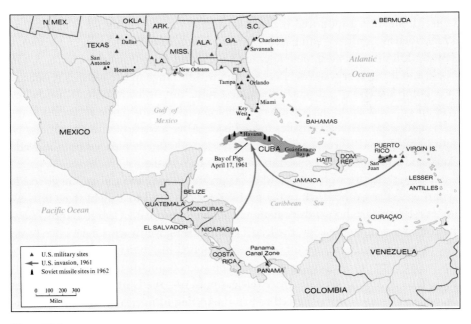

M A P 28.2
The United States and Cuba, 1961–1962

Fidel Castro's takeover in Cuba in 1959 brought cold-war tensions to the Caribbean. In 1961 the United States tried unsuccessfully to overthrow Castro's regime by supporting the Bay of Pigs invasion of Cuban exiles launched from Nicaragua and other points in the Caribbean. In 1962 a major confrontation with the Soviet Union occurred over Soviet missile sites in Cuba. The Soviets removed the missiles after President Kennedy ordered a naval blockade of the island, which lies just 90 miles south of Florida.

Already weakened by the Bay of Pigs invasion, U.S.-Soviet relations deteriorated further in June 1961 when Soviet Premier Khrushchev deployed soldiers to isolate communist-controlled East Berlin from the western sector of the city controlled by West Germany. With congressional approval Kennedy responded by adding 300,000 troops to the armed forces and promptly dispatching 40,000 of them to Europe. In mid-August, to stop the exodus of East Germans to the West, the Soviets ordered construction of the Berlin Wall, and East German guards began policing the border. Until it was dismantled in 1989 the Berlin Wall remained the supreme symbol of the cold war.

The climactic confrontation of the cold war came in October 1962. After the failed Bay of Pigs invasion the Kennedy administration increased economic pressure against Cuba and resumed covert efforts to overthrow the Castro regime. In response the Soviets stepped up military aid to Cuba, including the installation of nuclear missiles. In early October American reconnaissance planes photographed Soviet-built bases for intermediate-range ballistic missiles (IRBMs), which could reach U.S. targets as far as 2,200 miles away. Some of those weapons had already been installed, and more were on the way.

In a somber televised address on Monday, October 22, Kennedy confronted the Soviet Union, and announced that the United States would impose a "quarantine on all offensive military equipment" intended for Cuba. As the two superpowers went on full military alert, people around the world feared that the confrontation would end in nuclear war. Americans living within range of the missiles restocked their bomb shelters or calculated the fastest route out of town. When Khrushchev denounced the quarantine, tension mounted. But as the world held its breath, ships carrying the Soviet-made missiles turned back. After a week of tense negotiations, both Kennedy and Khrushchev made concessions: Kennedy pledged not to invade Cuba, and Khrushchev promised to dismantle the missile bases.

Although the risk of nuclear war was greater during the Cuban missile crisis than it was at any other time in the postwar period, it led to a slight thaw in U.S.-Soviet relations. In the words of national security advisor McGeorge Bundy, "having come so close to the edge, the leaders of the two governments have since taken care to keep away from the cliff." Kennedy softened his cold-war rhetoric and began to strive for peaceful coexistence. Soviet leaders, similarly chastened, were willing to talk. In August 1963 the three nuclear powers—the United States, the Soviet Union, and Great Britain—agreed to ban the testing of nuclear weapons in the atmosphere, in space, and underwater. Underground testing, however, was allowed to continue. The new emphasis on peaceful coexistence also led to the establishment of a Washington-Moscow telecommunications "hot line" in 1963 so that leaders could contact each other quickly during potential crises.

But no matter how often American leaders talked about opening channels of communication with the Soviets, the preoccupation with the Soviet military threat to American security remained a cornerstone of U.S. policy. Nor did Soviet leaders moderate their concern over the threat that they believed the United States posed to the survival of the USSR. The cold war, and the escalating arms race that accompanied it, would continue for another twenty-five years.

The expansive vision of presidential leadership that Kennedy and his advisors brought to the White House worked less well at home than it did abroad. Hampered by the lack of a popular mandate in the 1960 election, Kennedy could not mobilize public support for the domestic agenda of the New Frontier. A conservative coalition of southern Democrats and western and midwestern Republicans effectively stalled most liberal initiatives. More important, Kennedy was not nearly as impassioned about domestic reform as he was about foreign policy.

One program that did win both popular and congressional support was increased funding for the National Aeronautics and Space Administration (NASA), whose Mercury space program had begun in 1958. On May 5, 1961, just three months after Kennedy took office, Alan Shepard became the first American in space. (The Soviet cosmonaut Yuri Gagarin became the first person in space when he made a 108-hour flight in April 1961.) The following year, American astronaut John Glenn manned the first space mission to orbit the earth. At the height of American fascination with space flight Kennedy proposed that the nation commit itself to landing a man on the moon within the decade. To support this mission (accomplished in 1969), Kennedy persuaded Congress to greatly increase NASA's budget.

Kennedy's most striking domestic achievement was his use of modern economic theory to shape government fiscal policy. New Dealers had gradually moved away from the ideal of a balanced budget, turning instead to deliberate deficit spending to stimulate economic growth. In addition to relying on federal spending to create the desired deficit, Kennedy and his advisors proposed a reduction in income taxes. A tax cut, they argued, would put more money in the hands of taxpayers, who would spend it, thereby creating more jobs. For a time federal expenditures would exceed federal income, but after a year or two the expanding economy would raise American incomes and generate higher tax revenues.

Congress balked at this unorthodox proposal, and the measure failed to pass. But Lyndon Johnson pressed for it after Kennedy's assassination, signing it into law in February 1964. The Kennedy-Johnson tax cut—the Tax Reduction Act (1964)—marked a milestone in the use of fiscal policy to encourage economic growth, an approach that Republicans and other fiscal conservatives would later embrace.

Kennedy's interest in stimulating economic growth did not include a commitment to spending for domestic social needs, although he did not entirely ignore the liberal legislative agenda of Franklin Roosevelt and Harry Truman. Kennedy managed to push through legislation raising the minimum wage and expanding Social Security benefits. But on other issues—federal aid to education, wilderness preservation, federal investment in mass transportation, and medical insurance for the elderly—he ran into determined congressional opposition from both Republicans and dissenters in his own party.

JFK AND CIVIL RIGHTS

Perhaps the gravest failure of the Kennedy administration was its reluctance to act on civil rights—the most important domestic issue of the 1960s. Building on the strategy of nonviolent direct action pioneered by Martin Luther King Jr. and the Montgomery bus boycotters in the 1950s, a younger generation of activists in the 1960s initiated new, more assertive tactics such as sit-ins, freedom rides, and voter registration campaigns.

This new phase of the civil rights movement began in Greensboro, North Carolina, on February 1, 1960, when four black college students took seats at the "whites-only" lunch counter of a local Woolworth's, determined to "sit in" until they were served. Although the protesters were arrested, the sit-in tactic worked and quickly spread to other southern cities. A few months later Ella Baker, an adminis-trator with the Southern Christian Leadership Conference (SCLC) and a lifelong activist, helped to organize the Student Non-Violent Coordinating Committee (SNCC, known as "Snick") to facilitate student sit-ins. By the end of the year about 50,000 people had participated in sit-ins or other demonstrations, and 3,600 of them had been jailed. But lunch counters had been desegregated in 126 cities throughout the South (see American Voices, "A Badge of Honor").

The success of SNCC's unorthodox tactics encouraged the Congress of Racial Equality (CORE), an interracial group founded in 1942, to organize a series of *free-dom rides* in 1961 on interstate bus lines throughout the South to call attention to the continuing segregation of public transportation. The activists who rode the buses, mostly young and both black and white, were brutally attacked by white mobs in Anniston, Montgomery, and Birmingham, Alabama. Governor John Patterson refused to intervene, claiming, "I cannot guarantee protection for this bunch of rabble rousers."

Although the Kennedy administration generally opposed the freedom riders' activities, films of their beatings and the bus burning shown on the nightly news prompted Attorney General Robert Kennedy to send federal marshals to Alabama to restore order. Faced with Department of Justice intervention against those who defied the Interstate Commerce Commission's prohibition of segregation in inter-state vehicles and facilities, most southern communities quietly acceded to the changes. And civil rights activists learned that nonviolent protest could succeed if it provoked vicious white resistance and generated publicity. Only when forced to, it appeared, would the federal authorities act.

This lesson was confirmed in Birmingham, Alabama, when Martin Luther King Jr. and the Reverend Fred Shuttlesworth called for a protest against conditions in what King called "the most segregated city in the United States." In April 1963 thousands of black demonstrators marched downtown to picket Birmingham's department stores. They were met by Eugene ("Bull") Connor, the city's commissioner of public safety, who used snarling dogs, electric cattle prods, and high-pressure fire hoses to break up the crowd. Television cameras captured the scene for the evening news.

AMERICAN VOICES

A Badge of Honor

JOHN LEWIS

Twenty-year-old John Lewis, a student at American Baptist Theological Seminary in Nashville, was one of 500 students to participate in the 1960 sit-ins at the city's lunch counters. His oral account reveals the tactical planning that went into the students' efforts, the virulence of the resistance they encountered, and the spirit of commitment and courage that sustained civil rights activists. Lewis went onto join the Student Non-Violent Coordinating Committee (SNCC) and to participate in the Freedom Rides, Freedom Summer, and the March on Washington.

The first day nothing in terms of violence or disorder happened. This continued for a few more days and it continued day in and day out. Finally, on Saturday, February twenty-seventh, when we had about a hundred students prepared to go down—it was a very beautiful day in Nashville—we got a call from a local white minister who had been a real supporter of the movement. He said that if we go down on this particular day, he understood that the police would stand to the side and let a group of white hoodlums and thugs come in and beat people up, and then we would be arrested. We made a decision to go, and we all went to the same store. It was a Woolworth in the heart of the downtown area, and we occupied every seat at the lunch counter, every seat in the restaurant, and it did happen. A group of young white men came in and they started pulling and beating primarily the young women. They put lighted cigarettes down their backs, in their hair, and they were really beating people. In a short time police officials came in and placed all of us under arrest, and not a single member of the white group, the people that were opposing our sit-in, was arrested.

That was the first time that I was arrested. Growing up in the rural South, you learned it was not the thing to do. To go to jail was to bring shame and disgrace on the family. But for me it was like being involved in a holy crusade. It became a badge of honor. I think it was in keeping with what we had been taught in the workshops, so I felt very good, in the sense of righteous indignation, about being arrested, but at the same time I felt the commitment and dedication on the part of the students.

SOURCE: Henry Hampton and Steve Fayer, *Voices of Freedom: An Oral History of the Civil Rights Movement from the 1950s Through the 1980s* (New York: Bantam Books, 1991), p. 58.

President Kennedy, realizing that he could no longer postpone decisive action, decided to step up the federal government's role in civil rights. On June 11, 1963, Kennedy went on television to promise major legislation banning discrimination in public accommodations and empowering the Justice Department to enforce desegregation. Black leaders hailed the speech as the "Second Emancipation Proclamation," but for one person Kennedy's speech came too late. That night, Medgar

Racial Violence in Birmingham

When thousands of blacks marched through downtown Birmingham, Alabama, to protest racial segregation in April 1963, they were met with fire hoses and attack dogs unleashed by Police Chief "Bull" Connor. The violence, which was televised on the national evening news, shocked many Americans and helped build sympathy for the civil rights movement among northern whites. (Bill Hudson/Wide World Photos, Inc.)

Evers, president of the Mississippi chapter of the NAACP, was shot in the back and killed in his driveway in Jackson. The martyrdom of Evers became a spur to further action.

To rouse the conscience of the nation and to marshal support for Kennedy's bill, civil rights leaders adopted a tactic A. Philip Randolph had first suggested in 1941 (see Chapter 26): a massive march on Washington. Martin Luther King Jr. of the SCLC, Roy Wilkins of the NAACP, Whitney Young of the National Urban League, and the black socialist Bayard Rustin were the principal organizers. On August 28, 1963, about 250,000 black and white demonstrators—the largest crowd at any demonstration up to that time—gathered at the Lincoln Memorial. The march culminated in a memorable speech delivered, indeed preached, by King, in the evangelical style of the black church. He ended with an exclamation from an old Negro spiritual: "Free at last! Free at last! Thank God almighty, we are free at last!"

King's eloquence and the sight of blacks and whites marching solemnly together did more than any other event to make the civil rights movement acceptable to white Americans. The March on Washington marked the climax of the nonviolent phase of the civil rights movement and confirmed King's position, especially among white liberals, as the leading speaker for the black cause. In 1964 King won the Nobel Peace Prize for his leadership.

Despite the impact of the march on public opinion, it changed few congressional votes. Southern senators continued to block Kennedy's legislation by threatening a filibuster. Even more troubling was a new outbreak of violence by white extremists determined to oppose equality for blacks at all costs. In September a Baptist church in Birmingham was bombed, and four black Sunday school students were killed. The violence shocked the nation and stiffened the resolve of civil rights activists to escalate their demands for change. Two months later, President Kennedy was assassinated.

THE KENNEDY ASSASSINATION

Although the first two years of Kennedy's presidency had been plagued by foreign-policy crises and domestic inaction, many political observers believed that by 1963 Kennedy was maturing as a national leader. On November 22, 1963, Kennedy went to Texas. As he and his wife, Jacqueline, rode in an open car past the Texas School Book Depository in Dallas, he was shot through the head and neck by a sniper. Kennedy died a half hour later. (Whether accused killer Lee Harvey Oswald, a twenty-four-year-old loner who had spent three years in the Soviet Union, was the sole gunman is still a matter of controversy.) Before Air Force One left Dallas to take the president's body back to Washington, a grim-faced Lyndon Johnson was sworn in as president. Kennedy's stunned widow, still wearing her bloodstained pink suit, looked on.

Kennedy's youthful image, the trauma of his assassination, and the collective sense that Americans had been robbed of a promising leader contributed to a powerful mystique. This romantic aura has overshadowed what most historians agree was at best a mixed record. Kennedy exercised bold presidential leadership in foreign affairs, but his initiatives in Cuba and Berlin marked the height of superpower confrontation during the cold war. Moreover, his enthusiasm for fighting communism abroad had no domestic equivalent. Kennedy's proposals for educational aid, medical insurance, and other liberal reforms stalled, and his tax-cut bill languished in Congress until after his death. Perhaps his greatest domestic failure was his reluctance to act boldly on civil rights.

Lyndon B. Johnson and the Great Society

Lyndon Baines Johnson, a seasoned politician who was best at negotiating in the backrooms of power, was no match for the Kennedy style, but less than a year after assuming office Johnson won the 1964 presidential election in a landslide that far surpassed Kennedy's meager mandate in 1960. Johnson then used his astonishing energy and genius for compromise to bring to fruition many of Kennedy's stalled programs and more than a few of his own. Those legislative accomplishments— Johnson's "Great Society"—fulfilled and in many cases surpassed the New Deal liberal agenda of the 1930s.

THE MOMENTUM FOR CIVIL RIGHTS

On assuming the presidency Lyndon Johnson promptly turned the passage of civil rights legislation into a memorial to his slain predecessor—an ironic twist in light of Kennedy's lukewarm support for the cause. The Civil Rights Act, passed finally in June 1964, was a landmark in the history of American race relations. Its keystone, Title VII, outlawed discrimination in employment on the basis of race, religion, national origin, or sex. Another section barred discrimination in public accommodations. But while the act forced the desegregation of public facilities throughout the South, including many public schools, obstacles to black voting rights remained.

In 1964, with the Civil Rights Act on the brink of passage, black organizations and churches mounted a major civil rights campaign in Mississippi. Known as Freedom Summer, the effort drew several thousand volunteers from across the country, including many idealistic white college students. Freedom Summer workers established freedom schools, which taught black children traditional subjects as well as their own history, conducted a major voter registration drive, and organized the Mississippi Freedom Democratic Party, a political alternative to the all-white Democratic organization in Mississippi. White southerners reacted swiftly and violently to their efforts. Fifteen civil rights workers were murdered; only about 1,200 black voters were registered that summer.

The need for federal action to support voting rights became even clearer in March 1965, when Martin Luther King Jr. and other black leaders called for a massive march from Selma, Alabama, to the state capital in Montgomery to protest the murder of a voting-rights activist. As soon as the marchers left Selma, mounted state troopers attacked them with tear gas and clubs. The scene was shown on national television that night.

Calling the episode "an American tragedy," President Johnson redoubled his efforts to persuade Congress to pass the pending voting-rights legislation. In a televised speech to a joint session of Congress on March 15, quoting the best-known slogan of the civil rights movement, "We shall overcome," he proclaimed voting rights a moral imperative.

On August 6 Congress passed the Voting Rights Act of 1965, which suspended the literacy tests and other measures most southern states used to prevent blacks from registering to vote. The act authorized the attorney general to send federal examiners to register voters in any county where less than 50 percent of the voting-age population was registered. Together with the adoption in 1964 of the

Twenty-fourth Amendment to the Constitution, which outlawed the federal poll tax, and successful legal challenges to state and local poll taxes, the Voting Rights Act allowed millions of blacks to register and vote for the first time. Congress reauthorized the Voting Rights Act in 1970, 1975, and 1982.

In the South the results were stunning. In 1960 only 20 percent of blacks of voting age had been registered to vote; by 1964 the figure had risen to 39 percent, and by 1971 it was 62 percent. As Hartman Turnbow, a Mississippi farmer who risked his life to register in 1964, later declared, "It won't never go back where it was."

ENACTING THE LIBERAL AGENDA

Johnson's success in pushing through the 1965 Voting Rights Act stemmed in part from the 1964 election, in which he won the presidency in his own right by defeating the conservative Republican senator Barry Goldwater of Arizona. With his running mate, Senator Hubert H. Humphrey of Minnesota, Johnson achieved one of the largest margins in history, 61.1 percent of the popular vote. And Johnson's coattails were long—his sweeping victory brought democratic gains in both Congress and the state legislatures. Thus strengthened politically, he used this mandate not only to promote a civil rights agenda but also to bring to fruition what he called the "Great Society."

Like most New Deal liberals, Johnson took an expansive view of presidential leadership and the role of the federal government. Johnson's first major success came in education. The Elementary and Secondary Education Act, passed in 1965, authorized $1 billion in federal funds to benefit impoverished children. The same year the Higher Education Act provided the first federal scholarships for college students. The Eighty-ninth Congress also gave Johnson enough votes to enact the federal health insurance legislation first proposed by Truman. The result was two new programs: Medicare, a health plan for the elderly funded by a surcharge on Social Security payroll taxes, and Medicaid, a health plan for the poor paid for by general tax revenues.

Although the Great Society is usually associated with programs for the disadvantaged, many Johnson administration initiatives actually benefited a wide spectrum of Americans. Federal urban renewal and home mortgage assistance helped those who could afford to live in single-family homes or modern apartments. Medicare covered every elderly person eligible for Social Security, regardless of need. Much of the federal aid to education benefited the children of the middle class. Finally, the creation of the National Endowment for the Arts and the National Endowment for the Humanities in 1965 supported artists and historians in their efforts to understand and interpret the nation's cultural and historical heritage.

Another aspect of public welfare addressed by the Great Society was the environment. President Johnson pressed for expansion of the national park system, improvement of the nation's air and water, and increased land-use planning. At the insistence of his wife, Lady Bird Johnson, he promoted the Highway Beautification Act of 1965. His approach marked a significant break with past conservation efforts, which had tended to concentrate on maintaining natural resources and national wealth. Under Secretary of the Interior Stewart Udall, Great Society programs emphasized quality of life, battling the problem "of vanishing beauty, of increasing ugliness, of shrinking open space, and of an overall environment that is diminished daily by pollution and noise and blight."

Taking advantage of the Great Society's reform climate, liberal Democrats also brought about significant changes in immigration policy. The Immigration Act of 1965 abandoned the quota system of the 1920s that had discriminated against Asians and southern and Eastern Europeans, replacing it with more equitable numerical limits on immigration from Europe, Africa, Asia, and countries in the Western Hemisphere. Since close relatives of individuals who were already legal residents of the United States could be admitted over and above the numerical limits, the legislation led to an immigrant influx far greater than anticipated, with the heaviest volume coming from Asia and Latin America.

Perhaps the most ambitious part of Johnson's liberal agenda was the War on Poverty, based on his expectation that the Great Society could put "an end to poverty in our time." During Johnson's presidency, poor people made up about a fourth of the American population; three-fourths of the poor were white. The poor included isolated farmers and miners in Appalachia, blacks and Puerto Ricans in urban ghettos, Mexican Americans in migrant labor camps and urban barrios, Native Americans on reservations, women raising families on their own, and the abandoned and destitute elderly.

To reduce poverty the Johnson administration expanded long-established social insurance, welfare, and public works programs. It broadened the Social Security program to include more workers. Social welfare expenditures increased rapidly, especially for Aid to Families with Dependent Children (AFDC), public housing, rent subsidies, and food stamps. As during the New Deal these social welfare programs developed in piecemeal fashion, without central coordination.

The Great Society's showcase in the War on Poverty was the Office of Economic Opportunity (OEO), established by the omnibus Economic Opportunity Act of 1964. OEO programs produced some of the most innovative measures of the Johnson administration. Head Start provided free nursery schools to prepare disadvantaged preschoolers for kindergarten. The Job Corps, Upward Bound, and Volunteers in Service to America (VISTA), modeled on the Peace Corps, provided poor youths with training and jobs. And the Community Action Program encouraged the poor to demand "maximum feasible participation" in decisions that affected them.

By the end of 1965 the Johnson administration had compiled the most impressive legislative record of liberal reforms since the New Deal. It had put issues of poverty, justice, and access at the center of national political life, and it had expanded the federal government's role in protecting citizens' welfare. Yet the Great

Society never quite measured up to the extravagant promises made for it, and by the end of the decade many of its programs were under attack.

In part, the political necessity of bowing to pressure from various interest groups hampered Great Society programs. For example, the American Medical Association (AMA) used its influence to shape the Medicare and Medicaid programs, to ensure that Congress did not impose a cap on medical expenses. Its intervention produced escalating federal expenditures and contributed to skyrocketing medical costs. And Democratic-controlled urban political machines criticized VISTA and Community Action Program agents who encouraged poor people to demand the public services long withheld by unresponsive local governments. In response to such political pressure the Johnson administration gradually phased out the Community Action Program and instead channeled spending for housing, social services, and other urban poverty programs through local municipal governments.

Another inherent problem was the limited funding of Great Society programs. The annual budget for the War on Poverty was less than $2 billion. Despite the limited nature of the program, the statistical decline in poverty during the 1960s suggests that the Great Society was successful on some levels. From 1963 to 1968 the proportion of Americans living below the poverty line dropped from 20 percent to 13 percent. Among African Americans economic advancement was even more marked. In the 1960s the black poverty rate was cut in half, and millions of blacks moved into the middle class, some through federal jobs in antipoverty programs. But critics charged that the reduction in the poverty rate was due to the decade's booming economy, not to the War on Poverty. Another criticism was that while the nation's overall standard of living increased during this period, distribution of wealth was still uneven. The poor were better off in an absolute sense, but they remained far behind the middle class in a relative sense.

Other factors also hampered the success of the Great Society. Following in the steps of Roosevelt's New Deal coalition, Kennedy and Johnson had gathered an extraordinarily diverse set of groups—middle-class and poor; white and nonwhite; Protestant, Jewish, and Catholic; urban and rural—in support of an unprecedented level of federal activism. For a brief period between 1964 and 1966 the coalition held together. But inevitably the demands of certain groups—such as blacks' demands for civil rights and the urban poor's demands for increased political power—conflicted with the interests of other Democrats, such as white southerners and northern political bosses. In the end the Democratic coalition could not sustain a consensus on the purposes of governmental activism powerful enough to resist a growing backlash of conservatives who increasingly resisted expanded civil rights and social welfare legislation.

At the same time Democrats were plagued by disillusionment over the shortcomings of their reforms. In the early 1960s the lofty rhetoric of the New Frontier and the Great Society had raised unprecedented expectations for social change. But competition for federal largesse was keen, and the shortage of funds for the War on

Poverty left many promises unfulfilled, especially after 1965 when the escalation of the Vietnam War siphoned funding away from domestic programs. In 1966 the government spent $22 billion on the Vietnam War and only $1.2 billion on the War on Poverty. Ultimately, as Martin Luther King Jr. put it, the Great Society was "shot down on the battlefields of Vietnam."

T I M E L I N E

1944	Bretton Woods economic conference World Bank and International Monetary Fund (IMF) founded	1962	Michael Harrington's *The Other America* Cuban missile crisis
1947	Levittown, New York, built	1963	Betty Friedan's *The Feminine Mystique* Civil rights protest in Birmingham, Alabama
1952	Norman Vincent Peale's *The Power of Positive Thinking*		March on Washington Test-ban treaty prohibits U.S., Soviet, and British nuclear tests in air, space, or water.
1953–1958	Operation Wetback and Indian termination programs		John F. Kennedy assassinated; Lyndon B. Johnson assumes presidency.
1954	First McDonald's opens.	1964	Civil Rights Act Freedom Summer
1955	AFL and CIO merge. Disneyland opens.		Economic Opportunity Act inaugurates War on Poverty.
1956	National Interstate and Defense Highway Act Congress adds "In God We Trust" to coins. Allen Ginsberg's "Howl"		Johnson elected president in his own right and begins the Great Society program.
1957	Postwar baby boom peaks. Jack Kerouac's *On the Road*	1965	Immigration Act abolishes national quota system. Civil rights march from Selma to Montgomery
1959	"Kitchen debate" Fidel Castro leads Cuban revolution.		Voting Rights Act Medicare and Medicaid established
1960	Sit-ins in Greensboro, North Carolina John F. Kennedy elected president and begins New Frontier.		National Endowment for the Arts and National Endowment for the Humanities created
1961	Peace Corps established Freedom rides Bay of Pigs invasion crushed by Cuban army. Berlin Wall erected		

For Further Exploration

Two engaging introductions to postwar society are Paul Boyer, *Promises to Keep* (1995), and James T. Patterson, *Grand Expectations* (1996). Elaine Tyler May, *Homeward Bound* (1988), is the classic introduction to postwar family life. For youth culture see William Graebner, *Coming of Age in Buffalo* (1990). For insightful essays on the impact of television see Karal Ann Marling, *As Seen on TV* (1996). Powerful literary works of the period include Jack Kerouac, *On the Road* (1957); Allen Ginsberg, *Howl and Other Poems* (1996), and Arthur Miller, *Death of a Salesman* (1949). An excellent award-winning memoir of the Beat generation is Joyce Johnson, *Minor Characters* (1983). Good starting points for understanding Kennedy's presidency are Richard Reeves, *President Kennedy: Profile of Power* (1993), and David Halberstam, *The Best and the Brightest* (1972). For Lyndon Johnson see Robert Dallek, *Flawed Giant* (1998), and Doris Kearns, *Lyndon Johnson and the American Dream* (1976). There are many engaging accounts of the civil rights movement, including Henry Hampton and Steve Fayer's oral history, *Voices of Freedom* (1991), and Harvard Sitkoff, *The Struggle for Black Equality* (2nd ed., 1993).

The John F. Kennedy Library and Museum's site at <http://www.cs.umb.edu/~rwhealan/jfk/main.html> provides a large collection of records from Kennedy's presidency. The Reference Desk area contains frequently requested information, including transcripts and recordings of JFK's speeches, a database of his executive orders, and a number of other resources. The Avalon Project at the Yale Law School's site, "Foreign Relations of the United States: 1961–1963 Cuban Missile Crisis and Aftermath," at <http://www.yale.edu/lawweb/avalon/diplomacy/forrel/cuba/cubamenu.htm> contains almost 300 official documents related to the crisis, including State Department memoranda, records of telephone conversations, transcripts of conversations in the White House, and CIA reports. "Literary Kicks: The Beat Generation," at <http://www.charm.net/~brooklyn/LitKicks.html>, is an independent site created by New York writer Levi Asher devoted to the literature of the Beat generation. The site includes writings by Jack Kerouac, Allen Ginsberg, Neil Cassidy, and others; material on Beats, music, religion, and film; an extensive bibliography; biographical information; and photographs.

Chapter 29

WAR ABROAD AND AT HOME: THE VIETNAM ERA
1961–1975

In our excessive involvement in the affairs of other countries, we are not only living off our assets and denying our own people the proper enjoyment of their resources; we are also denying the world the example of a free society enjoying its freedom to the fullest. This is regrettable indeed for a nation that aspires to teach democracy to other nations.

—J. William Fulbright, 1966

On June 16, 1972, three hundred mourners assembled at Arlington National Cemetery for the funeral of John Paul Vann, a well-known Army lieutenant colonel who had died in a helicopter crash in Vietnam the week before. Though he supported the United States' commitment to the war, Vann had nonetheless publicly criticized the way it was being fought. Politicians and military leaders closely associated with the war effort—General William Westmoreland, Secretary of State William Rogers—were very much in evidence, but so were Daniel Ellsberg, a former Pentagon official who had publicly turned against the war, and Senator Edward Kennedy, another war opponent. Vann's family also showed the rifts over Vietnam. His wife, Mary Jane, requested her husband's favorite piece of music: the upbeat "Colonel Bogie March" from the film *The Bridge on the River Kwai* but added the haunting antiwar ballad "Where Have All the Flowers Gone?" to voice her own opposition to the war. One of his sons expressed his hatred of the war by tearing his draft card in two at the funeral, placing half of it on his father's casket. Although unusually public the Vann funeral provides a dramatic example of the ruptures the Vietnam War brought to families, institutions, and the American social fabric.

Vietnam spawned a vibrant antiwar protest movement, which intersected with a broader youth movement that questioned traditional American political and cultural values. The challenges posed by youth, together with the revival of feminism, the rise of the black and Chicano power movements, and explosive riots in the cities, produced a profound sense of social disorder at home. Vietnam split the Democratic Party and shattered the liberal consensus. The high monetary cost of the war diverted resources from domestic uses, spelling an end to the Great Society. Beyond its domestic impact the war wreaked extraordinary damage on the country of Vietnam and undermined U.S. credibility abroad. For the first time average Americans began to question their assumptions about the nation's cold-war objectives and the beneficence of American foreign policy.

Into the Quagmire, 1945–1968

Like many new nations that emerged from the dissolution of European empires after World War II, Vietnam was characterized by a volatile mix of nationalist sentiment, religious and cultural conflict, economic need, and political turmoil. The rise of communism there was just one phase of the nation's larger struggle, which would eventually climax in a bloody civil war. But American policymakers viewed these events through the lens of the cold war, interpreting them as part of an international communist movement toward global domination. Their failure to understand the complexity of Vietnam's internal conflicts led to a long and ultimately disastrous attempt to influence the course of the war.

AMERICA IN VIETNAM: FROM TRUMAN TO KENNEDY

Vietnam had been part of the French colony of Indochina since the late nineteenth century but had been occupied by Japan during World War II. When the Japanese surrendered in 1945, Ho Chi Minh and the Vietminh, the communist nationalist group that had led Vietnamese resistance to the Japanese, took advantage of the resulting power vacuum. With words drawn from the American Declaration of Independence, Ho proclaimed the establishment of the independent republic of Vietnam that September. The next year, when France rejected his claim and reasserted control over the country, an eight-year struggle that the Vietminh called the Anti-French War of Resistance ensued. Appealing to American anticolonial sentiment Ho called on President Truman to support the struggle for Vietnamese independence. But Truman ignored his pleas and instead offered covert financial support to the French, in hopes of stabilizing the politically chaotic region and rebuilding the French economy.

By the end of the decade cold-war developments had prompted the United States to step up its assistance to the French. After the Chinese revolution of 1949 the United States became concerned that China—along with the Soviet Union—might actively support anticolonial struggles in Asia and that newly independent countries might align themselves with the communists. At the same time Republican charges that the Democrats had "lost" China influenced Truman to take a firmer stand against perceived communist aggression in both Korea and Vietnam. Truman also wanted to maintain good relations with France, whose support was crucial to the success of the new NATO alliance. Finally, Indochina played a strategic role in

Secretary of State Dean Acheson's plans for an integrated Pacific Rim economy centered on a reindustrialized Japan.

For all these reasons, when the Soviet Union and the new Chinese leaders recognized Ho's republic early in 1950, the United States—along with Great Britain—recognized the French-installed puppet government of Bao Dai. Subsequently, both the Truman and the Eisenhower administrations provided substantial military support to the French in Vietnam. President Eisenhower argued that such aid was essential to prevent the collapse of all noncommunist governments in the area, in a chain reaction he called the *domino effect:* "You have a row of dominoes set up, you knock over the first one, and what will happen to the last one is the certainty that it will go over very quickly."

Despite joint French-American efforts the Vietminh forces gained strength in northern Vietnam. In the spring of 1954 they seized the isolated administrative fortress of Dienbienphu after a fifty-six-day siege. The spectacular victory gave the Vietminh negotiating leverage in the 1954 Geneva Accords, which partitioned Vietnam temporarily at the seventeenth parallel (see Map 29.1) and committed France to withdraw its forces from the area north of that line. The Accords also provided that within two years, in free elections, the voters in the two sectors would choose a unified government for the entire nation. The United States refused to sign the agreements and instead issued a separate protocol acknowledging the Accords and promising to "refrain from the threat or use of force to disturb them."

Eisenhower had no intention of allowing a communist victory in Vietnam's upcoming election. With the help of the CIA he made sure that a pro-American government took power in South Vietnam in June 1954, just before the accords were signed. Ngo Dinh Diem, an anticommunist Catholic who had spent eight years in the United States, returned to Vietnam as the premier of the French-backed South Vietnamese government. The next year, in a rigged election, Diem became president of an independent South Vietnam. Realizing that the popular Ho Chi Minh would easily win in both north and south, Diem then called off the reunification elections that were scheduled for 1956, a move the United States supported.

In March 1956 the last French soldiers left Saigon, the capital of South Vietnam, and the United States replaced France as the dominant foreign power in the region. American policymakers quickly asserted that a noncommunist South Vietnam was vital to U.S. security interests. In reality, Vietnam was too small a country to upset the international balance of power, and its communist movement was regional and intensely nationalistic rather than expansionist. Nevertheless, Eisenhower and subsequent U.S. presidents persisted in viewing Vietnam as part of the cold-war struggle to contain the communist threat to the free world. Between 1955 and 1961 the Eisenhower administration sent Diem an average of $200 million a year in aid and stationed approximately 675 American military advisers in Saigon. Having stepped up U.S. involvement there considerably, Eisenhower left office, passing the Vietnam situation to his successor, John F. Kennedy.

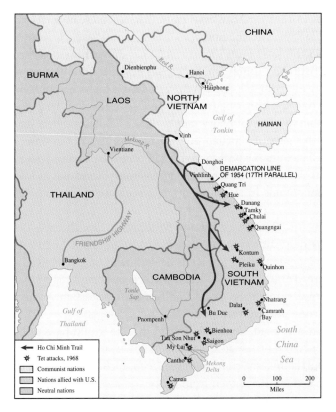

M A P 29.1
The Vietnam War, 1954–1975

The Vietnam War was a guerrilla war, fought in skirmishes and inconclusive encounters rather than decisive battles. Supporters of the National Liberation Front filtered into South Vietnam along the Ho Chi Minh Trail, which wound through Laos and Cambodia. In January 1968 Vietcong forces launched the Tet offensive, a surprise attack on several South Vietnamese cities and provincial centers. American vulnerability to these attacks served to undermine U.S. credibility and fueled opposition to the war.

President Kennedy saw Vietnam as an ideal testing ground for the counterinsurgency techniques that formed the centerpiece of his military policy (see Chapter 28). But he first had to prop up Diem's unpopular regime, which faced a growing military threat. In December 1960 the Communist Party in North Vietnam organized most of Diem's opponents in South Vietnam into a revolutionary movement known as the National Liberation Front (NLF). In response, Kennedy increased the number of American military "advisers" (an elastic term that included helicopter units and special forces), raising it to more than 16,000 by November 1963. To win the "hearts and minds" of Vietnamese peasants away from the insurgents and to increase agricultural production, he also sent economic development specialists. But

Kennedy refused to send combat troops to assist the South Vietnamese in what had become a guerrilla-style civil war with the north.

American aid did little good in South Vietnam. Diem's political inexperience and corruption, combined with his Catholicism in a predominantly Buddhist country, prevented him from creating a stable popular government. The NLF's guerrilla forces—called the Viet Cong by their opponents—made considerable headway against Diem's regime, using the revolutionary tactics of the Chinese leader Mao Zedong to blend into South Vietnam's civilian population "like fish in the water." They found a receptive audience among peasants who had been alienated by Diem's "strategic hamlet" program, which uprooted families and whole villages and moved them into barbed-wire compounds in a vain attempt to separate them from Ho Chi Minh's sympathizers.

Anti-Diem sentiment also flourished among Buddhists, who charged the government with religious persecution. Starting in May 1963 militant Buddhists staged a dramatic series of demonstrations against Diem, including several self-immolations that were recorded by American television crews. Diem's regime retaliated with raids on temples and mass arrests of Buddhist priests in August, prompting more antigovernment demonstrations.

As opposition to Diem deepened, Kennedy decided that he would have to be removed. Ambassador Henry Cabot Lodge Jr. let it be known in Saigon that the United States would support a military coup that had "a good chance of succeeding." On November 1, 1963, Diem was driven from office and assassinated by officers in the South Vietnamese army. America's role in the coup reinforced the links between the United States and the new regime in South Vietnam, making the prospect of withdrawal from the region less acceptable to U.S. policymakers.

Less than a month later Kennedy himself was assassinated. Although historians continue to debate whether Kennedy would have withdrawn American forces from Vietnam had he lived, his administration's actions clearly accelerated U.S. involvement. When Lyndon Johnson became president, he retained many of Kennedy's foreign policy advisers. Asserting that "I am not going to be the President who saw Southeast Asia go the way China went," he quickly declared he would maintain U.S. support for South Vietnam.

ESCALATION: THE JOHNSON YEARS

Diem's removal did not improve the efficiency or the popularity of the government in Saigon. Secretary of Defense Robert McNamara and other top advisers argued that only a rapid, full-scale deployment of U.S. forces could prevent the imminent defeat of the South Vietnamese. But Johnson would need at least tacit congressional support, perhaps even a declaration of war, to commit U.S. forces to an offensive strategy. During the summer of 1964 the president saw his opportunity. American naval forces were conducting surveillance missions off the North Vietnamese coast to aid South Vietnamese amphibious attacks. When the North Vietnamese resisted the attacks, President Johnson told the nation that on two separate occasions North Vietnamese torpedo boats had fired on American destroyers in international waters in the Gulf of Tonkin. At Johnson's request Congress authorized him to "take all necessary measures to repel any armed attack against the forces of the United States and to prevent further aggression." On August 7 the Gulf of Tonkin resolution passed in the Senate eighty-eight to two and in the House 416 to 0. Johnson's deceptive characterization of the unverified attack got him what he wanted—a sweeping mandate to conduct operations in Vietnam as he saw fit. The only formal approval of American intervention in Vietnam that Congress ever granted, the Tonkin resolution represented a significant expansion of presidential power.

Once congressional support was ensured and the 1964 elections had passed (see Chapter 28), the Johnson administration moved toward the Americanization of the war with Operation Rolling Thunder, a protracted bombing campaign. Begun in March 1965, by 1968 it had dropped a million tons of bombs on North Vietnam. Each B-52 sortie cost $30,000: by early 1966 the direct costs of the air war had exceeded $1.7 billion. From 1965 to 1973 the United States dropped three times as many bombs on North Vietnam, a country roughly the size of Texas, as had fallen on all of Europe, Asia, and Africa during World War II. The several hundred captured U.S. pilots downed in the raids then became pawns in prisoner-of-war negotiations with the North Vietnamese.

To the amazement of American advisers the bombings did not appear to impede the North's ability to wage war. The flow of troops and supplies to the South continued unabated as the North Vietnamese quickly rebuilt roads and bridges, moved munitions plants underground, and constructed networks of tunnels and shelters. Instead of destroying enemy morale and bringing the North Vietnamese to the bargaining table, Operation Rolling Thunder intensified their nationalism and will to fight.

A week after the launch of Operation Rolling Thunder the United States sent its first official ground troops into combat duty. Soon U.S. Marines were skirmishing with the enemy. Over the next three years the number of American troops in Vietnam grew dramatically. Although U.S. troops were accompanied by military forces from Australia, New Zealand, and South Korea, the war increasingly became an American war, fought for American aims. By 1966 more than 380,000 American soldiers were stationed in Vietnam; by 1967, 485,000; by 1968, 536,000.

The massive commitment of troops and air power threatened to destroy Vietnam's countryside. Besides the bombardment a defoliation campaign had seriously damaged agricultural production, undercutting the economic and cultural base of Vietnamese society. After one devastating but not unusual engagement a commanding officer reported, using the logic of the time, "It became necessary to destroy the town in order to save it." Graffiti on a plane that dropped defoliants read "Only you can prevent forests." (In later years defoliants such as Agent Orange were found to have highly toxic effects on both humans and the environment.) The destruction was not limited to North Vietnam; South Vietnam, America's ally, absorbed more than twice the bomb tonnage dropped on the North. In Saigon and other South Vietnamese cities the influx of American soldiers and dollars distorted local economies, spread corruption and prostitution, and triggered uncontrollable inflation and black-market activity.

Why did the dramatically increased American presence in Vietnam fail to turn the tide of the war? Some advisors argued that military intervention would accomplish little unless it was accompanied by reform in Saigon and increased popular support in the countryside. Other critics claimed that the United States never fully committed itself to a total victory—although what that term meant was never settled. Military strategy was inextricably tied to political considerations. For domestic reasons policymakers often searched for an elusive "middle ground" between all-out invasion (and the possibility of sparking a nuclear exchange between the two superpowers) and the politically unacceptable alternative of disengagement. Hoping to win a war of attrition, the Johnson administration assumed that American superiority in personnel and weaponry would ultimately triumph. But that limited commitment was never enough to ensure victory—however it was defined.

AMERICAN SOLDIERS' PERSPECTIVES ON THE WAR

Approximately 2.8 million Americans served in Vietnam. At an average age of only nineteen most of those servicemen and women were too young to vote or drink (the voting age was twenty-one until passage of the Twenty-sixth Amendment in 1971), but they were old enough to fight and die. Some were volunteers, including 7,000 women enlistees. Many others served because they were drafted. Until the nation shifted to an all-volunteer force in 1973, the draft stood as a concrete reminder of the government's impact on the lives of ordinary Americans. Blacks were drafted and died roughly in the same proportion as their share of the draft-age population (about 12 to 13 percent), although early in the war black casualty rates were significantly higher than average. Even more than in other recent wars, sons of the poor and the working class shouldered a disproportionate amount of the fighting, forming an estimated 80 percent of the enlisted ranks. Young men from more affluent backgrounds were more likely to avoid combat through student deferments, medical exemptions, and appointments to National Guard and reserve units— alternatives that made Johnson's Vietnam policy more acceptable to the middle class.

At first many draftees and enlistees shared common cold-war assumptions about the need to fight communism and the superiority of the American military. However, their experience in Vietnam quickly challenged simple notions of patriotism and the inevitability of victory. In "Nam" long days of boring menial work were punctuated by brief flashes of intense fighting. "Most of the time, nothing happened," a soldier recalled, "but when something did, it happened instantaneously and without warning." Rarely were there large-scale battles, only skirmishes; rather than front lines and conquered territory, there were only daytime operations in areas the Vietcong controlled at night.

Racism was a fact of everyday life. Because differentiating between friendly South Vietnamese and Vietcong sympathizers was difficult, many soldiers lumped

AMERICAN VOICES

A Vietnam Vet Remembers

DAVE CLINE

B *orn in 1947, Dave Cline grew up in a working-class family outside Buffalo, New York.*
Drafted by the army in 1967, Cline was eager to help fight communist aggression in
Vietnam. But after his arrival in Danang seven months later, his attitude toward the war
quickly changed. Cline described this transformation in an interview conducted in 1992.

I went to basic training at Fort Dix. . . . Down there, they used to give you basically two
raps on why you were going to Vietnam. One was that rap about we're going to help the
heroic South Vietnamese people. We're going to go fight for freedom [and repel] communist aggression. They'd show you the maps and stuff, the domino theory, the Red
Chinese are trying to engulf all of southeast Asia. The other rap was: killing communists
was your duty. . . .

First thing you do when you get in-country is, they give you these indoctrination classes
and they say, "Forget all that shit they told; you can't trust any of these people. They're not
really people anyway; they're gooks." . . . In other words: You see anyone with slant eyes,
that's your potential enemy—don't trust them. That sort of blows away any "help the
people" thing. . . .

I got wounded the last time out near the Cambodian border. This happened on
December 20, 1967. . . . The north Vietnamese launched a massive human wave attack. . . .

A guy came running up to my foxhole. We saw him coming from the next hole over
and we didn't know if it was an American retreating over to us or a Vietnamese, because
it was two in the morning. . . . I was sitting there with my rifle waiting to see, and all of a
sudden he stuck his rifle in. I saw the front side of an AK-47 and a muzzle flash, and then
I pulled my trigger. I shot him through the chest. I blacked out initially, but then I came
to and found a round went right through my knee. . . .

They carried me over to this guy I had shot. . . . He was dead. The sergeant started
giving me this pep talk, "Here's the gook you killed!" . . .

The kid looked about the same age as me. The first thing I started thinking was, Why
is he dead and I'm alive? . . .

Then after going into the hospital, I started thinking about that guy. I wonder if his
mother knows he's dead? I wonder if he had a girlfriend? Looking back, I think I was
retaining the sense that he was a human being.

SOURCE: Richard Stacewicz, *Winter Soldiers: An Oral History of the Vietnam Veterans Against the War*
(New York: Twayne, 1997), pp. 135–36, 140–41.

them together as "gooks." As a draftee noted of his indoctrination, "The only thing
they told us about the Vietcong was they were gooks. They were to be killed. Nobody
sits around and gives you their historical and cultural background. They're the
enemy. Kill, kill, kill" (see American Voices, "A Vietnam Vet Remembers").

Fighting and surviving under such conditions took its toll. One veteran explained that "The hardest thing to come to grips with was the fact that making it through Vietnam—surviving—is probably the only worthwhile part of the experience. It wasn't going over there and saving the world from communism or defending the country." Cynicism and bitterness were common. The pressure of waging war under such conditions drove many soldiers to seek escape in alcohol or drugs, which were cheap and readily available.

The women who served in Vietnam shared many of these experiences. As Women's Army Corp members (WACs), nurses, and civilians serving with organizations such as the United Service Organizations (USO), women volunteers witnessed death and mutilation on a massive scale. Though they tried to maintain a professional distance, as a navy nurse recalled, "It's pretty damn hard not getting involved when you see a nineteen- or twenty-year-old blond kid from the Midwest or California or the East Coast screaming and dying. A piece of my heart would go with each."

The Cold-War Consensus Unravels

In the twenty years following World War II, despite widespread affluence and confidence in the nation's cold-war leadership, there emerged a variety of challenges to the status quo. From the nonconforming Beats came a critical assault on corporate capitalism. Teenagers' embracing of rock 'n' roll defied the cultural norms of their elders. African Americans' boycotts, sit-ins, and freedom rides signaled a rising wind of protest about racial injustice. By 1965 such angry expressions of disaffection from mainstream America had multiplied dramatically. Criticism of the war in Vietnam mounted, as youthful protesters rebelled against traditional respect for the "system." The civil rights movement took on a more militant thrust and expanded beyond African Americans to other minority groups, while the feminist movement revived to challenge social values and the family structure itself. Together the various movements forced Americans to reassess basic assumptions about the nature of their society.

PUBLIC OPINION ON VIETNAM

President Kennedy and at first President Johnson enjoyed broad support for their conduct of foreign affairs. Both Democrats and Republicans approved Johnson's escalation of the war, and public opinion polls in 1965 and 1966 showed strong popular support for his policies. But in the late 1960s public opinion began to turn against the war. In July 1967 a Gallup poll revealed that for the first time a majority of Americans disapproved of Johnson's Vietnam policy and believed the war had reached a stalemate.

A Televised War

This harrowing scene from Saigon during the Tet offensive in 1968 depicts the head of the South Vietnamese National Police preparing to shoot a captured member of the Viet Cong. Telecast on U.S. network news, it was one of scores of disturbing images that flooded American living rooms during the Vietnam era and helped to sway public opinion against continued participation in what commentator Walter Cronkite called a "bloody experience" that would end in "stalemate." (AP/Wide World Photos)

Television had much to do with these attitudes. Vietnam was the first war in which television brought films of the fighting directly into the nation's living rooms. At the beginning of the conflict Americans watched footage of U.S. soldiers apparently advancing steadily through the countryside and heard reports of staggering Viet Cong losses and minimal U.S. casualties. Despite the glowing reports filed by the media and the administration on the progress of the war, by 1967 many administration officials had privately reached a more pessimistic conclusion. In November Secretary of Defense Robert McNamara sent a memo to the president arguing that continued escalation "would be dangerous, costly in lives, and unsatisfactory to the American people," but President Johnson continued to insist that victory in Vietnam was vital to U.S. national security and prestige. Journalists, especially those who had spent time in Vietnam, soon began to warn that the Johnson administration suffered from a "credibility gap." The administration, they charged, was concealing important and discouraging information about the war's progress. In February 1966 television coverage of hearings by the Senate Foreign Relations Committee (chaired by J. William Fulbright, an outspoken critic of the war) raised further questions about the administration's policy.

Economic developments put Johnson and his advisers even more on the defensive. In 1966 the federal deficit was $9.8 billion; in 1967 the Vietnam War cost the taxpayers $27 billion and the deficit jumped to $23 billion. Although the war consumed just 3 percent of the gross national product, its costs became more evident as the growing federal deficit nudged the inflation rate upward. Only in the summer of 1967 did Johnson ask for a 10 percent surcharge on individual and corporate income taxes, an increase that Congress did not approve until 1968. By then the inflationary spiral that would plague the U.S. economy throughout the 1970s was well under way.

Another major problem facing the Johnson administration was the growing strength and visibility of the antiwar movement. Between 1963 and 1965 peace activists in a variety of organizations staged periodic protests, vigils, and petition- and letter-writing campaigns against U.S. involvement in the war. After the escalation of combat in the spring of 1965 various antiwar coalitions, swelled by growing numbers of students, clergy, housewives, politicians, artists, and others opposed to the war, organized several mass demonstrations in Washington, bringing out 20,000 to 30,000 people at a time. A diverse lot, participants in these rallies shared a common skepticism about the means and aims of U.S. policy. The war was morally wrong, they argued, and antithetical to American ideals; the goal of an independent, anticommunist South Vietnam was unattainable; and American military involvement in Vietnam would not help the Vietnamese people.

STUDENT ACTIVISM AND THE COUNTERCULTURE

Although some of the most potent images of the 1960s show civil rights demonstrators, youthful protesters rebelling against the war in Vietnam, or "hippies" high on drugs and psychedelic music, American youth were not monolithic. Many young people, especially those in the working class, were critical of the more extreme expressions of rebellion. It was primarily college students—many of whom had been raised in a privileged environment, showered with consumer goods, and inculcated with faith in American institutions and leaders—who began to question U.S. foreign policy, racial injustice, and middle-class morals and conformity. Not all youth challenged authority in the 1960s, but those who did had a powerful impact.

In June 1962 forty students from Big Ten and Ivy League universities, disturbed by the gap they perceived between the ideals they had been taught to revere and the realities in American life, met in Port Huron, Michigan, to found Students for a Democratic Society (SDS). Tom Hayden wrote their manifesto, the Port Huron Statement, which expressed their disillusionment with the consumer culture and the gulf between the prosperous and the poor. These students rejected cold-war ideology and foreign policy, including but not limited to the Vietnam conflict. The founders of SDS referred to their movement as the "New Left" to distinguish themselves from the "Old Left"—communists and socialists of the 1930s and 1940s. Consciously adopting the activist tactics pioneered by members of the civil rights movement, they turned to grassroots organizing in cities and on college campuses.

The first major student protests erupted in the fall of 1964 at the University of California at Berkeley after administrators banned political activity near the Telegraph Avenue entrance, where student groups had traditionally distributed leaflets and recruited volunteers. In protest the major student organizations formed a coalition called the Free Speech Movement (FSM) and organized a sit-in at the administration building. The FSM owed a strong debt to the civil rights movement. Some students had just returned from Freedom Summer in Mississippi, radicalized by their experience. Mario Savio spoke for many of them:

> Last summer I went to Mississippi to join the struggle there for civil rights. This fall I am engaged in another phase of the same struggle, this time in Berkeley. The two battlefields may seem quite different to some observers, but this is not the case. The same rights are at stake in both places—the right to participate as citizens in a democratic society and to struggle against the same enemy. In Mississippi an autocratic and powerful minority rules, through organized violence, to suppress the vast, virtually powerless majority. In California, the privileged minority manipulates the university bureaucracy to suppress the students' political expression.

On a deeper level Berkeley students were challenging a university that in their view had grown too big and was too far removed from the major social issues of the day. Emboldened by the Berkeley movement students across the nation were soon protesting their universities' academic policies and then more passionately the Vietnam War.

The highly politicized activists of the New Left, who had developed a wide-ranging critique of American society, increasingly focused on the war, and they were joined by thousands of other students in protesting American participation in the Vietnam conflict. When President Johnson escalated the war in March 1965, faculty and students at the University of Michigan organized a teach-in against the war. Abandoning their classes, they debated the political, diplomatic, and moral aspects of the nation's involvement in Vietnam. Teach-ins quickly spread to other universities as students turned from their studies to protest the war.

Many protests centered on the draft, especially after the selective service system abolished student deferments in January 1966. To avoid the draft some young men enlisted in the National Guard or the reserves; others declared themselves conscientious objectors. Several thousand young men ignored their induction notices, risking prosecution for draft evasion. Others left the country, most often for Canada or Sweden. In public demonstrations of civil disobedience opponents of the war burned their draft cards, closed down induction centers, and on a few occasions broke into selective service offices.

As antiwar and draft protests multiplied students realized that their universities were deeply implicated in the war effort. In some cases as much as 60 percent

Columbia University Protests, 1968

At the height of the Vietnam War in 1968 Columbia University students launched a series of protests against military research contracts, university governance, and the construction of a gymnasium in a nearby Harlem neighborhood. (Steve Schapiro/Black Star)

of a university's research budget came from government contracts, especially those of the Defense Department. Protesters blocked recruiters from the Dow Chemical Company, the producer of napalm and Agent Orange. Arguing that universities should not train students for war, they demanded that the Reserve Officer Training Corps (ROTC) be removed from college campuses.

In the late 1960s student protesters joined the much larger antiwar movement of peace activists, housewives, religious leaders, and a few elective officials. After 1967 nationwide student strikes, mass demonstrations, and other organized protests became commonplace. In October 1967 more than 100,000 antiwar demonstrators marched on Washington, D.C., as part of "Stop the Draft Week." The event culminated in a "siege of the Pentagon," in which protesters clashed with police and federal marshals. Hundreds of people were arrested and several demonstrators beaten. Lyndon Johnson, who had once dismissed antiwar protesters as "nervous Nellies," rebellious children, or communist dupes, now had to face the reality of large-scale public opposition to his policies.

While the New Left took to the streets in protest, a growing number of young Americans embarked on a general revolution against authority and middle-class respectability. The "hippie"—attired in ragged blue jeans, tie-dyed T-shirt, beads, and army fatigues, with long, unkempt hair—symbolized the new counterculture, a youthful movement that glorified liberation from traditional social strictures.

Not surprisingly, given the importance of rock 'n' roll to 1950s' youth culture, popular music formed an important part of the counterculture. The folksinger Pete Seeger set the tone for the era's political idealism with songs such as the antiwar ballad "Where Have All the Flowers Gone?" Another folksinger, Joan Baez, gained national prominence for her rendition of the African American protest song "We Shall Overcome" and other folk and political anthems she performed at protest rallies in the mid-1960s. In 1963, the year of the Birmingham demonstrations and President Kennedy's assassination, Bob Dylan's "Blowin' in the Wind" reflected the impatience of people whose faith in "the system" was wearing thin.

Other winds of change in popular music came from the Beatles, four English working-class youths, who burst onto the American scene early in 1964. The Beatles' music, by turns lyrical and driving, was phenomenally successful, spawning a commercial and cultural phenomenon called Beatlemania. American youth's eager embrace of the Beatles deepened the generational divide between teenagers and their elders already set in motion by the popularity of rock 'n' roll in the 1950s. The Beatles also helped to pave the way for the more rebellious, angrier music of other British groups, notably the Rolling Stones, whose raunchy 1965 "(I Can't Get No) Satisfaction" not only signaled a new openness about sexuality but also made fun of the consumer culture ("He can't be a man 'cause he doesn't smoke the same cigarettes as me").

Drugs intertwined with music as a crucial element of the youth culture. The recreational use of drugs—especially marijuana and the hallucinogen lysergic acid diethylamide, popularly known as LSD, or "acid"—was celebrated in popular music. San Francisco bands, such as the Grateful Dead and the Jefferson Airplane, and musicians like the Seattle-born guitarist Jimi Hendrix developed a musical style known as "acid rock," which was characterized by long, heavily amplified guitar solos accompanied by psychedelic lighting effects. In August 1969, 400,000 young people journeyed to Bethel, New York, to "get high" on music, drugs, and sex at the three-day Woodstock Music and Art Fair. Despite torrential rain and numerous drug overdoses, most enjoyed the festival, which was heralded as the birth of the "Woodstock nation."

For a brief time adherents of the counterculture believed a new age was dawning. They experimented in communal living and glorified uninhibited sexuality. In 1967 the "world's first Human Be-In" drew 20,000 people to Golden Gate Park in San Francisco. The Beat poet Allen Ginsberg "purified" the site with a Buddhist ritual, and the LSD advocate Timothy Leary, a former Harvard psychology instructor, urged the gathering to "turn on to the scene, tune in to what is happening, and drop out." That summer—dubbed the "Summer of Love"—San Francisco's Haight-Ashbury, New York's East Village, and Chicago's Uptown neighborhoods swelled with young dropouts, drifters, and teenage runaways dubbed "flower children" by observers. Their faith in instant love and peace quickly turned sour, however, as they suffered bad drug trips, venereal disease, loneliness, and violence. Although many young people kept their distance from both the counterculture and the antiwar movement, to many adult observers it seemed that all of American youth were rejecting political, social, and cultural norms.

THE WIDENING STRUGGLE FOR CIVIL RIGHTS

The counterculture and the antiwar movement were not the only social movements to challenge the status quo in the 1960s. The frustration and anger of blacks boiled over in a new racial militance as the struggle moved outside the South and took on the more stubborn problems of entrenched poverty and racism. The rhetoric and tactics of the emerging black-power movement shattered the existing civil rights coalition and galvanized white opposition.

Once the system of legal, or *de jure,* segregation had fallen, the civil rights movement turned to the more difficult task of eliminating the *de facto* segregation, enforced by custom, that made blacks second-class citizens throughout the nation. Outside the South racial discrimination was less flagrant, but it was pervasive, especially in education, housing, and employment. Although the *Brown* decision outlawed separate schools, it did nothing to change the educational system in areas where schools were all-black or all-white because of residential segregation. Not until 1973 did federal judges begin to extend the desegregation of schools, which had begun in the South two decades earlier, to the rest of the country.

As civil rights leaders took on northern racism, the movement fractured along generational lines. Some younger activists, eager for confrontation and rapid social change, questioned the very goal of integration into white society. Black separatism, espoused by earlier black leaders such as Marcus Garvey in the 1920s (see Chapter 23), was revived in the 1960s by the Nation of Islam, a religious group with more than 10,000 members and many more sympathizers. Popularly known as the Black Muslims, the organization was hostile to whites and stressed black pride, unity, and self-help.

The Black Muslims' most charismatic figure was Malcolm X. A brilliant debater and spellbinding speaker, Malcolm X preached a philosophy quite different from Martin Luther King's. He advocated militant protest and separatism, though he condoned the use of violence only for self-defense. Hostile to the traditional civil rights organizations, he caustically referred to the 1963 March on Washington as the "Farce on Washington." In 1964, after a power struggle with the founder of the Black Muslims, Elijah Muhammed, Malcolm X broke with the Nation of Islam. Following a pilgrimage to Mecca and a tour of Africa, he embraced the liberation struggles of all colonized peoples. But before he could fully pursue his new agenda, he was assassinated while delivering a speech at the Audubon Ballroom in Harlem on February 21, 1965. Three Black Muslims were later convicted of his murder.

A more secular black nationalist movement emerged in 1966 when young black SNCC and CORE activists, following the lead of Stokely Carmichael, began to call for black self-reliance and racial pride under the banner of "Black Power." Amid growing distrust of white domination, SNCC effectively ejected its white members.

In the same year Huey Newton and Bobby Seale, two college students in Oakland, California, founded the Black Panthers, a militant self-defense organization dedicated to protecting local blacks from police violence. The Panthers' organization quickly spread to other cities, where members undertook a wide range of community organizing projects, including interracial efforts, but their affinity for Third World revolutionary movements and armed struggle became their most publicized attribute.

Among the most significant legacies of black power was the assertion of racial pride. Many young blacks insisted on using the term *Afro-American* rather than *Negro,* a term they found demeaning because of its historical association with slavery and racism. Rejecting white tastes and standards, blacks wore African clothing and hairstyles and helped to awaken interest in black history, art, and literature. By the 1970s many colleges and universities were offering programs in black studies.

The new black assertiveness alarmed many white Americans. They had been willing to go along with the moderate reforms of the 1950s and early 1960s but became wary when blacks began demanding immediate access to higher-paying jobs, housing in white neighborhoods, education in integrated schools, and increased political power. Another major reason for the erosion of white support was a wave of riots that struck the nation's cities. Lacking education and skills, successive generations of blacks had moved out of the rural South in search of work that paid an adequate wage. In the North many remained unemployed. Resentful of white landlords who owned the substandard housing they were forced to live in and white shopkeepers who denied them jobs in their neighborhoods, many blacks also hated police, whose violent presence in black neighborhoods seemed that of "an occupying army." Stimulated by the successes of southern blacks who had challenged whites and gotten results, young urban blacks expressed their grievances through their own brand of direct action.

The first "long hot summer" began in July 1964 in New York City, when police shot a young black criminal suspect in Harlem. Angry youths looted and rioted there for a week. Over the next four years the volatile issue of police brutality set off riots in dozens of cities. In August 1965 the arrest of a young black motorist in the Watts section of Los Angeles sparked six days of rioting that left thirty-four blacks dead. The riots of 1967 were the most serious (see Map 29.2), engulfing twenty-two cities in July and August. The most devastating outbreaks occurred in Newark and Detroit. Forty-three people were killed in Detroit alone, nearly all of them black, and $50 million worth of property destroyed. As in most of the riots, the arson and looting in Detroit targeted white-owned stores and property, but there was little physical violence against white people.

On July 29, 1967, President Johnson appointed a special commission to investigate the riots. The final report of the National Advisory Commission on Civil Disorders, released in March 1968, detailed the continuing inequality and racism of urban life. It also issued a warning: "Our nation is moving toward two societies, one black, one white—separate and unequal. . . . What white Americans have never

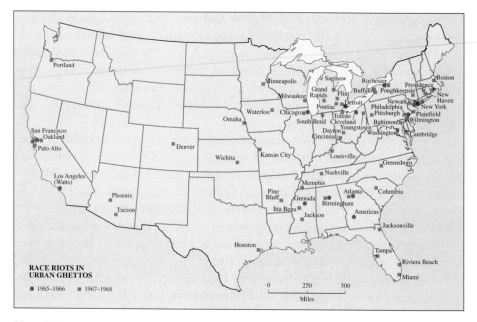

M A P 29.2
Racial Unrest in America's Cities, 1965–1968

American cities suffered through four "long hot summers" of rioting in the mid-1960s. In 1967, the worst year, riots broke out across the United States, including the South and West. Major riots did not usually occur in the same city two years in a row.

fully understood—but what the Negro can never forget—is that white society is deeply implicated in the ghetto. White institutions created it, white institutions maintain it, and white society condones it."

On April 4, 1968, barely a month after the Commission on Civil Disorders released its report, Martin Luther King Jr. was assassinated in Memphis, Tennessee, by James Earl Ray, a white ex-convict whose motive was unknown. King's death set off an explosion of urban rioting. Violence broke out in more than a hundred cities. With King's assassination the civil rights movement lost the one leader best able to stir the conscience of white America.

THE LEGACY OF THE CIVIL RIGHTS MOVEMENT

The 1960s brought permanent, indeed revolutionary, changes in American race relations. Jim Crow segregation was overturned, and federal legislation passed to ensure protection of black Americans' most basic civil rights. The enfranchisement of blacks in the southern states ended political control by all-white state Democratic Parties and allowed black candidates to enter the political arena. White candidates who had once been ardent segregationists began to court the black vote. In time Martin Luther King's greatness was recognized even among whites in the South; in 1986 his birthday became a national holiday.

Yet much remained undone. The more entrenched forms of segregation and discrimination persisted. African Americans, particularly those in the central cities, continued to make up a disproportionate number of the poor, the unemployed, and the undereducated. As the civil rights movement gradually splintered, its agenda remained unfinished.

Despite its limitations, the black civil rights movement provided a fresh and innovative model for social change. Although Mexican Americans had been working actively for civil rights since the 1930s (see Chapter 24), poverty, an uncertain legal status, and language barriers made their political mobilization difficult. That situation began to change when the Mexican American Political Association (MAPA) mobilized support for John F. Kennedy and in return Kennedy appointed several Mexican American leaders to posts in Washington. Over the next four years MAPA and other political organizations worked successfully to elect Mexican American candidates to Congress: in the House Edward Roybal of California and

Mourning Martin Luther King Jr.

Thousands of African Americans mourned the death of the country's foremost civil rights leader, Martin Luther King Jr., who had been assassinated in Memphis, Tennessee, on April 4, 1968. Among those who marched alongside King's casket, borne by a simple farm wagon pulled by mules, were future presidential candidate Jesse Jackson (in green) and future U.N. ambassador Andrew Young (at the left corner of the casket). During that week racial uprisings broke out in more than a hundred cities. (Wide World Photos, Inc.)

Henry González and Elizo de la Garza of Texas; in the Senate Joseph Montoya of New Mexico.

Younger Mexican Americans quickly grew impatient with MAPA, however. The barrios of Los Angeles and other western cities produced the militant Brown Berets, modeled on the Black Panthers (who wore black berets). Rejecting the assimilationist approach of their elders, 1,500 Mexican American students met in Denver in 1969 to hammer out a new nationalist political and cultural agenda. They proclaimed a new term, *Chicano,* to replace *Mexican American,* and later organized a new political party, La Raza Unida (The United Race), to promote Chicano interests and candidates. In California and other southwestern states students staged demonstrations and boycotts to press for bilingual education, the hiring of more Chicano teachers, and the creation of Chicano studies programs. By the 1970s dozens of such programs were offered at universities throughout the region.

Chicano strategists also pursued economic objectives. Working in the fields around Delano, California, the labor leader Cesar Chavez organized the United Farm Workers (UFW), the first union to represent migrant workers successfully. A 1965 grape pickers' strike and a nationwide boycott of table grapes brought Chavez and his union national publicity and won support from the AFL-CIO and from Senator Robert F. Kennedy of New York. Victory came in 1970 when California grape growers signed contracts recognizing the UFW.

North American Indians also found a model in the civil rights movement. Numbering nearly 800,000 in the 1960s, Indians were an exceedingly diverse group, divided by language, tribal history, region, and degree of integration into the mainstream of American life. But they shared an unemployment rate ten times the national average, as well as the worst poverty, the most inadequate housing, the highest disease rates, and the least access to education of any group in the United States.

As early as World War II the National Council of American Indians had lobbied for improvement of those conditions. In the 1960s some Indian groups became more assertive. Like the young militants in the black civil rights movement, they challenged the accommodationist approach of their elders. Proposing a new name for themselves—*Native Americans*—they organized protests and demonstrations to build support for their cause (see American Voices, "The Trail of Broken Treaties"). In 1968 several Chippewas from Minnesota organized the militant American Indian Movement (AIM), which drew its strength from the third of the Native American population who lived in "red ghettos" in cities throughout the West.

In February 1973, 200 Sioux organized by AIM leaders began an occupation of the tiny village of Wounded Knee, South Dakota, the site of an army massacre of the Sioux in 1890 (see Chapter 16). They were protesting the light sentences given to a group of white men convicted of killing a Sioux in 1972. To dramatize their cause the protesters took eleven hostages and occupied several buildings. But when a gun battle with the FBI left one protester dead and another wounded, the seventy-one-day siege collapsed. Although the new Native American activism helped to

AMERICAN VOICES
The Trail of Broken Treaties
MARY CROW DOG

*I*n November 1972, nineteen-year-old Mary Crow Dog traveled to Washington, D.C., with
several hundred other Sioux from the Rosebud and Pine Ridge reservations in South
Dakota. As she explains in her autobiography, their group was one of several caravans participating in a protest known as the Trail of Broken Treaties, which ended in a six-day occupation of the Bureau of Indian Affairs (BIA) headquarters. Their demands included restoration
of native lands and resources, reinstitution of the treaty-making rights of the Indian Nations,
and replacement of the BIA with an agency more attuned to their rights and cultures.

We had been promised food and accommodation, but due to government pressure many
church groups which had offered to put us up and feed us got scared and backed off. . . .

Somebody suggested, "Let's all go to the BIA." It seemed the natural thing to do, to go
to the Bureau of Indian Affairs building on Constitution Avenue. . . . It was "our" building after all. Besides, that was what we had come for, to complain about the treatment the
bureau was dishing out to us. . . . Next thing I knew we were in it. We spilled into the
building like a great avalanche. Some people put up a tipi on the front lawn. . . . The
building finally belonged to us and we lost no time turning it into a tribal village. . . .

We pushed the police and guards out of the building. . . . We had formulated twenty
Indian demands. These were all rejected by the few bureaucrats sent to negotiate with
us. . . . Soon we listened to other voices as the Occupation turned into a siege. I heard
somebody yelling, "The pigs are here." . . . A fight broke out between the police and our
security. Some of our young men got hit over the head with police clubs and we saw the
blood streaming down their faces. . . .

From then on, every morning we were given a court order to get out by six P.M. Come
six o'clock and we would be standing there ready to join battle. I think many brothers and
sisters were prepared to die right on the steps of the BIA building. . . .

In the end a compromise was reached. The government said . . . they would appoint
two high administration officials to seriously consider our twenty demands. . . . Of course,
our twenty points were never gone into afterward. . . . But morally it had been a great
victory. We had faced White America collectively, not as individual tribes. We had stood
up to the government and gone through our baptism of fire.

SOURCE: Mary Crow Dog, *Lakota Woman* (New York: Grove Weidenfeld, 1990), pp. 84–85, 88–91.

alienate many white onlookers, it did spur government action on tribal issues (see
Chapter 31).

Civil rights also sparked a new awareness among some predominantly white
groups. Homosexual men and women banded together to protest legal and social
oppression based on their sexual orientation. In 1969 the gay liberation movement

Wounded Knee Revisited

In 1973 members of the American Indian Movement staged a seventy-one-day protest at Wounded Knee, South Dakota, the site of the 1890 massacre of 200 Sioux by U.S. soldiers. The takeover was sparked by the murder of a local Sioux by a group of whites but quickly expanded to include demands for basic reforms in federal Indian policy and tribal governance. (UPI/Corbis-Bettmann)

was born in the "Stonewall riot" in New York City, when patrons of a gay bar fought back against police harassment. The assertion of gay pride that followed the incident drew heavily on the language and tactics of the civil rights movement. Activists took the new name of *gay* rather than *homosexual;* founded advocacy groups, newspapers, and political organizations to challenge discrimination and prejudice; and offered emotional support to those who "came out" and publicly affirmed their homosexuality. For gays as well as members of various ethnic and cultural groups, political activism based on heightened group identity represented one of the most significant legacies of the African American struggle.

THE REVIVAL OF FEMINISM

The black civil rights movement also helped to reactivate feminism, a movement that had been languishing since the 1920s. Just as the abolition movement had been the training ground for women's rights advocates in the nineteenth century, the black struggle became an inspiration for young feminists in the 1960s. But the revival of feminism also sprang from social and demographic changes that affected women young and old. By 1970, 42.6 percent of women were working, and four out of ten working women were married. Especially significant was the growth in the number of working women with preschool children—up from 12 percent in 1950 to 30 percent in 1970.

Another significant change was increased access to education for women. Immediately after World War II the percentage of college students who were women declined. The GI Bill gave men a temporary advantage in access to higher education. At the height of the baby boom many college women dropped out of school to marry and raise families. By 1960, however, the percentage of college students who were women had risen to 35 percent; in 1970 it reached 41 percent.

The meaning of marriage was changing, too. The baby boom turned out to be only a temporary interruption of a century-long decline in the birth rate. The introduction of the birth control pill, first marketed in 1960, and the intrauterine device (IUD) helped women control their fertility. Women had fewer children, and because of an increased life expectancy (seventy-five years in 1970—up from fifty-four years in 1920), they devoted proportionally fewer years to raising children. At the same time the divorce rate, which had risen slowly throughout the twentieth century, rose markedly as the states liberalized divorce laws. As a result of these changes traditional gender expectations were dramatically undermined. American women's lives now usually included work and marriage, often child rearing and a career, and possibly bringing up children alone after a divorce. Those changing social realities created a major constituency for the emerging women's movement of the 1960s.

Older, politically active professional women sought change by working through the political system. This group was galvanized in part by a report by the Presidential Commission on the Status of Women (1963), which documented the employment and educational discrimination women faced. More important than the report's rather conservative recommendations was the rudimentary nationwide network of women in public life that formed in the course of the commission's work.

Another spark that ignited the revival of feminism was Betty Friedan's pointed indictment of suburban domesticity, *The Feminine Mystique,* published in 1963. Women responded enthusiastically to Friedan's book—especially white, college-educated, middle-class women. The book sold 3 million copies and was excerpted in many women's magazines. *The Feminine Mystique* gave women a vocabulary with which to express their dissatisfaction and promoted women's self-realization through employment, continuing education, and other activities outside the home.

Like so many other constituencies in postwar America, women's rights activists looked to the federal government for help. Especially important was the Civil Rights Act of 1964, which had as great an impact on women as it did on blacks and other minorities. Title VII, which barred discrimination in employment on the basis of race, religion, national origin, or sex, eventually became a powerful tool in the fight against sex discrimination. At first, however, the Equal Employment Opportunity Commission (EEOC) avoided implementing it.

Dissatisfied with the Commission's reluctance to defend women's rights, Friedan and others founded the National Organization for Women (NOW) in 1966. Modeling itself on groups such as the NAACP, NOW aimed to be a civil rights organization for women. "The purpose of NOW," an early statement declared, "is to take action to bring women into full participation in the mainstream of American society now, exercising all the privileges and responsibilities thereof in truly equal partnership with men." Under Friedan, who served as NOW's first president, membership grew from 1,000 in 1967 to 15,000 in 1971. Men made up a fourth of NOW's early membership. The group is still the largest feminist organization in the United States.

Another group of new feminists, the women's liberationists, came to the women's movement through their civil rights work. White women had made up about half the students who went south with SNCC in the Freedom Summer project of 1964. These college women developed self-confidence and organizational skills working in the South, and they found role models in older southern women like Ella Baker, Anne Braden, and Virginia Foster Durr, who were prominent in the civil rights movement. Yet women volunteers also found they were expected to do all the cleaning and cooking at the Freedom Houses where SNCC volunteers lived.

After 1965 black militants made white women unwelcome in the civil rights movement. But when these women transferred their energies to the antiwar groups that were emerging in that period, they found the New Left equally male-dominated. When the antiwar movement adopted draft resistance as a central strategy, women found themselves marginalized. Those women who tried to raise feminist issues at conventions were shouted off the platform with jeers such as "Move on, little girl, we have more important issues to talk about here than women's liberation."

Around 1967 the contradiction between the New Left's lip service to egalitarianism and women's treatment by male leaders caused women radicals to realize that they needed their own movement. In contrast to groups such as NOW, which had traditional organizational structures and dues-paying members, these women formed loose collectives whose shifting membership often lacked any formal structure. They organized independently in five or six different cities, including Chicago, San Francisco, and New York.

Members of the women's liberation movement (or "women's lib," as it was dubbed by the somewhat hostile media) went public in 1968 in a protest at the Miss America Pageant. Their demonstration featured a "freedom trash can" into which they encouraged women to throw false eyelashes, hair curlers, brassieres, and girdles—all of which they branded as symbols of female oppression. An activity with a more lasting impact was consciousness raising—group sessions in which women shared their experiences of being female. Swapping stories about being passed over for a promotion, needing a husband's signature on a credit-card application, or enduring the whistles and leers of men while walking down the street helped participants to realize that their individual problems were part of a wider pattern of oppression. The slogan "The personal is political" became a rallying cry of the movement.

By 1970 a growing convergence of interests began to blur the distinction between women's rights and women's liberation. Radical women realized that key feminist goals—child care, equal pay, and abortion rights—could best be achieved in the political arena. At the same time more traditional activists developed a broader view of the women's movement, tentatively including divisive issues such as abortion and lesbian rights. Although the movement remained largely white and

Women's Liberation

Arguing that beauty contests were degrading to women, members of the National Women's Liberation Party staged a protest against the Miss America pageant held in Atlantic City, New Jersey, in September 1968. (Wide World Photos, Inc.)

middle class, feminists were beginning to think of themselves as part of a broad, growing, and increasingly influential social crusade that would continue to grow.

The Long Road Home, 1968–1975

In 1968, as Lyndon Johnson planned his reelection campaign, antiwar protests and rising battlefield casualties had begun to erode public support for a war that seemed to have no end. Moreover, since Diem's assassination in 1963 South Vietnam had undergone a confusing series of military coups and countercoups. In the spring of 1966 the Johnson administration pressured the unpopular South Vietnamese government to adopt democratic reforms, including a new constitution and popular elections. In September 1967 U.S. officials helped to elect General Nguyen Van Thieu president of South Vietnam. Thieu's regime, the administration hoped, would stabilize politics in South Vietnam, advance the military struggle against the communists, and legitimize the South Vietnamese government in the eyes of the American public.

1968: A YEAR OF SHOCKS

The administration's hopes evaporated on January 30, 1968, when the Viet Cong unleashed a massive, well-coordinated assault on major urban areas in South Vietnam. Known as the Tet offensive, the assault was timed to coincide with the lunar new year, a festive Vietnamese holiday. Viet Cong forces struck thirty-six of the forty-four provincial capitals and five of the six major cities, including Saigon, where they raided the supposedly impregnable U.S. embassy (see Map 29.1). In strict military terms the Tet offensive was a failure for the Viet Cong since it did not provoke the intended collapse of the South Vietnamese government. But its long-term effect was quite different. The daring attack made a mockery of official pronouncements that the United States was winning the war and swung American public opinion more strongly against the war. Just before the offensive a Gallup poll found that 56 percent of Americans considered themselves "hawks" (supporters of the war), while only 28 percent identified with the "doves" (opponents). Three months after Tet the doves outnumbered the hawks 42 to 41 percent. This turnaround in public opinion did not mean that a majority of Americans supported the peace movement, however. Many who called themselves doves had simply concluded that the war was unwinnable and were therefore opposed to it on pragmatic rather than moral grounds. As a housewife told a pollster, "I want to get out, but I don't want to give up."

The growing opposition to the war spilled over into the 1968 presidential campaign. Even before Tet, Senator Eugene J. McCarthy of Minnesota had entered the Democratic primaries as an antiwar candidate. President Johnson won the early New Hampshire primary, but McCarthy received a stunning 42.2 percent of the vote. His strong showing against the president reflected profound public dissatisfaction with the course of the war—even among those who were hawks.

Johnson realized that his political support was evaporating. On March 31 and at the end of an otherwise mundane televised address, he stunned the nation by announcing that he would not seek reelection. Johnson had already reversed his policy of incremental escalation of the war. Now he called a partial bombing halt and vowed to devote his remaining months in office to the search for peace. On May 10, 1968, preliminary peace talks between the United States and North Vietnam opened in Paris.

Just four days after Johnson's withdrawal from the presidential race, Martin Luther King Jr. was assassinated in Memphis. The ensuing riots in cities across the country left forty-three people dead. Soon afterward, students protesting Columbia University's plans for expanding into a neighboring ghetto and displacing its residents occupied several campus buildings. The brutal response of the New York City police helped to radicalize even more students. The next month a massive strike by students and labor unions toppled the French government. Student unrest seemed likely to become a worldwide phenomenon.

Then came the final painful tragedy of the year. Senator Robert Kennedy, who had entered the Democratic presidential primaries in March, had quickly become a front runner. On June 5, 1968, as he celebrated his victory in the California primary, he was shot dead by a young Palestinian who was thought to oppose Kennedy's pro-Israeli stance. Robert Kennedy's assassination shattered the dreams of many who had hoped that social change could be achieved by working through the political system. His death also weakened the Democratic Party. In his brief but dramatic campaign Kennedy had excited and energized the traditional members of the New Deal coalition, including blue-collar workers and black voters, in a way that the more cerebral Eugene McCarthy, who appealed mostly to the antiwar movement, never did.

The Democratic Party never fully recovered from Johnson's withdrawal and Kennedy's assassination. McCarthy's campaign limped along, while Senator George S. McGovern of South Dakota entered the Democratic race in an effort to keep the Kennedy forces together. Meanwhile, Vice President Hubert H. Humphrey lined up pledges from traditional Democratic constituencies—unions, urban machines, and state political organizations. Democrats found themselves on the verge of nominating not an antiwar candidate but a public figure closely associated with Johnson's war policies.

At the August Democratic nominating convention the political divisions generated by the war consumed the party. Most of the drama occurred not in the convention hall but outside on the streets of Chicago. Led by Jerry Rubin and Abbie Hoffman around 10,000 protesters descended on the city, calling for an end to the war, the legalization of marijuana, and the abolition of money. To mock those inside the convention hall, these "Yippies," as the group called themselves, nominated a pig for president. Their stunts, geared toward maximizing their media exposure, diverted attention from the more serious and far more numerous antiwar activists who had come to Chicago as convention delegates or volunteers.

Richard J. Daley, the Democratic mayor of Chicago, who had grown increasingly angry as protesters disrupted his convention, called out the police to break up the demonstrations. Several nights of skirmishes between protesters and police culminated on the evening of the nominations. In what an official report later described as a "police riot," patrolmen attacked protesters with Mace, tear gas, and clubs as demonstrators chanted, "The whole world is watching!" Television networks broadcast a film of the riot as the nominating speeches were being made, cementing a popular impression of the Democrats as the party of disorder. Inside the hall the Democrats dispiritedly nominated Hubert H. Humphrey, who chose Senator Edmund S. Muskie of Maine as his running mate. The delegates approved a middle-of-the-road platform that endorsed continued fighting in Vietnam while the administration explored diplomatic means of ending the conflict.

The disruptive Democratic convention unleashed a backlash against antiwar protesters. The general public did not differentiate between the disruptive antics of the Yippies and the more responsible behavior of those activists who were trying to work within the system. Polls showed overwhelming support for Mayor Daley and the police.

The turmoil surrounding the New Left and the antiwar movement strengthened support for proponents of "law and order," which became a conservative catch phrase for the next several years. Indeed, many Americans, though opposed to the war, were fed up with protest and dissent. Governor George C. Wallace of Alabama, a third-party candidate, skillfully exploited their growing disapproval of the antiwar movement by making student protests and urban riots his chief campaign issues. But Wallace, who in 1963 had promised to enforce "segregation now . . . segregation tomorrow . . . and segregation forever," also exploited the mounting backlash against the civil rights movement. Articulating the resentments of many working-class whites, he combined attacks on liberal intellectuals and government elites with strident denunciations of school desegregation and forced busing.

Even more than George Wallace, Richard Nixon tapped the increasingly conservative mood of the electorate. After his unsuccessful presidential campaign in 1960 and his loss in the California gubernatorial race in 1962, Nixon engineered an amazing political comeback and in 1968 won the Republican presidential nomination. He chose Spiro Agnew, the conservative governor of Maryland, as his running mate to attract southern voters, especially Wallace supporters, who opposed Democratic civil rights legislation. Nixon pledged to represent the "quiet voice" of the "great majority of Americans, the forgotten Americans, the nonshouters, the nondemonstrators."

Despite the Democratic debacle in Chicago the election was a close one. In the last weeks of the campaign Humphrey rallied by gingerly disassociating himself from Johnson's war policies. Then in a televised address on October 31 President Johnson announced a complete halt to the bombing of North Vietnam. Nixon countered by intimating that he had his own plan to end the war—although in reality no such plan existed. On election day Nixon received 43.4 percent of the vote to Humphrey's 42.7 percent, defeating him by a scant 510,000 votes out of the 73 million that were cast. Wallace finished with 13.5 percent of the popular vote. Though Nixon owed his election largely to the split in the Democratic coalition, the success of his southern strategy presaged the emergence of a new Republican majority. In the meantime, however, the Democrats retained a majority in both houses of Congress.

The closeness of the 1968 election suggested how polarized American society had become. Nixon appealed to a segment of society that came to be known as the *silent majority*—the hard-working, nonprotesting, generally white American. Although his victory suggested a growing consensus among voters who were "unblack, unpoor, and unyoung," heated protest and controversy would persist until the war ended.

NIXON'S WAR

Vietnam, long Lyndon Johnson's war, now became Richard Nixon's. At first Nixon sought to end the war by expanding its scope, as a means of pressuring the North Vietnamese to negotiate. But Nixon and his national security adviser, Henry

Kissinger, soon realized that the public would not support such an approach. Thus, shortly after Nixon took office, he sent a letter to the North Vietnamese leaders proposing mutual troop withdrawals. In March 1969, to convince North Vietnam that the United States meant business, Nixon ordered clandestine bombing raids on neutral Cambodia, through which the North Vietnamese had been transporting supplies and reinforcements.

When the intensified bombing failed to end the war, Nixon and Kissinger adopted a policy of Vietnamization. On June 8, 1969, Nixon announced that 25,000 American troops would be withdrawn by August and replaced by South Vietnamese forces. As the U.S. ambassador to Vietnam, Ellsworth Bunker, noted cynically, Vietnamization was just a matter of changing "the color of the bodies." Antiwar demonstrators denounced the new policy, which protected American lives at the expense of the Vietnamese but would not end the war. On October 15, 1969, in cities across the country, millions of Americans joined a one-day "moratorium" against the war. A month later more than a quarter of a million people mobilized in Washington in the largest antiwar demonstration to date.

To discredit his critics Nixon denounced student demonstrators as "bums" and stated that "North Vietnam cannot defeat or humiliate the United States. Only Americans can do that." Vice President Spiro Agnew attacked dissenters as "ideological eunuchs" and "nattering nabobs of negativism." Nixon staunchly insisted that he would not be swayed by the mounting protests against the war. During the November 1969 march on Washington the president barricaded himself in the White House and watched football on television.

On April 30, 1970, the bombing of Cambodia, which Nixon had kept secret from both the public and from Congress, culminated in an "incursion" into Cambodia by American ground forces to destroy enemy havens there. The invasion proved only a short-term setback for the North Vietnamese. More critically, the American action in Cambodia—along with the ongoing North Vietnamese intervention there—destabilized the country, exposing it to a takeover by the ruthless Khmer Rouge later in the 1970s.

When the *New York Times* uncovered the secret invasion of Cambodia, outrage led antiwar leaders to organize a national student strike. On May 4 at Kent State University outside Cleveland, panicky National Guardsmen fired into a crowd of students at an antiwar rally. Four people were killed and eleven more wounded. Only two of those who were killed had been attending the demonstration; the other two were just passing by on their way to class. Soon afterward National Guardsmen stormed a dormitory at Jackson State College in Mississippi, killing two black students. More than 450 colleges closed in protest, and 80 percent of all campuses experienced some kind of disturbance. In June 1970, immediately after the Kent State slayings, a Gallup poll identified campus unrest as the issue that most troubled Americans.

At the same time, however, dissatisfaction with the war continued to spread. Congressional opposition to the war, which had been growing since the Fulbright hearings in 1966, intensified with the invasion of Cambodia. In June 1970 the Senate expressed its disapproval by voting to repeal the Gulf of Tonkin resolution and by cutting off funding for operations in Cambodia. Even the soldiers in Vietnam were showing mounting opposition to their mission. The number of troops who refused to follow combat orders increased steadily, and thousands of U.S. soldiers deserted. Among the majority who fought on, many sewed peace symbols on their uniforms. In the heat of battle a number of overbearing junior officers were sometimes "fragged"—killed or wounded in grenade attacks by their own soldiers. At home members of a group called Vietnam Veterans Against the War turned in their combat medals at demonstrations outside the U.S. Capitol.

In 1971 Americans were appalled by revelations of the sheer brutality of the war when Lieutenant William L. Calley was court-martialed for atrocities committed in the village of My Lai. In March 1968 Calley and the platoon under his command had apparently murdered 350 Vietnamese villagers in retaliation for casualties sustained in an earlier engagement. The military court sentenced Calley to life in prison for his part in the massacre. Yet George Wallace and some congressional conservatives called him a hero. President Nixon had Calley's sentence reduced; he was paroled in 1974.

After a final outbreak of protest and violence following the incident at Kent State, antiwar activism began to ebb. The antiwar movement was weakened in part by internal divisions within the New Left. In the late 1960s SDS and other antiwar groups fell victim to police harassment, and Federal Bureau of Investigation (FBI) and Central Intelligence Agency (CIA) agents infiltrated and disrupted radical organizations. After 1968 the New Left splintered into factions, its energy spent. One radical faction broke off from SDS and formed the Weathermen, a tiny band of self-styled revolutionaries who embraced terrorist tactics that alienated more moderate activists.

Nixon's Vietnamization policy also played a role in the decline of antiwar protest by dramatically reducing the number of soldiers in combat. When Nixon took office, more than 543,000 American soldiers were serving in Vietnam; by the end of 1970 there were 334,000, and two years later there were 24,200. Nixon's promise to continue troop withdrawals, end the draft, and institute an all-volunteer army by 1973 further deprived the antiwar movement of important organizing issues, particularly on college campuses. Student commitment to social causes, however, did not disappear altogether. In the early 1970s many student activists refocused their energies on issues such as feminism and environmentalism.

DÉTENTE AND THE END OF THE WAR

At the same time Nixon had been prosecuting the war in Vietnam, ostensibly to halt the spread of communism, he had been formulating a new policy toward the Soviet Union and China. Known as *détente* (the French word for a relaxation of tensions), Nixon's policy was to seek peaceful coexistence with the two communist powers and to link his overtures of friendship with a plan to end the Vietnam War.

In his talks with Chinese and Soviet leaders Nixon urged them to reduce their military aid to the North Vietnamese as a means of pressuring the North Vietnamese to the negotiating table.

A lifelong anticommunist crusader, Nixon was better able to reach out to the two communist superpowers without arousing American mistrust than a Democratic president would have been. Since the Chinese revolution of 1949 the United States had refused to recognize the government of the People's Republic of China. Instead, the State Department had recognized the Nationalist Chinese government in Taiwan. Nixon moved away from that policy, reasoning that the United States could exploit the growing rift between the People's Republic of China and the Soviet Union. In February 1972 Nixon journeyed to China in a symbolic visit that set the stage for the establishment of formal diplomatic relations in 1979.

In a similar spirit Nixon journeyed to Moscow in May 1972 to sign the first Strategic Arms Limitations Treaty (SALT I) between the United States and the Soviet Union. Although SALT I fell far short of ending the arms race, it did limit the production and deployment of intercontinental ballistic missiles (ICBMs) and antiballistic missile systems (ABMs). The treaty also signified that the United States could no longer afford the massive military spending that would have been necessary to regain the nuclear and military superiority it had enjoyed immediately following World War II. By the early 1970s inflation, domestic dissent, and the decline in American hegemony had limited and reshaped American aims and options in international relations. Most of all Nixon hoped that a rapprochement with the Soviets would help to resolve the prolonged crisis in Vietnam.

The Paris peace talks had been in stalemate since 1968. Though the war had been "Vietnamized," and American casualties had decreased, the South Vietnamese military proved unable to hold its own. In late 1971, as American troops withdrew from the region, communist forces stepped up their attacks on Laos, Cambodia, and South Vietnam. The next spring North Vietnamese forces launched a major new offensive against South Vietnam. In April, as the fighting intensified, Nixon ordered B-52 bombing raids against North Vietnam, and a month later he approved the mining of North Vietnamese ports.

That spring the increased combat activity and growing political pressure at home helped revive the Paris peace negotiations. Nixon hoped to undercut antiwar critics by making concessions to the North Vietnamese in the peace talks. In October Henry Kissinger and the North Vietnamese negotiator Le Duc Tho reached a cease-fire agreement calling for the withdrawal of the remaining U.S. troops; the return of all American prisoners of war; and the continued presence of North Vietnamese troops in South Vietnam. Nixon and Kissinger also promised the North Vietnamese substantial aid for postwar reconstruction. On the eve of the 1972 presidential election Kissinger announced "peace is at hand," and Nixon returned to the White House with a resounding electoral victory (see Chapter 30).

The peace initiative, however, soon stalled when the South Vietnamese rejected the provision concerning North Vietnamese troop positions, and the North declined

Hanoi Devastated

The North Vietnamese capital of Hanoi sustained heavy damage from bombing raids by American B-52 jets. The most devastating raids occurred during the "Christmas bombings" in December 1972, just weeks before the Paris Peace Accords were signed.

(Marc Riboud/Magnum Photos, Inc.)

to compromise further. With negotiations deadlocked, Nixon stepped up military action once more. From December 17 to December 30, 1972, American planes subjected civilian and military targets in Hanoi and Haiphong to the most devastating bombing of the war, referred to in the press as the "Christmas bombings." Finally, on January 27, 1973, representatives of the United States, North and South Vietnam, and the Viet Cong signed a cease-fire in Paris. But the Paris Peace Accords, which differed little from the proposal that had been rejected in October, did not fulfill Nixon's promise of "peace with honor." Basically, they mandated the unilateral withdrawal of American troops in exchange for the return of American prisoners of war from North Vietnam. For most Americans that was enough.

Without massive U.S. military and economic aid and with North Vietnamese guerrillas operating freely throughout the countryside, the South Vietnamese government of General Nguyen Van Thieu soon fell to the more disciplined and popular communist forces. In March 1975 North Vietnamese forces launched a final offensive. Horrified American television viewers watched as South Vietnamese officials and soldiers struggled with American embassy personnel to board the last helicopters that would fly out of Saigon before North Vietnamese troops entered the city. On April 29, 1975, Vietnam was reunited, and Saigon was renamed Ho Chi Minh City in honor of the communist leader, who had died in 1969.

THE LEGACY OF VIETNAM

Spanning nearly thirty years, the Vietnam War occupied American administrations from Truman to Nixon's successor Gerald Ford. U.S. troops fought in Vietnam for more than eleven years, from 1961 to 1973. In human terms the nation's longest war exacted an enormous cost. Some 58,000 U.S. troops died, and another 300,000 were wounded. Even those who returned unharmed encountered a sometimes hostile or indifferent reception. Arriving home alone without the fanfare that had greeted soldiers of America's victorious wars, most Vietnam veterans found the transition to civilian life abrupt and disorienting. The psychological tensions of serving in Vietnam and the difficulty of reentry sowed the seeds of what is now recognized as *post-traumatic stress disorder*—recurring physical and psychological problems that often lead to divorce, unemployment, and suicide. Only in the 1980s did America begin to make its peace with those who had served in the nation's most unpopular war.

In Southeast Asia the damage was far greater. The war claimed an estimated 1.5 million Vietnamese lives and devastated the country's physical and economic infrastructure. Neighboring Laos and Cambodia also suffered, particularly Cambodia, where between 1975 and 1979 the Khmer Rouge killed an estimated 2 million Cambodians—a quarter of the population—in a brutal relocation campaign. All told, the war produced nearly 10 million refugees, many of whom immigrated to the United States. Among them were thousands of Amerasians, the offspring of American soldiers and Vietnamese women. Spurned by their fathers and by most Vietnamese, more than 30,000 Amerasians arrived in the 1990s.

The defeat in Vietnam prompted Americans to think differently about foreign affairs and to acknowledge the limits of U.S. power abroad. The United States became less willing to plunge into overseas military commitments, a controversial change that conservatives dubbed the "Vietnam syndrome." In 1973 Congress declared its hostility to undeclared wars like those in Vietnam and Korea by passing the War Powers Act, which required the president to report any use of military force within forty-eight hours and directed that without a declaration of war by Congress hostilities must cease within sixty days. On those occasions when Congress did agree to foreign intervention, as in the Persian Gulf War of 1990 to 1991, American leaders would insist on obtainable military objectives and carefully channeled information to the news media. In the future any foreign entanglement would be evaluated in terms of its potential to become "another Vietnam."

The Vietnam War also distorted American economic and social affairs. At a total price of over $150 billion, the war siphoned resources from domestic needs, added to the deficit, and fueled inflation (see Chapter 32). Lyndon Johnson's Great Society programs had been pared down, and domestic reform efforts slowed thereafter. Moreover, the war shattered the liberal consensus that had supported the Democratic coalition. Even more seriously, the conduct of the war—the lies about American successes on the battlefield, the questionable representation of events in the Gulf of Tonkin, the secret war in Cambodia—spawned a deep distrust of government among American citizens. The discrediting of liberalism, the increased

T I M E L I N E

1946–1954	France and Vietminh struggle for Vietnam.	1967	Hippie counterculture's Summer of Love
1950	United States begins sending military aid to French in Vietnam.		Antiwar protest in Washington, D.C.
1954	Vietminh defeat French at Dienbienphu. Geneva Accords temporarily partition Vietnam at seventeenth parallel.	1968	Tet offensive
			Lyndon Johnson withdraws from presidential race.
			Martin Luther King Jr. assassinated
1960	Ngo Dinh Diem president of pro-American Vietnamese government		Robert F. Kennedy assassinated
	Birth control pill first marketed		Riot at Democratic National Convention in Chicago
1962	Students for a Democratic Society (SDS) founded		Women's liberation movement emerges
			American Indian Movement (AIM) organized
1963	Militant Buddhists protest Diem.	1969	Stonewall riot leads to gay liberation movement.
	Diem assassinated		
	Bob Dylan's "Blowin' in the Wind"		Woodstock Music and Art Fair
	Presidential Commission on the Status of Women		Richard Nixon begins troop withdrawal.
1964	Free Speech Movement at Berkeley	1970	Nixon orders invasion of Cambodia.
	Gulf of Tonkin resolution approves U.S. intervention in Vietnam.		Killings at Kent State and Jackson State
			Lieutenant William L. Calley court-martialed for My Lai atrocities
1965	Malcolm X assassinated	1972	Nixon visits People's Republic of China.
	Operation Rolling Thunder mass bombings		SALT I Treaty with Soviet Union
	First U.S. combat troops arrive in Vietnam.		Christmas bombing of North Vietnam
	Six-day riot in Watts district of Los Angeles	1973	Paris Peace Accords
			War Powers Act
			AIM occupies village of Wounded Knee, South Dakota.
1966	National Organization for Women (NOW) founded	1975	Fall of Saigon

cynicism toward government, and the growing social turmoil that accompanied the war would continue into the next decade, paving the way for a resurgence of the Republican Party and a new mood of conservatism.

For Further Exploration

Two insightful overviews of the 1960s are David Farber, *The Age of Great Dreams* (1994), and Maurice Isserman and Michael Kazin, *America Divided: The Civil War of the 1960's* (1999). The period is unusually rich in compelling primary accounts. *Takin' It to the Streets,* edited by Alexander Bloom and Wini Breines (1995), offers an impressive array of documents that encompass the war, counterculture, civil rights, feminism, gay liberation, and other issues. Henry Hampton and Steve Fayer's oral history, *Voices of Freedom* (1991), and *The Autobiography of Malcolm X* (1995), cowritten with Alex Haley, provide insight into black power movements. Mary Crow Dog recounts her experiences as a Native American activist in *Lakota Woman* (1990). Memoirs of Vietnam are numerous. Secretary of Defense Robert McNamara offers an insider's view and belated apologia in *In Retrospect* (1995); in *An American Requiem: God, My Father, and the War That Came Between Us* (1996), the antiwar former priest James Carroll writes eloquently of the fissures Vietnam created in his family and the culture more generally; and Ron Kovic's *Born on the Fourth of July* (1976) is one soldier's powerful account of the war experience and its aftermath. Documents concerning the My Lai Massacre may be found in James S. Olson and Randy Roberts, eds., *My Lai* (1999).

"The Sixties Project," which is hosted by the University of Virginia at Charlottesville, offers personal narratives, special exhibits, and a bibliography of articles published in "Vietnam Generation," at <http://lists.village.virginia.edu/sixties/>. A useful Vietnam site is edited by Professor Vincent Ferraro of Mount Holyoke College and includes state papers and official correspondence from 1941 to the fall of Saigon, <http://www.mtholyoke .edu/acad/intrel/vietnam.htm>. The University of California Library's site, "Free Speech Movement: Student Protest–U.C. Berkeley, 1964–65," at <http://www.lib.berkeley.edu/ BANC/FSM/>, offers newsletters, oral histories, student newspaper accounts, legal defense material, and audio recordings, as well as good links to related sites. Historians at the University of Michigan maintain "A Study and Timeline of the Lakota Nation," at <http://www-personal.umich.edu/~jamarcus/>, which includes material on the American Indian Movement, the occupation of Wounded Knee in 1973, and the confrontation at the Bureau of Indian Affairs Office in 1972.

Chapter 30

THE LEAN YEARS
1969–1980

We've always believed in something called progress. We've always
had a faith that the days of our children would be better than our
own. Our people are losing that faith, not only in government itself
but in their ability as citizens to serve as the ultimate rulers and
shapers of our democracy.

—JIMMY CARTER, 1979

"The United States Steel Corporation announced yesterday that it
was closing 14 plants and mills in eight states. About 13,000 production and white-
collar workers will lose their jobs." "Weyerhaeuser Co. may trim about 1,000 salaried
employees from its 11,000 member workforce over the next year." "Philadelphia:
Food Fair Inc. plans to close 89 supermarkets in New York and Connecticut." Newspaper articles in the 1970s told the story of the widespread downsizing that cost
millions of workers their jobs when rising oil prices, runaway inflation, declining
productivity, and stagnating incomes caused the biggest economic downturn in
three decades. Beyond the individual hard-luck stories of demeaning low-paid jobs,
lost homes, forced relocations, broken marriages, and alcoholism, the economic uncertainties facing working- and middle-class Americans in this period created a
sense of disillusionment about the nation's future. Already reeling from the nation's
withdrawal from Vietnam and its implications for the United States' international
power, many people also grew disenchanted with their political leadership in the
1970s, as one public official after another, including President Richard Nixon, resigned for misconduct. In the wake of Nixon's resignation, the lackluster administrations of Presidents Gerald Ford and Jimmy Carter failed to provide the leadership
necessary to cope with the nation's economic and international insecurities—a failure that fed Americans' growing skepticism about government and its capacity to
improve people's lives.

Paradoxically, in the midst of this growing disaffection and skepticism, a commitment to social change persisted. Some of the social movements born in the
1960s, such as feminism and environmentalism, had their greatest impact in the
1970s. As former student radicals moved into the political mainstream, they took

their struggles with them, from streets and campuses into courts, schools, workplaces, and community organizations. But like the civil rights and antiwar movements of the 1960s, the social activism of the 1970s stirred fears and uncertainties among many Americans. Furthermore, the darkening economic climate of the new decade undercut the sense of social generosity that had characterized the 1960s, fueling a new conservatism that would become a potent political force by the decade's end.

The Nixon Years

Richard Nixon set the stage for the conservative political resurgence. His election gave impetus to a long-standing Republican effort to trim back the Great Society and shift some federal responsibilities back to the states. At the same time Nixon embraced the use of federal power—within limits—to uphold governmental responsibility for social welfare, environmental protection, and economic stability. The president's domestic accomplishments, however, as well as his international initiatives, were ultimately overshadowed by the Watergate scandal, which swept him from office in disgrace and undermined Americans' confidence in their political leaders.

THE REPUBLICAN DOMESTIC AGENDA

In a 1968 campaign pledge to "the average American," Nixon had vowed to "reverse the flow of power and resources from the states and communities to Washington and start power and resources flowing back . . . to the people." One hallmark of this approach was the 1972 revenue-sharing program, which distributed a portion of federal tax revenues to the states as block grants, to be spent as state officials saw fit. In later years revenue sharing would become a key Republican strategy for reducing federal social programs and federal bureaucracy.

Nixon also worked to scale down certain federal government programs that had grown dramatically during the two preceding administrations. He reduced funding for many War on Poverty programs and dismantled the Office of Economic Opportunity altogether in 1971. Urban renewal, pollution control, and other environmental initiatives suffered when Nixon *impounded* (refused to spend) billions of dollars appropriated for them by Congress. Nixon's lack of interest in extending the gains of the civil rights movement, as well as his effort, albeit unsuccessful, to reform the social welfare system further exemplified the Republicans' desire to roll back the consolidation of federal power that had characterized American political life since the New Deal.

Still, with Democratic majorities in both houses of Congress, Nixon needed to be flexible in legislative matters. He agreed to the growth of major entitlement programs, including Medicare, Medicaid, and Social Security. In 1970 he signed a bill establishing the Environmental Protection Agency (EPA), and in 1972 he approved legislation creating the Occupational Safety and Health Administration (OSHA) and the Consumer Products Safety Commission. Thus, his administration witnessed the expansion of federal power in numerous areas.

Nixon demonstrated his conservative social values most clearly in his appointments to the Supreme Court. The liberal thrust of the Court under the direction of Chief Justice Earl Warren (1953–1969) had disturbed many conservatives. Its *Brown v. Board of Education* decision in 1954 requiring the desegregation of public schools (see Chapter 27) was followed by other landmark decisions in the 1960s. The *Miranda v. Arizona* (1966) decision reinforced defendants' rights by requiring arresting officers to notify suspects of their legal rights. In *Baker v. Carr* (1962) and *Reynolds v. Sims* (1964) the Court put forth the doctrine of "one person, one vote," meaning that all citizens' votes should have equal weight, no matter where they lived. The ruling substantially increased the representation in state legislatures and Congress of both suburban and urban areas (with their concentrations of African American and Spanish-speaking residents) at the expense of rural regions. One of the most controversial decisions was *Engel v. Vitale* (1962), which banned organized prayer in public schools as a violation of the First Amendment. When Earl Warren retired in 1969, President Nixon took the opportunity to begin reshaping the court and nominated conservative Warren Burger to become chief justice. After some difficulties in getting nominees confirmed by the Senate, Nixon eventually named three other justices: Harry Blackmun (who proved more liberal than expected), Lewis F. Powell Jr., and William Rehnquist.

Nixon's appointees did not always hand down decisions the president approved, however. Despite attempts by the Justice Department to halt further desegregation in the face of determined white opposition, the Court ordered busing to achieve racial balance. In 1972 it issued restrictions on the implementation of capital punishment, though it did not rule the death penalty unconstitutional. And in the controversial 1973 case *Roe v. Wade* Justice Harry Blackmun wrote the decision that struck down laws prohibiting abortion in Texas and Georgia.

THE 1972 ELECTION

Nixon's reelection in 1972 was never much in doubt. In May the threat of a conservative third-party challenge from Alabama governor George Wallace ended abruptly when an assailant shot Wallace, paralyzing him from the waist down. With Wallace out of the picture Nixon's strategy of wooing southern white voters away from the Democrats got a boost. Nixon also benefited from the disarray of the Democratic Party. Divided over Vietnam and civil rights the Democrats were plagued by tensions between their newer, more liberal constituencies—women, minorities, and young adults—and the old-line officeholders and labor union leaders who had always dominated the party. Recent changes in the party's system of selecting delegates and candidates benefited the newer groups, and they helped to nominate Senator George McGovern of South Dakota, a noted liberal and an outspoken opponent of the Vietnam War.

McGovern's campaign quickly ran into trouble. On learning that his running mate, Senator Thomas F. Eagleton of Missouri, had undergone electroshock therapy for depression some years earlier, McGovern first supported him and then abruptly insisted that he quit the ticket. But McGovern's waffling on the matter made him appear weak and indecisive. Moreover, he was far too liberal for many traditional Democrats, who rejected his ill-defined proposals for welfare reform and his call for unilateral withdrawal from Vietnam.

Nixon's campaign took full advantage of McGovern's weaknesses. Although the president had failed to end the war, his Vietnamization policy had virtually eliminated American combat deaths by 1972. Henry Kissinger's premature declaration that "peace is at hand" raised voters' hopes for a negotiated settlement (see Chapter 29). Not only did those initiatives rob the Democrats of their greatest appeal—their antiwar stance—but a short-term upturn in the economy further favored the Republicans. Nixon won handily, receiving nearly 61 percent of the popular vote and carrying every state except Massachusetts and the District of Columbia. Yet the president failed to kindle strong loyalty in the electorate. Only 55.7 percent of eligible voters bothered to go to the polls, and the Democrats maintained control of both houses of Congress. A far graver threat to Nixon's leadership would emerge shortly after the election, when the news broke that the White House was implicated in the 1972 break-in at the Democratic National Committee's headquarters at the Watergate apartment complex in Washington, D.C.

WATERGATE

Though the Watergate scandal, one of the great constitutional crises of the twentieth century, began in 1972, its roots lay in the early years of Nixon's first administration. Obsessed with the antiwar movement, the White House had repeatedly authorized illegal surveillance—opening mail, tapping phones, arranging break-ins—of citizens such as Daniel Ellsberg, a former Defense Department analyst who had become disillusioned with the war. In 1971 Ellsberg had leaked the so-called Pentagon Papers to the *New York Times*. This secret study, commissioned by Secretary of Defense McNamara in 1967, detailed so many American blunders in Vietnam that, after reading it, McNamara had commented, "You know, they could hang people for what is in there." To discredit Ellsberg, White House underlings broke into his psychiatrist's office in an unsuccessful search for damaging personal information. When their break-in was revealed, the court dismissed the government's case against Ellsberg.

In another abuse of presidential power the White House had established a clandestine intelligence group known as the "plumbers" that was supposed to plug leaks of government information. The plumbers relied on tactics such as using the Internal Revenue Service to harass the administration's opponents, who were named on an "enemies list" drawn up by presidential counsel John Dean. One of the plumbers' major targets was the Democratic Party, whose front-running primary candidate in 1972, Senator Edmund Muskie of Maine, became the object of several of their "dirty tricks," including the distribution of phony campaign posters reading "Help Muskie in Busing More Children Now."

These secret and highly questionable activities were financed by massive illegal fund-raising efforts by Nixon's Committee to Re-Elect the President (known as CREEP). To obtain contributions from major corporations, Nixon's fund-raisers had used high-pressure tactics that included implied threats of federal tax audits if companies failed to cooperate. CREEP raised over $20 million, a portion of which was used to finance the plumbers' dirty tricks, including the Watergate break-in.

Early in the morning of June 17, 1972, police arrested five men carrying cameras, wiretapping equipment, and a large amount of cash and charged them with breaking into the Democratic National Committee's headquarters at the Watergate apartment complex in Washington, D.C. Two accomplices were apprehended soon afterward. Three of the men had worked in the White House or for CREEP, and four had CIA connections. Nixon later claimed that White House counsel John Dean had conducted a full investigation of the incident (no such investigation ever took place) and that "no one on the White House staff, no one in this administration, presently employed, was involved in this very bizarre incident."

Subsequent investigations revealed that shortly after the break-in the president had ordered his chief of staff, H. R. Haldeman, to instruct the CIA to tell the FBI not to probe too deeply into connections between the White House and the burglars. When the burglars were convicted in January 1973, John Dean, with Nixon's approval, tried to buy their continued silence with $400,000 in hush money and hints of presidential pardons.

The cover-up of the White House's involvement began to unravel when one of the convicted burglars began to talk. Two tenacious investigative reporters at the *Washington Post*, Carl Bernstein and Bob Woodward, exposed the attempt to hide the truth and traced it back to the White House. Reports of CREEP's "dirty tricks" and illegal fund-raising soon compounded the public's suspicions about the president. In February the Senate voted seventy-seven to zero to establish an investigative committee. Two months later Nixon accepted the resignations of Haldeman, Assistant Secretary of Commerce Jeb Stuart Magruder, and chief domestic advisor John Ehrlichman, all of whom had been implicated in the cover-up. He fired Dean, who had agreed to testify in the case in exchange for immunity from prosecution. In May the Senate Watergate committee began holding nationally televised hearings. In June Magruder testified before the committee, confessing his guilt and implicating former Attorney General John Mitchell, Dean, and others. Dean, in turn, implicated Nixon in the plot. Even more startling testimony from a Nixon aide revealed that Nixon had installed a secret taping system in the Oval Office.

The president steadfastly "stonewalled" the committee's demand that he surrender the tapes, citing executive privilege and national security. But Archibald Cox, a special prosecutor whom Nixon had appointed to investigate the case, successfully petitioned a federal court to order the president to hand the tapes over. Still Nixon refused to comply. After receiving additional federal subpoenas the following spring, Nixon finally released a heavily edited transcript of the tapes, peppered with the words "expletive deleted." Senate Republican leader Hugh Scott called the transcripts "deplorable, disgusting, shabby, immoral." Most suspicious was an eighteen-minute gap in the tape covering a crucial meeting between Nixon, Haldeman, and Ehrlichman on June 20, 1972—three days after the break-in.

The Watergate affair moved into its final phase when on June 30 the House of Representatives voted three articles of impeachment against Richard Nixon: obstruction of justice, abuse of power, and acting to subvert the Constitution. Two days later the Supreme Court ruled unanimously that Nixon could not claim executive privilege as a justification for refusing to turn over additional tapes. Under duress, on August 5 Nixon released the unexpurgated tapes, which contained evidence that he had ordered the cover-up as early as six days after the break-in. Facing certain conviction in a Senate trial, on August 9, 1974, Nixon became the first U.S. president to resign.

The next day Vice President Gerald Ford was sworn in as president. Ford, a former Michigan congressman and house minority leader, had replaced Vice President Spiro Agnew in 1973 after Agnew resigned under indictment for accepting

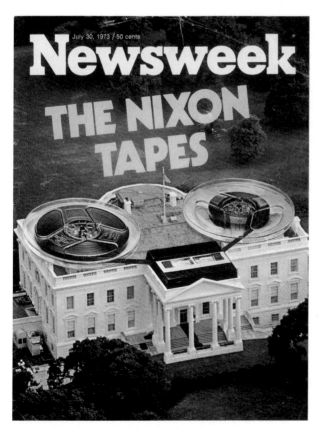

Watergate

In July 1973 White House aide Alexander Butterfield testified before the Senate Watergate Committee that all Oval Office telephone communications had been recorded on a secret taping system. Although Nixon tried in vain to suppress the tapes by claiming executive privilege, their eventual release—including statements directly implicating the president in the Watergate cover-up—led to Nixon's resignation in August of 1974.

kickbacks on construction contracts. The transfer of power proceeded smoothly. A month later, however, Ford stunned the nation by granting Nixon a "full, free, and absolute" pardon "for all offenses he had committed or might have committed during his presidency." Ford took that action, he said, to spare the country the agony of rehashing Watergate in a criminal prosecution. Twenty-five members of Nixon's administration went to prison, but he refused to admit guilt for what had happened, conceding only that he had made an error in judgment.

In response to the abuses of the Nixon administration and to contain the power of what the historian Arthur M. Schlesinger Jr. called "the imperial presidency," Congress adopted several reforms. In 1974 a strengthened Freedom of Information Act gave citizens greater access to files federal agencies had amassed on them. The Fair Campaign Practices Act of 1974 limited campaign contributions and provided for stricter accountability and public financing of presidential campaigns. Ironically, because the act allowed an unlimited number of political action committees (PACs) to donate up to $5,000 per candidate, corporations and lobbying groups found they could actually increase their influence by making multiple donations. By the end of the decade close to 3,000 PACs were playing an increasingly pivotal— and some would argue unethical—role in national elections.

Perhaps the most significant legacy of Watergate, however, was the wave of cynicism that swept the country in its wake. Beginning with Lyndon Johnson's "credibility gap" during the Vietnam War, public distrust of government had risen steadily with the disclosure of the secret bombing of Cambodia and the illegal surveillance and harassment of antiwar protesters and other political opponents. The saga of Watergate confirmed what many Americans had long suspected: that politicians were hopelessly corrupt and that the federal government was out of control (see American Voices, "Watergate Diary").

An Economy of Diminished Expectations

Economic difficulties compounded Americans' political disillusionment. Growing international demand for natural resources, particularly oil, coupled with unstable access to foreign oil supplies wreaked havoc with the American economy. At the same time foreign competitors successfully expanded their share of the world market, edging out American-made products. The resulting sharp downturn in the domestic economy marked the end of America's twenty-five-year dominance of the world economy.

ENERGY CRISIS

Until the mid-twentieth century the United States was the world's leading producer and consumer of oil. During World War II the nation had produced two-thirds of the world's oil, but by 1972 its share had fallen to only 22 percent, even though

AMERICAN VOICES

Watergate Diary

ELIZABETH DREW

*J*ournalist Elizabeth Drew kept a diary during the Watergate crisis. This passage, written *on August 5, 1974, shortly after President Nixon was forced to release some exceptionally damaging tape transcripts, explores the implications of the revelations for Americans' faith in the presidency.*

For those who believed that the President was aware of, and even directed, the cover-up, it must still be a shock to *read his conversation* about it. . . .

There is an inexplicable difference between the experiences of suspecting a lie and being whacked in the face with the evidence of one. Many Americans had become accustomed to thinking of the President as a liar, and had alternately suspended belief in, scoffed at, or become enraged at his statements. But I wonder whether the enormity of his lying has sunk in yet—whether we have, or can, come to terms with the thought that so much of what he said to us was just noise, words, and that we can no longer begin by accepting any of it as the truth. This is a total reversal of the way we were brought up to think about Presidents, a departure from deeply ingrained habits. One's mind resists the thought of our President as a faithless man, capable of looking at us in utter sincerity from the other side of the television camera and telling us multiple, explicit, barefaced lies. One is torn between the idea that people must be able to have some confidence in their leaders and the idea that in this day of image manipulation a certain skepticism may serve them well. I do not think there is much comfort to be taken from the fact that eventually Nixon's lies—like Johnson's—caught up with him. It took a long time, and a great deal of damage was done meanwhile.

SOURCE: Elizabeth Drew, *Washington Journal: The Events of 1973–1974* (New York: Random House, 1974), pp. 391–92.

domestic production had continued to rise. By the late 1960s the United States was buying more and more of its oil on the world market to keep up with shrinking domestic reserves and growing demand.

The imported oil came primarily from the Middle East, where production had increased a stupendous 1,500 percent in the twenty-five years following World War II. The rise of nationalism and the corresponding decline of colonialism in the postwar era had encouraged the Persian Gulf nations to wrest control from the European and American oil companies that once dominated petroleum exploration and production in that region. In 1960, joining with other oil-producing developing countries, they had formed the Organization of Petroleum Exporting Countries (OPEC). Just five of the founding countries—the Middle Eastern states of Saudi Arabia,

Kuwait, Iran, and Iraq, plus Venezuela—were the source of more than 80 percent of the world's crude oil exports. During the early 1970s when world demand climbed and oil reserves fell, they took advantage of market forces to maximize their profits. Between 1973 and 1975 OPEC raised the price of a barrel of oil from $3 to $12. By the end of the decade the price had peaked at $34 a barrel, setting off a round of furious inflation in the oil-dependent United States.

OPEC members also found that oil could be used as a weapon in global politics. In 1973 OPEC instituted an oil embargo against the United States, Western Europe, and Japan in retaliation for their aid to Israel during the Yom Kippur War, which had begun when Egypt and Syria invaded Israel. The embargo, which lasted until 1974, forced Americans to curtail their driving or spend long hours in line at the pumps; in a matter of months, gas prices climbed 40 percent. Since the U.S. automobile industry had little to offer except "gas-guzzlers" built to run on cheap fuel, Americans turned to cheaper, more fuel-efficient foreign cars manufactured in Japan and West Germany. Soon the auto industry was in a slump, weakening the American economy.

No Gas

During the energy crisis of 1973 and 1974 American motorists faced widespread gasoline shortages for the first time since World War II. Although gas was not rationed, gas stations were closed on Sundays, air travel was cut by 10 percent, and a national speed limit of 55 miles per hour was imposed.

(Tony Korody/Sygma)

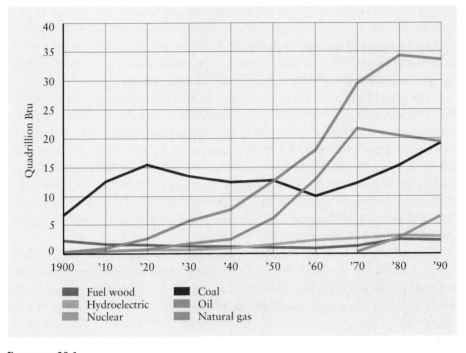

FIGURE 30.1
U.S. Energy Consumption, 1900–1990

Coal was the nation's primary source of energy until the 1950s, when oil and natural gas became the dominant fuels. The use of nuclear and hydroelectric power also rose substantially in the postwar era. Since the late 1970s fuel-efficient automobiles and conservation measures have reduced total energy use.

The energy crisis was an enormous shock to the American psyche. Suddenly Americans felt like hostages to economic forces that were beyond their control. As OPEC's leaders pushed prices higher and higher, they seemed to be able to determine whether Western economies would grow or stagnate. Despite an extensive public conservation campaign and a second gas shortage in 1979 caused by the Iranian revolution, Americans could not wean themselves from foreign oil. In fact, they used even more foreign oil after the energy crisis than they had before—a testimony to the enormous thirst of modern industrial and consumer societies for petroleum (see Figure 30.1).

ECONOMIC WOES

While the energy crisis dealt a swift blow to the U.S. economy, other developments had equally damaging results. The high cost of the Vietnam War and the Great Society had contributed to a steadily growing federal deficit and spiraling inflation. A business downturn in 1970 had led to rising unemployment and declining productivity. In the industrial sector the reviving economies of West Germany and Japan over time had reduced demand for American goods worldwide. As a result, in 1971 the dollar fell to its lowest level on the world market since 1949, and the United States posted its first trade deficit in almost a century.

That year Nixon took several bold steps to turn the economy around. To stem the decline in currency and trade, he suspended the Bretton Woods system that had been set up at the United Nations monetary conference in 1944 (see Chapter 28). Once again, the dollar would fluctuate in relation to the price of an ounce of gold. The change, which effectively devalued the dollar in hopes of encouraging foreign trade, represented a frank acknowledgment that America's currency was no longer the world's strongest. Nixon also instituted wage and price controls to curb inflation, and to boost the sluggish economy he offered a "full employment" budget for 1972, including $11 billion in deficit spending.

Though these measures brought a temporary improvement in the economy, the general decline persisted. Overall economic growth, as measured by the gross national product (GNP), had averaged 4.1 percent per year in the 1960s; in the 1970s it dropped to only 2.9 percent, contributing to a noticeable decline in most Americans' standard of living. At the same time galloping inflation forced consumer prices upward. Housing prices, in particular, rose rapidly: the average cost of a single-family home more than doubled in the 1970s, making home ownership inaccessible to a growing segment of the working and middle classes.

Young adults faced a constricted job market in the late 1970s, as a record number of baby boomers competed for a limited number of jobs. Unemployment peaked at around 9 percent in 1975 and hovered at 6 to 7 percent in the late 1970s. A devastating combination of inflation and unemployment—dubbed *stagflation*—bedeviled presidential administrations from Nixon to Reagan, whose remedies (such as deficit spending and tax reduction) failed to eradicate the double scourge.

American economic woes were most acute in the industrial sector, which entered a prolonged period of decline, or deindustrialization. Investors who had formerly bought stock in basic U.S. industries began to speculate on the stock market or put their money into mergers or foreign companies. Many U.S. firms relocated overseas, partly to take advantage of cheaper labor and production costs. By the end of the 1970s the hundred largest multinational corporations and banks were earning more than a third of their overall profits abroad.

The most dramatic consequences of deindustrialization occurred in the older industrial regions of the Northeast and Midwest, which came to be known as the Rust Belt. There the dominant images of American industry in the mid-twentieth century—huge factories such as Ford's River Rouge outside Detroit and the General Electric plant in Lynn, Massachusetts—were fast becoming relics. When a community's major employer closed down and left town, the devastating effect rippled through communities in America's heartland. Many workers moved to the cities of the Sun Belt, continuing the dramatic growth in that region that had begun after World War II.

Deindustrialization and the changing economic conditions that provoked it posed a critical problem for the labor movement. In the heyday of labor during the 1940s and 1950s American managers had often cooperated with unions; with profits high there was room for accommodation. But as foreign competition cut into corporate profits in the 1970s, industry became less willing to bargain, and the labor movement's power declined. In the 1970s union membership dropped from 28 to 23 percent of the American workforce. Facing conflict with labor, some employers simply moved their operations abroad, where they found a cheaper, more compliant workforce. In a competitive global environment, labor's prospects seemed dim.

Reform and Reaction in the 1970s

The nation's economic problems and growing cynicism about government led to deep public anxiety and resentment. Many Americans turned inward to private satisfactions, prompting the journalist Tom Wolfe to label the 1970s the "Me Decade." Yet such a label hardly does justice to a decade in which environmentalism, feminism, lesbian and gay rights, and other social movements blossomed. Furthermore, such characterizations neglect the growing social conservatism that was in part a response to such movements. In fact, the confluence of these trends produced a pattern of shifting crosscurrents that made the 1970s a complex transitional decade.

THE NEW ACTIVISM: ENVIRONMENTAL AND CONSUMER MOVEMENTS

After 1970 many baby boomers left the counterculture behind and settled down to pursue careers and material goods. But these young adults sought personal fulfillment as well. In a quest for physical well-being, millions of Americans began jogging, riding bicycles, and working out at the gym. The fitness craze coincided with a heightened environmental awareness that spurred the demand for pesticide-free foods and vegetarian cookbooks. For spiritual support some young people embraced the self-help techniques of the human-potential, or New Age, movement; others turned to religious cults such as the Hare Krishna, the Church of Scientology, and the Unification Church of Reverend Sun Myung Moon.

A few baby boomers continued to pursue the unfinished social and political agendas of the 1960s. Moving into law, education, social work, medicine, and other fields, these former radicals continued their activism on a grassroots level. Some joined the left wing of the Democratic Party; others helped to establish community-based organizations, including health clinics, food co-ops, and day-care centers. On the local level, at least, the progressive spirit of the 1960s lived on.

Many of these 1960s-style activists helped invigorate the environmental movement, which had been reenergized by the publication in 1962 of Rachel Carson's *Silent Spring*, a powerful analysis of the impact of pesticides on the food chain. Activists brought their radical political sensibilities to the environmental movement, using sit-ins and other protest tactics developed in the civil rights and antiwar movements to mobilize mass support and infuse the movement with new life. For example, they construed the search for alternative technologies (especially solar power) as a political statement against a corporate structure that was increasingly inhospitable to human-scale technology—and to humans, as well.

Other issues that galvanized public opinion included the environmental impact of industrial projects such as the Alaska pipeline and the harmful effects of chlorofluorocarbons and increased carbon dioxide levels on the earth's atmosphere. In January 1969 a huge oil spill off the coast of Santa Barbara, California, provoked an outcry, as did the discovery in 1978 that a housing development outside Niagara Falls, New York, had been built on a toxic waste site. The abnormally high rates of illness and birth defects recorded in this Love Canal neighborhood deepened public awareness of the culpability of business in generating environmental hazards.

Nuclear energy became the subject of citizen action in the 1970s, when rising prices and oil shortages led to the expansion of nuclear power, pitting environmental concerns against the need for alternative energy sources. By January 1974 forty-two nuclear power plants were in operation, and over a hundred more were planned. Suddenly the proliferation of nuclear power plants and reactors, which had gone largely unchallenged in the 1950s and 1960s, raised public concerns about safety. Community activists protested plans for new reactors, citing inadequate evacuation plans and the unresolved problem of the disposal of radioactive waste. Their fears seemed to be confirmed in March 1979 when a nuclear plant at Three Mile Island near Harrisburg, Pennsylvania, came critically close to a meltdown of its central core reactor. A prompt shutdown of the plant brought the problem under control before radioactive material seeped into the environment, but as a member of the panel that investigated the accident admitted, "We were damn lucky." Ultimately, Three Mile Island caused Americans to rethink the question of whether nuclear power could be a viable solution to the nation's energy needs. Grassroots activism, combined with public fear of the potential dangers of nuclear energy, convinced many utility companies to abandon nuclear power, despite its short-term economic advantages.

Americans' concerns about nuclear power, chemical contamination, pesticides, and other environmental issues helped to turn environmentalism into a mass movement. On the first Earth Day, April 22, 1970, 20 million citizens gathered in communities across the country to show their support for the endangered planet. Their efforts helped to create bipartisan support for a spate of new federal legislation. In 1969 Congress passed the National Environmental Policy Act, which required the developers of public projects to file an environmental impact statement. The next year Nixon established the Environmental Protection Agency (EPA) and signed the Clean Air Act, which toughened standards for auto emissions in order to reduce smog and air pollution. Two years later Congress banned the use of the pesticide DDT. And in 1973 the Endangered Species Act expanded the protection provided by the Endangered Animals Act of 1964, granting species such as snail darters and spotted owls protected status. Thus environmental protection joined social welfare, defense, and national security as targets of federal intervention.

The environmental movement did not go uncontested. The EPA-mandated fuel-economy standards for cars provoked criticism for threatening the health of the auto industry as it struggled to keep up with foreign competitors. Corporations resented environmental regulations, but so did many of their workers, who believed that tightened standards threatened their jobs and privileged nature over human beings. "IF YOU'RE HUNGRY AND OUT OF WORK, EAT AN ENVIRONMENTALIST" read one labor union's bumper sticker. In a time of rising unemployment and deindustrialization, activists clashed head-on with proponents of economic development, full employment, and global competitiveness.

The rise of environmentalism was paralleled by a growing movement to eliminate harmful consumer products and curb dangerous practices by American corporations. After decades of inertia, in the 1960s the consumer protection movement, which had originated in the Progressive Era (see Chapter 20), reemerged under the leadership of Ralph Nader, a young lawyer whose book *Unsafe at Any Speed* (1965) attacked General Motors for putting style ahead of safety and fuel economy in its engineering. His Public Interest Research Group, a national network of consumer groups that focused on issues ranging from product safety to consumer fraud and environmental pollution, became the model for dozens of other groups that emerged in the 1970s and afterward to combat the health hazards of smoking, unethical insurance and credit practices, and other consumer problems. With the establishment of the federal Consumer Products Safety Commission in 1972 Congress acknowledged the growing need for consumer protection.

CHALLENGES TO TRADITION: THE WOMEN'S MOVEMENT AND GAY RIGHTS ACTIVISM

Feminism proved the most enduring movement to emerge from the 1960s. In the next decade the women's movement grew more sophisticated, generating an array of services and organizations, from rape crisis centers and battered women's shelters to feminist health collectives and women's bookstores. In 1972 Gloria Steinem and other journalists founded *Ms.* magazine, the first consumer magazine aimed at a feminist audience. Formerly all-male bastions, such as Yale, Princeton, and the U.S. Military Academy, admitted women undergraduates for the first time, while the proportion of women attending graduate and professional schools rose markedly. Several new national women's organizations emerged, and established groups such as the National Organization for Women (NOW) continued to grow. In 1977, 20,000

The Expanding Women's Movement

By the late 1970s the feminist movement had broadened its base, attracting women of all ages and backgrounds, such as this delegate to the 1977 National Women's Conference in Houston, Texas. As the slogan on her hat implies, though, the movement was already on the defensive against right-wing claims that it undermined traditional values. (Bettye Lane)

women went to Houston for the first National Women's Conference. Their "National Plan of Action" represented a hard-won consensus on topics ranging from violence against women to homemakers' rights, the needs of older women, and, most controversially, abortion and other reproductive issues.

Women were also increasingly visible in politics and public life. The National Women's Political Caucus, founded in 1971, actively promoted the election of women to public office. Their success stories included Shirley Chisholm, Patricia Schroeder, and Geraldine Ferraro, all of whom served in Congress, and Ella Grasso, who won election as Connecticut's governor in 1974.

Women's political mobilization produced significant legislative and administrative gains. With the passage of Title IX of the Educational Amendments Act of 1972, which broadened the 1964 Civil Rights Act to include educational institutions, Congress prohibited colleges and universities that received federal funds from discriminating on the basis of sex, a change that particularly benefited women athletes. Another federal initiative was *affirmative action.* Originally instituted in 1966 under Lyndon Johnson's administration to redress a history of discrimination against nonwhites in employment and education, affirmative action procedures—hiring and enrollment goals and recruitment training programs—were extended to women the following year and gave many women, especially educated white ones, more opportunities for educational and career advancement. In 1972 Congress authorized child-care deductions for working parents; in 1974 it passed the Equal Credit Opportunity Act, which significantly improved women's access to credit.

The Supreme Court also significantly advanced women's rights. In several rulings the Court gave women more control over their reproductive lives by reading a right of privacy into the Ninth and Fourteenth Amendments' concept of personal liberty. In 1965 *Griswold v. Connecticut* had overturned state laws against the sale of contraceptive devices to married adults, an option that was later extended to single persons. In 1973, in *Roe v. Wade,* the Court struck down Texas and Georgia statutes that allowed an abortion only if the mother's life was in danger. According to this seven-to-two decision, states could no longer outlaw abortions performed during the first trimester of pregnancy.

Roe v. Wade nationalized the liberalization of state abortion laws, which had begun in New York in 1970, but also fueled the development of a powerful anti-abortion movement. Charging that the rights of a fetus took precedence over a woman's right to decide whether or not to terminate a pregnancy, abortion opponents worked to circumvent or overturn *Roe v. Wade.* In 1976 they convinced Congress to deny Medicaid funds for abortions for poor women, one of the opening rounds in a protracted legislative and judicial campaign to chip away at the *Roe* decision.

Another battlefront for the women's movement was the proposed Equal Rights Amendment (ERA) to the Constitution. The ERA, first introduced in Congress in 1923 by the National Woman's Party, stated in its entirety, "Equality of rights under the law shall not be denied or abridged by the United States or any State on the basis of sex." In 1970 feminists revived the amendment, which passed the House but died in the Senate. In the next session it passed both houses and was submitted to the states for ratification. But though thirty-four states quickly passed the ERA between 1972 and 1974, growing opposition by conservative groups slowed its momentum (see Map 30.1). By 1982 the amendment was dead.

The fate of the ERA and the battle over abortion rights showed that by the mid-1970s the women's movement was beginning to weaken. Increasingly its members were divided over issues of race, class, age, and sexual orientation. For many non-white and working-class women, the feminist movement seemed to stand for the interests of self-seeking white career women. At the same time, the women's movement faced growing social conservatism among Americans in general. Although 63 percent of women polled in 1975 said they favored "efforts to strengthen and change women's status in society," a growing minority of both sexes expressed concern over what seemed to be revolutionary changes in women's traditional roles.

Lawyer Phyllis Schlafly, long active in conservative causes, led the antifeminist backlash. Despite the active career she had pursued while raising five children,

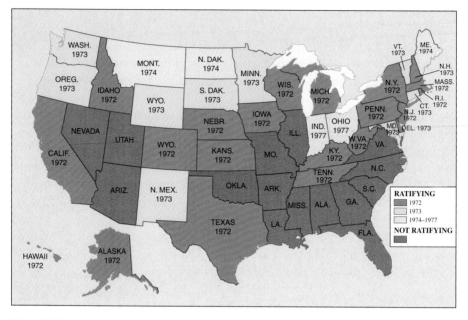

M A P 30.1
States Ratifying the Equal Rights Amendment

The Equal Rights Amendment quickly won support in 1972 and 1973 but then stalled. ERAmerica, a coalition of women's groups formed in 1976, lobbied extensively, particularly in Florida, North Carolina, and Illinois, but failed to sway the conservative legislatures in those states. After Indiana ratified in 1977, the amendment still lacked three votes toward the three-fourths majority needed to pass. Efforts to revive the ERA in the 1980s were unsuccessful.

Schlafly advocated traditional roles for women. Schlafly's STOP ERA organization claimed that the amendment would create a "unisex society" in which women could be drafted, homosexuals could be married, and separate toilets for men and women would be prohibited. (Feminists argued that those charges were groundless.) Alarmed, conservative women in grassroots networks mobilized, showing up at statehouses with home-baked bread and apple pies, symbols of their traditional domestic role. Their message, that women would lose more than they would gain if the ERA passed, resonated with many men and women, especially those who were troubled by the rapid pace of social change.

Although the feminist movement was on the defensive by the mid-1970s, women's lives showed no signs of returning to the patterns of the 1950s. Because of increasing economic pressures, the proportion of women in the paid workforce continued to rise, from 44 percent in 1970 to 51 percent in 1980. In their private lives, easier access to birth control permitted married and unmarried women to enjoy greater sexual freedom (although they also became more vulnerable to male sexual pressure). With a growing number of career options available to them, many women, particularly educated white women, stayed single or delayed marriage and child rearing. The birth rate continued its postwar decline, reaching an all-time low in the mid-1970s. At the same time, the divorce rate rose 82 percent in the 1970s, as more men and women elected to leave unhappy marriages.

Although such changes brought increased autonomy for many women, they also caused new hardships, particularly in poor and working-class families. Divorce left many women with low-paying jobs and inadequate child care. Meanwhile, more tolerant attitudes toward premarital sex, along with other social and economic factors, had contributed to rising teenage pregnancy rates. The rise in divorce and adolescent pregnancy produced a sharp increase in the number of female-headed families, contributing to the "feminization" of poverty. By 1980 women accounted for 66 percent of adults who lived below the poverty line, a development that fueled a growing wave of social reaction.

Another major focus of social activism, the gay liberation movement, achieved heightened visibility in the 1970s. Thousands of gay men and lesbians "came out," publicly proclaiming their sexual orientation (see American Voices, "A Gay Athlete Comes Out"). In New York's Greenwich Village, San Francisco's Castro, and other urban enclaves, growing gay communities gave rise to hundreds of new gay and lesbian clubs, churches, businesses, and political organizations. In 1973 the National Gay Task Force launched a campaign to include gay men and lesbians as a protected group under laws covering employment and housing rights. Such efforts were most successful on the local level; during the 1970s Detroit, Boston, Los Angeles, Miami, San Francisco, and other cities passed laws barring discrimination on the basis of sexual preference.

Like abortion and the ERA, gay rights came under attack from conservatives, who believed that granting gay lifestyles legal protection would encourage immoral behavior. When the Miami city council passed a measure banning discrimination against gay men and lesbians in 1977, the singer Anita Bryant led a campaign to repeal the law by popular referendum. Later that year voters overturned the measure by a two-to-one majority, prompting similar antigay campaigns around the country.

RACIAL MINORITIES

Although the civil rights movement was in disarray by the late 1960s, continued minority-group protests brought social and economic gains in the next decade. Native Americans realized some of the most significant changes. In 1971 the Alaska Native Land Claims Act restored 40 million acres to Eskimos, Aleuts, and other native peoples, along with $960 million in compensation. Most important, the federal government abandoned the tribal termination program of the 1950s (see Chapter 28). Under the Indian Self-Determination Act of 1974, Congress restored the tribes' right to govern themselves and gave them authority over federal programs on their reservations (see Map 30.2).

AMERICAN VOICES
A Gay Athlete Comes Out
DAVID KOPAY

For ten years David Kopay played professional football for the San Francisco Forty-Niners, Detroit Lions, Washington Redskins, New Orleans Saints, and Green Bay Packers. In 1975, at the end of his playing career, Kopay publicly acknowledged his homosexuality, creating a national furor in the sports world.

I always knew I was a bit different, but I kept it kind of quiet. I didn't think of myself as queer. In fact I couldn't even say that word for years and years. . . .

By the time I spoke out, I really had nothing left to lose. It felt like I didn't have a choice: I just had to do it. Then one morning in 1975 I saw an article in the *Washington Star* about homosexual athletes and why they had everything to lose. There was an interview in the article with Jerry Smith [Washington Redskins tight end who died of AIDS in 1986]. . . . I was at a time and place in my own coming out where I felt that if I was going to survive, I had to speak out. It was do that or maybe go crazy.

So I called Lynn Rosellini. . . . Everybody said there was going to be a terrible backlash against me when Lynn's article was published. But there wasn't a backlash against me personally: there was a backlash against all the television shows and radio stations that I went on. And the newspapers. The *Washington Star* said they had never received more negative mail for anything they'd ever done—hundreds of horrible hate letters. . . . The letters said things like, "It doesn't belong on the sports page as a model for our young boys and girls." "How could the *Washington Star* run an article like this?" I got letters that said, "I hope you never get a coaching job. Yours in Christ. Love. . . ." Just horrible things.

I never did get a coaching job. . . . I had to make a spot for myself somehow, so I wound up working with Perry Young for a year on my book, *The Dave Kopay Story*.

I think we knew we were doing something good. . . .

A lot of kids still write. They say that the book meant so much to them. They remember that it changed them a lot or made a difference.

SOURCE: Eric Marcus, *Making History* (New York: Harper Collins, 1992), pp. 275–77.

The busing of children to achieve school desegregation proved the most disruptive social issue of the 1970s. Progress in achieving the desegregation mandated by *Brown v. Board of Education of Topeka* had been slow. In the 1970s both the courts and the Justice Department pushed for more action, not just in the South but in other parts of the country. In *Milliken v. Bradley* (1974) the Supreme Court ordered cities with deeply ingrained patterns of residential segregation to use busing to integrate their classrooms. The decision sparked intense and sometimes violent opposition. In Boston in 1974 and 1975 the strongly Irish-Catholic working-class neighborhood of South Boston responded to the arrival of African American students from Roxbury with mob action reminiscent of that in Little Rock in 1957. Threatened by court-ordered busing, many white parents transferred their children to private schools or moved to the suburbs. The resulting "white flight" exacerbated the racial imbalance busing was supposed to redress. Some black parents also opposed busing, calling instead for better schools in predominantly black neighborhoods. By the late 1970s federal courts had begun to back away from their insistence on busing to achieve racial balance.

Almost as divisive as busing was the issue of affirmative action procedures, which had expanded opportunities for blacks and Latinos. The number of African American students enrolled in colleges and universities doubled between 1970 and 1977 to 1.1 million, or 9.3 percent of the total student enrollment. A small but growing number of African Americans moved into white-collar professions in corporations and universities. Others found new opportunities in civil service occupations such as law enforcement or entered apprenticeships in the skilled construction trades. Latinos experienced similar gains in education and employment. On the whole, however, both groups enjoyed only marginal economic improvement, since

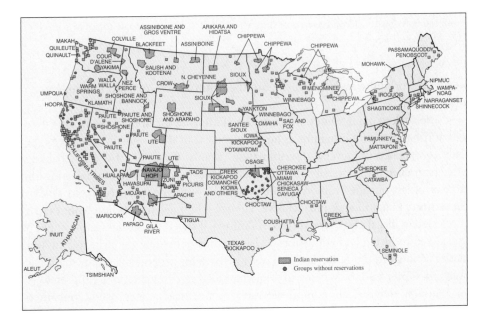

MAP 30.2
American Indian Reservations

Although Native Americans have been able to preserve small enclaves in the northeastern states, most Indian reservations are in the West. Beginning in the 1970s various nations filed land claims against federal and state governments.

An Antibusing Confrontation in Boston

Tensions over court-ordered busing ran high in Boston in 1976. When a black lawyer tried to cross the city hall plaza during an antibusing demonstration, he became a victim of Boston's climate of racial hatred and violence. This Pulitzer Prize–winning photograph by Stanley Forman for the Boston *Herald American* shows a protester trying to impale the man with a flagstaff. (Stanley Forman)

poor and working-class nonwhites bore the brunt of job loss and unemployment in the 1970s.

Nevertheless, many whites, who were also feeling the economic pinch, came to resent affirmative action programs as an infringement of their rights. White men especially complained of "reverse discrimination" against them. In 1978 Allan Bakke, a white man, sued the University of California Medical School at Davis for rejecting him in favor of less qualified minority candidates. The Supreme Court ruling in *Bakke v. University of California* was inconclusive. Though it branded the medical school's strict quota system illegal and ordered Bakke admitted, it stated that racial factors could be considered in hiring and admission decisions, thus upholding the principle of affirmative action. But the *Bakke* decision was a setback for proponents of affirmative action, and it prepared the way for subsequent efforts to eliminate those programs.

Though activists who supported racial minorities, women, gays, consumers, and the environment had distinct agendas, they also had much in common. They were part of "a rights revolution"—a wide-ranging movement in the 1960s and 1970s to bring issues of social justice and welfare to the forefront of public policy. Influenced by the Great Society's liberalism, they invariably turned to the federal government for protection of individual rights and—in the case of environmentalists—the world's natural resources. The activists of this period made substantial progress in widening the notion of the federal government's responsibilities, but by the end of the 1970s their movements faced growing opposition.

THE POLITICS OF RESENTMENT

Together with the rapidly growing antiabortion movement, the often vociferous public opposition to busing, affirmative action, gay rights ordinances, and the Equal Rights Amendment constituted a broad backlash against the social changes of the previous decade. Many Americans believed that their interests had been slighted by the rights revolution and resented a federal government that protected women who sought abortions or minorities who benefited from affirmative action. The economic changes of the 1970s, which left many working- and middle-class Americans with lower disposable incomes, rising prices, and higher taxes, further fueled what the conservative writer Alan Crawford has termed the "politics of resentment"—a grassroots revolt against "special-interest groups" (women, minorities, gays, and so on) and growing expenditures on social welfare. Special groups and programs, conservatives believed, robbed other Americans of educational and employment opportunities and saddled the working and middle classes with an extra financial burden.

One manifestation of the politics of resentment was a wave of local taxpayers' revolts. In 1978 California voters passed Proposition 13, a measure that reduced property taxes and eventually undercut local governments' ability to maintain schools and other essential services. Promising tax relief to middle-class homeowners and reduced funding for busing and other programs to benefit the poor— who were invariably viewed as nonwhite—Proposition 13 became the model for similar tax measures around the country in the late 1970s and 1980s.

The rising popularity of evangelical religion also fueled the conservative resurgence of the 1970s. Fundamentalist groups that fostered a "born-again" experience had been growing steadily since World War II, under the leadership of charismatic preachers such as Billy Graham. According to a Gallup poll conducted in 1976, some 50 million Americans—about a quarter of the population—were affiliated with evangelical movements. These groups set up their own school systems and newspapers. Through broadcasting networks like the Christian Broadcasting Network, founded by the Virginia preacher Pat Robertson, a new breed of televangelists such as Jerry Falwell built vast and influential electronic ministries.

Many of these evangelicals spoke out on a broad range of issues, denouncing abortion, busing, sex education, pornography, feminism, and gay rights and bringing their religious values to a wider public. In 1979 Jerry Falwell founded the Moral Majority, a political pressure group that promoted Christian "family values"—traditional gender roles, heterosexuality, family cohesion—and staunch anticommunism. The extensive media and fund-raising networks of the Christian right contributed to the organizational base for a larger conservative movement known as the New Right.

The New Right's constituency was complex. Conservatives of the early cold-war era had focused on resisting creeping socialism at home and abroad and were often identified with corporate business interests. In the 1970s they were joined not only by evangelical Christian groups but by "neoconservatives," intellectuals such as sociologist Nathan Glazier and Norman Podhoretz, editor of *Commentary* magazine, who had been associated with radical or liberal agendas in the past and now recanted their former political views vehemently. Articulate in their criticisms of affirmative action, the welfare state, and changing gender and sexual values, they helped to give conservative values a heightened respectability and reinforced much of the "politics of resentment." The New Right's diverse constituents shared a hostility toward a powerful federal government and a fear of declining social morality. Backed by wealthy corporate interests and using sophisticated computerized mass-mailing campaigns, a variety of New Right political groups mobilized thousands of followers and millions of dollars to support conservative candidates and causes.

Politics in the Wake of Watergate

It is not surprising that in the wake of Watergate many citizens had become cynical about the federal government and about politicians in general. "Don't vote. It only encourages them" read one bumper sticker during the 1976 campaign. Nixon's successors, Gerald Ford and Jimmy Carter, plagued by foreign-policy crises and continued economic woes, did little to restore public confidence. In the 1980 elections, voter apathy persisted, but Ronald Reagan's lopsided presidential victory signified a hope that the charismatic former actor could restore America's traditional values and its economic and international power.

FORD'S CARETAKER PRESIDENCY

During the two years Gerald Ford held the nation's highest office, he failed to establish his legitimacy as president. Ford's pardon of Nixon hurt his credibility as a political leader, but an even bigger problem was his handling of the economy, which was reeling from the inflation set in motion by the Vietnam War, rising oil prices, and the growing trade deficit. In 1974 the inflation rate soared to almost 12 percent, and in the following year the economy entered its deepest downturn since the Great Depression. Though many of the nation's economic problems were beyond the president's control, Ford's failure to take more vigorous action made him appear timid and powerless.

In foreign policy Ford was equally lacking in leadership. He maintained Nixon's détente initiatives by asking Henry Kissinger to stay on as secretary of state. Though Ford met with Soviet leaders hoping to hammer out the details of a SALT II (Strategic Arms Limitation Treaty) agreement, he made little progress. Ford and Kissinger also continued Nixon's policy of increasing support for the shah of Iran, ignoring the bitter opposition and anti-Western sentiment that the shah's policy of rapid modernization was provoking among the growing Muslim fundamentalist population in Iran.

JIMMY CARTER: THE OUTSIDER AS PRESIDENT

The 1976 presidential campaign was one of the blandest in years. President Ford chose as his running mate the conservative Senator Robert J. Dole of Kansas. The Democratic choice, James E. (Jimmy) Carter, governor of Georgia, shared the ticket with Senator Walter F. Mondale of Minnesota, who had ties to the traditional Democratic constituencies of labor, liberals, blacks, and big-city machines. Avoiding issues and controversy, Carter played up his role as a Washington outsider, pledging to restore morality to government. "I will never lie to you," he earnestly told voters. Carter won the election with 50 percent of the popular vote to Ford's 48 percent.

Despite his efforts to overcome the post-Watergate climate of skepticism and apathy, Carter never became an effective leader. His outsider strategy distanced him from traditional sources of power, and he did little to heal the breach. Shying away from established Democratic leaders, Carter turned to advisors and friends who had worked with him in Georgia, none of whom had national experience. When his budget director, Bert Lance, was questioned about financial irregularities at the Atlanta bank he had headed, Carter's campaign pledge to restore integrity and morality to the government rang hollow.

Inflation was Carter's major domestic challenge. When he took office, the nation was still recovering from the severe recession of 1975 and 1976. Carter embarked on a fiscal policy that eroded both business and consumer confidence. To counter inflation the Federal Reserve Board raised interest rates repeatedly; in 1980 they topped 20 percent, a historic high. A deep recession finally broke the inflationary spiral in 1982, a year after Carter left office.

The Carter administration expanded the federal bureaucracy in some cases and limited its reach in others. Carter enlarged the cabinet by creating the Departments of Energy and Education and approved new environmental protection measures, such as the $1.6 billion "Superfund" to clean up chemical pollution sites, as well as new park and forest lands in Alaska. But he continued President Nixon's efforts to reduce the scope of federal activities by reforming the civil service and deregulating the airline, trucking, and railroad industries. With deregulation prices often dropped, but the resulting cutthroat competition drove many firms out of business and encouraged corporate consolidation. Carter also failed in his effort to decontrol oil and natural gas prices as a spur to domestic production and conservation.

Carter's attempt to provide leadership during the energy crisis also faltered. He called energy-conservation efforts "the moral equivalent of war," but the media reduced the phrase to "MEOW." In early 1979 a revolution in Iran again raised oil prices, and gas lines again reminded Americans of their dependence on foreign oil.

That summer Carter's approval rating dropped to 26 percent—lower than Richard Nixon's during the worst part of the Watergate scandal.

In foreign affairs President Carter made human rights the centerpiece of his policy. He criticized the suppression of dissent in the Soviet Union—especially as it affected the right of Jewish citizens to emigrate—and withdrew economic and military aid from Argentina, Uruguay, Ethiopia, and other countries that violated human rights. Carter also established the Office of Human Rights in the State Department. Unable to change the internal policies of long-time U.S. allies who were serious violators of human rights, such as the Philippines, South Korea, and South Africa, he did manage to raise public awareness of the human-rights issue, making it one future administrations would have to address.

In Latin America Carter's most important contribution was the resolution of the lingering dispute over control of the Panama Canal. In a treaty signed on September 7, 1977, the United States agreed to turn over control of the canal to Panama on December 31, 1999. In return, the United States retained the right to send its ships through the canal in case of war, even though the canal itself would be declared neutral territory. Despite a conservative outcry that the United States was giving away more than it got, the Senate narrowly approved the treaty.

Though Carter had campaigned to free the United States from its "inordinate fear of Communism," relations with the Soviet Union soon became tense, largely because of problems surrounding arms-limitation talks. Eventually the Soviet leader Leonid Brezhnev signed SALT II (1979), but hopes for Senate ratification of the treaty collapsed when the Soviet Union invaded Afghanistan that December. In retaliation for this aggression, which Carter viewed as a threat to Middle Eastern oil supplies, the United States curtailed grain sales to the USSR and boycotted the 1980 summer Olympics in Moscow. (The Soviets returned the gesture by boycotting the 1984 summer games in Los Angeles.) When Carter left office in 1981, relations with the Soviet Union were worse than they had been when he took over.

President Carter achieved both his most stunning success and his greatest failure in the Middle East. Relations between Egypt and Israel had remained tense since the 1973 Yom Kippur War. In 1978 Carter helped to break the diplomatic stalemate by inviting Israel's prime minister Menachem Begin and Egyptian president Anwar al-Sadat to Camp David, the presidential retreat in Maryland. Two weeks of discussions and Carter's promise of additional foreign aid to Egypt persuaded Sadat and Begin to adopt a "framework for peace." The framework included Egypt's recognition of Israel's right to exist and Israel's return of the Sinai Peninsula, which it had occupied since 1967. Transfer of the territory to Egypt took place from 1979 to 1982.

Dramatically less successful was U.S. foreign policy toward Iran. Ever since the CIA had helped to install Muhammad Reza Pahlavi on the throne in 1953, the United States had counted Iran as a faithful ally in the troubled Middle East. Overlooking the repressive tactics of Iran's CIA-trained secret police, SAVAK, Carter followed in the footsteps of previous cold-war policymakers for whom access to Iranian

American Hostages in Iran

Images of blindfolded, hand-cuffed American hostages seized by Iranian militants at the American embassy in Teheran in November 1979 shocked the nation and created a foreign-policy crisis that eventually cost Jimmy Carter the presidency.

(Mingam/Liaison)

oil reserves and the shah's consistently anticommunist stance outweighed all other considerations.

Early in 1979, however, the shah's government was overthrown and driven into exile by a revolution led by fundamentalist Muslim leader Ayatollah Ruhollah Khomeini. In late October 1979 the Carter administration admitted the deposed shah, who was suffering from incurable cancer, to the United States for medical treatment. Though Iran's new leaders had warned that such an action would provoke retaliation, Henry Kissinger and other foreign-policy leaders had argued that the United States should assist the shah, both for humanitarian reasons and in return for his years of support for American policy. In response, on November 4, 1979, fundamentalist Muslim students under Khomeini's direction seized the U.S. embassy in Teheran, taking Americans there hostage in a flagrant violation of the principle of diplomatic immunity. The hostage takers demanded that the shah be returned to Iran for trial and punishment, but the United States refused. Instead, President Carter suspended arms sales to Iran, froze Iranian assets in American banks, and threatened to deport Iranian students in the United States.

For the next fourteen months the Iranian hostage crisis paralyzed Jimmy Carter's presidency. Night after night, humiliating pictures of blindfolded hostages appeared on television newscasts. The extensive media coverage, and Carter's insistence that the safe return of the fifty-two hostages was his top priority, enhanced the value of the hostages to their captors. An attempt to mount a military rescue of the hostages failed miserably in April 1980, six months into the crisis, because of helicopter equipment failures in the desert. The abortive rescue mission reinforced the public's view of Carter as a bumbling and ineffective executive.

THE REAGAN REVOLUTION

With Carter embroiled in the hostage crisis, the Republicans gained momentum by nominating former California governor Ronald Reagan. A movie actor in the late 1930s, the 1940s, and the early 1950s, Reagan had served as president of the Screen Actors Guild and had been active in the postwar anticommunist crusade in Hollywood. He had endorsed Barry Goldwater in 1964 and had begun his own political career shortly after, serving as governor of California from 1967 to 1975. After losing a bid for the Republican nomination in 1976, Reagan secured it easily in 1980 and chose former CIA director George Bush as his running mate.

In the final months of the campaign, Carter took on an embattled and defensive tone, while Reagan remained upbeat and decisive. The Republicans benefited from superior financial resources, which allowed them to make sophisticated use of television and direct-mail appeals. Reagan also had a powerful issue to exploit: the hostage stalemate. Calling the Iranians "barbarians" and "common criminals," he hinted that he would take strong action to win the hostages' return. More important, Reagan effectively appealed to the politics of resentment that flourished during the lean years of the 1970s. In a televised debate between the candidates, Reagan emphasized the economic plight of working- and middle-class Americans when he posed the rhetorical question, "Are you better off today than you were four years ago?"

In November Reagan won easily, with 51 percent of the popular vote to Carter's 41 percent. The landslide also gave the Republicans control of the Senate for the first time since 1954, though the Democrats maintained their hold on the House. Voter turnout, however, was at the lowest since the 1920s: only 53 percent of those eligible to vote went to the polls. Many poor and working-class voters stayed home. Nevertheless, the election confirmed the growth in the power of the Republican Party since Richard Nixon's victory in 1968.

The core of the Republican Party that elected Ronald Reagan remained the upper-middle-class white Protestant voters who supported balanced budgets, disliked government activism, feared crime and communism, and believed in a strong national defense. But new groups had gravitated toward the Republican vision: southern whites disaffected by big government and black civil rights gains; blue-collar workers, especially culturally conservative Catholics; young voters who identified themselves as conservatives; and residents in the West, especially those in the rapidly growing suburbs. By wooing these "Reagan Democrats," the Republican Party made deep inroads into Democratic territory, eroding that party's traditional coalition of southerners, blacks, laborers, and urban ethnics.

The New Right was another significant contributor to the Republican victory, especially the religious right, associated with groups like the Moral Majority, whose emphasis on traditional values and Christian morality dovetailed well with conservative Republican ideology. In 1980 these concerns formed the basis for the party's platform, which called for a constitutional ban on abortion, voluntary prayer in public schools, and a mandatory death penalty for certain crimes. The Republicans also demanded an end to court-mandated busing and for the first time in forty years opposed the Equal Rights Amendment. A key factor in the 1980 election, the New Right contributed to the rebirth of the Republican Party under Ronald Reagan.

On January 20, 1981, at the moment Carter turned over the presidency to Ronald Reagan, the Iranian government released the American hostages. After 444 days of captivity, the hostages returned home to an ecstatic welcome, a reflection of the public's frustration over their long ordeal. While most Americans continued to maintain "We're Number One," the hostage crisis in Iran came to symbolize the loss of America's power to control world affairs. Its psychological impact was enhanced by its occurrence at the end of a decade that had witnessed Watergate, the American defeat in Vietnam, and the OPEC embargo. To a great extent, the decline in American influence had been magnified by the unusual predominance the United States had enjoyed after World War II—an advantage that should not have been expected to last forever. The return of Japan and Western Europe to economic and political power, the control of vital oil resources by Middle Eastern countries, and the industrialization of some developing nations had widened the cast of characters on the international stage. Still, many Americans were unable to let go of the presumption of economic and political supremacy born in the postwar years. Ronald Reagan rode their frustrations to victory in 1980.

For Further Exploration

Peter N. Carroll, *It Seemed Like Nothing Happened* (1982), provides a general overview of the period. Gary Wills, *Nixon Agonistes* (rev. ed. 1990), judges Nixon to be a product of his times. For Watergate, a starting point are the books by the *Washington Post* journalists who broke the scandal, Carl Bernstein and Bob Woodward: *All the President's Men* (1974) and *The Final Days* (1976). Stanley Kutler, *Abuse of Power: The Nixon Tapes* (1997), is a collection of transcripts from the White House tapes relating to Watergate and other Nixon-era scandals. Gary Sick, a Jimmy Carter White House advisor on Iran, offers an insider's account of the hostage crisis in *All Fall Down: America's Tragic Encounter with Iran* (1986). Thomas Byrne Edsall with Mary D. Edsall, *Chain Reaction: The Impact of Race, Rights and Taxes on American Politics* (1991), examines some of the divisive social issues of the 1970s. J. Anthony Lukas, *Common Ground* (1985), tells the story of the Boston busing crisis through the biographies of three families. Barbara Ehrenreich examines the backlash against feminism in *Hearts of Men* (1984). A critical account of the New Right is *Thunder on the Right* (1980) by Alan Crawford.

For the Watergate scandal two useful sites are National Archives and Record Administration's "Watergate Trial Tapes and Transcripts" at <http://www.nara.gov/nixon/tapes/trial&transcripts.html>, which provides transcripts of the infamous tapes as well as other useful links to archival holdings concerning Richard Nixon's presidency. "Watergate" at <http://vcepolitics.com/watergate/> is a textual, visual, and auditory survey of Watergate.

T I M E L I N E

1968	Richard Nixon elected president		Freedom of Information Act strengthened
1969	Supreme Court Chief Justice Earl Warren retires, replaced by Warren Burger.		Fair Campaign Practices Act passed
		1974–1975	Busing controversy in Boston
1970	First Earth Day		
	Environmental Protection Agency established	1975–1976	Economic recession
1971	Pentagon Papers published	1976	Jimmy Carter elected president
1972	Watergate break-in at the Democratic National Committee's headquarters	1977	First National Women's Conference in Houston
	Title IX of the Educational Amendments Act		Voters overturn a Miami city council's gay rights measure.
	Congress passes Equal Rights Amendment.	1978	Carter brokers Camp David accords between Egypt and Israel.
	Occupational Safety and Health Administration (OSHA) and Consumer Products Safety Commission established		Proposition 13 reduces California taxes.
	Nixon reelected		*Bakke v. University of California* limits affirmative action.
	Ms. magazine founded		Discovery of the toxic waste site at Love Canal
1973	Spiro Agnew resigns; Gerald Ford appointed vice president	1979	Three Mile Island nuclear accident
	Roe v. Wade legalizes abortion.		Moral Majority founded
	OPEC oil embargo begins; gas shortages.		Second oil crisis triggered by revolution in Iran
	Endangered Species Act		Hostages seized at American embassy in Teheran, Iran
1974	*Milliken v. Bradley* mandates busing within cities.		USSR invades Afghanistan.
	Nixon resigns; Ford becomes president and pardons Nixon.	1980	Ronald Reagan elected president

Created by Australian political science professor Malcolm Farnsworth, the site's materials include a Nixon biography with speech excerpts, a Watergate chronology, an analysis of the significance of the "Deep Throat" informant, and an assessment of the Watergate legacy. Relevant links provide access to primary documents. The Oyez Project at Northwestern University at <http://oyez.nwu.edu/> is an invaluable resource for over 1,000 Supreme Court cases, with audio transcripts, voting records, and summaries. For this period, see, for example, its materials on *Roe v. Wade*, *Bakke v. University of California*, and *Griswold v. Connecticut*.

Chapter 31

A NEW DOMESTIC AND WORLD ORDER

1981–2000

The energizing slogans of the past—Making the World Safe for Democracy, the Domino Theory, the Evil Empire, the New World Order—ring hollow in light of present more sophisticated knowledge of history. When it comes to finding ways to deal with today's ambiguities and uncertainties, a new politics or a new leadership has not yet evolved.

—HAYNES JOHNSON, 1994

On November 9, 1989, millions of television viewers worldwide watched jubilant Germans swarm through the Berlin Wall after the East German government lifted all restrictions on passage between the eastern and western sectors of the city. The Berlin Wall, which had divided the city since 1961, was the foremost symbol of communist repression and the cold-war division of Europe. Over the years more than 400 East Germans had lost their lives trying to escape to the freedom of the other side. Now East and West Berliners, young and old, danced and mingled on what remained of the structure.

When the Berlin Wall came down, it brought communism's grip over Eastern Europe down with it. With the breakup of the Soviet Union in 1991, the cold war finally ended, but new sources of conflict soon threatened world peace. In the new world order the United States was increasingly linked to a global economy that directly affected American interest rates, consumption patterns, and job opportunities. At home, Americans grappled with racial, ethnic, and cultural conflict; crime and economic inequities; the shrinking role of the federal government; and disenchantment with political leaders' failure to solve many of the nation's pressing social problems.

The Reagan-Bush Years, 1981–1993

First elected at sixty-nine, Ronald Reagan was the oldest man ever to serve as president, yet he conveyed a sense of physical vigor. By capitalizing on his skills as an actor and a public speaker and by winning the support of the emerging New Right within the Republican Party, Reagan became one of the most popular presidents of the twentieth century. George Bush paled in comparison. His one term as president often seems indistinguishable from the two terms of his predecessor, in part because Bush was overshadowed by Reagan's extraordinary charisma but also because he followed the basic policies of the previous administration. Distrustful of the federal government, both Bush and Reagan turned away from the state as a source of solutions for America's social problems, calling into question almost half a century of governmental activism. "Government is not the solution to our problem," Reagan declared. "Government is the problem."

REAGANOMICS

The economic and tax policies that emerged under Reagan, quickly dubbed Reaganomics, were based on supply-side economics theory. According to the theory, high taxes siphoned off capital that would otherwise be invested, stimulating growth. Tax cuts would therefore promote investment, causing an economic expansion that would increase tax revenues. Together with cuts in government spending, especially on entitlement programs, tax cuts would also shrink the federal budget deficit. Critics charged that conservative Republicans deliberately cut taxes to force reductions in federal funding for the social programs that they abhorred.

The Economic Recovery Tax Act passed in 1981 reduced income tax rates by 25 percent over three years. The reductions were supposed to be linked to drastic cutbacks in federal expenditures. But while cuts were made in food stamps, unemployment compensation, and welfare programs such as Aid to Families with Dependent Children (AFDC), congressional resistance kept the Social Security and Medicare programs intact. The net impact of Reaganomics was to further the redistribution of income from the poor to the wealthy.

Another tenet of Reaganomics was that many federal regulations impeded economic growth and productivity. Insisting that a safety net existed for the truly needy, the administration moved to abolish or reduce federal regulation of the workplace, health care, consumer protection, and the environment. The responsibility and cost of such regulations were transferred to the states. One of the results of this policy was the deinstitutionalization of many of the mentally ill, forcing them onto the streets.

The money saved by these means—and more—was plowed into a five-year, $1.2 trillion defense buildup. This huge increase fulfilled Reagan's campaign pledge to "make America number one again." The B-1 bomber, which President Carter had canceled, was resurrected, and development of a new missile system, the MX, was begun. Reagan's most ambitious and controversial weapons plan, proposed in 1983, was the Strategic Defense Initiative (SDI), popularly known as "Star Wars." A computerized satellite and laser shield for detecting and intercepting incoming missiles, SDI would supposedly render nuclear war obsolete.

Reagan's programs benefited from the Federal Reserve Board's tight money policies, as well as a serendipitous drop in world oil prices, which reduced the disastrous inflation rates that had bedeviled the nation in the 1970s. Between 1980 and 1982 the inflation rate dropped from 12.4 percent to just 4 percent. Unfortunately, the Fed's tightening of the money supply also brought on the "Reagan recession" of 1981 and 1982, which threw some 10 million Americans out of work. But as the recession bottomed out in early 1983 the economy began to grow, and for the rest of the decade inflation remained low. Despite rather unexceptional growth in the gross national product the Reagan administration presided over the longest peacetime economic expansion in American history.

REAGAN'S SECOND TERM

This economic growth played a role in the 1984 elections. Reagan campaigned on the theme "It's Morning in America," suggesting that a new day of prosperity and pride was dawning. The Democrats nominated former vice president Walter Mondale of Minnesota to run against Reagan. With strong ties to labor unions, minority groups, and party leaders, Mondale epitomized the New Deal coalition that had dominated the Democratic Party since Roosevelt. To appeal to women voters, Mondale selected Representative Geraldine Ferraro of New York as his running mate—the first woman to run on a major party ticket. Nevertheless, Reagan won a landslide victory, carrying the entire nation except for Minnesota and the District of Columbia. Democrats, however, held onto the House and in 1986 would regain control of the Senate.

A major scandal marred Reagan's second term when in 1986 news leaked out that the administration had negotiated an arms-for-hostages deal with the revolutionary government of Iran—the same government Reagan had denounced during the 1980 hostage crisis. In an attempt to gain Iran's help in freeing some American hostages held by pro-Iranian forces in Lebanon, the United States had covertly sold arms to Iran. Some of the profits generated by the arms sales were diverted to the Contras, counterrevolutionaries in Nicaragua, whom the administration supported over the leftist regime of the Sandinistas. The covert diversion of funds, which was both illegal and unconstitutional, seemed to have been the brainstorm of Marine Lieutenant Colonel Oliver North, a National Security Council aide at the time. One key memo linked the White House to his plan. But when Congress investigated the mounting scandal in 1986 and 1987, White House officials testified that the president knew nothing about the diversion. Ronald Reagan's defense remained simple and consistent: "I don't remember."

The scandal bore many similarities to Watergate, including the possibility that the president had acted illegally. Early in Reagan's administration, one of his

Festive Times at the Reagan White House

Since Ronald and Nancy Reagan were both former actors, perhaps they thought of Fred Astaire and Ginger Rogers (see p. 703) when they struck this pose at a White House state dinner in May 1985. Some former White House staffers now suspect that Reagan was already showing signs of early Alzheimer's disease by that point.

(Photo by Harry Benson. Cover courtesy Vanity Fair. © 1985 by Condé-Nast Publications, Inc.)

critics had coined the phrase "Teflon presidency" to describe Reagan's resiliency: bad news didn't stick; it just rolled off. The public seemed untroubled that the president was often confused or ill informed or that he relied heavily on close advisors, especially his wife. Even the news that Nancy Reagan was in the habit of consulting an astrologer before planning major White House events failed to shake public confidence in the president. Reagan weathered "Iran-Contragate," but the scandal did weaken his presidency.

The president proposed no bold domestic policy initiatives in his last two years in office. He had promised to place drastic limits on the federal government and to give free-market forces freer reign. Despite reordering the federal government's priorities, he failed to reduce its size or scope. And although spending for most poverty programs had been cut, Social Security and other entitlement programs remained untouched. Despite Reagan's failure to achieve his goals, his spending cuts and antigovernment rhetoric shaped the terms of political debate for the rest of the century.

One of Reagan's most significant legacies was his conservative judicial appointments. In 1981 he had nominated Sandra Day O'Connor, the first woman ever to serve on the Supreme Court. In his second term he appointed two more justices,

Antonin Scalia (1986) and Anthony Kennedy (1988), both of whom were far more conservative than the moderate O'Connor. Justice William Rehnquist, a noted conservative, was elevated to chief justice in 1986. Under his leadership the Court, often by a five-to-four margin, chipped away at the Warren Court's legacy in decisions on individual liberties, affirmative action, and the rights of criminal defendants.

Ironically, though Reagan had promised to balance the budget by 1984, his most enduring legacy was the national debt, which tripled during his two terms. The huge deficit reflected the combined effects of increased military spending, tax reductions for high-income taxpayers, and Congress's refusal to approve deep cuts in domestic programs. By 1989 the national debt had climbed to $2.8 trillion—more than $11,000 for every American citizen.

The nation was also running an annual deficit in its trade with other nations. Exports had been falling since the 1970s, when American products began to encounter increasing competition in world markets. In the early 1980s a high exchange rate for dollars made U.S. goods more expensive for foreign buyers and imports more affordable for Americans. The budget and trade deficits contributed to a major shift in 1985: for the first time since 1915 the United States became a debtor rather than a creditor nation. Since then, with phenomenal speed, the United States has accumulated the world's largest foreign debt.

THE BUSH PRESIDENCY

George H. W. Bush won the Republican nomination in 1988 and chose for vice president a young conservative Indiana senator, Dan Quayle. In the Democratic primaries the contest was between Governor Michael Dukakis of Massachusetts and the charismatic civil rights leader Jesse Jackson, whose populist Rainbow Coalition had embraced the diversity of Democratic constituencies. Dukakis received the party's nomination and chose Senator Lloyd Bentsen of Texas as his running mate.

The 1988 campaign had a harsh tone: brief televised attack ads replaced meaningful discussion of the issues. The sound bite "Read My Lips: No New Taxes," drawn from George Bush's acceptance speech at the Republican convention, became the party's campaign mantra. In a television ad featuring Willie Horton, a black man convicted of murder who had killed again while on furlough from a Massachusetts prison, Republicans, pandering to voters' racist fears, charged Dukakis with being soft on crime. Dukakis, forced on the defensive, failed to mount an effective counterattack. Bush carried thirty-eight states, winning the popular vote by 53.4 percent to 45.6 percent. Only 50 percent of eligible voters went to the polls.

Some of the more significant domestic trends of the Bush era were determined by the judiciary rather than the executive branch. Under Reagan's appointees, the Supreme Court continued to move away from liberal activism toward a more conservative stance, especially on the issue of abortion. The 1989 *Webster v. Reproductive Health Services,* which upheld the right of states to limit the use of public funds and institutions for abortions, gave states more latitude in restricting abortions. The next year the Court upheld a federal regulation barring personnel at federally funded health clinics from discussing abortion with their clients. In 1992 the Court upheld a Pennsylvania law mandating informed consent and a twenty-four-hour waiting period before an abortion could be performed. But the justices also reaffirmed the "essential holding" in *Roe v. Wade:* women had a constitutional right to abortion.

In 1990 David Souter, a little-known federal judge from New Hampshire, easily won confirmation to the Supreme Court. But the next year a major controversy erupted over President Bush's nomination of Clarence Thomas, an African American conservative with little judicial experience. Just as Thomas's confirmation hearings were drawing to a close, a former colleague, Anita Hill, testified publicly that Thomas had sexually harassed her in the early 1980s. After widely watched and widely debated televised testimony by both Thomas and Hill before the all-male Senate Judiciary Committee, the Senate confirmed Thomas by a narrow margin. In the wake of the hearings national polls confirmed the pervasiveness of sexual harassment on the job: four out of ten women said that they had been the object of unwanted sexual advances from men at work.

Bush also had relatively little control over the economic developments that soon became a key issue. His campaign promise of a "kinder, gentler administration" was

A Woman of Conscience

Accusations by University of Oklahoma law professor Anita Hill that Supreme Court nominee Clarence Thomas had sexually harassed her sparked fierce debate. Many felt that had there been more women in the Senate, Hill's charges would have been treated more seriously. After the 1992 election women's representation did in fact increase to six women in the Senate and forty-seven in the House of Representatives.
(Markel/Gamma Liaison)

doomed by his predecessor's failed economic policies, especially the budget deficit. The Gramm-Rudman Act, passed in 1985, had mandated automatic cuts if budget targets were not met in 1991. Facing the prospect of a halt in nonessential government services and the layoff of thousands of government employees, Congress resorted to new spending cuts and one of the largest tax increases in history. Bush's failure to keep his "No New Taxes" promise earned him the enmity of Republican conservatives, which would dramatically hurt his chances for reelection in 1992.

Reagan's decision to shift the cost of many federal programs—including housing, education, public works, and social services—to state and local governments caused problems for Bush. In 1990 a recession began to erode state and local tax revenues. As incomes declined and industrial and white-collar layoffs increased, poverty and homelessness increased sharply. In 1991 unemployment approached 7 percent nationwide. To save money, state and local governments laid off workers even as demand for social services and unemployment compensation climbed.

Foreign Relations under Reagan and Bush

The collapse of détente during the Carter administration, after the Soviet invasion of Afghanistan, prompted Reagan's confrontational approach to what he called the "evil empire." Backed by Republican hard-liners and determined to reduce communist influence in developing nations, Reagan articulated some of the harshest anti-Soviet rhetoric since the 1950s. The collapse of the Soviet Union in 1991 removed that nation as a credible threat, but new post–cold-war challenges quickly appeared.

INTERVENTIONS IN DEVELOPING COUNTRIES AND THE END OF THE COLD WAR

Despite Reagan's rhetoric not all his international problems involved U.S.-Soviet confrontations. In 1983, after Israel invaded Lebanon, the U.S. Embassy in Beirut was bombed by anti-Israeli Muslim fundamentalists. A second bombing killed 239 Marine peacekeepers barracked in the city. Around the world terrorist assassins struck down Indira Gandhi in India and Anwar al-Sadat in Egypt. But it was the airplane hijackings and countless terrorist incidents in the Middle East that led Reagan to order air strikes against one highly visible source of terrorism, Muammar al-Qadhdhafi of Libya.

The administration reserved its most concerted attention for Central America. Halting what was seen as the spread of communism in that region became an obsession. In 1983 Reagan ordered the marines to invade the tiny Caribbean island of Grenada, claiming that its Cuban-supported communist regime posed a threat to other states in the region. Reagan's top priority, however, was to topple the leftist Sandinista government in Nicaragua. In 1981 the United States suspended aid to

Nicaragua, charging that the Sandinistas were supplying arms to rebels against a repressive right-wing regime in El Salvador. At the same time the CIA began to provide extensive covert support to the Nicaraguan opposition, the "Contras," whom Reagan called "freedom fighters." Congress, wary of the assumption of unconstitutional powers by the executive branch, responded in 1984 by passing the Boland Amendment, which banned the CIA and other intelligence agencies from providing military support to the Contras—a provision violated in the Iran-Contra affair.

Surprisingly, given Reagan's rhetoric, his second term brought a reduction in tensions with the Soviet Union. In 1985 Reagan met with the new Soviet premier, Mikhail Gorbachev, at the first superpower summit meeting since 1979. Two years later the two leaders agreed to eliminate all intermediate-range missiles based in Europe. Although a summit in Moscow in 1988 produced no further cuts in nuclear arms, the sight of the two first families attending the Bolshoi Ballet together and strolling amiably in Red Square exemplified the thaw in the cold war.

Under Bush's administration even more dramatic changes abroad brought an end to the cold war. In 1989 the grip of communism on Eastern Europe loosened and then let go completely in a series of mostly nonviolent revolutions that climaxed in the destruction of the Berlin Wall in November. Soon the Soviet Union itself began to succumb to the forces of change. The background for these dramatic upheavals was the changes set in motion by Soviet president Mikhail Gorbachev after 1985. Through his policies of *glasnost* (openness) and *perestroika* (economic restructuring), Gorbachev had signaled a willingness to tolerate significant changes. But Gorbachev, who was always more popular outside his country than at home, found that to call for the dismantling of an old system was easier than to build a new system.

On August 19, 1991, alarmed Soviet military leaders seized Gorbachev and attempted unsuccessfully to oust him. The failure of the coup broke the Communist Party's dominance over the Soviet Union. In December the Union of Soviet Socialist Republics formally dissolved itself to make way for an eleven-member Commonwealth of Independent States (CIS) (see Map 31.1). Gorbachev resigned, and Boris Yeltsin, president of the new state of Russia, the largest and most populous republic, became the preeminent leader in the region.

The suddenness of the collapse of the Soviet Union and the end of the cold war stunned America and the world. In the absence of bipolar superpower confrontations future international conflicts would arise from varied regional, religious, and ethnic differences. Suddenly the United States faced unfamiliar military and diplomatic challenges.

WAR IN THE PERSIAN GULF, 1990–1991

The first challenge surfaced in the Middle East. On August 2, 1990, Iraq, led by Saddam Hussein, invaded Kuwait, its small but oil-rich neighbor. In response President Bush sponsored a series of resolutions in the U.N. Security Council, con-

MAP 31.1
The Collapse of Communism in Eastern Europe and the Soviet Union

The end of the Soviet empire in Eastern Europe and the collapse of communism in the Soviet Union itself dramatically changed the borders of Europe and Central Asia. West and East Germany reunited, while the nations of Czechoslovakia and Yugoslavia, created by the 1919 Versailles treaty, divided into smaller states. The old Soviet Union produced fifteen new countries, of which eleven remained loosely bound in the Commonwealth of Independent States (CIS).

demning Iraq, calling for its withdrawal, and imposing an embargo and trade sanctions. When Hussein showed no signs of yielding, Bush prodded the international organization to create a legal framework for a military offensive against the man he called "the butcher of Baghdad." In November the Security Council voted to use force if Iraq did not withdraw by January 15. In a close fifty-two-to-forty-eight vote on January 12, the U.S. Senate authorized military action. Four days later President Bush announced to the nation that "the liberation of Kuwait has begun."

The forty-two-day war was a resounding success for the United Nations' coalition forces, which were predominantly American. Under the leadership of General Colin Powell, chairman of the Joint Chiefs of Staff, and the commanding general, H. Norman Schwarzkopf, Operation Desert Storm opened with a month of air strikes to crush communications, destroy armaments, and pummel Iraqi ground troops. A land offensive followed. Within days thousands of Iraqi troops had fled or surrendered, and the fighting quickly ended, although Hussein remained in power (see Map 31.2).

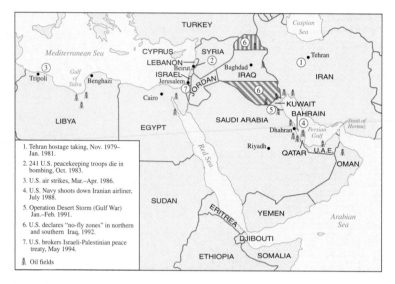

1. Tehran hostage taking, Nov. 1979–Jan. 1981.
2. 241 U.S. peacekeeping troops die in bombing, Oct. 1983.
3. U.S. air strikes, Mar.–Apr. 1986.
4. U.S. Navy shoots down Iranian airliner, July 1988.
5. Operation Desert Storm (Gulf War) Jan.–Feb. 1991.
6. U.S. declares "no-fly zones" in northern and southern Iraq, 1992.
7. U.S. brokers Israeli-Palestinian peace treaty, May 1994.

🛢 Oil fields

M A P 31.2
U.S. Involvement in the Middle East, 1980–1994

The United States has long played an active role in the Middle East, pursuing the twin goals of protecting Israel's security and ensuring a realiable supply of low-cost oil from the Persian Gulf states. By far the largest intervention came in 1991, when, under United Nations auspices, President Bush sent 540,000 American troops to liberate Kuwait from Iraq. The United States also played a major role in the 1994 agreement allowing for Palestinian self-rule in the Gaza Strip and parts of the West Bank.

Women at War

Women played key and visible roles in the Persian Gulf War, comprising approximately 10 percent of the American troops. Increasing numbers of women are choosing military careers, despite widespread reports of sexual harassment and other forms of discrimination.

(Luc Delahaye/SIPA Press)

Operation Desert Storm's success and the few U.S. casualties (145 Americans were killed in action) produced a euphoric reaction at home. For many the American victory over a vastly inferior fighting force seemed to banish the ghost of Vietnam. "By God, we've kicked the Vietnam syndrome once and for all," Bush gloated. The president's approval rating shot up precipitously but declined almost as quickly when a new recession showed that the easy victory had masked the country's serious economic problems.

Uncertain Times

Opinion polls taken in the early 1990s showed that Americans were deeply concerned about the future. They worried about crime in the streets, increases in poverty and homelessness, the decline of the inner cities, illegal immigration, the environment, the failure of public schools, the unresolved abortion issue, and AIDS. But above all they worried about their own economic security—whether they would be able to keep their jobs in an era of global competition. By the end of the decade, a vastly improved economic picture would lessen—but not erase—Americans' concerns for the future.

THE ECONOMY

Slow growth in productivity and growing inequality in income distribution were the most salient economic trends in the 1980s and early 1990s. From 1945 to 1973 productivity grew 2.8 percent annually, allowing the standard of living to double in one generation, but in the quarter-century after 1973 productivity increased less than 1 percent annually, barely enough to double the standard of living in eighty years. Americans also faced stagnating real income. In 1991 the typical family's real income was only 5 percent higher than it had been in 1973, and that increase was achieved mainly because multiple members of a household were employed and because all of them were working more hours.

At the same time that wage stagnation was squeezing the middle class, economic inequality increased: the rich got richer, the poor got poorer, and the middle class shrank. By 1996 the United States was the most economically stratified industrial nation in the world. Statistics from the Congressional Budget Office showed that the richest 1 percent of American families reaped most of the gains of Reaganomics. This trend continued in the 1990s: a federal survey released in January 2000 reported that the earnings of the top one-fifth of Americans grew 15 percent in the preceding decade, while the bottom one-fifth grew less than 1 percent.

Even relatively well-advantaged Americans felt a sense of diminished expectations, in part from changes in the job market. Following an established pattern, the number of minimum-wage service jobs continued to grow, while the number of union-protected manufacturing jobs was shrinking. For many—one-fifth of the labor force in 1994—part-time or temporary work was the only work that was available. Moreover, in the 1980s and 1990s the downsizing trend, in which companies deliberately shed permanent workers to cut wage costs, spread to middle management. From 1980 to 1995 IBM shrank its mostly white-collar workforce from 400,000 to 220,000—a 45 percent decrease. Although most laid-off middle managers eventually found new jobs, many took a large pay cut.

These economic trends put even more pressure on women to seek paid employment. In 1994, 58.8 percent of women were in the labor force, up from 38 percent in 1962, compared with 75.1 percent of men. The stereotypical nuclear family of employed father, homemaker wife, and children characterized less than 15 percent of U.S. households. Although women continued to make inroads in traditionally male-dominated fields—medicine, law, law enforcement, the military, and skilled trades—one out of five held a clerical or secretarial job, the same proportion as in 1950. Women's pay lagged behind men's; for black and Latino women the gender gap in pay was especially wide.

At the same time, the labor movement—hurt by downsizing, foreign competition, fear of layoffs, government hostility during the Reagan-Bush years, and its own failure to organize unskilled workers—continued to decline. The number of union members dropped from 20 million in 1978 to 16.2 million in 1998, representing only 13.9 percent of the labor force. Although union membership was more than one-third female and one-fifth black, union leadership remained overwhelmingly white and male.

Another major cause of diminished economic expectations was the widespread fear that American corporations were no longer competitive in the global marketplace. Americans viewed with alarm the economic success of Germany and Japan, the growing U.S. trade deficit, and the infusion of foreign workers and investment money into the United States. To compete American corporations adopted new technologies, including microelectronics, biotechnology, computers, and robots, and by the late 1990s saw their competitiveness return. Bethlehem Steel, which invested $6 billion to modernize its operations, for example, doubled its productivity between 1989 and 1997.

These developments contributed to a brightening national economic picture. By the late 1990s the United States led the world in information technology and had expanded productivity in manufacturing. By 1997 U.S. economic growth, measured at 4 percent, was among the healthiest in the world, while one of its most serious competitors in the 1980s, Japan, limped along with only a 1.1 percent growth rate. Working Americans benefited from these developments: new jobs were added to the economy at the rate of 213,000 per month in 1997, and unemployment dropped from 7.5 percent in 1992 to barely over 4 percent in the first half of 2000. A booming stock market, which daily seemed to reach new highs, fueled the wealth and retirement savings of middle- and upper-income Americans.

But there were downsides to the picture as well. Many stock-market analysts worried that a steep drop in the stock market might create a recession. Other experts warned that the consumer spending that was fueling economic growth was tied to growing debts. The median family indebtedness in 1998 was $33,300 in 1998, up from $23,400 in 1995. An economic downturn could have serious repercussions for overextended families' ability to repay their debts. Moreover, prosperity was not equally distributed. As former Secretary of Labor Robert Reich put it, "There are still millions of people desperately trying to stay afloat. One in five children lives in poverty. Forty-four million Americans have no health insurance. The average 50-year-old without a college education hasn't seen a wage or benefit increase in 20 years. But Americans are segregated by income as never before, so it is far easier to pretend the worse off don't exist. They're out of sight."

AN INCREASINGLY PLURALISTIC SOCIETY

Ethnic and racial diversity, always a source of conflict in American culture, became a defining theme of the 1990s. Between 1981 and 1996 almost 13.5 million immigrants entered the country. The greatest number of the newcomers were Latinos. Although Mexico continued to provide the largest group of Spanish-speaking immigrants, large numbers also arrived from El Salvador and the Dominican Republic. The 1986 Immigration Reform and Control Act (Simpson-Mazzoli Act), which granted amnesty to some immigrants, primarily benefited Mexicans and other Latinos who had entered the United States illegally before 1982. The Latino population grew at a rate of 18 percent in the 1990s to reach 31 million in 1999, making it the second-largest minority group in the United States after African Americans and the second fastest-growing after Asians. Once concentrated in California, Texas, and New Mexico, Latinos now lived in urban areas throughout the country and made up about 16 percent of the population of Florida and New York (see Map 31.3). Their growing numbers have increased their significance as consumers and voters and have led advertisers and politicians alike to vie for their loyalty.

Asia was the other major source of new immigrants. This migration, which increased almost 108 percent from 1980 to 1990, consisted mainly of people from China, the Philippines, Vietnam, Laos, Cambodia, Korea, India, and Pakistan. More than 700,000 Indochinese refugees came to escape upheavals in Southeast Asia in the decade following the Vietnam War. The first arrivals, many of them well educated, adapted successfully to their new homeland. Later refugees lacked professional or vocational skills and took low-paying jobs where they could find them.

The new immigrants' impact on the country's social, economic, and cultural landscape has been tremendous. In many places they have created thriving ethnic communities, such as Koreatown in Los Angeles. In the 1980s tens of thousands of Jews fleeing religious and political persecution in the Soviet Union created Little Odessa in Brooklyn, New York. Ethnic restaurants and shops have sprung up across the country, while some 300 specialized periodicals serve immigrant readers.

In 1990 the immigration quota was expanded to 700,000 per year (modified in 1995 to 675,000), with priority given to skilled workers and relatives of current

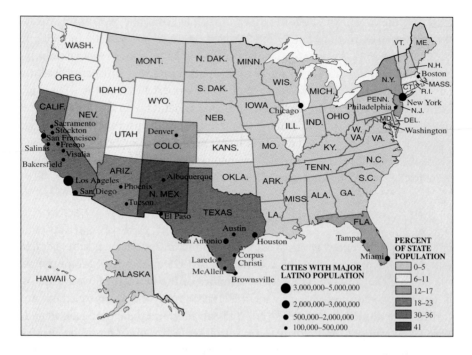

CITIES WITH MAJOR LATINO POPULATION
- 3,000,000–5,000,000
- 2,000,000–3,000,000
- 500,000–2,000,000
- 100,000–500,000

PERCENT OF STATE POPULATION
- 0–5
- 6–11
- 12–17
- 18–23
- 30–36
- 41

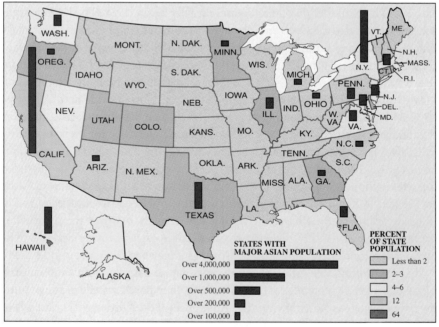

STATES WITH MAJOR ASIAN POPULATION
- Over 4,000,000
- Over 1,000,000
- Over 500,000
- Over 200,000
- Over 100,000

PERCENT OF STATE POPULATION
- Less than 2
- 2–3
- 4–6
- 12
- 64

M A P 31.3
Latino Population and Asian American Population, 1999

In 1999 Latinos made up over 11 percent of the U.S. population, and Asian Americans 4 percent. Demographers predict that Latinos will overtake African Americans as the largest minority group early in the twenty-first century and that by the year 2050 only about half the U.S. population will be composed of non-Latino whites.

residents. But by then the new immigrants had become scapegoats for all that was wrong with the United States. Though a 1997 study by the National Academy of Science reported that immigration has benefited the nation, adding some $10 billion a year to the economy, many American-born workers felt threatened by immigrants. The unfounded assumption that immigrants were lured to the United States by generous public services influenced provisions of a 1996 welfare reform act (see page 927), which severely curtailed legal immigrants' access to welfare benefits, especially food stamps. Also in 1996 Congress enacted legislation that increased the financial requirements for sponsors of new immigrants.

The most dramatic challenges to immigrants have emerged on the state level. In the 1980s California absorbed far more immigrants than any other state: more than a third of its population growth in that decade came from foreign immigration. In 1994 California voters overwhelmingly approved Proposition 187, a ballot initiative provocatively named "Save Our State," which barred undocumented aliens from public schools, nonemergency care at public health clinics, and all other state social services. The initiative also required law enforcement officers, school administrators, and social workers to report suspected illegal immigrants to the Immigration and Naturalization Service. Though opponents challenged the constitutionality of Proposition 187, anti-immigrant feeling soon spread to other parts of the country, becoming a hotly debated issue in the 1996 election (see American Voices, "The Undocumented Worker").

Though the National Academy of Sciences report did find that "some black workers have lost their jobs to immigrants," for the most part African Americans were not adversely affected by the new immigration. But in the cities African Americans and new immigrants were forced by economic necessity and entrenched segregation patterns to fight for space in decaying, crime-ridden ghettos, where unemployment rates sometimes hit 60 percent. Overcrowded and underfunded, inner-city schools had fallen into disrepair and were unable to provide a proper education.

In April 1992 the frustration and anger of impoverished urban Americans erupted in five days of race riots in Los Angeles. The worst civil disorder since the 1960s, the violence took sixty lives and caused $850 million in damage. The riot was set off by the acquittal (on all but one charge) of four white Los Angeles police officers accused of using excessive force in arresting a black motorist, Rodney King. A graphic amateur video showing the policemen kicking, clubbing, and beating King had not swayed the predominantly white jury. Three of the officers were later convicted on federal civil rights charges.

AMERICAN VOICES

The Undocumented Worker

Cuauhtémoc Mendez

*I*n this oral history, Cuauhtémoc Mendez, an immigrant construction worker, reflects on the controversial issue of undocumented Mexican workers—an issue that helped fuel anti-immigration sentiment in the 1980s and 1990s.

In the United States, to get rid of all the illegals, you don't need a border or the Immigration. Simply, if there is no work, what would the illegals do there? . . . For the United States it is a great advantage, because Mexican labor is very cheap. The illegal produces his product much cheaper, and they can sell it cheaper to the American people. In this sense the illegal helps the United States.

He also helps Mexico. All of the *mojados* bring money back. We don't take money out of Mexico. Those of us who work in the United States help our country more than the rich who send their Mexican money out. We support our country.

Normally the Mexican who goes to the United States goes to work in jobs that many Americans don't want. In the first place, it's hard work. I'm not going to say that they can't do the work, but they don't want to work for the same price as the Mexican. It's clear there is this contradiction, this antipathy toward the Mexican who is there illegally. They look at the *mojados* as scabs. The Chicanos and Mexican-Americans look at us from this perspective because they think we are the reason they don't have jobs. But it's not true. We are there at the convenience of the owners and bosses who want cheap labor, cheaper than they can get there. It isn't our fault. We have the necessity to work. I don't think it's a sin to subsist in another country that offers the opportunity to live a little better than is possible for us in Mexico.

SOURCE: Marilyn P. Davis, *Mexican Voices, American Dreams: An Oral History of Mexican Immigration to the United States* (New York: Holt, 1990), p. 110.

The Los Angeles riot exposed the cleavages in urban neighborhoods. Trapped in the nation's inner cities, many blacks resented recent immigrants who were struggling to get ahead and often succeeding. As a result some blacks had targeted Korean-owned stores during the arson and looting. Latinos were also frustrated by high unemployment and crowded housing conditions. According to the Los Angeles Police Department, Latinos accounted for more than half of those arrested and a third of those killed during the rioting. Thus the riots were not simply a case of black rage at white injustice; they contained a strong element of class-based protest against the failure of the American system to address the needs of all poor people.

New Immigrants

In the 1980s many Korean immigrants got their start by opening small grocery stores in urban neighborhoods. Their success sometimes led to conflicts with other racial groups, such as African Americans and Latinos, who were often their customers as well as competitors.

(Kay Chernush/The Image Bank)

One of the ways federal and state governments had tried to help poor blacks and Latinos was through the establishment of affirmative action programs in government hiring, contracts, and university admissions. In 1995, however, under pressure from the Republican governor, Pete Wilson, the Regents of the University of California voted to scrap the university's twenty-year-old policy of affirmative action, despite protests from the faculty and from university presidents. In the November 1996 elections the struggle over affirmative action was intensified by California's passage of Proposition 209, which banned all preference based on race or gender. As appeals worked their way through the federal courts and black and Latino enrollments declined, the University of California sought new admissions criteria that would circumvent the restrictions imposed by Proposition 209.

One reason affirmative action became a political issue in the 1990s was that many people, including prominent conservatives like George F. Will, William Bennett, and Patrick Buchanan, saw it as a threat to core American values. Lumping affirmative action together with multiculturalism—the attempt to represent the diversity of American society and its peoples—critics feared that all this counting by race, gender, sexual preference, and age would lead to a "balkanization," or fragmentation, of American society. Attempts to revise American history textbooks along multicultural lines aroused much anger, as did efforts by universities such as Stanford to revise college curricula to include the study of non-European cultures. Conservatives also took aim at the antiracist and antisexist regulations and speech codes that had been adopted by many colleges. Arguing for the need to protect First Amendment rights, conservatives derided the attempt to regulate hate speech as "politically correct" (PC).

BACKLASH AGAINST WOMEN'S AND GAY RIGHTS

Conservative critics also targeted the women's movement. In the widely read *Backlash: The Undeclared War on American Women* (1991), the journalist Susan Faludi described a powerful reaction against the gains American women had won in the 1960s and 1970s. Spearheaded by New Right leaders and aided by the media, conservatives held the women's movement responsible for every ill afflicting modern women, from infertility to rising divorce rates; yet polls showed strong support for many feminist demands, including equal pay, reproductive rights, and a more equitable distribution of household and child-care responsibilities.

The deep national divide over abortion, one of the main issues associated with feminism, continued to polarize the country. In the 1980s and 1990s harassment and violence toward those who sought or provided abortions became common. In 1994 two workers were murdered at two Massachusetts abortion clinics, and five people were wounded in the attacks. Although only a fraction of antiabortion activists supported such extreme acts, disruptive confrontational tactics had made receiving what was still a woman's legal right more dangerous.

Gay rights was another field of battle. As gays and lesbians gained legal protection against housing and job discrimination across the country, Pat Robertson, North Carolina senator Jesse Helms, and others denounced these civil rights gains as undeserved "special rights." To conservatives gay rights threatened America's traditional family values. In 1992 Coloradans passed a referendum (overturned by the Supreme Court in 1996) that barred local jurisdictions from passing ordinances protecting gays and lesbians. Across the nation "gay bashing" and other forms of violence against homosexuals continued.

A grim backdrop to gay men's struggle against discrimination was the AIDS epidemic. Acquired immune deficiency syndrome (AIDS) was first recognized by physicians in 1981 in the gay male population, and its cause identified as the human immunodeficiency virus (HIV). At first little government funding was directed toward AIDS research or treatment; critics charged that the lack of attention to the syndrome reflected society's antipathy toward gay men. Only when heterosexuals, such as hemophiliacs who had received the virus through blood transfusions, began to be affected did AIDS begin to gain significant public attention. The death of the film star Rock Hudson from AIDS in 1985 finally broke the barrier of public apathy. Another galvanizing moment came in 1991, when the basketball great Earvin "Magic" Johnson announced that he was HIV-positive.

As early as the mid-1980s AIDS cases had begun to increase among heterosexuals, especially intravenous drug addicts and their sexual partners, as well as bisexuals. Women now constitute the group with the fastest-growing incidence of HIV infection. To date more Americans have died of AIDS than were killed in the Korean and Vietnam Wars combined. Between 1995 and 1999, however, deaths from AIDS in the United States dropped 30 percent. This decline—in part the result of new treatment strategies using a combination of drugs, or a "cocktail"—has led to cau-

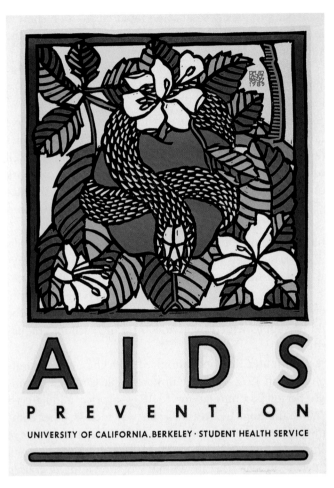

AIDS Awareness

This poster by David Lance Goines uses the image of the Garden of Eden to warn of the dangers of AIDS. By 1985, the year this poster appeared, 12,500 Americans had already died of AIDS, and the country began to confront the epidemic's human and medical costs. (David Lance Goines)

tious optimism about controlling the disease, though scientists warn that the drugs have not been effective for between 30 and 50 percent of patients. Moreover, the drugs' high costs limit their availability and make distribution particularly limited in poor nations. As AIDS deaths decline in developed countries like the United States, the epidemic reached crisis proportions in sub-Saharan Africa, which accounts for 24.5 million of the 34 million infections worldwide.

POPULAR CULTURE AND POPULAR TECHNOLOGY

Image was everything in the 1980s and 1990s—or so commentators said, pointing to rock stars Michael Jackson and Madonna and even to President Reagan. One strong influence on popular culture was MTV, a television channel that premiered in 1981 and featured short visual pieces accompanying popular songs. The MTV style—with its creative choreography, flashy colors, and rapid cuts—soon showed up in mainstream media and even political campaigns, which also adapted the 30-second sound bites common on television news shows to their own purposes. The national newspaper *USA Today*, which debuted in 1982, adapted the style, featuring eye-catching graphics, color photographs, and short, easy-to-read articles. Soon more staid newspapers followed suit.

At the same time new technology, especially satellite transmission and live "minicam" broadcasting, reshaped the television industry. Cable and satellite dishes were also increasingly available. By the mid-1990s viewers could choose from well over 100 channels, including upstarts such as Ted Turner's Cable News Network (CNN) and the Entertainment Sports Network (ESPN), an all-sports channel. Media, communications, and entertainment were big business, increasingly drawn into global financial networks, markets, and mergers.

Technology also reshaped the home in the late twentieth century. The 1980s saw the introduction of videocassette recorders (VCRs), compact disc (CD) players, cellular phones, and inexpensive fax machines. By 1993 more than three-quarters of American households had VCRs. Video was everywhere—stores, airplanes, tennis courts, operating rooms. With the introduction of camcorders, the family photo album could be supplemented by a video of a high school graduation, a marriage, or a birth.

But it was the personal computer that revolutionized both the home and office. The big breakthrough came in 1977 when the upstart Apple Computer Company offered the Apple II personal computer for $1,195—a price middle-class Americans could afford. When the Apple II became a runaway success, other companies scrambled to get into the market. IBM offered its first personal computer in the summer of 1981. Software companies such as Microsoft, whose founder Bill Gates is now the richest person in America, grew rapidly by providing operating systems and other software for the expanding personal computer market. By 1995, 37 percent of American households had at least one personal computer.

More than any other technological advance, the computer created the modern electronic office. Even the smallest business could keep all its records and do all its correspondence, billing, and other business on a single desktop machine. The very concept of the office was changing as a new class of telecommuters worked at home via computer, fax machine, and electronic mail. Today, new technologies utilizing fiberoptics, microwave relays, and satellites can transmit massive quantities of information to and from almost any place on earth, and even in outer space, via the information superhighway.

By 1999, almost 200 million people—80 million of them in the United States—used the Internet. At first scientists and other professionals, who communicated with their peers through electronic mail (e-mail), were the primary users of the Internet. But the debut of the World Wide Web in 1991 enhanced the commercial possibilities of the Internet. The web allowed companies, organizations, political campaigns, and even the White House to create their own "home pages," incorporating both visual and textual information. Businesses and entrepreneurs began to use the Internet to sell their products and services, leading critics to fear that the Net would become a big shopping mall.

Although theoretically available to all, the glories of cyberspace are still available mostly to those who can afford them: in 1997, 65 percent of Americans who used the Internet had incomes of $50,000 or more. But the trend may be changing. In 1998 only 25 percent of all households had access to cyberspace, but by 2000 the figure had grown to 50 percent. Additionally, programs to wire public schools and libraries should significantly increase access to the new technology.

The Clinton Presidency: Public Life Since 1993

If Americans hoped to make progress on the faltering economy and the deep social cleavages surrounding race, gender, and sexual orientation, they would need strong leadership. Yet low voter turnout and the strong showing of independent candidates in the 1992 presidential election signaled deep dissatisfaction with the American political system. In the ensuing years Americans' disaffection helped to continue the rollback of federal power begun by Reagan and Bush.

CLINTON'S FIRST TERM

As the 1992 election campaign got under way, the economy was the overriding issue, for the recession that had begun in 1990 showed no sign of abating. George Bush easily won renomination as the Republican candidate. To solidify the support of the New Right his running mate, J. Danforth (Dan) Quayle, spoke out strongly for "family values" and other conservative social agendas. William Jefferson (Bill) Clinton, the long-time governor of Arkansas, survived charges of marital infidelity and draft dodging, as well as questions about a dubious Arkansas real estate deal called Whitewater, to win the Democratic nomination. For his running mate he chose Albert (Al) Gore Jr., a second-term senator from Tennessee. At age forty-four Gore was a year and a half younger than Clinton, making the two men the first of the baby-boom generation to occupy the national ticket.

In the middle of the primary season the Texas billionaire H. Ross Perot, capitalizing on voters' desire for a change from politics as usual, announced he would run as an independent candidate. Although Perot dropped out of the race on the last day of the Democratic convention, he reentered it less than five weeks before the election, adding a well-financed wild card to an unusual election year.

The Democrats mounted an effective, aggressive campaign that highlighted Clinton's plans to solve domestic problems, especially in education, health care, and the economy. Gore added expertise on defense and environmental issues. Bush was hurt by the weak economy and especially by reneging on his "No New Taxes" pledge. On election day Clinton received 43 percent of the popular vote to Bush's 38 percent

Passing the Torch to the Baby Boomers

Baby boomer Bill Clinton, shown here campaigning in 1992, and his running mate Al Gore billed themselves as representing a "new generation of leadership." Born in 1946 and 1948, respectively, they came of age in the turbulent 1960s. Vietnam, not World War II or Korea, was the war that defined their generation. (Ira Wyman/Sygma)

and Perot's 19 percent. Although Perot did not win a single state, his popular vote was the highest for an independent candidate since Theodore Roosevelt's in 1912. The Democrats retained control of both houses of Congress, ending twelve years of divided government. But the narrowness of Clinton's victory and the public's perception that he did not really stand for anything did not augur well for his ability to lead the country.

The liberals who supported Clinton hoped that a Democratic presidency could erase the Reagan-Bush legacy and oversee the creation of a new Democratic social agenda. Initially, Clinton seemed to fulfill that promise. He nominated the liberal Ruth Bader Ginsberg for a seat on the Supreme Court; she was confirmed. The president also appointed Janet Reno as attorney general—the first woman to head the Department of Justice. Other trailblazing cabinet appointments included Secretary of Health and Human Services Donna E. Shalala and, in Clinton's second term, Secretary of State Madeline Albright. Clinton chose an African American, Ron Brown, as secretary of commerce, and two Latinos, Henry Cisneros and Frederico Peña, to head the Department of Housing and Urban Development (HUD) and the Department of Transportation, respectively.

Clinton's early legislative and administrative record was mixed. In early 1993 he signed into law the Family and Medical Leave Act, twice vetoed by Bush, which provided workers with up to twelve weeks of unpaid leave to tend to a newborn or an adopted child or to respond to a family medical emergency. But when Clinton tried to implement a campaign promise to lift the ban on gays serving in the armed forces, he ran into such ferocious opposition that he backed off, offering instead a weak compromise policy—"Don't ask, don't tell, don't pursue." The solution was an ineffective palliative at best, one that called into question Clinton's willingness to stand firm on issues of principle.

By the time Clinton took office, the economy had pulled out of the 1990 recession, enabling him to focus on other economic issues, especially the opening of foreign markets to U.S. goods. In 1992 President Bush had signed the North American Free Trade Agreement (NAFTA), in which the United States, Canada, and Mexico agreed to make all of North America a free-trade zone. Strongly supported by the business community, NAFTA was bitterly opposed by labor unions worried about the loss of jobs to lower-paid Mexican workers and by environmentalists concerned about the weak enforcement of antipollution laws south of the border. Nonetheless, with Clinton's support Congress narrowly passed NAFTA in November 1993. Another major development in international trade was the revision in 1994 of the General Agreement on Tariffs and Trade (GATT), which had been created at the end of World War II. The new provisions cut tariffs on many manufactured products and for the first time established regulations protecting intellectual property such as patents, copyrights, and trademarks on software, entertainment, and pharmaceuticals.

With the recession over, crime replaced the economy as a major concern among voters. In 1993 Congress passed the Brady Handgun Violence Prevention Act, over the opposition of the National Rifle Association. A much more wide-ranging piece of legislation was the Omnibus Violent Crime Control and Prevention Act (1994), which authorized $30.2 billion for stepped-up law enforcement, crime prevention, and prison construction and administration. The act also extended the death penalty to more than fifty federal crimes and banned the sale and possession of certain kinds of assault weapons. Responding to the deep anxieties Americans had about their economic security, Clinton had staked his political fortunes on his campaign promise of universal health care. Though the United States spent more on health care than any other country in the world, it remained the only major industrialized country not to provide national health insurance to all. Spiraling medical costs and rising insurance premiums had brought the health-care system to a crisis.

The president chose his wife, attorney Hillary Rodham Clinton, to head the task force that would draft the legislation—a controversial move since no first lady had ever played a formal role in policymaking. The resulting proposal was based on the idea of managed competition: market forces, not the government, would control health-care costs and expand citizen's access to health care. But even this mild form of social engineering ran into intense opposition from the well-financed pharmaceutical and insurance industries. By September 1994 congressional leaders were admitting that health reform was dead. In 1995 an estimated 40.3 million Americans—over 17 percent of the population under sixty-five—had no health insurance, and experts predicted that these statistics would climb.

Clinton seems never to have had the time to devote his full attention to pushing health reform through Congress. Three days before assuming office he had to commit his support to a missile attack President Bush had ordered on Iraq. In February foreign terrorists bombed the World Trade Center in New York City, and in April FBI agents made a misguided assault on the Branch Davidian compound in Waco, Texas. At the White House in September Israeli Prime Minister Yitzhak Rabin and Yasir Arafat, chairman of the Palestine Liberation Organization, signed an agreement allowing limited Palestinian self-rule in the Gaza Strip and Jericho. In October 1993, just after Clinton announced his health plan, twelve American soldiers were killed on a United Nations peacekeeping mission in Somalia. Constantly shifting from crisis to crisis, Clinton appeared to the American public to be vacillating, indecisive, and lacking in vision, especially in his handling of foreign affairs.

Nothing seemed more intractable than the problems that engulfed the former state of Yugoslavia, which had broken into five independent states in 1991. The province of Bosnia and Herzegovina, made up largely of Muslims and committed to a multiethnic state—Serb, Croat, and Muslim—had declared its independence in 1992. But Bosnian Serbs, supported financially and militarily by what remained of Yugoslavia, formed their own breakaway state and began a siege of the Bosnian capital, Sarajevo. In the countryside the Serbs launched a ruthless campaign of "ethnic cleansing," driving Bosnian Muslims and Croats from their homes and into concentration camps or shooting them in mass executions. More than 250,000 people were killed or reported missing after the outbreak of war in April 1992. After three years of unsuccessful efforts by the European powers to stop the carnage, President Clinton and Secretary of State Warren Christopher facilitated a peace accord in November 1995. A NATO-led peacekeeping force, backed by U.S. troops, would end the fighting, at least temporarily.

At the same time the end of cold-war superpower rivalry presented unexpected opportunities to resolve other long-standing conflicts. In Haiti the threat of a U.S. invasion in October 1993 led to the restoration of the exiled president, Jean-Bertrand Aristide, who had been ousted by a military coup in 1991. In South Africa the end of a fifty-year policy of racial separation was capped in May 1994 by the election of the rebel leader Nelson Mandela, who had spent twenty-seven years in prison for challenging apartheid, as the country's first black president. And in a move that was seen as the symbolic end to the American experience in Vietnam, the United States established diplomatic relations with Hanoi in July 1995, two decades after the fall of Saigon.

"THE ERA OF BIG GOVERNMENT IS OVER"

In the 1994 midterm elections Republicans gained fifty-two seats in the House of Representatives, which gave them a majority in the House as well as the Senate. In the House the centerpiece of the new Republican majority was the "Contract with America," a list of proposals that Newt Gingrich of Georgia, the new speaker of the house, vowed would be voted on in the first 100 days of the new session. The contract included constitutional amendments to balance the budget and set term limits for congressional office, $245 billion in tax cuts for individuals, tax incentives for small businesses, cuts in welfare and other entitlement programs, anticrime initiatives, and cutbacks in federal regulations. President Clinton, bowing to political reality, acknowledged in his State of the Union message in January 1996 that "the era of big government is over."

But the Republicans were frustrated in their commitment to cut taxes and balance the budget by the year 2002 because both practical and political considerations made many items in the budget immune to serious reductions. Interest on the national debt had to be paid. Defense spending had declined only slightly in the post–cold-war world. Since Social Security was considered untouchable, Congress looked to health care and discretionary spending as places to save.

In the fall of 1995 Congress passed a budget that cut $270 billion from projected spending on Medicare and $170 billion from spending on Medicaid over the next seven years. Other savings came from cuts in discretionary programs, including education and the environment. Clinton accepted Congress's resolve to balance the budget in seven years but, vowing to protect the nation from an "extremist" Congress, vetoed the budget itself. In the standoff that followed, nonessential departments of the government were forced to shut down twice for lack of funding, but polls showed that a majority of Americans held Congress, not the president, responsible. The budget that Clinton finally signed in April 1996 left Medicare and Social Security intact, though it did meet the Republicans' goal of cutting $23 billion from discretionary spending.

As part of the Contract with America, House Republicans were especially determined to cut welfare, a joint federal-state program that represented a fairly small part of the budget. To Republicans the program had become a prime example of misguided government priorities. The benefits of the main welfare program, Aid for Dependent Children (AFDC), were far from generous: the average annual welfare payment to families (including food stamps) was $7,740, well below the established poverty line. Still, in the 1990s both Democratic and Republican statehouses sought ways to change the behavior of welfare recipients by imposing work requirements or denying benefits for additional children born to women on AFDC. In August 1996, after vetoing two Republican-authored bills, President

Clinton, who had campaigned on a promise of welfare reform, signed into law the Personal Responsibility and Work Opportunity Act, a historic overhaul of federal entitlements. The 1996 law ended the federal guarantee of cash assistance to poor children by abolishing AFDC, required most adult recipients to find work within two years, set a five-year limit on payments to any one family, and gave states wide discretion in running their welfare programs.

The Republican takeover of Congress had one unintended consequence: it united the usually fractious Democrats behind the president. Unopposed in the 1996 primaries, Clinton was able to burnish his image as a moderate "New Democrat." His political fortunes were aided by the unpopularity of the Republican Congress following the government shutdowns. He also benefited from the continuing strength of the economy. Economic indicators released shortly before election day showed that the "misery index"—a combination of the unemployment rate and inflation—was the lowest it had been in twenty-seven years.

The Republicans settled on Senate Majority Leader Bob Dole of Kansas as their presidential candidate. Acceptable to both the conservative and the moderate wings of the party, Dole selected former representative Jack Kemp, a leading proponent of supply-side economics, as his running mate. Dole made a 15 percent across-the-board tax cut the centerpiece of his campaign, while Clinton emphasized an improved economy. Americans seemed to have made up their minds early about the candidates. With the lowest voter turnout since Calvin Coolidge won the presidency in 1924, Clinton became the first Democratic president since Franklin Roosevelt to win reelection. Republicans retained control in a majority of the nation's statehouses and in the House of Representatives and increased their majority in the Senate. Thus a key factor in Bill Clinton's second term would be the necessity, as a Democratic president working with a Republican-dominated Congress, of pursuing bipartisan policies or facing stalemate.

SECOND-TERM STALEMATES

In his 1998 State of the Union address Bill Clinton outlined an impressive program of federal spending for schools, tax credits for child care, a hike in the minimum wage, and protection for the beleaguered Social Security system. His ability to pursue this domestic agenda was seriously compromised, however, by a scandal that eventually led to his impeachment and by two international crises.

The first of these foreign crises emerged in Iraq, where Saddam Hussein was still in power despite his 1991 defeat in Operation Desert Storm and the United Nation's imposition of economic sanctions. In late 1997 Hussein ejected American members of a U.N. inspection team that was searching Iraqi sites for hidden "weapons of mass destruction," which included nuclear, biological, and chemical warfare materials. In response, the United States, with limited international support, began a military buildup in the Gulf. The threatened air strike against Iraq was averted when U.N. Secretary-General Kofi Annan brokered an agreement that temporarily put an end to the crisis. But in December 1998 the same issues led to an intense four-day joint U.S.-British bombing campaign, "Desert Fox." Neither that effort nor the missile strikes against Iraq that have continued to the present seem to have compromised the Iraqi's ability to build "weapons of mass destruction" or to have undercut Hussein's regime. At the same time international support for the United Nation's economic sanctions is eroding, fueled in part by humanitarian concerns about their impact on the Iraqi people. Growing pressure abroad and at home may force the United States to reconsider the use of economic sanctions as a diplomatic tool in Iraq.

The second major international crisis began in March 1999 in Kosovo, a province of the Serbian-dominated Federal Republic of Yugoslavia (FRY). There, NATO, strongly influenced by the United States, intervened to protect ethnic Albanians from the Serbians who were determined to drive them out of the region. Three months of bombing eventually forced the Serbians to agree to remove their troops from Kosovo and to agree to a multinational peacekeeping force. Yet, as in the Middle East, no long-term solutions were found to the problems generated by ethnic conflict. The brutal Serbian President Slobodan Milosevic was not pushed from office until 2000, the region was devastated and its people impoverished, and a year after the war most observers considered the war a "hollow triumph" for NATO and the United States. Both the Iraqi and Kosovo crises served as a potent reminder that despite its position as the most powerful nation in the world, the United States was limited in its ability to achieve its foreign-policy aims.

Although international events deflected President Clinton from his domestic agenda, far more damaging was the crisis that stemmed from a problem that had plagued him since 1992: allegations of sexual misconduct. In January 1998 attorneys representing Paula Jones, who claimed that the then governor Clinton had propositioned her when she was an Arkansas state employee, revealed that they planned to depose a former White House intern, Monica Lewinsky, about an alleged affair with President Clinton. Kenneth Starr, the independent counsel initially charged with investigating the Whitewater scandal, widened his investigation to explore whether Clinton or his aides had encouraged Lewinsky to lie in her statement. Clinton consistently denied having a sexual relationship with Lewinsky—both on national television and in deposition before a federal grand jury.

In September 1998, after Starr issued a report that concluded that the President had committed impeachable offenses, the House of Representatives began its inquiry. On December 20 the House narrowly approved two articles of impeachment against Clinton, one for perjury before a grand jury concerning his liaison with Lewinsky and a second for obstruction of justice, in which he was accused of encouraging others to lie in his behalf. Ironically, the evening of the House vote, a CBS news poll reported that 58 percent of its respondents opposed impeachment, while only 38 percent supported it.

Throughout the ensuing trial conducted by the Senate, Clinton's approval rating remained exceptionally high, perhaps because most Americans doubted the political motives of his attackers and almost certainly because a strong economy kept most citizens content with the president's performance, even if they disapproved of his personal morality. Finally, after a five-week trial and hours of televised debate, with Democrats voting solidly against impeachment and enough Republicans breaking with their party, the Senate acquitted Clinton on both charges. Like Andrew Johnson, the only other president to be impeached (see Chapter 15), Bill Clinton survived the process, but the scandal, the trial, and the profoundly partisan sentiments that surrounded it limited his ability to be an effective president and deepened public cynicism about politics and its practitioners.

For if Clinton had been hampered by the controversy, so too had Republicans. The November 1998 elections took place while the House was considering impeachment. Despite polls that indicated that Americans did not place much emphasis on the Lewinsky scandal, in many localities and on the national level Republican leaders made Clinton's moral character the focus of the campaign. The Democrats, in contrast, focused on issues like Social Security and education. They also employed vigorous get-out-the-vote drives, particularly among traditional Democratic constituencies—labor unions and African Americans. When the ballots were counted, for the first time since 1934 the party of the incumbent president gained seats—five— in a midterm election, shrinking the Republican majority in Congress to twelve. Although a variety of factors—including the improving economy—influenced voting patterns, many observers pointed to a backlash against the drive for impeachment. House leader Newt Gingrich admitted that "I totally underestimated the degree to which people would just get sick of 24-hour-a-day talk television and talk radio and then the degree to which this whole scandal became just sort of disgusting by sheer repetition." Ironically, it would be Gingrich who would be pushed from office, as the electoral debacle led to a revolt among Republicans that forced him to resign as Speaker of the House within a week of the election.

Because of the controversies surrounding Clinton and the weakened state of the Republicans, neither party was able to secure significant legislation. For the rest of Clinton's term, shoring up Social Security, addressing the high cost of medical care, and passing an effective gun-control law eluded the president and his supporters, while Republicans were stymied in their efforts to cut taxes and further roll back the federal government. The stalemate was exacerbated by politicians' focus on positioning themselves for the election of 2000. As Senator Joseph I. Lieberman, a Democrat from Connecticut, described the 106th Congress in November 1999, "This was not a session of great initiatives. . . . This was a session that was post-impeachment and preelection."

Lieberman was to become much better known when the Democratic Party nominated him as Vice President Al Gore's running mate for the 2000 presidential election. The Republicans chose Governor George W. Bush of Texas to head their ticket and Richard Cheney for their vice-presidential nominee. Although both Bush and Gore were considered moderate centrists, they had ideological differences over the role of the federal government and how best to use the large projected budget surpluses. Bush proposed a major tax cut that critics claimed would benefit primarily the wealthiest 10 percent of Americans, a partial privatization of Social Security, and the use of government-issued vouchers to pay for private education. Gore argued for using the surplus to shore up the Social Security funds, a tax break incentive for college tuition, and expansion of medicare. The two candidates disagreed on the abortion issue, with Bush opposing abortion and Gore supporting a woman's right to choose. While Pat Buchanan of the Reform Party fared poorly and was not able to make significant inroads among conservative Republicans, Ralph Nader, the Green Party representative, did appeal to many in the left wing of the Democratic Party who were disenchanted with Gore's centrist position. Nader received over two and a half million votes and detracted enough ballots from Gore in New Hampshire, New Mexico, and Florida to give those states to Bush. Nader's 97,419 votes in Florida (2 percent) contributed to making that state's presidential election a virtual tie between Bush and Gore.

As Florida hung in the balance, returns from the rest of the country showed that Gore had a lead of 337,000 in the popular vote and had won the District of Columbia and twenty states, mostly in the Northeast and Far West, with 267 electoral votes, while Bush had triumphed in twenty-nine states, mostly in the South and Midwest, with 246 electoral votes. In four states, however, fewer than 7,500 votes separated the two major candidates. In such a tight election, the results in Florida became crucial because the electoral college victory would come down to which candidate could claim that state's twenty-five electoral votes. It would take thirty-seven dramatic days to resolve the controversies surrounding the Florida vote and determine the new president, making the election one of the most remarkable in American history (see Map 31.4).

At stake were protested "butterfly ballots," which had apparently misled some Gore voters into voting for Buchanan, and "under votes," which resulted from antiquated voting machines and inattentive voters (see American Voices, "We Marched to Be Counted"). To make certain all votes were tabulated, Gore forces demanded hand recounts in several counties. How to evaluate dimpled, pregnant, and hanging "chads"—the tiny cardboard pieces punched from the ballot—became a hotly contested issue. On November 27, Florida Secretary of State Katherine Harris halted the recount process and declared Governor Bush the winner by a mere 537 votes. The struggle, however, continued. Twice Gore appealed to the Florida Supreme Court in an attempt to get a hand recount. When that court ordered the hand count to continue, Bush went to the United States Supreme Court, which then ordered it stopped. Finally on December 12, a deeply divided Supreme Court, in a 5–4 decision marked by acrimonious dissenting opinions, declared that the equal protection clause of the Fourteenth Amendment required that all ballots had to be counted in the same way and that time did not permit a statewide hand count. Justice

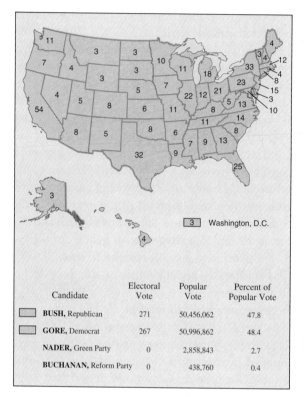

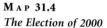
3   Washington, D.C.

Candidate	Electoral Vote	Popular Vote	Percent of Popular Vote
BUSH, Republican	271	50,456,062	47.8
GORE, Democrat	267	50,996,862	48.4
NADER, Green Party	0	2,858,843	2.7
BUCHANAN, Reform Party	0	438,760	0.4

MAP 31.4
The Election of 2000

This map makes the closeness of the 2000 presidential election graphically clear. Democrat Al Gore tallied 337,576 more popular votes than his opponent. Republican George W. Bush, drawing upon solid support in the South and Midwest, won in the electoral college by only four votes, thus securing the presidency.

Stephen G. Breyer in dissent angrily pointed out that the majority's opinion was clearly a political one that "runs the risk of undermining the public's confidence in the Court itself." On the following day, Vice President Gore gave his concession speech, and George W. Bush announced his victory to become the forty-third president.

MAKING SENSE OF THE LATE TWENTIETH CENTURY

The last two decades of the twentieth century brought enormous changes. In the international political arena, the end of the four-decade cold war had repercussions that are still evolving. The world appears to be returning to a situation in which power, both economic and military, is dispersed among a number of key players. The United States remains preeminent, but as the showdown in Iraq suggests, the nation's dominance in the new world order is offset by the limits to its power. Permanent peace in the Middle East or in other hot spots will undoubtedly prove elusive.

By the late 1990s the United States had dramatically improved its position in the world economy, but nonetheless decisions made beyond its borders continued to affect the daily lives of American workers, managers, and consumers. A startling 554-point drop in the stock market in November 1997—in part a reaction to se-

AMERICAN VOICES

We Marched to Be Counted

JOHN LEWIS

*E*merging from the furor over apparent voting irregularities in Florida in the 2000 presidential election is a concern that uncounted and disqualified voters were more likely to be poor people, especially African Americans. John Lewis, a civil rights activist (see p. 831) who had marched from Selma to Montgomery in 1965 to demonstrate for African American voting rights in Alabama, reflects on the relationship of the 1960s Civil Rights Movement to the Florida voting controversy. Lewis is now a congressman from Atlanta.

What's happening in Florida and in Washington is more than a game for pundits. The whole mess reminds African Americans of an era when we had to pass literacy tests, pay poll taxes, and cross every *t* and dot every *i* to get to be able to vote. . . . For all the political maneuvering and legal wrangling, many people have missed an important point: the story of the 2000 election is about more than George W. Bush and Al Gore. It's about the right to vote. And you cannot understand the true implications of this campaign and the subsequent litigation without grasping how deeply many minorities feel about the seemingly simple matter of the sanctity of the ballot box.

There is a lot of troubling new talk of "political profiling"—allegations that officials tried to suppress the black vote on Election Day and may be maneuvering now to make sure it isn't counted. There are reports that officials put new voting machines in white areas but not black ones and that African Americans were asked to present two, not just one, forms of identification to be allowed to vote. These charges should be looked into. But I like to believe that no one met in some smoke-filled room and said, "We're going to keep black voters out, we're going to keep Jewish voters out." . . .

My greatest fear today is that the perception our votes were not counted may usher in a period of great cynicism. On the other hand—and I bet this is more likely—it may give people a greater sense of the importance of voting and of vigilance. The vote, after all, is the real heart of the movement. Younger people shouldn't think civil rights was just about water fountains or stirring speeches on TV. Late in the summer of 1961, after the Freedom Rides, we realized it was not enough to integrate lunch counters and buses. We had to get the vote.

SOURCE: John Lewis, "We Marched to Be Counted," *Newsweek* (December 11, 2000), p. 38.

vere economic crises in several Asian countries—served as a potent reminder of just how interconnected the global economy had become.

Finally, in politics, several important trends developed. The intense media scrutiny of President Clinton's sexual behavior was just the most dramatic example of the way in which the private morality of public officials often took on more importance than political issues. The influence of the New Right ebbed and flowed, but throughout the period it made issues like abortion, gay rights, gun control,

George W. Bush

After a hotly contested ballot-counting controversy in the state of Florida that was ultimately resolved by the U.S. Supreme Court, Texas governor George W. Bush emerged victorious in the 2000 presidential race. Observers predicted that Bush, the first president since 1888 to have lost the popular vote while winning in the electoral college, also hampered by a fifty-fifty Republican-Democrat split in the Senate, would face many obstacles in implementing his programs. (AP/Wide World Photos)

affirmative action, the death penalty, and immigration potent political flash points that continued into the next century. Finally, a significant shift occurred in the ways that Americans and their leaders seem to think about government and the political system. Low voter turnout, the popularity of third-party candidates like H. Ross Perot and Ralph Nader, and the controversies surrounding President Clinton's impeachment, point to widespread cynicism with politics as usual. The failure of Congress and the president to make significant strides toward ensuring the future of Social Security, addressing the problem of health-care coverage and costs, or tackling other social problems effectively has left many Americans disenchanted with the nation's leadership and suspicious of the federal government in particular.

Despite Americans' nervousness about an unstable world characterized by ethnic conflict, civil wars, and the proliferation of "weapons of mass destruction," despite their reservations about a global economy and nations' increased interdependency, and despite their disappointment with their own politicians, Americans were relatively confident as the twentieth century ended. Economic prosperity—as unevenly distributed as it was—deflected serious discontent. Enthusi-

T I M E L I N E

Year	Event	Year	Event
1981	Sandra Day O'Connor nominated to Supreme Court MTV premieres. Beginning of AIDS epidemic IBM markets its first personal computer.		Clarence Thomas–Anita Hill Senate hearings Susan Faludi's *Backlash: The Undeclared War on American Women*
1981–1982	Recession	1992	Los Angeles riots Bill Clinton elected president Janet Reno appointed first woman to head Department of Justice
1981–1989	National debt triples.	1993	North American Free Trade Agreement (NAFTA) ratified Family and Medical Leave Act Brady Handgun Violence Prevention Act
1982	*USA Today* debuts.		
1983	Star Wars proposed	1994	Health-care reform fails. Omnibus Crime Control and Prevention Act Republicans gain control of Congress.
1984	Geraldine Ferraro becomes first woman on major party ticket. Reagan reelected		
1985	Gramm-Rudman Act requires balanced budget.	1995	Congress passes parts of Contract with America. University of California Regents vote to end affirmative action. U.S. troops enforce peace in Bosnia.
1986	Iran-Contra scandal Immigration Reform and Control Act		
1987	Stock market collapse	1996	Clinton reelected Madeline Albright appointed first woman to head Department of State
1988	George H. W. Bush elected president		
1989	*Webster v. Reproductive Health Services* limits abortion but upholds its legality. Berlin Wall destroyed	1998	Republicans' majority in Congress shrinks.
1990–1991	Persian Gulf War	1998–1999	Bill Clinton impeached and acquitted
1990–1992	Recession	1999	United States, with NATO, intervenes in Kosovo.
1991	Dissolution of Soviet Union ends cold war.	2000	George W. Bush elected president in contested election

asm about technology, especially the potential of the Internet, encouraged many to look forward to the twenty-first century with cautious optimism. But all that can be predicted with any assurance is that the dramatic changes in domestic and world realities will shape the future of the United States and the globe in the twenty-first century and beyond.

For Further Exploration

Two valuable overviews of the period are by Haynes Johnson: *Sleepwalking Through History: America in the Reagan Years* (1992) and *Divided We Fall: Gambling with History in the Nineties* (1995). For a firsthand account of the Republican agenda, see Newt Gingrich, *To Renew America* (1995). Richard A. Posner, *An Affair of State: The Investigation, Impeachment and Trial of President Clinton* (1999), stresses the legal issues involved in Bill Clinton's impeachment and acquittal. An engaging book that uses census data to counter the emphasis on American decline in the 1980s and 1990s is Reynolds Farley, *The New American Reality: Who We Are, How We Got There, Where We Are Going* (1996). On foreign policy Stephen Ambrose and Douglas Brinkley, *Rise of Globalism* (8th ed., 1997), offers a solid assessment. A lively collection of essays debating the new immigration is Nicolaus Mills, ed., *Arguing Immigration: The Debate over the Changing Face of America* (1994). On work, women, and families, see Arlie Hochschild, *The Second Shift: Working Parents and the Revolution at Home* (1989).

"The Gulf War" at <http://www.pbs.org/wgbh/pages/frontline/gulf/> is an online documentary treatment of the Gulf War conflict. A companion to the Gulf War documentary produced by the PBS series *Frontline,* the site includes maps, a chronology, interviews with decision-makers and soldiers from the various sides of the conflict, audio clips, and a section on weapons and technology. Jurist, the Law Professors' Network, provides a "Guide to Impeachment and Censure Materials Online" at <http://jurist.law.pitt.edu/impeach.htm#Public>, which offers extensive links to materials on the constitutional issues raised by impeachment and on public opinion polls, documents, and analysis specific to the Clinton impeachment.

The Gallup Organization has been conducting public opinion surveys since 1935. Its site at <http://www.gallup.com/index.html> provides access to recent polls on politics, family, religion, crime, and lifestyle. This searchable site is an invaluable guide to contemporary American opinion. The United States Census Bureau's web page at <http://www.census.gov/population/www/> offers a rich variety of data—on health insurance, racial and ethnic composition, poverty, work environment, and marriage and family—that offer insight into the major demographic changes transforming American society.

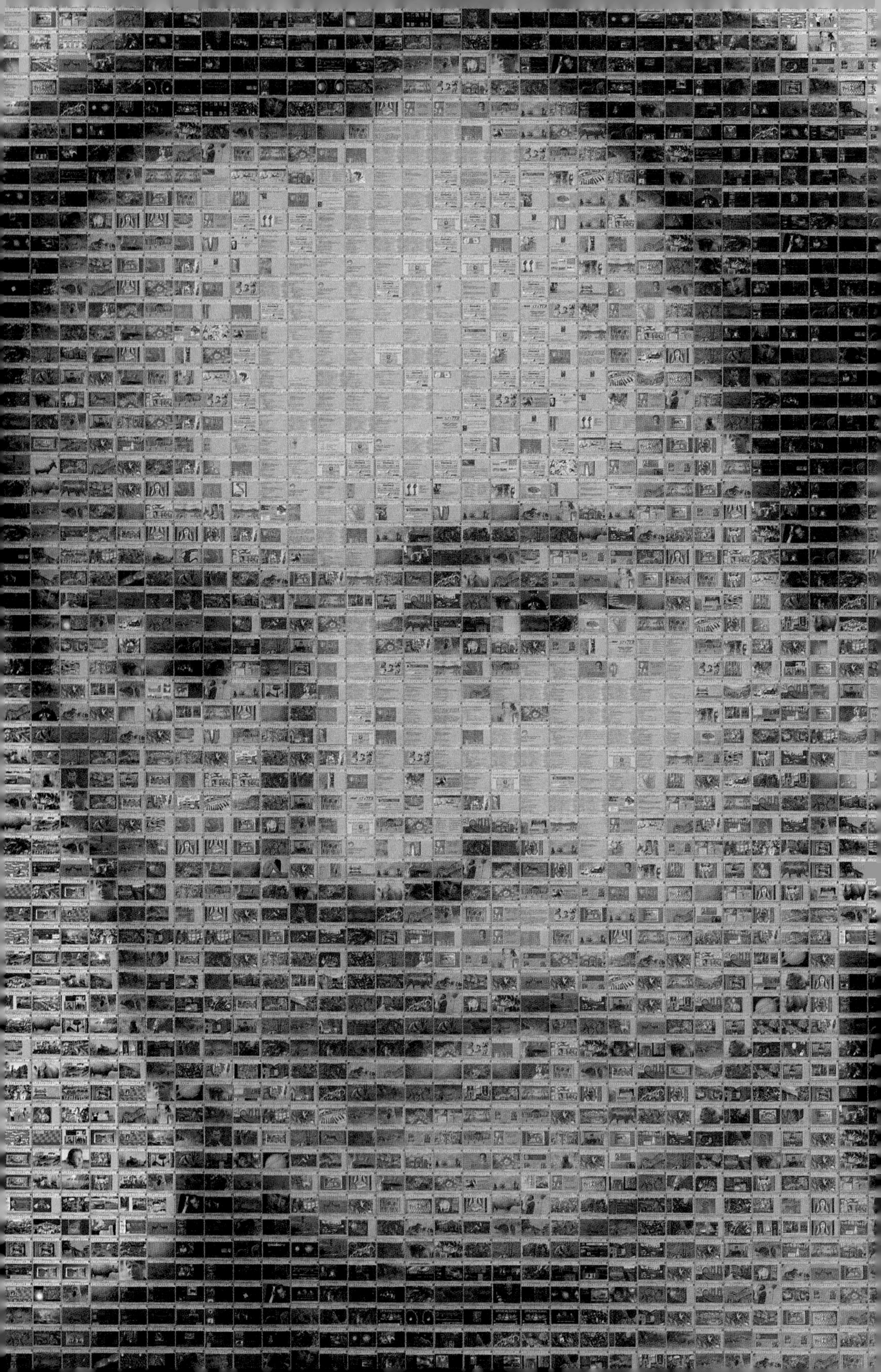

AMERICA AND THE WORLD AT 2001:

How Historians Interpret Contemporary Events and Their Legacy to the Future

IN A PREDAWN RAID on April 23, 2000, armed U.S. Immigration and Naturalization officers forcibly removed six-year-old Elián González from the home of his Miami, Florida, relatives and flew him to the waiting arms of his father, Cuban national Juan Miguel González. Powerful images of the terrified child during the raid as well as those picturing him beaming as he embraced his father, made front-page news and lead TV stories. The raid was the most dramatic event of a seven-month saga that began when the boy was rescued floating in an inner tube after his mother tragically drowned in an attempt to flee Castro's Cuba for the United States. His relatives in Miami claimed custody, and the politically powerful expatriate Cuban leadership there spearheaded a drive to prevent the Justice Department from returning the boy to his father in Cuba. The controversy ignited a media frenzy. Pictures of Elián enjoying the fruits of a consumer culture popped up everywhere. Conservatives invoked cold-war memories of the Cuban revolution, child psychologists aired their opinions on talk shows, the boy's Cuban grandmothers arrived in the United States to plead for his return, pollsters conducted repeated public-opinion surveys, Cubans in Miami demonstrated, Cubans in Cuba demonstrated, and political candidates weighed in, all reported in minute detail by the press. Yet this *mediathon*, as *New York Times* writer Frank Rich has termed the genre of "relentless hybrid of media circus, soap opera, and tabloid journalism," ground to a halt shortly after a U.S. federal court paved the way for Elián to return to Cuba in June. The story disappeared from national attention as quickly as it had surfaced.

The Original Webmaster

Tim Berners-Lee, here represented in a mosaic composed of 2,304 websites, was the brains behind the World Wide Web. (PhotomosaicTM by Robert Silvers/www.photomosaic.com)

For the textbook writer the Elián phenomenon invokes a recurring problem: What current events should be included in the closing chapter? Which will future historians view as having long-term significance, and which will they judge to be of little consequence? The answer in the González case will depend to a large extent on its aftermath. Many observers suggest that the Cuban expatriates' militant defiance of the Justice Department heightened public awareness of the exceptional political influence that the group has exerted on U.S. foreign policy. That recognition as well as new attention to the economic plight of Cubans under the thirty-nine-year U.S. embargo against the communist regime there might bolster efforts to normalize relations with Cuba. Future historians might also analyze the González case in the context of understanding the influence of Latinos in the nation's cultural and political life. Compared to the fewer than 1 million Cuban Americans in the country, Mexican Americans (20 million) and Puerto Ricans (7.7 million) have enjoyed significantly less political clout, but that trend is changing, and the Miami situation might provide a window into a broader story about politics in a pluralistic society. For the moment, Elián's inclusion in *America: A Concise History* is in limbo. Not yet in the final chapter, his story is given temporary status in this epilogue.

Writing history is about making choices by deciding what to include and what to leave out, and nowhere is this process more difficult than in writing of recent events. The key question for future editions of *America* is determining which occurrences will be thought significant enough to warrant inclusion in a broad synthesis of American history and culture and which will be judged mere blips on society's consciousness—things that seemed all-encompassing at the time but whose long-term significance paled. What the historian can offer is some sense from the past about how to think about the present, when all of us are bombarded with headlines and breaking stories and when our own reactions to major stories and events can cloud our ability to look at them objectively. Today's headlines do not always become tomorrow's history.

In a 1992 interview former President Richard M. Nixon stated bluntly, "In my view, history is never worth reading until it's fifty years old. It takes fifty years before you're able to come back and evaluate a man or a period of time." The mere passage of time does often help participants understand events and place them in their larger historical context. For example, we know much more about the origins of the cold war now that documents from the former Soviet Union and other former communist states are surfacing that present their side of the global conflict. And fifty years after the end of World War II Swiss banks are finally accounting for money deposited by Jews later killed in Hitler's concentration camps.

Yet if textbook writers took Nixon's advice literally, they would end their books just after World War II and the onset of the cold war. Of course this isn't desirable, and the enormous outpouring of excellent scholarship that informs Part Six of *America* demonstrates that it is indeed possible to assess and interpret historically events of the fairly recent past such as the cold war, the civil rights movement, the

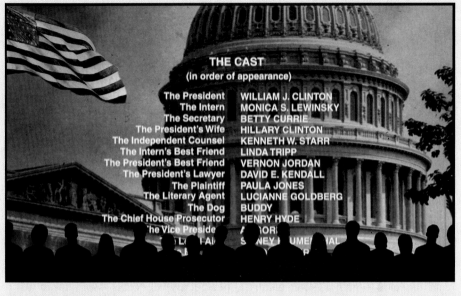

THE CAST
(in order of appearance)

The President	WILLIAM J. CLINTON
The Intern	MONICA S. LEWINSKY
The Secretary	BETTY CURRIE
The President's Wife	HILLARY CLINTON
The Independent Counsel	KENNETH W. STARR
The Intern's Best Friend	LINDA TRIPP
The President's Best Friend	VERNON JORDAN
The President's Lawyer	DAVID E. KENDALL
The Plaintiff	PAULA JONES
The Literary Agent	LUCIANNE GOLDBERG
The Dog	BUDDY
The Chief House Prosecutor	HENRY HYDE

The Impeachment Players

For more than a year the Monica Lewinsky story dominated the news, making household names of major and minor characters. Then, like a movie, it ended. Most Americans seemed relieved that the ordeal was over, telling pollsters that they were ready for Clinton and the country to move on. (Jesse Gordon/The New York Times. Reprinted with permission)

growth of suburbia, and the changing contours of the global economy. The closer that past gets to the present, the harder the task becomes. That does not mean, however, that historians have to cede the recent past or even contemporary events to journalists and television analysts.

What follows is an overview of the key areas in modern American life that we have traced throughout the book—politics, society and culture, economics, and foreign policy—at the historical moment when the twentieth century turned into the twenty-first. Think of this part of *America* as a historical document: how a group of American historians saw the challenges and promises of writing the contemporary history of their society as the year 2001 approached. Look at the choice of issues and methods to discover how historians gather and evaluate evidence, how they link individual events to larger patterns and themes, and yes, how they are often forced to revise their earlier conclusions or change their minds entirely.

POLITICS.   Unlike the last edition of *America*, we have been able to provide a brief discussion of President Bill Clinton's impeachment and acquittal, but even here it is premature to assess the lasting significance of the crisis. At this stage we can only draw on our understanding of the past to pose questions about its impact. For example, will the presidency be permanently undermined by the process, only the second time in America's history that a president has been impeached, or will the institution and the country prove as resilient as they did in 1974 after Richard Nixon's resignation to avoid imminent impeachment? Has the historic balance of power between the three branches of government been permanently upset by a partisan Congress pursuing an open-ended investigation of a sitting president of the opposite political party? What will be the effects of the impeachment proceedings on citizens' attitudes toward their elected representatives and Washington in general? These are some of the larger questions that will concern historians who evaluate this era in the years to come.

Yet it is quite possible that when historians assess the Clinton presidency and the politics of governance in the 1990s, the impeachment scandal, in hindsight, will be seen as less important than the way in which President Clinton helped move the Democratic Party to a more centrist position or presided over a flourishing economy. Writing in the heat of the moment robs historians of the ability to step back, gather evidence, and listen to and weigh different viewpoints—the tools of the historian's craft. But it is not always necessary to have Richard Nixon's proverbial fifty years to gain a better historical perspective on events—sometimes just a few years will do.

A good case in point is the 1994 election, in which Republicans won control of the House of Representatives for the first time in forty years with a campaign organized around an antigovernment theme spelled out in their "Contract with America." In the last edition of *America* we interpreted the electoral results as potentially dramatic, perhaps (although we intentionally fudged a bit here) signaling the end of the rise of the state, of "big government." Two years later Bill Clinton was re-elected, and in the 1998 election Democrats picked up five seats in the House (unprecedented for a party in power in an off-year election), and the architect of the 1994 Republican victory, Speaker of the House Newt Gingrich, resigned, not Bill Clinton. Not a single Washington pundit had predicted this startling turn of events. Suddenly the "Republican revolution" of 1994 looked less like a history-altering turning point than a minor political realignment.

Often these unexpected events—election upsets, assassinations, and natural disasters—can seem to change the course of history overnight. But historians need not place themselves at the mercy of fast-breaking news; instead, they can attempt to place events in their larger context and promise to revisit their assessment later to see if it has weathered the test of time. In other cases historians can draw on their knowledge of the past to identify contemporary issues likely to emerge as defining moments when they write about this period in the future.

One such issue, a major concern at the turn of the century, is what will happen when the baby boomers (Americans born between 1945 and 1963) begin to retire and collect Social Security. Perhaps when we look back at the early twenty-first century, one of the most critical markers will be whether the budget surplus that began in 1997 was used to shore up the ailing Social Security system. Current projections show Social Security running short of money to pay all promised benefits by 2032. As a result of these gloomy predictions many Americans are losing confidence that government pensions, one of the cornerstones of the American welfare state, will actually be available for them when they retire. The historical problem has been identified, but the solution remains for the future.

Another political issue that historians will be writing about in the future is health care. As the last chapter of *America* discusses, Clinton's 1994 plan for reform of the health-care system was considered too sweeping. An incremental, market-driven approach featuring managed care seemed better suited to the needs of the country, with the result that by 1998 almost two-thirds of the population (61 percent) belonged to some kind of health maintenance organization (HMO). But no sooner had managed care become the predominant method of dispensing health care than doubts set in. Complaints about restrictions on the kinds of care and services available—often fueled by heart-wrenching stories of patients denied access to potentially life-saving treatments by their cost-conscious HMOs—became so widespread that health-care advocates and politicians proposed a "Patient's Bill of Rights" to expand patient choice and make HMOs accountable for the quality of care provided. Furthermore, managed care had failed to reach the growing proportion of Americans (more than one-sixth of the population) who had no access to health insurance at all.

Another puzzle of contemporary politics that historians will have to address is what happened to the welfare system and its beneficiaries after Congress and the states passed sweeping changes in the 1990s, especially the 1996 federal law placing a five-year lifetime limit on assistance for single mothers and a two-year limit for adults without dependent children. Current welfare recipients would theoretically reach the end of their benefits at various points between 1998 and 2001, but welfare rolls were already dropping precipitously before the federal deadlines kicked in. For example, Wisconsin, which had developed one of the most ambitious "workfare" programs to get people off welfare, saw its number of cases drop from almost 80,000 in 1994 to just over 10,000 four years later.

And yet there was no consensus on what this drop meant or what had happened to the former welfare recipients. Were they able to use state employment services to develop skills and find jobs, or did they find jobs simply because the economy was booming? What will happen if the economy slows down and is unable to absorb all those who want to work, possibly throwing them back onto welfare or, worse, onto the streets to join the many thousands of already homeless Americans? Is the goal of workfare to help people find jobs in the private sector or merely to discourage the poor from applying for public assistance in the first place? Some answers will emerge when the time limits are reached; others will take longer to become clear. Only with the completion of substantive studies of what actually happened to former welfare recipients will historians have the data to mount an assessment of the success or failure of attempts, in President Clinton's words, to "end welfare as we know it." As with Social Security and health care, this task will be crucial to

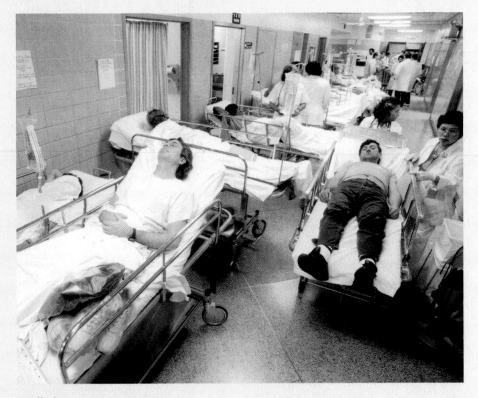

Gridlock

Although the escalating costs of medical care and prescription drugs dominate the headlines, a less well-known problem facing the country's health industry is the crisis in hospital
emergency rooms. Attempts to control costs have led hospital administrators to cut back
on Intensive Care Units, which have tended to shift the burden to emergency rooms, while
drug overdoses, AIDS-related crises, and urban violence have increased demand. It is poor,
uninsured Americans who most often turn to emergency rooms and who suffer the most from
the gridlock in these facilities, such as this one at Cook County Hospital in Chicago.
(Michael Melford)

understanding the evolution of the commitment of the state to public welfare, one
of the major themes of the twentieth century.

Finally, historians of turn-of-the-century politics may find in this period the
beginnings of changes in the political landscape. Will politicians' recognition of the
gender gap in voting and its impact on elections result in a marked increase in
the prominence of women in political life? Does the Democratic Party's nomination of Joseph Lieberman as the first Jewish candidate for vice president signal a
new openness in the national political arena? Will the Reform Party, founded by
Ross Perot, cease to be a magnet for Americans alienated from the two main parties? Will Ralph Nader's presidential campaign of 2000 mobilize Americans who are
critical of corporate power and concerned about the environment? And what about

The End of Welfare as We Know It?

Californian welfare recipients attend classes at a job-training center that reformers hope will give them skills to find work that will keep them off the welfare roles. It is still too soon to evaluate the long-term impact of the state and federal welfare reforms put in place in the 1990s. (Lava Jo Regan/Saba)

the dramatic November–December protests outside the 1999 World Trade Organization meeting in Seattle, where thousands of activists—from union organizers to environmentalists to students broadly concerned about the global concentration of corporate power—surprised and disrupted the city? As one protester explained, people "can't go to the polls and talk to these big conglomerates. So they had to take to the streets and talk to them." Does Seattle represent a "blip," or does it point to a mounting tide of impassioned activism, especially on the part of the young? Or will a more conservative approach to political change—the call for campaign finance reform—be implemented, and if so, will it have any impact on removing special interests from the political process?

Another series of far-reaching questions about American politics emerges from the chaos surrounding the Florida election results in 2000. As voters learned about hanging, dimpled, and pregnant "chads," they recognized that their voting procedures were fraught with the potential for machine error. At the very least, the publicity will put pressure on local and state agencies to improve the process by which citizens cast their ballots. But will more substantial results emerge from the Supreme Court's ruling in the first of George W. Bush's challenges to the Florida recount?

Taking It to the Streets

In November 1999 more than 200 members of the Sea Turtle Restoration project, dressed in sea turtle costumes, joined thousands of protesters against the World Trade Organization that was meeting in Seattle. Whether this impassioned coalition of environmentalists, labor activists, and critics of corporate capitalism represents the beginning of a sustained and powerful movement is just one of the many open questions for the future of American politics. (Wide World)

There, the Court, whose conservative majority has consistently emphasized state and local rights, seemingly reversed its position, arguing that variability in the way in which Florida's counties conducted elections and counted ballots undermined citizens' equal protection rights under the Fourteenth Amendment. Will this serve to discredit the Court in the future? As a result of the Court's decision, legal experts predict an avalanche of lawsuits designed to implement national voting standards, which could have a far-reaching impact. Furthermore, the messiness of the Florida case reinforced Al Gore's supporters' conviction that his victory had been stolen, a belief given much emotional weight by the fact that Gore won the popular vote by over 300,000 ballots. But Bush won where it counts—in the electoral college—with 270 votes to Gore's 266 (with one abstention), making him the first president since Benjamin Harrison (over Grover Cleveland in 1888) to gain the presidency while losing the popular vote. The day after the election newly elected

New York Senator Hillary Rodham Clinton was just one of a large chorus who called for eliminating the electoral college itself. Such a change would be difficult to accomplish because it involves amending the constitution, but if implemented, it could have a profound effect on the nation's political process and its political parties.

And finally, what long-term changes will the Internet bring to the practice of politics? Many observers credited the Internet for its ability to rally thousands of people to Seattle; in the future it may facilitate extraordinary mobilization of political support. Moreover, the Web, barely a factor in public life until the mid-1990s, is challenging established sources of news information, such as television or newspapers, as a major purveyor of information about important events. While the Internet promotes a broad transmission of information, the downside to this instant news is that much of it is circulated with minimal editorial controls or checks, leading to unsubstantiated statements and more than a few rumors. One of the tasks for future historians will be to sift fact from fiction in this proliferation of new sources of information.

A related factor is the way in which the media has turned the world into a global village, allowing billions around the world to tune in and watch a story unfolding live. (CNN's on-the-spot coverage of the Persian Gulf War in 1990–1991 was a major turning point in such coverage.) This explosion of information access coincided with what one critic has called the "growing tabloidization of American culture," a frenzy for gossip that blurred the lines between public and private. What does it say about contemporary American culture that we know more about the intimate details of the president's sexual habits than about nearly anyone else's but our own? These trends, building in the late twentieth century, will be hard to derail in the twenty-first.

SOCIETY AND CULTURE.   The future of many emerging trends is unclear, but reliable projections predict a changing racial makeup for American society. The U.S. Census Bureau predicts that in the year 2050, whites will make up 52.7 percent of the American population (down from 75.7 percent in 1990), with Latinos accounting for 21.1 percent, blacks 15 percent, and Asians 10.1 percent. If projected intermarriage is factored in (Latinos and Asians marry outside their racial groups much more frequently than blacks), the estimated white "majority" will probably slip to a white "minority." At the close of the twentieth century, already one out of twenty-five married couples were interracial, and at least 3 million children were of mixed-race parentage in the country. (This latter figure does not even include the millions of Latino mestizos as well as black Americans who have either European or American Indian ancestors.) Probably the best-known example of the country's increasingly multiracial heritage is golfer Tiger Woods, who used to call himself a "Cablinasian" to reflect his mix of Caucasian, black, Native American, and Asian heritages.

More immediately, in 2005 the United States will reach another demographic milestone: according to census projections Latinos will surpass African Americans

FATHER: Chinese, Irish,
French, German, Swedish
MOTHER: Italian, Irish, Japanese

The New Face of Race

In recognition that the "old labels of black and white cannot begin to capture the subtleties" of contemporary racial identity, in September 2000 *Newsweek* presented a special report, "Redefining Race in America." With one out of twenty-five married couples now interracial unions, this family represents a significant demographic trend. (Terrence T. Miele)

as the country's largest minority group, a development of great historical import. For most of the country's history racial issues have been seen literally as "black and white." The rising numbers of Latinos and Asian Americans will push the United States to reframe the American discourse on race. Whether these two groups join forces with African Americans will have large implications for civil rights organizations and divisive national issues like affirmative action. By contrast, if Latinos and Asians are seen more as "honorary whites" in a mostly white, mixed-race majority, then the historic black-nonblack dichotomy may even intensify. Americans have often talked about their society as a melting pot, and in the twentieth century they accepted a wide range of cultures and skin colors. Deep divisions accompanied the shift, however, and such acrimony (which died down temporarily in the

Have You Registered?

In an effort to mobilize the growing Latino population's participation in the democratic process, the Southwest Voter Registration Education Project has conducted more than 1,000 voter registration and education campaigns, like this one in Travis County, Texas.
(Bob Daemmrich Photography)

late 1990s) is likely to return periodically in the next century, especially during periods of economic or social conflict.

The changing nature of the American population is also having a decided impact on America's religious life. In a trend that also will likely continue into the next century, mainline (and often liberal) Protestant denominations such as Episcopalians, Methodists, and Presbyterians have been losing members since their baby-boom-era peak in the mid-1960s. The greatest growth for Protestants since the 1970s has been in the more conservative Southern Baptist Convention, which has become the largest religious organization in the United States after the Roman Catholic Church. At the same time changes in immigration laws have increased the ranks of Catholics as well as believers of faiths that had not previously been well represented in the United States, including larger numbers of American Muslims, Buddhists, and Hindus. A multiracial society is also increasingly a multireligious one.

Conversely, in a trend with wide-reaching implications, some American-based faiths have become so multinational that they no longer depend solely on American believers. The most striking example is the Church of Jesus Christ of Latter-Day Saints, or Mormons. In 1980 three-quarters of Mormonism's 4.6 million believers lived in the United States; by 1997 the church had 10 million followers,

Muslims at Prayer

The number of mosques and Islamic centers in the United States has more than doubled in the last twenty years to a total of 1,250. These men at a prayer service at the Islamic Center of Portland, Maine, are visual testimony to the growing diversity of American religious life. (Wide World)

the majority of them overseas. The Assemblies of God, a pentecostal denomination founded in Arkansas in 1914 whose believers seek to be filled with the Holy Spirit, also had more followers abroad than in the United States, especially in Brazil. Reflecting this new complexity of American religious life, one scholar observed, "It's a fun time to be a student of religion because there are a lot of interesting changes going on. We don't know where they're going to end up." That sums up the challenge of writing the history of contemporary America.

Another contemporary trend demanding attention is environmental consciousness. On the one hand, the United States has benefited from an increasingly active environmental movement. On April 26, 1995, when Americans came together for the twenty-fifth anniversary of Earth Day, they had much to celebrate. The nation's rivers and waterways were cleaner; air pollution had been reduced by a third; and lead emissions from fuel, a cause of retardation in children, had been cut by an astounding 98 percent. The bald eagle and the California condor had come back from the brink of extinction. By 1996 more than 7,000 communities across the country had established curb-side collection recycling programs. And in addition to addressing problems in their own communities, Americans were also becoming increasingly aware that environmental protection required action not just from the United States but from the global community as a whole. An important

Los Angeles by Night

The vast expanse that is the Los Angeles metropolitan area is especially striking at night, as captured by artist Peter Alexander. Yet think of the vast amounts of energy being consumed by those city lights. (James Corcoran Gallery, Santa Monica, CA)

precedent for international action on environmental issues was set by the Montreal Protocol (1987), in which thirty-four nations agreed to phase out ozone-damaging chlorofluorocarbons (CFCs) by 1999. In June 1992 delegates to the Earth Summit in Rio de Janeiro adopted a treaty on global warming, and in 1994 the United States joined sixty-three other countries in signing the Basel Convention, which banned the export of hazardous wastes from industrialized to developing countries. In the future, U.S. environmental policy would operate more and more within an international framework.

On the other hand, turn-of-the-century Americans continued to face serious ecological problems. Despite efforts to reduce urban smog, two out of five Americans lived in areas with unhealthy air. Many rivers and lakes were still unsafe for fishing and swimming. And one out of four Americans lived within four miles of toxic waste dumps, a trend with disproportionate effect on lower-income communities, constituting what activists term *environmental racism*.

Also alarming was the nation's growing energy use at the turn of the century, which calls into question how significant a realignment actually occurred as a result of the energy crisis of the 1970s. By the late 1990s Americans were using almost as much energy per capita as they had in 1973, wiping out practically all the savings that had occurred through conservation and efficiency in between. At century's end Americans consumed more than twice as much energy per person as Europeans or Japanese. (Only Canadians, with a larger percentage of heavy industry and a colder climate, consumed more worldwide.) The short-term reason for the turnaround is clear: a worldwide decline in oil prices made it cheaper and easier for Americans to live more energy intensively. Two symptoms of the shift were the growing popularity of sports utility vehicles and the trend toward larger, more appliance-laden houses. To meet these energy needs U.S. oil imports grew from 35 percent of total consumption in 1973 to about 50 percent in the late 1990s. Even though energy experts warned that a tightening of oil supplies and higher prices was inevitable—a prediction that came true in 2000—few changed their lifestyles by reducing energy consumption.

This change in mentality about the need for conservation and environmental protection also threatened to undercut the international progress made in the 1980s and 1990s on pressing ecological issues such as acid rain and depletion of the ozone layer. Yet these problems have not gone away. More evidence for global warming emerged in August 2000, when scientists reported the discovery that the ice cap at the North Pole had melted, leaving a mile-wide expanse of water for the first time in recorded history.

Other important issues that face the United States at 2001 are, like the environment, global ones. The AIDS epidemic is another international issue. According to a United Nations study in 1997, more than 34 million people worldwide suffered from AIDS or were infected with HIV, the virus that causes AIDS. The problem was especially acute in Africa, where 24 million were infected; in Botswana, a shocking 36 percent of adults were HIV positive. Rates were lower in Asia, Eastern Europe, and South America, but the disease was spreading there as well. In the United States, by contrast, the number of AIDS deaths dropped from over 30,000 in 1995 to 20,000 four years later, the result of potent—and expensive—drugs that allowed some infected people to manage the disease. But even after extensive public health campaigns, the number of new infections did not drop in the United States.

According to *USA Today* 75 percent of Americans believe that another major and deadly disease will appear by 2025. At the same time Americans seem to expect major miracles from medical science in the next century. Fueled by consumer demands for health information and a desire to live longer, healthier lives, the news

The Human Genome Project

This gel strip, which contains DNA fragments, was one of the experimental building blocks for the Human Genome Project. Originally launched in 1990, the project announced in June 2000 that scientists had succeeded in mapping the human genetic code. While many observers exulted over the possibilities for understanding and curing diseases based on this "Book of Life," others worried over ethical questions connected to potential genetic discrimination. (Photo Researchers)

media routinely treat advances in science and medicine as front-page news. In the June 2000 report on the "Genome Project," scientists announced that they had produced a "Book of Life" mapping the human genetic code, and commentators explored its medical implications for the treatment of disease as well as ethical questions about potential genetic discrimination. Less ambiguous was the response when the *New York Times* ran a feature story about a possible breakthrough in cancer research in 1998. Hopes soared that cancer might once and for all be conquered. "OUR BEST HOPE" ran one headline, with an accompanying article by a cancer-stricken journalist who stated, "Maybe we don't have to die." Doctors often learn about new drugs and procedures right along with their patients through newspaper accounts and drug company-sponsored advertisements; patients also surf the Internet for information about clinical trials of new treatments or experimental drugs for specific diseases. This democratization of medical knowledge empowers some consumers but at the cost of inflating hopes about untested drugs and procedures years away from marketability. And yet Americans' hope for the cure—for breast cancer, for AIDS, for Alzheimer's disease—continues unabated.

ECONOMICS.   Just as rapid-pace developments in the arenas of technology and science make it difficult for historians to assess recent events, dramatic changes in the economy in the last decade provide a good example of how quickly and unexpectedly our understanding of the nation's economic picture can be transformed. In 1989 it was widely accepted that Japan was rising and America was declining, or as the scholar Chalmers Johnson put it, "The cold war is over, and Japan won." Now the opposite appears to be true: the United States economy looks strong, almost invincible, and Asian economies are having difficulties. One seemingly safe conclusion is that when an economy is performing well, as was Japan's in the late 1980s and America's in the late 1990s, it temporarily hides all sorts of problems. As economist Laura D'Andrea Tyson observes, "In prosperous times we overstate the good and understate the bad." One of the most troubling "bad" trends is the growing disparity of wealth and opportunity that characterizes the American economy at the end of the century, with the very rich profiting the most from the recent period of prosperity.

And no matter how prosperous the United States might be, its fortunes are intimately tied to the performance of other nations' economies. The rapid growth of international corporations has eroded traditional barriers of nation states and led to increased concentration of the world's economic power, which at the very least has implications for working people who must compete in a global labor market. The late 1990s saw meltdown in Asia, with nine of Asia's thirteen major countries either in recession or depression by 1998, and the collapse of the Russian economy. As the world's economic troubles deepened, the new buzz word among politicians and economists was an updated version of the domino theory called *contagion*— the idea that if one country's economy was allowed to implode, it could set in motion an uncontrollable set of events around the world. The International Monetary Fund (IMF) and the World Bank, set up in the wake of World War II to ensure financial stability in world markets, responded by one costly rescue bailout after another of a shaky economy—Thailand, Indonesia, South Korea, and Russia. Fears surfaced that Brazil, Venezuela, or Mexico might be next.

As historians struggle to make sense of the global economic picture, they are hampered not just by the dramatic turn of events in Asia but also by the fact that many economic tenets no longer seem reliable. For example, since 1960 a widely accepted economic principle called the Phillips curve posited that there could be low inflation or low unemployment but not both. Yet the 1990s boom has seen inflation *and* unemployment drop to their lowest levels in generations. Another long-held economic tenet claimed that measures to lower the deficit would act as a drag on the economy, thereby slowing economic growth. To the contrary, in the 1990s the United States has experienced both significant deficit reduction and a period of sustained economic growth. In other words, many of the principles and tenets on which economists—and historians who rely on those economists—depend seem to have broken down. Perhaps the ups and downs of the past ten years will lead to the emergence of new economic laws, but for now we are all struggling to make sense of a complex and deeply interconnected world economy.

FOREIGN POLICY.   Just as complicated are the emerging contours of the post–cold-war world. Note that historians are still using the cold war as the organizing concept for the late twentieth century, even though it ended a decade earlier. Future textbooks will probably recognize the events of 1989 – 1991 in Eastern Europe and the Soviet Union as the defining watershed in the late twentieth century; certainly the years 1945 to 1991 would provide a logical periodization for Part Six in a future edition of America's History. Events since then—the last part of Chapter 31 and this epilogue—would in effect be the opening of a new Part Seven, as yet unnamed and (with apologies to the sports world) with themes and players to be announced later.

Despite the end of the cold war American foreign policy is still directed toward the goals that have shaped much of the twentieth century, such as desiring to contain major or potentially major nations that might appear as rivals. Thus the United States supported the expansion of NATO to include former communist bloc members Poland, Hungary, and the Czech Republic as a hedge against a resurgent Russia. Regarding China, the world's most populous country, the United States worried about China's nuclear capabilities and human-rights violations, yet the October 2000 agreement to establish Permanent Normal Trade Relations between the two nations was interpreted by U.S. leaders as a step toward promoting an American version of free-market capitalism and democracy in China. Protecting U.S. access to oil reserves worldwide remained a high priority, with the oil-rich Caspian region (wedged between Russia and Iran) emerging as the newest stage for diplomatic maneuvering.

On the eve of the twenty-first century, terrorism emerged as a central concern of U.S. foreign policy. A series of terrorist attacks, often directed at American citizens or embassies abroad but occasionally at targets in the United States (like the 1993 bombing of New York City's World Trade Center), had heightened America's sense of vulnerability. Even though the number of lives lost was relatively small (ninety-eight Americans were killed in foreign terrorist attacks between 1989 and 1998, less than are killed on average each year by lightning), driving the fear was the perception that terrorists posed a continuous, deadly, and invisible threat to American interests and installations throughout the world. As with cold-war fears of nuclear annihilation that sent schoolchildren ducking and covering under their desks, no one ever feels safe in a world where terrorists reign.

But unlike the cold war, a period when the Soviet Union was identified as America's main enemy, terrorist attacks cannot necessarily be traced to a single state or a single leader. Instead of a central headquarters like the Kremlin, loose organizations are dispersed throughout many countries. At the end of the twentieth

Terrorists Strike the USS Cole

A deadly reminder of the ever-present threat of terrorism came on October 12, 2000, when a suicide attack on the USS *Cole,* a navy guided-missile destroyer that was refueling in the Yemeni part of Aden, blew a huge hole in the ship's hull, killing seventeen sailors. The United States immediately lay the blame on Saudi exile Osama bin Laden. In Yemen, six suspects were arrested on suspicion of complicity in the attack. (U.S. Navy/TimePix)

century the strongest threats to American interests came from militant Islamic sects committed to a messianic vision of the end of Western influence in the Arab world and the ultimate destruction of the United States. Responsibility for attacks was often difficult to pin down—was it Hezbollah, Islamic Jihad, or Osama bin Laden's followers?—and bringing terrorists to international justice even harder. Retaliation can sometimes subdue opponents or can simply provoke further terrorism in a war of attrition.

While there are few rules or guidelines for a coming war against terrorism, the world began to feel confident that nuclear proliferation had been slowed or even halted as the century drew to an end. Then in 1998 India and Pakistan each defied world opinion by testing a nuclear device. In the immediate aftermath of World War II only the largest and most advanced countries could realistically hope to develop nuclear weapons, but fifty years later the capacity is spread much more broadly. Until India and Pakistan conducted their tests, only five countries had declared nuclear-weapons capability: the United States, Russia, Britain, France, and

China, although most observers believe that Israel had such capacity as well. In addition, Iran, Iraq, North Korea, and Libya were suspected of having secret nuclear-weapons programs. Especially worrisome about the Indian and Pakistani tests was these neighboring countries' long history of a bitter acrimony in one of the world's most populous and dangerous regions. International concerns about controlling nuclear weapons deepened in October 1999 when the U.S. Senate in a partisan battle refused to ratify the Comprehensive Test Ban Treaty (CTBT), a move widely interpreted as damaging to the nation's ability to exercise political and moral leadership in the drive to contain nuclear proliferation.

Small countries as well as terrorist organizations realize that they do not require a nuclear bomb to be taken seriously: short-range nuclear missiles, germ warfare, and poison gas can be just as effective and far cheaper. (This threat is sometimes abbreviated as "NBC"—nuclear, biological, and chemical weapons—or alternatively, weapons of mass destruction.) Much of the basic material and technology is available for purchase on the thriving world arms market, in which countries like the United States, France, Britain, and the former states of the Soviet Union are major dealers. Given this traffic in arms, it is fairly easy for intermediaries in the Middle East and other developing countries to buy what they need. It is said that highly destructive cruise missiles can be bought for approximately $10,000 apiece, making them in some ways the "poor man's nukes." Their potential danger increases when combined with the capacity for chemical and biological warfare. Unlike policing who has and who doesn't have the bomb, the containment of arms proliferation and suspected chemical and biological warfare is an even more complex task, as the United States has discovered in its dealings with Iraq and Saddam Hussein in the aftermath of the 1990–1991 Gulf War.

At the same time, destructive conflicts that have little to do with high-tech weaponry and everything to do with ethnicity, religion, and territory have flared up periodically in the aftermath of the cold war and threaten to do so for the foreseeable future. In the Middle East, violent attacks and counterattacks between Israelis and Palestinians in 2000–2001 shattered a Clinton-brokered peace plan, and the 2001 election of Likud Party leader Ariel Sharon as prime minister of Israel further dimmed hopes that a resolution of the differences between the two sides could be resolved peacefully. The Balkans especially continue to challenge U.S. policymakers, NATO leaders, and United Nations peacekeeping forces. Would the Yugoslavian province of Kosovo, which U.S. special envoy Richard Holbrooke in 1998 called "the most dangerous place in Europe," become the next Bosnia? Or would the Yugoslavian republic of Montenegro? Can genocides such as those that occurred in Bosnia and Rwanda be prevented?

The contemporary world can look like a scary place indeed, but rays of hope at the end of the twentieth century included the possible resolutions of problems that have long defied peaceful solutions: the hope that the 1998 Good Friday accords may finally bring peace to Ireland, or that U.S.-Cuban relations might improve in the wake of Pope John Paul II's visit to Cuba in 1998 despite the furor over

A Hero for Our Jaded Times

Nelson Mandela is that rare contemporary hero whose stature seems destined to be confirmed posthumously by history. In a valedictory address to the United Nations in 1998, Mandela spoke of his long personal journey:

> Born as the First World War came to a close and departing from public life as the world marks half a century of the Universal Declaration of Human Rights, I have reached that part of the long walk when the opportunity is granted, as it should be to all men and women, to retire to some rest and tranquility in the village of my birth.
>
> As I sit in Qunu and grow as ancient as its hills . . . I will continue to hope that Africa's renaissance will strike deep roots and blossom forever, without regard to the changing seasons. . . .
>
> Then would history and the billions throughout the world proclaim that it was right that we dreamed and that we toiled to give life to a workable dream.

(Louise Gubb/The Image Works)

the Elián González case. The end of apartheid in South Africa and that country's determination to come to grips with its past are surely among the twentieth century's most inspiring developments, as is the emergence of democratic countries from the former Soviet satellites in Eastern Europe. Along with globalization and the challenge of forging a post–cold-war foreign policy, these potential breakthroughs are part of the story of America and the world in 2001.

DOCUMENTS

THE DECLARATION OF INDEPENDENCE

The Unanimous Declaration of the Thirteen United States of America

When in the Course of human events, it becomes necessary for one people to dissolve the political bands which have connected them with another, and to assume among the Powers of the earth, the separate and equal station to which the Laws of Nature and of Nature's God entitle them, a decent respect to the opinions of mankind requires that they should declare the causes which impel them to the separation.

We hold these truths to be self-evident, that all men are created equal, that they are endowed by their Creator with certain unalienable rights, that among these are Life, Liberty, and the pursuit of Happiness. That to secure these rights, Governments are instituted among Men, deriving their just powers from the consent of the governed. That whenever any Form of Government becomes destructive of these ends, it is the Right of the People to alter or to abolish it, and to institute new Government, laying its foundation on such principles and organizing its powers in such form, as to them shall seem most likely to effect their Safety and Happiness. Prudence, indeed, will dictate that Governments long established should not be changed for light and transient causes; and accordingly all experience hath shown, that mankind are more disposed to suffer, while evils are sufferable, than to right themselves by abolishing the forms to which they are accustomed. But when a long train of abuses and usurpations, pursuing invariably the same Object evinces a design to reduce them under absolute Despotism, it is their right, it is their duty, to throw off such Government, and to provide new Guards for their future security. —Such has been the patient sufferance of these Colonies; and such is now the necessity which constrains them to alter their former Systems of Government. The history of the present King of Great Britain is a history of repeated injuries and usurpations, all having in direct object the establishment of an absolute Tyranny over these States. To prove this, let Facts be submitted to a candid world.

He has refused his Assent to Laws, the most wholesome and necessary for the public good.

He has forbidden his Governors to pass Laws of immediate and pressing importance, unless suspended in their operation till his Assent should be obtained; and, when so suspended, he has utterly neglected to attend to them.

He has refused to pass other Laws for the accommodation of large districts of people, unless those people would relinquish the right of Representation in the Legislature, a right inestimable to them and formidable to tyrants only.

He has called together legislative bodies at places unusual, uncomfortable, and distant from the depository of their public Records, for the sole purpose of fatiguing them into compliance with his measures.

He has dissolved Representative Houses repeatedly, for opposing with manly firmness his invasions on the rights of the people.

He has refused for a long time, after such dissolutions, to cause others to be elected; whereby the Legislative powers, incapable of Annihilation, have returned to the People at large for their exercise; the State remaining in the mean time exposed to all the dangers of invasion from without and convulsions within.

He has endeavoured to prevent the population of these States; for that purpose obstructing the Laws of Naturalization of Foreigners; refusing to pass others to encourage their migrations hither, and raising the conditions of new Appropriations of Lands.

He has obstructed the Administration of Justice, by refusing his Assent to Laws for establishing Judiciary powers.

He has made Judges dependent on his Will alone, for the tenure of their offices, and the amount and payment of their salaries.

He has erected a multitude of New Offices, and sent hither swarms of Officers to harass our People, and eat out their substance.

He has kept among us, in times of peace, Standing Armies without the Consent of our legislature.

He has combined with others to subject us to a jurisdiction foreign to our constitution, and unacknowledged by our laws; giving his Assent to their Acts of pretended Legislation:

For quartering large bodies of armed troops among us:

For protecting them, by a mock Trial, from Punishment for any Murders which they should commit on the Inhabitants of these States:

For cutting off our Trade with all parts of the world:

For imposing taxes on us without our Consent:

For depriving us of many cases, of the benefits of Trial by jury:

For transporting us beyond Seas to be tried for pretended offences:

For abolishing the free System of English Laws in a neighbouring Province, establishing therein an Arbitrary government, and enlarging its Boundaries so as to render it at once an example and fit instrument for introducing the same absolute rule into these Colonies:

For taking away our Charters, abolishing our most valuable Laws, and altering fundamentally the Forms of our Governments:

For suspending our own Legislatures, and declaring themselves invested with Power to legislate for us in all cases whatsoever.

He has abdicated Government here, by declaring us out of his Protection and waging War against us.

He has plundered our seas, ravaged our Coasts, burnt our towns, and destroyed the lives of our people.

He is at this time transporting large armies of foreign mercenaries to compleat the works of death, desolation, and tyranny, already begun with circumstances of Cruelty & perfidy scarcely paralleled in the most barbarous ages, and totally unworthy the Head of a civilized nation.

He has constrained our fellow Citizens taken Captive on the high Seas to bear Arms against their Country, to become the executioners of their friends and Brethren, or to fall themselves by their Hands.

He has excited domestic insurrections amongst us, and has endeavoured to bring on the inhabitants of our frontiers, the merciless Indian Savages, whose known rule of warfare, is an undistinguished destruction of all ages, sexes, and conditions.

In every stage of these Oppressions We have Petitioned for Redress in the most humble terms: Our repeated petitions have been answered only by repeated injury. A Prince, whose character is thus marked by every act which may define a Tyrant, is unfit to be the ruler of a free people.

Nor have We been wanting in attention to our British brethren. We have warned them from time to time of attempts by their legislature to extend an unwarrantable jurisdiction over us. We have reminded them of the circumstances of our emigration and settlement here. We have appealed to their native justice and magnanimity, and we have conjured them by the ties of our common kindred to disavow these usurpations, which, would inevitably interrupt our connections and correspondence. They too have been deaf to the voice of justice and of consanguinity. We must, therefore, acquiesce in the necessity, which denounces our Separation, and hold them, as we hold the rest of mankind, Enemies in War, in Peace Friends.

We, therefore, the Representatives of the United States of America, in General Congress, Assembled, appealing to the Supreme Judge of the world for the rectitude of our intentions, do, in the Name, and by Authority of the good People of these Colonies, solemnly publish and declare, That these United Colonies are, and of Right ought to be FREE AND INDE-PENDENT STATES; that they are Absolved from all Allegiance to the British Crown, and that all political connection between them and the State of Great Britain, is and ought to be totally dissolved; and that as Free and Independent States, they have full Power to levy War, conclude Peace, contract Alliances, establish Commerce, and to do all other Acts and Things which Independent States may of right do. And for the support of this Declaration, with a firm reliance on the Protection of Divine Providence, we mutually pledge to each other our Lives, our Fortunes, and our sacred Honor.

John Hancock

Button Gwinnett	George Wythe	James Wilson	Josiah Bartlett
Lyman Hall	Richard Henry Lee	Geo. Ross	Wm. Whipple
Geo. Walton	Th. Jefferson	Caesar Rodney	Saml. Adams
Wm. Hooper	Benja. Harrison	Geo. Read	John Adams
Joseph Hewes	Thos. Nelson, Jr.	Thos. M'Kean	Robt. Treat Paine
John Penn	Francis Lightfoot Lee	Wm. Floyd	Elbridge Gerry
Edward Rutledge	Carter Braxton	Phil. Livingston	Step. Hopkins
Thos. Heyward, Junr.	Robt. Morris	Frans. Lewis	William Ellery
Thomas Lynch, Junr.	Benjamin Rush	Lewis Morris	Roger Sherman
Arthur Middleton	Benja. Franklin	Richd. Stockton	Sam'el Hunington
Samuel Chase	John Morton	Jno. Witherspoon	Wm. Williams
Wm. Paca	Geo. Clymer	Fras. Hopkinson	Oliver Wolcott
Thos. Stone	Jas. Smith	John Hart	Matthew Thornton
Charles Carroll of Carrollton	Geo. Taylor	Abra. Clark	

THE ARTICLES OF CONFEDERATION AND PERPETUAL UNION

Between the states of New Hampshire, Massachusetts Bay, Rhode Island and Providence Plantations, Connecticut, New York, New Jersey, Pennsylvania, Delaware, Maryland, Virginia, North Carolina, South Carolina, Georgia.*

ARTICLE 1.

The stile of this confederacy shall be "The United States of America."

ARTICLE 2.

Each State retains its sovereignty, freedom and independence, and every power, jurisdiction, and right, which is not by this confederation expressly delegated to the United States, in Congress assembled.

ARTICLE 3.

The said states hereby severally enter into a firm league of friendship with each other for their common defence, the security of their liberties and their mutual and general welfare; binding themselves to assist each other against all force offered to, or attacks made upon them, or any of them, on account of religion, sovereignty, trade, or any other pretence whatever.

ARTICLE 4.

The better to secure and perpetuate mutual friendship and intercourse among the people of the different states in this union, the free inhabitants of each of these states, paupers, vagabonds, and fugitives from justice excepted, shall be entitled to all privileges and immunities of free citizens in the several states; and the people of each State shall have free ingress and regress to and from any other State, and shall enjoy therein all the privileges of trade and commerce, subject to the same duties, impositions, and restrictions, as the inhabitants thereof respectively; provided, that such restrictions shall not extend so far as to prevent the removal of property, imported into any State, to any other State of which the owner is an inhabitant; provided also, that no imposition, duties, or restriction, shall be laid by any State on the property of the United States, or either of them.

If any person guilty of, or charged with treason, felony, or other high misdemeanor in any State, shall flee from justice and be found in any of the United States, he shall, upon demand of the governor or executive power of the State from which he fled, be delivered up and removed to the State having jurisdiction of his offence.

Full faith and credit shall be given in each of these states to the records, acts, and judicial proceedings of the courts and magistrates of every other State.

---

*This copy of the final draft of the Articles of Confederation is taken from the *Journals,* 9:907–25, November 15, 1777.

ARTICLE 5.

For the more convenient management of the general interests of the United States, delegates shall be annually appointed, in such manner as the legislature of each State shall direct, to meet in Congress, on the 1st Monday in November in every year, with a power reserved to each State to recall its delegates, or any of them, at any time within the year, and to send others in their stead for the remainder of the year.

No State shall be represented in Congress by less than two, nor by more than seven members; and no person shall be capable of being a delegate for more than three years in any term of six years; nor shall any person, being a delegate, be capable of holding any office under the United States, for which he, or any other for his benefit, receives any salary, fees, or emolument of any kind.

Each State shall maintain its own delegates in a meeting of the states, and while they act as members of the committee of the states.

In determining questions in the United States, in Congress assembled, each State shall have one vote.

Freedom of speech and debate in Congress shall not be impeached or questioned in any court or place out of Congress: and the members of Congress shall be protected in their persons from arrests and imprisonments, during the time of their going to and from, and attendance on Congress, except for treason, felony, or breach of the peace.

ARTICLE 6.

No State, without the consent of the United States, in Congress assembled, shall send any embassy to, or receive any embassy from, or enter into any conference, agreement, alliance, or treaty with any king, prince, or state; nor shall any person, holding any office of profit or trust under the United States, or any of them, accept of any present, emolument, office or title, of any kind whatever, from any king, prince, or foreign state; nor shall the United States, in Congress assembled, or any of them, grant any title of nobility.

No two or more states shall enter into any treaty, confederation, or alliance, whatever, between them, without the consent of the United States, in Congress assembled, specifying accurately the purposes for which the same is to be entered into, and how long it shall continue.

No state shall lay any imposts or duties which may interfere with any stipulations in treaties entered into by the United States, in Congress assembled, with any king, prince, or state, in pursuance of any treaties already proposed by Congress to the courts of France and Spain.

No vessels of war shall be kept up in time of peace by any State, except such number only as shall be deemed necessary by the United States, in Congress assembled, for the defence of such State or its trade; nor shall any body of forces be kept up by any State, in time of peace, except such number only as, in the judgment of the United States, in Congress assembled, shall be deemed requisite to garrison the forts necessary for the defence of such State; but every State shall always keep up a well regulated and disciplined militia, sufficiently armed and accoutred, and shall provide, and constantly have ready for use, in public stores, a due number of field pieces and tents, and a proper quantity of arms, ammunition and camp equipage.

No State shall engage in any war without the consent of the United States, in Congress assembled, unless such State be actually invaded by enemies, or shall have received certain advice of a resolution being formed by some nation of Indians to invade such State, and the danger is so imminent as not to admit of a delay till the United States, in Congress assembled, can be consulted; nor shall any State grant commissions to any ships or vessels of war, nor letters of marque or reprisal, except it be after a declaration of war by the United States, in Congress assembled, and then only against the kingdom or state, and the subjects thereof, against which war has been so declared, and under such regulations as shall be established by the United States, in Congress assembled, unless such State be infested by pirates, in which case vessels of war may be fitted out for that occasion, and kept so long as the danger shall continue, or until the United States, in Congress assembled, shall determine otherwise.

ARTICLE 7.

When land forces are raised by any State for the common defence, all officers of or under the rank of colonel, shall be appointed by the legislature of each State respectively, by whom such forces shall be raised, or in such manner as such State shall direct; and all vacancies shall be filled up by the State which first made the appointment.

ARTICLE 8.

All charges of war and all other expences, that shall be incurred for the common defence or general welfare, and allowed by the United States, in Congress assembled, shall be defrayed out of a common treasury, which shall be supplied by the several states, in proportion to the value of all land within each State, granted to or surveyed for any person, as such land and the buildings and improvements thereon shall be estimated according to such mode as the United States, in Congress assembled, shall, from time to time, direct and appoint.

The taxes for paying that proportion shall be laid and levied by the authority and direction of the legislatures of the several states, within the time agreed upon by the United States, in Congress assembled.

ARTICLE 9.

The United States, in Congress assembled, shall have the sole and exclusive right and power of determining on peace and war, except in the cases mentioned in the 6th article; of sending and receiving ambassadors; entering into treaties and alliances, provided that no treaty of commerce shall be made, whereby the legislative power of the respective states shall be restrained from imposing such imposts and duties on foreigners as their own people are subjected to, or from prohibiting the exportation or importation of any species of goods or commodities whatsoever; of establishing rules for deciding, in all cases, what captures on land or water shall be legal, and in what manner prizes, taken by land or naval forces in the service of the United States, shall be divided or appropriated; or granting letters of marque and reprisal in times of peace; appointing courts for the trial of piracies and felonies committed on the high seas, and establishing courts for receiving and determining, finally, appeals in all cases of captures; provided, that no member of Congress shall be appointed a judge of any of the said courts.

The United States, in Congress assembled, shall also be the last resort on appeal in all disputes and differences now subsisting, or that hereafter may arise between two or more states concerning boundary, jurisdiction or any other cause whatever; which authority shall always be exercised in the manner following: whenever the legislative or executive authority, or lawful agent of any State, in controversy with another, shall present a petition to Congress, stating the matter in question, and praying for a hearing, notice thereof shall be given, by order of Congress, to the legislative of executive authority of the other State in controversy, and a day assigned for the appearance of the parties by their lawful agents, who shall then be directed to appoint, by joint consent, commissioners or judges to constitute a court for hearing and determining the matter in question; but, if they cannot agree, Congress shall name three persons out of each of the United States, and from the list of such persons each party shall alternately strike out one, the petitioners beginning, until the number shall be reduced to thirteen; and from that number not less than seven, nor more than nine names, as Congress shall direct, shall, in the presence of Congress, be drawn out by lot; and the persons whose names shall be so drawn, or any five of them, shall be commissioners or judges to hear and finally determine the controversy, so always as a major part of the judges who shall hear the cause shall agree in the determination; and if either party shall neglect to attend at the day appointed, without shewing reasons which Congress shall judge sufficient, or, being present, shall refuse to strike, the Congress shall proceed to nominate three persons out of each State, and the secretary of Congress shall strike in behalf of such party absent or refusing; and the judgment and sentence of the court to be appointed, in the manner before prescribed, shall be final and conclusive; and if any of the parties shall refuse to submit to the authority of such court, or to appear or defend their claim or cause, the court shall nevertheless proceed to pronounce sentence or judgment, which shall, in like manner, be final and decisive, the judgment or sentence and other proceedings begin, in either case, transmitted to Congress, and lodged among the acts of Congress for the security of the parties concerned: provided, that every commissioner, before he sits in judgment, shall take an oath, to be administered by one of the judges of the supreme or superior court of the State where the cause shall be tried, "well and truly to hear and determine the matter in question, according to the best of his judgment, without favour, affection, or hope of reward:" provided, also, that no State shall be deprived of territory for the benefit of the United States.

All controversies concerning the private right of soil, claimed under different grants of two or more states, whose jurisdictions, as they may respect such lands and the states which passed such grants, are adjusted, the said grants, or either of them, being at the same time claimed to have originated antecedent to such settlement of jurisdiction, shall, on the petition of either party to the Congress of the United States, be finally determined, as near as may be, in the same manner as is before prescribed for deciding disputes respecting territorial jurisdiction between different states.

The United States, in Congress assembled, shall also have the sole and exclusive right and power of regulating the alloy and value of coin struck by their own authority, or by that of the respective states; fixing the standard of weights and measures throughout the United States; regulating the trade and managing all affairs with the Indians not members of any of the states; provided that the legislative right of any State within its own limits be not infringed or violated; establishing and regulating post offices from one State to another throughout all the United States, and exacting such postage on the papers passing through the same as may be requisite to defray the expences of the said office; appointing all officers of the land forces in the service of the United States, excepting regimental officers; appointing all the officers of the naval forces, and commissioning all officers whatever in the service of the United States; making rules for the government and regulation of the said land and naval forces, and directing their operations.

The United States, in Congress assembled, shall have authority to appoint a committee to sit in the recess of Congress, to be denominated "a Committee of the States," and to consist of one delegate from each State, and to appoint such other committees and civil officers as may be necessary for managing the general affairs of the United States, under their direction; to appoint one of their number to preside; provided that no person be allowed to serve in the office of president more than one year in any term of three years; to ascertain the necessary sums of money to be raised for the service of the United States, and to appropriate and apply the same for defraying the public expences; to borrow money or emit bills on the credit of the United States, transmitting, every half year, to the respective states, an account of the sums of money so borrowed or emitted; to build and equip a navy; to agree upon the number of land forces, and to make requisitions from each State for in quota, in proportion to the number of white inhabitants in such State; which requisitions shall be binding; and thereupon, the legislature of each State shall appoint the regimental officers, raise the men, and cloathe, arm, and equip them in a soldier-like manner, at the expence of the United States; and the officers and men so cloathed, armed, and equipped, shall march to the place appointed and within the time agreed on by the United States, in Congress assembled; but if the United States, in Congress assembled, shall, on consideration of circumstances, judge proper that any State should not raise men, or should raise a smaller number than its quota, and that any other State should raise a greater number of men than the quota threof, such extra number shall be raised, officered, cloathed, armed, and equipped in the same manner as the quota of such State, unless the legislature of such State shall judge that such extra number cannot be safely spared out of the same, in which case they shall raise, officer, cloathe, arm, and equip as many of such extra number as they judge can be safely spared. And the officers and men so cloathed, armed, and equipped, shall march to the place appointed and within the time agreed on by the United States, in Congress assembled.

The United States, in Congress assembled, shall never engage in a war, nor grant letters of marque and reprisal in time of peace, nor enter into any treaties or alliances, nor coin money, nor regulate the value thereof, nor ascertain the sums and expences necessary for the defence and welfare of the United States, or any of them: nor emit bills, nor borrow money on the credit of the United States, nor appropriate money, nor agree upon the number of vessels of war to be built or purchased, or the number of land or sea forces to be raised, nor appoint a commander in chief of the army or navy, unless nine states assent to the same; nor shall a question on any other point, except for adjourning from day to day, be determined, unless by the votes of a majority of the United States, in Congress assembled.

The Congress of the United States shall have power to adjourn to any time within the year, and to any place within the United States, so that no period of adjournment be for a longer duration than the space of six months, and shall publish the journal of their proceedings monthly, except such parts thereof, relating to treaties, alliances or military operations, as, in their judgment, require secrecy; and the yeas and nays of the delegates of each State on any question shall be entered on the journal, when it is desired by any delegate; and the delegates of a State, or any of them, at his, or their request, shall be furnished with a transcript of the said journal, except such parts as are above excepted, to lay before the legislatures of the several states.

ARTICLE 10.

The committee of the states, or any nine of them, shall be authorized to execute, in the recess of Congress, such of the powers of Congress as the United States, in Congress assembled, by the consent of nine states, shall, from time to time, think expedient to vest them with; provided, that no power be delegated to the said committee, for the exercise of which, by the articles of confederation, the voice of nine states, in the Congress of the United States assembled, is requisite.

ARTICLE 11.

Canada acceding to this confederation, and joining in the measures of the United States, shall be admitted into and entitled to all the advantages of this union; but no other colony shall be admitted into the same, unless such admission be agreed to by nine states.

ARTICLE 12.

All bills of credit emitted, monies borrowed and debts contracted by, or under the authority of Congress before the assembling of the United States, in pursuance of the present confederation, shall be deemed and considered as a charge against the United States, for payment and satisfaction whereof the said United States and the public faith are hereby solemnly pledged.

ARTICLE 13.

Every State shall abide by the determinations of the United States, in Congress assembled, on all questions which, by this confederation, are submitted to them. And the articles of this confederation shall be inviolably observed by every State, and the union shall be perpetual; nor shall any alteration at any time hereafter be made in any of them, unless such alteration be agreed to in a Congress of the United States, and be afterwards confirmed by the legislatures of every State.

These articles shall be proposed to the legislatures of all the United States, to be considered, and if approved of by them, they are advised to authorize their delegates to ratify the same in the Congress of the United States; which being done, the same shall become conclusive.

THE CONSTITUTION OF THE UNITED STATES

We the People of the United States, in Order to form a more perfect Union, establish Justice, insure domestic Tranquility, provide for the common defence, promote the general Welfare, and secure the Blessings of Liberty to ourselves and our Posterity, do ordain and establish this Constitution for the United States of America.

ARTICLE I

Section 1
All legislative Powers herein granted shall be vested in a Congress of the United States, which shall consist of a Senate and a House of Representatives.

Section 2
The House of Representatives shall be composed of Members chosen every second Year by the People of the several States, and the Electors in each State shall have the Qualifications requisite for Electors of the most numerous Branch of the State Legislature.

No Person shall be a Representative who shall not have attained to the Age of twenty-five Years, and been seven Years a Citizen of the United States, and who shall not, when elected, be an Inhabitant of that State in which he shall be chosen.

Representatives and direct Taxes shall be apportioned among the several States which may be included within this Union, according to their respective Numbers, *which shall be determined by adding to the whole Number of free Persons, including those bound to Service for a Term of Years, and excluding Indians not taxed, three fifths of all other Persons.** The actual Enumeration shall be made within three Years after the first Meeting of the Congress of the United States, and within every subsequent Term of ten Years, in such Manner as they shall by Law direct. The Number of Representatives shall not exceed one for every thirty Thousand, but each State shall have at Least one Representative; and *until such enumeration shall be made, the State of New Hampshire shall be entitled to chuse three, Massachusetts eight, Rhode Island and Providence Plantations one, Connecticut five, New-York six, New Jersey four, Pennsylvania eight, Delaware one, Maryland six, Virginia ten, North Carolina five, South Carolina five, and Georgia three.*

When vacancies happen in the Representation from any State, the Executive Authority thereof shall issue Writs of Election to fill such Vacancies.

The House of Representatives shall chuse their Speaker and other Officers; and shall have the sole Power of Impeachment.

Section 3
The Senate of the United States shall be composed of two Senators from each State, *chosen by the Legislature thereof,*† for six Years; and each Senator shall have one Vote.

Immediately after they shall be assembled in Consequence of the first Election, they shall be divided as equally as may be into three Classes. The Seats of the Senators of the first

---

Note: The Constitution became effective March 4, 1789. Provisions in italics have been changed by constitutional amendment.

*Changed by Section 2 of the Fourteenth Amendment.

†Changed by Section 1 of the Seventeenth Amendment.

Class shall be vacated at the Expiration of the second Year, of the second Class at the Expiration of the fourth Year, and of the third Class at the Expiration of the sixth Year, so that one-third may be chosen every second Year; *and if Vacancies happen by Resignation, or otherwise, during the Recess of the Legislature of any State, the Executive thereof may make temporary Appointments until the next Meeting of the Legislature, which shall then fill such Vacancies.**

No person shall be a Senator who shall not have attained to the Age of thirty Years, and been nine Years a Citizen of the United States, and who shall not, when elected, be an Inhabitant of that State for which he shall be chosen.

The Vice President of the United States shall be President of the Senate, but shall have no Vote, unless they be equally divided.

The Senate shall chuse their other Officers, and also a President pro tempore, in the absence of the Vice President, or when he shall exercise the Office of President of the United States.

The Senate shall have the sole Power to try all Impeachments. When sitting for that Purpose, they shall be on Oath or Affirmation. When the President of the United States is tried, the Chief Justice shall preside: And no Person shall be convicted without the Concurrence of two thirds of the Members present.

Judgment in Cases of Impeachment shall not extend further than to removal from Office, and disqualification to hold and enjoy any Office of honor, Trust or Profit under the United States: but the Party convicted shall nevertheless be liable and subject to Indictment, Trial, Judgment and Punishment, according to Law.

Section 4

The Times, Places and Manner of holding Elections for Senators and Representatives, shall be prescribed in each State by the Legislature thereof, but the Congress may at any time by Law make or alter such Regulations, except as to the Places of Chusing Senators.

The Congress shall assemble at least once in every Year, and such Meeting *shall be on the first Monday in December, unless they shall by Law appoint a different Day.*†

Section 5

Each House shall be the Judge of the Elections, Returns and Qualifications of its own Members, and a Majority of each shall constitute a Quorum to do Business; but a smaller number may adjourn from day to day, and may be authorized to compel the Attendance of absent Members, in such Manner, and under such Penalties, as each House may provide.

Each House may determine the Rules of its Proceedings, punish its Members for disorderly Behavior, and, with the Concurrence of two thirds, expel a Member.

Each House shall keep a Journal of its Proceedings, and from time to time publish the same, excepting such Parts as may in their Judgment require Secrecy; and the Yeas and Nays of the Members of either House on any question shall, at the Desire of one-fifth of those Present, be entered on the Journal.

---

*Changed by Clause 2 of the Seventeenth Amendment.

†Changed by Section 2 of the Twentieth Amendment.

Neither House, during the Session of Congress, shall, without the Consent of the other, adjourn for more than three days, nor to any other Place than that in which the two Houses shall be sitting.

Section 6

The Senators and Representatives shall receive a Compensation for their Services, to be ascertained by Law, and paid out of the Treasury of the United States. They shall in all Cases, except Treason, Felony and Breach of the Peace, be privileged from Arrest during their Attendance at the Session of their respective Houses, and in going to and returning from the same; and for any Speech or Debate in either House, they shall not be questioned in any other Place.

No Senator or Representative shall, during the Time for which he was elected, be appointed to any civil Office under the Authority of the United States, which shall have been created, or the Emoluments whereof shall have been increased, during such time; and no Person holding any Office under the United States, shall be a Member of either House during his Continuance in Office.

Section 7

All Bills for raising Revenue shall originate in the House of Representatives; but the Senate may propose or concur with Amendments as on other Bills.

Every Bill which shall have passed the House of Representatives and the Senate, shall, before it becomes a Law, be presented to the President of the United States; If he approve he shall sign it, but if not he shall return it, with his Objections to that House in which it shall have originated, who shall enter the Objections at large on their Journal, and proceed to reconsider it. If after such Reconsideration two thirds of that House shall agree to pass the Bill, it shall be sent, together with the Objections, to the other House, by which it shall likewise be reconsidered, and if approved by two thirds of that House, it shall become a Law. But in all such Cases the Votes of both Houses shall be determined by Yeas and Nays, and the Names of the Persons voting for and against the Bill shall be entered on the Journal of each House respectively. If any Bill shall not be returned by the President within ten Days (Sundays excepted) after it shall have been presented to him, the Same shall be a Law, in like Manner as if he had signed it, unless the Congress by their Adjournment prevent its Return, in which Case it shall not be a Law.

Every Order, Resolution, or Vote to which the Concurrence of the Senate and the House of Representatives may be necessary (except on a question of Adjournment) shall be presented to the President of the United States; and before the Same shall take Effect, shall be approved by him, or being disapproved by him, shall be repassed by two thirds of the Senate and House of Representatives, according to the Rules and Limitations prescribed in the Case of a Bill.

Section 8

The Congress shall have Power To lay and collect Taxes, Duties, Imposts and Excises, to pay the Debts and provide for the common Defence and general Welfare of the United States; but all Duties, Imposts and Excises shall be uniform throughout the United States;

To borrow money on the credit of the United States;

To regulate Commerce with foreign Nations, and among the several States, and with the Indian Tribes;

To establish an uniform Rule of Naturalization, and uniform Laws on the subject of Bankruptcies throughout the United States;

To coin Money, regulate the Value thereof, and of foreign Coin, and fix the Standard of Weights and Measures;

To provide for the Punishment of counterfeiting the Securities and current Coin of the United States;

To establish Post Offices and post Roads;

To promote the Progress of Science and useful Arts, by securing for limited Times to Authors and Inventors the exclusive Right to their respective Writings and Discoveries;

To constitute Tribunals inferior to the supreme Court;

To define and punish Piracies and Felonies committed on the high Seas, and Offenses against the Law of Nations;

To declare War, grant Letters of Marque and Reprisal, and make Rules concerning Captures on Land and Water;

To raise and support Armies, but no Appropriation of Money to that Use shall be for a longer Term than two Years;

To provide and maintain a Navy;

To make Rules for the Government and Regulation of the land and naval Forces;

To provide for calling forth the Militia to execute the Laws of the Union, suppress Insurrections and repel Invasions;

To provide for organizing, arming, and disciplining the Militia, and for governing such Part of them as may be employed in the Service of the United States, reserving to the States respectively, the Appointment of the Officers, and the Authority of training the Militia according to the discipline prescribed by Congress;

To exercise exclusive Legislation in all Cases whatsoever, over such District (not exceeding ten Miles square) as may, by Cession of particular States, and the acceptance of Congress, become the Seat of Government of the United States, and to exercise like Authority over all Places purchased by the Consent of the Legislature of the State in which the Same shall be, for the Erection of Forts, Magazines, Arsenals, dock-Yards, and other needful Buildings;—And

To make all Laws which shall be necessary and proper for carrying into Execution the foregoing Powers, and all other Powers vested by this Constitution in the Government of the United States, or in any Department or Officer thereof.

Section 9

The Migration or Importation of such Persons as any of the States now existing shall think proper to admit, shall not be prohibited by the Congress prior to the Year one thousand eight hundred and eight but a tax or duty may be imposed on such Importation, not exceeding ten dollars for each Person.

The privilege of the Writ of Habeas Corpus shall not be suspended, unless when in Cases of Rebellion or Invasion the public Safety may require it.

No Bill of Attainder or ex post facto Law shall be passed.

No capitation, or other direct, Tax shall be laid, unless in Proportion to the Census or Enumeration herein before directed to be taken.*

---

*Changed by the Sixteenth Amendment.

No Tax or Duty shall be laid on Articles exported from any State.

No Preference shall be given by any Regulation of Commerce or Revenue to the Ports of one State over those of another: nor shall Vessels bound to, or from, one State, be obliged to enter, clear, or pay Duties in another.

No Money shall be drawn from the Treasury, but in Consequence of Appropriations made by law; and a regular Statement and Account of the Receipts and Expenditures of all public Money shall be published from time to time.

No Title of Nobility shall be granted by the United States: And no Person holding any Office of Profit or Trust under them, shall, without the Consent of the Congress, accept of any present, Emolument, Office, or Title, of any kind whatever, from any King, Prince, or foreign State.

Section 10

No State shall enter into any Treaty, Alliance, or Confederation; grant Letters of Marque and Reprisal; coin Money; emit Bills of Credit; make any Thing but gold and silver Coin a Tender in Payment of Debts; pass any Bill of Attainder, ex post facto Law, or Law impairing the Obligation of Contracts, or grant any Title of Nobility.

No State shall, without the Consent of the Congress, lay any Imposts or Duties on Imports or Exports, except what may be absolutely necessary for executing its inspection Laws: and the net Produce of all Duties and Imposts, laid by any State on Imports or Exports, shall be for the Use of the Treasury of the United States; and all such Laws shall be subject to the Revision and Control of the Congress.

No State shall, without the Consent of the Congress, lay any duty of Tonnage, keep Troops, or Ships of War in time of Peace, enter into any Agreement or Compact with another State, or with a foreign Power, or engage in War, unless actually invaded, or in such imminent Danger as will not admit of delay.

ARTICLE II

Section 1

The executive Power shall be vested in a President of the United States of America. He shall hold his Office during the Term of four Years, and, together with the Vice President, chosen for the same Term, be elected, as follows:

Each State shall appoint, in such Manner as the Legislature thereof may direct, a Number of Electors, equal to the whole Number of Senators and Representatives to which the State may be entitled in the Congress; but no Senator or Representative, or Person holding an Office of Trust or Profit under the United States, shall be appointed an Elector.

The Electors shall meet in their respective States, and vote by Ballot for two Persons, of whom one at least shall not be an Inhabitant of the same State with themselves. And they shall make a List of all the Persons voted for, and of the Number of Votes for each; which List they shall sign and certify, and transmit sealed to the Seat of the Government of the United States, directed to the President of the Senate. The President of the Senate shall, in the Presence of the Senate and House of Representatives, open all the Certificates, and the Votes shall then be counted. The Person having the greatest Number of Votes shall be the President, if such Number be a Majority of the whole Number of Electors appointed; and if there be more than one who have such Majority, and have an equal Number of Votes, then the House of Representatives shall immediately chuse by Ballot one of them for President; and if no Person have a Ma-

jority, then from the five highest on the List the said House shall in like Manner chuse the President. But in chusing the President, the Votes shall be taken by States, the Representation from each State having one Vote; a quorum for this Purpose shall consist of a Member or Members from two thirds of the States, and a Majority of all the States shall be necessary to a Choice. In every Case, after the Choice of the President, the Person having the greatest Number of Votes of the Electors shall be the Vice President. But if there should remain two or more who have equal Votes, the Senate shall chuse from them by Ballot the Vice President.*

The Congress may determine the Time of chusing the Electors, and the Day on which they shall give their Votes; which Day shall be the same throughout the United States.

No Person except a natural born Citizen, or a Citizen of the United States, at the time of the Adoption of this Constitution, shall be eligible to the Office of President; neither shall any Person be eligible to that Office who shall not have attained to the Age of thirty five Years, and been fourteen years a Resident within the United States.

In Case of the Removal of the President from Office, or of his Death, Resignation, or Inability to discharge the Powers and Duties of the said Office, the same shall devolve on the Vice President, *and the Congress may by Law provide for the Case of Removal, Death, Resignation, or Inability, both of the President and Vice President, declaring what Officer shall then act as President, and such Officer shall act accordingly, until the Disability be removed, or a President shall be elected.*†

The President shall, at stated Times, receive for his Services a Compensation, which shall neither be increased nor diminished during the Period for which he shall have been elected, and he shall not receive within that Period any other Emolument from the United States, or any of them.

Before he enter on the Execution of his Office, he shall take the following Oath or Affirmation:—"I do solemnly swear (or affirm) that I will faithfully execute the Office of President of the United States, and will to the best of my Ability, preserve, protect and defend the Constitution of the United States."

Section 2

The President shall be Commander in Chief of the Army and Navy of the United States, and of the Militia of the several States, when called into the actual Service of the United States; he may require the Opinion, in writing, of the principal Officer in each of the executive Departments, upon any Subject relating to the Duties of their respective Offices, and he shall have Power to Grant Reprieves and pardons for Offences against the United States, except in Cases of Impeachment.

He shall have Power, by and with the Advice and Consent of the Senate, to make Treaties, provided two thirds of the Senators present concur; and he shall nominate, and by and with the Advice and Consent of the Senate, shall appoint Ambassadors, other public Ministers and Consuls, Judges of the supreme Court, and all other Officers of the United States, whose Appointments are not herein otherwise provided for, and which shall be established by Law: but the Congress may by Law vest the Appointment of such inferior Officers, as they think proper, in the President alone, in the Courts of Law, or in the Heads of Departments.

---

*Superseded by the Twelfth Amendment.

†Modified by the Twenty-Fifth Amendment.

The President shall have Power to fill up all Vacancies that may happen during the Recess of the Senate, by granting Commissions which shall expire at the End of their next Session.

Section 3

He shall from time to time give to the Congress Information of the State of the Union, and recommend to their Consideration such Measures as he shall judge necessary and expedient; he may, on extraordinary Occasions, convene both Houses, or either of them, and in Case of Disagreement between them, with Respect to the Time of Adjournment, he may adjourn them to such Time as he shall think proper; he shall receive Ambassadors and other public Ministers; he shall take Care that the Laws be faithfully executed, and shall Commission all the Officers of the United States.

Section 4

The President, Vice President and all civil Officers of the United States, shall be removed from Office on Impeachment for, and Conviction of, Treason, Bribery, or other high Crimes and Misdemeanors.

Article III

Section 1

The judicial Power of the United States, shall be vested in one supreme Court, and in such inferior Courts as the Congress may from time to time ordain and establish. The Judges, both of the supreme and inferior courts, shall hold their Offices during good Behaviour, and shall, at stated Times, receive for their Services a Compensation, which shall not be diminished during their Continuance in Office.

Section 2

The judicial Power shall extend to all Cases, in Law and Equity, arising under this Constitution, the Laws of the United States, and Treaties made, or which shall be made, under their Authority;—to all Cases affecting Ambassadors, other public Ministers and Consuls;—to all Cases of admiralty and maritime Jurisdiction;—to Controversies to which the United States shall be a Party;—to Controversies between two or more States;—*between a State and Citizens of another State,**—between Citizens of different States;—between Citizens of the same State claiming Lands under Grants of different States, and between a State, or the Citizens thereof, and foreign States, Citizens or Subjects.

In all Cases affecting Ambassadors, other public Ministers and Consuls, and those in which a State shall be Party, the supreme Court shall have original Jurisdiction. In all the other Cases before mentioned, the supreme Court shall have appellate Jurisdiction, both as to Law and Fact, with such Exceptions, and under such Regulations as the Congress shall make.

---

*Restricted by the Eleventh Amendment.

The trial of all Crimes, except in Cases of Impeachment, shall be by Jury; and such Trial shall be held in the State where said Crimes shall have been committed; but when not committed within any State, the Trial shall be at such Place or Places as the Congress may by Law have directed.

Section 3

Treason against the United States, shall consist only in levying War against them, or in adhering to their Enemies, giving them Aid and Comfort. No Person shall be convicted of Treason unless on the Testimony of two Witnesses to the same overt Act, or on Confession in open Court.

The Congress shall have Power to declare the Punishment of Treason, but no Attainder of Treason shall work Corruption of Blood, or Forefeiture except during the Life of the Person attainted.

ARTICLE IV

Section 1

Full Faith and Credit shall be given in each State to the public Acts, Records, and judicial Proceedings of every other State. And the Congress may by general Laws prescribe the Manner in which such Acts, Records, and Proceedings shall be proved, and the Effect thereof.

Section 2

The Citizens of each State shall be entitled to all Privileges and Immunities of Citizens in the several States.

A Person charged in any State with Treason, Felony, or other Crime, who shall flee from Justice, and be found in another State, shall on demand of the executive Authority of the State from which he fled, be delivered up, to be removed to the State having Jurisdiction of the Crime.

No Person held to Service or Labour in one State, under the Laws thereof, escaping into another, shall, in Consequence of any Law or Regulation therein, be discharged from such Service or Labour, but shall be delivered up on Claim of the Party to whom such Service or Labour may be due.*

Section 3

New States may be admitted by the Congress into this Union; but no new State shall be formed or erected within the Jurisdiction of any other State; nor any State be formed by the Junction of two or more States, or parts of States, without the Consent of the Legislatures of the States concerned as well as of the Congress.

The Congress shall have Power to dispose of and make all needful Rules and Regulations respecting the Territory or other Property belonging to the United States; and nothing in this Constitution shall be so construed as to Prejudice any Claims of the United States, or of any particular State.

---

*Superseded by the Thirteenth Amendment.

Section 4

The United States shall guarantee to every State in this Union a Republican Form of Government, and shall protect each of them against Invasion; and on Application of the Legislature, or of the Executive (when the Legislature cannot be convened) against domestic Violence.

ARTICLE V

The Congress, whenever two thirds of both Houses shall deem it necessary, shall propose Amendments to this Constitution, or, on the Application of the Legislatures of two thirds of the several States, shall call a Convention for proposing Amendments, which, in either Case, shall be valid to all Intents and Purposes, as Part of this Constitution, when ratified by the Legislatures of three fourths of the several States, or by Conventions in three fourths thereof, as the one or the other Mode of Ratification may be proposed by the Congress; Provided that no Amendment which may be made prior to the Year One thousand eight hundred and eight shall in any Manner affect the first and fourth Clauses in the Ninth Section of the first Article; and that no State, without its Consent, shall be deprived of its equal Suffrage in the Senate.

ARTICLE VI

All Debts contracted and Engagements entered into, before the Adoption of this Constitution, shall be as valid against the United States under this Constitution, as under the Confederation.

This Constitution, and the Laws of the United States which shall be made in Pursuance thereof; and all Treaties made, or which shall be made, under the Authority of the United States, shall be the supreme Law of the Land; and the Judges in every State shall be bound thereby, any Thing in the Constitution or Laws of any State to the Contrary notwithstanding.

The Senators and Representatives before mentioned, and the Members of the several State Legislatures, and all executive and judicial Officers, both of the United States and of the several States, shall be bound by Oath or Affirmation, to support this Constitution; but no religious Test shall ever be required as a Qualification to any Office or public Trust under the United States.

ARTICLE VII

The Ratification of the Conventions of nine States shall be sufficient for the Establishment of this Constitution between the States so ratifying the Same.

Done in Convention by the Unanimous Consent of the States present the Seventeenth Day of September in the Year of our Lord one thousand seven hundred and Eighty seven and of the Independence of the United States of America the Twelfth. In Witness whereof We have hereunto subscribed our Names.

Go. Washington

President and deputy from Virginia

New Hampshire
John Langdon
Nicholas Gilman

Massachusetts
Nathaniel Gorham
Rufus King

Connecticut
Wm. Saml. Johnson
Roger Sherman

New York
Alexander Hamilton

New Jersey
Wil. Livingston
David Brearley
Wm. Paterson
Jona. Dayton

Pennsylvania
B. Franklin
Thomas Mifflin
Robt. Morris
Geo. Clymer
Thos. FitzSimons
Jared Ingersoll
James Wilson
Gouv. Morris

Delaware
Geo. Read
Gunning Bedford jun
John Dickenson
Richard Bassett
Jaco. Broom

Maryland
James McHenry
Dan. of St. Thos. Jenifer
Danl. Carroll

Virginia
John Blair
James Madison, Jr.

North Carolina
Wm. Blount
Richd. Dobbs Spaight
Hu Williamson

South Carolina
J. Rutledge
Charles Cotesworth
    Pickney
Pierce Butler

Georgia
William Few
Abr. Baldwin

AMENDMENTS TO THE CONSTITUTION

Amendment I [1791]*

Congress shall make no law respecting an establishment of religion, or prohibiting the free exercise thereof; or abridging the freedom of speech, or of the press; or the right of the people peaceably to assembley, and to petition the Government for a redress of grievances.

Amendment II [1791]

A well regulated Militia, being necessary to the security of a free State, the right of the people to keep and bear Arms shall not be infringed.

Amendment III [1791]

No Soldier shall, in time of peace, be quartered in any house, without the consent of the Owner, nor in time of war, but in a manner to be prescribed by law.

Amendment IV [1791]

The right of the people to be secure in their persons, houses, papers, and effects, against unreasonable searches and seizures, shall not be violated, and no Warrants shall issue, but upon probable cause, supported by Oath or affirmation, and particularly describing the place to be searched, and the persons or things to be seized.

Amendment V [1791]

No person shall be held to answer for a capital or otherwise infamous crime, unless on a presentment or indictment of a Grand Jury, except in cases arising in the land or naval forces, or in the Militia, when in actual service in time of War or public danger; nor shall any person be subject for the same offence to be twice put in jeopardy of life or limb; nor shall be compelled in any criminal case to be a witness against himself, nor be deprived of life, liberty, or property, without due process of law; nor shall private property be taken for public use, without just compensation.

Amendment VI [1791]

In all criminal prosecutions, the accused shall enjoy the right to a speedy and public trial, by an impartial jury of the State and district wherein the crime shall have been committed, which district shall have been previously ascertained by law, and to be informed of the nature and cause of the accusation; to be confronted with the witnesses against him; to have compulsory process for obtaining witnesses in his favor, and to have the Assistance of Counsel for his defence.

---

*The dates in brackets indicate when the amendments were ratified.

AMENDMENT VII [1791]

In suits at common law, where the value in controversy shall exceed twenty dollars, the right of trial by jury shall be preserved, and no fact tried by a jury, shall be otherwise reexamined in any Court of the United States, than according to the Rules of the common law.

AMENDMENT VIII [1791]

Excessive bail shall not be required, nor excessive fines imposed, nor cruel and unusual punishments inflicted.

AMENDMENT IX [1791]

The enumeration in the Constitution, of certain rights, shall not be construed to deny or disparage others retained by the people.

AMENDMENT X [1791]

The powers not delegated to the United States by the Constitution, nor prohibited by it to the States, are reserved to the States respectively, or to the people.

AMENDMENT XI [1798]

The Judicial power of the United States shall not be construed to extend to any suit in law or equity, commenced or prosecuted against one of the United States by Citizens of another State, or by Citizens or subjects of any foreign state.

AMENDMENT XII [1804]

The Electors shall meet in their respective States and vote by ballot for President and Vice-President, one of whom, at least, shall not be an inhabitant of the same State with themselves; they shall name in their ballots the person voted for as President, and in distinct ballots the person voted for as Vice-President, and they shall make distinct lists of all persons voted for as President, and of all persons voted for as Vice-President, and of the number of votes for each, which lists they shall sign and certify, and transmit sealed to the seat of the government of the United States, directed to the President of the Senate;—the President of the Senate shall, in the presence of the Senate and House of Representatives, open all the certificates and the votes shall then be counted;—The person having the greatest number of votes for President, shall be the President, if such number be a majority of the whole number of Electors appointed; and if no person have such majority, then from the persons having the highest numbers not exceeding three on the list of those voted for as President, the House of Representatives shall choose immediately, by ballot, the President. But in choosing the President, the votes shall be taken by States, the representation from each State having one vote; a quorum for this purpose shall consist of a member or members from two-thirds of the States, and a majority of all the States shall be necessary to a choice. And if the House of Representatives shall not choose a President whenever the right of choice shall devolve upon them, before *the fourth day of March* next following, then the Vice-President shall act as President, as in the case of the death or other constitutional disability of the President.*—The person having the greatest number of votes as Vice-President, shall be the Vice-President, if such number be a majority of the whole number of Electors appointed, and if no person have a majority, then from the two highest numbers on the list, the Senate shall choose the Vice-President; a quorum for the purpose shall consist of two-thirds of the whole number of Senators, and a majority of the whole number shall be necessary to a choice. But no person constitutionally ineligible to the office of President shall be eligible to that of Vice-President of the United States.

AMENDMENT XIII [1865]

Section 1
Neither slavery nor involuntary servitude, except as a punishment for crime whereof the party shall have been duly convicted, shall exist within the United States, or any place subject to their jurisdiction.

Section 2
Congress shall have power to enforce this article by appropriate legislation.

AMENDMENT XIV [1868]

Section 1
All persons born or naturalized in the United States, and subject to the jurisdiction thereof, are citizens of the United States and of the State wherein they reside. No State shall make or enforce any law which shall abridge the privileges or immunities of citizens of the United States; nor shall any State deprive any person of life, liberty, or property, without due process of law; nor deny to any person within its jurisdiction the equal protection of the laws.

Section 2
Representatives shall be apportioned among the several States according to their respective numbers, counting the whole number of persons in each State, excluding Indians not taxed. But when the right to vote at any election for the choice of electors for President and Vice-President of the United States, Representatives in Congress, the Executive and Judicial officers of a State, or the members of the Legislature thereof, is denied to any of the male inhabitants of such State, being twenty-one years of age, and citizens of the United States, or in any way abridged, except for participation in rebellion, or other crime, the basis of representation therein shall be reduced in the proportion which the number of such male citizens shall bear to the whole number of male citizens twenty-one years of age in such State.

Section 3
No person shall be a Senator or Representative in Congress, or elector of President and Vice-President, or hold any office, civil or military, under the United States, or under any State,

---

*Superseded by Section 3 of the Twentieth Amendment.

who, having previously taken an oath, as a member of Congress, or as an officer of the United States, or as a member of any State legislature, or as an executive or judicial officer of any State, to support the Constitution of the United States, shall have engaged in insurrection or rebellion against the same, or given aid or comfort to the enemies thereof. Congress may by a vote of two-thirds of each house, remove such disability.

Section 4
The validity of the public debt of the United States, authorized by law, including debts incurred for payment of pensions and bounties for services in suppressing insurrection or rebellion, shall not be questioned. But neither the United States nor any State shall assume or pay any debt or obligation incurred in aid of insurrection or rebellion against the United States, or any claim for the loss or emancipation of any slave; but all such debts, obligations and claims shall be held illegal and void.

Section 5
The Congress shall have power to enforce, by appropriate legislation, the provisions of this article.

Amendment XV [1870]

Section 1
The right of citizens of the United States to vote shall not be denied or abridged by the United States or by any State on account of race, color, or previous condition of servitude—

Section 2
The Congress shall have power to enforce this article by appropriate legislation.

Amendment XVI [1913]

The Congress shall have power to lay and collect taxes on incomes, from whatever source derived, without apportionment among the several States, and without regard to any census or enumeration.

Amendment XVII [1913]

The Senate of the United States shall be composed of two Senators from each State, elected by the people thereof, for six years; and each Senator shall have one vote. The electors in each State shall have the qualifications requisite for electors of the most numerous branch of the State legislatures.

When vacancies happen in the representation of any State in the Senate, the executive authority of such State shall issue writs of election to fill such vacancies: *Provided,* That the legislature of any State may empower the executive thereof to make temporary appointments until the people fill the vacancies by election as the legislature may direct.

This amendment shall not be so construed as to affect the election or term of any Senator chosen before it becomes valid as part of the Constitution.

AMENDMENT XVIII [1919]

Section 1
After one year from the ratification of this article the manufacture, sale, or transportation of intoxicating liquors within, the importation thereof into, or the exportation thereof from the United States and all territory subject to the jurisdiction hereof for beverage purposes hereby prohibited.

Section 2
The Congress and the several States shall have concurrent power to enforce this article by appropriate legislation.

Section 3
This article shall be inoperative unless it shall have been ratified as an amendment to the Constitution by the legislatures of the several States, as provided by the Constitution, within seven years from the date of submission hereof to the States by the Congress.*

AMENDMENT XIX [1920]

The right of citizens of the United States to vote shall not be denied or abridged by the United States or by any State on account of sex.

Congress shall have power to enforce this article by appropriate legislation.

AMENDMENT XX [1933]

Section 1
The terms of the President and Vice-President shall end at noon on the 20th day of January, and the terms of Senators and Representatives at noon on the 3d day of January, of the years in which such terms would have ended if this article had not been ratified; and the terms of their successors shall then begin.

Section 2
The Congress shall assemble at least once in every year, and such meeting shall begin at noon on the 3d day of January, unless they shall by law appoint a different day.

Section 3
If, at the time fixed for the beginning of the term of the President, the President elect shall have died, the Vice-President elect shall become President. If a President shall not have been chosen before the time fixed for the beginning of his term, or if the President elect shall have failed to qualify, then the Vice-President elect shall act as President until a President shall have qualified; and the Congress may by law provide for the case wherein neither a President elect nor a Vice-President elect shall have qualified, declaring who shall then act

---

*Repealed by Section 1 of the Twenty-First Amendment.

as President, or the manner in which one who is to act shall be selected, and such person shall act accordingly until a President or Vice-President shall have qualified.

Section 4
The Congress may by law provide for the case of the death of any of the persons from whom the House of Representatives may choose a President whenever the right of choice shall have devolved upon them, and for the case of the death of any of the persons from whom the Senate may choose a Vice-President whenever the right of choice shall have devolved upon them.

Section 5
Sections 1 and 2 shall take effect on the 15th day of October following the ratification of this article.

Section 6
This article shall be inoperative unless it shall have been ratified as an amendment to the Constitution by the legislatures of three-fourths of the several States within seven years from the date of its submission.

AMENDMENT XXI [1933]

Section 1
The eighteenth article of amendment to the Constitution of the United States is hereby repealed.

Section 2
The transportation or importation into any State, Territory, or possession of the United States for delivery or use therein of intoxicating liquors, in violation of the laws thereof, is hereby prohibited.

Section 3
This article shall be inoperative unless it shall have been ratified as an amendment to the Constitution by conventions in the several States, as provided in the Constitution, within seven years from the date of submission hereof to the States by the Congress.

AMENDMENT XXII [1951]

Section 1
No person shall be elected to the office of President more than twice, and no person who has held the office of President, or acted as President, for more than two years of a term to which some other person was elected President shall be elected to the office of the President more than once. But this Article shall not apply to any person holding the office of President when this Article was proposed by the Congress, and shall not prevent any person who may be holding the office of President, or acting as President, during the term within which this Article becomes operative from holding the office of the President or acting as President during the remainder of such term.

Section 2

This article shall be inoperative unless it shall have been ratified as an amendment to the Constitution by the legislatures of three-fourths of the several States within seven years from the date of its submission to the States by the Congress.

AMENDMENT XXIII [1961]

Section 1

The District constituting the seat of Government of the United States shall appoint in such manner as the Congress may direct:

A number of electors of President and Vice-President equal to the whole number of Senators and Representatives in Congress to which the District would be entitled if it were a State, but in no event more than the least populous State; they shall be in addition to those appointed by the States, but they shall be considered, for the purposes of the election of President and Vice-President, to be electors appointed by a State; and they shall meet in the District and perform such duties as provided by the twelfth article of amendment.

Section 2

The Congress shall have power to enforce this article by appropriate legislation.

AMENDMENT XXIV [1964]

Section 1

The right of citizens of the United States to vote in any primary or other election for President or Vice-President, for electors for President or Vice-President, or for Senator or Representative in Congress, shall not be denied or abridged by the United States or any State by reason of failure to pay any poll tax or other tax.

Section 2

The Congress shall have power to enforce this article by appropriate legislation.

AMENDMENT XXV [1967]

Section 1

In case of the removal of the President from office or of his death or resignation, the Vice-President shall become President.

Section 2

Whenever there is a vacancy in the office of the Vice-President, the President shall nominate a Vice-President who shall take office upon confirmation by a majority vote of both houses of Congress.

Section 3

Whenever the President transmits to the President pro tempore of the Senate and the Speaker of the House of Representatives his written declaration that he is unable to discharge the powers and duties of his office, and until he transmits to them a written declaration to the contrary, such powers and duties shall be discharged by the Vice-President as Acting President.

Section 4
Whenever the Vice-President and a majority of either the principal officers of the executive departments or of such other body as Congress may by law provide, transmit to the President pro tempore of the Senate and the Speaker of the House of Representatives their written declaration that the President is unable to discharge the powers and duties of his office, the Vice-President shall immediately assume the powers and duties of the office as Acting President.

Thereafter, when the President transmits to the President pro tempore of the Senate and the Speaker of the House of Representatives his written declaration that no inability exists, he shall resume the powers and duties of his office unless the Vice-President and a majority of either the principal officers of the executive department or of such other body as Congress may by law provide, transmit within four days to the President pro tempore of the Senate and the Speaker of the House of Representatives their written declaration that the President is unable to discharge the powers and duties of his office. Thereupon Congress shall decide the issue, assembling within forty-eight hours for that purpose if not in session. If the Congress, within twenty-one days after receipt of the latter written declaration, or, if Congress is not in session, within twenty-one days after Congress is required to assemble, determines by two-thirds vote of both Houses that the President is unable to discharge the powers and duties of his office, the Vice-President shall continue to discharge the same as Acting President; otherwise, the President shall resume the powers and duties of his office.

Amendment XXVI [1971]

Section 1
The right of citizens of the United States, who are eighteen years of age or older, to vote shall not be denied or abridged by the United States or by any state on account of age.

Section 2
The Congress shall have power to enforce this article by appropriate legislation.

Amendment XXVII [1992]

No law varying the compensation for services of the Senators and Representatives, shall take effect, until an election of Representatives shall have intervened.

APPENDIX

Territorial Expansion			
Territory	**Date Acquired**	**Square Miles**	**How Acquired**
Original states and territories	1783	888,685	Treaty of Paris
Louisiana Purchase	1803	827,192	Purchased from France
Florida	1819	72,003	Adams-Onís Treaty
Texas	1845	390,143	Annexation of independent country
Oregon	1846	285,580	Oregon Boundary Treaty
Mexican cession	1848	529,017	Treaty of Guadalupe Hidalgo
Gadsden Purchase	1853	29,640	Purchased from Mexico
Midway Islands	1867	2	Annexation of uninhabited islands
Alaska	1867	589,757	Purchased from Russia
Hawaii	1898	6,450	Annexation of independent country
Wake Island	1898	3	Annexation of uninhabited island
Puerto Rico	1899	3,435	Treaty of Paris
Guam	1899	212	Treaty of Paris
The Philippines	1899–1946	115,600	Treaty of Paris; granted independence
American Samoa	1900	76	Treaty with Germany and Great Britain
Panama Canal Zone	1904–1978	553	Hay–Bunau-Varilla Treaty
U.S. Virgin Islands	1917	133	Purchased from Denmark
Trust Territory of the Pacific Islands*	1947	717	United Nations Trusteeship

*A number of these islands have recently been granted independence: Federated States of Micronesia, 1990; Marshall Islands, 1991; Palau, 1994.

The Labor Force (thousands of workers)

Year	Agricul- ture	Mining	Manufac- turing	Construc- tion	Trade	Other	Total
1810	1,950	11	75	—	—	294	2,330
1840	3,570	32	500	290	350	918	5,660
1850	4,520	102	1,200	410	530	1,488	8,250
1860	5,880	176	1,530	520	890	2,114	11,110
1870	6,790	180	2,470	780	1,310	1,400	12,930
1880	8,920	280	3,290	900	1,930	2,070	17,390
1890	9,960	440	4,390	1,510	2,960	4,060	23,320
1900	11,680	637	5,895	1,665	3,970	5,223	29,070
1910	11,770	1,068	8,332	1,949	5,320	9,041	37,480
1920	10,790	1,180	11,190	1,233	5,845	11,372	41,610
1930	10,560	1,009	9,884	1,988	8,122	17,267	48,830
1940	9,575	925	11,309	1,876	9,328	23,277	56,290
1950	7,870	901	15,648	3,029	12,152	25,870	65,470
1960	5,970	709	17,145	3,640	14,051	32,545	74,060
1970	3,463	516	20,746	4,818	15,008	34,127	78,678
1980	3,364	979	21,942	6,215	20,191	46,612	99,303
1990	3,186	730	21,184	7,696	24,269	60,849	118,793
1998	3,378	620	20,733	8,518	27,203	71,011	131,463

SOURCE: *Historical Statistics of the United States, Colonial Times to 1970* (1975), 139; *Statistical Abstract of the United States, 2000,* Table 672.

Changing Labor Patterns

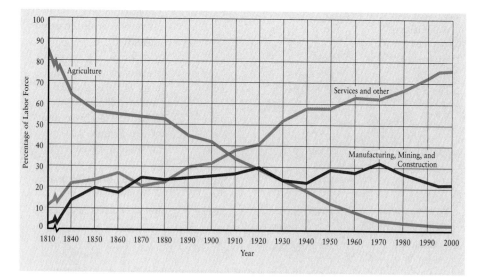

SOURCE: *Historical Statistics of the United States, Colonial Times to 1970* (1975), 139; *Statistical Abstract of the United States, 2000,* Table 672.

American Population

Year	Population	Percent Increase	Year	Population	Percent Increase
1610	350	—	1810	7,239,881	36.4
1620	2,300	557.1	1820	9,638,453	33.1
1630	4,600	100.0	1830	12,866,020	33.5
1640	26,600	478.3	1840	17,069,453	32.7
1650	50,400	90.8	1850	23,191,876	35.9
1660	75,100	49.0	1860	31,443,321	35.6
1670	111,900	49.0	1870	39,818,449	26.6
1680	151,500	35.4	1880	50,155,783	26.0
1690	210,400	38.9	1890	62,947,714	25.5
1700	250,900	19.2	1900	75,994,575	20.7
1710	331,700	32.2	1910	91,972,266	21.0
1720	466,200	40.5	1920	105,710,620	14.9
1730	629,400	35.0	1930	122,775,046	16.1
1740	905,600	43.9	1940	131,669,275	7.2
1750	1,170,800	29.3	1950	150,697,361	14.5
1760	1,593,600	36.1	1960	179,323,175	19.0
1770	2,148,100	34.8	1970	203,235,298	13.3
1780	2,780,400	29.4	1980	226,545,805	11.5
1790	3,929,214	41.3	1990	248,709,873	9.8
1800	5,308,483	35.1	2000	281,421,906	13.2

Note: These figures largely ignore the Native American population. Census takers never made any effort to count the Native American population that lived outside their political jurisdictions and compiled only casual and incomplete enumerations of those living within their jurisdictions until 1890. In that year the federal government attempted a full count of the Indian population: the Census found 125,719 Indians in 1890, compared with only 12,543 in 1870 and 33,985 in 1880.

SOURCE: *Historical Statistics of the United States, Colonial Times to 1970* (1975); *Statistical Abstract of the United States,* 1999; Bureau of the Census, 2001 <http://blue.census.gov/dmd/www/resapport/states/unitedstates.pdf>.

Presidential Elections

Year	Candidates	Parties	Percentage of Popular Vote	Electoral Vote	Percentage of Voter Participation
1789	**George Washington**	No party designations	*	69	
	John Adams†			34	
	Other candidates			35	
1792	**George Washington**	No party designations		132	
	John Adams			77	
	George Clinton			50	
	Other candidates			5	
1796	**John Adams**	Federalist		71	
	Thomas Jefferson	Democratic-Republican		68	
	Thomas Pinckney	Federalist		59	
	Aaron Burr	Democratic-Republican		30	
	Other candidates			48	
1800	**Thomas Jefferson**	Democratic-Republican		73	
	Aaron Burr	Democratic-Republican		73	
	John Adams	Federalist		65	
	Charles C. Pinckney	Federalist		64	
	John Jay	Federalist		1	
1804	**Thomas Jefferson**	Democratic-Republican		162	
	Charles C. Pinckney	Federalist		14	
1808	**James Madison**	Democratic-Republican		122	
	Charles C. Pinckney	Federalist		47	
	George Clinton	Democratic-Republican		6	
1812	**James Madison**	Democratic-Republican		128	
	De Witt Clinton	Federalist		89	
1816	**James Monroe**	Democratic-Republican		183	
	Rufus King	Federalist		34	
1820	**James Monroe**	Democratic-Republican		231	
	John Quincy Adams	Independent Republican		1	
1824	**John Quincy Adams**	Democratic-Republican	30.5	84	26.9
	Andrew Jackson	Democratic-Republican	43.1	99	
	Henry Clay	Democratic-Republican	13.2	37	
	William H. Crawford	Democratic-Republican	13.1	41	
1828	**Andrew Jackson**	Democratic	56.0	178	57.6
	John Quincy Adams	National Republican	44.0	83	
1832	**Andrew Jackson**	Democratic	54.5	219	55.4
	Henry Clay	National Republican	37.5	49	
	William Wirt	Anti-Masonic	8.0	7	
	John Floyd	Democratic	‡	11	
1836	**Martin Van Buren**	Democratic	50.9	170	57.8
	William H. Harrison	Whig		73	
	Hugh L. White	Whig		26	
	Daniel Webster	Whig	49.1	14	
	W. P. Mangum	Whig		11	
1840	**William H. Harrison**	Whig	53.1	234	80.2
	Martin Van Buren	Democratic	46.9	60	

*Prior to 1824, most presidential electors were chosen by state legislators rather than by popular vote.
†Before the Twelfth Amendment was passed in 1804, the electoral college voted for two presidential candidates; the runner-up became vice president.
‡Percentages below 2.5 have been omitted. Hence the percentage of popular vote might not total 100 percent.

Year	Candidates	Parties	Percentage of Popular Vote	Electoral Vote	Percentage of Voter Participation
1844	**James K. Polk**	Democratic	49.6	170	78.9
	Henry Clay	Whig	48.1	105	
	James G. Birney	Liberty	2.3		
1848	**Zachary Taylor**	Whig	47.4	163	72.7
	Lewis Cass	Democratic	42.5	127	
	Martin Van Buren	Free Soil	10.1		
1852	**Franklin Pierce**	Democratic	50.9	254	69.6
	Winfield Scott	Whig	44.1	42	
	John P. Hale	Free Soil	5.0		
1856	**James Buchanan**	Democratic	45.3	174	78.9
	John C. Frémont	Republican	33.1	114	
	Millard Fillmore	American	21.6	8	
1860	**Abraham Lincoln**	Republican	39.8	180	81.2
	Stephen A. Douglas	Democratic	29.5	12	
	John C. Breckinridge	Democratic	18.1	72	
	John Bell	Constitutional Union	12.6	39	
1864	**Abraham Lincoln**	Republican	55.0	212	73.8
	George B. McClellan	Democratic	45.0	21	
1868	**Ulysses S. Grant**	Republican	52.7	214	78.1
	Horatio Seymour	Democratic	47.3	80	
1872	**Ulysses S. Grant**	Republican	55.6	286	71.3
	Horace Greeley	Democratic	43.9		
1876	**Rutherford B. Hayes**	Republican	48.0	185	81.8
	Samuel J. Tilden	Democratic	51.0	184	
1880	**James A. Garfield**	Republican	48.5	214	79.4
	Winfield S. Hancock	Democratic	48.1	155	
	James B. Weaver	Greenback-Labor	3.4		
1884	**Grover Cleveland**	Democratic	48.5	219	77.5
	James G. Blaine	Republican	48.2	182	
1888	**Benjamin Harrison**	Republican	47.9	233	79.3
	Grover Cleveland	Democratic	48.6	168	
1892	**Grover Cleveland**	Democratic	46.1	277	74.7
	Benjamin Harrison	Republican	43.0	145	
	James B. Weaver	People's	8.5	22	
1896	**William McKinley**	Republican	51.1	271	79.3
	William J. Bryan	Democratic	47.7	176	
1900	**William McKinley**	Republican	51.7	292	73.2
	William J. Bryan	Democratic; Populist	45.5	155	
1904	**Theodore Roosevelt**	Republican	57.4	336	65.2
	Alton B. Parker	Democratic	37.6	140	
	Eugene V. Debs	Socialist	3.0		
1908	**William H. Taft**	Republican	51.6	321	65.4
	William J. Bryan	Democratic	43.1	162	
	Eugene V. Debs	Socialist	2.8		
1912	**Woodrow Wilson**	Democratic	41.9	435	58.8
	Theodore Roosevelt	Progressive	27.4	88	
	William H. Taft	Republican	23.2	8	
1916	**Woodrow Wilson**	Democratic	49.4	277	61.6
	Charles E. Hughes	Republican	46.2	254	
	A.L. Benson	Socialist	3.2		

Year	Candidates	Parties	Percentage of Popular Vote	Electoral Vote	Percentage of Voter Participation
1920	**Warren G. Harding**	Republican	60.4	404	49.2
	James M. Cox	Democratic	34.2	127	
	Eugene V. Debs	Socialist	3.4		
1924	**Calvin Coolidge**	Republican	54.0	382	48.9
	John W. Davis	Democratic	28.8	136	
	Robert M. La Follette	Progressive	16.6	13	
1928	**Herbert C. Hoover**	Republican	58.2	444	56.9
	Alfred E. Smith	Democratic	40.9	87	
1932	**Franklin D. Roosevelt**	Democratic	57.4	472	56.9
	Herbert C. Hoover	Republican	39.7	59	
1936	**Franklin D. Roosevelt**	Democratic	60.8	523	61.0
	Alfred M. Landon	Republican	36.5	8	
1940	**Franklin D. Roosevelt**	Democratic	54.8	449	62.5
	Wendell L. Willkie	Republican	44.8	82	
1944	**Franklin D. Roosevelt**	Democratic	53.5	432	55.9
	Thomas E. Dewey	Republican	46.0	99	
1948	**Harry S Truman**	Democratic	49.6	303	53.0
	Thomas E. Dewey	Republican	45.1	189	
1952	**Dwight D. Eisenhower**	Republican	55.1	442	63.3
	Adlai E. Stevenson	Democratic	44.4	89	
1956	**Dwight D. Eisenhower**	Republican	57.6	457	60.6
	Adlai E. Stevenson	Democratic	42.1	73	
1960	**John F. Kennedy**	Democratic	49.7	303	64.0
	Richard M. Nixon	Republican	49.5	219	
1964	**Lyndon B. Johnson**	Democratic	61.1	486	61.7
	Barry M. Goldwater	Republican	38.5	52	
1968	**Richard M. Nixon**	Republican	43.4	301	60.6
	Hubert H. Humphrey	Democratic	42.7	191	
	George C. Wallace	American Independent	13.5	46	
1972	**Richard M. Nixon**	Republican	60.7	520	55.5
	George S. McGovern	Democratic	37.5	17	
1976	**Jimmy Carter**	Democratic	50.1	297	54.3
	Gerald R. Ford	Republican	48.0	240	
1980	**Ronald W. Reagan**	Republican	50.7	489	53.0
	Jimmy Carter	Democratic	41.0	49	
	John B. Anderson	Independent	6.6	0	
1984	**Ronald W. Reagan**	Republican	58.4	525	52.9
	Walter F. Mondale	Democratic	41.6	13	
1988	**George H. W. Bush**	Republican	53.4	426	50.3
	Michael Dukakis	Democratic	45.6	111*	
1992	**William J. Clinton**	Democratic	43.7	370	55.1
	George H. W. Bush	Republican	38.0	168	
	H. Ross Perot	Independent	19.0	0	
1996	**William J. Clinton**	Democratic	49	379	49.0
	Robert J. Dole	Republican	41	159	
	H. Ross Perot	Reform	8	0	
2000	**George W. Bush**	Republican	47.9	271	N.A.
	Albert A. Gore	Democratic	48.4	266†	
	Ralph Nader	Green Party	2.7		

*One Dukakis elector cast a vote for Lloyd Bentsen.
†One Gore elector abstained.

CREDITS

CHAPTER 26

"Japanese Relocation." Excerpt from *Nisei Daughter* by Monica Sone. Copyright © 1953 by Monica Sone. Copyright © renewed 1981 by Monica Sone. Reprinted with the permission of Little, Brown and Company, Inc.

"An Army Nurse in Bataan." Excerpt from *American Women in a World at War: Contemporary Accounts from World War II* by Judy Barrett Litoff and David C. Smith, editors. Copyright © 1984 Garland Publishing, Inc. This excerpt was taken from *I Served on Bataan* by Juanita Redmond (J.P. Lippincott, 1943). Reprinted with permission of the publisher.

CHAPTER 27

"Resisting the Tactics of McCarthyism." Excerpt from *False Witness* by Melvyn Rader. Copyright ©1969 by Melvyn Rader. Reprinted with the permission of the University of Washington Press.

"Memories of a Cold War Childhood." Excerpt from *Born on the Fourth of July* by Ron Kovic. Copyright © 1976 by Ron Kovic. Reprinted with the permission of Pocket Books, a division of Simon & Schuster.

CHAPTER 28

"A Woman Encounters the Feminist Mystique." Excerpt from *The Fifties: A Women's Oral History* by Brett Harvey. Copyright © 1993 by Brett Harvey, editor. Copyright © 1993 by Brett Harvey. Reprinted with the permission of the author.

"A Badge of Honor." Excerpt from *Voices of Freedom: An Oral History of the Civil Rights Movement from the 1950s through the 1980s* by Henry Hampton and Steve Fayer. Copyright © 1990 by Blackside, Inc. Used by permission of Bantam Books, a division of Random House, Inc.

CHAPTER 29

"A Vietnam War Vet Remembers." Excerpt from *Winter Soldiers: An Oral History of the Vietnam Veterans against the War* by Richard Stacewicz. Copyright © 1997 by Richard Stacewicz. Reprinted with permission of Twayne Publishers, a division of Simon & Schuster.

CHAPTER 30

"Watergate Diary." Excerpt from *Washington Journal: The Events of 1973–1974* by Elizabeth Drew. Copyright © 1974 by Elizabeth Drew. Reprinted with the permission of Random House, Inc.

CHAPTER 31

"The Undocumented Worker." Excerpt from *Mexican Voices, American Dreams: An Oral History of Mexican Immigration in the United States* by Marilyn P. Davis. Copyright © 1990 by Marilyn P. Davis. Reprinted with permission of Henry Holt and Company, LLC.

INDEX

Note: Italic letters following page numbers refer to illustrations (*i*), maps (*m*), tables (*t*), and figures (*f*).

Abbott, Grace, 726
Abbott, Jacob, 556
Abernethy, Ralph, 801
abortion
 anti-abortion activities, 920
 informed consent/waiting period, 908
 New Right on, 900
 restriction by states (1989), 907–908
 Roe v. Wade, 876, 889, 908
abstract expressionism, 819
Abyssian Baptist Church, 686
accidents, and workers, 586, 586*i*
Acheson, Dean, 785, 842
acid rock, 853
"Acres of Diamonds" (Conwell), 554
Adams, Brooks, 608
Adams, Charles Francis, 525, 618
Adams, Samuel Hopkins, 593
Addams, Jane, 576, 579, 618
adolescent pregnancy, 891
advertising
 beginning of, 493, 494*i*
 of consumer goods (1920s), 672–673
 of consumer goods (1950s), 815
 slogans, 815
 television, 815
 to youth, 817
affirmative action, 893–894, 919
 and women, 888–889
Afghanistan, Soviet invasion, 898, 909
Africa/Africans, back-to-Africa movements, 534, 686
African American discrimination
 armed forces, 644–645*i*, 753, 792
 Black Codes, 431
 black resistance to. *See* civil rights movement
 discrimination outlawed, Civil Rights Act of 1964, 834
 employment discrimination, 755–756, 759
 Jim Crow, 532–534
 and Ku Klux Klan, 448–450
 lynching, 532, 657, 707–708*i*, 792, 799
 post–World War I, 657
 restrictive covenants, 793, 812
 Scottsboro case, 707
 separate but equal. *See* segregation
 Southern racism, forms of, 529–532
 urban African Americans, 560–562
 voting rights limitation, 531–532, 834
African Americans
 affirmative action, 893–894, 919
 back-to-Africa movements, 534, 686
 churches of. *See* black church
 city dwellers, 560–562, 823
 expatriates, 685
 in federal office, 736
 future population projections, 947
 and Great Depression, 700, 706–708
 Great Migration from South, 649
 and Great Society programs, 837
 Harlem Renaissance, 686
 –immigrant clashes, 917–918*i*
 in labor force, 498, 649, 755–756
 leadership, Reconstruction era, 442–443*i*
 in machine politics, 563
 music, 676, 817–819
 and New Deal, 736
 and Progressive Era, 587–589
 in Spanish-American War, 614, 616
 in sports, 678
 and suburban growth, 812
 voting rights, 440
 women, 500, 665
 World War I labor force, 649
Afrika Korps, 764
Afro-American, use of term, 855
Age of Innocence, The (Wharton), 685
Agency for International Development, 826
Agent Orange, 845, 852
Agnew, Spiro
 resignation of, 879–880
 as vice-president, 866–867
Agricultural Adjustment Act (AAA), 721–722, 728
Agricultural Marketing Act of 1929, 711
agriculture
 Chinese laborers, 481
 cooperatives, 536–537
 credit to farmers, 536–537, 599
 dry-farming methods, 470
 Dust Bowl migrations, 708–710
 economic problems (1920–1921), 667
 and Great Depression, 692–693, 706, 708–711, 714
 Great Plains, 469–470
 Hawaii, 603–604
 New Deal measures, 721–722, 729*t*, 736

agriculture (*cont.*)
  post–World War II, 822
  South after Reconstruction, 494–495*m*
  strikes, 710, 858
  wheat, 483, 667
Aguinaldo, Emilio, 616–618, 617*i*
AIDS, 920–921
  decrease in U.S., 952
  worldwide impact, 952
Aid to Families with Dependent Children, 836, 904, 927
air pollution, reduction in U.S., 950
Alabama, 602
Alabama
  Birmingham march, 830, 832*i*
  iron ore mining, 496
  Montgomery bus boycott, 800–801
  voting rights march, 834
Alaska Native Land Claims Act of 1971, 891
Albright, Madeleine K., 924
alcohol use
  immigrant population, 651
  Prohibition, 651–652
  during Prohibition, 683
  temperance activities, 524, 526–527
aldermen, 563
Aldrich, Nelson W., 594
Aleuts, 891
Alger, Horatio, 520, 520*i*, 703
Aliquippa, Pennsylvania, 546
Allen, Gracie, 704
Allen, Thomas, 442
Alliance for Progress, 826
Allies, World War I, 642–643
Alsberg, Henry, 740
Amalgamated Association of Iron and Steel Workers, 511
America First Committee, 749
American Automobile Association (AAA), 674
American Civil Liberties Union (ACLU), 683
American Commonwealth, The (Bryce), 516
American Communist Party, 707, 715–716
American Expeditionary Force (AEF), 641–643
American Express card, 814–815
American Federation of Labor (AFL), 510, 585–586, 649, 733
  merger with CIO, 811
American Indian Movement (AIM), 858–859
American Legion, 643
American Medical Association
  on health insurance issue, 791
  and Medicare/Medicaid costs, 837
American Mercury, 685
American Plan, 668
American Protective League, 653
American Railway Union (ARU), 512, 513
American Union against Militarism, 639
American Woman's Home, The (Beecher), 555
American Woman Suffrage Association, 441
Americanization policy, World War I, 652–653
amicus curiae, meaning of, 792
Amos 'n' Andy, 676, 704
amusement parks, 566–567*i*

anarchism, meaning of, 510
Ancona, Victor, 748
Anderson, Sherwood, 685
Angelou, Maya, 706
Annan, Kofi, 929
Anschutz, Thomas P., 504
Anthony, Susan B., 440–441
antiballistic missile systems (ABMs), 869
Anti-Comintern Pact, 748
Anti-French War of Resistance, 841
anti-imperialist cause, 618
Anti-Saloon League, 651
antitrust
  Clayton Act, 598
  good/bad trusts concept, 595
  Roosevelt trust-busting, 591–593, 595–596
  and rule of reason, 592, 595
  Sherman Act, 591–593
antiwar movement, Vietnam War, 850–854, 865–866
  avoiding draft, 851
  decline of, 868
  Democratic National Convention protest, 865–866
  Free Speech movement, 851
  Kent State massacre, 867
  Nixon obsession with, 877
  radical groups, 868
  student demonstrations, 851–852, 864, 867
  Students for a Democratic Society (SDS), 850–851, 868
  women in, 862
Apache Indians, 471
apartheid, 926, 958
Appalachian Mountains, migrants from, 822
Appalachian Trail, 739
Apple Computer, 922
Arapaho Indians, 462, 471
architecture. *See also* housing
  Chicago school, 547
  skyscrapers, 610
Arikara Indians, 462
Aristide, Jean-Bertrand, 926
Arkansas, school desegregation, 800–801, 800*i*
armed forces
  African American discrimination, 644–645*i*, 753, 792
  counterinsurgency, 825
  GI Bill, 757
  Green Berets, 825
  homosexuals in, 753, 925
  Japanese Americans in, 762
  Native Americans in, 753
  Navy, 607
  Vietnam War, 845–848
  women in, 753, 912*i*
  World War I, 643–644
  World War II, 753, 762
arms buildup. *See also* nuclear weapons
  Eisenhower era, 802, 805
  India/Pakistan, 956–957
  Reagan era, 904–905
  Soviet Union, 783, 802

arms control
  Comprehensive Test Ban Treaty, rejection by
    Congress, 957
  Eisenhower era, 805
  SALT I, 869
  SALT II, 896, 898
  Soviet/USSR summits, 910
  test ban of 1963, 828
Armstrong, Louis, 676
art
  abstract expressionism, 819
  museums/collections, 569
  New Deal projects, 739–741
Arthur, Chester A. (1830–1886)
  expansion of navy, 602–603
  as president, 517, 602–603
artisans
  immigrant, 498–499
  independent workers in industry, 502–504
arts. See cultural development
Asian Americans. See also specific groups by
    ethnicity
  ethnic groups of, 915
  future population projections, 947–948
  immigration in 1990s, 915–916m
assassinations
  Evers, Medgar, 831–832
  Garfield, James A., 517
  Kennedy, John F., 833
  Kennedy, Robert F., 864–865
  King, Martin Luther, Jr., 856–857i, 864
  Malcolm X, 854
  McKinley, William, 589, 620
Assemblies of God, 950
Astaire, Fred, 702, 703i
Astor, Mrs. William, 552
Aswan Dam, 803–804
Atlanta Compromise, 535
Atlantic Charter, 750, 764, 770
atomic bomb
  casualties of, 771
  Manhattan Project, 771
  World War II, 769m, 771
Atomic Energy Commission, 804i, 805
Auschwitz, concentration camp, 765
Australia, World War II, 767
Austria, 655
Austria-Hungary, World War I, 636
automobile
  consumer demand for, 673–674
  and energy crisis, 881–883
  environmental/safety issues, 887
  foreign market for, 668
  fuel-efficient cars, 882
  and highway construction, 813–814
  installment plans for, 672
  mass production in 1920s, 673–674
  Model T, 674
  sports utility vehicles, 952
  and suburban growth, 674, 679,
    813–814
  and vacations, 674, 815
aviation, Lindbergh's flight, 678

B1-bomber, 904
Babcock, Orville, 452
baby boom, 816
Backlash: The Undeclared War on American
    Women (Faludi), 920
Back to Bataan, 758
Baez, Joan, 853
Baker, Ella, 830, 862
Baker, Josephine, 685
Baker, Russell, 706
Baker v. Carr, 876
Bakke v. University of California, 894
balkanization, meaning of, 919
Baltimore & Ohio Railroad, 487
bank holiday, 720
Banking Act of 1863, 539
Banking Act of 1935, 723
banks
  collapse and Great Depression,
    692, 720
  Federal Reserve System, 598
  and global economy, 670
  international, 811, 954
  New Deal measures, 721, 723, 729t
  in 1920s, 667–668
Baptists, future view, 949
barbed wire, 638
Barnum, P.T., 569
barrios, 650
Barry, Leonora M., 508
Baruch, Bernard, 646–647
Baruch Plan, 781
baseball, 568, 676, 677
Basel Convention, 951
Batista, Fulgencio, 827
battleships, 607
Bay of Pigs invasion, 827–828, 827m
Beatles, 853
beat poets, 819–820
bebop, 819
Beecher, Catherine, 555
Beecher, Henry Ward, 564, 570
Begin, Menachem, 898
Belgians, 498
Belgium
  World War I, 636, 638
  World War II, 749, 765
Bell, Alexander Graham, 548
Bellow, Saul, 740
Bellamy, Edward, 575
Belleau Wood, Battle of, 642
Bennett, James Gordon, 568
Bennett, William, 919
Benny, Jack, 704, 815
Bentsen, Lloyd, 907
Bergen, Edgar, 704
Berger, Victor, 585, 653
Berle, Adolph Jr., 719
Berlin airlift, 782
Berlin Conference of 1884, 606
Berlin Wall
  creation of, 780, 828
  end of, 903

Berners-Lee, Tim, 939*i*
Bernstein, Carl, 878
Bessemer, Henry, 489
Bessemer converter, 489
Bethune, Mary McLeod, 736
Betty Crocker Hour, The, 704
Beveridge, Alfred J., 610
Big Band swing, 704
Big Foot, Chief, 473
big-stick policy, Roosevelt, 621
Billy the Kid, 740
biological warfare, 845, 852, 957
Bird, Caroline, 695
Birmingham, Alabama
    Baptist church bombing, 833
    civil rights protest, 830, 832*i*
birth control
    impact on gender expectations, 861
    legal freedoms, 699, 889
    Sanger as advocate for, 581, 699–700
Birth of a Nation, 587, 680
birth rate
    baby boom, 816
    decline (1970s), 891
    and Great Depression, 698–699
Black, Hugo, 729
black church
    in cities, 561–562
    Baptists, 444
    and civil rights movement, 801
    free blacks, 267, 444–445
    ministers as leaders, 444–445
    Reconstruction era influence, 444–445
Black Codes, 431
Blackfeet Indians, 462
Black Hills, 472, 476
blacklist, House Committee on Un-American
        Activities victims, 792–793
Blackmun, Harry, 876
Black Muslims, 854
Black Panthers, 855
black power, 854
Black Sox scandal, 678
Black Star Line, 686
Black Thursday (October 24, 1929), 692
Black Tuesday (October 29, 1929), 692
Blaine, James G., 519, 525, 603
Blair, Emily Newell, 666
Bland-Allison Act of 1878, 540
blitzkrieg, 749
"Blowin' in the Wind," 853
blue laws, 524
Blue Ridge Parkway, 739
Board of Governors, Federal Reserve System, 723
Bohemians, 559
Boland Amendment, 910
Bolsheviks, 642, 654–655, 658
bonds, railroad corporations, 490
Bonnin, Gertrude Simmons (Zitkala-Sa), 474
Bonsack, James A., 496
Bonus Army, 715
boodle, machine politics, 562–563

Book-of-the-Month Club, 676
Booth, John Wilkes, 429
bootleggers, 683
Borah, William E., 656
born-again Christians, 895
Bosnia
    Clinton actions, 926
    ethnic cleansing, 926
    and World War I, 636
Boston
    school busing issue, 892–893
    wealthy suburbs, 551
Boston Museum of Fine Arts, 569
Bourke-White, Margaret, 741
Bow, Clara, 675
Bowery, New York City, 568
Boxer Rebellion, 623
boxing, 678
Boyce, Ed, 514
boycotts. *See also* strikes
    Montgomery bus boycott, 800–801
    Olympic Games in Moscow, 898
    Pullman boycott, 511–513, 573
    secondary labor boycott, 512
    of segregated streetcars, 533–534
bracero, 821
Braden, Anne, 862
Bradley, Joseph P., 453
Brady Handgun Violence Prevention Act, 925
Brain Trust, FDR administration, 719
Brandeis, Louis D., 578–579
    as Wilson advisor, 598
breadlines, Great Depression, 696*i*
Brest-Litovsk, Treaty of, 642
Bretton Woods system, 884
Breyer, Stephen G., 932
Brezhnev, Leonid, 898
Bristow, Benjamin, 452
broker state, meaning of, 731
Brooklyn, New York, 564, 915
Brooklyn Dodgers, 791
Brooks, Phillip, 564
Brophy, John, 503
Brotherhood of Sleeping Car Porters, 756
Brown Berets, 858
Brown, Ron, 924–925
Brown v. Board of Education of Topeka, 799–800
Bruce, Blanche K., 442
Bruce, William, 680
Brush, Charles F., 548
Bryan, Charles W., 664
Bryan, William Jennings
    and election of 1896, 541–542*m*
    and election of 1900, 618
    and election of 1908, 594
    and Scopes monkey trial, 683–684*i*
    as secretary of state, 627–628
Bryant, Anita, 891
Bryce, James, 516, 604
Buchanan, Patrick, 919, 931
Buchenwald, concentration camp, 765
Buck, Pearl, 706

Buddhists, Vietnam protest, 844
buffalo, mass killing of, 462, 464–465i
Buford, 658
Bulgaria, World War I, 636
Bulge, Battle of the, 765
Bulkley, William Lewis, 588
Bull Moose Party, 596
Bundy, McGeorge, 828
Bunker, Ellsworth, 867
Bureau of Corporations, 591, 593
Bureau of Indian Affairs, 822, 859
Burger, Warren, 876
Burgess, John W., 587
Burkitt, Frank, 530–531
Burma, World War II, 767
Burns, George, 704
bus boycott, Montgomery, Alabama, 800–801
Bush, George (1924–)
    economic policy, 908–909
    election of 1988, 907
    election of 1992, 923–924
    Persian Gulf War, 910–913
    as president, 907–910, 923
    Supreme Court appointments, 908
    as vice-president, 900
Bush, George W. (1946–)
    election of 2000, 930–932
    election 2000 controversy, 931–934i,
        945–947
Bushnell, Horace, 570
busing, for school desegregation, 892–893
butterfly ballots, 931
Byrnes, James F., 730

cable TV, 922
Cahan, Abraham, 563
Cahill, Holger, 740
California
    agriculture in, 709–710
    Chinese in, 480–482
    cultural traditions, 482–484
    gold mining, 475–478, 476m
    Japanese in, 625
    migrants from Dust Bowl, 709–710
    migrants from Mexico, 478–479, 710–711
    migrants during World War II, 759
    natural resources, 484–485, 484i
    southern area development, 483–484
California condor, 950
Californios, 479
Calley, William L., 868
Cambodia
    Nixon bombing of, 867–868
    post-war effects, 871
Camp David accords, 898
Canby, Henry Seidel, 555
cancer research, 953
Cannon, "Uncle Joe," 595
Canwell committee, 795
capital goods, meaning of, 488
Capone, Al, 683
Capra, Frank, 704, 705i

Caribbean Islands
    Cuba, 610–615
    Puerto Rico, 613–614
    Roosevelt Corollary, 623
    U.S. involvement (1895–1924), 623–624m
Carmichael, Stokely, 854
Carnegie, Andrew, 489, 511, 520, 569, 618
carpetbaggers, 441–442
Carranza, Venustiano, 626
cars. *See* automobiles
Carson, Rachel, 885
Carter, Jimmy (James E.) (1924–)
    arms control, 898
    Camp David accords, 898
    deregulation, 897
    election of 1976, 897
    environmental programs, 897
    human rights activities, 898
    Iran hostage crisis, 899–900
    Latin America diplomacy, 898
    outsider approach of, 897
    as president, 897–899
Casablanca, 758
Cascade Mountains, 475
Castro, Fidel, 822, 827
categorical assistance, Social Security
    Act, 726
Catholic schools, federal funding issue, 524
Catholics. *See also* Roman Catholic Church
    anti-Catholic sentiment, 687–688
    challenges for American Catholics, 564
    as Democrats, 523
    future view, 949
    Irish, 564
Catt, Carrie Chapman, 580, 650
cattle ranching, 465–467, 479
"Celebrated Jumping Frog of Calaveras County,
    The" (Twain), 483
Central America
    El Salvador, 910
    Panama Canal, 603, 621i, 622
Central Intelligence Agency (CIA)
    cold war era, 802
    and Iran-Contra affair, 910
Central Pacific Railroad, 464, 481
Central Park, 550, 552
Cervera, Pascual, 613–614
Chamberlain, Neville, 748
Chambers, Whittaker, 793
Chaplin, Charlie, 672, 674–675
Chase, Salmon P., 439
Château-Thierry, Battle of, 642
Chautauqua movement, 569
Chávez, César, 710, 858
Checkers speech, Nixon, 797
Cheever, John, 740
chemical warfare, 845, 852, 957
Cheney, Richard, 931
Cherokee Indians, 471
Cheyenne Indians, 462, 471–472
Chiang Kai-Shek. *See* Jiang Jieshi (Chiang Kai-
    Shek)

Chicago, Burlington and Quincy Railroad, 491
Chicago, Illinois
 Appalachian migration to, 822
 African Americans in, 561
 Democratic National Convention riots (1968), 865–866
 as economic center, 470–471, 550–551
 fire of 1871, 549
 flower children, 853
 machine politics, 563
 mass transit, 547–548i
 meat center, 492–493
 race riots, 657
 skyscrapers, 547
 suburbs, 553
 wealthy area, 551
Chicago Art Institute, 569
Chicago River, 551
Chicago school, architecture, 547
Chicago World's Fair of 1893, 550
Chicano. See also Mexican Americans
 civil rights activities, 857–858
Chickasaw Indians, 471
child care, tax deductions, 889
child labor
 and family poverty, 502–503
 legal regulation, 502
children
 health care, federal program, 665
 latchkey, 759
 middle class, 556–557
China. See also People's Republic of China
 Boxer Rebellion, 623
 communism established, 784–788
 Japanese invasion, 747, 751
 and Korean War, 785–788, 786m
 trade agreement of 2000, 955
 World War II, 751, 764
Chinese
 anti-Chinese movement, 481–482, 680, 821
 immigration to U.S., 480–482
 as laborers, 481
Chinese Exclusion Act, 482, 821
Chinese Revolution of 1911, 625
Chinese Revolution of 1949, 841, 869
Chipewyan Indians, 858
Chisholm, Shirley, 888
chlorofluorocarbons, 886, 951
Choctaw Indians, 471
Chou En-lai. See Zhou Enlai (Chou En-lai)
Christian Broadcasting Network, 895
Christopher, Warren, 926
Churchill, Winston, and World War II, 750, 764, 770
Church of Jesus Christ of Latter-Day Saints. See Mormons
church and state, school prayer ban, 876
cigarettes, manufacturing in 1880s, 496
Cincinnati, Ohio
 Appalachian migrants, 822
 wealthy suburbs, 551

Cincinnati Red Stockings, 568
Cisneros, Henry, 925
cities
 African Americans in, 560–562, 823
 cultural activities, 569–571
 downtown areas, 546
 electric lights, 548
 ethnic communities, 559, 915
 gay life, 568
 immigrant settlement in, 559–560, 821–823
 industrial activities, 546
 Latino groups in, 821–822, 915
 leisure activities in, 566–569
 machine politics, 562–563
 mass transit, 547
 middle class in, 553
 Native American relocation to, 822
 newspapers of, 568–569
 parks, 550
 poor in, 549–550, 823
 population size (1920s), 679m
 population size (1950–1980), 813m
 race riots, 855–856m
 renewal projects, 823
 sex districts, 568, 651
 skyscrapers, 547
 tenement housing, 549–550
 wealthy in, 551–553
City Beautiful movement, 550
Civilian Conservation Corps (CCC), 721, 738, 757
civil rights
 African Americans. See civil rights movement
 Chicano movement, 857–858
 discrimination outlawed, 834
 group identity, 860
 Native American movement, 858–859
 Nineteenth Amendment, 650–651
 and politics of resentment, 895
 Thirteenth Amendment, 430
Civil Rights Act of 1866, 431, 435
Civil Rights Act of 1964, 834
 Title VII, 834, 861
civil rights movement
 African American self-help, 535
 Atlanta Compromise, 535
 Birmingham march, 830
 Black Panthers, 855
 black power, 854
 Brown decision, 799–800
 Congress of Racial Equality (CORE), 756, 830
 Double V campaign, 755
 Eisenhower administration, 799–801
 Evers assassination, 831–832
 freedom riders, 830
 Freedom Summer, 834
 Johnson administration, 834–835, 854–860
 Kennedy administration, 830–833
 King's assassination, 856–857i, 864
 King's leadership, 801, 830–834
 and McCarthy era, 793
 Malcolm X, 854
 March on Washington, 833

Montgomery bus boycott, 800–801
murder of civil rights workers, 834
National Association for the Advancement of
    Colored People (NAACP), 588–589, 756
National Urban League, 588–589
Niagara Movement, 588
post–World War II, 791–792
riots, 657, 707, 759–760, 855–856m
school desegregation, 800–801, 800i
Selma voting rights march, 834
Southern Christian Leadership Conference,
    801, 830
Student Non-Violent Coordinating Committee
    (SNCC), 830
white resistance tactics, 799, 830, 832–834, 832i
women in, 588, 665, 800
World War II era, 755–756
Civil Service Commission, creation of, 517
Civil Works Administration (CWA), 722–723
Clayton Antitrust Act of 1914, 598, 599
Clean Air Act of 1970, 887
Clemenceau, Georges, 655
Clemens, Samuel (Mark Twain), 483
Cleveland, Grover (1837–1908)
    on Cuban independence issue, 610
    election of 1884, 519, 525
    election of 1888 , 536, 946
    election of 1892, 536
    foreign policy, 607–608
    on Hawaii annexation, 604
    as president, 517
    and railroad workers' boycott, 512
    and silver issue, 540–541
Cleveland, Ohio, African Americans in, 561
Cliff-Dwellers, The (Fuller), 570–571
Cline, Dave, 847
Clinton, Hillary Rodham
    on electoral college, 947
    health care reform, 925–926
Clinton, William J. (1946–)
    anti-crime legislation, 925
    appointees of, 924–925
    Bosnia, 926
    budget balanced, 927
    election of 1992, 923–924i
    election of 1996, 928
    family-related legislation, 925
    foreign policy, 926–929
    health care reform, 925–926, 943
    history and assessment of, 941–942
    impeachment, 929–930
    independent council investigations, 929
    international trade, 925
    -Lewinsky matter, 929–930, 933, 941i
    as president, 924–930, 942–944
    and Republican Congress, 927–928, 930, 942
    and Social Security system, 927, 942–943
    unresolved issues of administration, 934
    welfare reform, 927–928, 943–944
closed shop, meaning of, 508
CNN (Cable News Network), 922
coal, steam-power, 489

coal mining, 489, 496
    and Great Depression, 667
Coeur d'Alene, Idaho, 476, 477
Cohan, George M., 641
Cohen, Lizabeth, 672
Colbert, Claudette, 758
cold war. See also Vietnam War
    Berlin airlift, 782
    Chinese communism, 784–788
    and Cuba, 827–828
    end of, 910
    Korean War, 785–788
    Marshall Plan, 782
    and Middle East, 803–805
    North Atlantic Treaty Organization (NATO), 783
    and Peace Corps, 826
    post–cold war foreign events, 910–913
    post–cold war foreign policy, 926–929
    post–World War II conflict, 778–781
    Truman Doctrine, 781–782
Cole, terrorist attack on, 956i
colleges/universities
    affirmative action, 893–894, 919
    African American studies programs, 855
    Chicano studies programs, 858
    Vietnam War protests, 851–852, 867
    and women, 888
Collier, John, 738
Collier's, 576, 593
Collier's Weekly, 676
Colorado, gold mining, 476, 477
Colorado plateau, 475
Colored Farmers' Alliance, 530
Columbia Broadcasting Service (CBS), 676
Columbia Plateau, 475
Columbia University, student protests, 852i, 864
Comanche Indians, 462
coming out, homosexuals, 891
Comintern (Third International), 658
Commission for Relief of Belgium, 713
Committee to Defend America, 749
Committee on Public Information (CPI), 652–653
Committee to Re-Elect the President (CREEP),
    878
common law, on monopolies, 591–592
Commonwealth of Independent States,
    910–911m
communism. See also cold war
    Berlin Wall, 780, 828, 903
    Central America, 910
    China, 784–788
    containment, 781–788
    Cuba, 827–828
    domino effect, 842
    McCarthyism, 792–796
    Red Scare, 658–659
    Russian Revolution, 642
    and U.S. arms development, 802
Communist Labor Party, 658
Community Action Program, 836, 837
compact disc (CD) players, 922

Comprehensive Test Ban Treaty, rejection by Congress, 957
computers, personal computer (PC), 922
concentration camps, 747–748, 765
Coney Island, 566
conglomerates, 810
Congress
    Mexican Americans in, 857–858
    women in, 641, 888
Congress of Industrial Organizations (CIO), 732–734, 757
    merger with AFL, 811
Congress of Racial Equality (CORE), beginning of, 756, 830
Conkling, Roscoe, 519–520, 525
Connor, Eugene "Bull," 830, 832i
conscription. See military draft
conservatism, New Right, 895–896
consumerism
    and advertising, 672–673, 815
    automobiles, 673–674
    and baby boom, 816
    consumer goods, meaning of, 488
    consumer protection legislation, 593, 887
    and Great Depression, 697–698
    household appliances, 672
    installment sales, 672
    Nader's activities, 887
    products of 1920s, 672
    rationing during World War II, 758–759
    and television ads, 815
Consumer Products Safety Commission, 876, 887
contagion, economic theory, 954
containment policy, 781–788
    formulation of, 781
    Marshall Plan, 782
    NATO, 783
    NSC-68 report, 784
    Truman Doctrine, 781–782
contraception. See birth control
Contract with America, 927, 942
Contras, 905–906, 910
Conwell, Russell H., 520, 554
Coolidge, Calvin (1872–1933)
    election of 1924, 663–664
    as president, 664–665, 670, 687
    as vice-president, 658, 663–664
cooperatives, farm, and populism, 536–537
Cooperstown, New York, 568
Copland, Aaron, 740
copper, mining of, 477, 479
Coral Sea, Battle of, 767, 769m
Corcoran Gallery of Art, 569
corporation, management of. See management
corporations
    conglomerates, 810
    diversification, 810
    downsizing, 914
    modern structure of, 667
    monopolies, 591–592
    oligopolies, 667
    railroad development, 490
    stock and bond sales, 490
    technological renovation in 1990s, 914
    vertical integration, 493
Corrigan, Michael A. (Archbishop), 564
corruption
    Black Sox scandal, 678
    government oil reserve leasing scandals, 664
    Iran-Contra affair, 905–906
    machine politics, 524–525, 562–563
    Progressive Era exposés, 576
    Wall Street, 723
    Watergate, 877–880
cotton, post–World War II, 822
Coughlin, Charles, 724
Council for Mutual Economic Assistance (COMECON), 783
Council of National Defense, 749
counterculture of 1960s, 852–853
    clothing of, 852
    drug use, 853
    music of, 853
counterinsurgency, 825
Country Club Plaza, 674
Court of International Justice, 670
Cousins, Norman, 700
cowboys, 465–466i
Cowell, Henry P., 494i
Cowperwood, Frank, 552
Cox, Archibald, 878
Cox, James M., 663
Coxey's Army, 540
Crane, Stephen, 469
Crawford, Alan, 895
Crazy Horse, 472
credit. See also debt
    consumer (1950s), 814–815
    consumer (1990s), 915
    credit cards, 814–815
    to farmers, 536–537, 599
    Great Depression, 697
    installment sales, 672
    women's access to, 889
Crédit Mobilier, 491
credit-ticket system, 481
Creek Indians, 471
Creel, George, 652
Crisis, The, 686
Croats, 926
cross-of-gold speech, 541
Crow Dog, Mary, 859
Crow Indians, 462
Cuba
    Bay of Pigs invasion, 827–828, 827m
    Cuban missile crisis, 828
    Elián González incident, 939–940, 958
    independence issue (1897), 610–615
    John Paul II visit, 957
    Platt amendment, 623
    and Spanish-American War, 610–615
    U.S. naval base, 746
Cubans, immigrants in U.S., 822

Cullen, Countee, 686
cultural development
  and cities, 569–571, 679–680
  counterculture of 1960s, 852–853
  Great Depression, 702–706, 741
  Great Society programs, 835
  Harlem Renaissance, 686
  high-culture activities, 569–571
  leisure activities, 566–569
  magazines, 555, 576, 676
  movies, 674–676, 702–704, 740–741, 758
  museums, 569
  music, 569, 675–676, 704, 740, 817–819
  New Deal era, 739–741
  newspapers, 568–569
  nonfiction works. See literature
  post–World War II, 815
  radio, 672, 676–677, 704
  television, 815
  theater, 566–567
  youth culture of 1950s, 817–820
Cummins, Albert B., 583
currency. See also money supply
  dollar devalued (1972), 884
  In God We Trust, 816
  sound money interests, 539
  state-issued, 539–540
Custer, George A., 472
Czechoslovakia
  creation of, 655
  Soviet takeover, 782–783
  World War II, 748–749
Czolgosz, Leon F., 589

Dachau, concentration camp, 765
Dai, Bao, 842
Dakota Territory, Native American relocation to, 471–474
Daley, Richard J., 865
Dallas, Texas, Kennedy assassination, 833
Damrosch, Leopold, 569
Dana, Charles A., 568
Danbury Hatters case, 585
Darrow, Clarence, and Scopes monkey trial, 683–684i
Darwin, Charles, 521, 608
Daughters of Bilitis, 818
Davis, David, 453
Davis, John W., 664
Davis, Maxine, 702
Dawes, Charles G., 670
Dawes Act of 1887, 473
Dawes Severalty Act of 1887, 738
Day, William R., 615
D-Day, 765, 767i
Dean, John, 877, 878
death, future view of disease, 952–954
de facto segregation, 854
de jure segregation, 854
De Leon, Daniel, 513
D. E. Loewe & Company, 585
debates, Kennedy-Nixon, 825

Debs, Eugene V., 512–513, 575, 653
  on World War I, 639
debt
  European and World War I, 655, 669–670
  federal deficit under Reagan, 907
dedicated machines, 505
defense industries, World War II, 754, 759
defense policy. See also arms control; nuclear weapons
  Eisenhower, 801–802
  Kennedy, 825
  Reagan, 904–905
deficit spending, during Great Depression, 730
deflation
  during Great Depression, 697
  meaning of, 488f
defoliants, Vietnam War, 845
deindustrialization
  economic effects, 884–885, 914–915
  and labor force, 884–885, 913
deinstitutionalization, of mentally ill, 904
Democracy in America (de Tocqueville), 516
Democratic national convention, riots of 1968, 865–866
Democratic Party
  African Americans, disenfranchising, 530–531
  and New Deal, 736, 742
  and the 1960s, 866–869
  post–Civil War status, 436
  Progressive Era, 594, 596–597
  and religious affiliation, 523
  in South, 529–530
  on states/national government, 518
Dempsey, Jack, 678
Denmark, World War II, 749
Denver, Colorado, 552
Department of Commerce, under Hoover, 663
Department of Education, 897
Department of Energy, 897
Department of Health, Education and Welfare (HEW), 798
depression
  of 1873, 451–452
  of 1893, 492, 536, 540–541
deregulation, Carter administration, 897
desegregation, public accommodations, 799–801, 834
Desert Fox, 929
Desire under the Elms (O'Neill), 685
détente, meaning of, 868
Detroit, Michigan, race riots of 1967, 855
Dewey, George, 613
Dewey, John, 653
Dewey, Thomas E., 757
DeWitt, John, 761
Dewson, Molly, 734
Diaz, Porfirio, 626
Dick Tracy, 704
Dickinson, G. Lowes, 569
Dies, Martin, 792
Diners Club, 814

discrimination. *See* African American
    discrimination; homosexuals; racism;
    women
disease. *See also* death
    AIDS, 952
    future view, 952–954
    malaria, 622
Disneyland, 815
Displaced Persons Act, 821
Distant Early Warning, 802
diversification, corporations, 810
Divine, Father, 707
Divine Peace Mission, 707
divorce
    effects for women, 861, 891
    during Great Depression, 698
    in 1950s, 816
Dixiecrats, 790
documentary films, 740–741
Dodge City, Missouri, 465
Dole, Robert J., 897–928
dollar diplomacy, 625
domestic servants, women, 500
Dominican Republic, 603, 670
domino effect, meaning of, 842
domino theory, 781–782
Dorr, Retha Childe, 526
Dorsey, Tommy, 704
Dos Passos, John, 685, 740
Doubleday, Abner, 568
Double V campaign, 755
Douglas, William O., 729
Dow Chemical Company, 852
Downing, Andrew Jackson, 553
downsizing, 914
downtown urban areas, 546
Dreiser, Theodore, 545, 552, 685
Drew, Elizabeth, 881
drought, Dust Bowl, 708–710
drugs, counterculture of 1960s, 853
dry-farming methods, 470
Du Bois, W.E.B., 535, 588, 686
Dual Alliance, 626
Duck Soup, 704
due process clause, purpose of, 522
Dukakis, Michael, 907
Duke, James B., 496
Dulles, John Foster, 802–803
Durr, Virginia Foster, 862
Dust Bowl, drought/migration of 1930s, 708–710
Dylan, Bob, 853

Eagleton, Thomas F., 877
Earth Day, 886, 950
Earth Summit, 951
eastern Europe
    Bosnia conflict, 926
    and end of communism, 910–911*m*
    Kosovo crisis, 929, 957
    NATO membership, 955
    post–World War I, 655
    post–World War II, 778–779, 782–783

    Soviet domination, 782–783
    World War II, 749, 764–765
East Germany
    Berlin Wall, 828, 903
    creation of, 780, 828
    as German Democratic Republic, 783
Eckford, Elizabeth, 800*i*
economic development
    business-government cooperation, 663–664, 667
    contagion concept, 954
    corporate capitalism, 667–668
    future view, 954–955
    international companies. *See* global economy
    mass marketing, 493
    new economic laws, 954–955
    post–World War I, 665–668
    post–World War II, 810–811
    and railroads, 492
    South, after Reconstruction, 494–495*m*
    and vertical integration, 493
    World War I era, 645–650
    World War II era, 752–755, 758–759
Economic Opportunity Act of 1964, 836
Economic Recovery Tax Act of 1981, 904
economy
    deflation, 488*f*
    and deindustrialization, 884–885
    federal deficit of 1980s, 907
    Keynesian, 730, 791
    monetary policy, 905
    Reaganomics, 904–905, 913
    recession, 666
    revenue sharing, 875
    stagflation, 884
    supply-side economics, 904–905
Ederle, Gertrude, 678
Edgar Thomson Works, 489
Edison, Thomas, 548
education
    and baby boom, 816
    and GI Bill, 811
    during Great Depression, 701
    Great Society programs, 835
    industrial education, 535
    middle class, 556–557
    public, 444
    second language learning issue, 524
    sex education, 651
    of women, 557, 888–889
Educational Amendments Act of 1972,
    Title IX, 888
Egypt
    Camp David peace accords, 898
    –Soviet Union relations, 803–804
    Yom Kippur War, 882
Ehrlichman, John, 878–879
Eighteenth Amendment
    Prohibition begins, 651–652
    repeal of, 683–684
Eisenhower, Dwight D. (1890–1969)
    arms control, 805
    CIA activities, 802

civil rights movement, 799–801
election of 1952, 796–797
and Middle East, 803–805
military-industrial complex, 805–806
New Look policy, 801–802
nuclear weapons development, 802, 805
and Vietnam, 842
World War II, 764–765, 796
Eisenhower Doctrine, 804–805
elderly. *See* older Americans
elections. *See* presidential elections
Electoral College
and presidential election of 1888, 536, 946
and presidential election of 2000, 931–932*m*,
946
electricity
incandescent light bulb, 548
lighting of cities, 548
rural electrification, New Deal, 739
electric trolley car, 547
Elementary and Secondary Education Act of
1965, 835
elevated transit (el), 547–548*i*
Eliot, T. S., 685
Elk Hills scandal, 664
Elkins Act, 593
Ellington, Duke, 676, 704
Ellison, Ralph, 740
Ellsberg, Daniel, 840, 877
El Paso, Texas, 478
El Salvador, 910, 915
embargo
Japan, World War II, 751
and Neutrality Act of 1935, 746–747
oil (1970s), 882
Emergency Banking Act, 721
employment discrimination
African Americans, 755–756, 759
legal end of, 834
women, 500, 735, 754
Endangered Animals Act of 1964, 887
Endangered Species Act of 1973, 887
energy crisis, 881–883
energy use
consumption (1900–1990), 883*f*
future view, 952
increased consumption (1990s), 952
Engel v. Vitale, 876
entente, meaning of, 627
entertainment business
McCarthyism, 792
movie studios, 674–675
entitlement programs. *See* welfare state
environmental impact statements (EIS), 886
environmental movement, 886–887
activists of, 886
Basel Convention, 951
Earth Summit, 951
environmental racism, 952
legislation, 886–887
Montreal protocol, 951
negative situations related to, 952

nuclear safety concerns, 886
progress of, 949
environmental programs
Carter era, 897
Great Society, 835–836
New Deal, 729*t*, 738–739
Nixon era, 876
Roosevelt (Teddy) era, 590
Environmental Protection Agency (EPA), 876
Equal Credit Opportunity Act of 1974, 889
Equal Employment Opportunity Commission
(EEOC), 861
Equal Rights Amendment (ERA), 889–890
Equal Rights Association, 441
Erdman Mediation Act of 1898, 573
Erie Railroad, 491
Eskimos, 891
espionage
Rosenberg case, 794
secret flights over USSR, 805
World War I targets, 653
Espionage Act of 1917, 653
ESPN (Entertainment Sports Network), 922
Estonia, 655
ethnic cleansing
Bosnia, 926
Kosovo, 929
ethnic diversity. *See also* immigration
alcohol and culture, 651
Americanization policy, World War I, 652–653
civil rights politics, 857–860
ethnic communities, 559, 915
future projections, 947–949
multiculturalism, 919, 947–948*i*
Europe
American expatriates to, 684–685
post–World War I, 654–656
socialism, 513
urban development, 550
World War I, 636–656
World War II, 747–751, 763–766*m*
evangelicalism
born-again Christians, 895
Moral Majority, 895
New Right, 895–896, 900–901
revival of 1970s, 895–896
Evans, Daniel J., 619
Evans, Walker, 741
Evers, Medgar, assassination of, 831–832
evolution
Darwin's theory, 521, 608
monkey trial, 683–684*i*
excess-profits tax, 646, 693
Exodusters, 469
expansionism, global
anti-imperialism of 1898, 618
Caribbean, 623
diplomacy, 602–604
economic factors, 604–607
global policy, 607–608
Hawaii, 603–604
ideology of, 608–609

expansionism, global (*cont.*)
  Manifest Destiny, 609
  Panama Canal, 621*i*, 622
expansionism, within America. *See* Southwest;
  West
Experimental Theater (Vassar), 740
exports, American. *See also* trade
  balance with imports (1870–1914), 606*t*
  to Canada and Europe (1875–1900), 606*t*

factory system. *See also* manufacturing
  inside contracting, 505
  scientific management, 505–506
Fairbanks, Douglas, 675
Fair Campaign Practices Act of 1974, 880
Fair Deal, Truman presidency, 790–792
Fair Employment Practices Committee (FEPC),
  756
Fair Labor Standards Act of 1938, 730, 743
Fall, Albert, 664
Faludi, Susan, 920
Falwell, Jerry, 895
family. *See also* marriage; women
  baby boom, 816
  divorce, 816, 861, 891
  dual-earner family, 501, 913
  and Great Depression, 697–702
  middle class, 554*i*, 555–557
  World War II era, 759
Family and Medical Leave Act of 1993, 925
family values, 895
Farewell to Arms, A (Hemingway), 685
Farmer, James, 756
Farmers' Alliance of the Northwest, 536
Farm Holiday Association, 714
farming. *See* agriculture
Farm Security Administration (FSA), 741
fast-food restaurants, 815
Father Knows Best, 815
Faubus, Orval, 800
Faulkner, William, 685
Fauset, Jessie, 686
Federal Art Project (FAP), 740
federal budget
  balanced under Clinton, 927
  deficit under Reagan, 907
federal bureaucracy
  New Deal expansion, 731
  World War II expansion, 752
Federal Communications Commission (FCC),
  media regulation, 815
Federal Council of Churches, 655
Federal Deposit Insurance Corporation (FDIC),
  creation of, 721
Federal Emergency Relief Administration
  (FERA), 722
Federal Farm Loan Act of 1916, 599
Federal Housing Administration, 812
Federal Music Project, 740
Federal One, 739–740
Federal Republic of Germany, 783
  West Germany as, 783
Federal Reserve Act of 1913, 598

Federal Reserve System
  Board of Governors, 723
  establishment of, 598
  and Great Depression, 693
  monetary policy, 905
  World War I, 646
Federal Theatre Project, 740
Federal Trade Commission (FTC)
  and antitrust cases, 663
  powers of, 598
Federal Writers' Project, 740
Feminine Mystique, The (Friedan), 817, 861,
  862
feminism. *See* women's movement
Fenway Park, 568
Ferdinand, Franz, 636
Ferraro, Geraldine, 888, 905
Fifteenth Amendment, disfranchisement and
  race, 532
  provisions of, 440
  women's movement on, 440–441
Finland, 655
fireside chats, 719, 721
Fiske, John, 608–609
Fithian, Philip
Fitzgerald, F. Scott, 685
Flanagan, Hallie, 740
flexible response policy, 825
Florida
  Sun Belt boom, 812–813, 885
  voting irregularities, presidential election 2000,
    931–934*i*, 945–947
Foch, Ferdinand, 642
Food Administration, 647
Food and Drug Administration (FDA), 593
Food for Peace program, 826
food stamps, 836, 927
Forbes, John Murray, 491
Forbes Field, 568
Ford, Gerald (1913–), as president, 879–880,
  896–897
Ford, Henry, 505, 667
  on World War I, 639
Ford Model T, 674
Ford Motor Company, 673–674, 673*i*
Fordney-McCumber Tariff of 1922, 670
Ford's Theater, 429
foreign policy. *See also* expansionism, global
  Cleveland administration, 607–608
  Clinton administration, 926–929
  isolationism, 602
  Manifest Destiny, 609
  Monroe Doctrine, 608
  post–World War I, 670–671
Forman, Stanley, 894
Forrest, Nathan Bedford, 448
Fort Hall, 463
Foster, William Z., 716
Fourteen Points, 654
Fourteenth Amendment
  due process clause, 522
  ratification of, 436
  separate but equal doctrine, 532, 799

France
  and Civil War, 602
  Franco-Prussian War of 1870, 626
  Morocco, dominance of, 627
  World War I, 636, 638, 642–643
  World War II, 749, 764–765
Franco, Francisco, 747
Franco-Prussian War of 1870, 626
Frankfurter, Felix, 575, 659, 729
Fraser River, 476
free blacks
  black church, influence of, 444–445
  discrimination against. *See* African American
    discrimination
  education for, 432*i*
  Freedmen's Bureau, 431–435
  political leaders, Reconstruction era, 442–443*i*
  resettlement, post–Civil War, 432–435
  sharecroppers, 445–448, 447*i*
  Southern violence against (Reconstruction
    era), 431, 435, 438*i*, 448–451
  wage labor after slavery, 433
Free Speech, 534
Free Speech movement, 851
Freed, Alan, 817–818
Freedman's Savings and Trust Company, 452
Freedmen's Bureau, 431–435
freedom riders, 830
Freedom Summer, 834
French colonization, Vietnam, 841–842
Freud, Sigmund, influence on literature, 685
Frick, Henry Clay, 511, 570
Friedan, Betty, 817, 861
Frost, Robert, 685
Fuel Administration, 647
Fulbright, J. William, 849
Fuller, Henry Blake, 570–571
Fundamentalism, 683–684

Gagarin, Yuri, 829
Gandhi, Indira, 909
gangs
  industrial laborers, 505
  Mexican American, 760
  slave work gangs, 433
Garfield, James A. (1831–1881)
  assassination of, 517
  election of 1880, 517
Garland, Hamlin, 558
garment workers
  Jews as, 501
  Triangle Shirtwaist Company fire, 583–584
  women's labor movement, 579–580
Garvey, Amy Jacques, 686
Garvey, Marcus, 686–687, 854
Gary, Elbert H., 593
Garza, Elizo de la, 858
gaslights, 548
gasoline
  energy crisis, 881–883
  World War II rationing, 759
Gates, Bill, 922
Gatling guns, 472

gay bashing, 920
Gay Divorcee, The, 702
gays. *See* homosexuals
Gellhorn, Martha, 741
gender roles
  birth control, effects on, 861
  and Great Depression, 697
  and homesteaders, 467, 469, 470*i*
  and Native Americans, 462
  and sex-typing of occupations, 500
General Agreement on Tariffs and Trade
  (GATT), 925
General Assembly, 770
General Electric, globalization of, 668
genetic research, Human Genome Project, 953
Geneva Accords, 842
*Gentle Measures in the Management and Training
  of the Young* (Abbott), 556
Gentlemen's Agreement, U.S. and Japan, 625, 680
George, David Lloyd, 655, 656
George, Henry, 481, 575
German Democratic Republic, East Germany, 783
Germany
  Berlin airlift, 782
  East Germany, creation of, 780, 828
  post–World War I debt, 655, 670
  West Germany, creation of, 783
  World War I, 636–642, 653, 655
  World War II, 747–749, 765–766
Geronimo, 472
Ghost Dance, 473
GI Bill, 757, 788, 811, 861
Gibson, Charles Dana, 556
Gibson girl, 556
Gilbert, John, 675
Gilded Age, The (Twain and Warner), 570
Gilman, Charlotte Perkins, 575, 581
Gingrich, Newt, 927, 930, 942
Ginsberg, Allen, 820, 853
Ginsburg, Ruth Bader, 924
glasnost, meaning of, 910
Glass, Carter, 597
Glass-Steagall Act, 721
Glazier, Nathan, 896
Gleason, Jackie, 815
Glenn, John, 829
global economy
  in 1920s, 668–671
  contagion theory, 954
  Dawes Plan, 670
  foreign manufacturing facilities, 604, 668–669
  Great Depression, 694
  and growth of corporations, 810–811
  U.S. decline in participation, 914
  and U.S. deindustrialization, 885
global warming, 951, 952
Godkin, Edwin L., 525, 551–552
Goines, David Lance, 921*i*
gold
  mining in California, 475–478, 476*m*
  mining Sioux sacred ground, 472
  standard for money, 540–541
Goldwater, Barry, 835

Gompers, Samuel, 509–510, 509*i*, 585, 618
Gone with the Wind, 706
González, Elián, 939–940, 958
Gonzalez, Henry, 858
Good Earth, The (Buck), 706
Good Friday accords, 957
Good Housekeeping, 555, 676
Goodman, Benny, 704
Good Neighbor Policy, 746
goods
    capital goods, 488
    consumer goods, 488
Gorbachev, Mikhail, 910
Gore, Albert, Jr.
    and election of 2000, 930–932
    election 2000 controversy, 931–934*i*, 945–947
    as vice president, 923
Gould, Jay, 491, 508
Grady, Henry W., 494
Graham, Billy, 816, 895
Gramm-Rudman Balanced Budget Act of
    1985, 909
Grange, Red, 678
Granger movement, 536
Grant, Ulysses S. (1822–1885)
    election of 1868, 440
    election of 1872, 451
    as president, 440, 449, 451–452
    and Reconstruction, 449, 451–452
    as Secretary of War, 438
grape pickers' strike, 858
Grapes of Wrath, The (Steinbeck), 709
Grasso, Ella, 888
Grateful Dead, 853
Great Atlantic and Pacific Tea Company (A&P),
    672
Great Basin, 475
Great Britain
    alliance of Roosevelt administration, 620–622
    and Civil War, 602
    and Panama Canal, 621, 622
    suffrage activities, 580
    World War I, 636, 639, 642–643
    World War II, 749–750, 764–765
Great Deflation, 488
Great Depression. *See also* New Deal
    African Americans during, 706–708
    and agriculture, 692–693, 706, 708–711, 714
    banks collapse, 692, 720
    causes of, 692–693
    consumerism during, 697–698
    declining industries, 693
    demographic trends, 698–699
    dust bowl migrations, 708–710
    education during, 701
    and gender roles, 697
    global scope of, 694
    Hoover presidency, 688, 694, 711–715
    Mexican Americans during, 710–711
    popular culture, 702–706
    Roosevelt elected, 715–716
    and sick industries, 667

    unemployment, 693–694, 716, 730
    violent outbreaks during, 714–715
    women during, 697, 699–701
    youth during, 701–702
Great Moments in History, 672
Great Northern Railroad, 491
Great Plains, 460–474
    agriculture, 469–470
    cattle raising, 465–467
    homesteading, 467–471
    Native Americans, 462–463, 471–474
    railroads, 464
Great Society, 833–838
    environmental programs, 835–836
    legislation, 835–836
    middle class, programs for, 835
    Nixon cuts to programs, 875
    shortcomings of, 837–838
    and welfare state, 836–837
Great Strike of 1877, 487
Great Train Robbery, The, 674
Greece, Truman Doctrine, 781–782
Greeley, Horace, 463
greenbacks, 540
Green Berets, 825
Green Party, 931
Greensboro, North Carolina, civil rights sit-in, 830
Grenada, 909
Griffith, Beatrice, 736
Griffith, D. W., 587
Guadalcanal Dairy, 758
Guam
    and Spanish-American War, 613–614
    World War II, 767
Guantanamo Bay, U.S. Naval base, 746
guerilla forces, Vietcong, 844, 846, 849*i*, 864
Guiteau, Charles, 517
Gulf of Tonkin Resolution, 845, 868
gun control, Clinton era, 925
guns
    high-velocity rifle, 637
    machine guns, 637
Guthrie, Oklahoma, 473
Guzman, Jacobo Arbenz, 802
Gypsies, and Holocaust, 747, 765

Hague Court, 627
Hague Peace Conference of 1899, 627
Haight-Ashbury, San Francisco, 853
Hairy Ape, The (O'Neill), 685
Haiti, 926
Haldeman, H.R., 878–879
Haley, Bill, 818
Halfbreeds, 525
Hanna, Mark, 541, 573, 589
Hanoi, 927
    Christmas bombing, 870, 870*i*
Hard, William, 576
Harding, Warren G. (1865–1923)
    election of 1920, 663
    as president, 663–664
Hare Krishnas, 885

Harlem, 561
  and Great Depression, 707
  Renaissance, 686
Harriman, Daisy, 666
Harris, Katherine, 931
Harrison, Benjamin (1833–1901)
  election of 1888, 536, 946
  foreign policy, 607
  as president, 518i
Harte, Bret, 483
hatters, 504
Hawaii
  annexation, 603–604, 613
  Pearl Harbor attack, 751, 767
Hawley, Ellis, 663
Hawley-Smoot Tariff of 1930, 670, 694
Hay, John, 623
Hayden, Tom, 850
Hayes, Rutherford B. (1822–1893)
  election of 1876, 452–453
  as president, 453, 487, 517
Haymarket Square Riot, 510
Hay-Pauncefote Agreement of 1901, 620
Haywood, "Big Bill," 514
Hazard of New Fortunes, A (Howells), 570
hazardous waste, 886, 951
health insurance
  AMA position on, 791
  Clinton health care reform, 925–926, 943
  federal program, 665
  Medicare and Medicaid, 836
Hearst, William Randolph, 568
hegemony, meaning of, 778
Helms, Jesse, 920
Hemingway, Ernest, 685
Hendrix, Jimi, 853
Hepburn Railway Act of 1906, 593
Hernandes, Harriet, 450
Herzegovina, and World War I, 636
Hetch Hetchy Valley, 485
Hewitt, George, 795
Hezbollah, 956
Hickock, Lorena, 741
Higher Education Act of 1965, 835
Highway Beautification Act of 1965, 836
highways
  building in 1920s, 674
  Great Society program, 836
  interstate, 1956, 798
  post–World War II development, 813–814
Hill, Anita, 908, 908i
Hill, James J., 491
Hilton, James, 706
Hine, Lewis, 586i
hippies, 852–853
Hirabayashi v. United States, 762
Hiroshima, atomic bomb, 769m, 771
Hirschfeld, Al, 794i
Hispanics. See Latinos
Hiss, Alger, 793
Hitler, Adolf
  death of, 765
  rise in power, 747
  World War II, 747–749, 765–766
Ho Chi Minh, 841, 842
Ho Chi Minh City, 871
Ho Chi Minh Trail, 843i
Hoar, George F., 617
Hoffman, Abbie, 865
Hohenberg, Duchess of, 636
Holbrooke, Richard, 957
Holiday Inn, 815
Holly, Buddy, 818
Hollywood, California, movies of the 1920s,
  674–676
Holmes, Oliver Wendell, Jr., 575, 653
Holocaust, 747–748, 765
  U.S. inaction in, 765
Home Insurance Building, 547
Home Owners Loan Corporation, 721
Home Rule, 639
Homestead, Pennsylvania, 511
Homestead Act of 1862, 467
homesteading, 467–471
Homestead strike, 511
homosexuals
  activism of, 859–860, 891
  AIDS, 920–921, 952
  coming out, 891
  communities, 891
  gay, use of term, 860
  gay bashing, 920
  gay rights in 1950s, 818–819
  gay rights opponents, 891
  and Holocaust, 747, 765
  meeting places for, 568
  in military, 753, 925
Honeymooners, The, 815
Hong Kong, World War II, 767
Hoover, Herbert (1874–1964)
  critics of, 713–715
  election of 1928, 687–688
  and Food Administration, 647
  on government-business pact, 663
  and Great Depression, 688, 694, 711–715
  as president, 688
Hoovervilles, 713–714i
Hopkins, Harry, 727
horsecar, 547
Horton, Willie, 907
hostage crisis, Iran, 899–900
House, Edward, 640
House Committee on Un-American Activities,
  792–793
household appliances, of 1920s, 672
housewives, 672, 817, 819i
housing
  Great Society programs, 835
  for poor, 549–550, 713–714i
  restrictive covenants, 792, 812
  suburban, 812–814
Howard, Oliver O., 433
Howe, Frederic, 541
Howe, Julia Ward, 441

Howe, Marie Jenny, 581
Howells, William Dean, 570
Huerta, Victoriano, 626
Hughes, Charles Evans, 640
Hughes, Langston, 685, 686, 706
Hull, Cordell, 746
Hull House, 579
Human Genome Project, 953, 953*i*
human rights, Carter presidency, 898
Humphrey, Hubert H. (1911–1978), 790
    and election of 1968, 865–866
    as vice-president, 835, 865
Hundred Days, New Deal, 720–723
Hungary, 655
Hurston, Zora Neale, 686, 740
Hussein, King of Jordan, 804
Hussein, Saddam, 910–911, 928–929, 957
Huston, John, 740
hydrogen bomb, 784, 802

Ickes, Harold, 719, 722
Il Progresso Italo-Americano, 559
immigrant groups
    Asians (1990s), 915–916*m*
    Chinese, 480–482
    crafts workers, 498
    Cubans, 822
    ethnic communities, 559, 915
    Filipinos, 821
    Hispanics, 915–916*m*
    Italians, 498, 500, 559–560
    Japanese, 482, 625
    Koreans, 821
    in labor force, 498–499, 710–711,
        821–822
    Mexicans, 479, 650, 710–711, 821
    mutual-aid societies of, 559–560
    poverty of first immigrants, 499
    Puerto Ricans, 821–822
    Russians, 469
    Scandinavians, 469
    Swedish, 468, 469
immigration. *See also* specific ethnic groups
    Americanization policy, World War I,
        652–653
    anti-immigration sentiments, 481–482, 680,
        917–919*i*
    to cities, 559–560, 821–823
    post–World War I, 682*f*
    wave of 1870–1914, 499*f*
immigration laws
    Chinese Exclusion Act, 482
    Immigration Act of 1965, 836
    National Origins Act, 680, 682
    of the 1920s, 680, 682
    post–World War II, 821
    quotas in 1990s, 915
Immigration Reform and Control Act of 1986,
    915
impeachment
    Clinton, 929–930
    Johnson, 439–440
imperial presidency concept, 880

imports to America. *See also* trade
    tariffs on, 518–519
incandescent light bulb, 548
income distribution
    and Great Depression, 693
    inequality in 1920s, 672
    inequality in 1990s, 913
income tax
    cuts (1964), 829
    Sixteenth Amendment, 646
independent counsel, Clinton issues, 929
independent workers, 502–504
India, nuclear capability, 956–957
Indian Reorganization Act of 1934, 738
Indian Rights Association, 473
Indian Self-Determination Act of 1974, 891
Indian Territory, Oklahoma, 472–474
individualism
    and acquisition of wealth, 520
    popular writings on, 520
    Social Darwinism, 521
industrial education, 535
industrial union, nature of, 513
Industrial Workers of the World (IWW), 514
    World War I suppression of, 653
inflation
    and Federal Reserve, 897
    and interest rate increase, 897
    post–Vietnam War, 883–884, 896
    post–World War I, 657, 665
    post–World War II, 788–789
    Vietnam War era, 850, 872
    World War I era, 649
Influence of Seapower upon History, The (Mahan),
    607
information superhighway, Internet, 922–923
In His Steps (Sheldon), 565
initiative, function of, 583
In Our Time (Hemingway), 685
In Re Jacobs, 522
inside contracting, 505
institutional economists, 574
intellectual movements
    Beats, 819–820
    expatriates, 684–685
    modernism, 685
    of the 1920s, 684–687
    progressive ideals, 574–581
    Social Darwinism, 521, 574, 608
    socialism, 513–514
intercontinental ballistic missiles, 802, 869
interest rates, and Federal Reserve, 897
intermediate-range ballistic missiles, 828, 910
International Bank for Reconstruction and
    Development (World Bank), 811
international companies, 668–669
International Labor Defense, 707
International Monetary Fund (IMF), 811, 954
International Telephone and Telegraph
    Corporation, 810
International Typographical Union, 508
Internet, 922–923
    impact on politics, 947

Interstate Commerce Act of 1887, 593
Interstate Commerce Commission, 593
    and segregation, 830
Interstate Highway Act of 1956, 798
Iran, 882
Iran-Contra affair, 905–906
Iran hostage crisis
    and Carter, 899–900
    and Reagan, 900–901
Iraq, 882
    Desert Fox, 929
    Persian Gulf War, 910–913
Ireland, John (Bishop), 564
Irish
    labor force, 498, 504
    machine politics, 563
    potato famine, 498
ironworkers, 504i
Islam
    Black Muslims, 854
    in Bosnia, 926
    growth in U.S., 950i
    Nation of Islam, 854
    terrorism and militant sects, 956
isolationism, post-Civil War, 602
Israel
    Camp David peace accords, 898
    creation of nation, 803
    violence of 2000–2001, 957
    Yom Kippur War, 882
Issei, 761
Italians, 498, 500, 559–560i
Italy
    World War I, 636
    World War II, 748, 764–765
It Happened One Night, 702
Iwo Jima, World War II, 768–769m

Jackson, Helen Hunt, 473, 483
Jackson, Jesse, 857i, 907
Jackson, Michael, 921
Jackson State College, student killings, 867
James, Henry, 570
James, William, 574–575, 618
Japan
    automobiles, 882
    Gentlemen's Agreement, 625, 680
    invasion of China, 747, 751
    Russo-Japanese War, 624
    Sino-Japanese War of 1894–1895, 606, 624
    World War I, 636
    World War II, 747, 751, 767–769
Japanese
    anti-Japanese sentiment, 482
    exclusion from U.S., 625, 680
    immigration to U.S., 625
Japanese Americans
    in armed forces, 762
    internment during World War II, 761–763i
jazz, 675–677i, 819
Jazz Age, 676, 686
Jazz Singer, The, 675–676
Jefferson Airplane, 853

Jenney, William, 547
Jewish Daily Forward, 559, 561
Jews
    anti-Semitism, 680, 747–748
    garment workers, 501
    Holocaust, 747–748, 765
    New York City, 559
    and Scottsboro case, 707
Jiang Jieshi (Chiang Kai-Shek), 784
Jihad, 956
Jim Crow
    African American resistance to, 533–534
    elements of, 532–534
jingoism, 610
Job Corps, 836
Joffre, Joseph, 641
John Paul II, Pope, 957
Johnson, Andrew (1808–1875), 430i
    attack on civil rights, 435–437
    impeachment of, 439–440
    as president, 429–440
    as vice-president, 421, 429–430
Johnson, C. H., 533
Johnson, Chalmers, 954
Johnson, Hiram W., 583, 656
Johnson, Hugh, 722
Johnson, Lady Bird, 836
Johnson, Lyndon B. (1908–1973). See also Great
        Society
    civil rights movement, 834–835, 854–860
    election of 1964, 833–835
    Great Society, 833–838
    as president, 833–838
    as vice-president, 824–825
    Vietnam War, 844–846, 848–850, 863–864
    Voting Rights Act of 1965, 834–835
    War on Poverty, 836–838
    withdrawal from 1968 election, 864
Jolson, Al, 675
Jones, Bobby, 678
Jones, Jacqueline, 701
Jones and Laughlin Steel Company, 546
Jones, Paula, 929
Jones Act of 1916, 619
Joseph, Chief, 471
journalism. See newspapers
J. P. Morgan & Co., 492, 541
judiciary. See Supreme Court
Jungle, The (Sinclair), 593
junta, 610
juvenile delinquency, World War II era,
        759–760

Kaiser Corporation, 759
kamikaze, 769
Kansas
    cattle ranching, 465
    homesteading, 467–471
    Swedish immigrants, 468–469
Kansas City, 550, 674
Kansas Pacific Railroad, 465i
Kawai, Kazuo, 681
Kearney, Denis, 482

Keaton, Buster, 674
Kelley, Florence, 578–579
Kellogg-Briand Peace Pact, 671
Kelly, Fanny, 462
Kemp, Jack, 928
Kennan, George F., 781
Kennedy, Anthony, 907
Kennedy, Edward, 840
Kennedy, Jacqueline, 833
Kennedy, John F. (1917–1963)
    assassination of, 833
    Bay of Pigs invasion, 827–828, 827m
    Berlin Wall, 828
    civil rights movement, 830–833
    on civil rights protests, 831
    Cuban Missile Crisis, 828
    economic policy, 829
    election of 1960, 824–825, 824m
    mystique versus leadership, 833
    New Frontier, 826i, 829
    and new politics, 825
    -Nixon debate, 825
    Peace Corps, 826, 826i
    space program, 829
    Vietnam War, 843–844
Kennedy, Robert F., 830, 858
    assassination of, 864–865
Kent State, antiwar protest killings, 867
Kerouac, Jack, 820
Kettle Hill, 614
Keynes, John Maynard, 730, 791
Khadafy, Muammar, 909
Khmer Rouge, 867, 871
Khomeini, Ayatollah Ruhollah, 899
Khrushchev, Nikita S., 801
    and East Germany, 828
Kim Il Sung, 784–785
King, Rodney, 917
King, Martin Luther, Jr., 830–834
    assassination of, 856–857i, 864
    Birmingham march, 830
    Nobel Peace Prize, 833
    and Selma voting rights march, 834
    Southern Christian Leadership Conference, 801
King's Canyon, 485
Kiowa Indians, 462
Kissinger, Henry, 896
    and Vietnam War, 867, 869, 877
Knickerbocker Trust Company, 597
Knights of Labor, 507–510
    goals/activities of, 507–508
    versus unions, 508–509
Knowland, William S., 785
Koehler, Karl, 748
Kooning, Willem de, 740
Kopay, David, 892
Koreans, immigration to U.S., 821, 915, 919i
Korean War, 785–788, 786m
    American forces, 785–788, 787i
    causes of, 785
Koreatown, 915
Korematsu v. United States, 762

Kosovo crisis, 929, 957
Kovic, Ron, 806
Ku Klux Klan (KKK), 448–450, 449i
    and Birth of a Nation, 587, 680
    civil rights movement era, 799
    groups targeted, 681
    klaverns, 681
    Reconstruction era, 448–450
    revival in 1920s, 680–682
    terrorist tactics of, 448–449, 451, 681, 833–834
    women in, 681
Ku Klux Klan Act of 1871, 449
Kuhn, Loeb & Co., 492
Kuwait, 882
    Persian Gulf War, 910–913

La Follette, Robert M., 582i, 656
    progressive position of, 574, 581–583,
        594–595, 664–665
La Raza Unida (The United Race), 858
labor force
    accidents and workers, 586, 586i
    African Americans, 498, 649, 755–756
    defense industries, World War II, 754, 759
    and deindustrialization, 884–885, 913
    immigrants, 498–499, 710–711, 821–822
    independent craft workers, 502–504
    mill workers, 495–496
    post-Reconstruction South, 495–497
    service sector, 913
    shifts in (1870–1900s), 498–502
    welfare capitalism, 668
    women in, 499–502, 504, 648i, 650, 699–701,
        754, 754i, 817, 860, 890–891, 914
    work culture, 504–505
    World War I era, 648–650
    World War II era, 754–756, 758–759
labor laws
    child labor, 502
    hours of workday, 510, 574–575, 578–579, 599
    minimum wage, 791, 829
    post–World War II, 789, 790
    Progressive Era laws, 583, 585
    under Wilson, 599
labor movement, 504–513. See also unions
    antilabor decisions, 585
    Haymarket Square Riot, 510
    Knights of Labor, 507–510
    Mexican Americans, 710, 858
    and New Deal, 726, 729t, 731–734
    Progressive Era, 585–586
    strikes, 511–513
    women's participation, 578–580, 710
    World War II era, 755
labor relations, and McCarthy era, 793
Laden, Osama bin, 956
Ladies' Home Journal, 555, 675
Lakota Indians. See Teton Indians
Lance, Bert, 897
Landon, Alfred M., 728
land ownership. See property ownership
Lange, Dorothea, 741

Langer, William L., 644
Laos, 869, 871
Latin America. *See also* Central America
  Carter diplomatic activities, 898
  diplomacy 1880s, 603
  Iran-Contra affair, 905–906
  Pan-Americanism, 603
  U.S. retreat in 1920s, 670
Latinos. *See also* specific groups by ethnicity
  affirmative action, 893–894
  in cities, 821–822, 915
  ethnic groups of, 915
  future population projections, 947–948
  immigration to U.S., 915–916*m*
Latvia, 655
Law of Civilization and Decay, The (Adams),
  608
Lawrence, William, 520
lead, mining of, 477
League of Nations, 654–656, 663, 670
  and World War II, 747
League of United Latin American Citizens
  (LULAC), 756
League of Women Voters, 665
Leahy, William D., 770
Leary, Timothy, 853
Lease, Mary Elizabeth, 537
Lebanon, 909
leisure activities
  of the 1920s, 678
  amusement parks, 566–567*i*
  cultural activities. *See* cultural development
  home entertainment, 705–706
  sports, 568, 678
  vacations by automobile, 674, 815
Lemke, William, 728
Lend-Lease Act, 750
Lenin, Vladimir Ilych, 642
Lesseps, Ferdinand de, 603
LeSueur, Meridel, 695
Levine, Lawrence W., 702
Levitt, Arthur, 812
Levittown, 812
Lewelling, Lorenzo Dow, 539
Lewinsky, Monica, 929, 941*i*
Lewis, John L., 732–733, 755, 831, 933
Lewis, Sinclair, 685
Leyte Gulf, Battle of, 767
Liberty League, 723
libraries, public, 569
Libya, 909
Lieberman, Joseph I., 930, 944
Life, 741
Liliuokalani, Queen of Hawaii, 604
limited liability, stockholders, 490
Lincoln, Abraham (1809–1865)
  assassination of, 429
  and Reconstruction, 428–429
Lindbergh, Charles, 678
  and World War II, 749
Lindgren, Ida, 468
literacy tests, 531–532, 834

literature
  African American writers, 686
  Freudian influenced, 685
  New Deal arts program, 740
  of the 1920s, 685
  of the 1950s, 819–820
  urban novels, 545, 570–571
  western theme, 483
Lithuania, 655
Little, Malcolm (Malcolm X), 854
Little Big Horn, Battle of, 472
Little Caesar, 703
Little Odessa, 915
Little Rock, Arkansas, desegregation enforced,
  800, 800*i*
Lloyd, Harold, 675
Lloyd, Henry Demarest, 539, 575
Lochner v. New York, 574–575
Locke, Alain, 686
Lodge, Henry Cabot, 615, 655–656
  on expansionism, 607, 610
Lodge, Henry Cabot, Jr., 844
Lôme, Dupuy de, 611
Lone Ranger, 704
Long, Huey, 724–725*i,* 728
Long, Stephen H., 463
Long Beach, California, 567*i*
Long Drive, 465
Look, 741
Looking Backward (Bellamy), 575
Lorentz, Pare, 741
Los Alamos, New Mexico, 771
Los Angeles, California, 484
  Mexicans in, 710–711, 760
  race riots of 1967, 855
  race riots of 1992, 917–918
los pobres, 479
Lost Horizon (Hilton), 706
Love Canal, 886
Lowell, Josephine Shaw, 576–577
Lower East Side, New York City, 559–560*i*
LSD (lysergic acid diethylamide), 853
Luce, Henry R., 785
"Luck of Roaring Camp, The" (Harte), 483
lumber industry, Southern, 496
Luna Park, 566
Lusitania, 639–640
Luxembourg, World War II, 749
lyceum movement, 569
lynching, African Americans, 532, 657, 707–708*i,*
  792, 799
Lynd, Helen Merrell and Robert, 662, 673, 697

McAdoo, William, 646
McAllister, Ward, 552
MacArthur, Douglas, 715, 784
  discharge by Truman, 787
  Korean War, 785–788, 786*m*
  World War II, 767
McCarran-Walter Act of 1952, 821
McCarthy, Charlie, 704
McCarthy, Eugene J., 864–865

McCarthy, Joseph, 792–796
McCarthyism, 792–796
    decline in support for, 793–794, 796
    and entertainment business, 792
    House Committee on Un-American
        Activities, 792–793
McClure's, 576
McDonald's restaurant, 815
McGovern, George S., 877
McGuire, Thomas B., 507
machine guns, 637
machine politics, 524–525
    bosses, 562–563
    cities, 562–563
    contributions of, 524–525, 562, 584–585
    examples of, 525
    Progressive Era, 585
    tactics of, 524–525, 562–563
machinists, 505
McKay, Claude, 686
McKinley, William (1843–1901)
    assassination of, 589, 620
    election of 1896, 541–542m
    election of 1900, 618
    Philippines acquisition, 615–620
    as president, 573
    Spanish-American War, 609–615
McKinley Tariff of 1890, 540, 604
McNamara, Robert, 844, 849, 877
McPherson, Aimee Semple, 682
MAD (Mutual Assured Destruction), 805
Madero, Francisco, 626
Madonna, 921
magazines
    African American, 686
    feminist, 887
    muckraker journalism, 576, 578
    news magazines, 922
    of 1920s, 676
    photojournalism, 741
    women's, 555, 675, 676
Maggie: A Girl of the Streets (Crane), 570
Magruder, Jeb Stuart, 878
Mahan, Alfred T., 607, 615
Maine, 611–612, 611i
malaria, Panama Canal, 622
Malaya, 669
    World War II, 767
Malcolm X, assassination of, 854
management
    middle, decline of, 914
    modern corporations, 667
    scientific management, 505–506, 668
    shop-floor, 505
Mandan Indians, 462–463
Mandela, Nelson, 958i
Manhattan. *See* New York City
Manhattan Project, 771
Manifest Destiny, and foreign policy, 609
manufacturing
    American natural resources for, 489
    automobiles, 673–674

deindustrialization, 884–885, 913
    foreign plants, 604, 668–669
    and growth of mining, 489
    mass production, 505
    plant closings, effects of, 884–885, 913–914
    post–World War I, 667
    steel, 489
    technology for, 489, 505
    World War II era, 753–754
Mao Zedong (Mao Tse-tung), 784–785, 844
Ma Perkins, 704
March of Time newsreels, 740–741
March on Washington, 833
Marcus, Joe, 732
marriage. *See also* family
    divorce, 861, 891
    during the 1950s, 816
    rate during Great Depression, 698
Marshall, Thurgood, civil rights movement,
        799
Marshall Plan, 782
Martin, Joseph J., 787
Marx, Karl, 513
Marx Brothers, 703–704
mass distribution, beginning of, 492–493
mass marketing, beginning of, 493
mass media
    and global events, 947
    magazines, 555, 576, 676
    mediathon concept, 939
    movies, 674–676, 702–704
    newspapers, 568–569, 576, 676
    and presidential election campaigns, 825, 907
    radio, 672, 676–677, 704
    television, 815
    and Vietnam War, 849, 849i
mass production
    automobiles, 673–674
    beginning of, 505
mass transit, 547–548i
Mattachine Society, 818
Maxim, Hiram, 637
Maximilian, Archduke, 602
meat business, impact of railroads, 492
Meat Inspection Act, 593
Me Decade, 885
Medicaid
    cuts to program, 927
    establishment of, 835
Medicare
    cuts to program, 927
    establishment of, 835
medicine men, 463
Mein Kampf (Hitler), 747
Mellon, Andrew W., 663, 693
Mencken, H. L., 685
mergers. *See also* antitrust
    of 1920s, 667
    trust-busting, 591–593
mestizo, 478
Metropolitan Museum of Art, 569
Meuse-Argonne campaign, 642

Mexican American Political Association (MAPA), 857–858
Mexican Americans
    in armed forces, 753
    Chicano movement, 857–858
    civil rights activism of, 756
    and Great Depression, 710–711
    labor activism of, 710–711
    and New Deal, 736–738
    World War I era, 650
    World War II era, 753, 756, 760
Mexicans
    deportation policy, 710
    immigrants to U.S., 478–479, 650, 680, 710–711, 821
    migrant workers, 710, 821
Mexico
    French seizure of, 602
    Mexican Revolution, 626
    Wilson administration, 625–626
    and World War I, 640
Miami, Florida, Cuban population, 822
Microsoft, 922
middle class
    family life, 554i, 555–557
    and Great Depression, 695
    and suburban growth, 554–555
Middle East
    Carter diplomatic activities, 898
    Cold War, 803–805
    Egypt conflict (1950s), 803–804
    Eisenhower Doctrine, 804–805
    and energy crisis, 881–883
    Israel-Palestine situation, 803, 882, 898, 957
    Jewish relocation to, 803
    oil resources (1950s), 805
    terrorism, 909, 956
Middletown (Lynd and Lynd), 662, 697
Midway Island, World War II, 767, 769m
migrant workers, Mexicans, 710, 821
military dictatorships, Cold War era, 802
military draft
    draft dodgers, 851
    Vietnam War, 846, 851–852
    World War I, 641
    World War II, 753
military-industrial complex, 805–806
    beginning of, 753
military service. See armed forces
Miller, Arthur, 740
Millicent v. Bradley, 892
Milosevic, Slobodan, 929
Milton, Massachusetts, 551
minerals. See also mining
    copper, 477, 479
    gold, 475–478
    iron ore, 489, 494–495m
    silver, 476m, 477
minimum wage, 791, 798, 829
mining
    accidents, 586
    Chinese workers, 481

codes/laws, 476
    gold mining in California, 475–478, 476m
    and Great Depression, 693
    growth and manufacturing, 489
    industrialization of, 477
    Mexican workers, 480i
    strikes, 590–591
    strip mining, 739
    Virginia City, 477
Minneconjou Indians, 473
Minnestoa, iron ore mining, 489
minority groups. See immigration; specific groups by ethnicity
Minow, Newton, 815
Miranda v. Arizona, 876
Miss America pageant, women's movement on, 863i
missiles
    intercontinental ballistic, 802
    intermediate-range ballistic, 828
    MX system, 904
Mississippi, Freedom Summer, 834
Mississippi Freedom Democratic Party, 834
Missouri Pacific Railroad, 465
Mitchell, John, 590, 878
Mitchell, Margaret, 706
Miyatake, Toyo, 763i
mobs. See also riots
    anti-Chinese, 482
    and school desegregation, 800
Modern Instance, A (Howells), 570
Moley, Raymond, 719, 721
Molotov, Vyacheslav, 764, 780
Mondale, Walter F., 897, 905
money supply, 539–541
    gold standard, 540–541
    monetary policy and Federal Reserve, 905
    pre–Civil War, 539–540
    silver issue, 540–541
    size issue, 539
Monitor, 602
monkey trial, 683–684i
monopolies. See also antitrust
    common law on, 591–592
    trust-busting, 591–593, 595–596
Monroe Doctrine, 608
Montana, mining centers, 477
Montenegro, 957
Montgomery, Alabama, bus boycott, 800–801
Montoya, Joseph, 858
Moody, Dwight L., 566
Moon, Sun Myung, 885
moonshine, 683
Moore, John Bassett, 620
Moore, Marianne, 685
Moral Majority, 895
    See also New Right
Morgan, John Pierpont, 569, 590, 592i
Morgenthau, Henry, Jr., 719
Mormons, globalization of, 949–950
Morocco, French dominance of, 627
mortgages, federally sponsored, 812, 835

Morton, Ferdinand "Jelly Roll," 676
Morton, Oliver, 436
Mossadegh, Muhammad, 802
movies
    Depression era, 702–704
    documentary, 740–741
    first films, 567
    in 1920s, 674–676
    silent films, 674–675
    with sound, 676
    World War II era, 758
Mr. Deeds Goes to Town, 704
Mr. Smith Goes to Washington, 704, 705*i*
Ms., 887
MTV, 921–922
muckrakers, 576, 578
Mugwumps, 525, 581, 618
Muhammad, Elijah, 854
Muir, John, 484–485, 590
Muller v. Oregon, 578–579, 598
multiculturalism
    and future population, 947–948*i*
    meaning of, 919
Mundt, Karl, 785
Munich Conference, 749
Murray, Robert, 658
Murrow, Edward R., 758
museums, 569
music
    acid rock, 853
    and African Americans, 676, 817–819
    Beatles, 853
    bebop, 819
    Big Band, 704
    jazz, 675–677*i*, 819
    New Deal arts program, 740
    orchestras, 569
    protest music, 853
    rhythm and blues, 818
    rock 'n' roll, 818, 853
Muskie, Edmund S., 865, 878
Muslims. *See* Islam
Mussolini, Benito, 747, 764
mustard gas, 638
mutual-aid societies, of immigrants, 559–560
MX missile system, 904*i*
My Lai Massacre, 868

Nader, Ralph
    consumer activism, 887
    and presidential election of 2000, 931, 944
Nagasaki, atomic bomb, 769*m*, 771
napalm, 852
Nasser, Gamal Abdel, 803
National Advisory Commission on Civil
    Disorders, 855–856
National Aeronautics and Space Administration
    (NASA), 829
National American Woman Suffrage Association
    (NAWSA), 580, 650
National Association for the Advancement of
    Colored People (NAACP)

beginning of, 588–589
    Brown decision, 799
    civil rights movement (1950s), 799–801
    magazine of, 686
    World War II era, 756
National Association of Colored Women's Clubs,
    588–589
National Association of Manufacturers, 791
National Association of Real Estate Boards, 791
National Baptist Convention, 444
National Broadcasting Company (NBC), 676
National Civil Rights Commission, 791–792
National Consumers' League, 578
National Council of American Indians, 858
National Defense Advisory Commission, 749
National Endowment for the Arts, 835
National Endowment for the Humanities, 835
National Environmental Policy Act of 1969,
    886–887
National Farmers' Alliance, 536
National Gay Task Force, 891
National Housing Act of 1937, 730, 743
National Housing Act of 1949, 791
National Industrial Recovery Act (NIRA), 722, 724
National Interstate and Defense Highway Act of
    1956, 813
National Labor Relations Act of 1935 (Wagner
    Act), 726, 789
National Labor Relations Board, 726
National League (baseball), 568
National Liberation Front (NLF), 843, 844
National Organization for Women (NOW),
    861–862, 887
national parks, California, 485
National Progressive Republican League, 595
National Recovery Administration (NRA), 722
National Rifle Association (NRA), on
    Brady Act, 925
National Security Council (NSC), 784
National Socialist (Nazi) Party, 747
National Union for Social Justice, 724
National Union Movement, 431, 436
National Urban League, 793, 832
    beginning of, 588–589
National War Labor Board (NWLB),
    648–649, 755
National Women's Conference, 888
National Women's Party, 650, 889
National Women's Political Caucus, 888
National Women's Suffrage Association, 441
National Women's Trade Union League, 579
National Youth Administration, 701, 757
Nation of Islam, 854
Native Americans
    in armed forces, 753
    assimilation to white culture, 474
    civil rights gains (1970s), 891
    civil rights movement (1970s), 858–859
    Great Plains, 462–463
    migration to cities, 822
    and New Deal, 738
    relocation of, 471–474

reservations, 471–474
spirituality of, 463, 473
Termination program, 822
women, 462
Wounded Knee, 473–474
Native Son (Wright), 740
nativism
immigration restriction, 680–682
and Ku Klux Klan (KKK), 680–682
natural resources
alternative energy sources, 886
increased energy consumption (1990s), 952
natural selection, 521
Navajo Code Talkers, 753
Navajo Indians, 471, 478
Naval War College, 602
Navy
battleships, 607
Civil War, 602
U.S. development of, 602–603, 607
Nazis
rise of, 747–748
World War II, 747–749, 765–766
Nebraska, homesteading, 467–471
Neel, Alice, 740
Negro, rejection of term, 855
Negro World, 686
Nestor, Agnes, 580
Netherlands, World War II, 749
Neutrality Act of 1935, 746–747
amended, 750
Nevada, Virginia City mining, 477
Nevelson, Louise, 740
New Age movement, 885
Newark, New Jersey, race riots of 1967, 855
New Deal
and African Americans, 736
Agricultural Adjustment Act (AAA), 721–722
and arts, 739–741
Banking Act of 1935, 723
Civil Works Administration (CWA), 722–723
Congressional opposition, 730, 756–757
criticisms of, 723–725
Emergency Banking Act, 721
environmental programs, 738–739
and federal bureaucracy, 731
Federal Emergency Relief Administration (FERA), 722
Hundred Days, 720–723
and labor relations, 726, 731–734
lasting contributions of, 741–743
legislation, listing of, 729*t*
and Mexican Americans, 736–738
National Labor Relations Act (Wagner Act), 726
National Recovery Administration (NRA), 722
and Native Americans, 738
packing Supreme Court, 728–730
Public Works Administration (PWA), 722
recession during, 730
Securities and Exchange Commission (SEC), 723
Social Security Act, 726

Tennessee Valley Authority (TVA), 721
use of term, 718
women during, 734–735
Works Progress Administration (WPA), 727
New Democrats, 928
New Era, 663, 688
New Freedom, 596–597
New Frontier, Kennedy presidency, 826*i*, 829
New Guinea, World War II, 767, 769
Newlands Reclamation Act of 1902, 590
New Left, 850–851, 868
New Look, Eisenhower policy, 801–802
New Mexico, 478–479
American-Hispanic conflict, 479
Hispanic-Indian relations, 478
Manhattan Project, 771
Spanish settlement, 478–479
New Nationalism, 596
New Negro, The (Locke), 686
New Orleans, jazz, 676
New Right
anti-feminism, 920
anti-gay, 920
influence in 1990s, 933–934
and Reagan, 900–901
values of, 895–896, 900–901
newspapers
African American, 686
foreign language, 559
magazine format, 922
muckrakers, 576, 578
syndicated columns, 676
tabloids, 676
urban papers, 568–569
yellow journalism, 569
Newton, Huey, 855
Newton, Massachusetts, 551
New York City
African Americans in, 560, 561, 822
cultural institutions, 569
entertainment activities, 566–569
immigrant groups, 559–560
lower East Side, 559–560*i*
machine politics, 563
mass transit, 547
Progressive Era labor laws, 583, 585
Puerto Ricans in, 822
race riots of 1967, 855
skyscrapers, 547
tenements, 549–550
wealthy in, 552, 569–570
World Trade Center bombing, 926, 955
New York Central Railroad, 491
New York Consumers' League, 577, 585
New York Herald, 568
New York Journal, 610, 611
New York State Factory Commission, 583
New York Sun, 568
New York World, 569, 610
New Yorker, 676
Nez Percé Indians, 471
Ngo Dinh Diem, 842–844, 863

Niagara Movement, 588
Nicaragua, 670
    and Bay of Pigs invasion, 827, 827m
    Iran-Contra affair, 905–906
    Sandinistas, 909
nickelodeons, 567
Nimitz, Chester W., 767
Nineteenth Amendment, 650–651
Nisei, 761
Nixon, Richard M. (1913–1994)
    arms control, 869
    Checkers speech, 797
    China visit, 869
    détente policy, 868
    economic problems, 883–885
    and election of 1960, 824–825
    election of 1968, 866
    election of 1972, 876–877
    on evaluation of history, 940
    Ford's pardon, 880
    -Kennedy debates, 825
    kitchen debate with Khrushchev, 809
    and McCarthy era, 793
    resignation of, 879
    social programs, 875–876
    social welfare cuts, 875
    as vice-president, 796–797, 809
    and Vietnam War, 866–871
    Watergate, 877–880
Nonaggression Pact of 1939, 749
Non-Partisan League, 734
Normandy, D-Day, 765, 767i
North, Oliver, 905
North American Free Trade Agreement
    (NAFTA), 925
North Atlantic Treaty Organization (NATO)
    creation of, 783
    former communist countries in, 955
North Carolina (state), civil rights sit-ins, 830
Northern Pacific Railroad, 464
North Pole, melting of ice cap, 952
Northern Securities Company, 591
Norton, Charles Eliot, 618
Norway, World War II, 749
Norwood (Beecher), 570
NSC-68 report, 784
nuclear power plants
    safety issues, 886
    waste issues, 886, 951
nuclear weapons
    atomic bomb, 769m, 771
    fallout casualties, 804i, 805
    flexible response policy, 825
    future view, 957
    hydrogen bomb, 784, 802
    India/Pakistan capability, 956–957
    missiles, 802, 828
    proliferation and U.S., 805
    and Star Wars, 905
nurses
    Vietnam War, 848
    World War II, 753, 768
Nye, Gerald P., 746

Occupational Safety and Health Administration
    (OSHA), 876
occupations
    gender-typing of, 500
    middle class, 553
    women, 499–502, 817, 914
O'Connor, Sandra Day, 906
Office of Economic Opportunity, 836, 875
Office of Human Rights, 898
Office of Indian Affairs, 471. See also Bureau of
    Indian Affairs
Office of Minority Affairs of the National Youth
    Administration, 736
Office of Price Administration (OPA), 788–789
Office of Price Administration and Civilian
    Supply, 759
Office of War Information, 758
Ohio River, 551
oil
    Caspian Sea region, 955
    embargo, 882
    energy crisis, 881–883
oil spills, 886
Okinawa, World War II, 768, 769m
Oklahoma, Native American relocation to, 472–474
Oklahoma City, Oklahoma, 473
Old Age Resolving Pension Plan, 724
older Americans
    and Great Depression, 695
    and Great Society, 835
    and New Deal, 724, 726
oligopolies
    function of, 667
    meaning of, 810
Olmsted, Frederick Law, 550
Olney, Richard, 573, 608
Olsen, Tillie, 740
Olympic Games, Moscow, boycott of, 898
Omaha Platform, 539
omnibus, 547
Omnibus Violent Crime Control and Prevention
    Act of 1994, 925
One Hundred Percent Americanism, 652–653
O'Neill, Eugene, 685
On the Road (Kerouac), 820
open door policy, Asia, 623–625
open shop, meaning of, 668
Operation Desert Storm, 911–913
Operation Rolling Thunder, 845
Operation Wetback, 821
orchestras, 569
Oregon, growth of, 477
Oregon Trail, 463
Organization of Petroleum Exporting Countries
    (OPEC), energy crisis, 881–883
organized crime, during Prohibition, 683
Origin of Species, The (Darwin), 521
Orlando, Vittorio, 655
Oswald, Lee Harvey, 833
"Outcasts of Poker Flat, The" (Harte), 483
Over the Rhine, 822
Ovington, Mary White, 588
Owens Valley, 485

Oxford Pledge, 701
ozone layer, 951
Ozzie and Harriet, 815

pachuco gangs, 760
Pacific Crest Trail, 739
pacifists
    pre–World War I, 638
    Vietnam War, 851
padrone, 499
Pago Pago, 604
Pahlavi, Muhammad Reza, 802, 898
Paige, Satchel, 678
Paiute Indians, 473
Pakistan, nuclear capability, 956–957
Palestine
    Israel divided from, 803
    violence of 2000–2001, 957
Palmer, A. Mitchell, 658–659
Palmer raids, 658
Panama Canal, 603, 621*i,* 622
    control issue, 898
Pan-American Union, 603
Pan Americanism, meaning of, 603
Panay, 751
Panic of 1873, 464
Panic of 1893, 492
Paris Peace Accords, 869–870
Paris, Treaty of 1899, 617
Parker, Alton B., 591
parks
    New Deal projects, 739
    urban parks, 550
Parks, Rosa, 800
patent medicines, consumer protection
        position, 593
Patterson, John, 830
Patton, George S., 715, 764
Paul, Alice, 580
Pawnee Indians, 462, 463
Pax Americana, 810
Payne-Aldrich Tariff Act of 1913, 595
Peace Corps, 826, 826*i*
Peale, Norman Vincent, 816
Pearce, Charles H., 444–445
Pearl Harbor, 603
    Japanese attack, 745, 751, 767, 833
Peña, Frederico, 925
Pendleton Civil Service Act of 1883, 517
Pennsylvania (state), coal mining, 489
Pennsylvania Railroad, 487, 489
pension system
    Civil War veterans, 587
    Social Security, 726, 942–944
Pentagon Papers, 877
Pentecostal movement, 950
People's Republic of China
    détente policy, 869
    establishment of, 784–785
perestroika, meaning of, 910
Perkins, Frances, 585, 719, 726, 734
Permanent Court of Arbitration, 627
Perot, H. Ross, 923–924, 944

Pershing, John J., 641–642
Persian Gulf War, 871, 911–913
    media coverage, 947
    Operation Desert Storm, 911–913, 928
    women in, 912*i*
personal computer (PC), 922
Personal Responsibility and Work Opportunity
        Act of 1996, 928
pesticides, 887
philanthropy, cultural institutions, founding of,
        569–570
Philippines
    Spanish-American War, 613, 615–620
    U.S. purchase of, 617
    war of 1899, 618
    World War II, 767, 769*m*
Phillips, David Graham, 576
Phillips curve, 954
phonograph, 676
photography, Depression era, 741
photojournalism, Depression era, 741
physical fitness movement, 885
Pickford, Mary, 675
Pike, James S., 451
Pike's Peak, 476
Pilgrim's Progress (Bunyan), 576
Pinchot, Forester Gifford, 594–595
Pinchot-Ballinger affair, 595
Pinckney, Thomas, 433
Pittsburgh, Pennsylvania, 489–499
*Plain Home Talk on Love, Marriage, and
        Parentage,* 556
plant closings, manufacturing, 884–885, 913–914
Platt, Orville, 604
Platt amendment, 623, 746
Pledge of Allegiance, 816
Plessy v. Ferguson, 532, 799
Plow That Broke the Plains, The, 741
Plunkitt, George Washington, 562–563
Plymouth Congregational Church, 564
Podhoretz, Norman, 896
poetry
    African American poets, 686, 706
    beats, 819–820
    of the 1920s, 685
Poland
    creation of, 655
    World War II, 749, 765
Polaris missile, 802
police brutality, and race riots, 855
police powers, of states, 521
Polish Americans, 499, 559, 564
Polish National Catholic Church of America, 564
political action committees (PACs), campaign
        contributions, 880
political parties
    Democratic Party. *See* Democratic Party
    Green Party, 931
    machine politics, 524–525
    party loyalty, factors in, 523–524, 523*f*
    Populist Party, 536, 538
    Progressive Party (Bull Moose Party), 581–583,
        594–596

political parties (*cont.*)
Reform Party, 931, 944
Republican Party. *See* Republican Party
Socialist Party of America, 513–514, 575
Pollock, Jackson, 740, 819
poll tax, 532
pollution, cities, 549
Populism, 514, 536–539, 537*m*
and African Americans, 530–532
development of, 536–537
end of, 531
free silver, 539, 541
ideology of, 538–539
and women, 537–538
Populist Party, 536, 538
Port Huron Statement, 850
Portland, Oregon, 477
post-traumatic stress disorder, Vietnam War
veterans, 871
Potsdam Conference, 780
Potter, Helen, 528
poverty
feminization of, 891
Great Society programs, 836–837
housing for poor, 549–550, 713–714*i*
Social Security system, 726
urban poor, 549–550, 823
Powderly, Terence V., 507
Powder River, 472
Powell, Colin, 911
Powell, Lewis F., Jr., 876
Power of Positive Thinking, The (Peale), 816
Powers, Francis Gary, 805
pragmatism, ideas of, 575
presidency, term limits, 824
presidential election campaigns
debates, 825
mass media, 825, 907
negative advertising, 907
political cartoons, 518*i*
reform legislation, 880
Watergate tactics, 878
presidential elections
Bush, George (1988 election), 907
Bush, George W. (2000 election), 930–932
Carter, Jimmy (1976 election), 897
Cleveland, Grover (1884 election), 519, 525
Cleveland, Grover (1892 election), 536
Clinton, William J. (1992 election), 923–924*i*
Clinton, William J. (1996 election), 928
Coolidge, Calvin (1924 election), 663–664
Eisenhower, Dwight D. (1952 election), 796–797
Garfield, James A. (1880 election), 517
Grant, Ulysses S. (1868 election), 440
Grant, Ulysses S. (1872 election), 451
Harding, Warren G. (1920 election), 663
Hayes, Rutherford B. (1876 election), 452–453
Harrison, Benjamin (1888 election), 536, 946
Hoover, Herbert (1928 election), 687–688
Johnson, Lyndon (1964 election), 833–835
Kennedy, John F. (1960 election), 824–825
McKinley, William (1896 election), 541–542*m*

McKinley, William (1900 election), 618
Nixon, Richard M. (1968 election), 866
Nixon, Richard M. (1972 election), 876–877
Reagan, Ronald (1980 election), 900
Reagan, Ronald (1984 election), 905
Roosevelt, Franklin D. (1932 election), 715–716
Roosevelt, Franklin D. (1936 election), 728
Roosevelt, Franklin D. (1940 election), 750
Roosevelt, Franklin D. (1944 election), 757
Roosevelt, Theodore (1904 election), 593
Taft, William Howard (1908 election), 594
Truman, Harry S. (1948 election), 789–790
Wilson, Woodrow (1912 election), 596–597
Wilson, Woodrow (1916 election), 640
presidio towns, 478
Presley, Elvis, 818, 820*i*
price controls, 884
Princip, Gavrilo, 636
Prioleau, George W., 616
Production Code Administration, 702
Progress and Poverty (George), 575
Progressive Era
and African Americans, 587–589
Bull Moose Party, 596
Democratic Party, 594, 596–597
direct democracy methods, 583
feminist movement, 576–581
intellectual roots of, 574–576
labor movement, 585–586
machine politics, 585
muckrakers, 576
Prohibition proponents, 651–652
Republican progressives, 594–596
Roosevelt presidency, 589–596
settlement houses, 576, 579
and social insurance, 587
urban liberalism, 583–587
Wilson presidency, 596–599
Prohibition
Eighteenth Amendment, 651–652
proponents of, 651–652
repeal of, 683–684, 721
in states, 651
Promontory Point, Utah, 510
propaganda, World War I, 652
property ownership
and free blacks, 445–448
versus tenancy, 496
and women, 443
Proposition 13, 895
Proposition 187, 917
Proposition 209, 919
prostitution, cities, 568
Protestantism
decline of, 949
evangelicalism, 896, 900
fundamentalism, 682–683
nativism of, 680
and Republican Party, 523
revivalism, 566
urban outreach, 564–565
protest music, 853

public accommodations
   desegregation, 799–801, 834
   segregation, 528–529, 532
Public Enemy, 703
Public Interest Research Group, 887
Public Works Administration (PWA), 722
Pueblo Indians, 478
Puerto Ricans, immigration to U.S., 821–822
Puerto Rico, and Spanish-American War,
   613–614
Pulitzer, Joseph, 568, 610
Pullman, George M., 511
Pullman, Illinois, 511
Pullman boycott, 511–513, 512*f,* 573
pump priming, 712
Pure Food and Drug Act of 1906, 593

Quaker Oats, 494*i*
Quayle, Dan, 907, 923
Quinn, Anthony, 758

racism. *See also* African American discrimination
   anti-immigration sentiments, 481–482, 680,
      917–918
   Chinese, 481–482
   Japanese, 625, 761–763
   nativism of 1920s, 680–682
Radar, Melvin, 796
Radical Republicans, 436–437
radicals
   antiwar movement, 868
   socialism, 513–514
   World War I era, 653
radio
   Depression era, 704
   music of 1950s, 817–818
   networks, 676
   programs of 1920s, 672, 676
railroads
   bankruptcy of companies, 492
   Chinese workers, 481
   corporations for development, 490
   developers, 491
   economic impact of, 492
   expansion (1870–1890), 489–492, 490*m*
   federal regulation, 573, 593
   integration of systems, 491–492
   land grants, 490
   refrigerator cars, 493
   strikes, 511–513
   westward expansion, 464
Railroad War Board, 647
Rainbow Coalition, 907
Ramona (Jackson), 483
Randolph, A. Philip, 639, 756, 832
Rankin, Jeanette, 641, 751
rapid transit, 547
Raskob, John J., 692
rationing, World War II, 758–759
Rauschenbusch, Walter, 575
Ray, James Earl, 856
Reader's Digest, 676

reading, during Great Depression, 705–706
Readjusters, 530
Reagan, Nancy, 906
Reagan, Ronald (1911–)
   arms buildup, 904–905
   election of 1980, 900
   election of 1984, 905
   foreign affairs, 909–910
   Iran-Contra affair, 905–906
   and Iran hostage crisis, 900–901
   labor and workers, 914
   legacy of, 907
   national debt/federal deficit, 907
   as president, 904–910
   Reaganomics, 904–905, 913
   Supreme Court appointments, 906–907
Reaganomics, 904–905, 913
recall, function of, 583
recession
   Asia, 1990s, 954
   Bush era, 909, 913–914
   Carter era, 897
   during New Deal, 730
   post–World War I, 666
   post–World War II, 811
   Reagan era, 897, 905
Reconstruction
   African American leaders, 442–443*i*
   civil rights legislation during, 435–436, 440
   end of, 487, 494
   Freedmen's Bureau, 431–435
   Grant Administration, 449, 451–452
   Johnson's plan, 429–430
   Lincoln's plan, 428–429
   Radical Republican Program, 441–444
   South, treatment of free blacks, 432–435
   Ten Percent Plan, 428–429
   Wade-Davis bill, 428–429
Reconstruction Finance Corporation (RFC),
   712–713
recreation. *See* leisure activities
recycling, 950
Red Cloud, 471
Red Cross, 650
Redmond, Juanita, 768
Red River Valley, 470, 472
Red Scare, 658–659
   immigrants as targets, 659, 680
   Palmer raids, 658
   Sacco-Vanzetti, 659
Red Shirts, 451
Redeemers, 529
Reform Party, 931, 944
Rehnquist, William, 876, 907
Reich, Robert, 915
Reid, Wallace, 675
religion and America
   and African Americans. *See* black church
   Catholicism, 564
   Evangelicalism, 895–896
   fundamentalism, 682–683
   future view, 949–950

religion and America (*cont.*)
  growth during 1950s, 816
  Judaism, 563–564
  and mass media, 816
  Moral Majority, 900
  multinational religions, 949–950
  Native American spirituality, 463, 473
  Prohibition proponents, 651
  Protestantism, 564–566
  revivalism, 566
  school prayer ban, 876
  Social Gospel, 575–576
  Southern Baptist Convention, 949
religious affiliation, and political party
    affiliation, 523*f*
Reno, Janet, 923
Republican Party
  and civil rights legislation, 435–436
  and Clinton era Congress, 927–928, 930, 942
  and election of 1980, 900
  Progressive Era, 594–596
  Radical Republicans, 436–437
  Reconstruction programs, 441–444
  and religious affiliation, 523
  in South, 529
  Stalwarts and Halfbreeds, 525
  on states/national government, 518
reservations, 471–474
  Dawes Act allotments, 473
  Indian resistance, 471–474
  locations (1850–1890), 471
  locations (1970s), 893*m*
  relocation of Native Americans to cities, 822
Reserve Office Training Corps (ROTC), 852
Resettlement Administration, 736
restrictive covenants, housing, 792, 812
Revels, Hiram R., 443*i*
Revenue Act of 1916, 663
Revenue Act of 1935, 728
Revenue Act of 1942, 752
revenue sharing, meaning of, 875
reverse discrimination, and affirmative action, 894
revivalism, urban settings, 566
Reynolds v. Sims, 876
Rich, Frank, 939
Rifle Clubs, 451
right to life, anti-abortion activities, 920
riots
  antiwar movement, 865–866
  gay activism, 860
  during Great Depression, 714–715
  race riots, 657, 707, 759, 855–856*m*, 917–918
Rise of David Levinsky, The (Cahan), 563–564
Rise of Silas Lapham, The (Howells), 570
River, The, 741
Robertson, Pat, 895, 920
Robinson, Edward G., 703
Robinson, Jackie, 791
rock 'n' roll
  of 1950s, 818
  of 1960s, 853
Rockefeller, John D., 493, 577*i*

Rockwell, Norman, 754
Rocky Mountains, 475
Rodeo, 740
Roe v. Wade, 876, 889, 908
Rogers, Ginger, 702, 703*i*
Rogers, William, 840
Rolling Stones, 853
Roman Catholic Church. *See* Catholics
Rommel, Erwin, 764
Roosevelt, Eleanor, 715
  on civil rights, 736, 755
  contributions of, 734–736, 735*i*
  on Great Depression, 695, 697
Roosevelt, Franklin Delano (1882–1945). *See also*
    New Deal
  advisors of, 719
  as assistant secretary of navy, 715
  death of, 770–771
  election of 1932, 715–716
  election of 1936, 728
  election of 1940, 750
  election of 1944, 757
  Good Neighbor Policy, 746
  leadership style of, 719
  paralysis of, 720*i*
  World War II, 750–752, 755–757, 764–765, 770
Roosevelt, Theodore (1858–1919)
  and 1904 election, 593
  American-British relations, 620–622
  Asian policy, 623–625
  big stick policy, 621
  Caribbean affairs, 623
  consumer protection, 593
  on expansionism, 607, 609
  Moroccan crisis, 627
  neutrality policy, 746–747
  New Nationalism, 596
  Panama Canal, 621*i*, 622
  pre–World War II events, 746–747
  presidency of, 589–596, 590*i*, 620–625
  progressive ideals of, 575–576
  railroad regulation, 593
  Roosevelt Corollary, 623
  in Spanish-American War, 612–614
  Spanish Civil War, 747
  Square Deal, 593, 594
  trust-busting, 591–593, 595–596
  as vice-president, 589
Roosevelt Corollary, 623
Roosevelt Field, 814
Root, Elihu, 623, 627
Root-Takahira Agreement, 625
Rosenberg, Ethel and Julius, 794
Rosie the Riveter, 754
Rough Riders, 613, 614
Roybal, Edward, 857
rubber, World War II shortage, 759
Rubin, Jerry, 865
Ruef, Abe, 583
rule of reason, in antitrust cases, 592, 595
Rural Electrification Administration, 739
Russell, Charles, 466*i*

Russell, Charles Edward, 578
Russia. *See also* Soviet Union
   Bolsheviks, 642, 654–655, 658
   economic collapse of 1990s, 954
   Russo-Japanese War, 624
   World War I, 636, 642
Russian Revolution, 642, 658
Russians, 469
Rust Belt, 884
Rustin, Bayard, 832
Ruth, Babe, 678

Sabbath, blue laws, 524
Sacco, Nicola, 659
Sackville-West, Lionel, 601
al-Sadat, Anwar, 898, 909
Safeway, 672
Saigon, renaming of, 871
St. Louis Post-Dispatch, 568
Samoan Islands, 604, 620
Sanchez, George, 711
Sandinistas, 909
San Francisco, California
   Chinese in, 481
   earthquake of 1906, 549
   growth of, 475, 478
   wealthy area, 551
San Francisco Zoo, 739
Sanger, Margaret, 581, 699–700
sanitation, cities, 551
San Joaquin Valley, 710
San Juan Hill, Battle of, 589, 614–615*i*
Sankey, Ira D., 566
Santa Fe, growth of, 478–479
Santa Fe Railroad, 464, 484
Santo Domingo (Dominican Republic), 603
Sarajevo, 926
   and World War I, 636
Sargent, John Singer, 558*i*
Saturday Evening Post, 672, 676, 754
Saudi Arabia, 881
Savage, Augusta, 686
SAVAK, 898
Save Our State, 917
Savio, Mario, 851
Scalawags, 441–442
Scalia, Antonin, 907
Scandinavians, 469, 498
Schechter v. United States, 724
Schenck, Charles T., 653
Schenck v. United States, 653
Schlafly, Phyllis, 889–890
Schneiderman, Rose, 501, 579
school desegregation
   Brown decision, 799–800
   busing for racial balance, 892–893
   enforcement of, 800–801*i*
school prayer ban, 876
school segregation
   Japanese, 625
   outlawed, Civil Rights Act of 1964, 834
schools. *See also* education

Schroeder, Patricia, 888
Schurz, Carl, 525, 618
Schwarzkopf, Norman, 911
scientific management, 505–506, 668
Scientology, 885
Scopes trial, 683
Scott, Hugh, 879
Scudder, Vida, 556
Seale, Bobby, 855
Seamen's Act of 1916, 599
Seattle, Washington, 477
   general strike of 1919, 657
Securities and Exchange Commission (SEC),
      creation of, 723
Security Council, 770
Sedalia, Missouri, 465
Sedition Act of 1918, 653
Seeger, Charles, 740
Seeger, Pete, 853
Seeger, Ruth Crawford, 740
segregation
   armed forces, 644–645*i*, 753, 792
   de facto, 854
   de jure, 854
   interstate transportation, 830
   Jim Crow laws, 532–534
   Montgomery bus boycott, 800–801
   outlawed, Civil Rights Act of 1964, 834
   public accommodations, 528–529, 532
   streetcar boycotts, 533–534
   Supreme Court support, 532
Selective Service Act of 1917, 641
Selma, Alabama, voting rights march, 834
Seminole Indians, 471
Seneca Indians, 738
separate-but-equal doctrine, 532, 799
Sequoia National Park, 485
Serbia, World War I, 636
Serbs, 499, 926, 929
service sector, growth of, 913
Servicemen's Readjustment Act of 1944 (GI Bill),
      757, 788, 811, 861
settlement houses, 576, 579
   African American, 588
severalty policy, Native Americans, 738
Seward, William H., 603
sex districts, cities, 568, 651
sex education, 651
sexual harassment, Hill/Thomas hearing,
      908, 908*i*
sexuality
   movies, 702
   women, 556
Seymour, Horatio, 440
Shahn, Ben, 741
Shalala, Donna E., 924
shantytowns, 713–714*i*
sharecropping, 445–448, 447*i*, 706, 736
Share Our Wealth Society, 724, 728
Sharon, Ariel, 957
Sheen, Fulton J., 816
sheep raising, 466–467

Sheldon, Charles M., 565
Shelley v. Kraemer, 792, 812
shelterbelts, 739
Shepard, Alan, 829
Sheppard-Towner Federal Maternity and Infancy
    Act, 665
Sheridan, Philip, 602
Sherman Antitrust Act of 1890, 591–593, 598
Sherman Silver Purchase Act of 1890, 541
Sherman, William Tecumseh, 453
Shibe Park, 568
shopping centers
    first, 674
    suburban malls, 814
Shuttlesworth, Fred, 830
Sicily, World War II, 764
Sierra Club, 485
Sierra Nevada mountains, 475, 484–485
"Significance of the Frontier in American History,
    The" (Turner), 609
silent majority, meaning of, 866
Silent Spring (Carson), 886
silver
    currency issue, 540–541
    free silver and Populists, 539, 541
    mining of, 476*m*, 477
Simpson-Mazzoli Act of 1986, 915
Since You Went Away, 758
Sinclair, Upton, 593
Singer Sewing Machine Company, 493,
    604–605*i*
single tax movement, 575
Sino-Japanese War of 1894–1895, 606, 624
Sioux Indians, Teton people, 462–463, 471–474
Sirhan, Sirhan, 865
Sister Carrie (Dreiser), 545
sitcoms, 815
sit-ins, civil rights, 830
Sitting Bull, 472
Six Companies, 481
Six Day War, 882
Sixteenth Amendment, provisions of, 646
skyscrapers, 547
Slavs, 498
    and Holocaust, 765
Smith, Alfred E., 583, 665, 687–688
Smith, Bessie, 676
Smith-Connally Labor Act of 1943, 755
social Darwinism
    and American individualism, 521
    and foreign expansion, 608
    and progressives, 574
Social Gospel, 575–576
social insurance
    Great Society programs, 836
    Progressive Era, 587
socialism
    in America, 513–514, 575
    in Europe, 513
    Industrial Workers of the World (IWW), 514
    socialist congressman, 585
Socialist Labor Party, 513

Socialist Party of America, 513–514, 575
Social Register, 552
Social Security Act, 726
Social Security system
    concern about future of, 942–943
    extension of, 791, 798, 829, 836
    and Medicare, 835
social work, settlement house roots, 579
socioeconomic status. *See also* poverty; wealth
    divisions of suburbanites, 553–555
Soil Conservation Service, 739
Sokoloff, Nicholas, 740
solar power, 886
Solomon Islands, World War II, 767, 769*m*
Sone, Monica, 762
Souls of Black Folk, The (Du Bois), 535, 588
Sound and the Fury, The (Faulkner), 685
Souter, David, 908
South
    Democratic Party in, 529–530
    economic comparison to North (1910), 497*t*
    economic development, post-Reconstruction,
        494–497, 495*m*
    lumber industry, 496
    after Reconstruction, 494–497, 495*m*
    Republican Party in, 529
    social group antagonism, 529–530
    tenant farmers, 496
South America. *See* Latin America
South and slavery/African Americans
    free blacks, 432–435
    Great Migration from South, 649
    Ku Klux Klan (KKK), 448–450, 449*i*
    racism, forms of, 529–532
    Sharecroppers, 445–448, 447*i*
    violence during Reconstruction, 431, 435, 438*i*,
        448–451
    white supremacy, 529–532
South Dakota
    Native Americans relocation to, 471
    Wounded Knee, 473–474, 858, 860*i*
Southeast Asia
    cold war. *See* Vietnam War
    immigrants from, 915
Southeast Asia Treaty Organization (SEATO), 802
Southern Baptist Convention, 949
Southern Christian Leadership Conference, 801
Southern Manifesto, 799
Southern Pacific Railroad, 464, 483–484, 583
Southern Tenant Farmers Union, 706
Southwest
    Hispanic-Indian relations, 478
    Mexican migration to, 479
    New Mexico, 478–479
Soviet Union. *See also* Russia
    arms control, 805
    Aswan Dam project, 803, 804
    –Cuba relations, 828
    détente policy, 869–870
    end of communism, 910, 911*m*
    and Korean War, 785
    nuclear weapons development, 783, 802, 893

post–World War II. *See* cold war
post–World War II problems, 778–781
space program, 798, 798*i*
U.S./Soviet summits, Reagan era, 910
World War II, 749, 763–764
space program
  Kennedy administration, 829
  NASA created, 798
  Soviet Union, 798, 798*i*
Spain
  and Cuba, 610–611
  Spanish-American War, 609–615, 746
  Spanish Civil War, 747
Spanish-American War, 609–615, 746
  beginning of, 612
  Cuban freedom issue, 610–615
  in Philippines, 613, 615–617
  Rough Riders, 613
Spanish Civil War, 747
Spanish colonization
  New Mexico, 478–479
  Texas, 478
Sparkman, John A., 797
speakeasies, 683
specie, 540
Spencer, Herbert, 521
Spirit of St. Louis, 678
spoils system, reform of, 517
sports
  baseball, 568
  boxing, 678
  football, 678
  golf, 678
  radio broadcasts, 676
  sex discrimination banned, 888
  tennis, 678
Sprague, Frank J., 547
Sputnik, 798
Square Deal, 593–594
stagflation, meaning of, 884
Stalin, Joseph
  death of, 801
  -Truman conflict, 780
  World War II, 764, 770
Stalingrad, Battle of, 764
Stalwarts, 525
stamp collecting, 705
Standard Oil Company, 493
  foreign affiliates, 604
  globalization of, 669
  trust-busting, 575–576, 591, 595
Stanton, Elizabeth Cady, 440–441
Starr, Ellen Gates, 579
Starr, Kenneth, 929
Star Wars, defense initiative, 905
state governments
  Populist view, 538–539
  takeover of federal programs, 928
states and federal government, due process clause, 522
States' Rights Party, 790
steam power, steam engines, 489

steam turbine, 489
steel
  Homestead strike, 511
  manufacturing of, 489
  uses of, 489
Steel Workers Organizing Committee (SWOC), 733*i*, 734
Steffens, Lincoln, 576
Stein, Gertrude, 685
Steinbeck, John, 709, 741
Steinem, Gloria, 887
Stephens, Alexander, 431
Stephenson, David, 681–682
Stevens, Wallace, 685
Stevenson, Adlai E., 797
Stimson, Henry, 752
stock, railroad corporations, 490, 492
stock market crash. *See also* Great Depression
  drop in 1997, 932–933
  of 1893, 536
  of 1929, 692–693
stockyards, 492
Stone, Lucy, 441
STOP ERA organization, 890
Stop the Draft Week, 852
Strategic Air Command, 802
Strategic Arms Limitations Treaty (SALT I), 869
Strategic Arms Limitations Treaty (SALT II), 896, 898
Strategic Defense Initiative (SDI), 905
streetcars, 547
strikes, 511–513
  agricultural, 710, 858
  automobile workers, 734
  employer anti-strike tactics, 510
  federal intervention, 512–513, 590, 714
  federal regulation, 573
  grape pickers, 858
  Homestead strike, 511
  miners, 590–591
  post–World War I, 657–658
  post–World War II, 789
  Pullman strike, 511–513, 512*i*, 573
  railroad workers, 487
  World War II era, 755
strip mining, 739
Students for a Democratic Society (SDS), 850–851, 868
Student Non-Violent Coordinating Committee (SNCC), 832
Student Strike against War, 701
submarine, U-boat, 639
suburbs
  African Americans in, 812
  automobile and growth of, 674, 679, 813–814
  malls/shopping centers, 674, 814
  middle class, 553–554
  post–World War II boom, 812–814
  social class divisions, 553–555
  wealthy, 553
  white flight to, 823
subway, 547

Suez Canal, 603, 803–804
suffrage. *See* voting rights; women's movement
sugar
    Hawaii, 603–604
    World War II rationing, 759
Sumatra, 669
Summer of Love, 853
Sumner, Charles, 436, 441
Sumner, William Graham, 521
Sun Also Rises, The (Hemingway), 685
Sun Belt
    post–World War II boom, 812–813, 885
    states of, 812–813
Sun Dance, 463
Sunday, Billy, 566, 682
Superfund, 897
Superman, 704
supermarkets, 672
supply-side economics, Reagan era, 904–905
Supreme Court
    abortion decisions, 876, 889, 907–908
    Bush (George) appointments, 907
    Clinton appointments, 924
    on due process, 522
    Nixon appointments, 876
    packing during New Deal, 728–730
    presidential election 2000 decision, 931–932,
        945–947
    Reagan appointments, 906–907
    on separate but equal, 532
    women on, 906, 924
Sutter's mill, 477
Swedish Americans, 468–469, 559
Swift, Gustavus F., 492–493
Swift & Co., 493
syndicalism, meaning of, 514
syndication, newspaper columns, 676
Syngman Rhee, 785
Syria, Six Day War, 882

tabloids, 676
Taft, William Howard (1857–1930)
    anti-civil rights position, 587
    election of 1908, 594
    as president, 594–596, 625, 627
Taft-Hartley Act, 789, 790
Taiwan, 787, 788, 869
Tammany Hall, 562–563
Tarbell, Ida, 576
Tardieu, Andre, 628
tariffs. *See also* taxation
    antiprotection view, 518–519
    high, of 1920s, 670
    McKinley Tariff, 540
    Progressives on, 594
    reform of 1913, 597
Tax Reduction Act of 1964, 829
taxation
    child-care deductions, 889
    and Great Depression, 693, 711
    income tax, 646
    income tax reduction (1964), 829

    increases under Bush, 909
    payroll deductions/tax withholding, 752
    Reconstruction era, 444
    tax cuts under Reagan, 904
    taxpayer revolts, 895
Taylor, Frederick W., 505–506, 668
Teapot Dome scandal, 664
technology
    Internet, 922–923
    manufacturing, 489, 505
    mass media of 1980s–1990s, 921–923
    personal computers (PC), 922
Teheran Conference, 764
tejanos, 479
telegraph, 464, 472
telephone, 548, 922
telephone operators, women as, 500, 502*i*
television
    advertising, 815
    cable TV, 922
    MTV, 921–922
    political events, 825, 865, 899, 900, 947
    presidential election campaigns, 825, 907
    rise of (1950s), 815
    sitcoms, 815
    televangelism, 895
    and VCRs, 922
    Vietnam War, 849, 849*i*, 871
Teller, Henry M., 612
temperance movement, women's activities,
        526–527*i*
tenancy
    sharecropping, 445–448
    South, 496
Tenderloin district, 568
Tenement House Law of 1901, 549–550
tenements, for urban poor, 549–550
Tennessee Coal and Iron Company, 595
Tennessee Valley Authority (TVA), 721, 738–739
Tenure of Office Act of 1867, 437, 439
term limits, presidency, 824
Termination program, 822
terrorism
    Cole incident, 956*i*
    Middle Eastern, 909, 956
    Weathermen, 868
Tet offensive, Vietnam War, 864
Teton Indians, 462–463
    culture of, 462–463
    gender roles, 462
    resistance to relocation, 471–474
    spirituality of, 463
Texas (colony), Spanish colonization, 478
Texas (state)
    cattle ranching, 465
    Mexican population (1900), 479
Texas Exchange, 536–537
textiles, South, after Reconstruction, 495–496
Thayer, Webster, 659
theater
    New Deal programs, 740
    vaudeville, 566–567

Their Eyes Were Watching God (Hurston), 740
Thieu, Nguyen Van, 863, 870
Third International (Comintern), 658
Third World
    foreign aid to, 826
    oil producing countries, 881–882
Thirteenth Amendment, 430
Thirty Seconds over Tokyo, 758
Tho, Le Duc, 869
Thomas, Clarence, 908
Thomas, Norman, 716
Thomas, Theodore, 569
Thompson, Virgil, 741
Thoughts for the Young Men of America, 520
Three Mile Island, 886
Three Soldiers, The (Dos Passos), 685
Thurmond, Strom, 790
Tilden Park, 739
Tilden, Bill, 678
Tillman, Benjamin R., 532
Time, 676
time-and-motion studies, 506
Titan, The (Dreiser), 552
tobacco, cigarette manufacturing, 496
Tocqueville, Alexis de, 516
Tojo, Hideki, 751
Toomer, Jean, 686
Top Hat, 702, 703*i*
Townsend Clubs, 724
Townsend, Francis, 724
Toynbee Hall, 579
Tracy, Benjamin F., 607
Tracy, Spencer, 758
trade
    deficit of 1980s, 907
    and expansionism, 604–606
    North American agreement (1993), 925
    of Teton Sioux, 463
    U.S. imports (1870–1914), 606*f*
Trail of Broken Treaties, 859
transportation
    ferry service, 551
    highways, 674, 798, 813–814
    mass transit, 547–548*i*
    railroads, 464, 489–492
    rapid transit, 547
travel, and automobile, 674, 815
Treasury notes, silver as basis, 540
trench warfare, 638, 638*i*, 644
Triangle Shirtwaist Company, 583–584
Tri-Partite Pact, 751
Triple Alliance, 626, 636
Triple Entente, 636
Triumphant Democracy (Carnegie), 520
trolley car, 547
Trotter, William Monroe, 588
True Story, 672
Truman Doctrine, 781–782
Truman, Harry S. (1884–1972)
    and atomic bomb, 771
    economic policy, 790–791
    election of 1948, 789–790

Fair Deal, 790–792
    labor relations, 789, 790
    leadership style of, 788
    McCarthyism, 792–796
    post–World War II. *See* cold war
    as president, 771, 778, 780–796
    -Stalin conflict, 780
    as vice-president, 757
    and Vietnam, 841–842
Trumbull, Lynn, 431–435
trusts. *See also* antitrust
    operation of, 501
    trust-busting, 591–593, 595–596
Tucson, Arizona, 478
Tugwell, Rexford, 719
Tunney, Gene, 678
Turkey
    Truman Doctrine, 782
    World War I, 636
Turnbow, Hartman, 835
Turner, Frederick Jackson, 609
Turner, Henry M., 433
Turner, Ted, 922
Tuskegee Institute, 535
Twain, Mark, 483, 559, 570
Twentieth Amendment, provision of, 716
Twenty-fourth Amendment, provisions of, 835
Twenty-second Amendment, provisions of, 824
Twenty-sixth Amendment, provisions of, 846
Tyson, Laura D'Andrea, 954

U-boat, 640
Udall, Stewart, 836
Underwood Tariff Act of 1913, 597
unemployment
    Great Depression, 693–694, 716, 730
    New Deal measures, 722–723, 726, 729*t*
    in 1970s, 884
    and plant closings, 884–885
unemployment compensation, beginning of, 809
Unification Church, 885
Union Pacific Railroad, 464, 491
Union Party, 728
Union of Soviet Socialist Republic (USSR). *See*
    Soviet Union
Union Stock Yards, 492
unions
    AFL-CIO merger, 811
    American Federation of Labor (AFL), 510,
        733
    closed shop, 508
    Congress of Industrial Organizations (CIO),
        732–734
    decline in membership, 885, 914
    first, 508
    goals of, 507–508
    Gompers influence, 509–510
    industrial union, 513
    trade unions, 507–508
    versus Knights of Labor, 508–509
    versus welfare capitalism, 668
United Automobile Workers (UAW), 734

United Cannery, Agricultural, Packing, and Allied Workers of America, 710
United Farm Workers (UFW), 858
United Fruit Company, 668–669*i*, 802
United Mine Workers, 590, 732, 755, 789
United Nations
  General Assembly, 770
  Security Council, 770
United Services Organization, 848
United States Steel Corporation, antitrust case, 595
United States v. One Package of Japanese Pessaries, 699
Universal Negro Improvement Association (UNIA), 686
universities. *See* colleges/universities
University of California, Berkeley
  affirmative action, 894, 919
  student protests, 851
Unsafe at Any Speed (Nader), 887
urban liberalism, 583–587
U'Ren, William, 583
U.S. Army Corps of Engineers, 622
U.S. Steel Corporation, 734
U.S. v. Northern Securities, 591
U.S. v. Standard Oil, 591, 595
U.S. v. Trans-Missouri, 591
USA Today, 922
Utah, growth of, 475
Ute Indians, 471

V-E (Victory in Europe) Day, 765
V-J (Victory over Japan) Day, 745
vacuum cleaner, 672
Vanderbilt, Cornelius, 491
Vanderbilt, George W., 570
Van Dusen, Larry, 698
Vann, John Paul, 840
Vanzetti, Bartolomeo, 659
vaqueros, 478
vaudeville, 566–567
Venezuela, 669, 882
Verdun, 642–643
Versailles, Treaty of 1919, 654–656
vertical integration, meaning of, 493
Veterans Administration, 812
victory gardens, 758
videocassette recorders (VCRs), 922
Vietminh, 841
Vietnam syndrome, 871
Vietnam War
  armed forces/combat experience, 845–848
  bombing halt, 866, 869–870
  Cambodia, bombing of, 867–868
  détente, 869–870
  economic factors, 850, 872
  Eisenhower administration, 842
  and election of 1968, 863–866
  failure for America, reasons for, 846, 864
  Gulf of Tonkin Resolution, 845
  impact of, 871–872

Johnson administration, 844–846, 848–850, 863–864
  Kennedy administration, 843–844
  and mass media, 849, 849*i*
  military draft, 846, 851–852
  My Lai Massacre, 868
  Nixon administration, 866–871
  Operation Rolling Thunder, 845
  protests. *See* antiwar movement, Vietnam War
  roots of, 841–844
  scope of (1954–1975), 843*m*
  Tet offensive, 864
  Truman and Vietnam policy, 841–842
  veterans, problems of, 871
  Vietcong, guerrilla forces, 844, 846, 849*i*, 864
  Vietnamization policy, 867–868
  withdrawal of American troops, 869–870
  women in, 846, 848
Vietnamese, immigration to U.S., 871, 915
voluntarism, 585
Volunteers in Service to America (VISTA), 836, 837
voter registration, African Americans (1960s), 835
voting irregularities, presidential election 2000, 931–934*i*, 945–947
voting rights
  Fifteenth Amendment, 440–441
  full legal rights, legislation for, 834–835
  granted for African Americans, 440
  granted for women, 650–651
  limitations for free blacks, 531–532, 834
  limitations for women, 526
  literacy tests, 531–532
  Nineteenth Amendment, 650–651
  poll tax, 530
  suffrage activities, 526, 580–581, 650–651
Voting Rights Act of 1965, 834–835
Voting Rights Act of 1970, 835

WAC (Women's Army Corps), 753
Wade-Davis bill, 428–429
wage discrimination
  free blacks, 433
  women, 500, 735, 754, 914
wages
  minimum wage, 791, 798, 829
  stagnation in 1990s, 913
  wage controls, 884
Wagner Act. *See* National Labor Relations Act
Wagner, Robert F., 583, 726
wagon trains, 463–464, 475
Wake Island, World War II, 767
Wallace, George C., 866, 868, 876
Wallace, Henry A., 719, 750, 757, 789–790
War Brides Act of 1945, 821
War Finance Corporation, 712
War Hawks, 612
War Industries Board (WIB), 646–647
War Manpower Commission, 754
War on Poverty, 836–838
  Nixon cuts to program, 875
War Powers Act of 1941, 752
War Powers Act of 1973, 871

War Production Board, 752
War Refugee Board, 765
War Relocation Authority (WRA), 761
War Revenue Bills of 1917 and 1918, 646
Ward, Lester F., 574
wards, machine politics, 562–563
Warner, Charles Dudley, 570
Warner, Sam Bass, 549
Warren, Earl, 789, 799
    judicial activism of, 876
Warsaw Pact, 783*i*, 801
Washington, Booker T.
    accommodationist position, 534–536
    African American criticism of, 588
Washington, D.C.
    African Americans in, 560
    March on Washington, 833
Washington Merry-Go-Round, 703
Washington Naval Arms Conference of 1921,
    671
Washington Post, Watergate story, 878
Washington State, growth of, 477
Waste Land, The (Eliot), 685
Watch on the Rhine, 758
Watergate, 877–880
    impact of, 880
    Nixon resignation, 879
    pre break-in events, 877–878
Watson, Tom, 530, 539, 541
Watts race riots, 855
WAVES (Women Appointed for Volunteer
    Emergency Service), 753
Wayne, John, 758
"We Shall Overcome," 853
wealth
    and philanthropy, 569–570
    and Protestants, 520, 564
    railroad developers, 491
    suburbs of, 553
    urban elite, 551–553
Wealth against Commonwealth (Lloyd), 575
weapons
    See also arms buildup; arms control
    B1 bomber, 904
    biological/chemical warfare, 845, 852, 957
    missiles, 802, 828, 904
    NSC-68 report, 784
    nuclear. *See* nuclear weapons
    post–Civil War, 472
    Vietnam War, 845
    World War I, 637
Weathermen, 868
Weaver, James B., 537
Webster v. Reproductive Health Services, 907
Wedemeye, Albert, 784
welfare capitalism, 668
welfare state
    Clinton reform, 927–928, 943–944
    Great Society programs, 836–837
    and illegal aliens, 917
    and New Deal, 726, 736, 741–742
    Reagan cuts, 904

social security, 726
    and women's movement, 579, 665
Welles, Orson, 740
Wells-Barnett, Ida, 534, 534*i*
Welsh Americans, 498
Wertheim, Frank, 704
West, Mae, 702
Western Federation of Miners (WFM), 514
West
    California, 482–485
    Chinese migration to, 480–482
    end of expansion, 609
    Great Plains, 460–474
    Hispanic population in (1848), 475
    Mexican migrants to, 479
    mining, 475–478, 476*m*
    Native American conflicts, 471–474
    natural environment, 461*m*
Western Trail, 467
West Germany, creation of, 783
Westinghouse, George, 491
Westmoreland, William, 840
Weyler, Valeriano, 609–610
Wharton, Edith, 552, 685
wheat, falling prices, 667
"Where Have All the Flowers Gone?," 853
Whiskey Ring, 452
White, William Allen, 749
White Citizens' Councils, 799
white flight, 823
White Sox, 678
white supremacy
    Ku Klux Klan (KKK), 448–450, 449*i*
    post–Civil War South, 529–532
    Progressive Era, 587–588
Whitewater affair, 929
Whitlock, Brand, 523, 585
Whyte, William, 811
Wickersham, George W., 595
Wilhelm II, Kaiser of Germany, 620
Wilhelm, Kaiser, 627
Wilkins, Roy, 832
Will, George F., 919
Willamette Valley, 463, 475, 477
Willard, Frances, 526–527
Williams, William Carlos, 685
Williams v. Mississippi, 532
Willkie, Wendell, 750
Wills, Helen, 678
Wilson, Charles E., 802
Wilson, Edith Bolling Galt, 656
Wilson, Pete, 919
Wilson, Woodrow (1856–1924)
    election of 1912, 596–597
    election of 1916, 640
    Federal Reserve System, 598
    Fourteen Points, 654
    Mexican Revolution, 626
    New Freedom, 596–597
    post–World War I, 647, 652, 654–656
    as president, 596–599, 625–627
    social policy, 598–599

Wilson, Woodrow (1856–1924) (cont.)
    suffrage for women, 650–651
    tariff reform, 597
    Treaty of Versailles, 654–656
    trust issue, 597
    World War I, 638–656
Winning of the West, The (Roosevelt), 609
Wisconsin, La Follette and Progressivism, 574,
    581–583, 594–595
Wissler, Clark, 463
Wobblies, 514
Wolfe, Tom, 885
women
    affirmative action, 888–889
    African American, 500, 665
    in antiwar movement, 862
    in armed forces, 753, 912i
    athletic participation, 888
    authors, 483, 817
    birth control, 581, 699–700, 861, 889
    Cabinet appointments, Clinton, 924
    Chinese immigrants, 481
    in civil rights movement, 588, 665, 800
    in Congress, 641, 888
    credit, access to, 889
    discrimination outlawed, 834, 861, 888
    divorce, 698, 861, 891
    education, 557, 888–889
    feminization of poverty, 891
    flappers, 675, 675i
    and Great Depression, 697, 699–701
    housewives, 672, 817, 819i
    in Ku Klux Klan (KKK), 681
    in labor force, 499–502, 504, 648i, 650,
        699–701, 754, 754i, 817, 860, 890–891,
        914
    in labor movement, 578–580, 710
    in male-dominated fields, 914
    Mexican American, 710
    middle class, 556–557
    Native American, 462
    New Deal era, 734–735
    and 1950s, 816–817
    occupations, 499–502, 817, 914
    Persian Gulf War, 912i
    political participation, 526–527, 641, 665, 924
    and Populism, 537–538
    Progressive Era activities, 576–581
    property ownership, 443
    settlement house movement, 579
    sexuality, 556
    Supreme Court judges, 906, 924
    temperance activities, 526–527i
    in unions, 508
    in Vietnam War, 846, 848
    voting limitations, 526
    voting rights granted, 650–651
    wage discrimination, 500, 735, 754, 861, 914
    war nurses, 753, 768, 848
    World War I workers, 648i, 650
    World War II workers, 754
Women's Army Corps (WACs), 848

Women's Christian Temperance Union (WCTU),
    526, 527i, 651
Women's Council of National Defense, 651
Women's International League for Peace and
    Freedom, 671
Women's Joint Congressional
    Committee, 665
Women's Land Army, 648i
women's movement
    abortion rights, 889
    conservative critics of 1990s, 920
    Equal Rights Amendment, 889–890
    feminine mystique concept, 817–818, 861
    feminism, birth of, 581
    labor reform, 578–580, 650, 710, 734–735
    leaders of, 817, 862
    National Organization for Women (NOW),
        861–862
    and New Left, 862
    Nineteenth Amendment, 650–651
    political mobilization activities, 861,
        888–889
    post-suffrage activities, 665
    separate spheres issue, 526
    struggle for suffrage, 440–441
    suffrage activities, 526, 580–581, 650–651
    women's liberation movement of 1960s,
        860–863
Women's Peace Party, 639
Woods, Tiger, 947
Woodstock Music and Art Fair, 853
Woodward, Bob, 878
Woolworth Building, 547
workers' compensation, beginning of, 587
Works Progress Administration (WPA),
    727, 730
World Bank, 811, 954
World Court, 670
World Series, 676, 678
World Trade Center bombing, 926, 955
World Trade Organization, Seattle protest, 945,
    946i, 947
World War I
    Allied victory, 642–643
    Allies, 636–637m
    antiradical activities, 653, 658–659
    Central Powers, 636–637m
    economic impact on U.S., 645–650
    global scope of, 636–637m
    labor force during, 648–650
    Lusitania crisis, 639–640
    military draft, 641
    military technology, 637–638, 644
    neutrality, proponents of, 639
    Prohibition established, 651–652
    propaganda, 652
    Russian Revolution, 642, 658
    suffrage victory, 650–651
    Treaty of Versailles, 654–656
    U.S. entry, 640
    U.S. military forces, 641–644
    war debt from, 655, 669–670

World War II
  atomic bomb, 769*m*
  beginning of, 748–750
  casualties of, 763
  citizen morale during, 758–759
  civil rights movement, 755–756
  D-Day, 765
  defense industries, 754, 759
  and election of 1944, 757
  financing of, 752–753
  goals and strategies, 764–769
  Holocaust, 747–748, 765
  internment of Japanese Americans, 761–763
  labor movement, 755
  migration/relocation of Americans, 759
  Pearl Harbor, 751, 767
  popular culture during, 758
  postwar conflicts, 778–781
  prewar events, 746–747
  rationing during, 758–759
  V-E (Victory in Europe) Day, 765
  V-J (Victory over Japan) Day, 745
  Yalta Conference, 770
World Wide Web, 922–923
Wounded Knee, 460, 473–474
  siege in 1973, 858, 860*i*
Wovoka, 473
Wright, Richard, 740

Yalta Conference, 770, 780
Yellow Bird, 473
yellow-dog contracts, function of, 510

yellow fever, 622
yellow journalism, 569
Yeltsin, Boris, 910
Yippies, 865
Yom Kippur War, 882
Yosemite National Park, 485
Yosemite Valley, 484
Young, Andrew, 857*i*
Young, Whitney, 832
Young Women's Christian Association (YWCA), 651
youth
  adolescence, period of, 557
  Great Depression era, 701–702
  juvenile delinquency, 759–760
  New Age movement, 885
  1950s rebellion, 818–819
  1950s teen culture, 817–820
  1960s counterculture, 852–853
  Vietnam War protest, 850–854, 865–866, 868
  work culture, 504
  World War II era, 759–760
  youth culture, 557
Yugoslavia, 655, 926
  Kosovo crisis, 929, 957

Zhou Enlai (Chou En-lai), 784
Zimmermann, Arthur, 640
Zimmermann telegram, 640
zinc, mining of, 477
Zitkala-Sa, 474
zoot suits, 760, 760*i*

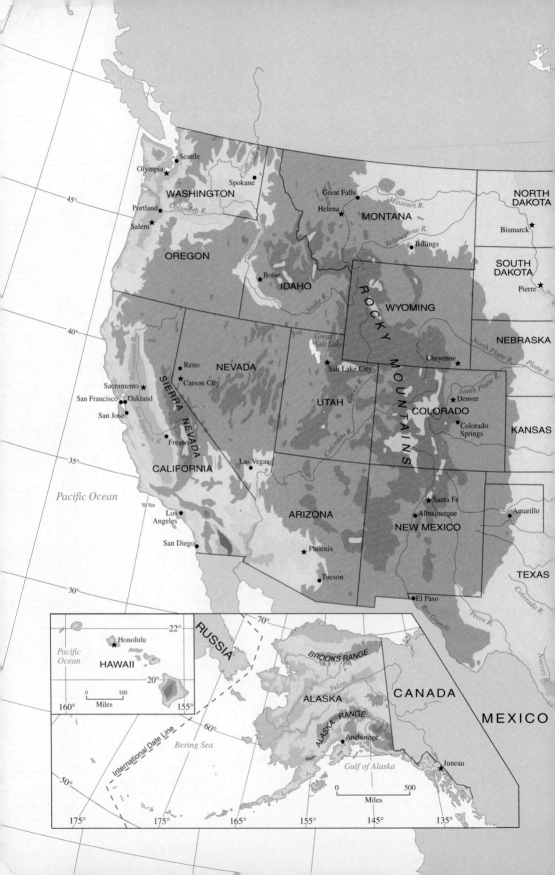

Seattle
Olympia
WASHINGTON
Spokane
Columbia R.
45°
Portland
Salem
OREGON
Columbia R.

Great Falls
Helena
MONTANA
Missouri R.
Yellowstone R.
Billings

NORTH
DAKOTA
Bismarck

SOUTH
DAKOTA
Pierre

Boise
IDAHO
Snake R.

WYOMING

ROCKY MOUNTAINS

40°
Great
Salt Lake

Cheyenne

North Platte R.
Platte R.
NEBRASKA

Reno
NEVADA
Carson City

Salt Lake City
Green R.

South Platte R.
Denver
COLORADO
Colorado
Springs

KANSAS

Sacramento
SIERRA NEVADA
San Francisco
Oakland
San Jose
Sacramento R.
San Joaquin R.
Fresno

UTAH

Colorado R.

35°
CALIFORNIA
Las Vegas

ARIZONA

Santa Fe
Albuquerque
Amarillo

NEW MEXICO

Los
Angeles
San Diego

Phoenix

TEXAS

Tucson

30°
Pacific Ocean

El Paso
Rio Grande
Pecos R.
Colorado R.
Nueces R.

22°
Honolulu
Pacific
Ocean
HAWAII
20°
0   100
Miles
160°   155°

RUSSIA
70°
BROOKS RANGE
Yukon R.
ALASKA
ALASKA RANGE
60°
Anchorage

CANADA

MEXICO

International Date Line

Bering Sea

Gulf of Alaska

Juneau

0   500
Miles

50°
175°   175°   165°   155°   145°   135°

CANADA

MINNESOTA

WISCONSIN

MICHIGAN

MAINE
Augusta
Burlington
Montpelier
VT. N.H.
Concord
Manchester
Portland
Albany
Boston
Providence
MASS.
CONN. R.I.
Hartford

Red River
of the North
Fargo
Duluth
L. Superior

St. Paul
Minneapolis
Sioux Falls
Milwaukee
Madison
Lansing
Detroit
Chicago
Gary

L. Huron
L. Michigan

L. Ontario
Buffalo
NEW YORK
L. Erie
Cleveland

IOWA
Des Moines
Omaha
Lincoln
Springfield

INDIANA
Indianapolis
Cincinnati
OHIO
Columbus
Wheeling
Pittsburgh

PENNSYLVANIA
Harrisburg
Newark
New York
Trenton
NEW
JERSEY
Philadelphia
Dover
Baltimore
MD.
Annapolis
DELAWARE
WASHINGTON D.C.

Topeka
Kansas
City
Jefferson
City
St. Louis
ILLINOIS
Frankfort
Louisville
KENTUCKY

WEST
VIRGINIA
Charleston
VIRGINIA
Richmond
Norfolk

Wichita
MISSOURI

Raleigh
NORTH
CAROLINA
Charlotte

APPALACHIAN MOUNTAINS

Oklahoma
City
ARKANSAS
Memphis
Knoxville
Nashville
TENNESSEE

SOUTH
CAROLINA
Columbia

Little Rock

Dallas
Fort
Worth
LOUISIANA
Jackson
Birmingham
Montgomery
ALABAMA
Atlanta
GEORGIA
Charleston

OKLAHOMA

austin
Houston
San Antonio
Baton Rouge
New Orleans
MISSISSIPPI
Tallahassee
Jacksonville

FLORIDA

Gulf of Mexico

Miami

Atlantic Ocean

BAHAMAS

67° Atlantic 66°
Ocean
San Juan
PUERTO RICO
Ponce
18°
Caribbean
Sea
0   500
Miles

CUBA

Red R.
Mississippi R.
Wisconsin R.
Missouri R.
Arkansas R.
Canadian R.
Tennessee R.
Ohio R.
Cumberland R.
Wabash R.
Illinois R.
Allegheny R.
Hudson R.
Potomac R.
Roanoke R.
Cape Fear R.
Santee R.
Chattahoochee R.
Alabama R.
Tombigbee R.
Sabine R.
Trinity R.
Brazos R.

Elevation
Feet   Meters
9,843   3,000
6,562   2,000
3,281   1,000
1,640   500
656   200
0   0
Below sea level   Below sea level

0   200   400
Miles

95°   90°   85°   80°   75°

Political divisions as of January 2001

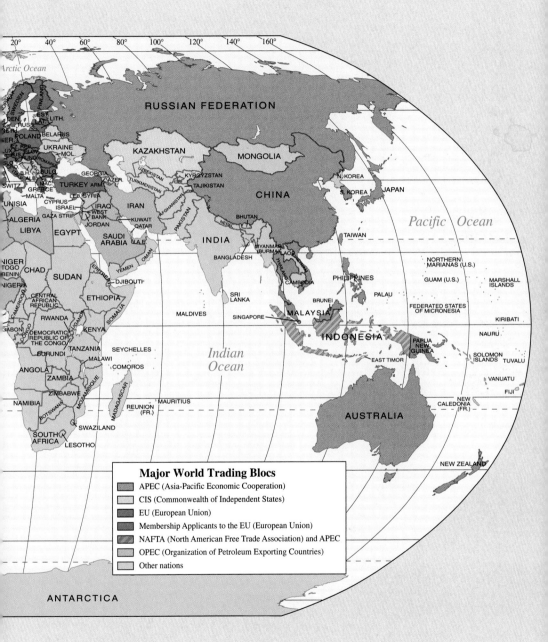

Major World Trading Blocs

- APEC (Asia-Pacific Economic Cooperation)
- CIS (Commonwealth of Independent States)
- EU (European Union)
- Membership Applicants to the EU (European Union)
- NAFTA (North American Free Trade Association) and APEC
- OPEC (Organization of Petroleum Exporting Countries)
- Other nations